enVision® Integrated

MATHEMATICS I

SAVVAS
LEARNING COMPANY

ISBN-13: 978-1418-28376-6
ISBN-10:   1418-28376-2

9 21

Contents in Brief

enVision Integrated MATHEMATICS I

Reviewers & Consultants

Mathematicians

David Bressoud, Ph.D.
Professor Emeritus of Mathematics
Macalester College
St. Paul, MN

Karen Edwards, Ph.D.
Mathematics Lecturer
Harvard University
Cambridge, MA

Teacher Reviewers

Jennifer Barkey
K-12 Math Supervisor
Gateway School District
Monroeville, PA

Miesha Beck
Math Teacher/Department Chair
Blackfoot School District
Blackfoot, ID

Joseph Brandell, Ph.D.
West Bloomfield High School
West Bloomfield Public Schools
West Bloomfield, MI

Andrea Coles
Mathematics Teacher
Mountain View Middle School
Blackfoot, ID

Julie Johnson
Mathematics/CS teacher (9 - 12)
Williamsville Central Schools
Williamsville, NY

Tamar McPherson
Plum Sr HS/Math Teacher
Plum School District
Pittsburgh, PA

Melisa Rice
Math Department Chairperson
Shawnee Public Schools
Shawnee, OK

Ben Wilson
Camille Casteel HS Teacher
Chandler Unified School District
Chandler, AZ

Erin Zitka
6-12 Math Coordinator
Forsyth County
Cumming, GA

Jeff Ziegler
Teacher
Pittsburgh City Schools
Pittsburgh, PA

Authors

Dan Kennedy, Ph.D
- Classroom teacher and the Lupton Distinguished Professor of Mathematics at the Baylor School in Chattanooga, TN
- Co-author of textbooks Precalculus: Graphical, Numerical, Algebraic and Calculus: Graphical, Numerical, Algebraic, AP Edition
- Past chair of the College Board's AP Calculus Development Committee.
- Previous Tandy Technology Scholar and Presidential Award winner

Eric Milou, Ed.D
- Professor of Mathematics, Rowan University, Glassboro, NJ
- Member of the author team for Pearson's **enVision**math**2.0** 6-8
- Member of National Council of Teachers of Mathematics (NCTM) feedback/advisory team for the Common Core State Standards
- Author of *Teaching Mathematics to Middle School Students*

Christine D. Thomas, Ph.D
- Professor of Mathematics Education at Georgia State University, Atlanta, GA
- Past-President of the Association of Mathematics Teacher Educators (AMTE)
- Past NCTM Board of Directors Member
- Past member of the editorial panel of the NCTM journal *Mathematics Teacher*
- Past co-chair of the steering committee of the North American chapter of the International Group of the Psychology of Mathematics Education

Rose Mary Zbiek, Ph.D
- Professor of Mathematics Education, Pennsylvania State University, College Park, PA
- Series editor for the NCTM *Essential Understanding* project

Contributing Author

Al Cuoco, Ph.D
- Lead author of CME Project, a National Science Foundation (NSF)-funded high school curriculum
- Team member to revise the Conference Board of the Mathematical Sciences (CBMS) recommendations for teacher preparation and professional development
- Co-author of several books published by the Mathematical Association of America and the American Mathematical Society
- Consultant to the writers of the Common Core State Standards for Mathematics and the PARCC Content Frameworks for high school mathematics

About :enVision Integrated
MATHEMATICS I

enVision® Integrated Mathematics I offers a carefully constructed lesson design to help you succeed in math.

Step 1 At the start of each lesson, you and your classmates will work together to come up with a solution strategy for the problem or task posed. After a class discussion, you'll be asked to reflect back on the processes and strategies you used in solving the problem.

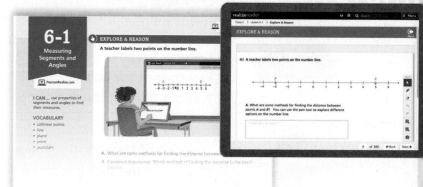

Step 2 Next, your teacher will guide you through new concepts and skills for the lesson.

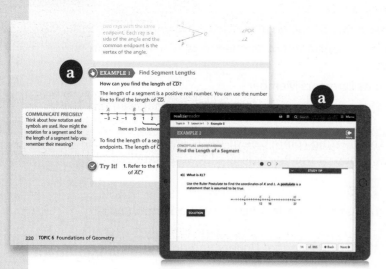

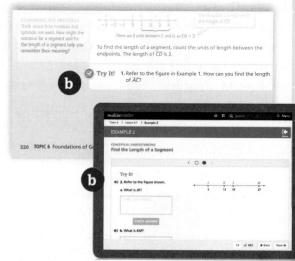

After each example **a**, you work out a problem called the **Try It! b** to solidify your understanding of these concepts.

In addition, you will periodically answer **Habits of Min**d **c** questions to refine your thinking and problem-solving skills.

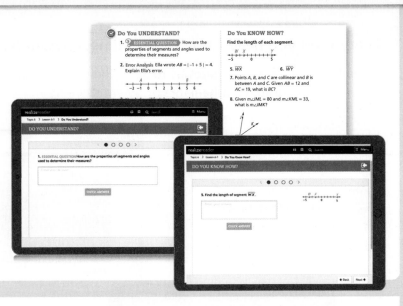

Step 2 cont.

This part of the lesson concludes with a Lesson Check that helps you to know how well you are understanding the new content presented in the lesson. With the exercises in the **Do You Understand?** and **Do You Know How?**, you can gauge your understanding of the lesson concepts.

Step 3

In Step 3, you will find a balanced exercise set with **Understand** exercises that focus on conceptual understanding, **Practice** exercises that target procedural fluency, and **Apply** exercises for which you apply concept and skills to real-world situations **d**.

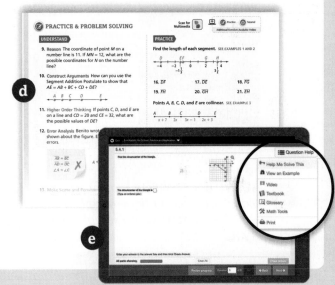

The **Assessment and Practice** **e** exercises offer practice for high stakes assessments. Your teacher may have you complete the assignment in your Student Edition, Student Companion, or online at SavvasRealize.com.

Step 4

Your teacher may have you take the Lesson Quiz after each lesson. You can take the quiz online or in print. To do your best on the quiz, review the lesson problems in that lesson.

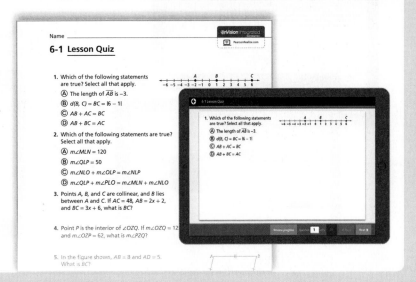

Digital Resources

Everything you need for math, anytime, anywhere.

SavvasRealize.com is your gateway to all of the digital resources for **enVision**® Integrated Mathematics I.

INTERACTIVE STUDENT EDITION

Log in to access your interactive student edition, called Realize Reader.

ANIMATION View and interact with real-world applications.

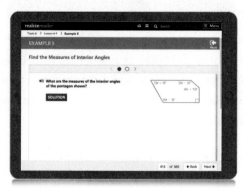

ACTIVITIES Complete *Explore & Reason*, *Model & Discuss*, *Critique & Explain* activities. Interact with *Examples* and *Try Its*.

PRACTICE

Practice what you've learned.

VIDEOS Watch clips to support Mathematical Modeling in 3 Acts Lessons and **enVision**® STEM Projects.

ASSESSMENT Show what you've learned.

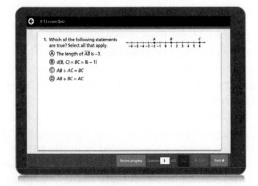

TUTORIALS Get help from Virtual Nerd, right when you need it.

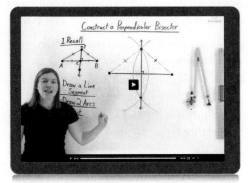

CONCEPT SUMMARY Review key lesson content through multiple representations.

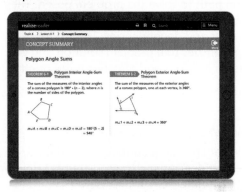

GLOSSARY Read and listen to English and Spanish definitions.

MATH TOOLS Explore math with digital tools and manipulatives.

Mathematical Practices and Processes

Problem Solving

Make sense of problems and persevere in solving them.

Proficient math thinkers are able to read through a problem situation and can put together a workable solution path to solve the problem posed. They analyze the information provided and identify constraints and dependencies. They identify multiple entries to a problem solution and will choose an efficient and effective entry point.

Consider these questions to help you make sense of problems.

- What am I asked to find?
- What are the quantities and variables? The dependencies and the constraints? How do they relate?
- What are some possible strategies to solve the problem?

Attend to precision.

Proficient math thinkers communicate clearly and precisely the approach they are using. They identify the meaning of symbols that they use and always remember to specify units of measure and to label accurately graphical models. They use mathematical terms precisely and express their answers with the appropriate degree of accuracy.

Consider these questions to help you attend to precision.

- Have I stated the meaning of the variables and symbols I am using?
- Have I specified the units of measure I am using?
- Have I calculate accurately?

Reasoning and Communicating

Reason abstractly and quantitatively.

Proficient math thinkers make sense of quantities in problem situations. They represent a problem situation using symbols or equations and explain what the symbols or equation represent in relationship to a problem situation. As they model a situation symbolically or mathematically, they explain the meaning of the quantities.

Consider these questions to help you reason abstractly and quantitatively.

- How can I represent the problem using equations or formulas?
- What do the numbers, variables, and symbols in the equation or formula represent?

Construct viable arguments and critique the reasoning of others.

Proficient math thinkers and problem solvers communicate their problem solutions clearly and convincingly. They construct sound mathematical arguments and develop and defend conjectures to explain mathematical situations. They make use of examples and counterexamples to support their arguments and justify their conclusions. When asked, they respond clearly and logically to the positions and conclusions of others, and compare two arguments, identifying any flaws in logic or reasoning that the arguments may contain. They ask questions to clarify or improve the position of a classmate.

Consider these questions to help you construct mathematical arguments.

- What assumptions can I make when constructing an argument?
- What conjectures can I make about the solution to the problem?
- What arguments can I present to defend my conjectures?

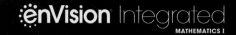

Representing and Connecting

Model with mathematics.

Proficient math thinkers use mathematics to represent a problem situation and make connections between a real-world problem situation and mathematics. They see the applicability of mathematics to solve every-day problems and explain how geometry can be used to solve a carpentry problem or algebra to solve a proportional relationship problem. They define and map relationships among quantities in a problem, using appropriate tools. They analyze the relationships and draw conclusions about the solutions.

Consider these questions to help you model with mathematics.

- What representations can I use to show the relationship among quantities or variables?
- What assumptions can I make about the problem situation to simplify the problem?

Use appropriate tools strategically.

Proficient math thinkers strategize about which tools are more helpful to solve a problem situation. They consider all tools, from paper and pencil to protractors and rulers, to calculators and software applications. They articulate the appropriateness of different tools and recognize which would best serve the needs for a given problem. They are especially insightful about technological tools and use them in ways that deepen or extend their understanding of concepts. They also make use of mental tools, such as estimation, to determine the appropriateness of a solution.

Consider these questions to help you use appropriate tools.

- What tool can I use to help me solve the problem?
- How can technology help me solve the problem?

Seeing Patterns and Generalizing

Look for and make use of patterns.

Proficient math thinkers see mathematical patterns in the problems they are solving and generalize mathematics principles from these patterns. They see complicated expressions or equations as single objects composed of many parts.

Consider these questions to help you see structure.

- Can I see a pattern in the problem or solution strategy?
- How can I use the pattern I see to help me solve the problem?

Look for generalizations.

Proficient math thinkers notice when calculations are repeated and can uncover both general methods and shortcuts for solving similar problems.

Consider these questions to help you look for regularity in repeated reasoning.

- Do I notice any repeated calculations or steps?
- Are there general methods that I can use to solve the problem?
- What can I generalize from one problem to another?
- How reasonable are the results that I am getting?

MATHEMATICAL PRACTICES AND PROCESSES

Key Concepts in Integrated Mathematics I

Proficiency with key concepts and skills of Integrated Mathematics I is often cited as a requisite for college- and career- readiness. These foundational concepts of algebraic and geometric thinking provide the gateway to advanced mathematics.

Listed below are the key concepts that you will be studying in **enVision Integrated Mathematics I.**

Solving Equations and Inequalities

- Equations and inequalities in two or more variables represent relationships between quantities. They can be used to model real-world situations.
- Rearranging an equation, using the same reasoning as in solving equations, reveals key information about a quantity of interest.
- Each step in solving an equation can be explained and justified mathematically.
- Properties of real numbers and equality hold for all types of equations. These properties, along with properties of inequality, can be applied to solve any equation or inequality.
- Equations and inequalities in two or more variables can represent constraints of the context they represent.
- A system of equations can have no solutions, one solution, or infinitely many solutions.
- A system of inequalities has infinitely many solutions.
- The solutions to equations and inequalities in two or more variables can be graphed in a coordinate plane.
- The solutions to equations and inequalities in two or more variables can be interpreted as viable or non-viable in relationship to the context represented.
- The graph of an equation in two variables is the set of all its solutions plotted in the coordinate plane.
- The graph of the solution to a linear inequality in two variables is a half-plane on a coordinate plane.
- The graph of the solution to a system of linear inequalities in two variables is the intersection of the corresponding half-planes.
- A system of linear equations can be solved by graphing the system or through algebraic manipulation.
- Linear equations can be solved algebraically through substitution or elimination.

A Study of Functions

- A function describes a relationship between two quantities. A function consists of inputs, called the domain, and outputs, called the range.
- A function can be written using function notation.
- A function can be rewritten in different forms. Each form reveals different information about the context it models.
- A function can be evaluated for inputs in its domain.
- A function can be represented in different ways: algebraically, in a graph, in a table, or by a verbal description.
- A function has parameters that can be interpreted in terms of the context it models.
- The domain and range of a function may be restricted based on the contextual situation.
- Key features of the graph of a function reveal information about the relationship between the two quantities that the function models.
- A table of values of a function has key features that reveal information about the relationship between the two quantities that the function models.
- The properties of two (or more) functions of the same type can be compared even when the functions are represented in different ways (algebraically, graphically, numerically in tables, or by verbal descriptions).

Linear Functions and Equations

- A linear function represents a situation in which one quantity changes at a constant rate per unit interval relative to another quantity.
- A linear function grows by equal differences over equal intervals.
- The graph of a linear function is a straight line that can show *x*- and *y*-intercepts.
- An arithmetic sequence is a type of linear function. It can be defined recursively or explicitly. It can be used to model a real-world situation.
- The domain of an arithmetic sequence is a subset of the integers.
- In a linear function, the slope represents the rate of change and the *y*-intercept represents a constant term. These parameters have meaning in the context of a situation or data set.
- Linear equations or functions can be used to represent and solve real-world and mathematical problems.
- A correlation coefficient represents the goodness of fit of a data set to a linear model.

Key Concepts in Integrated Mathematics I

Exponential Functions and Equations

- An exponential function grows by equal factors over equal intervals.
- An exponential function represents a situation in which a quantity grows or decays by a constant rate per unit interval relative to another.
- A geometric sequence is a type of exponential function. It can be defined recursively or explicitly. It can be used to model a real-world situation.
- The domain of a geometric sequence is a subset of the integers.
- The graph of an exponential function shows x- and y-intercepts, when appropriate, and end behavior.
- A quantity that increases exponentially eventually exceeds a quantity increasing linearly or quadratically.
- The parameters of an exponential function reveal important information about the context that the function represents.
- The properties of exponents can be used to interpret expressions for exponential functions.
- The properties of exponents can be used to transform expressions for exponential functions.

Foundations of Geometry

- The foundation of geometry is based on undefined notions of point, line, plane, distance along a line, and distance around a circular arc.
- Postulates and axioms are assumed to be true; whereas theorems and corollaries need to be proven.
- Theorems and corollaries about lines, angles, and figures can be proven using postulates, axioms, definitions, and other theorems.
- Two lines with the same slope are parallel while two lines whose slopes are opposite reciprocals are perpendicular.
- The coordinates of a polygon in a coordinate grid can be used to compute perimeters of polygons and areas of triangles and rectangles.
- Some geometric theorems can be proven algebraically by using coordinates of figures in a coordinate plane.
- Inductive reasoning is a tool to develop conjectures.
- Deductive reasoning is a way to formally construct a valid argument.
- Using laws of logic aids in the process of determining the validity of a statement.

Angle Relationships

- If the measure of one angle formed when a pair of parallel lines is cut by a transversal is known, then the measures of the other angles can be determined.
- Special angle pair measurements can be used to prove that two lines are parallel.

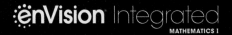

Congruence

- Transformations in the plane take points in the plane as inputs and give other points as outputs.
- Some transformations, such as translations, reflections, and rotations preserve distance and angle.
- A series of transformations can carry a given figure onto another.
- The definition of congruence in terms of rigid motions can be used to determine whether two figures are congruent.
- Two triangles are congruent if and only if corresponding pairs of sides and corresponding pairs of angles are congruent.
- The criteria for triangle congruence – Angle-Side-Angle, Side-Angle-Side, and Side-Side-Side – follow from the definition of congruence in terms of rigid motions.
- Congruence criteria for triangles can be used to solve problems and to prove relationships in geometric figures.

Statistics

- Data can be represented using a variety of displays. Some data can be plotted on the real number line to create dot plots, histograms, and box plots.
- The shape of the data distribution reveals key information about the center and spread of the data set. It can also reveal extreme outliers in the data set.
- Comparing the shapes of the data distribution for two different data sets reveals important information about the data sets.
- Two-way frequency tables can be used to summarize categorical data for two categories.
- The relative frequencies – joint, marginal, and conditional relative frequencies – of a data set can be interpreted to reveal possible associations or trends in the data.
- Data on two quantitative variables can be represented in a scatter plot. The scatter plot can show how the variables are related.
- A function can be fit to a data set. The function fitted to a data set can be used to solve problems in the context of the data. The function is often linear or exponential.
- The context of a data set may suggest the type of function that fits the data.
- The fit of a function to a data set can be informally assessed by plotting and analyzing residuals.
- Correlation suggests that the behavior of one variable is linked to the behavior of a second variable. Causation indicates that the behavior of one variable is caused by the behavior of a second variable.

TOPIC 4

Systems of Linear Equations and Inequalities

Exponents and Exponential Functions

Foundations of Geometry

Parallel and Perpendicular Lines

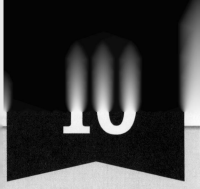

TOPIC 1

Solving Equations and Inequalities

? TOPIC ESSENTIAL QUESTION

What general strategies can you use to solve simple equations and inequalities?

Topic Overview

enVision® STEM Project:
Design a Smartphone

1-1 Solving Linear Equations

1-2 Solving Equations with a Variable on Both Sides

1-3 Literal Equations and Formulas

1-4 Solving Inequalities in One Variable

Mathematical Modeling in 3 Acts:
Collecting Cans

1-5 Compound Inequalities

1-6 Absolute Value Equations and Inequalities

Topic Vocabulary

- compound inequality
- formula
- identity
- literal equation

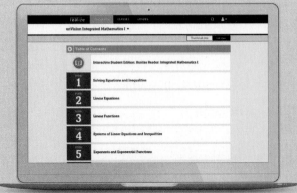

Digital Experience

INTERACTIVE STUDENT EDITION
Access online or offline.

ACTIVITIES Complete *Explore & Reason, Model & Discuss*, and *Critique & Explain* activities. Interact with Examples and Try Its.

ANIMATION View and interact with real-world applications.

PRACTICE Practice what you've learned.

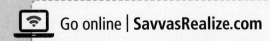 Go online | **SavvasRealize.com**

▶ Collecting Cans

Many schools and community centers organize canned food drives and donate the food collected to area food pantries or homeless shelters.

A teacher may hold a contest for the student who collects the most cans. The teacher will track the number of cans each student brings in. Sometimes students have their own ways of keeping track. You'll see how some students kept track in the Mathematical Modeling in 3 Acts lesson.

TOPIC 1

VIDEOS Watch clips to support *Mathematical Modeling in 3 Acts Lessons* and **enVision® STEM Projects**.

CONCEPT SUMMARY Review key lesson content through multiple representations.

ASSESSMENT Show what you've learned.

A-Z GLOSSARY Read and listen to English and Spanish definitions.

TUTORIALS Get help from *Virtual Nerd*, right when you need it.

MATH TOOLS Explore math with digital tools and manipulatives.

Did You Know?

The average American teenager spends about **9 hours each day** on a digital device.

● **90%** of Americans own a cellphone
● **64%** of Americans own a smartphone

In general, people keep their cellphones on and with them at all times.

1 GB ≈ **250 songs** ≈ **435 photos** ≈ **5 mins of HD video**

How Teens Spend Their Screen Time

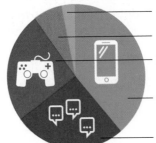

- **3%** creating digital content
- **7%** other
- **25%** playing games or browsing the Internet
- **39%** watching video, listening to music, or reading
- **26%** using social media

▶ Your Task: Design a Smartphone

Smartphones are many things to many people. You and your classmates will decide what a new smartphone will be able to do, how you want it to look and feel, and how much storage it should have.

📶 Go Online | SavvasRealize.com

1-1

Solving Linear Equations

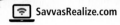 SavvasRealize.com

I CAN... create and solve linear equations with one variable.

👆 **MODEL & DISCUSS**

Joshua is going kayaking with a group during one of his vacation days. In his vacation planning, he budgeted $50 for a kayak rental.

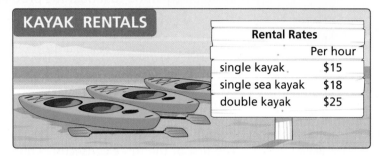

KAYAK RENTALS	Rental Rates	
		Per hour
	single kayak	$15
	single sea kayak	$18
	double kayak	$25

A. How can Joshua determine the number of hours he can rent a kayak for himself? Describe two different options.

B. Joshua found out that there is a $25 nonrefundable equipment fee in addition to the hourly rates. How does this requirement change the mathematics of the situation?

C. **Look for Relationships** How do the processes you used for parts A and B differ? How are they the same?

❓ **ESSENTIAL QUESTION**   How do you create equations and use them to solve problems?

CONCEPTUAL UNDERSTANDING

👆 **EXAMPLE 1**   Solve Linear Equations

What is the value of x in the equation $\frac{2(x+4)}{3} - 8 = 32$?

VOCABULARY
Remember, a *variable* is an unknown quantity, or a quantity that can vary. An *equation* is a mathematical statement with two expressions set equal to each other. A *solution of an equation* is a value for the variable that makes the equation a true statement.

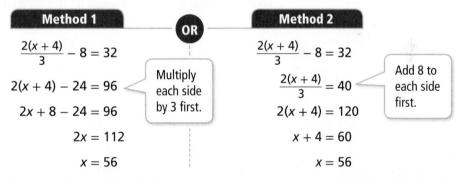

Method 1		OR	Method 2	

Method 1

$$\frac{2(x+4)}{3} - 8 = 32$$

$$2(x+4) - 24 = 96$$ Multiply each side by 3 first.

$$2x + 8 - 24 = 96$$

$$2x = 112$$

$$x = 56$$

Method 2

$$\frac{2(x+4)}{3} - 8 = 32$$

$$\frac{2(x+4)}{3} = 40$$ Add 8 to each side first.

$$2(x+4) = 120$$

$$x + 4 = 60$$

$$x = 56$$

Each solving method yields the same solution. Is one method better than the other?

Look at how the expression on the left side of the original equation is built up from x.

$$x \rightarrow x+4 \rightarrow 2(x+4) \rightarrow \frac{2(x+4)}{3} \rightarrow \frac{2(x+4)}{3} - 8$$

Notice how Method 2 applies these steps in reverse to isolate x. This is often a good strategy and can lead to simpler solution methods.

☑ **Try It!**   **1.** Solve the equation $4 + \frac{3x-1}{2} = 9$. Explain the reasons why you chose your solution method.

👆 **EXAMPLE 2** **Solve Consecutive Integer Problems**

The sum of three consecutive integers is 132. What are the three integers?

Write an equation to model the problem. Then solve.

$$x + (x + 1) + (x + 2) = 132$$

$$3x + 3 = 132$$

The three integers are consecutive, so each is 1 greater than the previous.

Combine like terms.

$$3x + 3 - 3 = 132 - 3$$

$$\frac{3x}{3} = \frac{129}{3}$$

$$x = 43$$

STUDY TIP
You can check the solution by substituting the value in the original equation.

The first of the three consecutive numbers is 43.
The three consecutive numbers whose sum is 132 are 43, 44, 45.

☑ **Try It!** **2.** The sum of three consecutive odd integers is 57. What are the three integers?

APPLICATION 👆 **EXAMPLE 3** **Use Linear Equations to Solve Mixture Problems**

A lab technician needs 25 liters of a solution that is 15% acid for a certain experiment, but she has only a solution that is 10% acid and a solution that is 30% acid. How many liters of the 10% and the 30% solutions should she mix to get what she needs?

Formulate ◀ Write an equation relating the number of liters of acid in each solution. Represent the total number of liters of one solution with a variable, like x. Then the total number of liters of the other solution must be $25 - x$.

25 L of 15% solution = x L of 10% solution + $(25 - x)$ L of 30% solution

$$(0.15)(25) = 0.10x + 0.30(25 - x)$$

Compute ◀

$$3.75 = 0.1x + 7.5 - 0.3x$$

$$3.75 - 7.5 = 0.1x - 0.3x + 7.5 - 7.5$$

Subtract 7.5 from each side

$$-3.75 = -0.2x$$

$$3.75 = 0.2x$$

$$\frac{3.75}{0.2} = \frac{0.2x}{0.2}$$

Divide each side by 0.2.

$$18.75 = x$$

Interpret ◀ Since x represents the number of liters of the 10% acid solution, the lab technician should use 18.75 liters of the 10% solution. Since $25 - x$ represents the number of liters of the 30% acid solution, she should use $25 - 18.75$, or 6.25 liters of the 30% solution.

☑ **Try It!** **3.** If the lab technician needs 30 liters of a 25% acid solution, how many liters of the 10% and the 30% acid solutions should she mix to get what she needs?

APPLICATION   **EXAMPLE 4**   **Use Linear Equations to Solve Problems**

Four friends use an online coupon to get discounts on concert tickets. They spent $312 for the four tickets. What was the price of one ticket without the discount?

Your online order is complete.

Your order details are shown below for your reference.

ORDER # 328
Sec B, Row 10, Seats 13-16

	Quantity	Price
Tickets	4	?
Discount	$15.00	4 x $15.00
Order Total		**$312**

Step 1 Write an equation to represent the problem situation.

Let p represent the original ticket price.

4 • original ticket price minus $15 = $312

$$4(p - 15) = 312$$

> **COMMON ERROR**
> Subtract 15 from the price of each ticket, not from the total cost of four undiscounted tickets.

Step 2 Solve the equation.

$$4(p - 15) = 312$$
$$\frac{4(p - 15)}{4} = \frac{312}{4}$$
$$p - 15 = 78$$
$$p - 15 + 15 = 78 + 15$$
$$p = 93$$

The ticket price without the discount was $93.

 Try It!   **4.** The same four friends buy tickets for two shows on consecutive nights. They use a coupon for $5 off each ticket. They pay a total of $416 for 8 tickets. Write and solve an equation to find the original price of the tickets.

 **EXAMPLE 5** **Solve Work and Time Problems**

LaTanya will walk her bike from her house to the bike shop, which is 1.5 mi from her house, to get the bike fixed. She expects to wait 30 min for the repair. Then she will ride her bike home. Can she be home in one hour?

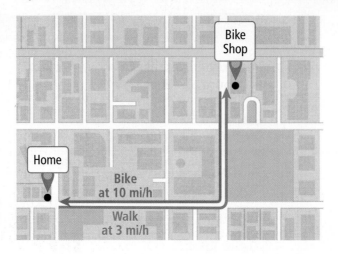

Step 1 Write an equation to represent the situation.

Time walking + Time at the shop + Time biking = Total time

$$\frac{1.5 \text{ miles}}{3 \text{ miles per hour}} + \frac{1}{2} \text{ hour} + \frac{1.5 \text{ miles}}{10 \text{ miles per hour}} = t$$

The equation $\frac{1.5}{3} + \frac{1}{2} + \frac{1.5}{10} = t$ represents the situation.

MAKE SENSE AND PERSEVERE
Look for relationships between the distance traveled and the rate when you write the equation.

Step 2 Solve for t.

$$\frac{1.5}{3} + \frac{1}{2} + \frac{1.5}{10} = t$$

$$(30)\frac{1.5}{3} + (30)\frac{1}{2} + (30)\frac{1.5}{10} = 30t$$

> Multiply each side by the least common denominator.

$$15 + 15 + 4.5 = 30t$$

$$\frac{34.5}{30} = \frac{30t}{30}$$

$$1.15 = t$$

It will take LaTanya 1.15 h, or 1 h 9 min to get home after leaving to get her bike repaired. She will need more than 1 h.

 Try It! **5.** LaTanya leaves her house at 12:30 P.M. and bikes at 12 mi/h to Marta's house. She stays at Marta's house for 90 min. Both girls walk back to LaTanya's house along the same route at 2.5 mi/h. They arrive at LaTanya's house at 3:30 P.M. How far is Marta's house from LaTanya's house?

Go Online | SavvasRealize.com

CONCEPT SUMMARY Create and Solve Linear Equations

Use the following information about Kelsey's visit to the flower shop.

- Kelsey bought some roses and tulips.
- She bought twice as many tulips as roses.
- Roses cost $5 each.
- Tulips cost $2 each.
- Kelsey spent $36 total.

How many of each kind of flower did Kelsey buy?

WORDS ▶ Write an equation to represent the situation.

| Cost of Roses | + | Cost of Tulips | = Total Cost |

(Cost of One Rose)(Number of Roses) + (Cost of One Tulip)(Number of Tulips) = Total Cost

ALGEBRA ▶ $\$5 \cdot x + \$2 \cdot 2x = \$36$

$$5x + 4x = 36$$
$$9x = 36$$
$$x = 4$$

Kelsey bought 4 roses and 8 tulips.

Do You UNDERSTAND?

1. **ESSENTIAL QUESTION** How do you create equations and use them to solve problems?

2. **Reason** What is a first step to solving for x in the equation $9x - 7 = 10$? How would you check your solution?

3. **Use Structure** For an equation with fractions, why is it helpful to multiply both sides of the equation by the LCD?

4. **Error Analysis** Venetta knows that 1 mi ≈ 1.6 km. To convert 5 mi/h to km/h, she multiplies 5 mi/h by $\frac{1 \text{ mi}}{1.6 \text{ km}}$. What error does Venetta make?

Do You KNOW HOW?

Solve each equation.

5. $4b + 14 = 22$

6. $-6k - 3 = 39$

7. $15 - 2(3 - 2x) = 46$

8. $\frac{2}{3}y - \frac{2}{5} = 5$

9. Terrence walks at a pace of 2 mi/h to the theater and watches a movie for 2 h and 15 min. He rides back home, taking the same route, on the bus that travels at a rate of 40 mi/h. The entire trip takes 3.5 h. How far along this route is Terrence's house from the theater? Explain.

UNDERSTAND

10. Use Structure What could be a first step to solving the equation $3x + -0.5(x + 3) + 4 = 14$? Explain.

11. Make Sense and Persevere The sum of four consecutive integers is -18. What is the greatest of these integers?

12. Error Analysis Describe and correct the error a student made when solving the equation $4 = -2(x - 3)$. What is the correct solution?

$$4 = -2(x - 3)$$
$$4 = -2x - 6$$
$$4 + 6 = -2x - 6 + 6$$
$$10 = -2x$$
$$\frac{10}{-2} = \frac{-2x}{-2}$$
$$-5 = x \quad ✗$$

13. Communicate Precisely Parker ran on a treadmill at a constant speed for the length of time shown. How many miles did Parker run? Explain.

6.00 mph   27:39 time

14. Reason The Division Property of Equality says that for every real number a, b, and c, if $a = b$ and $c \neq 0$, then $\frac{a}{c} = \frac{b}{c}$. Why does the property state that $c \neq 0$?

15. Higher Order Thinking Tonya's first step in solving the equation $\frac{1}{2}(2y + 4) = -6$ is to use the Distributive Property on the left side of the equation. Deon's first step is to multiply each side by 2. Which of these methods will result in an equivalent equation? Explain.

PRACTICE

Solve each equation. SEE EXAMPLES 1 AND 2

16. $-4x + 3x = 2$

17. $7 = 5y - 13 - y$

18. $7m - 4 - 9m - 36 = 0$

19. $-2 = -5t + 10 + 2t$

Solve each equation. SEE EXAMPLES 3 AND 4

20. $2(2x + 1) = 26$

21. $-2(2z + 1) = 26$

22. $92 = -4(2r - 5)$

23. $10(5 - n) - 1 = 29$

24. $-(7 - 2x) + 7 = -7$

25. $200 = 16(6t - 3)$

Solve each equation. SEE EXAMPLE 5

26. $\frac{1}{2}x + 2 = 1$

27. $\frac{3}{2}x - \frac{2}{3}x = 2$

28. $\frac{1}{5}(k - 3) = \frac{3}{4}$

29. $\frac{7}{60} = \frac{5}{24}w + \frac{11}{12}$

30. $\frac{3m}{4} - \frac{m}{12} = \frac{7}{8}$

31. $1{,}290 = \frac{h}{10} + \frac{h}{5}$

Solve each equation.

32. $0.1r - 1 = 0.65$

33. $1.2n + 0.68 = 5$

34. $0.025(q + 2) = 2.81$

35. $-0.07p - 0.6 = 5$

36. $1.037x + 0.02x + 25 = 30.285$

37. $-0.85t - 0.85t - 3.9 = -8.15$

38. A bee flies at 20 feet per second directly to a flowerbed from its hive. The bee stays at the flowerbed for 15 minutes, then flies directly back to the hive at 12 feet per second. It is away from the hive for a total of 20 minutes. SEE EXAMPLE 5

a. What equation can you use to find the distance of the flowerbed from the hive?

b. How far is the flowerbed from the hive?

APPLY

39. Reason A fastpitch softball player signs a six-year contract. Her agent expects that she will earn $1,000,000 over the next six years. If the agent is right, how many bonus payments, on average, should the pitcher expect each year? Explain.

40. Make Sense and Persevere There are nine water bottles in Devin's refrigerator. He adds three full boxes of water bottles to the refrigerator. Then he adds two more boxes that each have 1 fewer bottle than a full box. When he is done, there are 67 bottles in the refrigerator. Write and solve an equation to find the number of bottles in a full box.

41. Construct Arguments Yuson used her calculator to solve the equation $\frac{4}{5}x - 8 = 3$. She entered the following on her screen and got an incorrect answer. How could she use parentheses to find the correct answer? Explain. What is the correct answer?

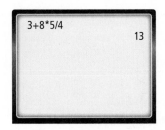

42. Communicate Precisely A scientist makes an acid solution by adding drops of acid to 1.2 L of water. The final volume of the acid solution is 1.202 L. Assuming the volume of each drop is 0.05 mL, how many drops were added to the water? About what percent of the solution is acid? Round to the nearest hundredth of a percent.

ASSESSMENT PRACTICE

43. Anna bought 8 tetras and 2 rainbow fish for her aquarium. The rainbow fish cost $6 more than the tetras. She paid a total of $37. Which of the following are true? Select all that apply.

Ⓐ The cost of 4 tetras is the same as the cost of a rainbow fish.

Ⓑ One rainbow fish plus 5 tetras cost $21.

Ⓒ An equation to find the cost r, in dollars, of a rainbow fish is $8r + 2(r + 6) = 37$

Ⓓ Reducing the number of rainbow fish by 1 would result in a total cost of $28.50.

Ⓔ An equation to find the cost t, in dollars, of a tetra t is $8t + 2t + 6 = 37$.

44. SAT/ACT What is the solution of $1,200 - 5(3x + 30) = 600$?

Ⓐ 30   Ⓑ 50   Ⓒ 150   Ⓓ 200   Ⓔ 250

45. Performance Task A mason will lay rows of bricks to build a wall. The mason will spread $\frac{3}{8}$ inch of mortar on top of all but the last row of bricks. The finished wall will be $1\frac{1}{8}$ inch less than 4 feet high.

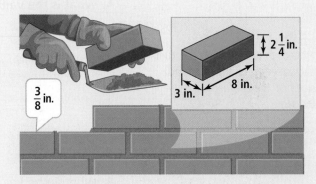

Part A The mason wants to lay the bricks so that the shortest edge of each brick is vertical. How many rows of bricks are needed? Show your work.

Part B Suppose the mason decides to lay bricks so that the 3-inch edge is vertical. If the mason lays the same number of rows of bricks that were used for the wall described in Part A, how high will this wall be?

1-2

Solving Equations With a Variable on Both Sides

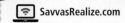 SavvasRealize.com

I CAN... write and solve equations with a variable on both sides to solve problems.

VOCABULARY
• identity

Activity   Assess

EXPLORE & REASON

Some friends want to see a movie that is showing at two different theaters in town. They plan to share three tubs of popcorn during the movie.

	Theater A	Theater B
Ticket Price	$14.50	$13.00
Popcorn	$5.75	$6.75

A. Construct Arguments Which movie theater should the friends choose? Explain.

B. For what situation would the total cost at each theater be exactly the same? Explain.

C. There are different methods to solving this problem. Which do you think is the best? Why?

ESSENTIAL QUESTION

How do you create equations with a variable on both sides and use them to solve problems?

EXAMPLE 1 Solving Equations With a Variable on Both Sides

A. What is the value of x in the equation shown?

$$3x - 10 + 4x = -2(x - 4) + 9$$

Combine like terms.

$$7x - 10 = -2x + 8 + 9$$ — Distribute the -2.

$$7x + 2x = 8 + 9 + 10$$ — Collect like terms on the same side of the equation.

$$9x = 27$$

$$\frac{9x}{9} = \frac{27}{9}$$

$$x = 3$$

STUDY TIP
It does not matter if you add 10 to each side first or add $2x$ to each side first. Either order will result in the same equation, $9x = 27$.

B. What is the value of n in the equation shown?

$$\frac{1}{2}(n - 4) - 7 = -2n + 6$$

$$\frac{1}{2}(n - 4) = -2n + 13$$ — Multiply each side by 2 to eliminate the fraction.

$$n - 4 = -4n + 26$$

$$n + 4n = 26 + 4$$ — Collect like terms on the same side of the equation.

$$5n = 30$$

$$n = 6$$

Try It! 1. Solve each equation.

a. $100(z - 0.2) = -10(5z + 0.8)$ **b.** $\frac{5}{8}(16d + 24) = 6(d - 1) + 1$

👆 **EXAMPLE 2** ▷ Understand Equations With Infinitely Many or No Solutions

A. What is the value of x in $4x + 6 = 2(2x + 3)$?

Use algebra tiles to represent and solve $4x + 6 = 2(2x + 3)$.

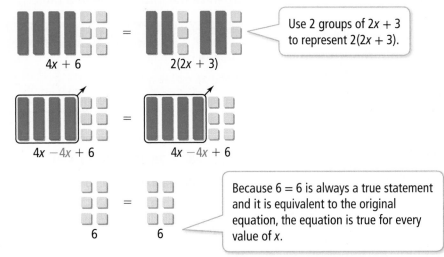

Use 2 groups of $2x + 3$ to represent $2(2x + 3)$.

$4x + 6$ $2(2x + 3)$

$4x - 4x + 6$ $4x - 4x + 6$

Because $6 = 6$ is always a true statement and it is equivalent to the original equation, the equation is true for every value of x.

6   6

The equation $4x + 6 = 2(2x + 3)$ is true for all values of x.

An equation that is true for all values of the variables is an **identity**.

B. What is the value of x in $6x - 5 = 2(3x + 4)$?

Solve for x.

$$6x - 5 = 2(3x + 4)$$
$$6x - 5 = 6x + 8$$
$$6x - 6x - 5 = 6x - 6x + 8$$
$$-5 = 8$$

Maintain the equality by subtracting $6x$ from each side.

There is no value of x that makes the equation true. Therefore, the equation has no solution.

> **VOCABULARY**
> Since this equation is true for all values of the variable, it is sometimes referred to as having *infinitely many solutions*.

> **STUDY TIP**
> Recall that you can assign a value to the variable in an equation to check whether the equation is true.

 Try It!   **2.** Solve each equation. Is the equation an identity? Explain.

    a. $t - 27 = -(27 - t)$

    b. $16(4 - 3m) = 96\left(-\dfrac{m}{2} + 1\right)$

APPLICATION   **EXAMPLE 3**   Solve Mixture Problems

Arabica coffee costs $28 per pound and Robusta coffee costs $8.75 per pound. How many pounds of Arabica coffee must you mix with 3 pounds of Robusta coffee to make a blend that costs $15.50 per pound?

Organize the information in a table.

USE APPROPRIATE TOOLS
How are tables helpful in organizing quantities to represent situations algebraically?

	Price ($/lb)	·	Amount (lb)	=	Total cost ($)
Arabica coffee	28.00		a		$28a$
Robusta coffee	8.75		3		26.25
Coffee blend	15.50		$a + 3$		$15.5(a + 3)$

Write an equation to represent the situation.

$$28a + 26.25 = 15.5(a + 3)$$
$$28a + 26.25 = 15.5a + 46.5$$
$$28a - 15.5a = 46.5 - 26.25$$
$$12.5a = 20.25$$
$$a = 1.62$$

You must mix 1.62 pounds of Arabica coffee with 3 pounds of Robusta coffee to make a blend that costs $15.50 per pound.

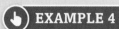 **Try It!**   **3.** How many pounds of Arabica coffee should you mix with 5 pounds of Robusta coffee to make a coffee blend that costs $12.00 per pound?

APPLICATION   **EXAMPLE 4**   Use Equations to Solve Problems

Cameron pays $0.95 per song with his current music service. A new music download service charges $0.89 per song with a $12 joining fee. Should Cameron switch to the new service?

Formulate ◄ Write an equation to represent when the cost for any number of songs, s, is the same for both services.

New music service = Cameron's current music service
$$0.89s + 12 = 0.95s$$

Compute ◄ Solve the equation to find the number of songs at which the cost for each option will be the same.

$$0.89s - 0.89s + 12 = 0.95s - 0.89s$$
$$12 = 0.06s$$
$$\frac{12}{0.06} = \frac{0.06s}{0.06}$$
$$200 = s$$

Interpret ◄ The cost of the two options will be the same for 200 songs.

If Cameron plans to purchase more than 200 songs, he should switch to the new service because it will cost less than his current service.

Music Downloads

Current Plan

$0.95 per song

New Plan

$12.00
TO JOIN

$0.89 per song

CONTINUED ON THE NEXT PAGE

Try It! 4. Cameron's friend tells him of another service that has a $15 joining fee but charges $0.80 per song. At what number of songs does this new service become a less expensive option than Cameron's current service?

 CONCEPT SUMMARY Solve Equations with a Variable on Both Sides

Linear equations can be used to solve mathematical and real-world problems.

WORDS ▸ You can use properties of equality to solve an equation with variables on both sides. Equations can have one solution, infinitely many solutions, or no solution.

NUMBERS ▸

$3x - 6 = 3(x - 2)$

$3x - 6 = 3x - 6$

$3x - 3x - 6 = 3x - 3x - 6$

$-6 = -6$

The equation is true for all values of x. It is an identity. It has infinitely many solutions.

$3x - 2 = 3x - 6$

$3x - 3x - 2 = 3x - 3x + 6$

$-2 = 6$

The equation is not true for any value of x. It has no solutions.

 Do You UNDERSTAND?

1. **? ESSENTIAL QUESTION** How do you create equations with a variable on both sides and use them to solve problems?

2. **Vocabulary** Why does it make sense to describe an equation that has infinitely many solutions as an *identity*?

3. **Error Analysis** Isabel says that the equation $x - 2 = -(x - 2)$ has no solution because a number can never be equal to its opposite. Explain the error Isabel made.

4. **Look For Relationships** You are solving an equation with a variable on each side. Does the side on which you choose to isolate the variable affect the solution? Why might you choose one side over the other?

Do You KNOW HOW?

Solve each equation.

5. $5(2x + 6) = 8x + 48$

6. $-3(8 + 3h) = 5h + 4$

7. $2(y - 6) = 3(y - 4) - y$

8. $8x - 4 = 2(4x - 4)$

9. For how many games is the total cost of bowling equal for the two bowling establishments?

Family Bowling		
Cost (dollars)	Game	4.00
	Shoes	1.00

Knight Owl Bowling		
Cost (dollars)	Game	3.75
	Shoes	2.00

UNDERSTAND ▶

10. Reason Do only equations with variables on both sides ever have no solution? Or can an equation with the variable on one side have no solution? Justify your answer.

11. Generalize How do you know whether an equation is an identity? How many solutions does an identity have? Explain.

12. Error Analysis Describe and correct any error a student may have made when solving the equation $0.15(y - 0.2) = 2 - 0.5(1 - y)$.

$0.15(y - 0.2) = 2 - 0.5(1 - y)$
$0.15y - 0.3 = 2 - 0.5 + 0.5y$
$0.15y - 0.3 = 1.5 + 0.5y$
$(100)(0.15y - 0.3) = 100(1.5 + 0.5y)$
$15y - 30 = 150 + 50y$
$15y - 30 - 15y - 150 = 150 + 50y$
$\qquad\qquad - 15y - 150$
$-180 = 35y$
$-\dfrac{180}{35} = y$

13. Reason When Nicky tried to solve an equation using properties of equality, she ended up with the equation $-3 = -3$. What equation might she have tried to solve? What is the solution of the equation?

14. Mathematical Connections The triangle shown is isosceles. Find the length of each side and the perimeter.

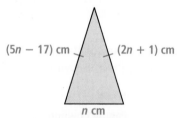

$(5n - 17)$ cm $\qquad (2n + 1)$ cm

n cm

15. Higher Order Thinking The equation shown has a missing value.

$$-2(2x - \blacksquare) + 1 = 17 - 4x$$

a. For what missing value is the equation an identity?

b. For what missing value(s), if any, does the equation have exactly one solution?

c. For what missing value(s), if any, does the equation have no solution?

PRACTICE ▶

Solve each equation. SEE EXAMPLES 1–3

16. $5x - 4 = 4x$

17. $7x = 8x + 12$

18. $27 - 3x = 3x + 27$

19. $34 - 2x = 7x$

20. $5r - 7 = 2r + 14$

21. $-x = 7x - 56$

22. $5(n - 7) = 2(n + 14)$

23. $6w - 33 = 3(4w - 5)$

24. $3(x - 2) = 9x$

25. $6(x + 5) = 3x$

26. $\dfrac{4x + 6}{2} = \dfrac{3x - 15}{3}$

27. $\dfrac{q + 1}{2} = \dfrac{q - 1}{3}$

28. $2c + 3 = 2c + 3$

29. $12b + 9 = 12b + 11$

30. $x - 27 = -(27 - x)$

31. $4(x + 9) = x + 9$

32. $16(4 - 3m) = 96\left(-\dfrac{m}{2} + 1\right)$

33. $6y - 8 = 2(3y - 4)$

34. $5(5t + 1) = 25t - 7$

35. $-3k + 4 = -2 - 6k$

36. $\dfrac{1}{4}(2(x - 1) + 10) = x$

37. $\dfrac{6x + 8}{2} - 4 = 3x$

38. $3y = \dfrac{8 - 12y}{4} + 2$

39. $0.25t = 0.25 - t$

40. $0.625(x + 10) - 10 = 0$

Solve each problem. SEE EXAMPLE 4

41. Tavon has a $50 gift card that loses $2 for each 30-day period it is not used. He has a $40 card that loses $1.50 for each 30-day period it is not used.

a. Write and solve an equation for the number of 30-day periods until the value of the gift cards will be equal.

b. What will the value of each card be when they have equal value?

42. A cereal box manufacturer changes the size of the box to increase the amount of cereal it contains. The equations $12 + 7.6n$ and $6 + 8n$, where n is the number of smaller boxes, are both representative of the amount of cereal that the new larger box contains. How many smaller boxes equal the same amount of cereal in the larger box?

12 oz ? oz

APPLY

43. Model With Mathematics Arthur wants to buy an item that costs p dollars before tax. Using a 6% sales tax rate, write two different expressions that represent the price of the item after tax. Show that the two expressions are equal.

44. Model With Mathematics Two window washers start at the heights shown. One is rising, the other is descending. How long does it take for the two window washers to reach the same height? Explain.

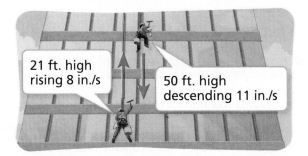

21 ft. high rising 8 in./s

50 ft. high descending 11 in./s

45. Construct Arguments Jamie will choose between two catering companies for an upcoming party. Company A charges a set-up fee of $500 plus $25 for each guest. Company B charges a set-up fee of $200 plus $30 per guest.

a. Write expressions that you can use to determine the amount each company charges for g guests.

b. Jamie learns that the $500 set-up fee for Company A includes payment for 20 guests. The $25 per guest charge is for every guest over the first 20. If there will be 50 guests, which company will cost the least? Explain.

46. Construct Arguments A two-year prepaid membership at Gym A costs $250 for the first year plus $19 per month for the second year. A two-year prepaid membership at Gym B costs $195 for the first year plus $24 per month for the second year. Leah says the cost for both gym memberships will be the same after the 11th month of the second year. Do you agree? Explain.

47. Model With Mathematics A red balloon is 40 feet above the ground and rising at 2 ft/s. At the same time, a blue balloon is at 60 feet above the ground and descending at 3 ft/s. What will the height of the balloons be when they are the same height above the ground?

ASSESSMENT PRACTICE

48. Which equations have no solution? Select all that apply.

Ⓐ $x - 9 = 2(x - 3) + 12$

Ⓑ $5(-2x + 7) + 3 = -10x + 38$

Ⓒ $\frac{1}{2}(6x - 4) = 3(x - 2)$

Ⓓ $0.01x + 0.001 = \frac{1}{100}(x + 10)$

Ⓔ $3(x + 2) + 1 = x + 2(4 + x)$

49. SAT/ACT Which equation is an identity?

Ⓐ $\frac{9x}{15} + 27 = \frac{9x}{15} + \frac{27}{15}$

Ⓑ $3\left(\frac{x}{2} + 16\right) - 16 = \frac{3}{2}x$

Ⓒ $-4(3 - 2x) = -12 - 8x$

Ⓓ $-5\left(\frac{x}{15} - 16\right) - 30 = 50 - \frac{1}{3}x$

Ⓔ $36\left(\frac{3}{4}x - 2\right) + 72 = -72 + 27x$

50. Performance Task Benito and Tyler are painting opposite sides of the same fence. Tyler has already painted $19\frac{1}{2}$ feet of his side of the fence when Benito starts painting.

Benito: Painting rate 15 ft/min

Tyler: Painting rate 11 ft/min

150 ft

Part A How long will it take for the two sides of the fence to have an equal number of feet painted? How many feet will be painted on Benito's side of the fence when the two sides have an equal number of feet painted?

Part B Tyler claims that because he started painting first, he will finish painting his side of the fence before Benito finishes painting his side. Is this true? Explain.

Part C The painter who finishes first gets to rest while the other painter finishes. How long will the painter who finishes first get to rest? Explain.

1-3
Literal Equations and Formulas

 SavvasRealize.com

I CAN... rewrite and use literal equations to solve problems.

VOCABULARY
- formula
- literal equation

👆 MODEL & DISCUSS

Nora drew a nonsquare rectangle. Then she drew the length of each side from end to end to make a line segment to represent the perimeter.

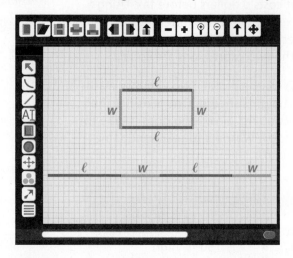

A. Write an equation that represents the perimeter of the model shown.

B. Rearrange the order of the sides so you can represent the perimeter with a different equation. Is this equation equivalent to your first equation?

C. Use Structure How many different ways can you express the relationship in parts A and B? Are any of them more useful than others?

❓ ESSENTIAL QUESTION

How is rewriting literal equations useful when solving problems?

CONCEPTUAL UNDERSTANDING

👆 EXAMPLE 1 ▸ Rewrite Literal Equations

Janet wants to calculate the time it takes to earn a certain amount of interest on a principal amount in an investment with simple interest. What equation can she use?

A **formula** is an equation that states a relationship between one quantity and one or more other quantities. Use the simple interest formula, $I = prt$, and solve for t. The formula $I = prt$ is a **literal equation** because letters represent both variables and known constants.

> I = interest
> p = principle
> r = interest rate
> t = time

VOCABULARY
One definition of *literal* is *of, relating to, or expressed in letters*. A literal equation is an equation expressed in letters, or variables.

$$I = prt$$

$$\frac{I}{pr} = \frac{prt}{pr}$$

$$\frac{I}{pr} = t$$

> You use properties of equality to solve literal equations for a variable just as you do linear equations.

When she writes the equation this way, she can use what she knows (I, p, and r) to calculate what she needs (t).

☑️ Try It!   **1.** What equation can Janet use to calculate the principal amount?

      Go Online | SavvasRealize.com

EXAMPLE 2   Use Literal Equations to Solve Problems

In a half hour, Sarah is meeting her friends at the lake, 6 mi from her house. At what average speed must she ride her bike to get there on time?

Step 1 Solve the distance formula for r.

$$d = rt$$

> Remember, distance = rate • time.

$$\frac{d}{t} = r$$

Step 2 Find the average speed, or rate, at which Sarah must ride her bike to be on time.

$$\frac{d}{t} = r$$

$$\frac{6}{0.5} = r$$

> Substitute 6 for d and 0.5 for t.

$$12 = r$$

Sarah needs to ride her bike at an average speed of 12 mi/h to get to the lake on time.

 Try It!   **2.** Sarah is going to the store 2.5 mi away. She has only 15 min to get there before they close. At what average speed must she ride to get to the store before they close?

EXAMPLE 3   Rewrite a Formula

A worker at a framing store is making a rectangular frame. He knows that the perimeter of the frame is 144 in. and the length is 40 in. How can he determine the width of the frame?

Step 1 Rewrite the perimeter formula $P = 2\ell + 2w$ in terms of w.

$$P - 2\ell = 2\ell + 2w - 2\ell$$

$$\frac{P - 2\ell}{2} = \frac{2w}{2}$$

$$\frac{P - 2\ell}{2} = w$$

40 in.

w

The perimeter formula in terms of w is $w = \frac{P - 2\ell}{2}$.

Step 2 Use the literal equation to solve for w when P is 144 and ℓ is 40.

$$w = \frac{P - 2\ell}{2}$$

$$w = \frac{144 - 2(40)}{2}$$

$$w = \frac{144 - 80}{2} = 32$$

The width of the frame is 32 in.

 Try It!   **3.** Write the formula for the area of a triangle, $A = \frac{1}{2}bh$ in terms of h. Find the height of a triangle when $A = 18$ in.^{2} and $b = 9$ in.

APPLICATION  **EXAMPLE 4** **Apply Formulas**

According to Teo's bread recipe, he should bake the bread at 190°C for 30 minutes. His oven measures temperature in °F. To what temperature in °F should he set his oven?

$C = \frac{5}{9}(F - 32)$

190° C

Formulate ◀ Rewrite the formula to find the Fahrenheit temperature that is equal to 190°C.

Compute ◀ **Step 1** Solve for F.

$$C = \frac{5}{9}(F - 32)$$

$$\frac{9}{5} \cdot C = \frac{9}{5} \cdot \frac{5}{9}(F - 32)$$

> Dividing by a fraction is the same as multiplying by its reciprocal.

$$\frac{9}{5}C = F - 32$$

$$\frac{9}{5}C + 32 = F - 32 + 32$$

$$\frac{9}{5}C + 32 = F$$

Step 2 Use the formula for F to find the Fahrenheit temperature equivalent to 190°C.

$$\frac{9}{5}C + 32 = F$$

$$\frac{9}{5}(190) + 32 = 374$$

Interpret ◀ Teo should set the oven to 374°F.

☑ **Try It!** **4.** The high temperature on a given winter day is 5°F. What is the temperature in °C?

CONCEPT SUMMARY Literal Equations and Formulas

WORDS Literal equations can use letters for both constants and variables. A formula is a kind of literal equation where one quantity is related to one or more other quantities.

To solve for a particular variable in a literal equation, you rewrite the equation, isolating the variable.

ALGEBRA The volume of a rectangular prism is given by the following formula.

$$V = \ell wh$$

To find a formula for h, the height of the prism, solve for h.

$$V = \ell hw$$

$$\frac{V}{\ell w} = \frac{\ell hw}{\ell w} \quad \text{Divide each side by } \ell w.$$

$$\frac{V}{\ell w} = h$$

$$h = \frac{V}{\ell w}$$

Do You UNDERSTAND?

1. **ESSENTIAL QUESTION** How is rewriting literal equations useful when solving problems?

2. **Communicate Precisely** How is solving $2x + c = d$ similar to solving $2x + 1 = 9$ for x? How are they different? How can you use $2x + c = d$ to solve $2x + 1 = 9$?

3. **Vocabulary** Explain how literal equations and formulas are related.

4. **Error Analysis** Dyani began solving the equation $g = \frac{x-1}{k}$ for x by adding 1 to each side. Explain Dyani's error. Then describe how to solve for x.

Do You KNOW HOW?

Solve each literal equation for the given variable.

5. $y = x + 12$; x

6. $n = \frac{4}{5}(m + 7)$; m

7. Use your equation from Exercise 6 to find m when $n = 40$.

8. William got scores of q_1, q_2, and q_3 on three quizzes.

   a. Write a formula for the average x of all three quizzes.

   b. William got an 85 and an 88 on the first two quizzes. What formula can William use to determine the score he needs on the third quiz to get an average of 90? What score does he need?

UNDERSTAND

9. **Mathematical Connections** Some two-step equations can be written in the form $ax + b = c$, where a, b, and c are constants and x is the variable.

   a. Write the equation $ax + b = c$ in terms of x.

   b. Use the formula to solve $3x + 7 = 19$ and $\frac{1}{2}x - 1 = 5$.

10. **Make Sense and Persevere** The flag of the Bahamas includes an equilateral triangle. The perimeter of the triangle is $P = 3s$, where s is the side length. Solve for s. Use your formula to find the dimensions of the flag in feet and the area in square feet when the perimeter of the triangle is 126 inches.

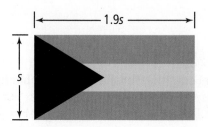

11. **Error Analysis** Describe and correct the error a student made when solving $kx + 3x = 4$ for x.

$$kx + 3x = 4$$
$$kx + 3x - 3x = 4 - 3x$$
$$kx = 4 - 3x$$
$$\frac{kx}{k} = \frac{4 - 3x}{k}$$
$$x = \frac{4 - 3x}{k} \quad ✗$$

12. **Higher Order Thinking** Given the equation $ax + b = c$, solve for x. Describe each statement as *always*, *sometimes*, or *never* true. Explain your answer.

   a. If a, b, c, are whole numbers, x is a whole number.

   b. If a, b, c, are integers, x is an integer.

   c. If a, b, c, are rational numbers, x is a rational number.

PRACTICE

Solve each equation for the indicated variable.
SEE EXAMPLES 1 AND 2

13. $\frac{b}{c} = a$; c 14. $k = a - y$; y

15. $dfg = h$; f 16. $w = \frac{x}{a - b}$; x

17. $2x + 3y = 12$; y 18. $2n = 4x + 2y$; n

19. $abc = \frac{1}{2}$; b 20. $y = \frac{3}{5u} + 5$; u

21. $8(x - a) = 2(2a - x)$; x

22. $12(m + 3x) = 18(x - 3m)$; m

23. $V = \frac{1}{3}\pi r^2 h$; h

24. $V = \frac{1}{3}\pi r^2(h - 1)$; h

25. $y(a - b) = c(y + a)$; y

26. $x = \frac{3(y - b)}{m}$; y

27. $F = -\frac{Gm}{r^2}$; G

28. Use the area formula $A = \ell w$ to write a formula for the length ℓ of the baking sheet shown.
SEE EXAMPLE 3

A = 117 in.^{2}

29. You can determine the approximate temperature in degrees Fahrenheit by counting the number of times a cricket chirps in one minute. Then multiply that by 7, divide by 30, and add 40. SEE EXAMPLE 4

   a. Write a formula for estimating the temperature based on the number of cricket chirps.

   b. Write a new formula for the number of chirps you would expect in one minute at a given Fahrenheit temperature.

   c. Use the formula to find the number of chirps in one minute when the temperature is 89°F.

APPLY

30. Model With Mathematics Water boils at different temperatures at different elevations. The boiling temperature of water is 212°F at sea level (0 ft) but drops about 1.72°F for every 1,000 feet of elevation. Write a formula for the boiling point at a given elevation. Then solve the formula for the elevation when the boiling point for water is 190°F.

31. Reason In the National Hockey League, the goalie may not play the puck outside the isosceles trapezoid behind the net. The formula for the area of a trapezoid is $A = \frac{1}{2}(b_1 + b_2)h$.

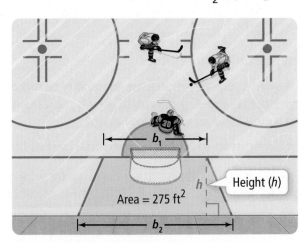

Area = 275 ft²
Height (h)

a. Solve the formula for either base, b_1 or b_2.

b. Use the formula to find the length of the base next to the goal given that the height of the trapezoid is 11 ft and the base farthest from the goal is 28 ft.

c. How can you find the distance d of each side of the base that extends from the goal given that the goal is 6 ft long? What is the distance?

32. Use Appropriate Tools The formula for cell D2 is shown in the spreadsheet. Use the data shown in row 3 to write a formula for cell A3.

= A2*B2*C2

	A	B	C	D
1	length	width	height	volume
2	3	4	5	60
3	■	10	12	600
4	6	12	13	936

✓ ASSESSMENT PRACTICE

33. Given the proportion $\frac{a}{b} = \frac{c}{d}$, solve for c.

34. SAT/ACT The formula for the area of a sector of a circle is $A = \frac{\pi r^2 s}{360}$. Which formula shows s expressed in terms of the other variables?

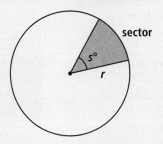

sector

$s°$

r

Ⓐ $s = \frac{\pi r^2 A}{360}$

Ⓑ $s = \frac{360}{\pi r^2 A}$

Ⓒ $s = 360\pi r^2 A$

Ⓓ $s = \frac{360 A}{\pi r^2}$

Ⓔ $s = \frac{A}{360\pi r^2}$

35. Performance Task A manufacturer can save money by making a can that maximizes volume and minimizes the amount of metal used. For a can with radius r and height h, this goal is reached when $2\pi r^3 = \pi r^2 h$.

Part A Solve the equation for h. How is the height related to the radius for a can that meets the manufacturer's goal?

Part B The area of a label for a can is $A = 2\pi rh$. Use your result from Part A to write a formula giving the area of a label for a can that meets the manufacturer's goals.

1-4

Solving Inequalities in One Variable

🔊 SavvasRealize.com

I CAN... solve and graph inequalities.

👆 **MODEL & DISCUSS**

Skyler competes in the high jump event at her school. She hopes to tie or break some records at the next meet.

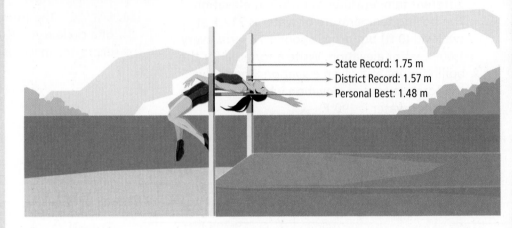

State Record: 1.75 m
District Record: 1.57 m
Personal Best: 1.48 m

A. Write and solve an equation to find *x*, the number of meters Skyler must add to her personal best to tie the district record.

B. **Look for Relationships** Rewrite your equation as an inequality to represent the situation where Skyler *breaks* the district record. How is the value of *x* in the inequality related to the value of *x* in the equation?

C. How many meters does Skyler need to add to her personal best to break the state record?

❓ **ESSENTIAL QUESTION**   How are the solutions of an inequality different from the solutions of an equation?

👆 **EXAMPLE 1** > **Solve Inequalities**

Solve $-4(3x - 1) + 6x \geq 16$ and graph the solution.

$$-4(3x - 1) + 6x \geq 16$$

$$-12x + 4 + 6x \geq 16$$

$$-12x + 4 - 4 + 6x \geq 16 - 4$$

> Apply the properties of inequalities to solve for *x*.

$$-12x + 6x \geq 12$$

$$-6x \geq 12$$

$$\frac{-6x}{-6} \leq \frac{12}{-6}$$

> Remember that the direction of the inequality symbol is reversed when both sides of the inequality are multiplied or divided by negative values.

$$x \leq -2$$

STUDY TIP
Recall that when you graph the solution of an inequality on a number line, you use an open circle if the inequality symbol is < or >, and a closed circle if the inequality symbol is ≤ or ≥.

Graph the solution.

-2 0

✅ **Try It!**   **1.** Solve each inequality and graph the solution.

a. $-3(2x + 2) < 10$ **b.** $2(4 - 2x) > 1$

 EXAMPLE 2 Solve an Inequality With Variables on Both Sides

Solve $3.5x + 19 \geq 1.5x - 7$. Then graph the solution.

Solve the inequality.

$$3.5x + 19 \geq 1.5x - 7$$

$$3.5x - 1.5x + 19 - 19 \geq 1.5x - 1.5x - 7 - 19$$

$$2x \geq -26$$

$$x \geq -13$$

> Collect like terms on the same side of the inequality.

Graph the solution.

☑ Try It! **2.** Solve $2x - 5 < 5x - 22$. Then graph the solution.

CONCEPTUAL UNDERSTANDING ⟶

 EXAMPLE 3 Understand Inequalities With Infinitely Many or No Solutions

A. Solve $-3(2x - 5) > -6x + 9$.

$$-3(2x - 5) > -6x + 9$$

$$-6x + 15 > -6x + 9$$

$$-6x + 6x + 15 > -6x + 6x + 9$$

$$15 > 9$$

The original inequality is equivalent to $15 > 9$, a true statement. What does this mean?

Using the same steps above, you can show that the inequality is true for any value of x. So all real numbers are solutions of the inequality.

B. Solve $4x - 5 < 2(2x - 3)$.

$$4x - 5 < 2(2x - 3)$$

$$4x - 5 < 4x - 6$$

$$4x - 4x - 5 < 4x - 4x - 6$$

$$-5 < -6$$

LOOK FOR RELATIONSHIPS
Consider the definition of the solution to an inequality. What would the graph of an inequality with no solution look like?

Since the inequality results in a false statement ($-5 < -6$), any value of x you substitute in the original inequality will also result in a false statement.

This inequality has no solution.

☑ Try It! **3.** Solve each inequality.

> **a.** $-2(4x - 2) < -8x + 4$
>
> **b.** $-6x - 5 < -3(2x + 1)$

APPLICATION    **EXAMPLE 4** **Use Inequalities to Solve Problems**

Derek wants to order some roses online. For what number of roses is it less expensive to order from Florist A? From Florist B?

Florist A:
$4.75 per blue rose
plus $40
delivery charge.

Florist B:
$5.15 per red rose
plus $25
delivery charge.

Formulate ◀ Write an inequality to compare the total cost of x roses from each florist.

The cost of x roses at Florist A is less than the cost of x roses at Florist B.

$$4.75x + 40 \qquad\qquad < \qquad\qquad 5.15x + 25$$

Compute ◀ Solve for x.

$$4.75x + 40 < 5.15x + 25$$

Set up the inequality to find the number of roses it would take for Florist A to be less expensive.

$$4.75x - 4.75x + 40 < 5.15x - 4.75x + 25$$

$$40 - 25 < 0.4x + 25 - 25$$

$$\frac{15}{0.4} < \frac{0.4x}{0.4}$$

$$37.5 < x$$

Interpret ◀ The solution is all real numbers greater than 37.5. However, the number of roses must be a whole number.

If Derek plans to buy 38 or more roses, then Florist A is less expensive.
If Derek plans to buy 37 or fewer roses, then Florist B is less expensive.

 Try It! **4.** If Florist B increases the cost per rose to $5.20, for what number of roses is it less expensive to order from Florist A? From Florist B?

CONCEPT SUMMARY Solving Inequalities in One Variable

WORDS To solve inequalities, use the Properties of Inequalities to isolate the variable.

The solution of an inequality is the set of all real numbers that makes the inequality true. Some inequalities are true for all real numbers (like $x + 3 < x + 7$), but others have no solutions (like $x + 7 < x + 3$).

ALGEBRA

$$-5(2x - 3) \le 34$$

$$-10x + 15 \le 34$$

$$-10x + 15 - 15 \le 34 - 15$$

$$-10x \le 19$$

$$\frac{-10x}{-10} \ge \frac{19}{-10}$$

> Reverse the inequality when multiplying or dividing by a negative number.

$$x \ge -1.9$$

Do You UNDERSTAND?

1. **ESSENTIAL QUESTION** How are the solutions of an inequality different from the solutions of an equation?

2. **Reason** How is dividing each side of $x > 0$ by a negative value different from dividing each side by a positive value?

3. **Vocabulary** Give an example of two inequalities that are *equivalent inequalities*. Explain your reasoning.

4. **Error Analysis** Rachel multiplied each side of $x \ge 2$ by 3. She wrote the result as $3x \le 6$. Explain the error Rachel made.

Do You KNOW HOW?

Solve each inequality and graph the solution.

5. $\frac{1}{2}x < 6$

6. $-4x \ge 20$

7. $8 \le -4(x - 1)$

8. $3x - 2 > 4 - 3x$

9. Lourdes plans to jog at least 1.5 miles. Write and solve an inequality to find x, the number of hours Lourdes will have to jog.

3.75 MPH

UNDERSTAND

10. Construct Arguments Let a, b, and c be real numbers, $c \neq 0$. Show that each of the following statements is true.

a. If $a > b$ and $c < 0$, then $ca < cb$.

b. If $a > b$ and $c < 0$, then $\frac{a}{c} < \frac{b}{c}$.

11. Use Structure For each of the graphs below, write an inequality that the graph represents. Explain your reasoning.

a.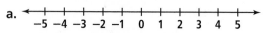

b.

12. Construct Arguments Describe and correct the error a student made when solving the inequality shown.

$3x - 1 > 5$
$3x - 1 + 1 > 5 + 1$ Add 1 to each side.
$3x > 6$ Simplify.
$\frac{3x}{3} < \frac{6}{3}$ Divide each side by 3.
$x < 2$ Simplify.

13. Mathematical Connections Jake's solution to the equation $-4(2x - 3) = 36$ is shown.

$$-4(2x - 3) = 36$$
$$-8x + 12 = 36$$
$$-8x + 12 - 12 = 36 - 12$$
$$-8x = 24$$
$$\frac{-8x}{-8} = \frac{24}{-8}$$
$$x = -3$$

How is the solution to $-4(2x - 3) > 36$ similar to and different from the solution shown?

14. Higher Order Thinking Suppose each side of the inequality $a - b < 0$ is multiplied by c.

a. If $c < 0$ and $c(a - b) > 0$, write an inequality to represent the relationship between a and b.

b. If $c < 0$, is $c(a - b)$ always greater than 0? Explain your reasoning.

PRACTICE

Solve each inequality and graph the solution.
SEE EXAMPLES 1 AND 4

15. $x + 9 > 15$

16. $-\frac{1}{5}x > -10$

17. $5x + 15 \leq -10$

18. $-0.3x < 6$

19. $6x \geq -0.3$

20. $-3x > 15$

21. $\frac{1}{4}x > \frac{1}{2}$

22. $x - 8.4 \leq 2.3$

23. $2.1x \geq 6.3$

24. $-2.1x + 2.1 < 6.3$

25. $-\frac{3}{8}x - 20 + 2x > 6$

26. $\frac{2}{3}x + 14 - 3x > -7$

27. $0.5x - 4 - 2x \leq 2$

28. $4x + 1 + 2x \geq 5$

Match each inequality to the graph that represents its solution. Explain your reasoning. SEE EXAMPLE 1

29. $-2(3x - 1) > 20$

A.

30. $2(1 - 3x) < 20$

B.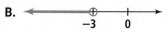

31. $-2(1 - 3x) > 16$

C.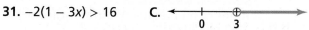

32. $2(3x - 1) < 16$

D.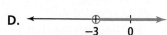

Solve each inequality. SEE EXAMPLE 2

33. $2x + 5 < 3x + 4$

34. $2(7x - 2) > 9x + 6$

Solve each inequality and tell whether it has infinitely many or no solutions. SEE EXAMPLE 3

35. $\frac{3}{4}x + \frac{3}{4} - \frac{1}{2}x \geq -1$

36. $\frac{1}{4}x + 3 - \frac{7}{8}x < -2$

37. $-5(2x + 1) < 24$

38. $4(3 - 2x) \geq -4$

39. $7.2x + 6 \leq 2.4x$

40. $-2x - 5 \geq 3x - 25$

41. $2x + 12 > 2(x + 6)$

42. $0.5x + 8 < 2x - 4$

A solution is graphed for each inequality below. Describe the changes that need to be made, if any, to each graph. SEE EXAMPLE 3

43. $3x - 24 \leq -2(2x - 30)$

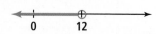

44. $-2(x - 5) \geq -2x + 10$

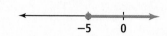

PRACTICE & PROBLEM SOLVING

APPLY

45. Make Sense and Persevere Luke and Aisha are traveling on the same road, in the same direction. Luke is driving at a rate of 50 mi/h, and Aisha is driving at a rate of 55 mi/h. Write and solve an inequality to find when Aisha will be ahead of Luke on the highway. Let x represent time in hours.

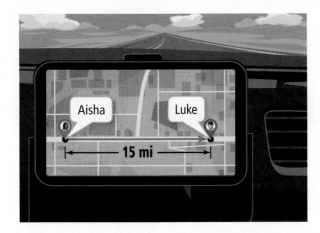

46. Make Sense and Persevere An office manager is selecting a water delivery service. Acme H_2O charges a $15 fee and $7.50 per 5-gallon jug. Best Water charges a $24 fee and $6.00 per 5-gallon jug. How many 5-gallon jugs will the office have to buy each month for the cost of Best Water to be less than that of Acme H_2O?

47. Model With Mathematics Charlie can spend up to $8 on lunch. He wants to buy a tuna sandwich, a bottle of apple juice, and x pounds of potato salad. Write and solve an inequality to find the possible numbers of pounds of potato salad he can buy.

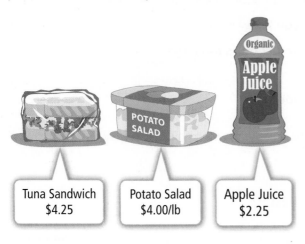

Tuna Sandwich
$4.25

Potato Salad
$4.00/lb

Apple Juice
$2.25

ASSESSMENT PRACTICE

48. Match each inequality with the equivalent inequality.

A. $-\frac{1}{2}x > -\frac{3}{2}$ **I.** $x < 3$

B. $\frac{1}{2}x > \frac{3}{2}$ **II.** $x > 3$

C. $\frac{3}{2}x > \frac{1}{2}$ **III.** $x > \frac{1}{3}$

D. $-\frac{3}{2}x > -\frac{1}{2}$ **IV.** $x < \frac{1}{3}$

49. SAT/ACT Which of the following is the solution of $0.125x + 1 - 0.25x < -3$?

Ⓐ $x < -0.5$

Ⓑ $x < 0.5$

Ⓒ $x > 0.5$

Ⓓ $x < 32$

Ⓔ $x > 32$

50. Performance Task Students have organized a three-day walkathon to raise money for charity. The average walking speeds of four participants are given in the table below.

Name	Walking Speed (mi/h)
Elijah	3.2
Aubrey	3
Mercedes	2.4
Steve	3.5

Part A Write and solve an inequality to determine how many hours it would take Steve to walk at least 21 mi on Day 1.

Part B At the beginning of Day 2, Mercedes is 2 mi ahead of Elijah. Write and solve an inequality to determine the hours x when Elijah will be behind Mercedes.

Part C At the beginning of Day 3, Elijah starts walking at the marker for Mile 42, and Aubrey starts walking at the marker for Mile 42.5. Write and solve an inequality to determine the hours when Elijah is ahead of Aubrey.

Collecting Cans

Many schools and community centers organize canned food drives and donate the food collected to area food pantries or homeless shelters.

A teacher may hold a contest for the student who collects the most cans. The teacher will track the number of cans each student brings in. Sometimes students have their own ways of keeping track. You'll see how some students kept track in the Mathematical Modeling in 3 Acts lesson.

Scan for
Multimedia

ACT 1 — Identify the Problem

1. What is the first question that comes to mind after watching the video?

2. Write down the main question you will answer about what you saw in the video.

3. Make an initial conjecture that answers this main question.

4. Explain how you arrived at your conjecture.

5. Write a number that you know is too small.

6. Write a number that you know is too large.

ACT 2 — Develop a Model

7. Use the math that you have learned in this Topic to refine your conjecture.

ACT 3 — Interpret the Results

8. Is your refined conjecture between the highs and lows you set up earlier?

1-5

Compound Inequalities

SavvasRealize.com

I CAN... write and solve compound inequalities.

VOCABULARY
• compound inequality

🖐 EXPLORE & REASON

Hana has some blue paint. She wants to lighten the shade, so she mixes in 1 cup of white paint. The color is still too dark, so Hana keeps mixing in 1 cup of white paint at a time. After adding 4 cups, she decides the color is too light.

plus 4 c white paint
plus 1 c white paint

A. Explain in words how much paint Hana should have added initially to get the shade she wants.

B. Model With Mathematics Represent your answer to part A with one or more inequalities.

C. Hana decides that she likes the shades of blue that appear in between adding 1 cup and 4 cups of white paint. How can you represent the number of cups of white paint that yield the shades Hana prefers?

❓ ESSENTIAL QUESTION   What are compound inequalities and how are their solutions represented?

CONCEPTUAL UNDERSTANDING

🖐 EXAMPLE 1   Understand Compound Inequalities

How can you use inequalities to describe the sets of numbers graphed below?

A.

−3   0   2

The graph shows the solutions of two inequalities. The two inequalities form a *compound inequality*. A **compound inequality** is made up of two or more inequalities.

Write an inequality to represent the solutions shown in each part of the graph.

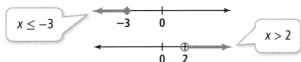
$x \leq -3$
−3   0
$x > 2$
0   2

The compound inequality that describes the graph is $x \leq -3$ or $x > 2$.

B.

−4   0 1

The solutions shown in the graph are greater than or equal to −4. They are also less than 1. Write two inequalities to represent this.

$x \geq -4$
−4   0 1
$x < 1$
−4   0 1

The compound inequality that describes the graph is $-4 \leq x$ and $x < 1$. You can also write this as $-4 \leq x < 1$.

MAKE SENSE AND PERSEVERE
There is no number that can be less than −3 AND greater than 2. So it makes sense to use OR to write the compound inequality.

☑ Try It!   1. Write a compound inequality for the graph.

−2   0   6

EXAMPLE 2   Solve a Compound Inequality Involving *Or*

Solve the compound inequality $5x + 7 < 13$ or $-4x + 3 > 11$. Graph the solution.

Solve each inequality.

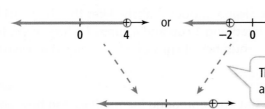

$$5x - 7 < 13 \qquad \text{or} \qquad -4x + 3 > 11$$
$$5x - 7 + 7 < 13 + 7 \qquad\qquad -4x + 3 - 3 > 11 - 3$$
$$5x < 20 \qquad\qquad\qquad -4x > 8$$
$$\frac{5x}{5} < \frac{20}{5} \qquad\qquad\qquad \frac{-4x}{-4} < \frac{8}{-4}$$
$$x < 4 \qquad\qquad\qquad x < -2$$

COMMON ERROR
You may think that there should be two parts in the graph of the solutions. However, the solution to $x < -2$ is a subset of the solution to $x < 4$, so $x < 4$ is the complete solution.

The final graph is all points that appear in *either* solution above.

The solution is $x < 4$, which is the set of all real numbers less than 4.

☑ Try It!   **2.** Solve the compound inequality $-3x + 2 > -7$ or $2(x - 2) \geq 6$. Graph the solution.

EXAMPLE 3   Solve a Compound Inequality Involving *And*

What is the solution of $-12 \leq 7x + 9 < 16$?

Solve each inequality.

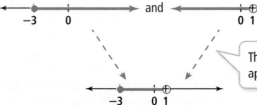

$$-12 \leq 7x + 9 \qquad \text{and} \qquad 7x + 9 < 16$$
$$-12 - 9 \leq 7x + 9 - 9 \qquad\qquad 7x + 9 - 9 < 16 - 9$$
$$-21 \leq 7x \qquad\qquad\qquad 7x < 7$$
$$\frac{-21}{7} \leq \frac{7x}{7} \qquad\qquad\qquad \frac{7x}{7} < \frac{7}{7}$$
$$-3 \leq x \qquad\qquad\qquad x < 1$$

The final graph is all points that appear in *both* solutions above.

The solution is $x \geq -3$ and $x < 1$, or $-3 \leq x < 1$.

☑ Try It!   **3.** Solve the compound inequality $-2(x + 1) < 4$ and $4x + 1 \leq -3$. Graph the solution.

APPLICATION

EXAMPLE 4 **Solve Problems Involving Compound Inequalities**

Enrique plans a diet for his dog, River. River consumes between 510 and 540 Calories per day.

If River eats $1\frac{1}{2}$ servings of dog food each day, how many treats can she have?

320 calories per serving

15 calories per treat

Formulate ◀ Model the situation with a compound inequality.

Let x represent the number of treats River can have each day.

Write an expression to represent River's total daily Calories.

$1\frac{1}{2}$ servings at 320 Cal. per serving plus x treats at 15 Cal. per treat

　　　480　　　　　　　　　　+　　　　　　　$15x$

Write a compound inequality for the number of dog treats each day.

at least 510 Calories　　　　　　at most 540 Calories

$$510 \leq 480 + 15x \leq 540$$

Compute ◀ Solve the compound inequality.

$$510 \leq 480 + 15x \leq 540$$

$$510 - 480 \leq 480 + 15x - 480 \leq 540 - 480$$

$$30 \leq 15x \leq 60$$

$$\frac{30}{15} \leq \frac{15x}{15} \leq \frac{60}{15}$$

$$2 \leq x \leq 4$$

The solution is $2 \leq x \leq 4$.

Interpret ◀ River can have at least 2 and at most 4 treats each day.

☑ **Try It!**　4. Suppose River has new treats that are 10 Calories each. How many of the new treats can she have and remain in her Calorie range?

WORDS	The solution of a compound inequality involving or includes the solutions of one inequality as well as the solutions of the other inequality.	The solution of a compound inequality involving and includes only solutions of both inequalities where they coincide.
ALGEBRA	$x < a$ or $x > b$	$x > a$ and $x < b$ $a < x < b$
GRAPHS		

Do You UNDERSTAND?

1. **ESSENTIAL QUESTION** What are compound inequalities and how are their solutions represented?

2. **Look for Relationships** When $a < b$, how is the graph of $x > a$ and $x < b$ similar to the graph of $x > a$? How is it different?

3. **Vocabulary** A *compound* is defined as a *mixture*. Make a conjecture as to why the term *compound inequality* includes the word *compound*.

4. **Error Analysis** Kona graphed the compound inequality $x > 2$ or $x > 3$ by graphing $x > 3$. Explain Kona's error.

Do You KNOW HOW?

Write a compound inequality for each graph.

5.

6.

Solve each compound inequality and graph the solution.

7. $4x - 1 > 3$ and $-2(3x - 4) \geq -16$

8. $2(4x + 3) \geq -10$ or $-5x - 15 > 5$

9. Nadeem plans to ride her bike between 12 mi and 15 mi. Write and solve an inequality to model how many hours Nadeem will be riding.

PRACTICE & PROBLEM SOLVING

Scan for Multimedia

 Practice · Tutorial

Additional Exercises Available Online

UNDERSTAND

10. Look for Relationships The compound inequality $x > a$ and $x > b$ is graphed below. How is the point labeled c related to a and b?

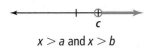

$x > a$ and $x > b$

11. Error Analysis Describe and correct the error a student made graphing the compound inequality $x \geq 2$ and $x > 4$.

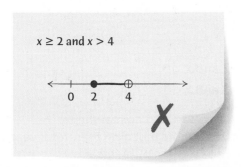

$x \geq 2$ and $x > 4$

12. Generalize Suppose that $a < b$. Select from the symbols $>$, $<$, $\geq$, and $\leq$, as well as the words *and* and *or*, to complete the compound inequality below so that its solution is all real numbers.

$$x \ \blacksquare \ a \ \blacksquare \ \blacksquare \ x \ \blacksquare \ b$$

13. Higher Order Thinking Let a and b be real numbers.

a. If $a > b$, how is the graph of $x > a$ and $x > b$ different from the graph of $x > a$ or $x > b$?

b. If $a < b$, how is the graph of $x > a$ and $x > b$ different from the graph of $x > a$ or $x > b$?

c. If $a = b$, how is the graph of $x > a$ and $x > b$ different from the graph of $x > a$ or $x > b$?

14. Mathematical Connections Consider the solutions of the compound inequalities.

$$4 < x < 8 \qquad 2 < x < 11$$

Describe each solution as a set. Is one set a subset of the other? Explain your answer.

PRACTICE

Write a compound inequality for each graph.
SEE EXAMPLE 1

15. ⊕——+—⊕——
    −2   0 1

16. ——◆——————◆—+—
      −5   −1 0

17. ——◆——+—⊕———
      −0.5   0 0.25

18. ——◆————◆—+—
      −1.2   −0.4 0

Solve each compound inequality and graph the solution. SEE EXAMPLES 2 AND 3

19. $2x + 5 > -3$ and $4x + 7 < 15$

20. $2x - 5 > 3$ or $-4x + 7 < -25$

21. $2x - 5 > 3$ and $-4x + 7 < -25$

22. $-x + 1 > -2$ or $6(2x - 3) \geq -6$

23. $-x + 1 > -2$ and $6(2x - 3) \geq -6$

24. $-\frac{5}{8}x + 2 + \frac{3}{4}x > -1$ or $-3(x + 25) > 15$

The value for the area A of each figure is given. Write and solve a compound inequality for the value of x in each figure. SEE EXAMPLE 4

25. $35 \geq A \geq 25$ **26.** $9 \leq A \leq 12$

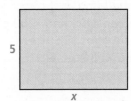

Write a compound inequality to represent each sentence below. SEE EXAMPLE 4

27. A quantity x is at least 10 and at most 20.

28. A quantity x is either less than 10 or greater than 20.

29. A quantity x is greater than 10 and less than 20.

APPLY

30. Reason Fatima plans to spend at least $15 and at most $20 on sketch pads and pencils. If she buys 2 sketch pads, how many pencils can she buy while staying in her price range?

Sketch Pad
$3.25 each

Pencil
$0.75 each

31. Make Sense and Persevere A peanut company ships its product in a carton that weighs 20 oz when empty. Twenty bags of peanuts are shipped in each carton. The acceptable weight for one bag of peanuts is between 30.5 oz and 33.5 oz, inclusive. If a carton weighs too much or too little, it is opened for inspection. Write and solve a compound inequality to determine x, the weights of cartons that are opened for inspection.

32. Model With Mathematics Volunteers at an animal shelter are building a rectangular dog run so that one shorter side of the rectangle is formed by the shelter building as shown. They plan to spend between $100 and $200 on fencing for the sides at a cost of $2.50 per ft. Write and solve a compound inequality to model the possible length of the dog run.

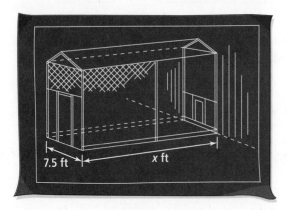

7.5 ft x ft

ASSESSMENT PRACTICE

33. Which of the following compound inequalities have the solution $x < 3$? Select all that apply.

Ⓐ $3x + 5 < 6$ or $-2x + 9 > 3$

Ⓑ $3x + 5 < 6$ and $-2x + 9 > 3$

Ⓒ $3x - 5 < 10$ and $-2x + 9 > 3$

Ⓓ $3x + 5 < 6$ or $-2x + 9 < 3$

Ⓔ $3x - 5 < 10$ or $-2x + 9 > 3$

34. SAT/ACT What is the solution of $0.2x - 4 - 2x < -0.4$ and $3x + 2.7 < 3$?

Ⓐ $x < -2$

Ⓑ $x < 0.1$

Ⓒ $x < 1$

Ⓓ $x > -2$ and $x < 0.1$

Ⓔ $x > -2$ and $x < 1$

35. Performance Task An animal shelter categorizes donors based on their total yearly donation, as shown in the table.

Donor Category	Total Yearly Donation
Bronze	$< \$100$
Silver	$\geq \$100$ and $< \$500$
Gold	$\geq \$500$ and $< \$1,000$
Platinum	$\geq \$1,000$

Part A Keenan donates the same amount each month. Write and solve a compound inequality for the monthly donation that will put him in the Gold category.

Part B Libby donated $50 during the first month of the year. If she makes three additional donations of equal amounts during the year, how much will she need to donate each time to be in the Silver category?

Part C Paula originally planned to donate $50 each month. After reviewing her budget, she decides that she must reduce her planned donation. By what amount can she reduce her original planned monthly donation of $50 so that she will be in the Silver category?

1-6

Absolute Value Equations and Inequalities

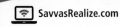
SavvasRealize.com

I CAN... write and solve absolute value equations and inequalities.

🖑 MODEL & DISCUSS

Amelia is participating in a 60-mile spin-a-thon. Her spin bike keeps track of the simulated number of miles she travels. She plans to take a 15-minute break within 5 miles of riding 30 miles.

Amelia spins at a constant 22 mph.

Spin-a-thon Schedule	
Event	**Time**
Start spinning	10:00 A.M.
Stop for break	▪
Resume spinning	▪

A. Write a compound inequality that models the number of miles Amelia spins before taking a break.

B. How is the number of miles Amelia spins before she takes a break related to the amount of time before she takes a break?

C. Make Sense and Persevere About how many hours will Amelia spin before she takes a break? Discuss how you could use your mathematical model to complete the spin-a-thon schedule.

❓ ESSENTIAL QUESTION

Why does the solution for an absolute value equation or inequality typically result in a pair of equations or inequalities?

🖑 EXAMPLE 1 Understand Absolute Value Equations

A. What is the value of x in $7 = |x| + 2$?

Solve for x by isolating the absolute value expression on one side of the equation.

STUDY TIP
The absolute value of a number is its distance from 0 on a number line.

$$7 = |x| + 2$$
$$7 - 2 = |x| + 2 - 2$$ ← Use the Subtraction Property of Equality.
$$5 = |x|$$

Both −5 and −5 are 5 units away from 0.

The solutions are $x = -5$ and $x = 5$.

Check the solutions.

$7 \stackrel{?}{=} |-5| + 2$	$7 \stackrel{?}{=} |5| + 2$
$\stackrel{?}{=} 5 + 2$	$\stackrel{?}{=} 5 + 2$
$= 7\checkmark$	$= 7\checkmark$

CONTINUED ON THE NEXT PAGE

EXAMPLE 1 CONTINUED

CONTINUED ON THE NEXT PAGE

USE STRUCTURE

When solving an absolute value equation in the form $|ax + b| = c$, use two different equations to find the solutions, $ax + b = c$ and $ax + b = -c$.

B. What is the value of x in $|2x - 3| = 1$?

Write and solve equations for the two possibilities:

$2x - 3$ is positive.

$$2x - 3 = 1$$
$$2x - 3 + 3 = 1 + 3$$
$$2x = 4$$
$$\frac{2x}{2} = \frac{4}{2}$$
$$x = 2$$

$2x - 3$ is negative.

$$2x - 3 = -1$$
$$2x - 3 + 3 = -1 + 3$$
$$2x = 2$$
$$\frac{2x}{2} = \frac{2}{2}$$
$$x = 1$$

The expression inside the absolute value symbol can be positive or negative. So the expression $2x - 3$ can be equal to 1 or −1.

The solutions are $x = 2$ and $x = 1$.

C. What is the value of x in $3|x + 6| + 8 = 5$?

Step 1 Isolate the absolute value expression.

$$3|x + 6| + 8 - 8 = 5 - 8$$
$$3|x + 6| = -3$$
$$\frac{3|x + 6|}{3} = \frac{-3}{3}$$

Step 2 Solve for x.

$$|x + 6| = -1$$

The absolute value of a number is a distance and cannot be negative.

This equation has no solution.

 Try It! **1.** Solve each equation.

a. $6 = |x| - 2$ **b.** $2|x + 5| = 4$ **c.** $|3x - 6| = 12$

EXAMPLE 2 **Apply an Absolute Value Equation**

STUDY TIP

You can use an absolute value equation to model a quantity "plus or minus" another quantity.

The cruising speed of Kennedy's boat is 25 mi/h. She plans to cruise at this speed for the distances shown in the diagram.

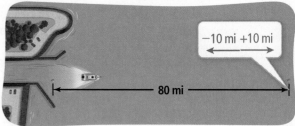

−10 mi +10 mi

80 mi

Not to scale

A. What equation models the number of hours x that Kennedy will travel?

The distance Kennedy actually travels

$$|25x - 80| = 10$$

10 miles from the 80-mile point

Final distance from the 80-mile point

Go Online | SavvasRealize.com

EXAMPLE 2 CONTINUED

B. What are the minimum number and maximum number of hours Kennedy will travel?

Write and solve equations for the two possibilities.

If Kennedy travels plus 10 miles, the absolute value expression is positive.

$$25x - 80 = 10$$
$$25x - 80 + 80 = 10 + 80$$
$$25x = 90$$
$$\frac{25x}{25} = \frac{90}{25}$$
$$x = 3.6$$

If Kennedy travels minus 10 miles, the absolute value expression is negative.

$$25x - 80 = -10$$
$$25x - 80 + 80 = -10 + 80$$
$$25x = 70$$
$$\frac{25x}{25} = \frac{70}{25}$$
$$x = 2.8$$

The solutions are $x = 3.6$ and $x = 2.8$.

Kennedy will travel at least 2.8 hours and at most 3.6 hours.

 Try It! 2. What will be the minimum and maximum time that Kennedy will travel if she resets her cruising speed to 20 mi/h?

CONCEPTUAL
UNDERSTANDING

 EXAMPLE 3 **Understand Absolute Value Inequalities**

What are the solutions of an absolute value inequality?

COMMON ERROR
Remember to look at the $>$ and $<$ symbols when solving absolute value inequalities. Inequalities with absolute value have to be set up differently to solve if it is an "and" situation vs. an "or" situation.

Solve and graph two absolute value inequalities.

A.

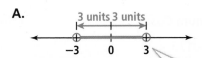

The distance between x and 0 must be less than 3, so the values 3 units to the right and 3 units to the left are solutions.

$|x| < 3$

$|x| < 3$ is equivalent to the compound inequality $x < 3$ *and* $x > -3$, which can also be written as $-3 < x < 3$.

B.

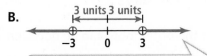

The distance between x and 0 must be greater than 3. So positive values of x must be greater than 3, and negative values of x must be less than -3.

$|x| > 3$

$|x| > 3$ is equivalent to the compound inequality $x < -3$ *or* $x > 3$.

 Try It! 3. Solve and graph the solutions of each inequality.

a. $|x| > 15$ **b.** $|x| \leq 7$

APPLICATION   👆 **EXAMPLE 4**   **Write an Absolute Value Inequality**

Members of the debate team are traveling to a tournament, where they will stay in a hotel for 4 nights. The total cost for each member must be within $20 of $175. Which of the hotels shown can they consider?

Hotel Room Costs*

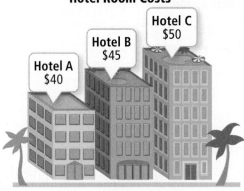

*Per person per night

Formulate ◀ Write an absolute value inequality to represent the situation.

Let x be the cost per night of a hotel room.

The difference between total cost and $175 is less than or equal to $20.

$$|4x - 175| \qquad\qquad \leq \qquad\qquad 20$$

Compute ◀ Solve the inequality to find the maximum and minimum hotel cost for each team member.

Maximum Cost	**Minimum Cost**
$4x - 175 \leq 20$	$4x - 175 \geq -20$
$4x - 175 + 175 \leq 20 + 175$	$4x - 175 + 175 \geq -20 + 175$
$4x \leq 195$	$4x \geq 155$
$\dfrac{4x}{4} \leq \dfrac{195}{4}$	$\dfrac{4x}{4} \geq \dfrac{155}{4}$
$x \leq 48.75$	$x \geq 38.75$

Interpret ◀ The cost of the hotel room can be between $38.75 and $48.75, inclusive.

The debate team can consider Hotel A or Hotel B.

 Try It!   **4.** If the debate team increased their limit to $200 plus or minus $20, would they be able to afford Hotel D at $55 per night? Explain.

CONCEPT SUMMARY Absolute Value Equations and Inequalities

WORDS	Absolute Value Equations	Absolute Value Inequalities
	To solve an absolute value equation, isolate the absolute value expression. Then write two equations and solve.	If an inequality uses < or ≤ and these symbols point to the variable in the solution, the solution uses "and". If an inequality uses > or ≥ and these symbols point to the variable in the solution, the solution uses "or".

ALGEBRA

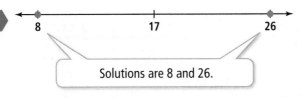

$2|x - 17| = 18$

$|x - 17| = 9$

$x - 17 = -9 \qquad x - 17 = 9$

$x = 8 \qquad\qquad x = 26$

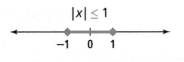

$|x| \leq 1$

$x \geq -1$ and $x \leq 1$

$|x| > 2$

$x < -2$ or $x > 2$

DIAGRAMS

Solutions are 8 and 26.

$|x| \leq 1$

$|x| > 2$

Do You UNDERSTAND?

1. **ESSENTIAL QUESTION** Why does the solution for an absolute value equation or inequality typically result in a pair of equations or inequalities?

2. **Reason** How is solving an absolute value equation similar to solving an equation that does not involve absolute value? How is it different?

3. **Vocabulary** Describe how you would explain to another student why the *absolute value* of a number cannot be negative.

4. **Error Analysis** Yumiko solved $|x| > 5$ by solving $x > -5$ and $x < 5$. Explain the error Yumiko made.

Do You KNOW HOW?

Solve each absolute value equation.

5. $5 = |x| + 3$

6. $|2x - 8| = 16$

Solve each absolute value inequality. Graph the solution.

7. $|3x - 6| \geq 9$

8. $|4x - 12| \leq 20$

9. On a road trip, Andrew plans to use his cruise control for 125 mi, plus or minus 20 mi. Write and solve an equation to find the minimum and maximum number of hours for Andrew's road trip.

PRACTICE & PROBLEM SOLVING

Scan for Multimedia

Practice Tutorial

Additional Exercises Available Online

UNDERSTAND

10. **Make Sense and Persevere** Sasha is solving the absolute value equation $|2x| + 4 = 8$. What is the first step she should take?

11. **Use Structure** The absolute value inequality $5 \leq |x| - n$ is graphed below. What is the value of n?

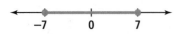

12. **Error Analysis** Describe and correct the error a student made when solving $2|x| < 16$.

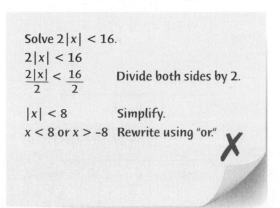

Solve $2|x| < 16$.
$2|x| < 16$
$\dfrac{2|x|}{2} < \dfrac{16}{2}$ Divide both sides by 2.

$|x| < 8$ Simplify.
$x < 8$ or $x > -8$ Rewrite using "or."

13. **Mathematical Connections** Jack wants to model a situation where the perimeter of the rectangle below is 6 ft plus or minus 1.5 ft.

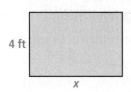

4 ft

x

Because he is modeling a length "plus or minus" another length, he decides to use an absolute value equation for his model. Do you agree with his decision? Explain your reasoning.

14. **Higher Order Thinking** Let a, b, c, and x be real numbers.

a. How is solving $|ax| + b = c$ different from solving $|ax + b| = c$?

b. How is solving $|ax| + b \leq c$ different from solving $|ax + b| \geq c$?

PRACTICE

Solve each absolute value equation. SEE EXAMPLE 1

15. $2 = |x| - 1$

16. $|x| - 4 = 9$

17. $14 = |x| + 2$

18. $|x| + 4 = -9$

19. $|-2x + 8| = 20$

20. $|x - 4| = 9$

21. $2|x + 8| = 20$

22. $2|x - 8| = 20$

23. $5|x + 3| + 8 = 6$

24. $3|x - 2| - 8 = 7$

Write and solve an absolute value equation for the minimum and maximum times for an object moving at the given speed to travel the given distance. (Figures are not to scale.) SEE EXAMPLE 2

25. 5 mi/h

−2.5 mi +2.5 mi

10 mi

26. 10 ft/s

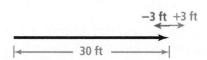

−3 ft +3 ft

30 ft

Solve each absolute value inequality. Graph the solution. SEE EXAMPLES 3 AND 4

27. $2 \leq |x| - 8$

28. $-2 > |x| - 8$

29. $|x| + 5 \geq 10$

30. $|x| + 2.4 < 3.6$

31. $|2x + 5| \geq 9$

32. $|2x - 5| < 9$

33. $-2|x + 4| \leq -6$

34. $-2|2x + 4| + 10 > -6$

Match each absolute value inequality to the graph that represents its solution. Explain your reasoning. SEE EXAMPLES 3 AND 4

35. $3|x| - 2 \leq 10$ A.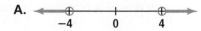
−4   0   4

36. $2|x| - 1 < 7$ B.
−4   0   4

37. $3|2x| + 1 > 25$ C.
−4   0   4

38. $2|4x| - 7 \geq 25$ D.
−4   0   4

Go Online | SavvasRealize.com

PRACTICE & PROBLEM SOLVING

APPLY

39. Make Sense and Persevere A company manufactures cell phone cases. The length of a certain case must be within 0.25 mm of 125 mm, as shown (figure is not to scale). All cases with lengths outside of this range are removed from the inventory. How could you use an absolute value inequality to represent the lengths of all the cases that should be removed? Explain.

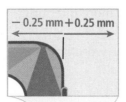

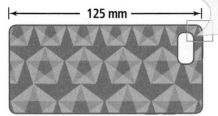

40. Construct Arguments Ashton is hosting a banquet. He plans to spend $400, plus or minus $50, at a cost of $25 per guest. Solve $|25x - 400| = 50$ to find the maximum and minimum number of guests. If there can be up to 7 guests at each table, what is the minimum number of tables Ashton should reserve so that every guest has a seat?

41. Model With Mathematics Hugo is pumping regular gas into his truck. Write and solve an absolute value equation to represent how many gallons of gas will be pumped when the total is $25 plus or minus $0.50.

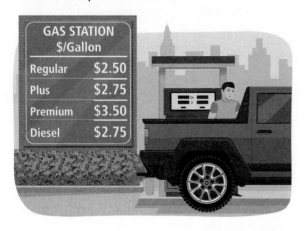

ASSESSMENT PRACTICE

42. Arrange steps in the solution to $2|x - 3| + 4 < 12$ in the correct order.

A. $-1 < x < 7$

B. $2|x - 3| + 4 < 12$

C. $2|x - 3| < 8$

D. $-4 < x - 3 < 4$

E. $|x - 3| < 4$

43. SAT/ACT What is the solution of $|4x - 6| = 2$?

Ⓐ $x = 1, x = 2$

Ⓑ $x = -1, x = 2$

Ⓒ $x = 1, x = -2$

Ⓓ $x = -1, x = -2$

Ⓔ $x = -2, x = 2$

44. Performance Task A road sign shows a vehicle's speed as the vehicle passes.

Part A The sign blinks for vehicles traveling within 5 mi/h of the speed limit. Write and solve an absolute value inequality to find the minimum and maximum speeds of an oncoming vehicle that will cause the sign to blink.

Part B Another sign blinks when it detects a vehicle traveling within 2 mi/h of a 35 mi/h speed limit. Write and solve an absolute value inequality to represent the speeds of the vehicles that cause the sign to blink.

Part C The sign is programmed to blink using absolute value inequalities of the form $|x - a| \leq b$ and $|x - a| \geq b$. Which of these formulas is used to program the sign for cars traveling either 5 mi/h above or below the 20 mi/h speed limit? What are the values of a and b? Explain.

Topic Review

1. What general strategies can you use to solve simple equations and inequalities?

Vocabulary Review

Choose the correct term to complete each sentence.

2. An equation rule for a relationship between two or more quantities is a(n) _____.

3. A combination of two or more inequalities using the word *and* or the word *or* is a(n) _____.

4. An equation where letters are used for constants and variables is a(n) _____.

5. An equation that is true for all values of the variable is a(n) _____.

- compound inequality
- formula
- identity
- literal equation

Concepts & Skills Review

LESSON 1-1 ▶ **Solving Linear Equations**

Quick Review

You can use properties of equality to solve linear equations. Use the Distributive Property and combine like terms, when needed.

Example

Solve $\frac{2}{3}(6x - 15) + 5x = 26$.

$$\frac{2}{3}(6x - 15) + 5x = 26$$

$4x - 10 + 5x = 26$ · · · · · · Distributive Property

$9x - 10 = 26$ · · · · · · · Combine like terms.

$9x - 10 + 10 = 26 + 10$ · · · · · Add 10 to each side.

$9x = 36$ · · · · · · · · · Simplify.

$\frac{9x}{9} = \frac{36}{9}$ · · · · · · · · · Divide each side by 9.

$x = 4$ · · · · · · · · · · Simplify.

Practice & Problem Solving

6. **Use Structure** What property would you use first to solve $\frac{1}{2}x - 6 = 10$? Explain.

Solve each equation.

7. $3(2x - 1) = 21$

8. $100 = 8(4t - 5)$

9. $\frac{5}{8} = \frac{3}{4}b - \frac{7}{12}$

10. $1.045s + 0.068 = 15.743$

11. **Model With Mathematics** The price for an adult movie ticket is $1\frac{1}{3}$ more than a movie ticket for a child. Ines takes her daughter to the movie, buys a box of popcorn for $5.50, and spends $26.50. Write and solve an equation to find the prices for each of their movie tickets.

Quick Review

To solve equations with a variable on both sides, rewrite the equation so that all the variable terms are on one side of the equation and the constants are on the other. Then solve for the value of the variable.

Example

Solve $5x - 48 = -3x + 8$.

$$5x - 48 = -3x + 8$$

$5x - 48 + 3x = -3x + 8 + 3x$ ····· Add $3x$ to each side.

$8x - 48 = 8$ ················ Simplify.

$8x - 48 + 48 = 8 + 48$ ······· Add 48 to each side.

$8x = 56$ ················· Simplify.

$\dfrac{8x}{8} = \dfrac{56}{8}$ ············· Divide each side by 8.

$x = 7$ ················ Simplify.

Practice & Problem Solving

12. Error Analysis Describe and correct any errors a student may have made when solving the equation $0.6(y - 0.2) = 3 - 0.2(y - 1)$.

$$0.6(y - 0.2) = 3 - 0.2(y - 1)$$
$$0.6y - 0.12 = 3.2 - 0.2y$$
$$100(0.6y - 0.12) = 10(3.2 - 0.2y)$$
$$60y - 12 = 32 - 2y$$
$$60y - 12 + 12 + 2y = 32 + 12 - 2y + 2y$$
$$62y = 42$$
$$y = \frac{21}{31}$$

Solve each equation.

13. $21 - 4x = 4x + 21$

14. $6b - 27 = 3(5b - 2)$

15. $0.45(t + 8) = 0.6(t - 3)$

16. Construct Arguments Aaron can join a gym that charges $19.99 per month, plus an annual $12.80 fee, or he can pay $21.59 per month. He thinks the second option is better because he plans to use the gym for 10 months. Is Aaron correct? Explain.

Quick Review

You can use properties of equality to solve literal equations for a specific variable. You can use the rewritten equation as a formula to solve problems.

Example

Find the height of a cylinder with a volume of 1,650 cm³ and a radius of 6 cm.

Rewrite the formula for the volume of a cylinder in terms of h.

$$A = \pi r^2 h$$

$$\frac{A}{\pi r^2} = \frac{\pi r^2 h}{\pi r^2}$$

$$\frac{A}{\pi r^2} = h$$

Find the height of the cylinder. Use 3.14 for pi.

$$h = \frac{A}{\pi r^2}$$

$$h = \frac{1,650}{(3.14)(6)^2} = \frac{1,650}{(3.14)(36)} = \frac{1,650}{113.04} \approx 14.60$$

The height of the cylinder is about 14.60 cm.

Practice & Problem Solving

17. **Error Analysis** Describe and correct the error a student made when solving $a = \frac{3}{4}(b + 5)$ for b.

$$a = \frac{3}{4}(b + 5)$$

$$\frac{4}{3}a = \frac{3}{4}(b + 5)\frac{4}{3}$$

$$\frac{4}{3}a = b + 5$$

$$b = \frac{4}{3}a + 5$$

Solve each equation for the given variable.

18. $xy = k$; y 19. $a = \frac{2}{b} + 3c$; c

20. $6(2c + 3d) = 5(4c - 3d)$; d

21. **Model With Mathematics** The formula for average acceleration is $a = \frac{V_f - V_i}{t}$, where V_f is the final velocity, V_i is the initial velocity, and t is the time in seconds. Rewrite the equation as a formula for the final velocity, V_f. What is the final velocity when a person accelerates at 2 ft/s² for 5 seconds after an initial velocity of 4 ft/s?

Quick Review

The same strategies used for solving multistep equations can be used to solve multistep inequalities. When multiplying or dividing by a negative value, reverse the inequality symbol.

Example

Solve −2(6x + 5) ≤ 74. Graph the solution.

$$-2(6x + 5) \leq 74$$

$$-12x - 10 \leq 74 \quad \text{·········· Distributive Property}$$

$$-12x - 10 + 10 \leq 74 + 10 \quad \text{······· Add 10 to each side.}$$

$$\frac{-12x}{-12} \geq \frac{84}{-12} \quad \text{······· Divide each side by −12.}$$

$$x \geq -7 \quad \text{········· Simplify.}$$

The solution is $x \geq -7$.

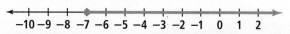

Practice & Problem Solving

22. **Use Structure** Write an inequality that represents the graph.

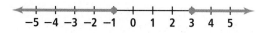

Solve each inequality and graph the solution.

23. $x + 8 > 11$

24. $4x + 3 \leq -6$

25. $2.4x - 9 < 1.8x + 6$

26. $3x - 8 \geq 4(x - 1.5)$

27. **Make Sense and Persevere** Neil and Yuki run a data entry service. Neil starts at 9:00 A.M. and can type 45 words per minute. Yuki arrives at 10:30 A.M. and can type 60 words per minute. Write and solve an inequality to find at what time Yuki will have typed more words than Neil. Let x represent the time in minutes.

LESSON 1-5 ▸ Compound Inequalities

Quick Review

When a compound inequality uses the word *and*, the solution must make both inequalities true. If a compound inequality uses the word *or*, the solution must make at least one of the inequalities true.

Example

Solve $-24 < 4x - 4 < 4$. Graph the solution.

Separate the inequality and solve each separately.

$$-24 < 4x - 4 \qquad\qquad 4x - 4 < 4$$
$$-24 + 4 < 4x - 4 + 4 \qquad 4x - 4 + 4 < 4 + 4$$
$$-20 < 4x \qquad\qquad 4x < 8$$
$$-5 < x \qquad\qquad x < 2$$

The solution is $x > -5$ and $x < 2$, or $-5 < x < 2$.

Practice & Problem Solving

28. Construct Arguments Describe and correct the error a student made graphing the compound inequality $x > 3$ or $x < -1$.

Solve each compound inequality and graph the solution.

29. $2x - 3 > 5$ or $3x - 1 < 8$

30. $x - 6 \leq 18$ and $3 - 2x \geq 11$

31. $\frac{1}{2}x - 5 > -3$ or $\frac{2}{3}x + 4 < 3$

32. $3(2x - 5) > 15$ and $4(2x - 1) > 10$

33. Model With Mathematics Lucy plans to spend between $50 and $65, inclusive, on packages of beads and packages of charms. If she buys 5 packages of beads at $4.95 each, how many packages of charms at $6.55 can Lucy buy while staying within her budget?

LESSON 1-6 ▸ Absolute Value Equations and Inequalities

Quick Review

When solving an equation or an inequality that contains an absolute value expression, you must consider both the positive and negative values of the absolute value expression.

Example

What is the value of x in $|4x + 7| < 43$?

Write and solve inequalities for the two cases.

$4x + 7$ is positive. $4x + 7$ is negative.

$$4x + 7 < 43 \qquad\qquad 4x + 7 > -43$$
$$4x + 7 - 7 < 43 - 7 \qquad 4x + 7 - 7 > -43 - 7$$
$$4x < 36 \qquad\qquad 4x > -50$$
$$x < 9 \qquad\qquad x > -12.5$$

The solution is $-12.5 < x < 9$.

Practice & Problem Solving

34. Make Sense and Persevere Thato is solving the absolute value equation $|3x| - 5 = 13$. What is the first step he should take?

Solve each absolute value equation or inequality.

35. $3 = |x| + 1$

36. $4|x - 5| = 24$

37. $3 > |x| - 6$

38. $|2x - 3| \leq 12$

39. Make Sense and Persevere A person's normal body temperature is 98.6°F. According to physicians, a person's body temperature should not be more than 0.5°F from the normal temperature. How could you use an absolute value inequality to represent the temperatures that fall outside of normal range? Explain.

? TOPIC ESSENTIAL QUESTION

Why is it useful to have different forms of linear equations?

Topic Overview

Topic Vocabulary

- parallel lines
- perpendicular lines
- point-slope form
- reciprocal
- slope-intercept form
- standard form of a linear equation
- *y*-intercept

Digital Experience

INTERACTIVE STUDENT EDITION Access online or offline.

ACTIVITIES Complete *Explore & Reason, Model & Discuss,* and *Critique & Explain* activities. Interact with Examples and Try Its.

ANIMATION View and interact with real-world applications.

PRACTICE Practice what you've learned.

 Go online | **SavvasRealize.com**

▶ How Tall is Tall?

The world's tallest person in recorded history was Robert Wadlow. He was 8 feet 11.1 inches tall! Only 5% of the world population is 6 feet 3 inches or taller. What percent of the population would you guess is 7 feet or taller?

We usually use standard units, such as feet and inches or centimeters, to measure length or height. Did you ever wonder why? In the Mathematical Modeling in 3 Acts lesson you'll consider some interesting alternatives.

VIDEOS Watch clips to support *Mathematical Modeling in 3 Acts Lessons* and **enVision**® *STEM Projects.*

CONCEPT SUMMARY Review key lesson content through multiple representations.

ASSESSMENT Show what you've learned.

GLOSSARY Read and listen to English and Spanish definitions.

TUTORIALS Get help from *Virtual Nerd*, right when you need it.

MATH TOOLS Explore math with digital tools and manipulatives.

Did You Know?

It takes 8 minutes 19 seconds for the sun's rays to travel 93 million miles to Earth. The amount of solar energy that hits Earth in **1 hour** is enough to meet the energy demands of the world's population for **1 year**.

In 2004, about **15,000 homes** in the United States had solar panels. By the end of 2014, about **600,000 homes** had solar panels.

2004

2014

• 1,500 homes

What Is **Roof Pitch**?

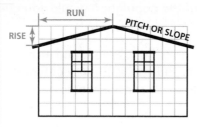

RUN

RISE

PITCH OR SLOPE

Roof pitch is closely related to **slope**. This roof's pitch is equivalent to 3 : 12, which means the roof rises (or falls) 3 inches for every horizontal foot.

The steepness, or pitch, of a roof affects many things, including the installation of solar panels and how much snow the roof can handle.

Solar panels are a collection of solar cells. Solar cells **convert sunlight to electricity**. The solar cells in a solar panel are arranged so that solar energy travels along a specific path.

▶ Your Task: Design a Pitched Roof

You and your classmates will analyze roofs to determine their pitch. Then you will design a roof with a pitch that is appropriate for installing solar panels.

2-1

Slope-Intercept Form

SavvasRealize.com

I CAN... write and graph linear equations using slope-intercept form.

VOCABULARY
• slope-intercept form
• y-intercept

👆 **MODEL & DISCUSS**

Alani wants to buy a $360 bicycle. She is considering two payment options. The image shows Option A, which consists of making an initial down payment then smaller, equal-sized weekly payments. Option B consists of making 6 equal payments over 6 weeks.

Full Price | Down payment | Week 1 | Week 2 | Week 3 | Week 4 | Week 5

Weekly Bike Payments

A. What factors should Alani take into consideration before deciding between Option A and Option B?

B. Communicate Precisely Suppose Alani could modify Option A and still pay off the bike in 5 weeks. Describe the relationship between the down payment and the weekly payments.

❓ **ESSENTIAL QUESTION**   **What information does the slope-intercept form of a linear equation reveal about a line?**

👆 **EXAMPLE 1** ▶ **Graph a Linear Equation**

What is the graph of $y = \frac{4}{5}x + 2$?

The equation is in slope-intercept form. You can use the slope and y-intercept to graph the line.

$$y = \frac{4}{5}x + 2$$

Step 1 Identify the y-intercept in the equation.

The y-intercept is 2, so plot the point (0, 2).

USE STRUCTURE
Think about the relationship between the value of the leading coefficient and the slope of the line.

Step 2 Use the slope to plot a second point.

$$m = \frac{4}{5} = \frac{\text{vertical change}}{\text{horizontal change}}$$

Start at (0, 2), move 4 units up and 5 units to the right to locate a second point. Plot the point (5, 6).

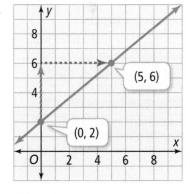

Step 3 Draw a line through the points.

☑ **Try It!**   **1.** Sketch the graph of $y = -\frac{3}{4}x - 5$.

 EXAMPLE 2 **Write an Equation from a Graph**

What is the equation of the line in slope-intercept form?

Step 1 Find the slope between two points on the line.

The line passes through (0, 1) and (4, −2).

$$\text{slope} = \frac{y_2 - y_1}{x_2 - x_1} = \frac{-3}{4}$$

Step 2 Find the y-intercept.

The line intersects the y-axis at (0, 1), so the y-intercept is 1.

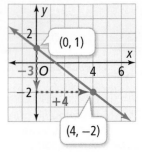

Step 3 Write the equation in the form $y = mx + b$.

Substitute $-\frac{3}{4}$ for m and 1 for b.

The equation of the line in slope-intercept form is $y = -\frac{3}{4}x + 1$.

> **STUDY TIP**
> If you can approximate the y-intercept by looking at the graph, you can use it as one of the two points for finding the slope.

✓ **Try It!** **2.** Write the equation of the line in slope-intercept form.

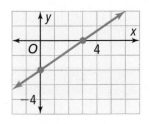

CONCEPTUAL UNDERSTANDING

 EXAMPLE 3 **Understand Slope-Intercept Form**

How can you find an equation of a line that passes through two points if neither of them is the y-intercept?

Consider the line that passes through the points (−1, −2) and (3, 4).

Step 1 Find the slope of the line.

$$m = \frac{4 - (-2)}{3 - (-1)} = \frac{3}{2}$$

Step 2 Use the slope and one point to find the y-intercept.

$4 = \frac{3}{2}(3) + b$ ········· Substitute $\frac{3}{2}$ for m and (3, 4) for (x, y) in $y = mx + b$.

$4 = \frac{9}{2} + b$ ········· Simplify.

$-\frac{1}{2} = b$ ········· Solve for b.

Step 3 Use the slope and the y-intercept to write the equation

$y = \frac{3}{2}x + \left(-\frac{1}{2}\right)$ ········· Substitute $\frac{3}{2}$ for m and $-\frac{1}{2}$ for b.

The equation in slope-intercept form of the line that passes through (−1, −2) and (3, 4) is $y = \frac{3}{2}x - \frac{1}{2}$.

> **COMMON ERROR**
> You may think that a point with two negative coordinates means that the slope will be negative. Keep in mind that the slope depends on both points, so there is no way to determine the sign of the slope from one point.

✓ **Try It!** **3.** Write the equation in slope-intercept form of the line that passes through the points (5, 4) and (−1, 6).

Go Online | SavvasRealize.com

APPLICATION   **EXAMPLE 4**   **Interpret Slope and *y*-Intercept**

Allie received a gift card for her local coffee shop. Every time she goes to the shop, she gets a medium coffee. The graph shows the gift card balance at two points. How can Allie determine the number of medium coffees she can buy with the gift card if she does not know the original value of the card?

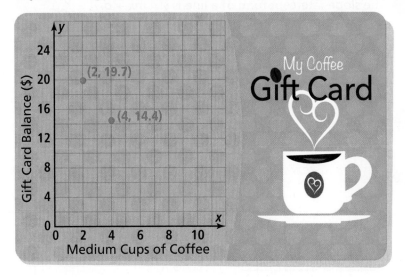

Step 1   Interpret the meaning of the two points.

(2, 19.7): After buying 2 coffees, Allie had $19.70 left on the gift card.

(4, 14.4): After buying 4 coffees, Allie had $14.40 left on the gift card.

Step 2   Find the slope. Then interpret the meaning of the slope.

Use the points (2, 19.7) and (4, 14.4).

$$m = \frac{19.7 - 14.4}{2 - 4}$$

$$= -2.65$$

The slope is −2.65, which means that the balance on the gift card decreases by $2.65 each time Allie buys a medium coffee. The cost of a medium coffee is $2.65.

Step 3   Use one point and the slope to find the *y*-intercept. Then interpret its meaning.

$$y = mx + b$$

$$19.7 = -2.65(2) + b$$

$$25 = b$$

The *y*-intercept is 25. It represents the original value of the gift card.

To determine the number of medium coffees she can buy with the gift card, Allie can divide $25 by $2.65. She can purchase 9 medium coffees with the gift card.

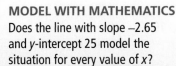
MODEL WITH MATHEMATICS
Does the line with slope −2.65 and *y*-intercept 25 model the situation for every value of *x*?

 Try It!   **4.** Use information from Example 4 to write the equation in slope-intercept form. Find the *x*-intercept of the graph of the equation. What does the *x*-intercept mean in terms of the situation?

CONCEPT SUMMARY Slope-Intercept Form of a Linear Equation

WORDS The slope-intercept form of a linear equation is used when the slope and the *y*-intercept of a line are known.

ALGEBRA The slope-intercept form of a line is $y = mx + b$.

slope   *y*-intercept

NUMBERS $y = \frac{2}{3}x + 1$ $y = -2x - 1$

GRAPH

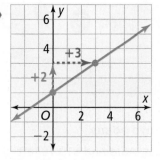

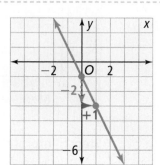

The line has a slope of $\frac{2}{3}$. The *y*-intercept is 1.

The line has a slope of −2. The *y*-intercept is −1.

Do You UNDERSTAND?

1. **ESSENTIAL QUESTION** What information does the slope-intercept form of a linear equation reveal about a line?

2. **Communicate Precisely** How are the graphs of $y = 2x + 1$ and $y = -2x + 1$ similar? How are they different?

3. **Error Analysis** To graph $y = \frac{2}{3}x + 4$, Emaan plots one point at (0, 4) and a second point 2 units right and 3 units up at (2, 7). He then draws a line through (0, 4) and (2, 7). What error did Emaan make?

4. **Make Sense and Persevere** When writing the equation of a line in slope-intercept form, how can you determine the value of m in $y = mx + b$ if you know the coordinates of two points on the line?

Do You KNOW HOW?

Sketch the graph of each equation.

5. $y = 2x - 5$ 6. $y = -\frac{3}{4}x + 2$

Identify the slope and *y*-intercept of the line for each equation.

7. $y = -5x - \frac{3}{4}$ 8. $y = \frac{1}{4}x + 5$

Write the equation of each line in slope-intercept form.

9.
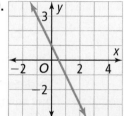

10.
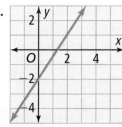

11. A line that passes through (3, 1) and (0, −3)

12. A line that passes through (−1, −5) and (4, −2)

UNDERSTAND

13. Use Structure Aisha and Carolina each sketch a graph of the linear equation $y = -\frac{3}{4}x + 2$. Aisha uses the equation $y = \frac{-3}{4}x + 2$ to sketch the graph, and Carolina uses the equation $y = \frac{3}{-4}x + 2$.

   a. Explain how this leads them to use different steps to construct their graphs.

   b. Will the two graphs look the same? Explain.

14. Make Sense and Persevere Line g passes through the points $(-2.6, 1)$ and $(-1.4, 2.5)$, as shown. Find the equation of the line that passes through $(0, -b)$ and $(c, 0)$.

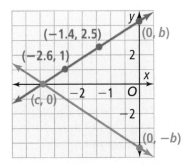

15. Error Analysis Describe and correct the error a student made when graphing the linear equation $y = -\frac{3}{4}x - 6$.

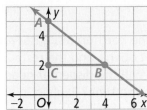

   1. Plot the y-intercept at $(0, 6)$.
   2. Plot a second point 3 units down and 4 units right from $(0, 6)$ at $(4, 3)$.
   3. Connect the points with a line.

   ✗

16. Mathematical Connections The points $A(0, 5)$, $B(4, 2)$ and $C(0, 2)$ form the vertices of a right triangle in the coordinate plane. What is the equation of the line that forms the hypotenuse?

17. Higher Order Thinking The line $y = -0.5x + b$ passes through the points $(1, 5.5)$, $(3, p)$, $(4, 4)$, and $(7, n)$. Find b, n, and p.

PRACTICE

Sketch the graph of each equation. SEE EXAMPLE 1

18. $y = \frac{3}{8}x + 5$

19. $y = -\frac{1}{2}x + 3$

20. $y = -2x + 3$

21. $y = 3x - 6$

22. $y = -\frac{3}{5}x + 4$

23. $y = \frac{5}{2}x - \frac{1}{2}$

Write the equation of each line in slope-intercept form. SEE EXAMPLE 2

24.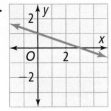

25.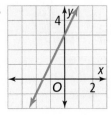

26.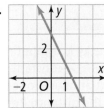

27.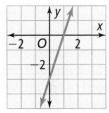

Write the equation of the line that passes through the given points. SEE EXAMPLE 3

28. $(0, 1)$ and $(2, 2)$

29. $(-2, -1)$ and $(0, -5)$

30. $(4, 0)$ and $(0, 2)$

31. $(-2, -6)$ and $(1, 2)$

32. $\left(\frac{3}{8}, 0\right)$ and $\left(\frac{5}{8}, \frac{1}{2}\right)$

33. $(2, 1.5)$ and $(0, 4.5)$

34. Jordan will hike the trail shown at a rate of 4 mi/h. Write a linear equation to represent the distance Jordan still has to walk after x hours. What does the y-intercept of the equation represent? SEE EXAMPLE 4

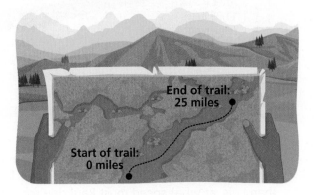

End of trail: 25 miles

Start of trail: 0 miles

APPLY

35. Make Sense and Persevere Naomi wants to buy a new computer for $840. She is considering two payment plans that require weekly payments. Which plan will pay for the computer faster? Explain.

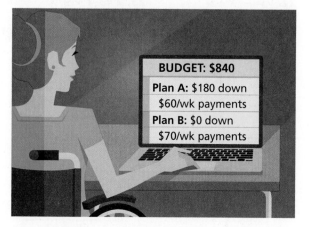

BUDGET: $840

Plan A: $180 down
$60/wk payments

Plan B: $0 down
$70/wk payments

36. Model With Mathematics Becky is competing in an 8-mi road race. She runs at a constant speed of 6 mi/h. Write an equation in slope-intercept form to represent the distance Becky has left to run.

37. Construct Arguments Luis and Raul are riding their bicycles to the beach from their respective homes. Luis proposes that they leave their respective homes at the same time and plan to arrive at the beach at the same time. The diagram shows Luis's position at two points during his ride to the beach.

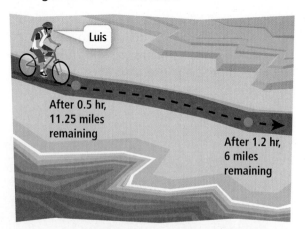

Luis

After 0.5 hr,
11.25 miles
remaining

After 1.2 hr,
6 miles
remaining

Write an equation in slope-intercept form to represent Luis's ride from his house to the beach. If Raul lives 5 miles closer to the beach than Luis, at what speed must Raul ride for the plan to work?

ASSESSMENT PRACTICE

38. Which of the following statements about the graph of $y = \frac{3}{4}x - 1$ are true? Select all that apply.

Ⓐ The slope of the line is -1.

Ⓑ The line intersects the point $\left(0, -\frac{3}{4}\right)$.

Ⓒ The line intersects the point $(0, 1)$.

Ⓓ The y-intercept is -1.

Ⓔ The slope of the line is $\frac{3}{4}$.

Ⓕ The y-intercept is $\frac{3}{4}$.

39. SAT/ACT What is the equation of the line that has a slope of -3 and a y-intercept of 2?

Ⓐ $y = 2x - 3$

Ⓑ $y = 2x + 3$

Ⓒ $y = -3x + 2$

Ⓓ $y = -3x - 2$

Ⓔ $y = -3x - 3$

40. Performance Task After filling the ketchup dispenser at the snack bar where she works, Kelley measures the level of ketchup during the day at different hourly intervals.

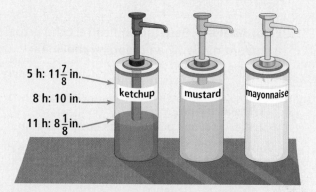

5 h: $11\frac{7}{8}$ in.

8 h: 10 in.

11 h: $8\frac{1}{8}$ in.

ketchup   mustard   mayonnaise

Part A Assuming the ketchup is used at a constant rate, write a linear equation that can be used to determine the level of ketchup in the dispenser after x hours.

Part B How can you use the equation from Part A to find the level of ketchup when the dispenser is full?

Part C If Kelley fills the ketchup dispenser just before the restaurant opens, and the restaurant is open for 18 hours, will the dispenser need to be refilled before closing time? Explain.

2-2

Point-Slope Form

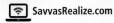
SavvasRealize.com

I CAN... write and graph linear equations in point-slope form.

VOCABULARY
• point-slope form

CRITIQUE & EXPLAIN

Paul and Seth know that one point on a line is (4, 2) and the slope of the line is −5. Each student derived an equation relating *x* and *y*.

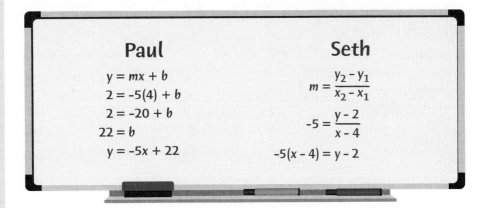

Paul

$y = mx + b$
$2 = -5(4) + b$
$2 = -20 + b$
$22 = b$
$y = -5x + 22$

Seth

$m = \dfrac{y_2 - y_1}{x_2 - x_1}$

$-5 = \dfrac{y - 2}{x - 4}$

$-5(x - 4) = y - 2$

A. Do the two equations represent the same line? Construct a mathematical argument to support your answer.

B. Make Sense and Persevere Generate a table of values for each equation. How can you reconcile the tables with the equations?

? ESSENTIAL QUESTION

What information does the point-slope form of a linear equation reveal about a line?

CONCEPTUAL UNDERSTANDING

EXAMPLE 1   Understand Point-Slope Form of a Linear Equation

A. How can you write the equation of a line using any points on a line?

Use the slope formula to find the slope using a specific point (x_1, y_1) and any point (x, y).

COMMUNICATE PRECISELY
What mathematical notation is important in this example?

$$m = \frac{y_2 - y_1}{x_2 - x_1}$$

$$m = \frac{y - y_1}{x - x_1}$$

> Substitute x for x_2 and y for y_2.

$$m(x - x_1) = \frac{y - y_1}{x - x_1}(x - x_1)$$

$$m(x - x_1) = y - y_1$$

> Multiply both sides of the equation by $(x - x_1)$.

$$y - y_1 = m(x - x_1)$$

You can write the equation of a line using any point, (x_1, y_1), and the slope, m, in **point-slope form**, $y - y_1 = m(x - x_1)$.

B. Why is it helpful to have point-slope form in addition to slope-intercept form?

Using point-slope form allows you to write the equation of a line without knowing the *y*-intercept. You can use any two points on the line to write the equation.

 Try It!   **1.** Describe the steps needed to find the *y*-intercept of the graph using point-slope form.

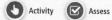
EXAMPLE 2   **Write an Equation in Point-Slope Form**

A. A line with a slope of $\frac{1}{2}$ passes through the point (3, –2). What form can you use to write the equation of the line? What is the equation in that form?

The slope and a point on the line are known, so use point-slope form.

$$y - y_1 = m(x - x_1)$$

$$y - (-2) = \frac{1}{2}(x - 3)$$

> Substitute 3 for x_1, –2 for y_1, and $\frac{1}{2}$ for m.

$$y + 2 = \frac{1}{2}(x - 3)$$

The equation in point-slope form is $y + 2 = \frac{1}{2}(x - 3)$.

MAKE SENSE AND PERSEVERE
Explain why it might not be helpful to apply the Distributive Property to right side of the equation.

B. What is the equation of the line that passes through (–4, 1) and (2, 3).

Find the slope of the line using the two given points.

$$m = \frac{y_2 - y_1}{x_2 - x_1}$$

$$= \frac{3 - 1}{2 - (-4)}$$

> Substitute (2, 3) for (x_2, y_2) and (–4, 1) for (x_1, y_1).

$$= \frac{1}{3}$$

Use the slope and one point to write the equation.

$$y - y_1 = m(x - x_1)$$

> Substitute 2 for x_1, 3 for y_1, and $\frac{1}{3}$ for m.

$$y - 3 = \frac{1}{3}(x - 2)$$

The equation in point-slope form is $y - 3 = \frac{1}{3}(x - 2)$.

STUDY TIP
You can use either point as (x_1, y_1). You just need to be careful to substitute the x- and y-coordinates from the same point.

Try It!   **2.** Write an equation of the line that passes through (2, –1) and (–3, 3).

EXAMPLE 3   **Sketch the Graph of a Linear Equation in Point-Slope Form**

What is the graph of $y - 3 = -\frac{2}{3}(x + 1)$?

Step 1   Identify a point on the line from the equation and plot it.

$$y - 3 = -\frac{2}{3}(x + 1)$$

$$y - 3 = -\frac{2}{3}(x - (-1))$$

> The point is (–1, 3).

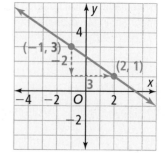

COMMON ERROR
You may think that the x-coordinate of the point is 1. Remember that point-slope form uses $x - x_1$ which in this case is $x - (-1)$.

Step 2   Use the slope to plot a second point.

$$m = \frac{-2}{3} = \frac{\text{vertical change}}{\text{horizontal change}}$$

Move 2 units down and 3 units right from the first point. Plot the point (2, 1).

Step 3   Sketch a line through the points.

Try It!   **3.** Sketch the graph of $y + 2 = \frac{1}{2}(x - 3)$.

APPLICATION

EXAMPLE 4 Apply Linear Equations

An event facility has a banquet hall that can hold up to 250 people. The price for a party includes the cost of the room rental plus the cost of a meal for each guest. Marissa is planning an event for 75 people. She has budgeted $1,200 for the party. Will it be enough?

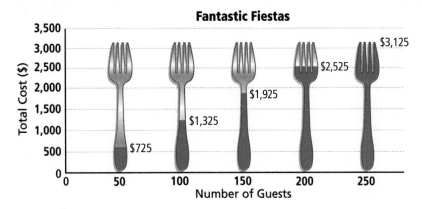

Fantastic Fiestas

Formulate ◀ Determine which form of a linear equation is more useful.

The number of guests and the total costs represent different data points on a line. The point-slope form is more useful.

Compute ◀ The slope represents the cost of each meal. Use the two points (50, 725) and (100, 1,325) to find the slope.

$$m = \frac{y_2 - y_1}{x_2 - x_1}$$

$$= \frac{1,325 - 725}{100 - 50} \quad \text{......... Substitute (50, 725) for } (x_1, y_1) \text{ and (100, 1,325) for } (x_2, y_2).$$

$$= 12$$

The slope is 12, so each meal costs $12.

Use point-slope form to find the cost of the event for 75 guests.

$$y - y_1 = m(x - x_1)$$

$$y - 725 = 12(x - 50) \quad \text{........ Substitute 50 for } x_1, 725 \text{ for } y_1, \text{ and 12 for } m.$$

$$y - 725 = 12(75 - 50) \quad \text{..... Substitute 75 for } x.$$

$$y = 300 + 725 \quad \text{....... Simplify and solve for } y.$$

$$y = 1,025$$

When x = 75, y = 1,025. The cost of the event for 75 guests is $1,025.

Interpret ◀ Since Marissa budgeted $1,200 for her event she will have enough money.

☑ **Try It!** 4. Rewrite the point-slope form equation from Example 4 in slope-intercept form. What does the y-intercept represent in terms of the situation?

CONCEPT SUMMARY Point-Slope Form of a Linear Equation

WORDS	The point-slope form of a linear equation is useful when you know the slope and at least one point on the line.

ALGEBRA	$y - y_1 = m(x - x_1).$

NUMBERS	$y - 4 = \frac{3}{5}(x - 2)$
	$y - 6 = -\frac{3}{4}(x + 5)$

GRAPH

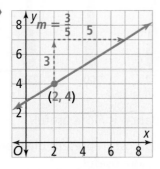

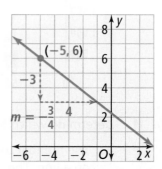

✓ Do You UNDERSTAND?

1. **? ESSENTIAL QUESTION** What information does the point-slope form of a linear equation reveal about a line?

2. **Use Structure** If you know a point on a line and the slope of the line, how can you find another point on the line?

3. **Error Analysis** Denzel identified (3, 2) as a point on the line $y - 2 = \frac{2}{3}(x + 3)$. What is the error that Denzel made?

4. **Generalize** You know the slope and one point on a line that is not the y-intercept. Why might you write the equation in point-slope form instead of slope-intercept form?

Do You KNOW HOW?

Write the equation of the line in point-slope form that passes through the given point with the given slope.

5. (1, 5); $m = -3$ 6. (−4, 3); $m = 2$

Write an equation of the line in point-slope form that passes through the given points.

7. (4, 2) and (1, 6)   8. (−2, 8) and (7, −4)

9. Write the equation $y - 6 = -5(x + 1)$ in slope-intercept form.

10. Write the equation of the line in point-slope form.

a.
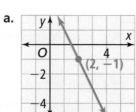

b.
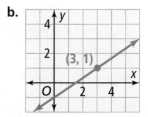

UNDERSTAND

11. Use the graph of the line shown.

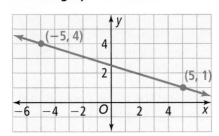

a. Write a point-slope form of the equation for the line shown.

b. Estimate the value of the y-intercept of the line.

c. **Construct Arguments** Use proportional reasoning to support your conjecture about the value of the y-intercept.

d. Rewrite the point-slope form of the equation in slope-intercept form to check your conjecture.

12. **Error Analysis** Describe and correct the error a student made when graphing $y + 5 = -\frac{3}{4}(x - 8)$.

1. Plot a point at (-5, 8).
2. Plot a point 3 units down and 4 units right from (-5, 8) at (-1, 5).
3. Connect the points with a line.

13. **Higher Order Thinking** In slope-intercept form $y = mx + b$, the y-intercept is located at (0, b).

a. What equation do you get when you substitute (0, b) for (x_1, y_1) in point-slope form $y - y_1 = m(x - x_1)$?

b. How are the slope-intercept and the point-slope forms related?

PRACTICE

Write the equation in point-slope form of the line that passes through the given point with the given slope. SEE EXAMPLES 1, 2, AND 3

14. (3, 1); $m = 2$

15. (2, -2); $m = -4$

16. (2, -8); $m = -\frac{3}{4}$

17. (-1, 4); $m = \frac{2}{3}$

18. $(-\frac{1}{2}, 2)$; $m = -1$

19. (3.5, 7.5); $m = 1.5$

Write the equation of the line in point-slope form. SEE EXAMPLES 2 AND 3

20.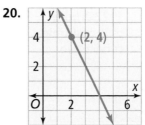

21.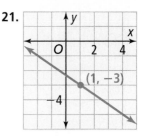

Write an equation of the line in point-slope form that passes through the given points. SEE EXAMPLE 2

22. (2, 4) and (3, 6)

23. (-1, -7) and (2, -4)

24. (3, -5) and (1, -8)

25. (-4, 12) and (-7, -3)

26. (-4, -2) and (1, 6)

27. $(3, -\frac{1}{2})$ and $(1, \frac{3}{2})$

Sketch the graph of each equation. SEE EXAMPLE 3

28. $y + 2 = -3(x + 2)$

29. $y - 2 = 4(x - 1)$

30. $y + 1 = \frac{3}{2}(x - 1)$

31. $y - 3 = \frac{2}{5}(x + 1)$

32. $y - 1 = \frac{5}{4}(x + 2)$

33. $y + 5 = \frac{1}{2}(x + 3)$

Write an equation of the line in point-slope form that passes through the given points in each table. Then write each equation in slope-intercept form. SEE EXAMPLE 4

34.

x	y
15	100
20	115
25	130
30	145
35	160

35.

x	y
-4	-21
-2	-18
0	-15
2	-12
4	-9

APPLY

36. Model With Mathematics Liam rented a pedal board for 5.5 hours and paid a total of $93.75. What is an equation in point-slope form that models the cost of renting a pedal board for x hours? How can Liam use the equation to find the one-time service charge?

PEDAL BOARD RENTAL

$12.50/hour plus one-time service fee

37. Make Sense and Persevere Emery borrowed money from her brother to buy a new phone, and is paying off a fixed amount each week. After 2 weeks, she will owe $456, and after 5 weeks, she will owe $228.

a. What was the original amount Emery borrowed?

b. How much does she pay each week?

c. How useful are equations in point-slope and slope-intercept forms for answering each question?

38. Generalize The total price of a printing job at Incredible Invites includes the cost per invitation plus a one-time set-up fee.

| 25 invitations $100 | 50 invitations $140 | 75 invitations $180 | 100 invitations $220 |

Write equations in point-slope and slope-intercept forms to model the situation. What part of the equations represents the cost per invitation? Which form is easier to use to find information about the set-up fee? Explain.

ASSESSMENT PRACTICE

39. The line $y - 5 = \frac{9}{7}(x + 4)$ is graphed in the coordinate plane.

By inspecting the equation, you can see the graph of the line has a slope of _____ and passes through the point _____ .

Using the point and the slope, you can plot a second point _____ and then graph the line through the two points.

40. SAT/ACT A line with a slope of −2 passes through the point (3, −2). Which of the following is the equation of the line?

Ⓐ $y + 2 = -2(x - 3)$ Ⓑ $y - 2 = -2(x - 3)$

Ⓒ $y - 2 = -2(x + 3)$ Ⓓ $y + 2 = 2(x - 3)$

Ⓔ $y - 2 = 2(x + 3)$

41. Performance Task A railway system on a hillside moves passengers at a constant rate to an elevation of 50 m. The elevations of a train are given for 2 different locations.

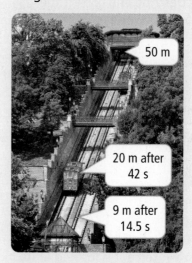

50 m

20 m after 42 s

9 m after 14.5 s

Part A Write an equation in point-slope form to represent the elevation of the train in terms of time. How can you use the equation to find the rate of increase in elevation of the train in meters per second?

Part B At what elevation does the train start initially? Write a linear equation in a form that gives the information as part of the equation. Explain your reasoning.

Activity   Assess

I CAN... write and graph linear equations in standard form.

VOCABULARY
• standard form of a linear equation

Jae makes a playlist of 24 songs for a party. Since he prefers country and rock music, he builds the playlist from those two types of songs.

A. Determine two different combinations of country and rock songs that Jae could use for his playlist.

B. Plot those combinations on graph paper. Extend a line through the points.

C. **Model With Mathematics** Can you use the line to find other meaningful points? Explain.

Playlist	
Country 1	Rock 14
Country 2	Country 15
Rock 3	Country 16
Rock 4	Rock 17
Country 5	Rock 18
Rock 6	Country 19
Country 7	Rock 20
Rock 8	Country 21
Rock 9	Rock 23
Country 10	Country 24
Rock 11	Country 25
Country 12	Country 26

? ESSENTIAL QUESTION   What information does the standard form of a linear equation reveal about a line?

CONCEPTUAL UNDERSTANDING

EXAMPLE 1   **Understand Standard Form of a Linear Equation**

A. Hanna will spend $150 on music festival tickets. Reserved seat tickets cost $25 and general admission tickets cost $10. How can you represent the situation with a linear equation?

Let x = reserved seat tickets   Let y = general admission tickets

money spent on reserved seat tickets	money spent on general admission tickets	total budget

$25 \cdot x$ $+$ $10 \cdot y$ $= 150$

VOCABULARY
Remember, *integers* are rational numbers with no fractional or decimal part.

The equation, $25x + 10y = 150$ is in standard form. The **standard form of a linear equation** is $Ax + By = C$, where A, B, and C are integers, and A and B are not both equal to 0.

B. What information does the standard form give you that the slope-intercept form does not?

Compare equivalent slope-intercept and standard forms for the situation in Part A.

REASON
What is the relationship between the sign of the slope and the quantities in the problems?

Slope-Intercept Form	**AND**	**Standard Form**
$y = -2.5x + 15$		$25x + 10y = 150$

Hanna can buy 15 general admission tickets if she buys no reserved seat tickets.

Hanna can spend $150. This is the constraint.

When the equation is in slope-intercept form, you can determine the y-intercept by inspection. To find the x-intercept you still need to solve for $y = 0$.

When the equation is in standard form, you can determine the constraint by inspection.

CONTINUED ON THE NEXT PAGE

EXAMPLE 1 CONTINUED

  Activity Assess

 Try It! **1.** Is it easier to find the *x*-intercept of the graph of the equations in Part B using slope-intercept or standard form? Explain.

EXAMPLE 2 **Sketch the Graph of a Linear Equation in Standard Form**

What is the graph of $3x - 2y = 9$?

To sketch a graph of a linear equation in standard form, find the *x*- and *y*-intercepts.

Step 1 Find the intercepts.

To find the *x*-intercept, substitute 0 for *y* and solve for *x*.

$$3x - 2y = 9$$
$$3x - 2(0) = 9$$
$$3x = 9$$
$$x = 3$$

The *x*-intercept is 3.

To find the *y*-intercept, substitute 0 for *x* and solve for *y*.

$$3x - 2y = 9$$
$$3(0) - 2y = 9$$
$$-2y = 9$$
$$y = -4.5$$

The *y*-intercept is −4.5.

Step 2 Sketch a graph of the line.

Plot the *x*-intercept at (3, 0).
Plot the *y*-intercept at (0, −4.5).

Sketch the line that passes through the intercepts.

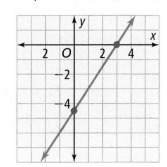

 Try It! **2.** Sketch the graph of $4x + 5y = 10$.

EXAMPLE 3 **Relate Standard Form to Horizontal and Vertical Lines**

A. What does the graph of $Ax + By = C$ look like when $A = 0$?

Graph the line of $2y = 6$.

$$2y = 6$$
$$y = 3$$

The equation $y = 3$ does not include *x*, so *x* has no effect on the *y*-values. The value of *y* is 3 for every *x*-value, so the graph of $y = 3$ is a horizontal line.

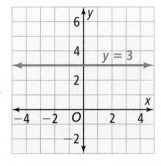

In the coordinate plane, an equation in one variable means that the other variable has no effect on the equation or the graph.

When $A = 0$, the graph of $Ax + By = C$ is a horizontal line.

> **STUDY TIP**
> In a one-variable system, the graph of $y = 3$ is a point on a number line. In a two-variable system, the graph of $y = 3$ or $x = 3$ is a line on the coordinate plane.

CONTINUED ON THE NEXT PAGE

 Go Online | SavvasRealize.com

EXAMPLE 3 CONTINUED

B. What does the graph of $Ax + By = C$ look like when $B = 0$?

Graph the linear equation $3x = -6$.

$$3x = -6$$

$$x = -2$$ — The value of x is -2, regardless of the value of y.

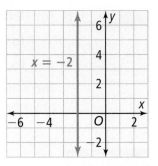

USE APPROPRIATE TOOLS
Can you use slope-intercept or point-slope forms to generate equations for vertical and horizontal lines?

When $B = 0$, the graph of the $Ax + By = C$ is a vertical line.

 Try It! **3.** Sketch the graph of each equation.

    a. $3y = -18$ **b.** $4x = 12$

APPLICATION **EXAMPLE 4** **Use the Standard Form of a Linear Equation**

Tamira is making trail mix. She has $40 to spend on a mixture of almonds and cashews and wants about the same amount of almonds as cashews. How can she determine how many pounds of each kind of nut to buy?

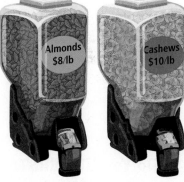

Formulate ◄ Write and graph an equation to represent the situation.

price of almonds • x pounds + price of cashews • y pounds = $40

$$8 \cdot x \quad + \quad 10 \cdot y \quad = 40$$

Compute ◄ Find the x- and y-intercepts of $8x + 10y = 40$.

$$8x + 10(0) = 40 \qquad\qquad 8(0) + 10y = 40$$

$$x = 5 \qquad\qquad\qquad y = 4$$

Graph the segment between the intercepts.

Interpret ◄ Tamira can use the graph of the equation to help her determine the amount of almonds and cashews to buy. Each point on the line represents a combination of almonds and cashews that costs a total of $40.

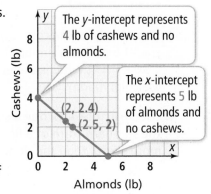

Tamira can buy 2 lb of almonds and 2.4 lb of cashews or 2.5 lb of almonds and 2 lb of cashews for $40.

 Try It! **4.** How does the equation change if Tamira has $60 to spend on a mixture of almonds and cashews? How many pounds of nuts can she buy if she buys only cashews? Only almonds? A mixture of both?

CONCEPT SUMMARY Standard Form of a Linear Equation

| **WORDS** | The standard form of a linear equation is useful |

- to find the x- and y-intercepts easily.
- to write the equation of a vertical or horizontal line.

The x-intercept is the value of x when $y = 0$, and the y-intercept is the value of y when $x = 0$.

| **ALGEBRA** | $Ax + By = C$, where A, B, and C are integers, and A and B are not both equal to 0. |

| **NUMBERS** | $2x - 3y = -3$ |

| **GRAPH** |

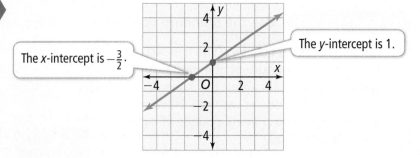

The x-intercept is $-\frac{3}{2}$.

The y-intercept is 1.

Do You UNDERSTAND?

1. **ESSENTIAL QUESTION** What information does the standard form of a linear equation reveal about a line?

2. **Communicate Precisely** How is the standard form of a linear equation similar to and different from the slope-intercept form?

3. **Error Analysis** Malcolm says that $y = -1.5x + 4$ in standard form is $1.5x + y = 4$. What is the error that Malcolm made?

4. **Use Structure** Describe a situation in which the standard form of a linear equation is more useful than the slope-intercept form.

Do You KNOW HOW?

Use the x- and y-intercepts to sketch a graph of each equation.

5. $x + 4y = 8$

6. $3x - 4y = 24$

7. $5x = 20$

8. $-3y = 9$

9. Deondra has $12 to spend on a mixture of green and red grapes. What equation can she use to graph a line showing the different amounts of green and red grapes she can buy for $12?

PRACTICE & PROBLEM SOLVING

UNDERSTAND

10. Use Structure If $C = 24$, what values of A and B complete $Ax + By = C$ for each graph? Write the standard form for each equation.

a. 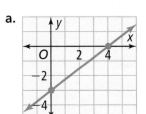 b.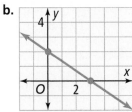

11. Construct Arguments Darren graphs the linear equations $y = -\frac{2}{5}x + 3$ and $2x + 5y = 15$. The graphs look identical so he believes that the equations represent the same line. What mathematical argument can he construct to show that the two forms are equivalent?

12. Error Analysis Describe and correct the error a student made finding the intercepts of the graph of the line $4x - 6y = 12$.

> 1. $4(0) - 6y = 12$
> 2. $6y = 12$, so $y = 2$; the y-intercept is 2.
> 3. $4x - 6(0) = 12$
> 4. $4x = 12$, so $x = 3$; the x-intercept is 3. ✗

13. Mathematical Connections Point A is one vertex of triangle ABC. Point B is the x-intercept of $6x - 4y = -12$ and point C is the y-intercept. What are points B and C? Sketch the triangle in the coordinate plane.

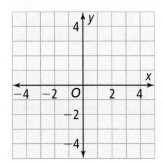

14. Higher Order Thinking Consider the line represented by the equation $5x + 2y = 10$. How is the slope of the line related to values of A, B, and C in standard form $Ax + By = C$?

PRACTICE

Identify the x- and y-intercepts of the graph of each equation. SEE EXAMPLES 1 AND 2

15. $2x + 5y = 10$ **16.** $3x - 4y = -24$

17. $10x + 5y = 120$ **18.** $2x - y = 8$

Sketch the graph of each equation. SEE EXAMPLE 2

19. $2x - 4y = 8$ **20.** $3x + 5y = 15$

21. $3x - 6y = -12$ **22.** $8x + 12y = -24$

Which line matches each equation? SEE EXAMPLE 2

23. $4x + 4y = -8$

24. $3x - 2y = -6$

25. $x + 2y = 2$

26. $3x - y = 3$

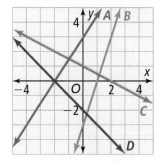

How is the graph of each equation related to standard form $Ax + By = C$? SEE EXAMPLE 3

27. 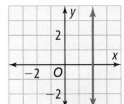 **28.**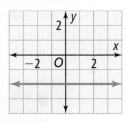

Sketch the graph of each equation. SEE EXAMPLE 3

29. $4x = 10$ **30.** $-6y = 3$

31. $3y = -15$ **32.** $-9x = -27$

Write each equation in standard form.

33. $y = 4x - 18$ **34.** $y = 2x + \frac{3}{7}$

35. $y = -\frac{1}{2}x - 10$ **36.** $y - 1 = \frac{2}{3}(x + 6)$

Write an equation in standard form of the line that passes through the given points.

37. $(0, 2)$ and $(8, 0)$ **38.** $(6, 0)$ and $(0, 4)$

39. $(3, 0)$ and $(0, -7)$ **40.** $(2, -3)$ and $(2, 9)$

APPLY

41. Model With Mathematics Keisha is catering a luncheon. She has $30 to spend on a mixture of Cheddar cheese and Swiss cheese. How many pounds of cheese can Keisha get if she buys only Cheddar cheese? Only Swiss cheese? A mixture of both cheeses? What linear equation in standard form can she use to model the situation?

Cheddar Cheese $3/lb

Swiss Cheese $5/lb

42. Model With Mathematics Gregory can buy 4 pounds of wheat flour for $8 and 5 pounds of rye flour for $20. He has $12 to spend on a flour mixture. What linear equation in standard form can Gregory use to model the situation?

43. Make Sense and Persevere Paxton, a summer camp counselor, has a budget of $300 to spend on caps and T-shirts for a summer camp.

$20.00

$12.00

What equation can Paxton use to determine the number of caps and T-shirts he can order for $300? If Paxton sketched a graph of the linear equation, would every point on the graph represent a possible solution? Explain.

ASSESSMENT PRACTICE

44. Which of the following equations has the same graph as $2x + 3y = 12$? Select all that apply.

Ⓐ $y = -\frac{2}{3}x + 4$

Ⓑ $x + \frac{3}{2}y = 6$

Ⓒ $y - 2 = -\frac{2}{3}(x - 3)$

Ⓓ $-2x - 3y = -12$

Ⓔ $y - 2 = -\frac{2}{3}x + 4$

45. SAT/ACT What is $\frac{3}{8}x + \frac{2}{3}y = 5$ written in standard form?

Ⓐ $y = -\frac{9}{16}x + \frac{15}{2}$

Ⓑ $y + \frac{3}{2} = -\frac{9}{16}(x - 16)$

Ⓒ $\frac{3}{8}x + \frac{2}{3}y = 5$

Ⓓ $3x + \frac{16}{3}y = 40$

Ⓔ $9x + 16y = 120$

46. Performance Task Fatima has a total of $8 to spend to make fruit smoothies. She will use two types of fruit. The table shows the cost of each type of fruit per cup.

Fruit	Cost per cup ($)
Mango	0.50
Pineapple	0.75
Strawberry	1.00

Part A What are the possible combinations of ingredients that Fatima can buy? Write a linear equation in standard form to model how many cups of fruit she can buy for each possible mixture.

Part B What are the possible amounts of fruit, in cups, that she can buy for each mixture in Part A?

Part C Fatima will add 1 cup of liquid for every cup of fruit to complete the smoothies. If she needs at least 24 cups of smoothies, which mixtures will allow her to make enough and still stay within her budget? Explain your reasoning.

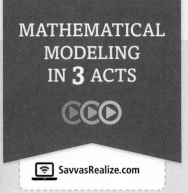

MATHEMATICAL MODELING IN **3** ACTS

 SavvasRealize.com

How Tall Is Tall?

The world's tallest person in recorded history was Robert Wadlow. He was 8 feet 11.1 inches tall! Only 5% of the world population is 6 feet 3 inches or taller. What percent of the population would you guess is 7 feet or taller?

We usually use standard units, such as feet and inches or centimeters, to measure length or height. Did you ever wonder why? In the Mathematical Modeling in 3 Acts lesson you'll consider some interesting alternatives.

Scan for
Multimedia

ACT 1 **Identify the Problem**

1. What is the first question that comes to mind after watching the video?
2. Write down the main question you will answer about what you saw in the video.
3. Make an initial conjecture that answers this main question.
4. Explain how you arrived at your conjecture.
5. Write a number that you know is too small.
6. Write a number that you know is too large.
7. What information will be useful to know to answer the main question? How can you get it? How will you use that information?

ACT 2 **Develop a Model**

8. Use the math that you have learned in this Topic to refine your conjecture.

ACT 3 **Interpret the Results**

9. Is your refined conjecture between the highs and lows you set up earlier?
10. Did your refined conjecture match the actual answer exactly? If not, what might explain the difference?

2-4

Parallel and Perpendicular Lines

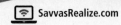 SavvasRealize.com

I CAN... write equations of parallel lines and perpendicular lines.

VOCABULARY
- parallel lines
- perpendicular lines
- reciprocal

EXPLORE & REASON

Graph these three equations using a graphing calculator.

A. Look for Relationships Choose any two of the lines you graphed. How are they related to each other?

B. Does your answer to Part A hold for any two lines? Explain.

C. Write another set of three or more equations that have the same relationships as the first three equations.

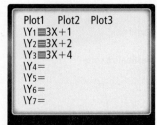

```
Plot1   Plot2   Plot3
\Y1=3X+1
\Y2=3X+2
\Y3=3X+4
\Y4=
\Y5=
\Y6=
\Y7=
```

? ESSENTIAL QUESTION

How can the equations of lines help you identify whether the lines are parallel, perpendicular, or neither?

EXAMPLE 1 Write an Equation of a Line Parallel to a Given Line

What is the equation of the line in slope-intercept form that passes through the point (8, 9) and is parallel to the graph of $y = \frac{3}{4}x - 2$?

COMMUNICATE PRECISELY
Explain why it is necessary to use the term nonvertical when discussing slopes of parallel lines.

Parallel lines are lines in the same plane that never intersect. Nonvertical lines that are parallel have the same slope but different y-intercepts.

Step 1 Identify the slope of the given line.

$$y = \frac{3}{4}x - 2$$

The slope is $\frac{3}{4}$. The slope of a parallel line will be the same.

Step 2 Start with point-slope form. Use the given point and the slope of the parallel line.

$$y - y_1 = m(x - x_1)$$

$$y - 9 = \frac{3}{4}(x - 8)$$

$$y - 9 = \frac{3}{4}x - 6$$ ← Change point-slope form to slope-intercept form.

$$y = \frac{3}{4}x + 3$$

The equation of the line is $y = \frac{3}{4}x + 3$.

 Try It! **1.** Write the equation of the line in slope-intercept form that passes through the point (−3, 5) and is parallel to $y = -\frac{2}{3}x$.

Go Online | SavvasRealize.com

CONCEPTUAL
UNDERSTANDING   **EXAMPLE 2**   **Understand the Slopes of Perpendicular Lines**

A. How can you create two perpendicular lines?

Perpendicular lines are lines that intersect to form right angles.

Draw two identical right triangles as shown.

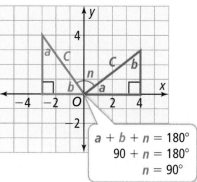

Because the angle sum for each triangle is 180° and the right angle is 90°, the sum of angles *a* and *b* in each triangle must be 90°. Angles *b*, *n*, and *a* form a straight angle of 180° at the origin, so *n* must equal 90°.

$$a + b + n = 180°$$
$$90 + n = 180°$$
$$n = 90°$$

The hypotenuses (*C*) of the right triangles intersect at a right angle, so the lines that include them are perpendicular to each other.

B. How do the slopes of perpendicular lines compare?

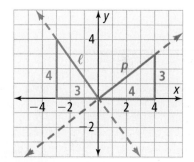

Compute the slopes of lines ℓ and *p*.

Line ℓ: $m = \dfrac{4 - 0}{-3 - 0} = -\dfrac{4}{3}$

Line *p*: $m = \dfrac{3 - 0}{4 - 0} = \dfrac{3}{4}$

> **VOCABULARY**
> Another way to state the definition is as follows: the product of reciprocals is 1.
> $$\frac{3}{4} \cdot \frac{4}{3} = 1$$

The numbers $\dfrac{4}{3}$ and $\dfrac{3}{4}$ are reciprocals. The **reciprocal** of a number is 1 divided by that number. The reciprocal of *x* is $\dfrac{1}{x}$ when $x \neq 0$.

Reciprocal of $\dfrac{3}{4}$ is $1 \div \dfrac{3}{4} = 1 \cdot \dfrac{4}{3}$

$$= \dfrac{4}{3}.$$

So, the slopes of perpendicular lines are *opposite reciprocals*. Opposite reciprocals have a product of −1.

For example, $-\dfrac{4}{3} \cdot \dfrac{3}{4} = -\dfrac{12}{12} = -1$.

Try It!   **2.** Why does it make sense that the slopes of perpendicular lines have opposite signs?

EXAMPLE 3 Write an Equation of a Line Perpendicular to a Given Line

What is the equation of the line that passes through the point (1, 7) and is perpendicular to the graph of $y = -\frac{1}{4}x + 11$?

Step 1 Use the slope of the given line to determine the slope of the line that is perpendicular.

$$y = -\frac{1}{4}x + 11 \qquad m = -\frac{1}{4}$$

The slope of a line perpendicular to the given line is the opposite reciprocal of $-\frac{1}{4}$. Use $\frac{4}{1}$, or 4, as the slope of the new line.

MAKE SENSE AND PERSEVERE
Think about the usefulness of the different forms of a linear equation to decide which form to use.

Step 2 Start with point-slope form. Use the given point and the slope of the perpendicular line.

$$y - y_1 = m(x - x_1)$$
$$y - 7 = 4(x - 1)$$

Substitute 1 for x_1, 7 for y_1 and 4 for m.

The graph of $y - 7 = 4(x - 1)$ passes through the point (1, 7) and is perpendicular to the graph of $y = -\frac{1}{4}x + 11$.

 Try It! 3. Write the equation of the line that passes through the point (4, 5) and is perpendicular to the graph of $y = 2x - 3$.

EXAMPLE 4 Classify Lines

Are the graphs of the equations $3y = -4x + 6$ and $y = -\frac{3}{4}x - 5$ parallel, perpendicular, or neither?

Step 1 Identify the slope of each line.

$$3y = -4x + 6 \qquad\qquad y = -\frac{3}{4}x - 5$$

Rewrite the equation of the line in slope-intercept form.

$$\frac{3y}{3} = \frac{-4x + 6}{3}$$
$$y = -\frac{4}{3}x + 2 \qquad\qquad y = -\frac{3}{4}x - 5$$

The slopes of the lines are $-\frac{4}{3}$ and $-\frac{3}{4}$.

COMMON ERROR
You may confuse the slopes of perpendicular lines. The slopes of perpendicular lines are opposite reciprocals, not reciprocals.

Step 2 Compare the slopes of the lines.

The slopes of the lines, $-\frac{4}{3}$ and $-\frac{3}{4}$, are neither the same nor opposite reciprocals.

The graphs of the equations $3y = -4x + 6$ and $y = -\frac{3}{4}x - 5$ are neither parallel nor perpendicular.

 Try It! 4. Are the graphs of the equations *parallel, perpendicular,* or *neither*?

a. $y = 2x + 6$ and $y = \frac{1}{2}x + 3$

b. $y = -5x$ and $25x + 5y = 1$

APPLICATION  **EXAMPLE 5** **Solve a Real-World Problem**

A landscaper plans to install two new paths in a park. The new Fountain Path will be perpendicular to the East Path and lead to the fountain. The new Picnic Path will be parallel to the Fountain Path and pass through the picnic area. What are the equations in point-slope form that represent the new paths?

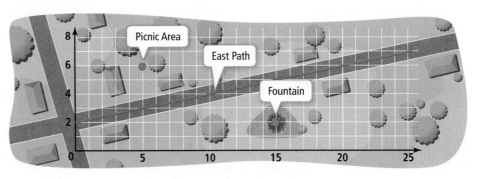

Formulate ◀ Find the slope of the line that represents the East Path. Then determine equations for the two new pathways.

The East Path passes through (0, 2) and (5, 3).

$$m = \frac{3-2}{5-0} = \frac{1}{5}$$

The slope of the line representing the East Path is $\frac{1}{5}$.

Compute ◀ Find an equation for the Fountain Path.

> The slope is the opposite reciprocal of the slope of the East Path.

$y - 2 = -5(x - 15)$ ◁ The fountain is located at the point (15, 2).

Find the equation of the Picnic Path.

> The slope is the same as the slope of the Fountain Path.

$y - 6 = -5(x - 5)$ ◁ The picnic area is located at the point (5, 6).

Interpret ◀ Equation of the line of the Fountain Path: $y - 2 = -5(x - 15)$

Equation of the line of the Picnic Path: $y - 6 = -5(x - 5)$

 Try It! **5.** The equation $y = 2x + 7$ represents the North Path on a map.

　　　　a. Find the equation for a path that passes through the point (6, 3) and is parallel to the North Path.

　　　　b. Find the equation for a path that passes through the same point but is perpendicular to North Path.

CONCEPT SUMMARY Parallel Lines and Perpendicular Lines

	Parallel Lines	Perpendicular Lines
WORDS	The graphs of two equations are parallel if the slopes are the same.	The graphs of two equations are perpendicular if the slopes are opposite reciprocals.

NUMBERS

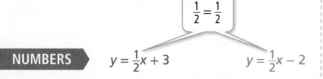

$$\frac{1}{2} = \frac{1}{2}$$

$y = \frac{1}{2}x + 3 \qquad y = \frac{1}{2}x - 2$

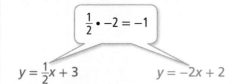

$$\frac{1}{2} \cdot -2 = -1$$

$y = \frac{1}{2}x + 3 \qquad y = -2x + 2$

GRAPHS

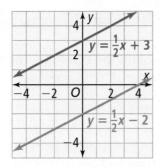

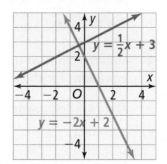

Do You UNDERSTAND?

1. **ESSENTIAL QUESTION** How can the equations of lines help you identify whether the lines are parallel, perpendicular, or neither?

2. **Error Analysis** Dwayne stated that the slope of the line perpendicular to $y = -2x$ is 2. Describe Dwayne's error.

3. **Vocabulary** Describe the difference between the slopes of two parallel lines and the slopes of two perpendicular lines.

4. **Use Structure** Is there one line that passes through the point (3, 5) that is parallel to the lines represented by $y = 2x - 4$ and $y = x - 4$? Explain.

Do You KNOW HOW?

The equation $y = -\frac{3}{4}x + 1$ represents a given a line.

5. Write the equation for the line that passes through (−4, 9) and is parallel to the given line.

6. Write the equation for the line that passes through (6, 6) and is perpendicular to the given line.

Are the graphs of the equations parallel, perpendicular, or neither?

7. $x - 3y = 6$ and $x - 3y = 9$

8. $y = 4x + 1$ and $y = -4x - 2$

9. What equation represents the road that passes through the point shown and is perpendicular to the road represented by the red line?

(1, 0)

UNDERSTAND

10. **Use Structure** A line passes through points $A(n, 4)$ and $B(6, 8)$ and is parallel to $y = 2x - 5$. What is the value of n?

11. **Error Analysis** Describe and correct the error the student made when writing the equation of the line that passes through $(-8, 5)$ and is perpendicular to $y = 4x + 2$.

$$y - 5 = \frac{1}{4}(x - (-8))$$

$$y - 5 = \frac{1}{4}x + 2$$

$$y - 5 + 5 = \frac{1}{4}x + 2 + 5$$

$$y = \frac{1}{4}x + 7 \quad ✗$$

12. **Reason** The graphs of $4x + 12y = 8$ and $y = mx + 5$ are perpendicular. What is the value of m?

13. **Mathematical Connections** Rectangles have four right angles and opposite sides that are parallel.

a. Is the figure shown a rectangle? Explain.

b. If not, how could the points change so it would be a rectangle?

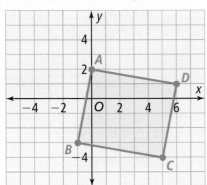

14. **Higher Order Thinking** Explain how you can determine whether the graphs of $5x - 3y = 2$ and $5x - 3y = 8$ are parallel without doing any calculations.

PRACTICE

Write the equation of the line that passes through the given point and is parallel to the given line. SEE EXAMPLE 1

15. $(5, -4)$; $y = \frac{1}{5}x - 4$ 16. $(2, 7)$; $3x - y = 5$

17. $(-3, 2)$; $y = -4$ 18. $(6, 4)$; $2x + 3y = 18$

19. Use the slopes of lines A and B to show that they are perpendicular to each other. SEE EXAMPLE 2

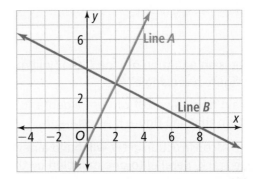

Write the equation of the line that passes through the given point and is perpendicular to the given line. SEE EXAMPLES 3 AND 5

20. $(-6, -3)$; $y = -\frac{2}{5}x$ 21. $(0, 3)$; $3x - 4y = -8$

22. $(-2, 5)$; $x = 3$ 23. $(4, 3)$; $4x - 5y = 30$

Are the graphs of each pair of equations parallel, perpendicular, or neither? SEE EXAMPLE 4

24. $y = 2x + 1$ 25. $y = \frac{1}{2}$
    $2x - y = 3$ $y = -3$

26. $x = 4$ 27. $-2x + 5y = -4$
    $y = 4$ $y = -\frac{5}{2}x + 6$

28. Copy and complete the table.

	Equation	Slope of a parallel line	Slope of a perpendicular line
a.	$y = \frac{1}{2}x + 6$		
b.	$x = -4.2$		
c.	$3x + 4y = 3$		
d.	$y = 3$		
e.	$y = x$		

APPLY

29. Use Structure An artist is drawing up plans for a mural. She wants to include a rectangle in her design.

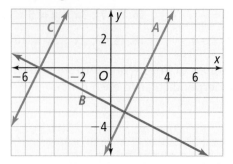

a. What is an equation of Line D that will make the figure a rectangle?

b. Explain how the artist can use algebra to confirm that the figure is a rectangle.

30. Reason A construction crew will build a new railroad track, parallel to one modeled by the line, which passes through the point $(8, 5)$. What equation models the path of the new track?

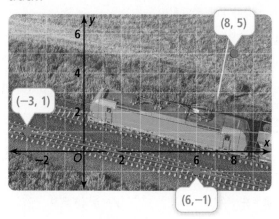

31. Make Sense and Persevere Elijah and Aubrey have summer jobs. Elijah deposits the same amount of money in his account every week. The equation $y = 125x + 72$ represents his bank balance any given week of the summer. Aubrey also deposits the same amount into her account every week. At the end of the third week she has $398. At the end of the sixth week she has $773.

a. Write an equation to represent Aubrey's bank balance any given week of the summer.

b. Would the graph of the equation for Aubrey's balance be parallel to the graph of Elijah's balance? Explain.

c. What do the parallel graphs mean in terms of the situation?

ASSESSMENT PRACTICE

32. Which of the following lines is perpendicular to $y = \frac{1}{4}x - 3$? Select all that apply.

Ⓐ $y = 4x$ Ⓑ $4x - y = -2$

Ⓒ $y = -4x + 6$ Ⓓ $8x - 2y = 3$

Ⓔ $y = 4x + 9$

33. SAT/ACT A line passing through $(6, a)$ and $(9, -4)$ is parallel to $2x - 3y = 6$. What is the value of a?

Ⓐ -6 Ⓑ -3

Ⓒ -2 Ⓓ 3

Ⓔ 6

34. Performance Task A video game is designed to model the path of a laser. A laser is placed at $(2, -1)$ and is aimed at Mirror 1. Other mirrors are placed as shown. Each mirror is placed so the light will reflect at a $90°$ angle.

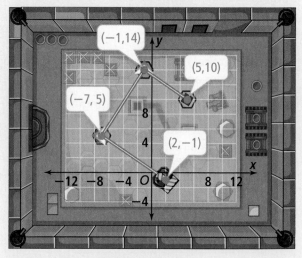

Part A After reflecting off of all three mirrors, where will the light cross the y-axis?

Part B Write an equation to model the path of the light between the following:

a. Laser and Mirror 1

b. Mirror 1 and Mirror 2

c. Mirror 2 and Mirror 3

d. Mirror 3 and y-axis

Part C Change the placement of the mirrors so that the laser light hits a target in Quadrant IV. Give the coordinates of the mirrors and the equations of lines that the path of the light would follow.

Topic Review

1. Why is it useful to have different forms of linear equations?

Vocabulary Review

Choose the correct term to complete each sentence.

2. The slopes of two perpendicular lines are opposite _____.

3. The _____ of a linear equation is $Ax + By = C$, where A, B, and C are integers.

4. Nonvertical lines that are _____ have the same slope and different y-intercepts.

5. The _____ of a linear equation is $y = mx + b$.

6. You can write the equation of a line using any point (x_1, y_1) and the slope, m, in _____, $y - y_1 = m(x - x_1)$.

- parallel
- perpendicular
- point-slope form
- reciprocals
- slope-intercept form
- standard form
- y-intercept

Concepts & Skills Review

LESSON 2-1	Slope-Intercept Form

Quick Review

The **slope-intercept form** of a linear equation is $y = mx + b$, where m is the slope of the line and the y-intercept is b. The slope-intercept form is useful when the slope and the y-intercept of the line are known.

Example

Write the equation of the line in slope-intercept form that passes through (0, 4) and (2, 3).

$m = \dfrac{4 - 3}{0 - 2}$ ·········· Use the slope formula.

$\quad = -\dfrac{1}{2}$

$b = 4$ ·········· The line intersects y-axis at (0, 4).

$y = mx + b$ ···· Write the equation in slope-intercept form.

$y = -\dfrac{1}{2}x + 4$ ··· Substitute $-\dfrac{1}{2}$ for m and 4 for b.

Practice & Problem Solving

Sketch the graph of each equation.

7. $y = 3x - 1$

8. $y = -1.5x + 3.5$

Write the equation of the line in slope-intercept form that passes through the given points.

9. (2, 0) and (4, 6)

10. (−1, 8) and (5, −2)

11. **Model With Mathematics** Ricardo wants to buy a new tablet computer that costs $1,150. He will make a down payment of $250 and will make monthly payments of $50. Write an equation in slope-intercept form that Ricardo can use to determine how much he will owe after x months.

LESSON 2-2 ▸ Point-Slope Form

Quick Review

The **point-slope form** of a linear equation is $y - y_1 = m(x - x_1)$, where m is the slope and (x_1, y_1) is a specific point and (x, y) is any point on the line. The point-slope form is useful when you know the slope and a point that is not $(0, b)$.

Example

Write the equation of the line in point-slope form that passes through the points (2, 2) and (5, 1).

$m = \dfrac{y_2 - y_1}{x_2 - x_1}$ ⋯⋯⋯⋯ Find the slope of the line.

$\quad = \dfrac{1 - 2}{5 - 2}$ ⋯⋯⋯⋯ Substitute (5, 1) for (x_2, y_2) and (2, 2) for (x_1, y_1).

$\quad = -\dfrac{1}{3}$

$y - y_1 = m(x - x_1)$ ⋯⋯⋯ Write the equation in point-slope form.

$y - 2 = -\dfrac{1}{3}(x - 2)$ ⋯⋯ Substitute $-\dfrac{1}{3}$ for m and (2, 2) for (x_1, y_1).

Practice & Problem Solving

Write the equation in point-slope form of the line that passes through the given point with the given slope.

12. $(4, -2); m = 0.5$

13. $(-2, 5); m = -3$

Write an equation in point-slope form of the line that passes through the given points.

14. (3, 1) and (−5, −2) **15.** (1.5, 4) and (−2.5, 6)

16. Reason Jeffrey purchased a card for $180 that gives him 20 visits to a new gym and includes a one-time fee for unlimited use of the sauna. After 5 visits, Jeff has $123.75 left on the card, and after 11 visits, he has $74.25 left on the card. Write an equation that Jeffrey can use to determine the cost of each visit and the fee for the sauna use.

LESSON 2-3 ▸ Standard Form

Quick Review

The **standard form** of a linear equation is $Ax + By = C$, where A, B, and C are integers. The standard form is useful for graphing vertical and horizontal lines, for finding the x- and y-intercepts, and for representing certain situations in terms of constraints.

Example

What are the x- and y-intercepts of the line $3x - 4y = 24$?

Substitute 0 for y and solve for x.

$3x - 4(0) = 24$

$\quad\quad x = 8$

Then substitute 0 for x and solve for y.

$3(0) - 4y = 24$

$\quad\quad y = -6$

The x-intercept is 8 and the y-intercept is −6.

Practice & Problem Solving

17. If $C = 15$, what values of A and B complete $Ax + By = C$ for the graph shown? Write the standard form of the equation.

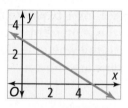

Write each equation in standard form.

18. $y = 4x - 5$ **19.** $y - 3 = 5(4 - x)$

Determine the x- and y-intercepts of each line.

20. $5x - 3y = 30$ **21.** $x + 3y = 24$

22. Model With Mathematics Jung-Soon has $25 to spend on prizes for a game at the school fair. Lip balm costs $1.25 each, and mini-notebooks cost $1.50 each. Write a linear equation that can be used to determine how many of each prize she can buy.

Quick Review

Two nonvertical lines are **parallel** if they have the same slope, but different y-intercepts. Vertical lines are parallel if they have different x-intercepts. Two nonvertical lines are **perpendicular** if their slopes are opposite reciprocals. A vertical line and a horizontal line are perpendicular if they intersect and form right angles.

Example

Are the graphs of the equations $4y = 2x - 5$ and $y = -2x + 7$ parallel, perpendicular, or neither?

Determine the slope of each line.

$$4y = 2x - 5 \qquad y = -2x + 7$$

$$\frac{4y}{4} = \frac{2x - 5}{4}$$

$$y = \frac{1}{2}x - \frac{5}{4}$$

The slopes of the lines are $\frac{1}{2}$ and -2, so the graphs of the equations are perpendicular lines.

Practice & Problem Solving

23. The graphs of $3x + 9y = 15$ and $y = mx - 4$ are parallel lines. What is the value of m?

Write the equation for the line that passes through the given point and is parallel to the given line.

24. $(2, 1)$; $y = -3x + 8$ 25. $(-3, -1)$; $x - 2y = 5$

Write the equation for the line that passes through the given point and is perpendicular to the given line.

26. $(1, 7)$; $x - 4y = 8$ 27. $(-2, 6)$; $y = 0.5x - 3$

Are the graphs of the given pairs of equations parallel, perpendicular, or neither?

28. $y = \frac{1}{4}x - 8$ 29. $3y + 2x = 9$

    $2x + y = 5$ $y = -\frac{2}{3}x - 4$

TOPIC 3

Linear Functions

? TOPIC ESSENTIAL QUESTION

How can linear functions be used to model situations and solve problems?

Topic Overview

enVision® STEM Project:
Planning a Recycling Drive

3-1 Relations and Functions

3-2 Linear Functions

3-3 Transforming Linear Functions

Mathematical Modeling in 3 Acts:
The Express Lane

3-4 Arithmetic Sequences

3-5 Scatter Plots and Lines of Fit

3-6 Analyzing Lines of Fit

Topic Vocabulary

- arithmetic sequence
- causation
- common difference
- continuous
- correlation coefficient
- discrete
- domain
- explicit formula
- extrapolation
- function
- function notation
- interpolation
- line of best fit
- linear function
- linear regression
- negative association
- negative correlation
- no association
- one-to-one
- positive association
- positive correlation
- range
- recursive formula
- relation
- residual
- sequence
- term of a sequence
- transformation
- translation
- trend line

Digital Experience

 INTERACTIVE STUDENT EDITION Access online or offline.

 ACTIVITIES Complete *Explore & Reason, Model & Discuss*, and *Critique & Explain* activities. Interact with Examples and Try Its.

 ANIMATION View and interact with real-world applications.

 PRACTICE Practice what you've learned.

 Go online | SavvasRealize.com

MATHEMATICAL MODELING IN 3 ACTS ⊝⊂▷

▶ The Express Lane

Some supermarkets have self-checkout lanes. Customers scan their items themselves and then pay with either cash or credit when they have finished scanning all of the items. Some customers think these lanes are faster than the checkout lanes with cashiers, but others don't like having to bag all of their purchases themselves.

What's your strategy for picking a checkout lane at the grocery store? Think about this during the Mathematical Modeling in 3 Acts lesson.

▶ **VIDEOS** Watch clips to support *Mathematical Modeling in 3 Acts Lessons* and enVision® *STEM Projects.*

CONCEPT SUMMARY Review key lesson content through multiple representations.

☑ **ASSESSMENT** Show what you've learned.

A-Z **GLOSSARY** Read and listen to English and Spanish definitions.

TUTORIALS Get help from *Virtual Nerd*, right when you need it.

MATH TOOLS Explore math with digital tools and manipulatives.

Did You Know?

Glass, aluminum, and other metals can be melted over and over again **without a loss in quality**. Paper can be recycled up to six times, with its quality decreasing each time.

Americans throw away **25,000,000 plastic bottles every hour**. If those bottles were recycled, they would offset the environmental impact of 625 round-trip flights between New York and London.

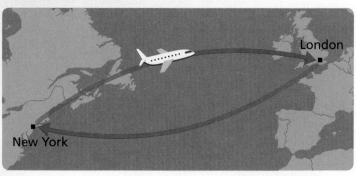

1 million recycled phones

35,274 lb of copper

772 lb of silver

75 lb of gold

33 lb of palladium

How Recycling Offsets CO$_2$ Production

RECYCLE	SAVE
1 ton of plastic	1 ton of CO$_2$
1 ton of paper	3 tons of CO$_2$
1 ton of metal	3 tons of CO$_2$
3 tons of glass	1 ton of CO$_2$

▶ Your Task: Planning a Recycling Drive

About 75% of the trash Americans generate is recyclable, but only about 30% gets recycled. You and your classmates will plan a recycling drive at your school to increase the amount of trash that gets recycled.

3-1
Relations and Functions

I CAN... determine whether a relation is a function.

VOCABULARY
• continuous
• discrete
• domain
• function
• one-to-one
• range
• relation

EXPLORE & REASON

The desks in a study hall are arranged in rows like the horizontal ones in the picture.

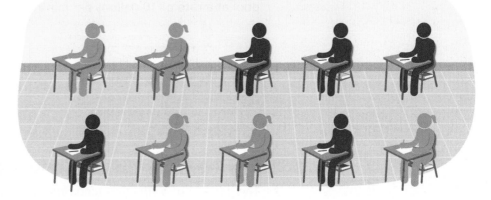

A. What is a reasonable number of rows for the study hall? What is a reasonable number of desks?

B. Look for Structure What number of rows would be impossible? What number of desks would be impossible? Explain.

C. What do your answers to Parts A and B reveal about what the graph of rows to desks looks like?

? ESSENTIAL QUESTION   What is a function? Why is domain and range important in defining a function?

EXAMPLE 1   Recognize Domain and Range

What are the domain and the range of the function?

x	1	2	3	4	5	⟵ inputs
y	11	12	13	13	13	⟵ outputs

A **relation** is a set of ordered pairs. A **function** is a relation in which each input is assigned to exactly one output. The **domain** of a function is the set of inputs. The **range** of a function is the set of outputs. By convention, inputs are *x*-values and outputs are *y*-values.

The domain of this function is the set of *x*-values, {1, 2, 3, 4, 5}. The range is the set of *y*-values, {11, 12, 13}.

Try It!   **1.** Identify the domain and the range of each function.

a.
x	2	3	4	5	6
y	0	1	2	3	4

b.
x	−3	−1	1	3	4
y	1	3	−2	2	6

CONCEPTUAL
UNDERSTANDING

👆 **EXAMPLE 2** — Analyze Reasonable Domains and Ranges

A. A function can model each situation. What is a reasonable domain and range of each function?

A hose fills a 10,000-gallon swimming pool at a rate of 10 gallons per minute.

A restaurant needs to order chairs for its tables. One table can accommodate four chairs.

> A reasonable domain is from 0 minutes to the time it takes to fill the pool. A reasonable range is from 0 to 10,000 gallons, the capacity of the pool.

> A reasonable domain is from 0 tables to the number of tables needed. A reasonable range is multiples of 4 from 0 to 4 times the number of tables needed.

B. Is the domain for each situation continuous or discrete?

The domain of a function is **continuous** when it includes all real numbers. The graph of the function is a line or curve.

The domain of a function is **discrete** when it consists of just whole numbers or integers. The graph of the function is a series of data points.

Sketch a graph of each situation.

> The volume of water in the pool can be determined at any point in time, for any value of x.

> The number of tables and chairs must be whole numbers. There cannot be parts of tables or chairs.

MAKE SENSE AND PERSEVERE
What do the relationships in the two situations have in common?

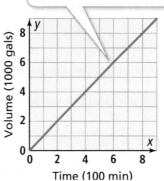

The domain is continuous.

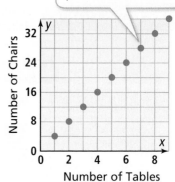

The domain is discrete.

 Try It! **2.** Analyze each situation. Identify a reasonable domain and range for each situation. Explain.

a. A bowler pays $2.75 per game.

b. A car travels 25 miles using 1 gallon of gas.

 EXAMPLE 3 **Classify Relations and Functions**

Is each relation a function? If so, is it one-to-one or not one-to-one?

A function is **one-to-one** if no two elements of the domain map to the same element in the range. When two or more elements of the domain map to the same element of the range, the function is **not one-to-one**.

A. {(1, 2), (5, 6), (7, –1), (8, 0)}

The relation is a function. Every element of the domain {1, 5, 7, 8} maps to exactly one element of the range {–1, 0, 2, 6}.

Since none of the range values are shared, the function is one-to-one.

COMMON ERROR
Two or more elements of the domain of a function can map to one element of the range, but two or more elements of the range, can not map to only one element of the domain.

B.

The relation is a function. Every element of the domain maps to exactly one element of the range.

Since more than one element in the domain maps to a single element in the range, the function is not one-to-one.

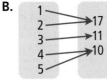 **Try It!** **3.** Is each relation a function? If so is it one-to-one or not one-to-one?

a.
b.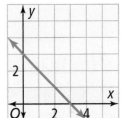

APPLICATION **EXAMPLE 4** **Identify Constraints on the Domain**

The diagram shows shipping charges as a function of the weight of several online orders. Based on the situation, what constraints, if any, are on the domain of the function?

REASON
Think about the relationship between elements in the domain and the elements in the range.

An order must have a weight greater than zero, so the domain of the function is confined to values greater than 0.

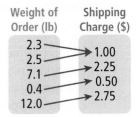

Weight of Order (lb)	Shipping Charge ($)
2.3	1.00
2.5	2.25
7.1	0.50
0.4	2.75
12.0	

 Try It! **4.** Margaret has a monthly clothes budget of $50. She maps the amount of money she spends each month to the number of items of clothing she buys. What constraints are there on the domain?

WORDS A **relation** is any set of ordered pairs.

A relation is a **function** when each input, or element in the domain, has exactly one output, or element in the range.

TABLE

x	−5	−2	−1	2	4
y	0	4	−3	4	−1

Each element in the domain is associated with exactly one element in the range.

NUMBERS {(−5, 0), (−2, 4), (−1, −3), (2, 4), (4, −1)}

The domain is the set of x-values.
The range is the set of y-values.

DIAGRAM

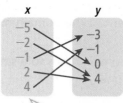

Each element in the domain is assigned one element in the range.

GRAPH

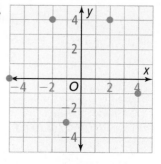

Do You UNDERSTAND?

1. **ESSENTIAL QUESTION** What is a function? Why is domain and range important when defining a function?

2. **Vocabulary** Maya is tracking the amount of rainfall during a storm. Describe the *domain* and *range* for this situation. Include *continuous* or *discrete* in your description.

3. **Reason** What can you conclude about the domain and the range of a function if a vertical line at $x = 5$ passes through 2 points? 1 point? No points? Explain.

4. **Error Analysis** Felipe states that every relation is a function, but not every function is a relation. Explain Felipe's error.

Do You KNOW HOW?

5. Use the graph to determine the domain and range of this relation. Is the relation a function?

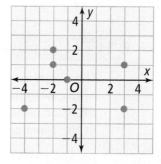

6. For the set of ordered pairs shown, identify the domain and range. Does the relation represent a function?

{(1, 8), (5, 3), (7, 6), (2, 2), (8, 4), (3, 9), (5, 7)}

7. Each day Jacob records the number of laps and the distance he walks, in miles, on a track. Graph the relation and determine whether the distance that Jacob walks is a function of the number of laps.

{(3, 0.75), (6, 1.5), (9, 2.25), (2, 0.5), (7, 1.75), (10, 2.5), (4, 1)}

PRACTICE & PROBLEM SOLVING

 Scan for Multimedia

Practice · Tutorial

Additional Exercises Available Online

 UNDERSTAND

8. **Use Structure** Identify the domain and range of each function.

a.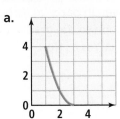

b.

9. **Construct Arguments** If the domain of a relation is all whole numbers between 2.5 and 7.5, and the range contains 6 different values, can you determine whether the relation is a function? Explain your reasoning.

10. **Error Analysis** A student was asked to name all values of *n* that make the relation a function. Correct the error.

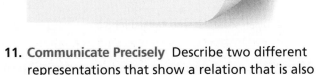

{(2, 8), (6, 0), (4, 2), (2n, n)}
n can be any value except 2, 6, or 4.

✗

11. **Communicate Precisely** Describe two different representations that show a relation that is also a function. Explain.

12. **Higher Order Thinking** Relations mapping domain values to range values can be described as *one-to-one* or *not one-to-one*.

a. If one *x*-value maps to many *y*-values (*one-to-many*), does the relation represent a function? If the *x*- and *y*-values are reversed, does the relation represent a function? Explain.

b. If the relation is *not one-to-one*, does the relation represent a function? If the *x*- and *y*-values are reversed, does the relation represent a function? Explain.

c. If the relation is *one-to-one*, does the relation represent a function? If the *x*- and *y*-values are reversed, does the relation represent a function? Explain.

 PRACTICE

Identify the domain and range of each relation. Is the relation a function? Explain. SEE EXAMPLES 1 AND 3

13.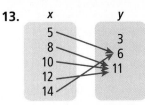

14.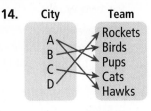

Analyze each situation. Identify a reasonable domain and range for each situation. SEE EXAMPLE 2

15. An airplane travels at 565 mph.

16. Tickets to a sporting event cost $125 each.

17. An average person consumes 2,000 Calories each day.

Determine whether each relation is a function. If yes, classify the function as one-to-one or not one-to-one. SEE EXAMPLE 3

18.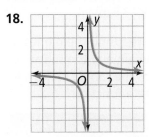

19.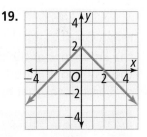

20.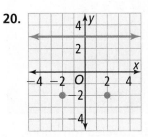

21.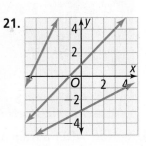

Identify any constraints on the domain. SEE EXAMPLE 4

22. Cameron earns an hourly wage at his job. He makes a table of the number of hours he works each week and the amount of money he earns.

23. Every day Isabel swims 10 to 20 laps in a 50-meter pool. She tracks the numbers of laps she swims and how long it takes her to complete the lap, in minutes.

APPLY

24. Model With Mathematics The table shows the number of minutes Drew spends in each class for two weeks.

Class	Week 1 Time (min)	Week 2 Time (min)
English	60	60
Math	90	60
History	45	45
Biology	45	45
Biology Lab	0	60

a. For Drew's week 1 classes, identify the domain and range. Is the relation a function? Explain.

b. For Drew's week 2 classes, identify the domain and range. Is the relation a function? Explain.

c. Is Drew's class time for week 2 a function of his class time for week 1? Explain.

25. Make Sense and Persevere Using the names of the emoticons as the domain and the shapes of the emoticons' mouths as the range, make a list of 5 emoticons that make a function.

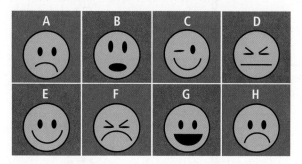

26. Reason After a train has traveled for $\frac{1}{2}$ hour, it increases its speed and travels at a constant rate for $1\frac{1}{2}$ hours.

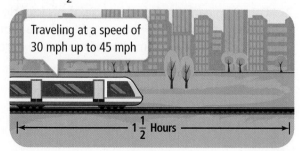

Traveling at a speed of 30 mph up to 45 mph

$1\frac{1}{2}$ Hours

a. What is the domain? What is the range?

b. How can you represent the relationship between time traveled and speed?

c. Why did you choose this representation?

ASSESSMENT PRACTICE

27. The graph shows students' study times and their scores on a recent exam. Determine whether each of the data points given in parts (a) through (e) can be added to the graph so the graph still represents a function. Select **Yes** or **No**.

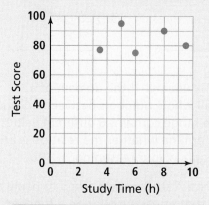

	Yes	No
a. Pilar scored 85 and studied for 8 h.	☐	☐
b. Naida scored 97 and studied for 9 h.	☐	☐
c. Alex scored 77 and studied for 4.5 h.	☐	☐
d. Damian scored 80 and studied for 7.5 h.	☐	☐
e. Dylan scored 90 and studied for 6 h.	☐	☐

28. SAT/ACT For a relation, where y is a function of x, and $y = 4$ when $x = 6$; which of the following does not represent another possible mapping in the relation?

Ⓐ $x = 3$ maps to $y = 2$

Ⓑ $x = 1$ maps to $y = 6$

Ⓒ $x = 0$ maps to $y = 0$

Ⓓ $x = 4$ maps to $y = 6$

Ⓔ $x = 6$ maps to $y = 2$

29. Performance Task City Tours rents bicycles for $10 an hour with a maximum daily fee of $100.

Part A Make a table that show the cost for renting a bicycle for 1, 3, 11, and 20 hours.

Part B Is cost a function of time? Explain.

Part C Is time a function of cost? Explain.

3-2

Linear Functions

I CAN... identify, evaluate, graph, and write linear equations.

VOCABULARY

• function notation
• linear function

EXPLORE & REASON

The flowchart shows the steps of a math puzzle.

A. Try the puzzle with 6 different integers.

B. Record each number you try and the result.

C. Make a prediction about what the final number will be for any number. Explain.

D. Use Structure Would your prediction be true for all numbers? Explain.

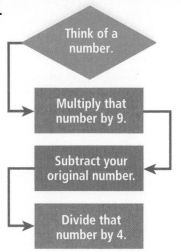

Think of a number.

Multiply that number by 9.

Subtract your original number.

Divide that number by 4.

ESSENTIAL QUESTION How can you identify a linear function?

CONCEPTUAL UNDERSTANDING

EXAMPLE 1 Evaluate Functions in Function Notation

A. How can you represent a function rule?

Write the equation $y = 5x + 1$ using function notation.

Remember that a function is a rule that takes an input, or an element in the domain, and maps it to an output, or an element in the range.

COMMUNICATE PRECISELY
Function names are not restricted to f. What advantages are there to giving letter names to functions when modeling real-world situations?

Function notation is a method for writing variables as a function of other variables. The variable y, becomes a function of x, meaning the variable x is used to find the value of y. This helps distinguish between different functions. You can use the relationship between variables to solve problems and make predictions.

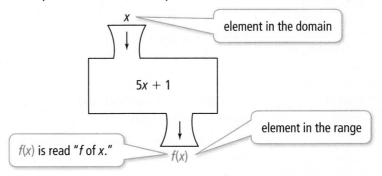

x → element in the domain

$5x + 1$

$f(x)$ is read "f of x." $f(x)$ → element in the range

COMMUNICATE PRECISELY
$f(x)$ describes both the function that is being used, f, and the input value, x.

The function f is defined in function notation by $f(x) = 5x + 1$.

CONTINUED ON THE NEXT PAGE

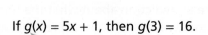
EXAMPLE 1 CONTINUED

B. What is the value of $g(x) = 5x + 1$ when $x = 3$?

Evaluate $g(x) = 5x + 1$ for $x = 3$.

> Substitute the input, 3, for every instance of x in the function.

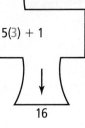

3

$5(3) + 1$

16

If $g(x) = 5x + 1$, then $g(3) = 16$.

> Function notation can use letters other than f. Other commonly used letters are g and h.

 Try It!   **1. Evaluate each function for $x = 4$.**

     a. $g(x) = -2x - 3$ **b.** $h(x) = 7x + 15$

EXAMPLE 2   **Write a Linear Function Rule**

The cost to make 4 bracelets is shown in the table.

How can you determine the cost to make any number of bracelets?

Step 1 Examine the relationship between the values in the table.

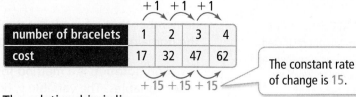

number of bracelets	1	2	3	4
cost	17	32	47	62

$+1 \ +1 \ +1$

$+15 \ +15 \ +15$

> The constant rate of change is 15.

The relationship is linear.

Step 2 Write a function using slope-intercept form for the rule.

$$f(x) = mx + b$$
$$f(x) = 15x + b$$

Step 3 Find the value of b.

$$17 = 15(1) + b$$
$$2 = b$$

> Substitute any ordered pair from the table.

You can use the function $f(x) = 15x + 2$ to determine the cost to make any number of bracelets.

The function $f(x) = 15x + 2$ is a linear function because the rule, $15x + 2$, is the same as the rule of the linear equation $y = 15x + 2$.

COMMON ERROR
You may think that the domain and range are all real numbers because the function $f(x) = 15x + 2$ has a domain and range of all real numbers. However, you need to consider the situation when determining the domain and range of a particular scenario.

 Try It!   **2. Write a linear function for the data in each table using function notation.**

a.

x	1	2	3	4
y	6.5	13	19.5	26

b.

x	1	2	3	4
y	1	4	7	10

APPLICATION   👆 **EXAMPLE 3**   **Analyze a Linear Function**

A. **Tamika records the outside temperature at 6:00 A.M. The outside temperature increases by 2°F every hour for the next 6 hours. If the temperature continues to increase at the same rate, what will the temperature be at 2:00 P.M.?**

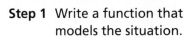

Step 1 Write a function that models the situation.

2°F increase each hour

$f(x) = 2x - 3$ ← temperature at 6:00 A.M.

Step 2 Sketch a graph of the function.

The range of this function is the set of reasonable temperatures in °F greater than –3.

Use slope-intercept form to graph the equation.

$f(x) = 2x - 3$

Step 3: Find the value of y when $x = 8$.

$y = 2(8) - 3$
$= 13$

Assuming the temperature continues to increase at the same rate, the temperature at 2:00 p.m. will be 13°F.

The graph of $f(x) = 2x - 3$ is a line. A **linear function** is a function whose graph is a line.

MODEL WITH MATHEMATICS
What makes a function a good model over a given domain?

B. **Does using a linear function realistically represent the temperature for the domain of $0 < x < 24$? Explain.**

The graph of $f(x) = 2x - 3$ has a slope of 2, which represents the temperature rising 2°F each hour. However, when the sun sets it is unlikely that the temperature will continue to rise. The linear function is realistic for only a portion of the day.

 Try It!   **3.** Sketch the graph of each function.

a. $f(x) = -x + 1$ b. $g(x) = 3x + 1$

APPLICATION

EXAMPLE 4   Use Linear Functions to Solve Problems

A chairlift starts 0.5 mi above the base of a mountain and travels up the mountain at a constant speed. How far from the base of the mountain is the chairlift after 10 minutes?

The chairlift travels 6 miles per hour. It takes 15 minutes to reach the top.

0.5 miles from base.

Formulate ◀ Write a linear function to represent the distance the chairlift travels from the base of the mountain.

Let t = time in minutes.

$$\frac{6 \text{ miles}}{\text{hour}} \times \frac{1 \text{ hour}}{60 \text{ minutes}} = \frac{0.1 \text{ mile}}{\text{minute}}$$

The speed of the chairlift is in miles per hour, so convert the speed to miles per minute.

distance traveled = rate of the chairlift • time traveling + distance from the base

$\quad d(t) \qquad = \qquad 0.1 \qquad • \qquad t \qquad + 0.5$

Compute ◀ The distance of the chairlift from the base of the mountain at any time is represented by the linear function, $d(t) = 0.1t + 0.5$.

Evaluate the function for $t = 10$.

$$d(t) = 0.1(10) + 0.5$$
$$= 1 + 0.5$$
$$= 1.5$$

Interpret ◀ After 10 minutes, the chairlift will be 1.5 miles up the mountainside.

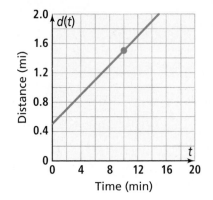

Try It!   4. In Example 4, how would the function, graph, and equation change if the speed is 4 mph? What is the effect on the domain?

Concept Summary   Assess

CONCEPT SUMMARY Linear Function Representations

WORDS Linear functions are represented by words, rules, tables, or graphs. Function notation tells us the name of a function and the input variable.

ALGEBRA $f(x) = -2x + 1$

"f of x"

TABLE

x	−2	−1	0	1	2
f(x)	5	3	1	−1	−3

The table shows the domain and range of the function.

GRAPH The graph of the function $f(x) = -2x + 1$ is the graph of the linear equation $y = -2x + 1$.

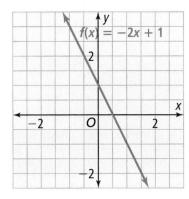

Do You UNDERSTAND?

1. **ESSENTIAL QUESTION** How can you identify a linear function?

2. **Communicate Precisely** Give a real-world example of a function that is linear and one that is not linear. Explain.

3. **Vocabulary** What is the difference between a *linear function* and a linear equation?

4. **Error Analysis** The cost of using a game facility is $1 for every 12 minutes. Talisa writes the function for the cost per hour as $f(x) = 12x$. Explain Talisa's error.

Do You KNOW HOW?

Evaluate each function for x = 2 and x = 6.

5. $f(x) = 4x - 3$

6. $f(x) = -(x - 2)$

7. Sketch the graph of $f(x) = \frac{1}{2}x + 5$.

8. What function models the height of the periscope lens at time t? If the periscope reaches its maximum height after ascending for 22 seconds, what is the maximum height in feet?

24 inches above the surface

ascends at 6 inches per second

UNDERSTAND

9. Use Structure The two points on the graph are given by the function f.

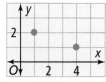

a. Use the two points to find the equation that represents the function f.

b. What is f(6)?

10. Higher Order Thinking Consider the functions $g(x) = 2x + 1$ and $h(x) = 2x + 2$ for the domain $0 < x < 5$.

a. Without evaluating or graphing the functions, how do the ranges compare?

b. Graph the two functions and describe each range over the given interval.

11. Make Sense and Persevere Customers at a deli can buy an unlimited amount of potato salad. The customer is not charged for the weight of the container.

a. The table shows the weight of the container with food and the cost. If 1 oz = 0.0625 lb, what is the price per pound of the potato salad? What is the weight of the container in pounds? What is the weight of the container and potato salad in pounds?

Weight (oz)	5	7	9	11	13
Cost ($)	▦	1	2	3	4

b. If the store had not accounted for the weight of the container, how much would the customer be charged for the container? Is the cost of the container the same, or does it vary by how much potato salad is purchased? Explain.

12. Error Analysis Describe and correct the error a student made when finding the function rule for the data in the table.

x	1	2	3	4
y	10	19	28	37

When x increases by 1, y increases by 9 each time. When x = 1, y = 10. So y = 9x + 10. ✗

PRACTICE

Find the value of f(5) for each function.
EXAMPLE 1

13. $f(x) = 6 + 3x$

14. $f(x) = -2(x + 1)$

15. $f(a) = 3(a + 2) - 1$

16. $f(h) = -\frac{h}{10}$

17. $f(m) = 1 - 4\left(\frac{m}{2}\right)$

18. $f(m) = 2(m - 3)$

Write a linear function for the data in each table.
SEE EXAMPLE 2

19.

x	0	1	2	3	4
y	−1	4	9	14	19

20.

x	0	1	2	3	4
y	4	1.5	−1	−3.5	−6

21.

x	−2	−1	0	1	2
y	2	$\frac{1}{2}$	−1	$-2\frac{1}{2}$	−4

Sketch the graph of each linear function.
SEE EXAMPLE 3

22. $g(x) = x - 3$

23. $h(x) = 3 - x$

24. $f(x) = \frac{1}{2}(x - 1)$

25. $f(x) = 0.75(10 - x) + 1$

Use the graph for Exercises 26 and 27. SEE EXAMPLE 3

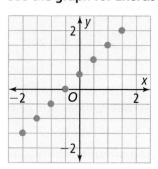

26. Is the function shown a linear function? Explain.

27. Describe the domain and range of the function.

28. Katrina buys a 64-ft roll of fencing to make a rectangular play area for her dogs. Use $2(l + w) = 64$ to write a function for the length, given the width. Graph the function. What is a reasonable domain for the situation? Explain. SEE EXAMPLE 4

APPLY

29. Model With Mathematics A staff gauge measures the height of the water level in a river compared to the average water level. At one gauge the river is 1 ft below its average water level of 10 ft. It begins to rise by a constant rate of 1.5 ft per hour.

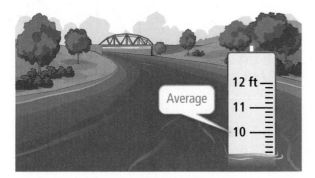

12 ft
Average
11
10

a. Graph the linear function to show the change in the water level over time.

b. Will the river reach a level of 7 ft above normal after 5 hours? Explain.

30. Use Structure Ramona's Garage charges the following labor rates. All customers are charged for at least 0.5 hr.

Ramona's Garage					
Hours	0.5	1	1.5	2	2.5
Labor	$60	$90	$120	$150	$180

a. Write a linear function for the data in the table.

b. A repair job took 4 h and 15 min and required $390 in parts. What is the total cost?

31. Reason A snack bar at an outdoor fair is open from 10 A.M. to 5:30 P.M. and has 465 bottles of water for sale. Sales average 1.3 bottles of water per minute.

a. Graph the number of bottles remaining each hour as a function of time in hours. Find the domain and range.

b. At this rate, what time would they run out of water? How many bottles of water are needed at the start of the next day? Explain.

ASSESSMENT PRACTICE

32. Consider the function $f(x) = 3(x - 1) - 0.4(9 - x)$. Match each expression with its equivalent value.

I. $f(2) + f(4)$ A. 3.4

II. $f(5)$ B. 3.6

III. $f(7) - f(6)$ C. 7.2

IV. $f(3)$ D. 10.4

33. SAT/ACT Determine a linear function from the data in the table. Which point is not part of the function?

x	f(x)
0	180
1	174
2	168
3	162
4	156

Ⓐ (12, 108)

Ⓑ (30, 0)

Ⓒ (−15, 270)

Ⓓ (21, 54)

Ⓔ (9, 120)

34. Performance Task Manuel calculates the business costs and profits to produce *n* hiking backpacks. Manuel's profit is his revenue minus expenses.

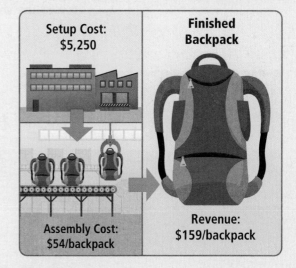

Setup Cost: $5,250

Finished Backpack

Assembly Cost: $54/backpack

Revenue: $159/backpack

Part A Write a function to represent the profit Manuel makes selling *n* backpacks.

Part B Graph the profit function. What is a reasonable domain for this function for one year if his revenue is between $4,000 and $30,000? Is the function discrete or continuous? Explain.

Part C How much is his profit if he sells 43 backpacks? Explain.

3-3

Transforming Linear Functions

SavvasRealize.com

I CAN... transform linear functions.

VOCABULARY
- transformation
- translation

Activity   Assess

CRITIQUE & EXPLAIN

Avery states that the graph of *g* is the same as the graph of *f* with every point shifted vertically. Cindy states that the graph of *g* is the same as the graph of *f* with every point shifted horizontally.

A. Give an argument to support Avery's statement.

B. Give an argument to support Cindy's statement.

C. Look for Relationships What do you know about linear equations that might support either of their statements?

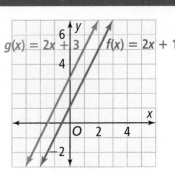

ESSENTIAL QUESTION How does modifying the input or the output of a linear function rule transform its graph?

APPLICATION

EXAMPLE 1   Vertical Translations of Linear Functions

The positions of 2 baby sea turtles making their way to the water after hatching from their eggs is recorded. They move at the same speed, with Byron starting 2 ft ahead of Frank's starting point.

A. What function represents each turtle's position as they make their way toward the shore?

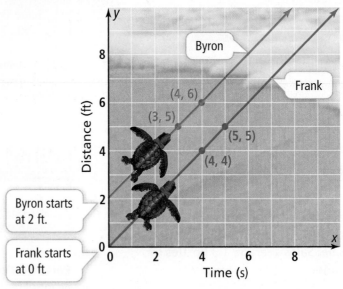

Find the speed of each turtle by finding the slope of each line.

Frank: $m = \frac{5-0}{5-0} = 1$ 　　　　 Byron: $m = \frac{6-2}{4-0} = 1$

Both turtles are moving at 1 ft/s.

The function $f(x) = x$ represents Frank's distance from his starting point, and $g(x) = x + 2$ represents Byron's distance from his starting point.

CONTINUED ON THE NEXT PAGE

　　　　　Go Online | SavvasRealize.com

EXAMPLE 1 CONTINUED

B. What happens to the graph of a function when you add a constant to its output?

Compare Byron's and Frank's graph.

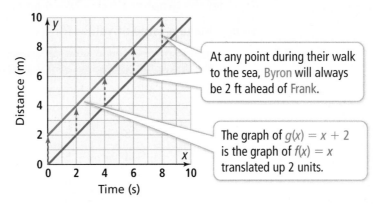

At any point during their walk to the sea, Byron will always be 2 ft ahead of Frank.

The graph of $g(x) = x + 2$ is the graph of $f(x) = x$ translated up 2 units.

LOOK FOR RELATIONSHIPS
Look for relationships between the value of k and whether the vertical translation is up or down.

Adding a constant k to the output of a linear function *translates* the graph vertically by k units.

 Try It! **1.** Let $f(x) = -4x$.

  a. How does the graph of $g(x) = -4x - 3$ compare with the graph of f?

  b. How does the graph of $g(x) = -4x + 1.5$ compare with the graph of f?

DEFINITION

A **transformation** of a function f maps each point of its graph to a new location. One type of transformation is a *translation*. A **translation** shifts each point of the graph of a function the same distance. A translation may be horizontal or vertical.

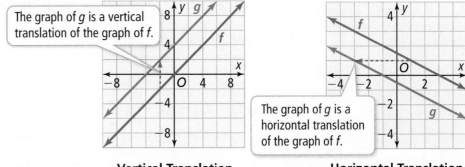

The graph of g is a vertical translation of the graph of f.

The graph of g is a horizontal translation of the graph of f.

Vertical Translation   **Horizontal Translation**

CONCEPTUAL
UNDERSTANDING   **EXAMPLE 2**   Horizontal Translations of Linear Functions

How does adding a constant k to the input of a linear function affect its graph?

Consider the graphs of $f(x) = 2x - 4$ and $g(x) = 2(x + 5) - 4$.

Step 1   Make a table of values for $f(x) = 2x - 4$ and $g(x) = 2(x + 5) - 4$.

x	$f(x) = 2x - 4$	$x + 5$	$g(x) = 2(x + 5) - 4$
−4	−12	1	$2(1) - 4 = -2$
−3	−10	2	$2(2) - 4 = 0$
−2	−8	3	$2(3) - 4 = 2$
0	−4	5	$2(5) - 4 = 6$
1	−2	6	$2(6) - 4 = 8$
2	0	7	$2(7) - 4 = 10$
3	2	8	$2(8) - 4 = 12$

Step 2   Graph the functions $f(x) = 2x - 4$ and $g(x) = 2(x + 5) - 4$.

The graph of g is the graph of f translated 5 units to the left.

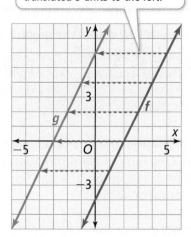

COMMON ERROR
You may think that a positive value of k in $g(x) = 2(x + k) - 4$ shifts the graph in a positive direction, to the right. However, a positive value of k shifts the graph to the left.

Adding a constant k to the input of the function translates the graph horizontally by k units.

 Try It!   **2.** Let $f(x) = 3x + 7$.

     a. How does the graph of $g(x) = 3(x - 4) + 7$ compare with the graph of f?

     b. How does the graph of $g(x) = 3(x + 9.5) + 7$ compare with the graph of f?

👆 **EXAMPLE 3** **Stretches and Compressions of Linear Functions**

A. How does multiplying the output of a linear function affect its graph?

Compare the graphs of $f(x) = x + 1$ and $g(x) = 4(x + 1)$.

x	f(x) = x + 1	g(x) = 4(x + 1)
−3	−2	−8
−2	−1	−4
−1	0	0
0	1	4
1	2	8

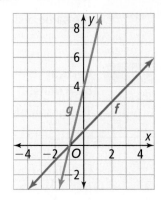

GENERALIZE

Is it always true that for a linear function f, the graphs of f and kf would have different y-intercepts?

The graph of g is vertical stretch of the graph of f, by a scale factor of 4. The slope and y-intercept are scaled by the same factor.

Multiplying the output of a linear function f by k scales its graph vertically. If $k > 1$, the transformed graph is a **vertical stretch**. If $0 < |k| < 1$ the transformed graph is a **vertical compression**.

B. How does multiplying the input of a linear function affect its graph?

Compare the graphs of $f(x) = x + 1$ and $g(x) = (3x) + 1$.

x	f(x) = x + 1	g(x) = (3x) + 1
0	1	1
1	2	4
2	3	7
3	4	10
6	7	19

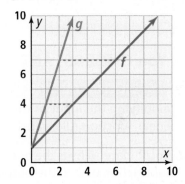

The graph of g is horizontal compression of the graph of f, by a scale factor of 3. The slope is changed by the same factor, but the y-intercept is unchanged.

Multiplying the input of a linear function f by k scales its graph horizontally. If $k > 1$, the transformed graph is a **horizontal compression**. If $0 < |k| < 1$ the transformed graph is a **horizontal stretch**.

 Try It! **3.** Let $f(x) = x - 2$.

  a. How does the graph of $g(x) = 0.25(x - 2)$ compare with the graph of f?

  b. How does the graph of $g(x) = 0.5x - 2$ compare with the graph of f?

	Translations		Stretches and Compressions	
WORDS	Translations shift each point of the graph the same distance horizontally or vertically.		Stretches and compressions scale the graph either horizontally or vertically.	
ALGEBRA	**Vertical by k units:** The graph of $g(x) = \left(\frac{1}{2}x - 2\right) + k$ is a vertical translation of $f(x) = \frac{1}{2}x - 2.$	**Horizontal by k units:** The graph of $g(x) = -2(x + k) + 2$ is a horizontal translation of $f(x) = -2x + 2.$	**Vertical by scale factor k:** The graph of $g(x) = k(-x + 2)$ is a stretch of $f(x) = -x + 2$ when $k > 1.$	**Horizontal by scale factor k:** The graph of $g(x) = k(-x) + 2$ is a compression of $f(x) = -x + 2$ when $k > 1.$

GRAPHS

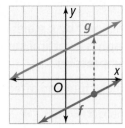 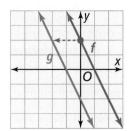 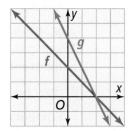 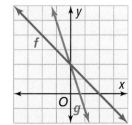

Do You UNDERSTAND?

1. **ESSENTIAL QUESTION** How does modifying the input or the output of a linear function rule transform its graph?

2. **Vocabulary** Why is the addition or subtraction of k to the output of a function considered a *translation*?

3. **Error Analysis** The addition or subtraction of a number to a linear function always moves the line up or down. Describe the error with this reasoning.

4. **Use Structure** Why does multiplying the input of a linear function change only the slope while multiplying the output changes both the slope and the y-intercept?

Do You KNOW HOW?

Given $f(x) = 4x + 1$, describe how the graph of g compares with the graph of f.

5. $g(x) = 4(x + 3) + 1$ 6. $g(x) = (4x + 1) + 3$

Given $f(x) = x + 2$, describe how setting $k = 4$ affects the slope and y-intercept of the graph of g compared to the graph of f.

7. $g(x) = 4(x + 2)$ 8. $g(x) = (4x) + 2$

9. The minimum wage for employees of a company is modeled by the function $f(x) = 7.25x$. The company decided to offer a signing bonus of $75. How does adding this amount affect a graph of an employee's earnings?

UNDERSTAND

10. Reason Describe the transformation of the function $f(x) = \frac{1}{2}x - 2$ that makes the slope 2 and the y-intercept –8.

11. Look for Relationships Why do translations produce parallel lines?

12. Error Analysis A student graphs $f(x) = 3x - 2$. On the same grid they graph the function g which is a transformation of f made by subtracting 4 from the input of f. Describe and correct the error they made when graphing g.

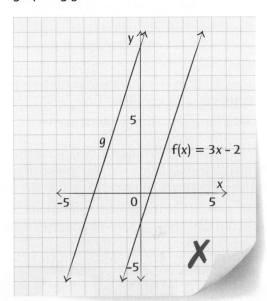

13. Look for Relationships Let $f(x) = \frac{1}{2}x - 3$. Suppose you subtract 6 from the input of f to create a new function g, then multiply the input of function g by 4 to create a function h. What equation represents h?

14. Use Structure Describe each transformation. Then write the equation of the transformed function.

$f(x) = 2x + 1 \qquad g(x) = \frac{1}{3}x + 2$

	Transformation	Description	Function
a.	$f(x) - 5$		
b.	$g(x) + 4$		
c.	$3g(x)$		
d.	$\frac{1}{2}f(x)$		

PRACTICE

Given $f(x) = 3x + 5$, describe how the graph of g compares with the graph of f.
SEE EXAMPLES 1, 2, AND 3

15. $g(x) = (3x + 5) + 8$ **16.** $g(x) = (3x + 5) - 4$

17. $g(x) = 3(x + 10) + 5$ **18.** $g(x) = 3(x - 1) + 5$

19. $g(x) = 3(0.1x) + 5$ **20.** $g(x) = 5(3x + 5)$

21. $g(x) = 3(2x) + 5$ **22.** $g(x) = 8(3x + 5)$

Given $f(x) = 2x + 3$, describe how the value of k affects the slope and y-intercept of the graph of g compared to the graph of f. SEE EXAMPLE 3

23. $g(x) = 3(2x + 3)$ **24.** $g(x) = 2(0.5x) + 3$

25. $g(x) = \frac{1}{6}(2x + 3)$ **26.** $g(x) = 2\left(\frac{1}{8}\right)x + 3$

27. $g(x) = (2x + 3) - 3$ **28.** $g(x) = 2(x + 0.5) + 3$

Find the value of k for each function g. Then describe the graph of g as a transformation of the graph of f.

29.

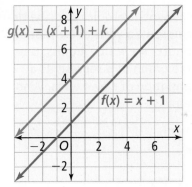

30.

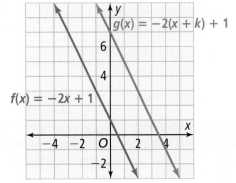

APPLY

31. Mathematical Connections The cost of renting a landscaping tractor is a $100 security deposit plus the hourly rate.

TRACTOR
FOR RENT
$40/hour

a. The function f represents the cost of renting the tractor. The function g represents the cost if the hourly rate were doubled. Write each function.

b. How would the slope and y-intercept of the graph g compare to the slope and y-intercept of the graph of f?

32. Construct Arguments Veronica said the graph of g below represents a vertical translation of the function $f(x) = x + 1$ by 4 units. Dawn argued that the graph of g represents a horizontal translation of f by 4 units. Who is correct? Explain.

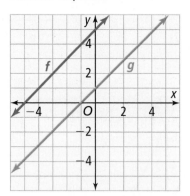

33. Higher Order Thinking The graph of a linear function f has a negative slope. Describe the effect on the graph of the function if the transformation has a value of $k < 0$.

a. adding k to the outputs of f

b. adding k to the inputs of f

c. multiplying the outputs of f by k

d. multiplying the inputs of f by k

ASSESSMENT PRACTICE

34. How is the graph of the function $g(x) = \frac{2}{5}x + 6$ transformed from the graph of the function $f(x) = \frac{2}{5}x$?

Ⓐ Moved up 6 units

Ⓑ Moved down 6 units

Ⓒ Moved left 6 units

Ⓓ Moved right 6 units

35. SAT/ACT Which of the following describes the differences between the graph of f and the graph of the output of f multiplied by 3?

Ⓐ The slope changes by a factor of 3; the y-intercept does not change.

Ⓑ Both the slope and y-intercept change by a factor of 3.

Ⓒ The slope does not change; the y-intercept changes by a factor of 3.

Ⓓ Neither the slope nor y-intercept change.

36. Performance Task The science club members are using transformations on coordinate grids to track the movement of constellations in the sky.

Choose one side of the constellation depicted below and describe a series of transformations to move the side.

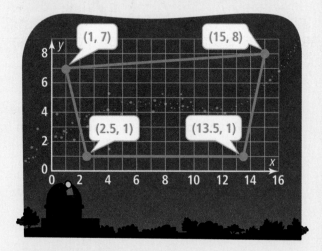

Copy and complete the table to record the motion.

Transformation	Function

MATHEMATICAL MODELING IN **3** ACTS

SavvasRealize.com

▶ The Express Lane

Some supermarkets have self checkout lanes. Customers scan their items themselves and then pay with either cash or credit when they have finished scanning all of the items. Some customers think these lanes are faster than the checkout lanes with cashiers, but others don't like having to bag all of their purchases themselves.

What's your strategy for picking a checkout lane at the grocery store? Think about this during the Mathematical Modeling in 3 Acts lesson.

Scan for Multimedia

ACT 1 ▸ Identify the Problem

1. What is the first question that comes to mind after watching the video?

2. Write down the main question you will answer about what you saw in the video.

3. Make an initial conjecture that answers this main question.

4. Explain how you arrived at your conjecture.

5. What information will be useful to know to answer the main question? How can you get it? How will you use that information?

ACT 2 ▸ Develop a Model

6. Use the math that you have learned in this Topic to refine your conjecture.

ACT 3 ▸ Interpret the Results

7. Did your refined conjecture match the actual answer exactly? If not, what might explain the difference?

3-4
Arithmetic Sequences

 SavvasRealize.com

I CAN... identify and describe arithmetic sequences.

VOCABULARY
- arithmetic sequence
- common difference
- explicit formula
- recursive formula
- sequence
- term of a sequence

EXPLORE & REASON

A fashion designer is designing a patterned fabric.

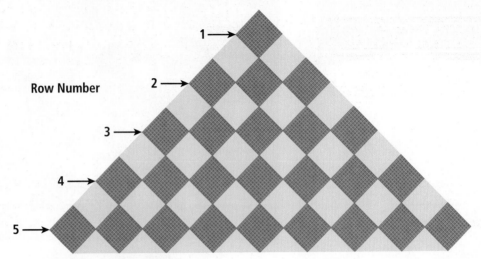

Row Number

A. Copy and complete the table.

Row number	1	2	3	4	5
Number of Patterned Squares in the Row	1	▪	5	▪	▪
Total Number of Patterned Squares	1	▪	9	▪	▪

B. Use Structure What number patterns do you see in the rows of the table?

? ESSENTIAL QUESTION
How are arithmetic sequences related to linear functions?

CONCEPTUAL UNDERSTANDING

EXAMPLE 1 Connect Sequences and Functions

A. Is the ordered list 26, 39, 52, 65, 78 an arithmetic sequence?

A **sequence** is an ordered list of numbers that often forms a pattern. Each number is a **term of the sequence**. In an **arithmetic sequence**, the difference between any two consecutive terms is a constant called the **common difference**.

Find the differences between pairs of consecutive terms.

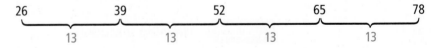

There is a common difference of 13, so this is an arithmetic sequence.

CONTINUED ON THE NEXT PAGE

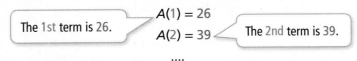

EXAMPLE 1 CONTINUED

B. How are sequences related to functions?

You can think of a sequence as a function where the domain is restricted to the natural numbers and the range is the terms of the sequence.

For the sequence 26, 39, 52, 65, 78,

Let n = the term number in the sequence.

Let $A(n)$ = the value of the nth term of the sequence.

REASON
Why are the values of n restricted?

The 1st term is 26. ⟶ $A(1) = 26$

$A(2) = 39$ ⟵ The 2nd term is 39.

....

C. How do you represent sequences using subscript notation?

Subscript notation is commonly used to describe sequences.

$a_2 = 39$ ⟵ The 2nd term is 39.

You can use either function or subscript notation to represent sequences.

 Try It! **1.** Is the domain of the function in Part B of Example 1 continuous or discrete? Explain.

DEFINITION

Recursive, in mathematics, means to repeat a process over and over again, using the output of each step as the next input. A recursive formula relates each term of a sequence to the previous term. It is composed of an initial value and a rule for generating the sequence.

The **recursive formula** for an arithmetic sequence is:

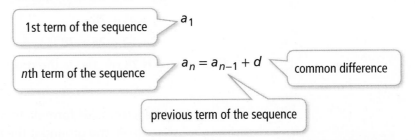

1st term of the sequence ⟶ a_1

nth term of the sequence ⟶ $a_n = a_{n-1} + d$ ⟵ common difference

previous term of the sequence

A recursive formula describes the pattern of a sequence and can be used to find the next term in a sequence.

👆 **EXAMPLE 2** **Apply the Recursive Formula**

A. What is a recursive formula for the height above the ground of the nth step of the pyramid shown?

Each step is 26 cm tall.

COMMON ERROR
Be careful not to assume that the first term and the common difference are the same in all arithmetic sequences. It is true for this sequence but not for all sequences.

Use the recursive formula.

$$a_1 = 26$$
$$a_n = a_{n-1} + 26$$

Since each step is the same height, d is 26.

The formula $a_n = a_{n-1} + 26$ gives the height above the ground of the nth step with $a_1 = 26$.

B. Use the recursive formula to find the height above the ground of the 3rd step.

Find the height above the ground of the 2nd step.

$$a_1 = 26$$
$$a_2 = a_1 + 26$$
$$a_2 = 26 + 26 = 52$$

Use a_1 to find a_2.

Find the height above the ground of the 3rd step.

$$a_2 = 52$$
$$a_3 = a_2 + 26$$
$$a_3 = 52 + 26 = 78$$

Use a_2 to find a_3.

The 3rd step is 78 cm above the ground.

 Try It! **2.** Write a recursive formula to represent the total height of the nth stair above the ground if the height of each stair is 18 cm.

DEFINITION

An **explicit formula** expresses the nth term of a sequence in terms of n.

The explicit formula for an arithmetic sequence is:

$$a_n = a_1 + (n - 1)d$$

common difference

first term of the sequence

term number

 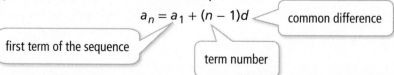

APPLICATION

EXAMPLE 3 Apply the Explicit Formula

A. The cost of renting a bicycle is given in the table. How can you represent the rental cost using an explicit formula?

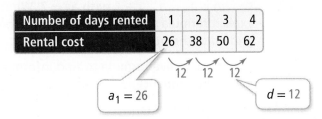

Number of days rented	1	2	3	4
Rental cost	26	38	50	62

12 12 12

$a_1 = 26$ $d = 12$

To find the rental cost for n days, write an explicit formula for the nth term of the sequence.

Use the explicit formula.

$a_n = 26 + (n - 1)12$ .... Substitute 26 for a_1 and 12 for d.

$ = 26 + 12n - 12$ .... Distributive Property

$ = 14 + 12n$ .... Simplify.

The explicit formula $a_n = 14 + 12n$ gives the rental cost for n days.

B. What is the cost of renting the bicycle for 10 days?

Use the explicit formula to find the 10th term in the sequence.

$a_n = 14 + 12n$

$a_{10} = 14 + 12(10)$ ⟵ Substitute 10 for n.

$\phantom{a_{10}} = 134$

The 10th term in sequence is 134. It costs $134 to rent the bicycle for 10 days.

C. How is the explicit formula of an arithmetic sequence related to a linear function?

The formula $a_n = 14 + 12n$ shows that the cost, a_n, is a function of the number of days, n, the bicycle is rented.

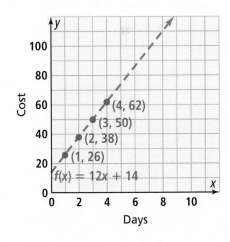

COMMON ERROR
You might think that the initial value of the sequence and the y-intercept of the graph of the equivalent linear function are the same, but they will not be the same if the initial value of the sequence is not zero.

You can write this as a linear function, $f(x) = 12x + 14$, or as an equation in slope-intercept form, $y = 12x + 14$. The common difference, 12, corresponds to the slope of the graph.

 Try It! **3.** The cost to rent a bike is $28 for the first day plus $2 for each day after that. Write an explicit formula for the rental cost for n days. What is the cost of renting the bike for 8 days?

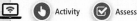

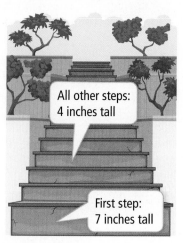

EXAMPLE 4 > **Write an Explicit Formula From a Recursive Formula**

The recursive formula for the height above the ground of the nth step of the stairs shown is $a_n = a_{n-1} + 4$ with $a_1 = 7$. What explicit formula finds the height above the ground of the nth step?

Use the recursive formula to find information about the sequence.

$$a_1 = 7$$

$$a_n = a_{n-1} + 4$$ ⟵ common difference

Write the explicit formula.

$$a_n = a_1 + (n - 1)d$$

$$a_n = 7 + (n - 1)4$$ ·········· Substitute 7 for a_1 and 4 for d.

The explicit formula $a_n = 7 + (n - 1)4$ can be used to find the height above the ground of the nth step.

All other steps:
4 inches tall

First step:
7 inches tall

Try It! **4.** Write an explicit formula for each arithmetic sequence.

a. $a_n = a_{n-1} - 3$; $a_1 = 10$ **b.** $a_n = a_{n-1} + 2.4$; $a_1 = -1$

EXAMPLE 5 > **Write a Recursive Formula From an Explicit Formula**

The explicit formula for an arithmetic sequence is $a_n = 1 + \frac{1}{2}n$.

What is the recursive formula for the sequence?

Step 1 Identify the common difference.

$$a_n = 1 + \frac{1}{2}n$$

$$d = \frac{1}{2}$$

Step 2 Find the first term of the sequence.

$$a_n = 1 + \frac{1}{2}n$$

$$a_1 = 1 + \frac{1}{2}(1)$$ ·········· Substitute 1 for n.

$$a_1 = \frac{3}{2}$$ ·········· Simplify.

Step 3 Write the recursive formula.

$$a_n = a_{n-1} + d$$

$$a_n = a_{n-1} + \frac{1}{2}$$ ·········· Substitute $\frac{1}{2}$ for d.

STUDY TIP
When writing a recursive formula for an arithmetic sequence, include the value of the first term, a_1.

The recursive formula for the sequence is:

first term: $a_1 = \frac{3}{2}$; nth term: $a_n = a_{n-1} + \frac{1}{2}$

Try It! **5.** Write a recursive formula for each explicit formula.

a. $a_n = 8 + 3n$ **b.** $a_n = 12 - 5n$

CONCEPT SUMMARY Arithmetic Sequences

WORDS An arithmetic sequence is a sequence of numbers that follows a pattern. The difference between two consecutive terms is a constant called the common difference.

FORMULAS

Recursive Formula	**Explicit Formula**
Used to describe a sequence and find the next few terms	Used to find a specific term in the sequence
$a_n = a_{n-1} + d$	$a_n = a_1 + (n-1)d$

$a_n = a_{n-1} + d$

- *n*th term of the sequence
- previous term of the sequence
- common difference

$a_n = a_1 + (n-1)d$

- *n*th term of the sequence
- first term of the sequence
- common difference

The first term of the sequence is a_1.

NUMBERS

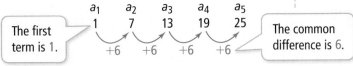

1, 7, 13, 19, 25, . . .

Use the recursive formula to describe the sequence and find the next two terms.

$$a_n = a_{n-1} + 6$$

	a_1	a_2	a_3	a_4	a_5
	1	7	13	19	25

The first term is 1.

+6 +6 +6 +6

The common difference is 6.

$a_6 = a_5 + 6$
$= 25 + 6$
$= 31$

$a_7 = a_6 + 6$
$= 31 + 6$
$= 37$

The next two terms are 31 and 37.

Use the explicit formula to find the 15th term in the sequence.

$$a_n = 1 + (n-1)6$$
$$a_{15} = 1 + (14)6$$
$$a_{15} = 85$$

Do You UNDERSTAND?

1. **ESSENTIAL QUESTION** How are arithmetic sequences related to linear functions?

2. **Error Analysis** A student uses the explicit formula $a_n = 5 + 3(n - 1)$ for the sequence 3, 8, 13, 18, 23, ... to find the 12th term. Explain the error the student made.

3. **Vocabulary** When is a *recursive formula* more useful than an *explicit formula* for an arithmetic sequence?

4. **Communicate Precisely** Compare and contrast a recursive formula and an explicit formula for an arithmetic sequence.

Do You KNOW HOW?

Tell whether or not each sequence is an arithmetic sequence.

5. 15, 13, 11, 9, . . .   6. 4, 7, 10, 14, . . .

Write a recursive formula for each sequence.

7. 81, 85, 89, 93, 97, . . .

8. 47, 39, 31, 23, 15, . . .

9. An online store charges $5 to ship one box and $10 to ship two boxes. Write an explicit formula for an arithmetic sequence to represent the amount the online store charges to ship *n* boxes. Use the explicit formula to determine how much the online store charges when shipping 11 boxes.

UNDERSTAND

10. Make Sense and Persevere What can you tell about the terms of an arithmetic sequence when the common difference is negative?

11. Mathematical Connections How does the domain of an arithmetic sequence compare to the domain of a linear function? Explain.

12. Error Analysis Describe and correct the error a student made in identifying the common difference of the following sequence: 29, 22, 15, 8, 1, ...

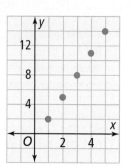

The common difference of the sequence is 7, since 29 – 22 = 7, 22 – 15 = 7, 15 – 8 = 7, and 8 – 1 = 7. ✗

13. Reason Given the common difference and the first term of an arithmetic sequence, which formula – the recursive or explicit formula – would be more useful to determine a_{500}? Explain. Would your answer change if you knew the value of term a_{499}? Explain.

14. Reason The graph of an arithmetic sequence is shown. Write a recursive formula for the arithmetic sequence if the y-value of each point is increased by 3.

15. Use Structure Does an explicit formula for a sequence make sense assuming $n = 2.5$? Explain.

16. Higher Order Thinking Consider the following recursive formula which describes the Fibonacci sequence.

$$a_1 = 1, a_2 = 1$$
$$a_{(n+1)} = a_n + a_{(n-1)}$$

a. Find the first 6 terms of the sequence.

b. Is the Fibonacci sequence an arithmetic sequence? Explain.

PRACTICE

Tell whether or not each sequence is an arithmetic sequence. If it is, give the common difference, d. SEE EXAMPLE 1

17. 1, 15, 29, 43, 57, . . . **18.** 77, 64, 51, 38, 25, . . .

19. 1, −2, 3, −4, 5, . . . **20.** 3, 6, 9, 12, 15, . . .

21. 3, 6, 9, 15, 18, . . . **22.** 37, 34, 31, 29, 26, . . .

23. 93, 86, 79, 72, 65, . . . **24.** 45, 54, 63, 72, 81, . . .

Write a recursive formula and an explicit formula for each arithmetic sequence. SEE EXAMPLES 2 AND 3

25. 12, 19, 26, 33, 40, . . . **26.** −4, 5, 14, 23, 32, . . .

27. 62, 57, 52, 47, 42, . . . **28.** −15, −6, 3, 12, 21, . . .

29. 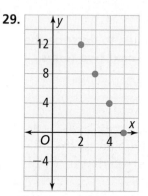 **30.**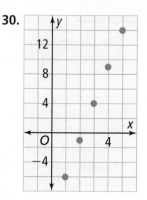

Write an explicit formula for each recursive formula. SEE EXAMPLE 4

31. $a_n = a_{n-1} + 15; a_1 = 8$

32. $a_n = a_{n-1} + 6; a_1 = 9$

33. $a_n = a_{n-1} - 2; a_1 = -1$

34. $a_n = a_{n-1} - 21; a_1 = 56$

35. $a_n = a_{n-1} + 1; a_1 = 12$

36. $a_n = a_{n-1} - 7; a_1 = -3$

Write a recursive formula for each explicit formula and find the first term of the sequence. SEE EXAMPLE 5

37. $a_n = 10 + 8n$ **38.** $a_n = 108 - n$

39. $a_n = -29 + 12n$ **40.** $a_n = 35 + 52n$

41. $a_n = \frac{7}{2} - 3n$ **42.** $a_n = 7 + \frac{1}{4}n$

APPLY

43. Make Sense and Persevere The lowest and leftmost note on a piano keyboard is an A. The next lowest A is seven white keys to the right. This pattern continues. Write an explicit formula for an arithmetic sequence to represent the position of each A key on the piano, counting from the left. If a piano has 52 white keys, in what position is the key that plays the highest A?

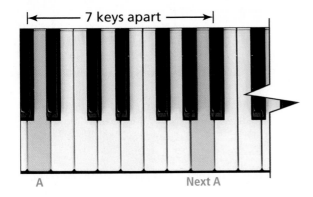

|← 7 keys apart →|

A   Next A

44. Make Sense and Persevere After the first raffle drawing, 497 tickets remain. After the second raffle drawing, 494 tickets remain. Assuming that the pattern continues, write an explicit formula for an arithmetic sequence to represent the number of raffle tickets that remain after each drawing. How many tickets remain in the bag after the seventh raffle drawing?

45. Reason In a video game, you must score 5,500 points to complete level 1. To move through each additional level, you must score an additional 3,250 points. What number would you use as a_1 when writing an arithmetic sequence to represent this situation? What would n represent? Write an explicit formula to represent this situation. Write a recursive formula to represent this situation.

PICK A LEVEL!

1 — SCORE TO COMPLETE 5,500
2 — SCORE TO COMPLETE 8,750
3 — SCORE TO COMPLETE 12,000

ASSESSMENT PRACTICE

46. Fill in the blanks to complete the explicit formula that corresponds to the sequence shown.

14, 23, 32, 41, 50, . . .

$a___ = $ _____ $+$ _____ n

47. SAT/ACT Which sequence is an arithmetic sequence?

Ⓐ 1, 3, 5, 7, 11, . . .

Ⓑ 4, 6, 9, 13, 18, . . .

Ⓒ 8, 15, 22, 29, 36, . . .

Ⓓ 3, 6, 12, 24, 48, . . .

48. Performance Task A city sets up 14 rows of chairs for an outdoor concert. Each row has 2 more chairs than the row in front of it.

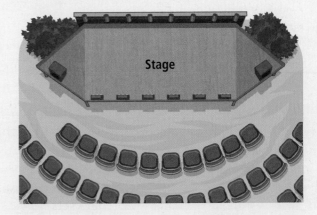

Stage

Part A Write a recursive formula to represent the number of chairs in the nth row.

Part B Write an explicit formula to represent the number of chairs in the nth row.

Part C Graph the sequence for the first 5 rows.

Part D What linear function represents the sequence? Which represents this situation best, this linear function or one of the formulas you wrote? Explain.

3-5

Scatter Plots and Lines of Fit

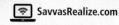
SavvasRealize.com

I CAN... use a scatter plot to describe the relationship between two data sets.

VOCABULARY
- negative association
- negative correlation
- no association
- positive association
- positive correlation
- trend line

MODEL & DISCUSS

Nicholas plotted data points to represent the relationship between screen size and cost of television sets. Everything about the televisions is the same, except for the screen size.

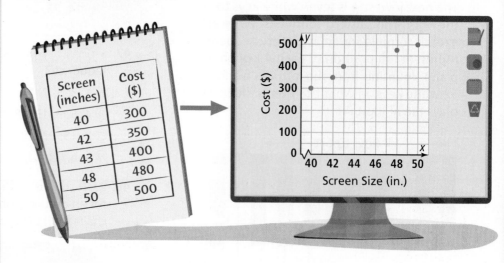

Screen (inches)	Cost ($)
40	300
42	350
43	400
48	480
50	500

A. Describe any patterns you see.

B. What does this set of points tell you about the relationship of screen size and cost of the television?

C. Reason Where do you think the point for a 46-inch television would be on the graph? How about for a 60–inch TV? Explain.

? ESSENTIAL QUESTION   How can you use a scatter plot to describe the relationship between two data sets?

CONCEPTUAL UNDERSTANDING

EXAMPLE 1   Understand Association

A. What is the relationship between the hours after sunrise, x, and the temperature, y, shown in the scatter plot?

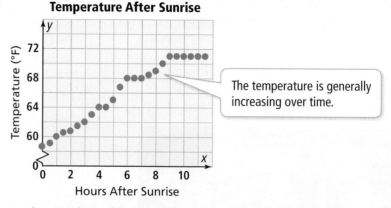

COMMON ERROR
You may think that since the points do not line up exactly, there is no relationship. However, when looking for an association, you are looking for a general trend.

The temperature is generally increasing over time.

As the number of hours after sunrise increases, so does the temperature.

When y-values tend to increase as x-values increase, the two data sets have a **positive association**.

CONTINUED ON THE NEXT PAGE

EXAMPLE 1 CONTINUED

B. **What is the relationship between the hours after sunset, *x*, and the temperature, *y*, shown in the scatter plot?**

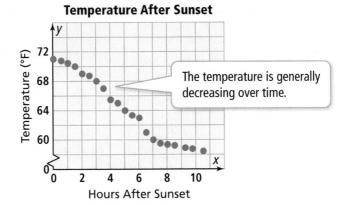

Temperature After Sunset

The temperature is generally decreasing over time.

As the number of hours after sunset increases, the temperature decreases.

When *y*-values tend to decrease as *x*-values increase, the two data sets have a **negative association**.

C. **What is the relationship between the hours after sunset, *x*, and the amount of rain, *y*, shown in the scatter plot?**

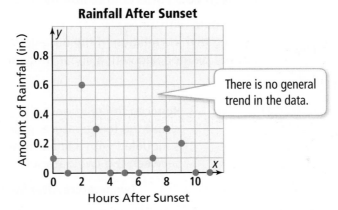

Rainfall After Sunset

There is no general trend in the data.

There is no relationship between the amount of rainfall and the number of hours after sunset.

When there is no general relationship between *x*-values and *y*-values, the two data sets have **no association**.

 Try It! **1.** Describe the type of association each scatter plot shows.

a.
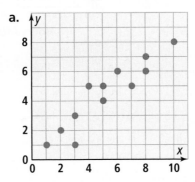

b.
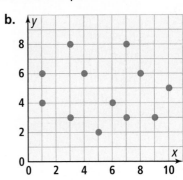

APPLICATION  **EXAMPLE 2** Understand Correlation

How can the relationship between the hours after sunrise, *x*, and the temperature, *y*, be modeled?

The data points on the scatter plot approximate a line. Sketch a trend line that best fits the data to determine whether a linear function can model the relationship.

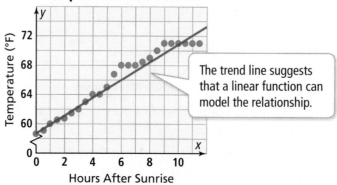

Temperature After Sunrise

The trend line suggests that a linear function can model the relationship.

The scatter plot suggests a linear relationship. There is a **positive correlation** between hours after sunrise and the temperature.

When data with a negative association are modeled with a line, there is a **negative correlation**. If the data do not have an association, they can not be modeled with a linear function.

COMMON ERROR
You might think that negative correlation means that the data are not well correlated, but it refers only to the direction of the association.

 Try It! 2. How can the relationship between the hours after sunset, *x*, and the temperature, *y*, be modeled? If the relationship is modeled with a linear function, describe the correlation between the two data sets.

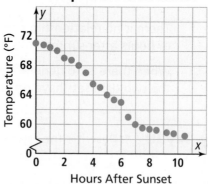

Temperature After Sunset

EXAMPLE 3   Write the Equation of a Trend Line

What trend line models the data in the scatterplot?

A **trend line** models the data in a scatter plot by showing the general direction of the data. A trend line fits the data as closely as possible.

Step 1   Sketch a trend line for the data.

A trend line approximates a balance of points above and below the line.

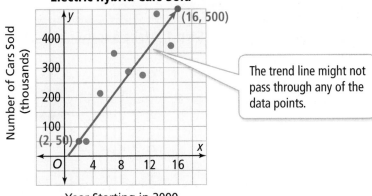

Electric Hybrid Cars Sold

(16, 500)

The trend line might not pass through any of the data points.

(2, 50)

Year Starting in 2000

Step 2   Write the equation of this trend line.

Select two points on the trend line to find the slope.

$$m = \frac{500 - 50}{16 - 2} \approx 32.1$$

(2, 50) and (16, 500) are two points on the trend line.

Use the slope and one of the points to write the equation in slope-intercept form.

$$y - 50 = 32.1(x - 2)$$

$$y = 32.1x - 14.2$$

Use the point-slope formula.

The trend line that models the data is $y = 32.1x - 14.2$.

This trend line is one of many possible trend lines.

 Try It!   **3. a.** What trend line, in slope-intercept form, models the data from the Example 2 Try It?

b. Explain why there could be no data points on a trend line, yet the line models the data.

APPLICATION   🖑 **EXAMPLE 4**   Interpret Trend Lines

The table shows the amount of time required to download a 100-megabyte file for various Internet speeds. Assuming the trend continues, how long would it take to download the 100-megabyte file if the Internet speed is 75 kilobytes per second?

Internet Speed (kilobytes/s (KB/s))	35	40	45	50	55	60
Time to Download 100 Megabytes (min)	6.65	5.82	5.17	4.65	4.23	3.88

Step 1 Make a scatter plot of the data and sketch a trend line.

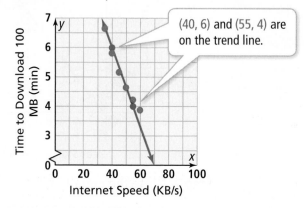

(40, 6) and (55, 4) are on the trend line.

REASON
When a scatterplot has a break in the *y*-axis, can you visually interpret a trend line across the entire range?

Step 2 Find the equation of the trend line.

Select two points on the trend line to find the slope:
(40, 6) and (55, 4)

$$m = \frac{6 - 4}{40 - 55} = \frac{2}{-15} \approx -0.13$$

Use the slope and one of the points to write the equation for the trend line.

$$y - 6 = -0.13(x - 40)$$
$$y = -0.13x + 11.2$$

Write the equation in slope-intercept form.

The equation of the trend line is $y = -0.13x + 11.2$.

Step 3 Use the equation of the linear model to find the *y*-value that corresponds to $x = 75$.

$$y = -0.13x + 11.2$$
$$= -0.13(75) + 11.2$$
$$= 1.45$$

Substitute 75 for *x*.

The download time would be 1.45 s.

✅ **Try It!**   **4.** What is the *x*-intercept of the trend line? Is that possible in a real-world situation? Explain.

CONCEPT SUMMARY Scatter Plots and Trend Lines

TABLE **Positive Association**

x	1	2	3	4	5	6	7
y	2	3	3	4	6	7	7

Negative Association

x	1	2	2	4	5	6	6
y	7	7	5	4	3	3	1

GRAPHS **Positive Correlation**

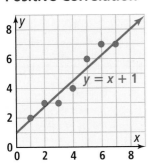

$y = x + 1$

Negative Correlation

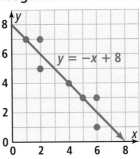

$y = -x + 8$

Do You UNDERSTAND?

1. **ESSENTIAL QUESTION** How can you use a scatter plot to describe the relationship between two data sets?

2. **Error Analysis** A student claims that if y-values are not increasing as x-values increase, then the data must show a negative association. Explain the error the student made.

3. **Vocabulary** In a scatter plot that shows a *positive association*, describe how y-values change as x-values increase.

4. **Make Sense and Persevere** Does a trend line need to pass through all the points in a scatter plot? Explain.

5. **Communicate Precisely** Describe how the point-slope formula is useful when writing the equation for a trend line.

Do You KNOW HOW?

Describe the type of association between x and y for each set of data. Explain.

6.

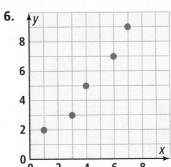

7.

x	4	6	7	9	10
y	9	7	5	3	3

8. The table shows the hours of studying, x, and a person's test score, y. What is the equation of a trend line that models the data? What does the slope of your trend line represent?

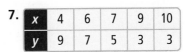

Hours of Studying	6	7	7	8	9
Test Score	77	80	83	87	92

Scan for Multimedia

Practice Tutorial

Additional Exercises Available Online

UNDERSTAND

9. **Reason** Can you use any two of the given data points in a scatter plot to write an equation for a trend line? Explain.

10. **Look for Relationships** Describe the slope of a trend line that models the data in a scatter plot with positive correlation. Describe the slope of a trend line that models the data in a scatter plot with negative correlation.

11. **Error Analysis** Describe and correct the error a student made in describing the association of the data in the table.

x	19	18	17	17	15	13	11
y	3	6	7	8	10	11	12

The data in the table show positive association because y is increasing.

12. **Higher Order Thinking** Would a trend line be a good fit for these data? Explain.

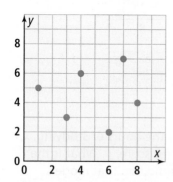

13. **Reason** Describe a set of data that has neither a positive nor a negative association, but that does have a valid trend line.

14. **Mathematical Connections** How could finding the y-intercept of a trend line for a data set help you determine the usefulness of the trend line as a model?

PRACTICE

Describe the type of association each scatter plot shows. SEE EXAMPLE 1

15.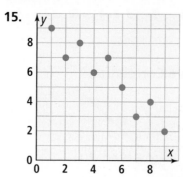

16.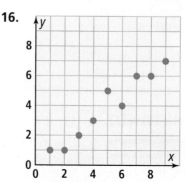

For each table, make a scatter plot of the data. Describe the type of association that the scatter plot shows. SEE EXAMPLE 2

17.
x	y
2	4
3	4
3	6
5	8
6	10

18.
x	y
1	9
2	7
5	3
6	2
6	1

19.
x	y
3	1
4	9
7	2
8	8
10	3

For each table, make a scatter plot of the data. Draw a trend line and write its equation.
SEE EXAMPLES 3 AND 4

20.
x	y
2	3
4	6
5	5
7	7
8	9
8	8

21.
x	y
3	9
5	8
5	6
6	5
6	6
8	3

22.
x	y
1	1
2	3
3	5
3	6
5	8
6	9

Go Online | SavvasRealize.com

APPLY

23. **Make Sense and Persevere** A student is tracking the growth of some plants. What type of association do you think the data would show? Explain.

Days Since Germination

24. **Model With Mathematics** When planting trees for reforestation purposes, different densities result in different numbers of trees per acre. The following table shows the recommended spacing in square feet and the corresponding trees per acre. What trend line models the data shown in the table? What do the slope and y-intercept of the trend line represent?

Spacing (ft²), x	Trees per Acre, y
60	726
64	680
70	622
72	605
80	544
81	530
84	519
90	484
96	454
100	435

25. **Make Sense and Persevere** The table shows the maximum recommended viewing distances y, in feet, for an HDTV with screen size x, in inches. What trend line models the data shown in the table? What does the slope of the trend line represent?

x	40	43	50	55	60
y	8.3	9	10.4	11.5	12.5

ASSESSMENT PRACTICE

26. When two data sets have a negative association, the y-values tend to _____ when the x-values _____.

27. **SAT/ACT** Which equation could represent a possible trend line for the data in the scatter plot?

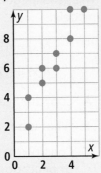

Ⓐ $y = -2x + 1$ Ⓑ $y = 2x + 1$

Ⓒ $y = -2x - 1$ Ⓓ $y = 2x - 1$

28. **Performance Task** A store records the price of kites in dollars, x, and the number of kites, y, sold at each price.

Kite Style	Price	Quantity
	$10.00	25
	$12.00	23
	$15.00	20
	$22.00	18
	$30.00	15

Part A Make a scatter plot of the data.

Part B What trend line models the data? What does the slope of the trend line represent?

Part C What factors other than price could influence the number of kites sold? Could you use any of these factors to make another scatter plot? Explain.

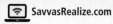
3-6

Analyzing Lines of Fit

SavvasRealize.com

I CAN... find the line of best fit for a data set and evaluate its goodness of fit.

VOCABULARY

- causation
- correlation coefficient
- extrapolation
- interpolation
- line of best fit
- linear regression
- residual

EXPLORE & REASON

The scatter plot shows the number of beachgoers each day for the first six days of July. The head lifeguard at the beach uses the data to determine the number of lifeguards to schedule based on the weather forecast.

The head lifeguard compares two linear models:

$$g(x) = 13x + 25$$
$$h(x) = 12x + 30$$

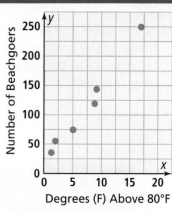

A. Copy the scatter plot and graph the linear functions on the same grid.

B. What is a reasonable domain for each function? Explain.

C. Construct Arguments Which model is the better predictor of the number of beachgoers based on the temperature above 80°F? Defend your model.

? ESSENTIAL QUESTION

How can you evaluate the goodness of fit of a line of best fit for a paired data set?

EXAMPLE 1   Find the Line of Best Fit

What is the equation of the line of best fit for the data in the table?

x	1	2	5	8	9	17
y	30	55	75	120	145	250

A **linear regression** is a method used to calculate the **line of best fit**. A line of best fit is the trend line that most closely matches the data.

Step 1 Enter the data into a graphing calculator.

Step 2 Perform a linear regression.

Use the Linear Regression function. The values of *a* and *b* from the linear regression – the slope and the *y*-intercept – are displayed.

a is the slope.
b is the *y*-intercept.

```
     LinReg
   y=ax+b
   a=13.55882353
   b=17.58823529
   r²=.9909817911
   r=.9954806834
```

Step 3 Write the equation of the line of best fit. Substitute 13.56 for *a* and 17.59 for *b*.

$$y = 13.56x + 17.59$$

The equation for the line of best fit for the data is $y = 13.56x + 17.59$.

CONTINUED ON THE NEXT PAGE

EXAMPLE 1 CONTINUED

 Try It! 1. Use the linear regression function to find the equation of the line of best fit for the data in the table.

x	1	2	4	5	7	8	9
y	5.4	6.1	8.1	8.5	10.3	10.9	11.5

CONCEPTUAL UNDERSTANDING

 EXAMPLE 2 Understand Correlation Coefficients

What does the correlation coefficient reveal about the quantities in a bivariate data set?

When you perform a linear regression using technology, you are also given the correlation coefficient. The **correlation coefficient**, represented by *r*, is a number between −1 and 1 that indicates the direction and strength of the linear relationship between two quantitative variables in a **bivariate data set**, a set of data that uses two variables.

When the correlation coefficient is close to 1, there is a strong positive correlation between the two variables. That is, as the values of *x* increase, so do the values of *y*.

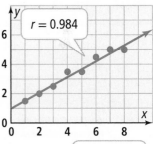

When the correlation coefficient is close to 0, there is a weak correlation between the two variables.

When the correlation coefficient is close to −1, there is a strong negative correlation between the two variables.

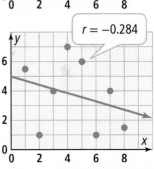

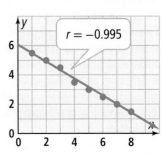

 Try It! 2. What does each correlation coefficient reveal about the data it describes?

    a. *r* = 0.1   **b.** *r* = −0.6

CONCEPT Residuals

A **residual** is the difference between the y-value of a data point and the corresponding y-value from the line of best fit, or the predicted y-value.

residual = actual y-value − predicted y-value

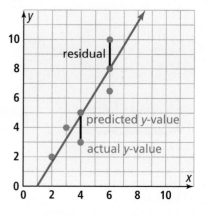

A residual plot shows how well a linear model fits the data set. If the residuals are randomly distributed on either side of the x-axis and clustered close to the x-axis, then the linear model is likely a good fit.

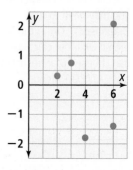

APPLICATION   **EXAMPLE 3**   **Interpret Residual Plots**

Student enrollment at Blue Sky Flight School over 8 years is shown. The owner used linear regression to determine the line of best fit. The equation for the line of best fit is $y = -35x + 1208$. How well does this linear model fit the data?

Step 1 Evaluate the equation for each x-value to find the predicted y-values.

Step 2 Calculate the differences between the actual and predicted y-values for each x-value.

Step 3 Plot the residual for each x-value.

COMMON ERROR

The appearance of a residual plot does not correspond to a positive or negative correlation. The data shown might be misinterpreted as data with no correlation, but it has a negative correlation that is seen when the actual data points are plotted.

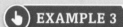

Blue Sky Flight School

	Year (x)	Students (y)	Predicted value	Residual
1				
2	Year (x)	Students (y)	Predicted value	Residual
3	0	1,235	1,208	27
4	1	1,178	1,173	5
5	2	1,115	1,138	−23
6	3	1,102	1,103	−1
7	4	1,020	1,068	−48
8	5	1,050	1,033	17
9	6	1,003	998	5
10	7	978	963	15

CONTINUED ON THE NEXT PAGE

EXAMPLE 3 CONTINUED

Enrollment

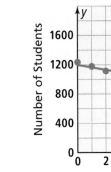

Residual Plot

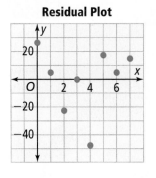

USE APPROPRIATE TOOLS
Why is it helpful to make a plot when analyzing residuals?

The scatter plot with the line of best fit suggests that there is a negative correlation between years and enrollment.

The residual plot shows the residuals randomly distributed above and below the x-axis and somewhat clustered close to the x-axis. The linear model is likely a good fit for the data.

 Try It! 3. The owner of Horizon Flight School also created a scatter plot and calculated the line of best fit for her enrollment data shown in the table. The equation of the line of best fit is $y = 1.44x + 877$. Find the residuals and plot them to determine how well this linear model fits the data.

Year (x)	0	1	2	3	4	5	6	7
Students (y)	832	872	905	928	903	887	863	867

Enrollment

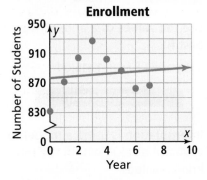

APPLICATION

EXAMPLE 4 Interpolate and Extrapolate Using Linear Models

The graphic shows regional air travel data recorded by a domestic airline company. How can you use the data to estimate the number of air miles people flew in 2003? If the trend in air travel continues, what is a reasonable estimate for the number of miles that people will fly in 2030?

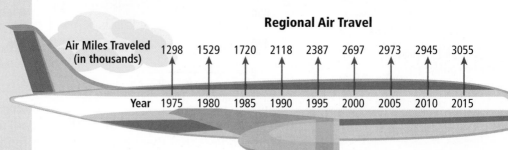

Regional Air Travel

Air Miles Traveled (in thousands)	1298	1529	1720	2118	2387	2697	2973	2945	3055
Year	1975	1980	1985	1990	1995	2000	2005	2010	2015

Formulate

Plot the data points on a scatter plot. Using technology, perform a linear regression to determine the line of best fit for the data. For the x-values, use number of years since 1975.

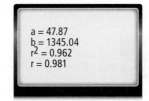

a = 47.87
b = 1345.04
r^2 = 0.962
r = 0.981

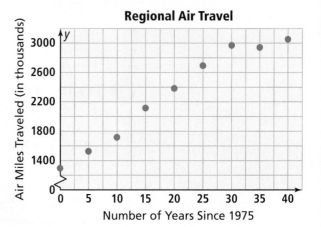

Regional Air Travel

Compute

Use the values of a and b (from the linear regression) to write the line of best fit.

$$y = 47.87x + 1345.04$$

Interpolation	OR	**Extrapolation**

Interpolation is using a model to estimate a value within the range of known values.

Interpolate to estimate the miles people flew in 2003, or 28 years after 1975.

$$y = 47.87(28) + 1345.04 = 2{,}685.4$$

Extrapolation is using a model to make a prediction about a value outside the range of known values.

Extrapolate to predict the miles that people will fly in 2030, 55 years after 1975.

$$y = 47.87(55) + 1345.04 = 3{,}977.89$$

Interpret

The model predicts that people flew a total of 2,685 thousand air miles on the airline in 2003, and that people will fly a total of 3,978 thousand air miles in 2030. This prediction is not as reliable as the estimate for 2003 because the trend may not continue.

 Try It! **4.** Using the model from Example 4, estimate the number of miles people flew on the airline in 2012.

EXAMPLE 5   **Correlation and Causation**

A. A student found a positive correlation between the number of hours of sleep his classmates got before a test and their scores on the test. Can he conclude that he will do well on the test if he goes to bed early?

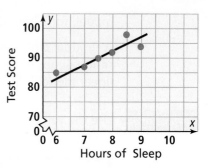

Causation describes a cause-and-effect relationship. A change in the one variable causes a change in the other variable.

To determine whether two variables have a causal relationship, you have to carry out an experiment that can control for other variables that might influence the relationship between the two target variables.

The student cannot conclude that he will do well if he goes to bed early. Other variables, like the time spent studying or proficiency with the content, could affect how well he does on the test.

B. A lifeguard notices that as the outside temperature rises, the number of people coming to the beach increases. Can she conclude that the change in temperature results in more people going to the beach?

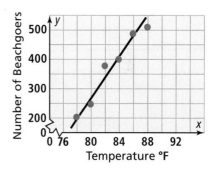

She did not carry out an experiment or control for other variables that might affect the relationship. These include weather forecast and time of year.

She cannot conclude that the only reason that more people come to the beach is the outside temperature.

 Try It!   **5.** The number of cars in a number of cities shows a positive correlation to the population of the respective city. Can it be inferred that an increase of cars in a city leads to an increase in the population? Defend your response.

CONCEPT SUMMARY Linear Models, Lines of Best Fit, and Residuals

WORDS A linear regression is a method for finding the line of best fit, or a linear model, for a bivariate data set.

A residual plot reveals how well the linear model fits the data set. If the residuals are fairly symmetrical around and clustered close to the *x*-axis, the linear model is likely a good fit.

ALGEBRA Use the values of *a* and *b* from the linear regression to write the equation for the line of best fit. The equation is $y = 0.542x + 1$.

```
LinReg
y=ax+b
a=.5416666667
b=1
r²=.9688779689
r=.9843159904
```

The correlation coefficient, *r*, describes the relationship between the two variables in a bivariate data set. It is a number between −1 and 1.

GRAPHS

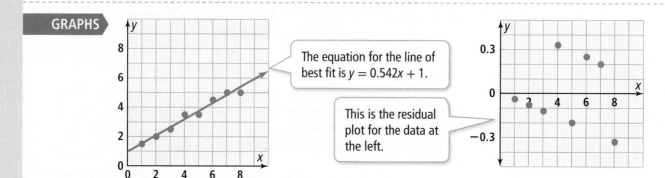

The equation for the line of best fit is $y = 0.542x + 1$.

This is the residual plot for the data at the left.

Do You UNDERSTAND?

1. **ESSENTIAL QUESTION** How can you evaluate the goodness of fit of a line of best fit for a paired data set?

2. **Vocabulary** Describe the difference between *interpolation* and *extrapolation*.

3. **Error Analysis** A student says that a correlation coefficient of −0.93 indicates that the two quantities of a data set have a weak correlation. Explain the error the student made.

4. **Look for Relationships** A student found a strong correlation between the age of people who run marathons and their marathon time. Can the student say that young people will run marathons faster than older people? Explain.

Do You KNOW HOW?

Use the table for Exercises 5 and 6.

x	10	20	30	40	50
y	7	11	14	20	22

5. Use technology to determine the equation of the line of best fit for the data.

6. Make a residual plot for the line of best fit and the data in the table. How well does the linear model fit the data?

7. The table shows the number of customers *y* at a store for *x* weeks after the store's grand opening. The equation for the line of best fit is $y = 7.77x + 38.8$. Assuming the trend continues, what is a reasonable prediction of the number of visitors to the store 7 weeks after its opening?

x	1	2	3	4	5	6
y	46	53	65	71	75	86

PRACTICE & PROBLEM SOLVING

UNDERSTAND

8. Make Sense and Persevere Two quantities of a data set have a strong positive correlation. Can the line of best fit for the data set have a correlation coefficient of 0.25? Explain.

9. Error Analysis Describe and correct the error a student made in determining the equation for the line of best fit for the data in the table.

x	3	6	9	12	15	18	21
y	4	17	28	40	55	67	72

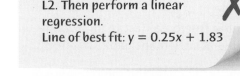

Enter y data in L1 and x data in
L2. Then perform a linear
regression.
Line of best fit: y = 0.25x + 1.83 ✗

10. Higher Order Thinking Which is likely to be more accurate: an estimate through interpolation or a prediction through extrapolation? Explain.

11. Generalize Describe how the values of *a* and *b* in a linear model are related to the data being modeled.

12. Look for Relationships How can you use the graph of the line of best fit to make predictions about future behaviors of the quantities of the data set?

13. Construct Arguments Arthur and Tavon each calculated lines of best fit for their last five math tests. Based on the residual plots, Arthur states that his scores are more closely aligned to a linear model than Tavon's scores. Make a mathematical argument to support or refute Arthur's claim.

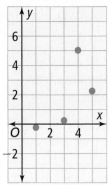
Arthur's Residual Plot

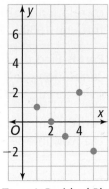
Tavon's Residual Plot

PRACTICE

Use technology to perform a linear regression to determine the equation for the line of best fit for the data. Estimate the value of *y* when *x* = 19.
SEE EXAMPLES 1 AND 4

14.

x	y
12	35
14	39
16	41
18	44
20	48

15.

x	y
16	105
20	83
24	62
28	34
32	15

Describe the type of correlation indicated by each correlation coefficient. SEE EXAMPLE 2

16. $r = -0.89$

17. $r = 0.94$

18. $r = 0.23$

19. $r = -0.19$

Make a residual plot for each linear model and the data set it represents. How well does each model fit its data set? SEE EXAMPLE 3

20. $y = 0.14x + 12.8$

21. $y = -0.58x + 25.2$

x	y
10	12
15	16
20	18
25	17
30	15

x	y
10	19
15	17
20	14
25	10
30	8

Construct an argument for each scenario given.
SEE EXAMPLE 5

22. The average monthly heating bills for houses in a neighborhood are positively correlated to the number of pets in the house. Can it be inferred that the number of pets in a household causes an increase in average monthly heating bills? Explain.

23. A person's level of education is positively correlated to the salary the person earns. Can it be inferred that a person with a doctorate degree will always earn more than a person with a bachelor's degree? Explain.

APPLY

24. Make Sense and Persevere Temperatures at different times of day are shown. How can you describe the relationship between temperature and time? Would a linear model be a good fit for the data? Explain.

12 P.M., 76 °F

8 A.M., 69 °F   4 P.M., 79 °F

4 A.M., 66 °F   8 P.M., 72 °F

12 A.M., 67 °F   12 A.M., 67 °F

25. Model With Mathematics The table shows the number of miles people in the U.S. traveled by car annually from 1975 to 2015. The equation for the line of best fit is $y = 0.048x + 1.345$, where x is the number of years since 1975. What does the slope represent? Estimate the number of miles people in the U.S. traveled in 2007. What is a reasonable prediction for the number of miles people in the U.S. will travel in 2022?

Year	Vehicle-Miles Traveled in U.S. (in trillions)
1975	1.298
1980	1.529
1985	1.720
1990	2.118
1995	2.387
2000	2.697
2005	2.973
2010	2.945
2015	3.055

26. Make Sense and Persevere The table shows the file size y in megabytes of photos taken at different resolutions x in megapixels. The equation for the line of best fit is $y = 0.3x$. Use this equation to create a residual plot. What does the residual plot tell you about the data?

x	4	5	6	7	8	10	12
y	1.2	1.5	1.8	2.1	2.4	3.0	3.6

ASSESSMENT PRACTICE

27. Characterize the relationship of the two variables of different data sets represented by the correlation coefficients shown.

   a. $r = -0.91$ **c.** $r = 0.87$

   b. $r = 0.54$ **d.** $r = 0.07$

28. SAT/ACT Students who eat breakfast are more likely to do well in school. Which of the following can be inferred from this relationship?

Ⓐ The two events are causally related.

Ⓑ The more often a student eats breakfast, the better the student will do in school.

Ⓒ Without more evidence, it cannot be determined whether the correlation is causal.

Ⓓ Providing free breakfast to all students will close the achievement gap.

29. Performance Task Use the table to answer the questions.

THE DAILY NEWS

NEWSPAPERS DECLINING!

Year	Daily Newspapers in U.S.
1940	1,878
1950	1,772
1960	1,763
1970	1,748
1980	1,745
1990	1,611
2000	1,480
2010	1,382

Part A Use technology to determine the equation for the line of best fit and the correlation coefficient for the data from 1940 through 1980.

Part B Find the line of best fit and the correlation coefficient for the data from 1940 through 2010.

Part C Compare the correlation coefficients of the two data sets. What do they indicate?

Topic Review

1. How can linear functions be used to model situations and solve problems?

Vocabulary Review

Choose the correct term to complete each sentence.

2. When *y* tends to increase as *x* increases, the two data sets have a _____.

3. A(n) _____ is the difference between an actual and a predicted data value.

4. A(n) _____ is an ordered list of numbers that often forms a pattern.

5. A trend line that most closely models the relationship between two variables displayed in a scatter plot is the _____.

6. The _____ measures the strength and direction of the relationship between two variables in a linear model.

- arithmetic sequence
- correlation coefficient
- line of best fit
- linear regression
- positive association
- residual
- sequence
- term of a sequence
- trend line

Concepts & Skills Review

LESSON 3-1 Relations and Functions

Quick Review

A **function** is a relation in which every input, or element of the **domain**, is associated with exactly one output, or element of the **range**.

Example

Identify the domain and range of the ordered pairs in the table. Do the ordered pairs represent a function? Justify your response.

x	−2	0	3	5	9
y	−3.5	−1.5	1.5	3.5	7.5

The domain is {−2, 0, 3, 5, 9}. The range is {−3.5, −1.5, 1.5, 3.5, 7.5}.

Each element of the domain is associated with exactly one element of the range, so the ordered pairs represent a function.

Practice & Problem Solving

Identify the domain and range of each relation. Is the relation a function? Explain.

7. {(4, 1), (2, 3), (0, 4), (5, 3)}

8.

x	−1	−5	4	0	2
y	−5	−2	0	3	2

Reason For 9 and 10, would a reasonable domain include all real numbers? Explain.

9. A person drinks *n* ounces of a 20-ounce bottle of a sports drink.

10. A printer prints *p* pages at a rate of 25 pages per minute.

Construct Arguments What constraints, if any, are there on the domain? Explain.

11. An airplane ascends to a cruising altitude at the rate of 1,000 ft/min for *m* minutes.

12. The value of an automobile in *d* dollars decreases by about 10% each year.

LESSON 3-2 — Linear Functions

Quick Review

A **linear function** is a function whose graph is a straight line. It represents a linear relationship between two variables. A linear function written in **function notation** is $f(x) = mx + b$ and $f(x)$ is read "f of x."

Example

A taxi company charges $3.50 plus $0.85 per mile. What linear function can be used to determine the cost of a taxi ride of x miles? How much would a 3.5-mile taxi ride cost?

Let d = distance of the taxi ride.

Cost of taxi ride = cost × distance + fee

$$f(d) = 0.85d + 3.5$$

Use the function to determine the cost of a 3.5-mile ride.

$$f(3.5) = (0.85)(3.5) + 3.5$$
$$= 6.475$$

The cost of a 3.5-mile taxi ride is $6.48.

Practice and Problem Solving

Evaluate each function for the elements in the domain {–4, –2, 0, 2, 4}.

13. $f(x) = 2x - 1$ **14.** $f(t) = -3(t - 2)$

15. Make Sense and Persevere Melissa runs a graphic design business. She charges by the page, and has a setup fee. The table shows her earnings for the last few projects. What is her per-page rate, and what is her setup fee?

Cost ($)	185	335	485	635
Page totals	2	4	6	8

16. Use Structure Tia's Computer Repair Shop charges the labor rates shown for computer repairs. What linear function can she use to determine the cost of a repair that takes 5.5 hours and includes $180 in parts?

Hours	1	1.5	2	2.5
Labor ($)	85	127.5	170	212.5

LESSON 3-3 — Transforming Linear Functions

Quick Review

A **transformation** of a function f maps each point of its graph to a new location. A **translation** shifts each point of the graph of a function the same distance horizontally, vertically, or both. **Stretches** and **compressions** scale each point of a graph either horizontally or vertically.

Example

Let $f(x) = 2x - 1$. If $g(x) = (2x - 1) + 3$, how does the graph of g compare to the graph of f?

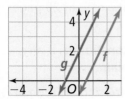

The graph of g is the translation of the graph of f three units up.

Practice & Problem Solving

Given the function $f(x) = x$, how does the addition or subtraction of a constant to the output affect the graph?

17. $f(x) = x - 2$ **18.** $f(x) = x + 5$

Given $f(x) = 4x - 5$, describe how the graph of g compares with the graph of f.

19. $g(x) = 4(x - 3) - 5$ **20.** $g(x) = 2(4x - 5)$

21. Reason Given $f(x) = -3x + 9$, how does multiplying the output of f by 2 affect the slope and y-intercept of the graph?

22. Model With Mathematics A hotel business center charges $40 per hour to rent a computer plus a $65 security deposit. The total rental charge is represented by $f(x) = 40x + 65$. How would the equation change if the business center increased the security deposit by $15?

LESSON 3-4 ▶ Arithmetic Sequences

Quick Review

A **sequence** is an ordered list of numbers that often follows a pattern. Each number is a **term of the sequence**. In an **arithmetic sequence**, the difference between any two consecutive terms is a constant called the **common difference, d**.

The **recursive formula** is used to describe the sequence and find the next term in a sequence from a given term. The **explicit formula** is used to find a specific term of the sequence.

Example

What is the 12th term in the sequence shown?

$-8, -5.5, -3, -0.5, 2.0, \ldots$

Determine the recursive formula to describe the sequence.

The common difference, d, is 2.5.

$$a_1 = -8$$
$$a_n = a_{n-1} + 2.5$$

Use the explicit formula to find the 12th term.

$$a_{12} = -8 + (12 - 1)2.5$$
$$a_{12} = 19.5$$

The 12th term of the sequence is 19.5.

Practice & Problem Solving

Tell whether each sequence is an arithmetic sequence. If it is, give the common difference. If it is not, explain why.

23. 48, 45, 41, 38, 34,…

24. −6, 5, 16, 27, 38,…

Write a recursive formula for each arithmetic sequence.

25. 2, 6, 10, 14, 18,…

26. −5, −8.5, −12, −15.5, −19,…

27. **Reason** A table of data of an arithmetic sequence is shown. Use the explicit formula for the arithmetic sequence to find the 15th term.

x	1	2	3	4	5
y	8	13	18	23	28

28. **Make Sense and Persevere** Gabriela is selling friendship bracelets for a school fundraiser. After the first day, she has 234 bracelets left. After the second day, she has 222 left. Assuming the sales pattern continues and it is an arithmetic sequence, how many bracelets will Gabriela have left to sell after the fifth day?

Quick Review

A paired data set (or a bivariate data set) has a **positive association** when y-values tend to increase as x-values increase and a **negative association** when y-values tend to decrease as x-values increase. When the relationship between the paired data can be modeled with a linear function, a **line of best fit** represents the relationship. The paired data are positively correlated if y-values increase as x-values increase and negatively correlated if y-values decrease as x-values increase.

Example

Yama takes a course to improve his typing speed. The scatter plot shows his progress over six weeks. What is the relationship between the number of weeks and Yama's typing speed?

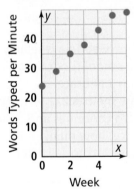

As the number of weeks of practice increases, so does the number of words typed per minute. The scatter plot shows a positive association that is approximately linear suggesting a positive correlation between weeks and words typed per minute.

Practice & Problem Solving

Describe the type of association each scatter plot shows.

29.
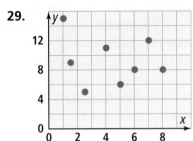

30.
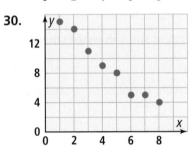

31. **Reason** Where should the line of best fit be in relationship to the points plotted on a scatter plot?

Use Appropriate Tools For each table, make a scatter plot of the data. If the data suggest a linear relationship, draw a trend line and write its equation.

32.

x	y
2	5
4	8
6	12
8	14
10	18

33.

x	y
3	40
6	36
8	31
12	27
15	24

34. **Model With Mathematics** The table shows the recommended distance of a light source y in feet, from the wall for different ceiling heights x in feet. What is the equation of the trend line that models the data shown in the table? What does the slope of the trend line represent?

x	8	9	10	11	12
y	20	27	33	40	48

Quick Review

Linear regression is a method used to calculate line of best fit. The **correlation coefficient** indicates the direction and strength of the linear relationship between two variables.
A **residual** reveals how well a linear model fits the data set. You can use the line of best fit to estimate a value within a range of known values (**interpolation**) or predict a value outside the range of known values (**extrapolation**).

Example

The scatter plot shows the percentage of American adults with a high school diploma or higher from 1940 to 2010. Based on the residual plot below the scatter plot, how appropriate is the linear model for the data?

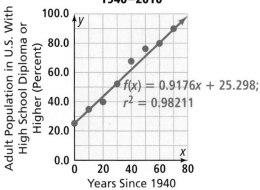

Educational Attainment 1940–2010

$f(x) = 0.9176x + 25.298;$
$r^2 = 0.98211$

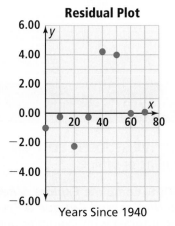

Residual Plot

Years Since 1940

The residual plot shows the residuals distributed above and below the x-axis and clustered somewhat close to the x-axis. The linear model is likely a good fit for the data.

Practice & Problem Solving

Use technology to perform a linear regression to determine the equation for the line of best fit for the data. Estimate the value of y when x = 25.

35.

x	y
20	9
22	12
24	16
26	20
28	23

36.

x	y
6	85
12	81
18	75
24	69
30	63

37. **Reason** How are interpolation and extrapolation similar? How are they different?

38. **Model With Mathematics** The table shows the winning times for the 100-meter run in the Olympics since 1928. What is the equation of the line of best fit for the data? What do the slope and y-intercept represent? Estimate the winning time in 2010, and predict the winning time in 2020.

Year	Time (s)	Year	Time (s)
1928	10.80	1980	10.25
1932	10.30	1984	9.99
1936	10.30	1988	9.92
1948	10.30	1992	9.96
1952	10.40	1996	9.84
1956	10.50	2000	9.87
1960	10.20	2004	9.85
1964	10.00	2008	9.69
1968	9.95	2012	9.63
1972	10.14	2016	9.81
1976	10.06		

TOPIC 4

Systems of Linear Equations and Inequalities

? TOPIC ESSENTIAL QUESTION

How do you use systems of linear equations and inequalities to model situations and solve problems?

Topic Overview

enVision® STEM Project:
Growing Grain

4-1 Solving Systems of Equations by Graphing

4-2 Solving Systems of Equations by Substitution

4-3 Solving Systems of Equations by Elimination

4-4 Linear Inequalities in Two Variables

Mathematical Modeling in 3 Acts:
Get Up There!

4-5 Systems of Linear Inequalities

Topic Vocabulary

- linear inequality in two variables
- solution of an inequality in two variables
- solution of a system of linear inequalities
- system of linear inequalities

Digital Experience

INTERACTIVE STUDENT EDITION Access online or offline.

ACTIVITIES Complete *Explore & Reason, Model & Discuss*, and *Critique & Explain* activities. Interact with Examples and Try Its.

ANIMATION View and interact with real-world applications.

PRACTICE Practice what you've learned.

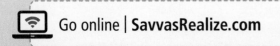

Go online | **SavvasRealize.com**

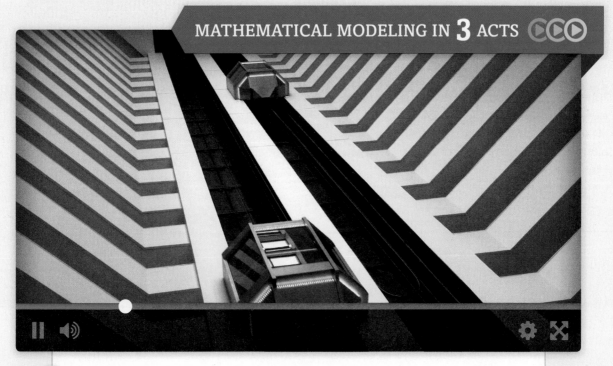

▶ Get Up There!

Have you ever been to the top of a skyscraper? If so, you probably didn't take the stairs. You probably took an elevator. How long did it take you to get to the top? Did you take an express elevator?

Express elevators travel more quickly because they do not stop at every floor. How much more quickly can you get to the top in an express elevator? Think about this during the Mathematical Modeling in 3 Acts lesson.

VIDEOS Watch clips to support *Mathematical Modeling in 3 Acts Lessons* and **enVision® STEM Projects.**

CONCEPT SUMMARY Review key lesson content through multiple representations.

ASSESSMENT Show what you've learned.

GLOSSARY Read and listen to English and Spanish definitions.

TUTORIALS Get help from *Virtual Nerd*, right when you need it.

MATH TOOLS Explore math with digital tools and manipulatives.

Did You Know?

American farmers produce enough meat and grain for the United States plus extra to export to other countries. Farms use about 53.5 billion gallons of groundwater each day for irrigation.

Peak Water Demands

Corn	July
Wheat	May and June
Soybeans	August

Corn is easier to grow than wheat and hardier in northern climates.

In 2012, soybeans became the biggest crop in the United States, with four times the acreage as in 1992. More soybeans are grown in the United States than in any other country.

 **1 bushel of wheat** = = **1 million individual kernels of wheat** = **42 pounds of white flour**  = **60 pounds of whole-wheat flour**  = **42 one and a half-pound loaves of white bread**

▶ Your Task: Growing Grain

You and your classmates will make decisions about growing crops on a farm. How much of each crop will you plant, and why?

🛜 Go Online | SavvasRealize.com

4-1

Solving Systems of Equations by Graphing

SavvasRealize.com

I CAN... use graphs to find approximate solutions to systems of equations.

🖐 **EXPLORE & REASON**

Juan and Leo were supposed to meet and drive ATVs on a trail together. Juan is late so Leo started without him.

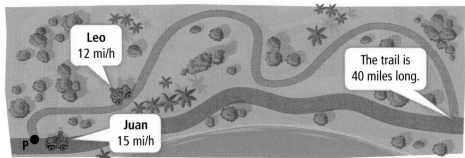

Leo
12 mi/h

The trail is 40 miles long.

Juan
15 mi/h

P

Not drawn to scale

A. Write an equation for Leo's distance from the starting point after riding for *x* hours. Write an equation for Juan's distance from the starting point if he starts *h* hours after Leo.

B. Model With Mathematics Suppose $h = 1$. How can you use graphs of the two equations to determine who finishes the trail first?

C. How much of a head start must Leo have to finish the trail at the same time as Juan?

? ESSENTIAL QUESTION   How can you use a graph to illustrate the solution to a system of linear equations?

CONCEPTUAL UNDERSTANDING

🖐 **EXAMPLE 1**   Solve a System of Equations by Graphing

What is the solution of the system of equations? $y = -2x - 4$
$y = 0.5x + 6$

Use a graph to solve this system of equations.

Step 1 Graph both equations.

Step 2 Find the point of intersection. Since the point of intersection lies on both lines, it is a solution to both equations.

The two lines intersect at $(-4, 4)$.

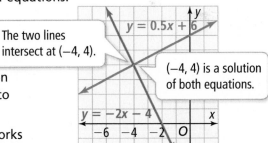

$(-4, 4)$ is a solution of both equations.

STUDY TIP
Substitute the *x*-coordinate for *x* and the *y*-coordinate for *y*.

Step 3 Check that the solution works for both equations.

$y = -2x - 4$ $y = 0.5x + 6$

$4 \stackrel{?}{=} -2(-4) - 4$ $4 \stackrel{?}{=} 0.5(-4) + 6$

$4 \stackrel{?}{=} 8 - 4$ $4 \stackrel{?}{=} -2 + 6$

$4 = 4 ✓$ $4 = 4 ✓$

Since there are no other points of intersection the system of equations has exactly one solution, $(-4, 4)$.

 Try It!   **1.** Use a graph to solve each system of equations.

a. $y = \frac{1}{2}x - 2$ **b.** $y = 2x + 10$

$y = 3x - 7$ $y = -\frac{1}{4}x + 1$

EXAMPLE 2 Graph Systems of Equations With Infinitely Many Solutions or No Solution

What is the solution of each system of equations? Use a graph to explain your answer.

A. $15x + 5y = 25$
   $y = 5 - 3x$

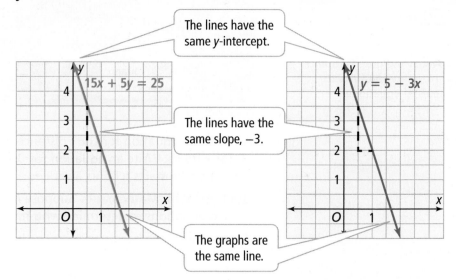

The lines have the same y-intercept.

The lines have the same slope, -3.

The graphs are the same line.

All ordered pairs on the line are solutions of both equations, so all points on the line are solutions to the system of equations. There are infinitely many solutions to the system.

B. $y - 2x = 6$
   $-4x + 2y = 8$

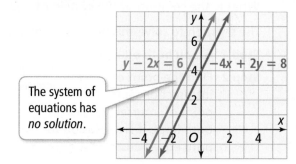

The system of equations has *no solution*.

The lines are parallel, so there is no point of intersection. Therefore, there is no solution to this system of equations.

 Try It! 2. Use a graph to solve each system of equations.

a. $y = \frac{1}{2}x + 7$
   $4x - 8y = 12$

b. $3x + 2y = 9$
   $\frac{2}{3}y = 3 - x$

APPLICATION **EXAMPLE 3** **Write a System of Equations**

Monisha and Holly have 14 more days to finish reading the same novel for class. Monisha plans to read 9 pages each day, while Holly plans to read 20 pages each day. Assuming Holly and Monisha both maintain their reading plan, when will Holly catch up with Monisha? Who will finish reading the novel first?

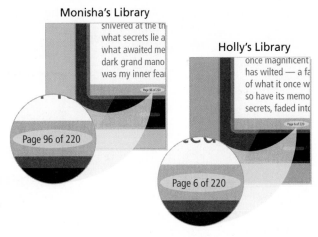

Formulate ◀ Write a system of equations to represent Holly's and Monisha's reading paces.

Monisha: Total pages = 96 pages already read + 9 pages/day • x days

$$y = 96 + 9x$$

Holly: Total pages = 6 pages already read + 20 pages/day • x days

$$y = 6 + 20x$$

Compute ◀ Graph the system of equations. Find the point where the graphs intersect.

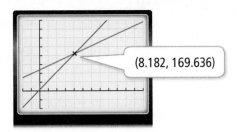

(8.182, 169.636)

Interpret ◀ After a little more than 8 days of reading, Monisha will have read $96 + 9(8.182) \approx 170$ pages.

Holly will have read $6 + 20(8.182) \approx 170$ pages. So, Holly will catch up with Monisha in a little over 8 days.

Since the book is 220 pages long, and Holly is reading at a faster rate, she will finish reading the novel before Monisha.

☑ **Try It!** 3. Suppose Monisha reads 10 pages each day instead.

    a. How will that change the length of time it takes for Holly to catch up with Monisha?

    b. Will Holly still finish the novel first? Explain.

👆 **EXAMPLE 4** ⟩ **Solve a System of Equations Approximately**

What is the solution of the system of equations?

$$y = 2x - 3$$
$$y = -5x + 6$$

Step 1 Use a graphing utility to graph both equations. Find the point of intersection.

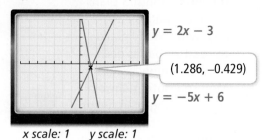

$y = 2x - 3$

(1.286, −0.429)

$y = -5x + 6$

x scale: 1   y scale: 1

Step 2 Check the values of *x* and *y* in each equation to see if they satisfy both equations.

$y = 2x - 3$	$y = -5x + 6$
$-0.429 \overset{?}{=} 2(1.286) - 3$	$-0.429 \overset{?}{=} -5(1.286) + 6$
$-0.429 \overset{?}{=} 2.572 - 3$	$-0.429 \overset{?}{=} -6.43 + 6$
$-0.429 \neq -0.428$	$-0.429 \neq -0.43$

> The solutions obtained by graphing are close to, but not equal to, the actual solutions.

REASON

What would happen if you substituted the exact solution into the system of equations?

The solution obtained by graphing, (1.286, −0.429) is correct to three decimal places, but it is not an exact solution. What is the exact solution? Consider which *x*-value gives you the same *y*-value in each equation.

Set the expressions for *y* equal to each other and solve for *x*.

$$2x - 3 = -5x + 6$$
$$2x + 5x = 6 + 3$$
$$7x = 9$$
$$x = \frac{9}{7}$$
$$= 1.\overline{285714}$$

> The *y*-values in both equations are equal when $x = \frac{9}{7}$.

Now substitute for *x* in either equation to find *y*.

$y = 2x - 3$	$y = -5x + 6$
$= 2\left(\frac{9}{7}\right) - 3$	$= -5\left(\frac{9}{7}\right) + 6$
$= \frac{18}{7} - 3$	$= \frac{-45}{7} + 6$
$= \frac{-3}{7}$	$= \frac{-3}{7}$
$= -0.\overline{428571}$	$= -0.\overline{428571}$

The exact solution is $\left(\frac{9}{7}, -\frac{3}{7}\right)$. You will see more methods for finding exact solutions in later lessons.

☑ **Try It!** **4.** What solution do you obtain for the system of equations by graphing? What is the exact solution?

$$y = 5x - 4$$
$$y = -6x + 14$$

CONCEPT SUMMARY Graphing to Solve Systems of Equations

WORDS	A system of linear equations may have one solution . . .	. . . infinitely many solutions . . .	. . . or no solution.
ALGEBRA	$y = -x + 9$ $y = \frac{3}{5}x + 3$	$y = -x + 9$ $2y = -2x + 18$	$y = -x + 9$ $y = -x + 12$
GRAPHS	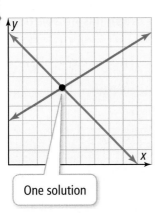 One solution	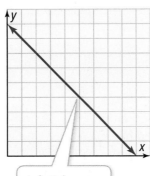 Infinitely many solutions	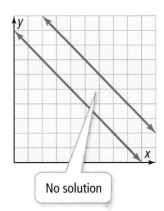 No solution

Do You UNDERSTAND?

1. **ESSENTIAL QUESTION** How can you use a graph to illustrate the solution to a system of linear equations?

2. **Model With Mathematics** How does the graph of a system of equations with one solution differ from the graph of a system of equations with infinitely many solutions or no solution?

3. **Reason** Why is the point of intersection for a system of equations considered its solution?

4. **Error Analysis** Reese states that the system of equations has no solution because the slopes are the same. Describe Reese's error.
$$y = -3x - 1$$
$$3x + y = -1$$

Do You KNOW HOW?

Solve each system of equations by graphing.

5. $y = 2x + 5$
$y = -\frac{1}{2}x$

6. $y = -\frac{2}{3}x + 2$
$2x + 3y = 6$

7. Juanita is painting her house. She can either buy Brand A paint and a paint roller tray or Brand B paint and a grid for the paint roller. For how many gallons of paint would the price for both options be the same? If Juanita needs 15 gallons of paint, which is the better option?

| 1-gallon can: **$27/gallon** | 1 paint roller tray: **$3** | 1-gallon can: **$25/gallon** | 1 grid for paint roller: **$5** |

✏ PRACTICE & PROBLEM SOLVING

UNDERSTAND

8. Use Structure Describe the solution set for the system of equations that includes the equation of the line shown and each equation below.

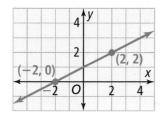

a. $y = \frac{1}{2}x - 3$

b. $2x + y = 6$

c. $x - 2y = -2$

9. Look for Relationships Write an equation in slope-intercept form that would have infinitely many solutions in a system of equations with $5x - 2y = 8$.

10. Communicate Precisely Copy and complete the table by writing the word *same* or *different* to show how the slope and *y*-intercept of each equation relate to the number of solutions in a system of two linear equations.

Number of solutions	Slopes	y-intercepts
One solution	■	■
Infinitely many solutions	■	■
No solution	■	■

11. Error Analysis Describe and correct the error a student made in finding the solution of the system of equations.

$y + 3x = 9$
$y = 3x + 9$

> There are an infinite number of solutions since the coefficients of the variables and the constants are the same. ✗

12. Higher Order Thinking The solution of a system of equations is (3, 2). One of the equations in the system is $2x + 3y = 12$. Write an equation in slope-intercept form that could be the second equation in the system.

PRACTICE

Solve each system of equations by graphing.
SEE EXAMPLE 1

13. $y = -2x - 2$
$y = 3x - 7$

14. $y = x$
$y = 2x$

15. $x + y = -5$
$y = \frac{1}{2}x - 2$

16. $3x + 2y = -3$
$2x - 3y = -15$

Determine whether each system of equations shown in the graph has *no solution* or *infinitely many solutions*. SEE EXAMPLE 2

17.

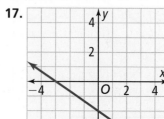

18.

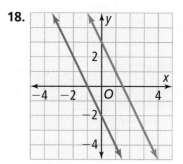

Write and solve a system of equations for the given situation. SEE EXAMPLE 3

19. Roshaun has saved $150 and continues to add $10 each week. Keegan starts with $0 and saves $25 each week.

a. In how many weeks will they have the same amount of money?

b. What amount of money will they each have saved?

Solve each system of equations by graphing. Round your answers to the thousandths, if necessary. SEE EXAMPLE 4

20. $y = 5x + 1$
$y = 2x + 6$

21. $y = -6x + 5$
$y = 4x + 3$

22. $y = 9x + 2$
$y = -3x - 4$

23. $y = \frac{1}{3}x + 9$
$y = -\frac{3}{4}x + 4$

APPLY

24. Use the graph to determine the solution for the system of equations.

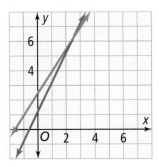

a. **Reason** How does the graph show that the solution of the system of equations has an *x*-value between 2 and 3?

b. What is the approximate solution of the system of equations?

25. **Model With Mathematics** Gabriela considers buying fleece jackets from Anastasia's Monograms or Monograms Unlimited. Anastasia's charges a one time design fee and a price per jacket. Monograms Unlimited only charges a price per jacket.

Anastasia's Monograms

Design fee: $15
Price per Jacket: $32

☆ | SAVE TO | ADD TO BAG

Monograms Unlimited

Price per Jacket: $35
Design fee: $0

ADD TO BAG

a. Write and solve a system of equations to represent the cost for a jacket from each company.

b. What does the solution mean?

c. Gabriela needs to buy 10 jackets. Which company should she choose? How does the graph help her decide? Explain.

26. **Reason** How do you know when the solution to a system of equations is a precise answer and when it is an approximate answer?

ASSESSMENT PRACTICE

27. Consider the system of equations.

$$y = \frac{3}{4}x + 2$$

$$3x + 4y = 8$$

The graph of the system of equations has _____ line(s) and the solution of the system is _____.

28. **SAT/ACT** Select which is the solution of the system of equations.

$$y = -3x - 3$$

$$y = -0.5x + 2$$

Ⓐ (0, 2)   Ⓑ (−1, 0)

Ⓒ (−1, 2)   Ⓓ (−2, 3)

29. **Performance Task** The lines that form the three sides of the triangle can be grouped into three different systems of two linear equations.

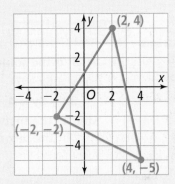

Part A Describe the system of equations that has each solution.

a. (2, 4)

b. (−2, −2)

c. (4, −5)

Part B Replace the solution (4, −5) to make an acute triangle. What are the coordinates of the new triangle?

Part C Describe the system of equations that will produce each of the new coordinates.

4-2

Solving Systems of Equations by Substitution

 SavvasRealize.com

I CAN... solve a system of equations using the substitution method.

 **MODEL & DISCUSS**

Rochelle is conducting an experiment on cells of Elodea, a kind of water plant. To induce plasmolysis at the correct rate, she needs to use an 8% saline solution, but she has only the solutions shown on hand.

Solution A
10% saline

Solution B
5% saline

A. If Rochelle mixes the two solutions to get 1,000 mL of an 8% saline solution, which will she use more of? Explain.

B. How can Rochelle determine the amount of each solution she needs to make the 8% saline solution?

C. Use Appropriate Tools Are there any methods for solving this problem other than the one you used in part B? Explain.

❓ ESSENTIAL QUESTION   How do you use substitution to solve a system of linear equations?

CONCEPTUAL UNDERSTANDING

EXAMPLE 1 ▸ Solve Systems of Equations Using Substitution

What is the solution of the system of equations?

$$y = 6x + 7$$
$$3x - 8y = 4$$

Step 1 The first equation is already solved for y, so substitute $6x + 7$ for y in the second equation.

$$3x - 8y = 4$$
$$3x - 8(6x + 7) = 4 \quad \longleftarrow \text{Substitute } 6x + 7 \text{ for } y.$$

COMMON ERROR
The value of the variable can be an expression, so be sure to use parentheses when substituting an expression for the value of a variable.

Step 2 Solve for x.

$$3x - 8(6x + 7) = 4$$
$$3x - 48x - 56 = 4$$
$$-45x - 56 = 4$$
$$-45x = 60$$
$$x = -\frac{4}{3}$$

Step 3 Substitute $-\frac{4}{3}$ for x in one of the equations and solve for y.

$$y = 6x + 7$$
$$y = 6\left(-\frac{4}{3}\right) + 7$$
$$y = -8 + 7$$
$$y = -1$$

This system of equations has exactly one solution, $\left(-\frac{4}{3}, -1\right)$.

CONTINUED ON THE NEXT PAGE

EXAMPLE 1 CONTINUED

Step 4 Check by substituting the values into each of the original equations.

$$y = 6x + 7 \qquad\qquad 3x - 8y = 4$$

$$(-1) \stackrel{?}{=} 6\left(-\frac{4}{3}\right) + 7 \qquad\qquad 3\left(-\frac{4}{3}\right) - 8(-1) \stackrel{?}{=} 4$$

$$-1 \stackrel{?}{=} -8 + 7 \qquad\qquad -4 + 8 \stackrel{?}{=} 4$$

$$-1 = -1 \checkmark \qquad\qquad 4 = 4 \checkmark$$

☑ **Try It!**   **1.** Use substitution to solve each system of equations.

a. $x = y + 6$
$x + y = 10$

b. $y = 2x - 1$
$2x + 3y = -7$

 EXAMPLE 2   **Compare Graphing and Substitution Methods**

A vacation resort offers surfing lessons and parasailing. If a person takes a surfing lesson and goes parasailing, she will pay a total of $175. On Friday, the resort collects a total of $3,101 for activities. How much does each activity cost?

$x + y = 175 \qquad 20x + 16y = 3,101$

> Let x be the price of a surfing lesson per person. Let y be the price of parasailing per person.

16 people go parasailing.

20 people take surfing lessons.

Method 1

Solve the system of equations by graphing.

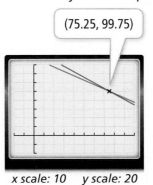

(75.25, 99.75)

x scale: 10   y scale: 20

REASON

How could you show that (75, 100) is a good estimate for the solution of the system?

Check your answer.

$$x + y = 175$$

$$75.25 + 99.75 \stackrel{?}{=} 175$$

$$175 = 175 \checkmark$$

$$20x + 16y = 3,101$$

$$20(75.25) + 16(99.75) \stackrel{?}{=} 3,101$$

$$1,505 + 1,596 \stackrel{?}{=} 3,101$$

$$3,101 = 3,101 \checkmark$$

Surfing lessons cost $75.25 and parasailing lessons cost $99.75.

CONTINUED ON THE NEXT PAGE

EXAMPLE 2 CONTINUED

Method 2

Solve the system of equations by substitution.

Step 1 Solve one of the equations for either x or y.

$$x + y = 175$$
$$x + y - y = 175 - y$$
$$x = 175 - y$$

Step 2 Substitute for x and solve for y.

$$20x + 16y = 3{,}101$$
$$20(175 - y) + 16y = 3{,}101 \quad \longleftarrow \boxed{\text{Substitute } 175 - y \text{ for } x.}$$
$$-4y = -399$$
$$y = 99.75$$

Step 3 Substitute 99.75 for y in one of the equations and solve for x.

$$x + y = 175$$
$$x + 99.75 = 175$$
$$x = 75.25$$

Step 4 Check by substituting the values for x and y into each of the original equations.

$$x + y = 175 \qquad\qquad 20x + 16y = 3{,}101$$
$$75.25 + 99.75 \overset{?}{=} 175 \qquad 20(75.25) + 16(99.75) \overset{?}{=} 3{,}101$$
$$175 = 175 \checkmark \qquad\qquad 1{,}505 + 1{,}596 \overset{?}{=} 3{,}101$$
$$3{,}101 = 3{,}101 \checkmark$$

It costs \$75.25 to take a surfing lesson and \$99.75 to go parasailing.

STUDY TIP
Remember that after solving one equation for a variable, you need to substitute the solution into the other equation in the system of equations.

✅ **Try It!**   **2.** On Saturday, the vacation resort offers a discount on water sports. To take a surfing lesson and go parasailing costs \$130. That day, 25 people take surfing lessons, and 30 people go parasailing. A total of \$3,650 is collected. What is the discounted price of each activity?

EXAMPLE 3   **Systems With Infinitely Many Solutions or No Solution**

What is the solution of each system of equations?

A. $y = 3x + 1$
$\quad 6x - 2y = -2$

$$6x - 2y = -2$$
$$6x - 2(3x + 1) = -2 \quad \longleftarrow \boxed{\text{Substitute } 3x + 1 \text{ for } y \text{ and then simplify.}}$$
$$6x - 6x - 2 = -2$$
$$-2 = -2$$

The statement $-2 = -2$ is an identity, so the system of equations has infinitely many solutions. Both equations represent the same line. All points on the line are solutions to the system of equations.

CONTINUED ON THE NEXT PAGE

EXAMPLE 3 CONTINUED

B. $5x - y = -4$

$y = 5x - 4$

$5x - y = -4$

$5x - (5x - 4) = -4$ ← Substitute $5x - 4$ for y and then simplify.

$5x - 5x + 4 = -4$

$4 = -4$

REASON
When the result of solving a system of equations is a false statement, there are no values of x and y that satisfy both equations.

The statement $4 = -4$ is false, so the system of equations has no solution.

 Try It! **3.** Solve each system of equations.

a. $x + y = -4$

$y = -x + 5$

b. $y = -2x + 5$

$2x + y = 5$

APPLICATION  **EXAMPLE 4** **Model Using Systems of Equations**

Nate starts a lawn-mowing business. In his business he has expenses and revenue. Nate's expenses are the cost of the lawn mower and gas, and his revenue is $25 per lawn. At what point will Nate's revenue exceed his expenses?

Lawnmower: $200

Gasoline: $2 per lawn

Formulate ◄ Write a system of linear equations to model Nate's expenses and revenue.

In both equations, let y represent the dollar amount, either of expenses or revenue. Let x represent the number of lawns Nate mows.

Nate's expenses: $y = 2x + 200$ ← Nate has an initial expense of $200 and then an additional expense of $2 per lawn.

Nate's revenue: $y = 25x$

Compute ◄ Substitute for y in one of the equations.

$y = 2x + 200$

$25x = 2x + 200$

$23x = 200$

$x \approx 8.7$

Interpret ◄ Since x is the number of lawns Nate mows, he needs to mow 8.7 lawns before his expenses and revenue are equal. However, Nate is hired to mow whole lawns and not partial lawns, so he will need to mow 9 lawns.

Nate will need to mow 9 lawns before his revenue exceeds his expenses.

 Try It! **4.** Funtime Amusement Park charges $12.50 for admission and then $0.75 per ride. River's Edge Park charges $18.50 for admission and then $0.50 per ride. For what number of rides is the cost the same at both parks?

CONCEPT SUMMARY Solve by Graphing and by Substitution

GRAPHING
$$x + y = 5.5$$
$$8x - 4y = 3.5$$

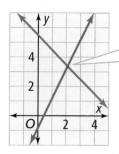

The point of intersection is about (2.1, 3.4).

SUBSTITUTION
$$x + y = 5.5$$
$$8x - 4y = 3.5$$

Solve for one variable.

$$x + y = 5.5$$
$$x = 5.5 - y$$

Substitute for x.

$$8x - 4y = 3.5$$
$$8(5.5 - y) - 4y = 3.5$$
$$44 - 8y - 4y = 3.5$$
$$-12y = -40.5$$
$$y = 3.375$$

Substitute for y.

$$x + y = 5.5$$
$$x + 3.375 = 5.5$$
$$x = 2.125$$

Do You UNDERSTAND?

1. **ESSENTIAL QUESTION** How do you use substitution to solve a system of linear equations?

2. **Use Appropriate Tools** When is using a graph to solve a system of equations more useful than the substitution method?

3. **Error Analysis** Simon solves a system of equations, in x and y, by substitution and gets an answer of $5 = 5$. He states that the solution to the system is all of the points (x, y) where x and y are real numbers. Describe Simon's error.

4. **Use Structure** When solving a system of equations using substitution, how can you determine whether the system has one solution, no solution, or infinitely many solutions?

Do You KNOW HOW?

Use substitution to solve each system of equations.

5. $y = 6 - x$
   $4x - 3y = -4$

6. $x = -y + 3$
   $3x - 2y = -1$

7. $-3x - y = 7$
   $x + 2y = 6$

8. $6x - 3y = -6$
   $y = 2x + 2$

9. A sports store sells a total of 70 soccer balls in one month and collects a total of $2,400. Write and solve a system of equations to determine how many of each type of soccer ball were sold.

Limited Edition soccer ball $65.00	Pro NSL soccer ball $15.00

Go Online | SavvasRealize.com

PRACTICE & PROBLEM SOLVING

UNDERSTAND

10. Use Structure When given a system of equations in slope-intercept form, which is the most efficient method to solve: graphing or substitution? Explain.

11. Look for Relationships After solving a system of equations using substitution, you end up with the equation $3 = 2$. What is true about the slope and y-intercepts of the lines in the system of equations?

12. Error Analysis Describe and correct the error a student made in finding the number of solutions of the system of equations.

$x - 2y = -4$
$5x - 3y = 1$

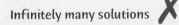

$x = 2y - 4$
$5x - 3y = 1$

$2y - 4 - 2y = -4$
$-4 = -4$

Infinitely many solutions

13. Use Structure When using substitution to solve systems of equations that have no solution or infinitely many solutions, the variables are the same on both sides. How is the solution determined by the constants in the equations?

14. Model With Mathematics The perimeter of a rectangle is 124 cm. The length is six more than three times the width. What are the dimensions of the rectangle?

15. Mathematical Connections Two angles are complementary. One angle is six more than twice the other. What is the measure of each angle?

16. Higher Order Thinking One equation in a system of equations is $5x - 2y = -4$.

a. Write the second equation in the system of equations that would produce a graph with parallel lines.

b. Write the second equation in the system of equations that would produce a graph with one line.

PRACTICE

Use substitution to solve each system of equations.
SEE EXAMPLE 1

17. $y = 2x - 4$
$3x - 2y = 1$

18. $y = 3x - 8$
$y = 13 - 4x$

19. $y = 2x - 7$
$9x + y = 15$

20. $y = -\frac{1}{2}x$
$2x + 2y = 5$

21. $x = 3y - 4$
$2x - 3y = -2$

22. $x + 2y = -10$
$y = -\frac{1}{2}x + 2$

Consider the system of equations. SEE EXAMPLE 2
$x + y = 5$
$2x - y = -2$

23. Solve the system of equations by graphing.

24. Solve the system of equations using the substitution method.

25. Which method do you prefer in this instance? Explain.

Identify whether each system of equations has infinitely many solutions or no solution.
SEE EXAMPLE 3

26. $4x + 8y = -8$
$x = -2y + 1$

27. $2x - 3y = 6$
$y = \frac{2}{3}x - 2$

28. $2x + 2y = 6$
$4x + 4y = 4$

29. $2x + 5y = -5$
$y = -\frac{2}{5}x - 1$

Write and solve a system of equations for the situation. SEE EXAMPLE 4

30. At a hot air balloon festival, Mohamed's balloon is at an altitude of 40 m and rises 10 m/min. Dana's balloon is at an altitude of 165 m and descends 15 m/min.

a. In how many minutes will both balloons be at the same altitude?

b. What will be the altitude?

31. Richard and Teo have a combined age of 31. Richard is 4 years older than twice Teo's age. How old are Richard and Teo?

APPLY

32. Reason The sum of two numbers is 4. The larger number is 12 more than three times the smaller number. What are the numbers?

33. Use Structure In a basketball game, the Bulldogs make a total of 21 shots. Some of the shots are 2-point shots while others are 3-point shots. The Bulldogs score a total of 50 points. How many 2-point and 3-point shots did they make?

34. Make Sense and Persevere Stay Fit gym charges a membership fee of $75. They offer karate classes for an additional fee.

KARATE
Members:
$3 per class

Non-members:
$8 per class

a. How many classes could members and non-members take before they pay the same amount?

b. How much would they pay?

35. Model With Mathematics Abby uses two social media sites. She has 52 more followers on Site A than on Site B. How many followers does she have on each site?

Social Media Site A

Abby's Studio1
@abbystudiooone.com

0 photos | 0 followers | following

@abbystudiooone.com my new photo and art studio is now open!

Follow

700 total followers for both social media sites.

Social Media Site B

Abby's Blog
@abbysphotos.com

0 photos | 0 followers | following

Follow

NEW POST - Edits - Settings

ASSESSMENT PRACTICE

36. What are the x- and y-coordinates of the solution for the system of equations?

$x = -y + 4$

$2x + 3y = 4$

x-coordinate = _____

y-coordinate = _____

37. SAT/ACT Describe the solution of the system of equations.

$2x - 5y = -5$

$y = \frac{2}{5}x - 2$

Ⓐ No solution

Ⓑ Infinitely many solutions

Ⓒ (10, 5)

Ⓓ (5, 3)

38. Performance Task Each side of a triangle lies along a line in a coordinate plane. The three lines that contain these sides are represented by the given equations.

Equation 1: $x - 2y = -4$

Equation 2: $2x + y = -3$

Equation 3: $7x - 4y = 12$

Part A Write three systems of equations that can be used to determine the vertices of the triangle.

Part B What are the coordinates of the vertices?

Part C Is this a right triangle? Explain.

4-3

Solving Systems of Equations by Elimination

I CAN... solve systems of linear equations using the elimination method.

CRITIQUE & EXPLAIN

Sadie and Micah used different methods to solve the system of equations.

$$y = 2x + 3$$
$$4x - y = 5$$

Sadie's work	Micah's work
$4x - (2x + 3) = 5$ $4x - 2x - 3 = 5$ $2x - 3 = 5$ $2x = 8$ $x = 4$ $y = 2(4) + 3 = 11$ **The solution is (4, 11).**	$y = 2x + 3$ and $y = 4x - 5$ $2x + 3 = 4x - 5$ $8 = 2x$ $x = 4$ $y = 2(4) + 3$ $y = 11$ **The solution is (4, 11).**

A. In what ways are Sadie's and Micah's approaches similar? In what ways are they different?

B. Are both Sadie's and Micah's approaches valid solution methods? Explain.

C. Reason Which method of solving systems of equations do you prefer when solving, Sadie's method, or Micah's method? Explain.

ESSENTIAL QUESTION

Why does the elimination method work when solving a system of equations?

EXAMPLE 1   Solve a System of Equations by Adding

What is the solution to the system of equations?

$$x + y = 7$$
$$2x - y = 2$$

You can add equations to get a new equation that is easier to solve.

Match like terms.
$$\begin{array}{r} x + y = 7 \\ + 2x - y = 2 \\ \hline 3x + 0 = 9 \end{array}$$
Write the sums of like terms below.

This method works because of the Addition Property of Equality.

COMMON ERROR
You may think that you need to add the same expression to each side of the equation. However, since $2x - y = 2$, adding one of the expressions to each side of the equation is still adding an equivalent value to each side of the equation.

$$x + y = 7$$
$$x + y + (2x - y) = 7 + 2$$
$$(x + 2x) + (y - y) = 7 + 2$$
$$3x + 0 = 9$$

Since $2x - y$ and 2 are equal, you can add $2x - y$ to the left side and 2 to the right side.

Look carefully at the last two steps. They are the same as adding like terms in the original system of equations.

$$\begin{array}{r} x + y = 7 \\ + 2x - y = 2 \\ \hline 3x + 0 = 9 \end{array}$$

$$(x + 2x) + (y - y) = 7 + 2$$
$$3x + 0 = 9$$

CONTINUED ON THE NEXT PAGE

EXAMPLE 1 CONTINUED

So $3x = 9$, or $x = 3$. Now substitute 3 for x in either of the two equations in the system of equations.

$$x + y = 7$$
$$3 + y = 7$$
$$y = 4$$

The solution to the system of equations is (3, 4).

 Try It! **1.** Solve each system of equations.

a. $2x - 4y = 2$ **b.** $2x + 3y = 1$
$-x + 4y = 3$ $-2x + 2y = -6$

CONCEPTUAL UNDERSTANDING **EXAMPLE 2** **Understand Equivalent Systems of Equations**

What is the solution to the system of equations?
$$x + 3y = 7$$
$$2x + 2y = 6$$

Before adding equations, multiply each side of one of the equations by a constant that makes either the x or y terms opposites.

$x + 3y = 7$ Multiply by -2. $-2(x + 3y) = -2 \cdot 7$
$2x + 2y = 6$ $2x + 2y = 6$

MAKE SENSE AND PERSEVERE
The two equations have the same solution because of the Multiplication Property of Equality.

The result is an *equivalent system* that has the same solution as the original system. This is because the first equation has the same solution after multiplying each side by the same nonzero value.

Now solve by adding the equations.

$$-2x - 6y = -14$$
$$+\ 2x + 2y = 6$$
$$\overline{0 - 4y = -8}$$

> Distribute the -2 on each side before adding.

So $-4y = -8$, or $y = 2$. Now substitute 2 for y in either of the two equations in the system.

$$x + 3y = 7$$
$$x + 3(2) = 7$$
$$x = 1$$

The solution to the system is (1, 2).

 Try It! **2.** Solve each system of equations.

a. $x + 2y = 4$ **b.** $2x + y = 2$
$2x - 5y = -1$ $x - 2y = -5$

APPLICATION →

👆 **EXAMPLE 3**   Apply Elimination

A florist is making regular bouquets and mini bouquets. The florist has 118 roses and 226 peonies to use in the bouquets. How many of each type of bouquet can the florist make?

> Each regular bouquet has 5 roses and 11 peonies.

> Each mini bouquet has 3 roses and 5 peonies.

Formulate ◄   Let x be the number of regular bouquets and y be the number of mini bouquets.

Roses: $5x + 3y = 118$

Peonies: $11x + 5y = 226$

Compute ◄   Multiply each equation by constants to eliminate one variable.

$5x + 3y = 118$ Multiply by 5. ➤ $25x + 15y = 590$

$11x + 5y = 226$ Multiply by −3. ➤ $-33x - 15y = -678$

$$-8x + 0 = -88$$

> Add the equations to eliminate y.

$$x = 11$$

> There are many ways to do this. In this case, 15 is the LCM of 3 and 5.

Solve for y. $5(11) + 3y = 118$

> Substitute 11 for x and solve for y.

$$55 + 3y = 118$$
$$3y = 63$$
$$y = 21$$

The solution is (11, 21).

Interpret ◄   The florist has enough roses and peonies to make 11 regular and 21 mini bouquets.

 Try It!   **3.** Before the florist has a chance to finish the bouquets, a large order is placed. After the order, only 85 roses and 163 peonies remain. How many regular bouquets and mini bouquets can the florist make now?

👆 **EXAMPLE 4**   **Choose a Method of Solving**

What is the solution of the system of equations?

A. $y = x + 13$

$2x + 7y = 10$

Since the first equation is already solved for one of the variables, you can easily substitute $x + 13$ for y.

$2x + 7(x + 13) = 10$

$9x + 91 = 10$ $\qquad\qquad$ $y = -9 + 13$

$9x = -81$ $\qquad\qquad$ $y = 4$

$x = -9$

The solution is $(-9, 4)$.

B. $8x - 2y = -8$

$5x - 4y = 17$

The coefficient of y in the second equation is an integer multiple of the coefficient of y in the first equation. This makes it easy to eliminate the y variable.

> **STUDY TIP**
> Since the coefficients of the y-terms have the same sign, multiply by a negative number.

$8x - 2y = -8$ $\boxed{\text{Multiply by } -2.}$ ➤ $-16x + 4y = 16$

$5x - 4y = 17$ $\qquad\qquad\qquad\qquad$ $\underline{5x - 4y = 17}$

$\boxed{\text{Add the equations.}}$ $\qquad\qquad$ $-11x + 0 = 33$

$\qquad\qquad\qquad\qquad\qquad\qquad$ $x = -3$ $\boxed{\text{Solve for } x.}$

Now solve for y.

$5(-3) - 4y = 17$

$-15 - 4y = 17$

$-4y = 32$

$y = -8$

To use the substitution method, you would have to solve for one of the variables first. Because of the structure of the equations, elimination is an easier method.

The solution is $(-3, -8)$.

☑ **Try It!**   **4.** What is the solution of each system of equations? Explain your choice of solution method.

a. $6x + 12y = -6$ $\qquad\qquad\qquad$ **b.** $3x - 2y = 38$

$\qquad$ $3x - 2y = -27$ $\qquad\qquad\qquad\qquad$ $x = 6 - y$

CONCEPT SUMMARY Elimination vs. Substitution

	Substitution	Elimination
WORDS	When one equation is already solved for one variable, or if it is easy to solve for one variable, use substitution.	When you can multiply one or both equations by a constant to get like coefficients that are opposite, use elimination.

ALGEBRA

Substitution:

$$3x + y = 8$$
$$x = 2y - 2$$

$$3(2y - 2) + y = 8$$
$$6y - 6 + y = 8$$
$$7y = 14$$
$$y = 2$$

$$x = 2(2) - 2$$
$$= 2$$

Elimination:

$3x - 7y = 16$ — Multiply by 5. → $15x - 35y = 80$
$5x - 4y = 19$ — Multiply by -3. → $-15x + 12y = -57$

$$0 - 23y = 23$$
$$y = -1$$

$$3x - 7(-1) = 16$$
$$3x = 9$$
$$x = 3$$

☑ Do You UNDERSTAND?

1. **ESSENTIAL QUESTION** Why does the elimination method work when solving a system of equations?

2. **Error Analysis** Esteban tries to solve the following system.

   $$7x - 4y = -12$$
   $$x - 2y = 4$$

   His first step is to multiply the second equation by 3.

   $$7x - 4y = -12$$
   $$3x - 6y = 12$$

   Then he adds the equations to eliminate a term. What is Esteban's error?

3. **Construct Arguments** How can you determine whether two systems of equations are equivalent?

4. **Mathematical Connections** The sum of 5 times the width of a rectangle and twice its length is 26 units. The difference of 15 times the width and three times the length is 6 units. Write and solve a system of equations to find the length and width of the rectangle.

Do You KNOW HOW?

Solve each system of equations.

5. $4x - 2y = -2$
   $3x + 2y = -12$

6. $3x + 2y = 4$
   $3x + 6y = -24$

7. $4x - 3y = -9$
   $3x + 2y = -11$

8. $x - 3y = -4$
   $2x - 6y = 6$

9. Ella is a landscape photographer. One weekend at her gallery she sells a total of 52 prints for a total of $2,975. How many of each size print did Ella sell?

Small: $50

Large: $75

PRACTICE & PROBLEM SOLVING

UNDERSTAND

10. Use Structure How does the structure of a system of equations help you choose which solution method to use?

11. Generalize Consider the system of equations.

$$Ax + By = C$$
$$Px + Qy = R$$

If the system has infinitely many solutions, how are the coefficients A, B, C, P, Q, and R related? If the system has no solution, how are the coefficients related?

12. Use Appropriate Tools Write and solve a system of equations for the graph shown.

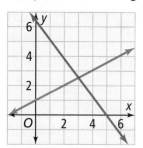

13. Error Analysis Describe and correct the error a student made in finding the solution to the system of equations.

$$2x - y = -1$$
$$x - y = -4$$

$2x - y = -1$
$-1(x - y) = -4$

$2x - y = -1$
$-x + y = -4$
$x = -5$

$2(-5) - y = -1$
$-10 - y = -1$
$-y = 9$

The solution is $(-5, -9)$.

14. Use Structure Explain the advantages of using substitution to solve the system of equations instead of elimination.

$$x = 6 + y$$
$$48 = 2x + 2y$$

PRACTICE

Solve each system of equations. SEE EXAMPLES 1 AND 3

15. $x - y = 4$
$2x + y = 5$

16. $x - 2y = -2$
$3x + 2y = 30$

17. $3x + 2y = 8$
$x + 4y = -4$

18. $x - 2y = 1$
$2x + 3y = -12$

19. $7x - 4y = -12$
$x - 2y = 4$

20. $5x + 6y = -6$
$7x - 3y = -54$

21. $2x + 5y = -20$
$3x - 2y = -11$

22. $4x - 3y = 17$
$2x - 5y = 5$

Is each pair of systems of equations equivalent? Explain. SEE EXAMPLE 2

23. $3x - 9y = 5$ $6x - 9y = 10$
$6x + 2y = 18$ $6x + 2y = 18$

24. $4y + 2x = -7$ $4y + 2x = -7$
$2y - 6x = 8$ $4y - 12x = 16$

25. $5x + 3y = 19$ $10x + 6y = 38$
$2x + 4y = 20$ $10x + 20y = 100$

Write and solve a system of equations to model each situation. SEE EXAMPLE 3

26. Two pizzas and four sandwiches cost $62. Four pizzas and ten sandwiches cost $140. How much does each pizza and sandwich cost?

27. At a clothing store, 3 shirts and 8 hats cost $65. The cost for 2 shirts and 2 hats is $30. How much does each shirt and hat cost?

Solve each system. Explain your choice of solution method. SEE EXAMPLE 4

28. $6x - 5y = -1$
$6x + 4y = -10$

29. $8x - 4y = -4$
$x = y - 4$

30. $5x - 2y = -6$
$3x - 4y = -26$

31. $2x - 3y = 14$
$5x + 4y = 12$

PRACTICE & PROBLEM SOLVING

APPLY

32. Construct Arguments DeShawn and Chris are solving the following system of equations.

$$x - 4y = -8$$
$$3x + 4y = 0$$

DeShawn says that the first step should be to add the two equations to eliminate y. Chris says that the first step should be to multiply the first equation by -3 so you can eliminate the x-terms.

Who is correct? Explain.

33. Generalize Describe a system of equations where each solution method would be the most efficient to use.

a. Graphing

b. Substitution

c. Elimination

34. Model With Mathematics Two groups of friends go to a baseball game. Each group plans to share the snacks shown. What is the price of one drink and one pretzel?

3 drinks and 2 pretzels: **$16.00**

5 drinks and 5 pretzels: **$31.25**

35. Higher Order Thinking Determine the value of n that makes a system of equations with a solution that has a y-value of 2.

$$5x + 6y = 32$$
$$2x + ny = 18$$

36. A group of 30 students from the senior class charters a bus to an amusement park. The total amount they spend on the bus and admission to the park for each student is $1,770.

A group of 50 students from the junior class also go to the amusement park, but they require two buses. If the group from the junior class spent $3,190 in total, how much does it cost to charter one bus?

ASSESSMENT PRACTICE

37. Solve the system of equations using elimination. Complete the solution of the system of equations.

$$4x + 3y = 6$$
$$2x - 5y = 16$$

$x =$ _____ and $y =$ _____

38. SAT/ACT A rental company can set up 3 small tents and 1 large tent in 115 min. They can set up 2 small tents and 2 large tents in 130 min. How much time is required to set up a small tent?

Ⓐ 15 min

Ⓑ 25 min

Ⓒ 35 min

Ⓓ 40 min

39. Performance Task At Concessions Unlimited, four granola bars and three drinks cost $12.50. Two granola bars and five drinks cost $15.00.

At Snacks To Go, three granola bars and three drinks cost $10.50. Four granola bars and two drinks cost $10.00.

Part A Write a system of equations for each concession stand that models the price of its items.

Part B Solve each system of equations. What do the solutions represent?

Part C You decide to open a new concessions stand and sell granola bars and drinks. Determine a price for each item that differ from the prices at Snacks To Go. Then write a system of equations to model the prices at your snack bar.

4-4

Linear Inequalities in Two Variables

SavvasRealize.com

I CAN... graph solutions to linear inequalities in two variables.

VOCABULARY
- linear inequality in two variables
- solution of a linear inequality in two variables

👆 **MODEL & DISCUSS**

A flatbed trailer carrying a load can have a maximum total height of 13 feet, 6 inches. The photograph shows the height of the trailer before a load is placed on top. What are the possible heights of loads that could be carried on the trailer?

5 ft

A. What type of model could represent this situation? Explain.

B. Will the type of model you chose show all the possible heights of the loads without going over the maximum height? Explain.

C. Reason Interpret the solutions of the model. How many solutions are there? Explain.

❓ **ESSENTIAL QUESTION**   How does the graph of a linear inequality in two variables help you identify the solutions of the inequality?

CONCEPTUAL UNDERSTANDING

👆 **EXAMPLE 1**   Understand an Inequality in Two Variables

A. What is the solution of the inequality $y \leq x - 1$?

STUDY TIP
You used substitution to test whether an ordered pair is a solution of an equation. You can do the same to test whether an ordered pair is a solution of an inequality.

The inequality $y \leq x - 1$ is an example of a **linear inequality in two variables**. It has the same form as a linear equation but uses an inequality symbol. The **solution of a linear inequality in two variables** is all ordered pairs (x, y) that make the inequality true.

You can plot these ordered pairs on a coordinate plane to understand the solution of the inequality.

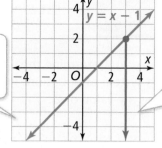

When $y = x - 1$, the solutions are all points on the red line.

The y-value of every point on the blue ray is less than or equal to $x - 1$ for each x.

Now imagine drawing the blue ray for *every* x-value.

The solution of the inequality is all points on the line (called a *boundary line*) and in the shaded region.

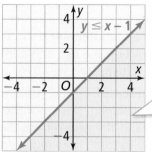

All the blue rays together form the shaded region.

CONTINUED ON THE NEXT PAGE

EXAMPLE 1 CONTINUED

B. What is the solution of the inequality $y > x - 1$?

The process for finding the solution of $y > x - 1$ is similar to finding the solution of $y \leq x - 1$. For each x, find all values of y that are greater than $x - 1$.

COMMON ERROR
You may think that the graph of any line is solid, but for inequalities it is only a solid line when the inequality symbol is $\geq$ or $\leq$.

Since the inequality uses *greater than*, shade *above* the line.

$y > x - 1$

The boundary line is a dashed line to indicate that points on it are *not* part of the solution.

The solution of the inequality is all points in the shaded region.

☑ **Try It!** 1. Describe the graph of the solutions of each inequality.

a. $y < -3x + 5$ **b.** $y \geq -3x + 5$

APPLICATION

 EXAMPLE 2 Rewrite an Inequality to Graph It

The Science Club sells T-shirts and key chains to raise money. How many T-shirts and key chains could they sell to meet or exceed their goal?

Formulate ◄ Let x represent the number of T-shirts sold and y represent the number of key chains sold. The total amount of money they make must equal or exceed $500.

$$10x + 2y \geq 500$$

Compute ◄ Solve the inequality for y.

$$10x + 2y \geq 500$$
$$2y \geq -10x + 500$$
$$y \geq -5x + 250$$

Graph the inequality.

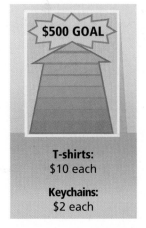

$500 GOAL

T-shirts:
$10 each

Keychains:
$2 each

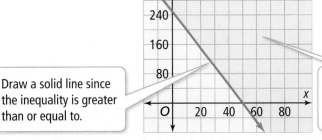

Draw a solid line since the inequality is greater than or equal to.

Shade above the line since the slope-intercept form of the inequality uses $\geq$.

Interpret ◄ Any point in the shaded region or on the boundary line is a solution of the inequality. However, since it is not possible to sell a negative number of T-shirts or key chains, you must exclude negative values for each.

☑ **Try It!** 2. Will the Science Club meet their goal if they sell 30 T-shirts and 90 key chains? Explain in terms of the graph of the inequality.

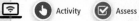

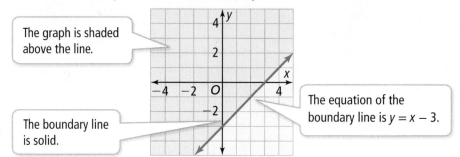

EXAMPLE 3 Write an Inequality From a Graph

What inequality does the graph represent?

Determine the equation of the boundary line.

The graph is shaded above the line.

The boundary line is solid.

The equation of the boundary line is $y = x - 3$.

LOOK FOR RELATIONSHIPS
The graph gives you information about the inequality. What does the solid line tell you about the inequality?

The graph is shaded above the boundary line and the boundary line is solid, so the inequality symbol is $\geq$.

The inequality shown by the graph is $y \geq x - 3$.

☑ **Try It!** **3.** What inequality does each graph represent?

a.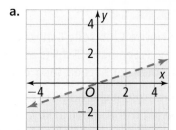

b.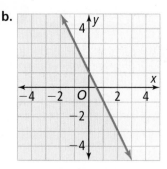

EXAMPLE 4 Inequalities in One Variable in the Coordinate Plane

What is the graph of the inequality in the coordinate plane?

A. $x \geq 3$?

You have graphed the solution of a one-variable inequality on a number line.

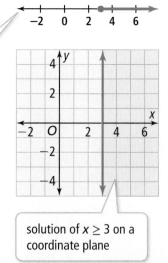

solution of $x \geq 3$ on a number line

You can write $x \geq 3$ as $x + 0 \cdot y \geq 3$. The inequality is true for all y, whenever $x \geq 3$.

Imagine stacking copies of the solution on the number line on top of each other, one for each y-value. The combined solutions graphed on the number line make up the shaded region on the coordinate plane.

solution of $x \geq 3$ on a coordinate plane

CONTINUED ON THE NEXT PAGE

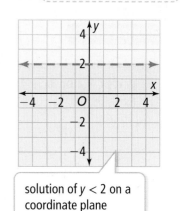

EXAMPLE 4 CONTINUED

B. $y < 2$?

You can graph the solution of the inequality on a vertical number line.

> solution of $y < 2$ on a vertical number line

Notice that the solution on the number line matches the shaded area for any vertical line on the coordinate grid. This is because x can be any number, and the inequality will still be $y < 2$.

> solution of $y < 2$ on a coordinate plane

LOOK FOR RELATIONSHIPS
How are the open circle and the dashed line similar?

 Try It! **4.** Graph each inequality in the coordinate plane.

a. $y > -2$ **b.** $x \leq 1$

CONCEPT SUMMARY Linear Inequalities in Two Variables

ALGEBRA $y \geq -\frac{3}{5}x + 1$ $y < -\frac{3}{5}x + 1$

GRAPH

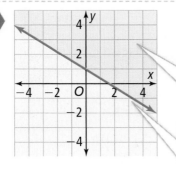

> Solutions are points in the shaded region.

> Solutions are also points on the solid line.

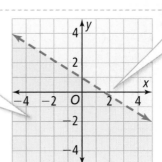

> No solutions are on the dashed line.

 ## Do You UNDERSTAND?

1. **ESSENTIAL QUESTION** How does the graph of a linear inequality in two variables help you identify the solutions of the inequality?

2. Communicate Precisely How many solutions does a linear inequality in two variables have?

3. Vocabulary In what form do you write one of the *solutions of an inequality in two variables*?

4. Error Analysis A student claims that the inequality $y < 1$ cannot be graphed on a coordinate grid since it has only one variable. Explain the error the student made.

Do You KNOW HOW?

Tell whether each ordered pair is a solution of the inequality $y > x + 1$.

5. $(0, 1)$ **6.** $(3, 5)$

Graph each inequality in the coordinate plane.

7. $y \geq 2x$ **8.** $y < x - 2$

9. What inequality is shown by the graph?

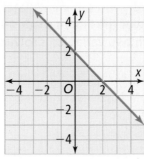

✎ PRACTICE & PROBLEM SOLVING

Scan for Multimedia

UNDERSTAND

10. Look for Relationships Which inequality, $y > \frac{3}{4}x - 2$ or $3x - 4y < 8$, is shown by the graph? Explain.

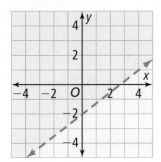

11. Error Analysis Describe and correct the error a student made in determining whether the ordered pair (1, 1) is a solution of the inequality $y \leq -4x + 5$.

$y \leq -4x + 5$
$1 \leq -4(1) + 5$
$1 \leq -4 + 5$
$1 \leq 1$

Since 1 is not less than 1, the inequality is not true. So, (1, 1) is not a solution of the inequality. **✗**

12. Higher Order Thinking What is the graph of the inequality $x < y + 3$? How is this graph different from the graph of the inequality $y < x + 3$?

13. Reason Write an inequality in two variables for which (3, 7) and (−2, 3) are solutions.

14. Mathematical Connections Compare the graph of a linear inequality $x < 4$ on a number line with its graph on a coordinate plane. How are they similar?

15. Generalize Explain why you can immediately determine which side of the line to shade when an inequality in two variables is solved for y.

PRACTICE

Graph each inequality in the coordinate plane.
SEE EXAMPLES 1, 2 AND 4

16. $y \geq -2x + 3$

17. $y < x - 6$

18. $y \leq \frac{2}{3}x - 1$

19. $y > x - 2$

20. $y < -0.5x + 2$

21. $y \geq 1.5x - 4$

22. $2x > 12$

23. $-2y \leq 6$

What inequality is shown by each graph?
SEE EXAMPLE 3

24.

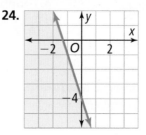

25.

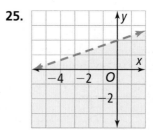

26.

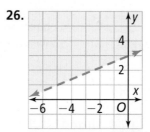

27.

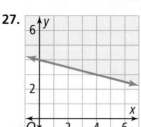

PRACTICE & PROBLEM SOLVING

APPLY

28. **Make Sense and Persevere** A school has $600 to buy molecular sets for students to build models.

a. Write and graph an inequality that represents the number of each type of molecular set the school can buy.

Large Kit $23

Small Kit $12

b. Suppose the school decides to buy 20 of the large kits. How many of the small kits can the school now afford?

29. **Model With Mathematics** A freight elevator can hold a maximum weight of 2,500 pounds. A 180-pound person has a load of boxes to deliver. Some of the boxes weigh 25 pounds each and some weigh 60 pounds each.

a. Write and graph an inequality that represents the number of boxes the elevator can hold in one trip if the person is not in the elevator.

b. Write and graph an inequality that represents the number of boxes the elevator can hold in one trip if the person rides in the elevator.

c. Compare the graphs of the two inequalities.

30. **Make Sense and Persevere** A soccer team holds a banquet at the end of the season. The team needs to seat at least 100 people and plans to use two different-sized tables. A small table can seat 6 people, and a large table can seat 8 people. Write a linear inequality that represents the numbers of each size table the team needs. Graph the inequality. If the school has 5 small tables and 9 large tables, will this be enough for the banquet?

ASSESSMENT PRACTICE

31. Choose *Yes* or *No* to tell whether each ordered pair is a solution of the inequality $y > 7x - 3$.

	Yes	No
a. (2, 15)	☐	☐
b. (−3, −15)	☐	☐
c. (0, −3)	☐	☐
d. (1, 5)	☐	☐

32. **SAT/ACT** What inequality is shown by the graph?

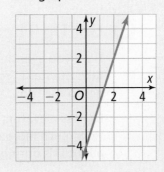

Ⓐ $y > 3x - 4$ Ⓒ $y \geq 3x - 4$
Ⓑ $y > 4x - 3$ Ⓓ $y \geq 4x - 3$

33. **Performance Task** A phone has a certain amount of storage space remaining. The average photo uses 3.6 MB of space and the average song uses 4 MB of space.

Storage   115 MB Free space

▪ Other ▪ Photos ▪ Movies ▪ Apps ▪ Songs

Part A Write a linear inequality to represent how many additional photos *x* and songs *y* the phone can store.

Part B Graph the inequality. Describe how the number of photos that are stored affects the number of songs that can be stored.

Part C Does the graph make sense outside of the first quadrant? Explain.

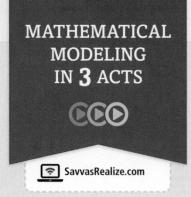

▶ Get Up There!

Have you ever been to the top of a skyscraper? If so, you probably didn't take the stairs. You probably took an elevator. How long did it take you to get to the top? Did you take an express elevator?

Express elevators travel more quickly because they do not stop at every floor. How much more quickly can you get to the top in an express elevator? Think about this during the Mathematical Modeling in 3 Acts lesson.

Scan for Multimedia

ACT 1 ▶ Identify the Problem

1. What is the first question that comes to mind after watching the video?

2. Write down the main question you will answer about what you saw in the video.

3. Make an initial conjecture that answers this main question.

4. Explain how you arrived at your conjecture.

5. What information will be useful to know to answer the main question? How can you get it? How will you use that information?

ACT 2 ▶ Develop a Model

6. Use the math that you have learned in this Topic to refine your conjecture.

ACT 3 ▶ Interpret the Results

7. Did your refined conjecture match the actual answer exactly? If not, what might explain the difference?

4-5

Systems of Linear Inequalities

SavvasRealize.com

I CAN... graph and solve a system of linear inequalities.

VOCABULARY
• solution of a system of linear inequalities
• system of linear inequalities

EXPLORE & REASON

The graph shows the equations
$y = x - 1$ and $y = -2x + 4$.

A. Choose some points above and below the line $y = x - 1$. Which of them are solutions to $y > x - 1$? Which are solutions to $y < x - 1$?

B. Choose some points above and below the line $y = -2x + 4$. Which of them are solutions to $y > -2x + 4$? Which are solutions to $y < -2x + 4$?

C. Look for Relationships The two lines divide the plane into four regions. How can you describe each region in terms of the inequalities in parts A and B?

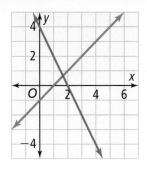

? ESSENTIAL QUESTION   How is the graph of a system of linear inequalities related to the solutions of the system of inequalities?

CONCEPTUAL UNDERSTANDING

EXAMPLE 1   Graph a System of Inequalities

What are the solutions to the system of linear inequalities?

A. $y > x - 2$
$y \leq -x + 1$

A **system of linear inequalities** is made up of two or more linear inequalities. **Solutions of a system of linear inequalities** are ordered pairs that make *all* of the inequalities true.

Look at the solutions of each inequality separately.

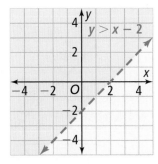   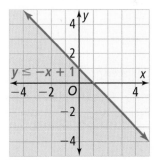

COMMON ERROR
Points on the solid boundary line for $y \leq -x + 1$ are solutions of the system only when they are also in the region representing the solutions to $y > x - 2$.

Now find points that are solutions to *both* inequalities.

> Points in the overlapping region are in *both* shaded regions.

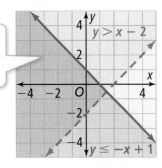

The solutions of the system of linear inequalities are the ordered pairs where the regions overlap.   **CONTINUED ON THE NEXT PAGE**

EXAMPLE 1 CONTINUED

B. $y \geq -x + 2$
$y < -x - 2$

Graph each inequality.

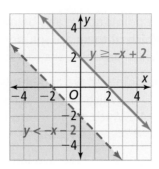

Since the slopes of the boundary lines are equal and their y-intercepts are different, they are parallel, and do not intersect.

The graphs do not overlap, so there is no solution to this system of inequalities.

 Try It!   **1.** Graph each system of inequalities.

  a. $y < 2x$
  $y > -3$

  b. $y \geq -2x + 1$
  $y > x + 2$

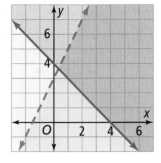

EXAMPLE 2   **Write a System of Inequalities From a Graph**

USE STRUCTURE
What information can you determine from the graphs of the lines? What information can you determine from the shaded region of the graph?

What system of inequalities is shown by the graph?

Determine the equation of each line using the slope and y-intercept.

The slope of the red boundary line is 2 and it has a y-intercept of 3.

The slope of the blue boundary line is -1 and it has a y-intercept of 4.

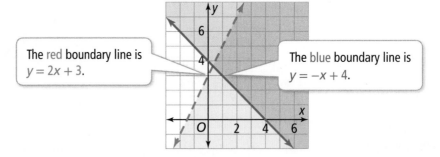

The red boundary line is $y = 2x + 3$.

The blue boundary line is $y = -x + 4$.

The solutions to the system are below the dashed red line, so one inequality is $y < 2x + 3$.

The solutions to the system are above the solid blue line, so the other inequality is $y \geq -x + 4$.

The graph shows the system of inequalities, $y < 2x + 3$ and $y \geq -x + 4$.

CONTINUED ON THE NEXT PAGE

EXAMPLE 2 CONTINUED

Activity   Assess

Try It!   2. What system of inequalities is shown by each graph?

a.

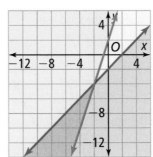

b.

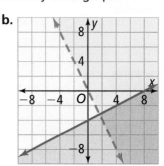

APPLICATION

👆 **EXAMPLE 3**   Use a System of Inequalities

Malia has $500 to purchase water bottles and pairs of socks for a fundraiser for her school's cross-country team. She needs to buy a total of at least 200 items without buying too many of just one item. What graph shows the possible numbers of water bottles and pairs of socks that Malia should buy?

Formulate ◀

Let x represent the number of water bottles and y represent the number of pairs of socks that Malia buys.

Write a system of inequalities.

$x + y \geq 200$ ················· Malia needs to buy *at least* 200 items.

$2x + 3y \leq 500$ ············· Malia can spend *at most* $500.

Compute ◀

Graph the system of inequalities.

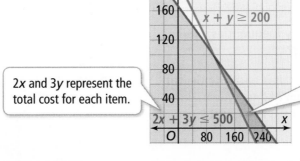

2x and 3y represent the total cost for each item.

All the points where both shaded regions overlap are solutions of the system of inequalities.

Interpret ◀

Malia could buy any combination of numbers of water bottles and pairs of socks represented by points in the overlapping region. However, she should be careful to choose a number of each item close to what she expects to sell. For example, she could buy 250 water bottles and 0 pairs of socks, but a more even distribution of items might be preferable.

 Try It!   3. Use the graph in Example 3 to determine if Malia can buy 75 water bottles and 100 pairs of socks. Explain.

CONCEPT SUMMARY Systems of Linear Inequalities

ALGEBRA $y < x + 1$ ········· All points below the dashed line

$y \geq 2x - 2$ ········· All points above the solid line

GRAPH

The line is dashed so the points on the line are not included in the solution.

The line is solid so the points on the line may be included in the solution.

The solution of the system of linear inequalities is the shaded region.

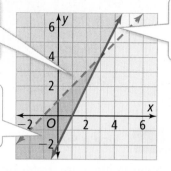

☑ Do You UNDERSTAND?

1. **ESSENTIAL QUESTION** How is the graph of a system of linear inequalities related to the solutions of the system of inequalities?

2. **Error Analysis** A student says that (0, 1) is a solution to the following system of inequalities.

    $y > x$
    $y > 2x + 1$

    She says that (0, 1) is a solution because it is a solution of $y > x$. Explain the error that the student made.

3. **Vocabulary** How many inequalities are in a *system of inequalities*?

4. **Use Appropriate Tools** Is it easier to describe the solution of a system of linear inequalities in words or to show it using a graph? Explain.

Do You KNOW HOW?

Identify the boundary lines for each system of inequalities.

5. $y > -3x + 4$
   $y \leq 8x + 1$

6. $y < -6x$
   $y \geq 10x - 3$

Graph each system of inequalities.

7. $y \leq -3x$
   $y < 2$

8. $y \geq x - 4$
   $y < -x$

9. What system of inequalities is shown by the graph?

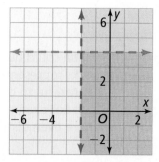

🛜 **Go Online** | SavvasRealize.com

PRACTICE & PROBLEM SOLVING

UNDERSTAND

10. Look for Relationships How does a real-world situation that is best described by a system of linear inequalities differ from a real-world situation that is best described by a single linear inequality?

11. Error Analysis Describe and correct the error a student made in writing the system of inequalities represented by the graph shown below.

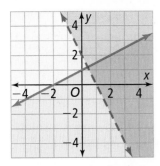

The red boundary line is $y = 0.5x + 1$.
Since the line is solid, use $\leq$ or $\geq$.
The blue boundary line is $y = -2x + 2$.
Since the line is dashed, use $<$ or $>$.

$y \leq 0.5x + 1$
$y < -2x + 2$ ✗

12. Mathematical Connections How is a system of two linear inequalities in two variables similar to a system of two linear equations in two variables? How is it different?

13. Reason In Example 3, the inequality made sense only in the first quadrant. What two inequalities could you add to the system to indicate this? Explain.

14. Higher Order Thinking Can you write a system of three inequalities that has no solutions? Explain.

15. Reason Could the solutions of a system of inequalities be a rectangular region? If so, give an example.

PRACTICE

Graph each system of inequalities.
SEE EXAMPLES 1 AND 3

16. $y < 2x + 1$
  $y \leq -x - 4$

17. $y \leq 3x - 2$
  $y > x - 2$

18. $y \geq -\frac{1}{2}x + 1$
  $y > x + 3$

19. $y < \frac{1}{3}x$
  $y \geq -4x + 1$

20. $2x + 3y < 5$
  $y \geq 2x - 3$

21. $x + 4y > 3$
  $x - y \leq 2$

22. $y > 0.3x + 2$
  $y < -0.2x + 1$

23. $y \leq 0.25x - 4$
  $y \geq -x - 3$

24. $y < -2x - 5$
  $4x - y < 3$

25. $-6x + 4y \geq 8$
  $y < -x - 1$

26. $x > 1$
  $y < 2x - 3$
  $y > x$

27. $y \leq -3x$
  $y > -x - 2$
  $y > 2$

What system of inequalities is shown by each graph? SEE EXAMPLES 2 AND 3

28.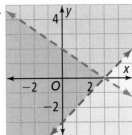

29.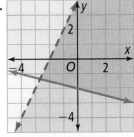

30.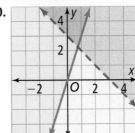

31.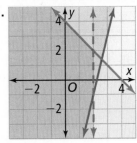

APPLY

32. Make Sense and Persevere A group of at most 10 people wants to purchase a combination of seats in Section A and Section B, but does not want to spend more than $450. Graph the system of inequalities that represents the possible ticket combinations they could buy. List three possible combinations they could buy.

STADIUM SEATING

Section A	$50
Section B	$40
Section C	$25
Section D	$15

33. Model With Mathematics Kendra earns $10 per hour babysitting and $15 per hour providing tech support. Her goal is to save at least $1,000 by the end of the month while not working more than 80 hours. Write and graph a system of inequalities that shows how many hours Kendra could work at each job to meet her goal. What is the fewest number of hours she could work and still meet her goal?

34. Make Sense and Persevere Alex knits hats and scarves to sell at an art fair. He can make at most 20 hats and 30 scarves, but no more than 40 items altogether, in time for the art fair. Write and graph a system of inequalities that shows the possible numbers of hats and scarves Alex can bring to the art fair if he wants to bring at least 25 items. How do the solutions change if he wants to make more hats than scarves? Explain.

35. Construct Arguments Shannon and Dyani graph the following system of inequalities.

$$y \geq \frac{1}{2}x - 1$$
$$x - y > 1$$

Which graph is correct? Explain.

Shannon's graph   **Dyani's graph**

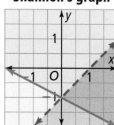   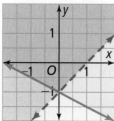

ASSESSMENT PRACTICE

Use the graph to answer Exercises 36 and 37.

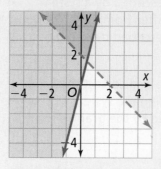

36. Fill in the blanks to complete the system of inequalities shown by the graph.

y ___ $-x +$ ___
y ___ $4x$

37. SAT/ACT Which of the following is a solution of the system of inequalities shown in the graph?

Ⓐ (3, 2)   Ⓒ (−1, 4)

Ⓑ (−3, 2)   Ⓓ (1, −4)

38. Performance Task A person is planning a weekly workout schedule of cardio and yoga. He has at most 12 hours per week to work out. The amounts of time he wants to spend on cardio and yoga are shown.

Part A Write a system of linear inequalities to represent this situation.

Part B Graph the system of inequalities. Is there a minimum number of hours the person will be doing cardio? Explain.

Topic Review

1. How do you use systems of linear equations and inequalities to model situations and solve problems?

Vocabulary Review

Choose the correct term to complete each sentence.

2. A(n) _____ is made up of two or more inequalities.

3. A(n) _____ is an inequality that is in the same form as a linear equation in two variables, but with an inequality symbol instead of an equal sign.

4. A(n) _____ is an ordered pair that makes all of the inequalities in the system true.

5. The _____ is the set of all ordered pairs that satisfy the inequality.

- linear inequality in two variables
- solution of an inequality in two variables
- solution of a system of linear inequalities
- system of linear inequalities

Concepts & Skills Review

LESSON 4-1	Solving Systems of Equations by Graphing

Quick Review

Systems of equations can have one solution, infinitely many solutions, or no solution. Graphing a system of linear equations can result in either an approximate solution or an exact solution.

Example

What is the solution of the system of equations? Use a graph.

$y = 3x - 1$
$y = -2x + 3$

The graph intersects at one point, so the system of linear equations has one solution. Find the point of intersection. The graph intersects at (0.8, 1.4).

Check that the solution works for both equations.

$y = 3x - 1$ $y = -2x + 3$

$1.4 \stackrel{?}{=} 3(0.8) - 1$ $1.4 \stackrel{?}{=} -2(0.8) + 3$

$1.4 = 1.4 ✓$ $1.4 = 1.4 ✓$

The system of equations has one solution at (0.8, 1.4).

Practice & Problem Solving

Approximate the solution of each system of equations by graphing.

6. $y = 5x + 4$
   $y = -3x - 8$

7. $y = -3x - 7$
   $y = 1.5x + 4$

8. **Use Structure** Describe the solution set of the system of equations made by the equation $y = 1.5x + 4.5$ and the graphed line.

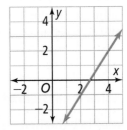

9. **Model With Mathematics** Kiyo is considering two catering companies for a party. A+ Food charges $35 per person and $75 to setup. Super Cater charges $38 per person with no setup fee. Write and solve a system of equations to represent the charges for catering by each company. Which company should Kiyo use if she expects 28 guests?

Solving Systems of Equations by Substitution

Quick Review

To use substitution to solve a system of equations, isolate the variable in one equation and substitute its value into the other equation. Solve for the variable. Then use that value to solve for the other variable.

Example

Solve the system of equations.
$$y = 3x - 5$$
$$4x - 2y = 8$$

Substitute $3x - 5$ for y and solve for x.

$$4x - 2y = 8$$
$$4x - 2(3x - 5) = 8$$
$$4x - 6x + 10 = 8$$
$$-2x = -2$$
$$x = 1$$

Substitute 1 for x in either equation and solve for y.

$$y = 3x - 5$$
$$= 3(1) - 5$$
$$= -2$$

The solution of the system of equations is $(1, -2)$.

Practice & Problem Solving

Use substitution to solve each system of equations.

10. $y = 5x - 2$
    $3x - 5y = 4$

11. $y = 2x - 3$
    $y = 8 - 2x$

12. $x = 4y - 8$
    $3x - 6y = 12$

13. $y = 2.5x - 8$
    $3x + 5y = 12$

Identify whether each system of equations has infinitely many solutions or no solution.

14. $3y = 3x - 9$
    $y - 2 = x$

15. $3x - 4y = 12$
    $\frac{3}{4}x = y + 3$

16. **Mathematical Connections** A room has a perimeter of 40 feet. The length is 4 less than 2 times the width. What are the dimensions of the room?

17. **Model With Mathematics** Benson has 58 more boxed action figures than collector pins. In total he has 246 collectible items. How many of each type of collectible item does Benson own?

Solving Systems of Equations by Elimination

Quick Review

To use elimination to solve a system of equations, multiply one or both equations by a number so that the coefficient of one variable in both equations is the same or opposite. Then add or subtract to eliminate one variable, and solve for the remaining variable.

Example

Solve the system of equations.
$$4x - 3y = 12$$
$$5x - 6y = 18$$

Multiply the first equation by -2 and add the two equations to eliminate y and solve for x.

$4x - 3y = 12$ | Multiply by -2. | $-8x + 6y = -24$
$5x - 6y = 18$ | | $\underline{5x - 6y = 18}$
| | $-3x = -6$
| | $x = 2$

Substitute 2 for x into either equation and solve for y.

$$5(2) - 6y = 18$$
$$y = -\frac{4}{3}$$

The solution of the system of equations is $\left(2, -\frac{4}{3}\right)$.

Practice & Problem Solving

Solve each system of equations.

18. $2x - y = -2$
    $3x - 2y = 4$

19. $5x - 2y = 10$
    $4x + 3y = -6$

Is each pair of systems equivalent? Explain.

20. $2x - 3y = 14$
    $5x - 2y = 8$

    $4x - 6y = 28$
    $-15x + 6y = -24$

21. $3x - 4y = -6$
    $2x + 5y = 1$

    $6x - 8y = 12$
    $6x + 15y = 3$

22. **Generalize** Do you always have to multiply one or both equations to use elimination? Explain.

23. **Model With Mathematics** Carmen and Alicia go to the office supply store to purchase packs of pens and paper. Carmen bought 5 packs of paper and 3 packs of pens for $36.60. Alicia bought 6 packs of paper and 6 packs of pens for $53.40. What is the price of one pack of paper and one pack of pens?

LESSON 4-4 — Linear Inequalities in Two Variables

Quick Review

A **linear inequality in two variables** is an inequality that is in the same form as a linear equation in two variables but with an inequality symbol instead of an equal sign. A **solution of a linear inequality in two variables** is an ordered pair that satisfies the inequality.

Example

What inequality is shown by the graph?

The slope of the line is 1 and its *y*-intercept is 2. Therefore, the equation of the line is $y = x + 2$. The boundary line is solid, and all values of *x* and *y* that make the inequality true lie on the line or above the line. The inequality shown by the graph is $y \geq x + 2$.

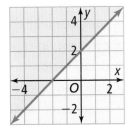

Practice & Problem Solving

Use the graph to tell whether each ordered pair is a solution of the inequality $y \geq 2x - 3$.

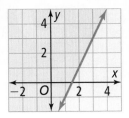

24. (2, 5)

25. (3, −1)

26. (−2, 4)

Graph the inequality in the coordinate plane.

27. $y > 4x - 9$

28. $y \leq 1.5x + 4$

29. **Reason** Write an inequality in two variables for which (2, 5) and (−3, −1) are solutions.

30. **Make Sense and Persevere** Renaldo has a budget of $500 to buy gift boxes for a party. Large boxes cost $65 and small boxes cost $35. Write and graph an inequality that represents the number of each type of gift box that Renaldo can buy. If Renaldo buys 6 small gift boxes, how many large gift boxes can he afford to buy?

LESSON 4-5 — Systems of Linear Inequalities

Quick Review

A **system of linear inequalities** is made up of two or more inequalities. The **solutions of a system of linear inequalities** is the set of all ordered pairs that satisfy the inequalities in the system.

Example

What system of inequalities is shown by the graph? Describe the solutions of the system of inequalities.

Determine the equation of each line using the slope and *y*-intercept.

Points below the red dashed line satisfy the inequality $y < 3x - 1$. Points above the blue dashed line satisfy the inequality $y > -4x + 5$.

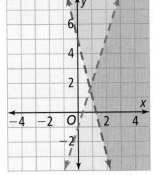

The solutions to the system lie in the region where the graphs overlap.

Practice & Problem Solving

Graph each system of inequalities.

31. $y < 2x + 3$
    $y \leq -3x + 1$

32. $y \geq 4x$
    $y < -x - 5$

33. **Generalize** What two inequalities can you add to any system of inequalities to indicate that only answers in the first quadrant make sense?

34. **Model With Mathematics** Olivia makes and sells bracelets and necklaces. She can make up to 60 pieces per week, but she can only make up to 40 bracelets and 40 necklaces. Write and graph a system of inequalities that shows the combination of bracelets and necklaces that she can make if she wants to sell at least 30 items per week. If necklaces sell for $80 each and bracelets sell for $5 each, what is the most money she can make in a week? Explain.

? TOPIC ESSENTIAL QUESTION

How do you use exponential functions to model situations
and solve problems?

Topic Overview

Topic Vocabulary

- asymptote
- compound interest
- constant ratio
- decay factor
- exponential decay
- exponential function
- exponential growth
- geometric sequence
- growth factor
- rational exponent

Digital Experience

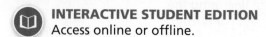

INTERACTIVE STUDENT EDITION
Access online or offline.

ACTIVITIES Complete *Explore & Reason,
Model & Discuss*, and *Critique & Explain*
activities. Interact with Examples and Try Its.

ANIMATION View and interact with
real-world applications.

PRACTICE Practice what
you've learned.

 Go online | SavvasRealize.com

▶ Big Time Pay Back

Most people agree that investing your money is a good idea. Some people might advise you to put money into a bank savings account. Other people might say that you should invest in the stock market. Still others think that buying bonds is the best investment option.

Is a bank savings account a good way to let your money grow? Just how much money can you make from a savings account? In the Mathematical Modeling in 3 Acts lesson, you'll see an intriguing situation about an investment option.

VIDEOS Watch clips to support *Mathematical Modeling in 3 Acts Lessons* and **enVision®** *STEM Projects.*

CONCEPT SUMMARY Review key lesson content through multiple representations.

ASSESSMENT Show what you've learned.

GLOSSARY Read and listen to English and Spanish definitions.

TUTORIALS Get help from *Virtual Nerd*, right when you need it.

MATH TOOLS Explore math with digital tools and manipulatives.

Did You Know?

Moore's Law predicts advancements in many digital electronics, stating that growth is exponential.

Moore's Law, 1965 (projected for 10 years): The number of transistors in a chip will double approximately every 12 months.

Moore's Law, amended 1975 (projected for 10 years): The number of transistors in a chip will double approximately every 24 months.

If you applied Moore's Law to space travel, a trip to the moon would take one minute.

Corollary to Moore's Law: For a chip of fixed size, the transistors will decrease in size by 50% every 24 months.

Transistor   Integrated Circuit   Microprocessor

If cars and transistors shrank at the same rate, today's cars would be the size of ants.

ⓥ Your Task: Predict the Future Using Moore's Law

You and your classmates will predict the features of a cellular phone released 3 years from now, and decide whether or not Moore's Law is sustainable for the next 20 years.

5-1

Rational Exponents and Properties of Exponents

 SavvasRealize.com

I CAN... use properties of exponents to solve equations with rational exponents.

VOCABULARY
• rational exponent

CRITIQUE & EXPLAIN

Students are asked to write an equivalent expression for 3^{-3}.

Casey and Jacinta each write an expression on the board.

A. Who is correct, Casey or Jacinta? Explain.

B. Reason What is the most likely error that was made?

Casey

$3^{-3} = -27$

Jacinta

$3^{-3} = \frac{1}{27}$

? ESSENTIAL QUESTION   What are the properties of rational exponents and how are they used to solve problems?

CONCEPTUAL UNDERSTANDING

👆 EXAMPLE 1   **Write Radicals Using Rational Exponents**

What does $3^{\frac{1}{2}}$ equal?

You can think of exponentiation as repeated multiplication.

$3^2 = 3 \cdot 3$ .... Multiply 3 by itself 2 times.

$3^3 = 3 \cdot 3 \cdot 3$ .... Multiply 3 by itself 3 times.

$3^4 = 3 \cdot 3 \cdot 3 \cdot 3$ .... Multiply 3 by itself 4 times.

etc.

But what does $3^{\frac{1}{2}}$ mean? You cannot multiply 3 by itself $\frac{1}{2}$ times. Since interpreting exponents as repeated multiplication does not work in this case, you have to *define* a new meaning for expressions like $3^{\frac{1}{2}}$.

GENERALIZE

The Power of a Power Property says that $(a^m)^n = a^{mn}$ for all integers m and n.

Whatever the new definition is, you want it to obey the same rules of exponents that you know for integers, such as the Power of a Power Property.

$$\left(3^{\frac{1}{2}}\right)^2 = 3^{\frac{1}{2} \cdot 2} = 3^1 = 3$$

When you square $3^{\frac{1}{2}}$ ...   ... the result is 3.

You know that a number whose square is 3 is $\sqrt{3}$. So in order to define raising a number to the $\frac{1}{2}$ power in a way that makes sense, define $3^{\frac{1}{2}}$ to be $\sqrt{3}$.

You can define the meaning of other rational exponents in a similar way. If the nth root of a is a real number and m is an integer, then $a^{\frac{1}{n}} = \sqrt[n]{a}$, and $a^{\frac{m}{n}} = \sqrt[n]{a^m} = (\sqrt[n]{a})^m$.

☑ Try It!   **1.** What does $2^{\frac{1}{3}}$ equal? Explain.

EXAMPLE 2 Use the Product of Powers Property to Solve Equations With Rational Exponents

What is the solution of $\left(3^{\frac{x}{2}}\right)\left(3^{\frac{x}{3}}\right) = 3^9$?

Rewrite the left side of the equation with one exponent.

$$\left(3^{\frac{x}{2}}\right)\left(3^{\frac{x}{3}}\right) = 3^9$$

$$3^{\frac{x}{2} + \frac{x}{3}} = 3^9 \quad\cdots\cdots\cdots\cdots \text{ Product of Powers Property}$$

$$3^{\frac{3x}{6} + \frac{2x}{6}} = 3^9 \quad\cdots\cdots\cdots\cdots \text{ Write the exponents with a common denominator.}$$

$$3^{\frac{5x}{6}} = 3^9$$

$$\frac{5x}{6} = 9 \quad\cdots\cdots\cdots\cdots \text{ The bases are the same, so set the exponents equal.}$$

$$\frac{6}{5}\left(\frac{5x}{6}\right) = \frac{6}{5}(9) \quad\cdots\cdots\cdots\cdots \text{ Multiply both sides by } \frac{6}{5}.$$

$$x = \frac{54}{5}$$

The solution is $\frac{54}{5}$.

STUDY TIP
To multiply two powers with a common base, keep the common base and add the exponents.

Try It! 2. What is the solution of $\left(2^{\frac{x}{4}}\right)\left(2^{\frac{x}{6}}\right) = 2^3$?

EXAMPLE 3 Use the Power of a Power Property to Solve Equations With Rational Exponents

A. What is the solution of $27^{x-4} = 3^{2x-6}$?

$$27^{x-4} = 3^{2x-6}$$

$$(3^3)^{x-4} = 3^{2x-6} \quad\cdots\cdots\cdots\cdots \text{ Rewrite 27 with a base of 3.}$$

$$3^{3x-12} = 3^{2x-6} \quad\cdots\cdots\cdots\cdots \text{ Power of a Power Property}$$

$$3x - 12 = 2x - 6 \quad\cdots\cdots\cdots\cdots \text{ Write the exponents as an equation.}$$

$$3x - 12 - 3x = 2x - 6 - 3x$$

$$-12 = -x - 6$$

$$-12 + 6 = -x - 6 + 6$$

$$-6 = -x$$

$$6 = x$$

The solution is 6.

STUDY TIP
To find the power of a power, keep the base and multiply the exponents.

B. What is the solution of $\left(\frac{1}{125}\right)^{-\frac{x}{2}} = \left(\frac{1}{25}\right)^{-\frac{x}{3} - 2}$?

Step 1 Rewrite the equation so both sides have the same base.

$$\left(\frac{1}{125}\right)^{-\frac{x}{2}} = \left(\frac{1}{25}\right)^{-\frac{x}{3} - 2}$$

$$(5^{-3})^{-\frac{x}{2}} = (5^{-2})^{-\frac{x}{3} - 2} \quad\longleftarrow \text{ Rewrite } \frac{1}{125} \text{ and } \frac{1}{25} \text{ as powers of 5.}$$

$$5^{\frac{3x}{2}} = 5^{\frac{2x}{3} + 4} \quad\cdots\cdots\cdots\cdots \text{ Power of a Power Property}$$

CONTINUED ON THE NEXT PAGE

EXAMPLE 3 CONTINUED

Step 2 Write the exponents as an equation and solve.

$$\frac{3x}{2} = \frac{2x}{3} + 4$$

$$6\left(\frac{3x}{2}\right) = 6\left(\frac{2x}{3} + 4\right)$$

$$9x = 4x + 24$$

$$9x - 4x = 4x + 24 - 4x$$

$$5x = 24$$

$$\frac{5x}{5} = \frac{24}{5}$$

$$x = 4.8$$

The solution is $x = 4.8$.

COMMON ERROR
Remember to distribute across both terms when multiplying.

 Try It! **3.** What is the solution of each equation?

a. $256^{x+2} = 4^{3x+9}$ **b.** $\left(\frac{1}{8}\right)^{\frac{x}{2}-1} = \left(\frac{1}{4}\right)^{\frac{x}{3}}$

APPLICATION   ● **EXAMPLE 4**   **Use the Power of a Product Property to Solve Equations With Rational Exponents**

Adam is setting up for an outdoor concert. He places three square blankets near the band as shown in the picture. What is the area of Blanket C?

Formulate ◀

Area	=	length	•	width
12	=	$8^{\frac{1}{2}}$	•	$x^{\frac{1}{2}}$

Area of the grass rectangle   Side length of Blanket B   Side length of Blanket C

Compute ◀   Solve for x, the area of Blanket C.

$$12 = \left(8^{\frac{1}{2}}\right)\left(x^{\frac{1}{2}}\right)$$

$$12 = (8x)^{\frac{1}{2}}$$
> Multiply the bases and keep the exponent.

$$12^2 = \left[(8x)^{\frac{1}{2}}\right]^2$$

$$144 = 8x$$
> Square both sides.

$$\frac{144}{8} = \frac{8x}{8}$$

$$18 = x$$

Blanket A

Blanket B
8 yd²

Blanket C
x yd²

12 yd²

Interpret ◀   The area of Blanket C is 18 yd².

Check Compare the product of $\sqrt{18}$ and $\sqrt{8}$ to the rectangular area of 12.

$$(\sqrt{8})(\sqrt{18}) = \left(8^{\frac{1}{2}}\right)\left(18^{\frac{1}{2}}\right)$$

$$= (8 \cdot 18)^{\frac{1}{2}} = 144^{\frac{1}{2}}$$

$$= 12$$

 Try It! **4.** When the side length of Blanket A is multiplied by $2^{\frac{1}{2}}$ the result is 6 yards. Find the area of Blanket A.

APPLICATION

 EXAMPLE 5 Use the Quotient of Powers Property to Solve Equations With Rational Exponents

Terrarium A and Terrarium B are cubes. The side length of Terrarium A is twice the side length of Terrarium B. What is the value of x?

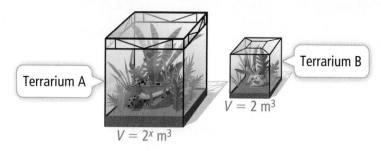

Terrarium B

Terrarium A

$V = 2 \text{ m}^3$

$V = 2^x \text{ m}^3$

Step 1 Write a proportion using the side lengths.

$$\frac{(2^x)^{\frac{1}{3}}}{2^{\frac{1}{3}}} = 2$$ ◄— The ratio of the side lengths is 2.

$$\frac{2^{x \cdot \frac{1}{3}}}{2^{\frac{1}{3}}} = 2$$

Step 2 Use properties of exponents to simplify.

$$\frac{2^{\frac{x}{3}}}{2^{\frac{1}{3}}} = 2$$

$$2^{\frac{x}{3} - \frac{1}{3}} = 2$$ ◄— Quotient of Powers Property

$$2^{\frac{x-1}{3}} = 2$$

$$2^{\frac{x-1}{3}} = 2^1$$ ◄— Write 2 with an exponent.

Step 3 Equate the exponents and solve for x.

$$\frac{x-1}{3} = 1$$

$$x - 1 = 3$$

$$x = 4$$

The value of x is 4.

> **STUDY TIP**
> To divide two powers with the same base, keep the common base and subtract the exponents.

☑ **Try It!** **5.** What is the value of x if the side length of Terrarium A is four times the side length of Terrarium B?

CONCEPT SUMMARY Rational Exponents and Properties of Exponents

WORDS If the nth root of a is a real number and m is an integer, then

$$a^{\frac{1}{n}} = \sqrt[n]{a} \qquad\qquad a^{\frac{m}{n}} = \sqrt[n]{a^m} = (\sqrt[n]{a})^m$$

ALGEBRA	Power of a Power	Power of a Product	Product of Powers	Quotient of Powers
	$(a^m)^n = a^{mn}$	$(ab)^m = a^m \cdot b^m$	$a^m \cdot a^n = a^{m+n}$	$\dfrac{a^m}{a^n} = a^{m-n},\ a \neq 0$

NUMBERS

$$\left(256^{\frac{1}{4}}\right)^{\frac{1}{2}} = 256^{\frac{1}{4} \cdot \frac{1}{2}}$$
$$= 256^{\frac{1}{8}}$$
$$= 2$$

$$(4 \times 9)^{\frac{1}{2}} = 4^{\frac{1}{2}} \cdot 9^{\frac{1}{2}}$$
$$= 2 \cdot 3$$
$$= 6$$

$$16^{\frac{1}{4}} \times 16^{\frac{1}{4}} = 16^{\frac{1}{4} + \frac{1}{4}}$$
$$= 16^{\frac{2}{4}}$$
$$= 16^{\frac{1}{2}}$$
$$= 4$$

$$\frac{8^{\frac{2}{3}}}{8^{\frac{1}{3}}} = 8^{\frac{2}{3} - \frac{1}{3}}$$
$$= 8^{\frac{1}{3}}$$
$$= 2$$

Do You UNDERSTAND?

1. **ESSENTIAL QUESTION** What are the properties of rational exponents and how are they used to solve problems?

2. **Communicate Precisely** A square has an area of 15 ft². What are two ways of expressing its side length?

3. **Look for Relationships** If $3^x = 3^y$, what is the relationship between x and y?

4. **Error Analysis** Corey wrote $\sqrt[3]{4^2}$ as $4^{\frac{3}{2}}$. What error did Corey make?

5. **Reason** When is it useful to have rational exponents instead of radicals?

6. **Vocabulary** How are *rational exponents* different than whole number exponents? How are they the same?

Do You KNOW HOW?

Write each radical using rational exponents.

7. $\sqrt{7}$

8. $\sqrt{15}$

9. $\sqrt[3]{6^4}$

10. $\sqrt[3]{2^3}$

11. $\sqrt[4]{2^4}$

12. $\sqrt{8^3}$

Solve each equation.

13. $\left(2^{\frac{x}{3}}\right)\left(2^{\frac{x}{2}}\right) = 2^5$

14. $\left(4^{\frac{x}{2}}\right)\left(4^{\frac{x}{5}}\right) = 4^8$

15. $64^{x+1} = 4^{x+7}$

16. $16^{(x-3)} = 2^{(x-6)}$

17. $\left(\frac{1}{243}\right)^{-\frac{x}{3}} = \left(\frac{1}{9}\right)^{-\frac{x}{2}+1}$

18. $\left(\frac{1}{36}\right)^{(x-4)} = \left(\frac{1}{216}\right)^{x+1}$

UNDERSTAND

19. **Make Sense and Persevere** Describe two ways to express the edge length of a cube with a volume shown.

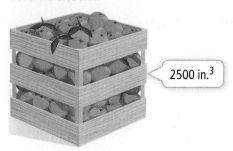

2500 in.³

20. **Construct Arguments** Explain why $5^{\frac{4}{3}}$ must be equal to $\sqrt[3]{5^4}$ if the Power of a Power Property holds for rational exponents.

21. **Error Analysis** Describe and correct the error a student made when starting to solve the equation $8^{x+3} = 2^{2x-5}$.

$$8^{x+3} = 2^{2x-5}$$
$$(2^3)^{x+3} = 2^{2x-5}$$
$$2^{3x+3} = 2^{2x-5}$$
$$\vdots$$

✗

22. **Construct Arguments** The Power of a Quotient rule is $\left(\frac{a}{b}\right)^m = \frac{a^m}{b^m}$, $b \neq 0$. Will this rule work with rational exponents if $\frac{a}{b}$ is a positive number? Give an example to support your argument.

23. **Higher Order Thinking** The Zero Exponent Property is $a^0 = 1$, $a \neq 0$.

   a. How could you use properties of exponents to explain why $a^0 = 1$?

   b. How could the Zero Exponent Property be applied when solving equations with rational exponents?

24. **Use Structure** Consider the expression $\sqrt{\sqrt{625}}$.

   a. Write the radical using rational exponents.

   b. Describe two different ways to evaluate the expression.

   c. Simplify the expression from part (b).

PRACTICE

Write each radical using rational exponents.
SEE EXAMPLE 1

25. $\sqrt{3}$

26. $\sqrt[3]{7}$

27. $\sqrt[5]{3^2}$

28. $\sqrt[4]{2^{-5}}$

29. $\sqrt[3]{a^2}$

30. $\sqrt{b^a}$

Solve each equation. SEE EXAMPLES 2–5

31. $\left(5^{\frac{x}{3}}\right)\left(5^{\frac{x}{4}}\right) = 5^5$

32. $\left(2^{\frac{x}{2}}\right)\left(4^{\frac{x}{2}}\right) = 2^6$

33. $\left(3^{\frac{x}{2}+1}\right) = \left(3^{-\frac{5x}{2}}\right)$

34. $625^{2x-3} = 25^{3x-2}$

35. $\left(\frac{1}{243}\right)^{-\frac{x}{3}} = \left(\frac{1}{9}\right)^{-\frac{x}{2}+1}$

36. $8^{\frac{-x}{3}} = 4$

37. $49^{\frac{x}{4}-1} = 343^{\frac{x}{3}}$

38. $3 = \left(5^{\frac{1}{2}}\right)\left(x^{\frac{1}{2}}\right)$

39. $2 = \left(4^{\frac{1}{3}}\right)\left(2^{\frac{x}{3}}\right)$

40. $\frac{27^{\frac{1}{4}}}{3^{\frac{x}{4}}} = 1$

41. $5^{-\frac{2}{3}} = \frac{125^{\frac{x}{3}}}{25^{\frac{4}{3}}}$

42. $\frac{6^{\frac{1}{4}}}{36^{-\frac{x}{2}}} = 1$

For each partial solution, identify the property of exponents that is used. SEE EXAMPLES 2–4

43.

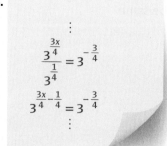

$$36^{\frac{x}{3}+3} = 216^{\frac{x}{5}}$$
$$(6^2)^{\frac{x}{3}+3} = (6^3)^{\frac{x}{5}}$$
$$6^{\frac{2x}{3}+6} = 6^{\frac{3x}{5}}$$
$$\vdots$$

44.

$$\vdots$$
$$\frac{3^{\frac{3x}{4}}}{3^{\frac{1}{4}}} = 3^{-\frac{3}{4}}$$
$$3^{\frac{3x}{4}-\frac{1}{4}} = 3^{-\frac{3}{4}}$$
$$\vdots$$

APPLY

45. Use Appropriate Tools The formula for the volume V of a sphere is $\frac{4}{3}\pi r^3$. What is the radius of the basketball shown?

$V = 392$ in.^{3}

46. Use Structure A singing contest eliminates contestants after each round. To find the number of contestants in the next round, raise the number of contestants in the current round to the power of $\frac{6-n}{7-n}$, where n is the number of the current round.

47. Make Sense and Persevere Photos A, B, and C are all square photos. The area of Photo C is the same as a rectangular photo whose length is the side length of Photo A and whose width is the side length of Photo B. Use the properties of rational exponents to write and solve an equation to find the side length of Photo A to two decimal places.

Photo A	Photo B	Photo C
Area = x cm²	Area = 72 cm²	Area = 110 cm²

ASSESSMENT PRACTICE

48. Match each expression with its equivalent expression.

I. $\sqrt[4]{2^5}$ **A.** $2^{\frac{1}{5}}$

II. $\sqrt{5}$ **B.** $2^{\frac{5}{4}}$

III. $\sqrt[5]{2^4}$ **C.** $2^{\frac{4}{5}}$

IV. $\sqrt[5]{2}$ **D.** $5^{\frac{1}{2}}$

49. SAT/ACT What is the value of x in $27^{\frac{x}{2}} = 3^{x-1}$?

Ⓐ -3

Ⓑ -2

Ⓒ $\frac{1}{3}$

Ⓓ 2

Ⓔ 3

50. Performance Task It is possible to write any positive integer as the sum of powers of 2 with whole number exponents. For example, you can write 75 in the following manner.

$$2^0 + 2^1 + 2^3 + 2^6 = 75$$

Part A Use the equation above to write 75 as the sum of powers of 8, using rational exponents. What are possible values for a, b, c and d?

$$8^a + 8^b + 8^c + 8^d = 75$$

Part B How can you modify the equation you wrote in part A to express 75 as sum of powers of 16?

$$16^a + 16^b + 16^c + 16^d = 75$$

Part C Given that a, b, c, and d are rational numbers, for what types of integer values of x is the following equation true? Explain your answer.

$$x^a + x^b + x^c + x^d = 75$$

5-2

Exponential Functions

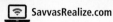
SavvasRealize.com

I CAN... describe and graph exponential functions.

VOCABULARY
- asymptote
- constant ratio
- exponential function

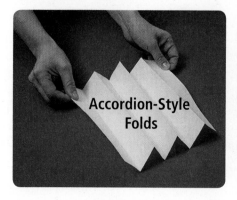

EXPLORE & REASON

Use two pieces of $8\frac{1}{2}$ in.-by-11 in. paper. Fold one of the pieces of paper accordion-style for five folds. Fold the other in half for five folds. After each fold, unfold each piece of paper and count the total number of rectangular sections.

Accordion-Style Folds

Half Folds

A. Find the pattern relating the number of folds to the number of sections for each folding style. What do you notice?

B. Make Sense and Persevere Explain why the two different folded styles of paper produce different results.

? ESSENTIAL QUESTION

What are the characteristics of exponential functions?

CONCEPTUAL UNDERSTANDING

🖐 **EXAMPLE 1** Key Features of $f(x) = 2^x$

A. What does the graph of $f(x) = 2^x$ look like?

The table and graph show $f(x) = 2^x$.

x	$f(x) = 2^x$
−2	$\frac{1}{4}$
−1	$\frac{1}{2}$
0	1
1	2
2	4
3	8

As x-values approach −∞, y-values approach 0.

The y-intercept is 1.

COMMON ERROR
The graph of $f(x) = 2^x$ does not have a y-value of exactly 0, so it does not have an x-intercept.

B. What are the characteristics of the graph of $f(x) = 2^x$?

The graph of $f(x) = 2^x$ is continuous between and beyond the x-values shown, so the domain is all real numbers.

CONTINUED ON THE NEXT PAGE

EXAMPLE 1 CONTINUED

The function gets closer and closer to the *x*-axis, but never quite reaches it. When a function approaches a line in this manner, the line is called an **asymptote.**

The asymptote of *f* is $y = 0$. The range is $y > 0$.

Try It!   **1.** Identify the key features of the function $f(x) = b^x$ for $b = 2$ and $b = \frac{1}{2}$.

APPLICATION   **EXAMPLE 2**   **Graph Exponential Functions**

A network administrator uses the function $f(x) = 5^x$ to model the number of computers a virus spreads to after *x* hours. If there are 1,000 computers on the network, about how many hours will it take for the virus to spread to the entire network?

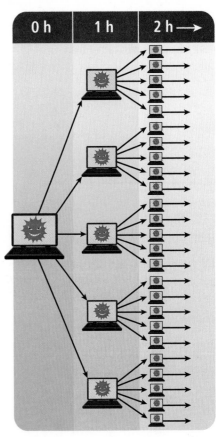

0 h   1 h   2 h →

Step 1 Make a table.

x	$f(x) = 5^x$
0	1
1	5
2	25
3	125
4	625
5	3,125

Step 2 Graph the function.

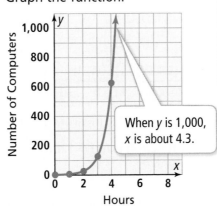

When *y* is 1,000, *x* is about 4.3.

STUDY TIP
When graphing an exponential function, choose a scale for the vertical axis so that the relevant domain is shown.

Step 3 Use a calculator to check if your answer, $5^{4.3} = 1{,}012.91$, is close to 1,000. ✓

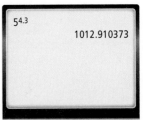

$5^{4.3}$

1012.910373

It will take the virus about 4.3 hours to spread to the entire network.

Try It!   **2.** How long will it take for the virus to spread to 50,000 computers?

CONCEPT Exponential Function

An **exponential function** is the product of an initial amount and a **constant ratio** raised to a power. Exponential functions are modeled using $f(x) = a \cdot b^x$, where a is a nonzero constant, $b > 0$, and $b \neq 1$.

$$f(x) = a \cdot b^x$$

a is the initial amount.

b is the constant ratio.

EXAMPLE 3   Write Exponential Functions

STUDY TIP
Note that exponential functions have constant ratios rather than differences.

A. What is the written form of the function represented by the table?

x	f(x)
0	4
1	12
2	36
3	108
4	324

The initial amount is 4.

$12 \div 4 = 3$
$36 \div 12 = 3$
$108 \div 36 = 3$ The constant ratio is 3.
$324 \div 108 = 3$

In $f(x) = a \cdot b^x$, substitute 4 for a and 3 for b.
The function is $f(x) = 4(3)^x$.

B. What is the written form of the function represented by the graph?

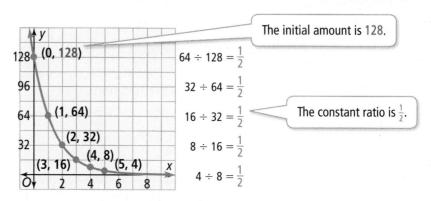

The initial amount is 128.

$64 \div 128 = \frac{1}{2}$
$32 \div 64 = \frac{1}{2}$
$16 \div 32 = \frac{1}{2}$ The constant ratio is $\frac{1}{2}$.
$8 \div 16 = \frac{1}{2}$
$4 \div 8 = \frac{1}{2}$

In $f(x) = a \cdot b^x$, substitute 128 for a and $\frac{1}{2}$ for b.
The function is $f(x) = 128\left(\frac{1}{2}\right)^x$.

 Try It!   **3.** Write an exponential function for each set of points.

     a. (0, 3), (1, 12), (2, 48), (3, 192), and (4, 768)

     b. (0, 2,187), (1, 729), (2, 243), (3, 81), and (4, 27)

APPLICATION   **EXAMPLE 4**   **Compare Linear and Exponential Functions**

Talisha is offered two pledge options for donating to a charity. Which option will increase the pledge amount faster over time?

Option A: $100 for the first week, and each week after that the amount increases by $25

Week	Payment ($)
0	100
1	125
2	150
3	175
4	200
5	225

Initial value

+25
+25
+25
+25
+25

Constant increase

Option B: $1 for the first week, and each week after that the amount triples

Week	Payment ($)
0	1
1	3
2	9
3	27
4	81
5	243

Initial value

×3
×3
×3
×3
×3

Constant ratio

CONSTRUCT ARGUMENTS
Will an exponential model with a base greater than 1 always have a greater rate of change over time? Explain.

Option A is a linear function and increases at a constant rate.

Since the ratio of consecutive terms in Option B is constant, the exponential function will increase faster over time.

 Try It! **4.** Identify each function as linear or exponential. Explain.

   a. $f(x)$ equals the number of branches at level x in a tree diagram, where at each level each branch extends into 4 branches.

   b. $f(x)$ equals the number of boxes in row x of a stack in which each row increases by 2 boxes.

CONCEPT SUMMARY Exponential Functions

Exponential Functions are modeled using $f(x) = a \cdot b^x$, where a is the initial amount and b is the constant ratio.

	$b > 1$	$0 < b < 1$
ALGEBRA	$f(x) = 2(3)^x$	$f(x) = 81\left(\frac{2}{3}\right)^x$

TABLES

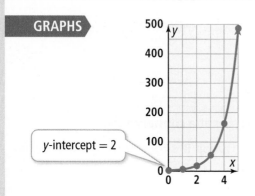

x	f(x)
0	2
1	6
2	18
3	54
4	162
5	486

$\times 3$ between each

x	f(x)
0	81
1	54
2	36
3	24
4	16
5	10.7

$\times \frac{2}{3}$ between each

GRAPHS

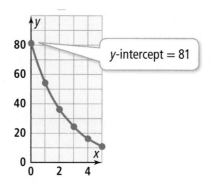

y-intercept $= 2$

y-intercept $= 81$

Do You UNDERSTAND?

1. **ESSENTIAL QUESTION** What are the characteristics of exponential functions?

2. **Look for Relationships** How can you tell whether the graph of a function of form $f(x) = ab^x$ where $a > 0$ will increase or decrease from left to right?

3. **Make Sense and Persevere** Why is $b \neq 1$ a condition for $f(x) = ab^x$?

4. **Error Analysis** Martin says that $f(x) = 2(4)^x$ starts at 4 and has constant ratio of 2. What error did Martin make? Explain.

Do You KNOW HOW?

Graph each function.

5. $f(x) = 3^x$

6. $f(x) = \left(\frac{1}{4}\right)^x$

Write each exponential function.

7.

x	f(x)
0	4
1	2
2	1
3	$\frac{1}{2}$
4	$\frac{1}{4}$

8.

x	f(x)
0	3
1	6
2	12
3	24
4	48

Scan for Multimedia

Practice   Tutorial

Additional Exercises Available Online

UNDERSTAND

9. **Make Sense and Persevere** An exponential function of form $f(x) = b^x$ includes the points (2, 16), (3, 64), and (4, 256). What is the value of b?

10. **Reason** Is $y = 0$ the asymptote of all functions of the form $f(x) = ab^x$? Explain your reasoning.

11. **Error Analysis** Describe and correct the error a student made in writing an exponential function.

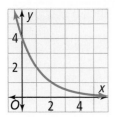

Starting value = 6
Constant ratio = $\frac{1}{3}$
$f(x) = 6(\frac{1}{3})^x$
$f(x) = 2^x$ ✗

12. **Use Structure** The function $f(x) = 4\left(\frac{1}{2}\right)^x$ is graphed below. Describe how the graph would change for $a > 4$ and $1 < a < 4$.

13. **Higher Order Thinking** The exponential function $f(x) = 2^x$ increases as x increases. Do all exponential functions behave this way? Use algebraic reasoning to support your answer.

14. **Use Structure** What happens to the graph of an exponential function when the initial value, a, is less than 0? Explain.

PRACTICE

Identify the key features of each exponential function. SEE EXAMPLE 1

15. $f(x) = 4^x$

16. $f(x) = \left(\frac{1}{3}\right)^x$

Graph each exponential function. SEE EXAMPLE 2

17. $f(x) = 0.5^x$

18. $f(x) = 6^x$

19. $f(x) = 2(3)^x$

20. $f(x) = 4\left(\frac{1}{2}\right)^x$

Write each exponential function. SEE EXAMPLE 3

21.

x	f(x)
0	2
1	8
2	32
3	128
4	512

22.

x	f(x)
0	4
1	$\frac{4}{3}$
2	$\frac{4}{9}$
3	$\frac{4}{27}$
4	$\frac{4}{81}$

23.

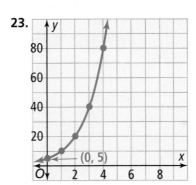

Tell whether each function is linear or exponential. Explain your reasoning. SEE EXAMPLE 4

24.

x	f(x)
0	5
1	9
2	13
3	17
4	21

25.

x	f(x)
0	216
1	36
2	6
3	1
4	$\frac{1}{6}$

APPLY

26. Make Sense and Persevere Write an exponential function to model earthquake intensity as a function of a Richter Scale number. How can you use your function to compare the intensity of the 1811 New Madrid and 1906 San Francisco earthquakes?

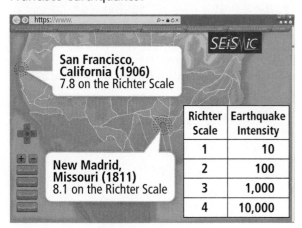

San Francisco, California (1906)
7.8 on the Richter Scale

New Madrid, Missouri (1811)
8.1 on the Richter Scale

Richter Scale	Earthquake Intensity
1	10
2	100
3	1,000
4	10,000

27. Model With Mathematics A television show will be canceled if the estimated number of viewers falls below 2.5 million by Week 10. Use the graph to write an exponential function to model the situation. If this pattern continues, will the show be canceled?

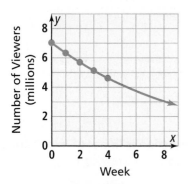

28. Make Sense and Persevere The table shows the number of algae cells in pool water samples. A pool will turn green when there are 24 million algae cells or more. Write and graph an exponential function to model the expected number of algae cells as a function of the number of days. If the pattern continues, in how many days will the water turn green?

Day	Number of Algae Cells
0	2000
1	10,000
2	50,000
3	250,000
4	1,250,000

ASSESSMENT PRACTICE

29. Consider the function $f(x) = 3(5)^x$.

The y-intercept is _____.

The asymptote is _____.

The domain is _____.

The range is _____.

30. SAT/ACT What is the y-intercept of $f(x) = 8\left(\frac{1}{2}\right)^x$?

Ⓐ 0

Ⓑ $\frac{1}{2}$

Ⓒ 1

Ⓓ 2

Ⓔ 8

31. Performance Task A gardener can increase the number of dahlia plants in an annual garden by either buying new bulbs each year or dividing the existing bulbs to create new plants. The table shows the expected number of bulbs for each method.

Year	Buy New Bulbs	Divide Existing Bulbs
0	6	6
1	56	12
2	106	24
3	156	48
4	206	96

Part A For each method, write a function to model the expected number of plants for each year.

Part B Use your functions to find the expected number of plants in 10 years for each method.

Part C How does the expected number of plants in five years compare to the expected number of plants in 15 years? Explain how these patterns could affect the method the gardener decides to use.

5-3

Exponential Growth and Decay

I CAN... use exponential functions to model situations and make predictions.

VOCABULARY

- compound interest
- decay factor
- exponential decay
- exponential growth
- growth factor

EXPLORE & REASON

Cindy is buying a new car and wants to learn how the value of her car will change over time. Insurance actuaries predict the future value of cars using depreciation functions. One such function is applied to the car whose declining value is shown at the right.

A. Describe how the value of the car decreases from year to year.

B. **Model With Mathematics** What kind of function would explain this type of pattern?

C. Given your answer to Part B, what is needed to find the function the actuary is using? Explain.

Years After Purchase	Value
0 yr	$10,000
1 yr	$8,520
2 yr	$7,213
3 yr	$6,100
4 yr	$5,210

? ESSENTIAL QUESTION

What kinds of situations can be modeled with exponential growth or exponential decay functions?

CONCEPTUAL UNDERSTANDING

EXAMPLE 1   Exponential Growth

The population of Hillville grows at an annual rate of 15%. What will the estimated population of Hillville be in five years?

> You can model **exponential growth** with a function $f(x) = a \cdot b^x$, where $a > 0$ and $b > 1$.

$$f(x) = a \cdot b^x$$

$$f(x) = a(1 + r)^x$$

> An exponential growth function has a **growth factor** that is equal to 1 plus the growth rate.

Welcome To HILLVILLE

Population: 5,000

MODEL WITH MATHEMATICS
In an exponential growth situation, the change in y is always proportional to the value of y itself; that is, with greater y-values, the function increases more rapidly. What other exponential growth situations can you think of?

Step 1 Write the exponential growth function that models the expected population growth.

Let $x =$ time in years, $a =$ initial amount, and $r =$ growth rate.

$f(x) = a(1 + r)^x$

$\quad = 5,000(1 + 0.15)^x$

$\quad = 5,000(1.15)^x$

The function is $f(x) = 5,000(1.15)^x$.

CONTINUED ON THE NEXT PAGE

EXAMPLE 1 CONTINUED

Step 2 Find the expected population in 5 years.

$$f(5) = 5,000(1.15)^5$$

$$\approx 10,056.79$$

In 5 years, the population is expected to be about 10,057.

COMMON ERROR
You may incorrectly record a decimal number when you are finding "how many" people. Remember that the number of people should be a whole number.

 Try It! **1.** The population of Valleytown is also 5,000, with an annual increase of 1,000. Can the expected population for Valleytown be modeled with an exponential growth function? Explain.

CONCEPT Interest

Interest is calculated in two ways: simple interest and compound interest.

Simple interest is interest paid only on the principal.

Compound interest is interest that is paid both on the principal and on the interest that has already been paid. The compound interest formula is an exponential growth function.

Compound Interest Formula

$$A = P\left(1 + \frac{r}{n}\right)^{nt}$$

A = amount paid
P = principal amount
r = rate of interest
n = number of times per year the interest is compounded
t = time in years

LOOK FOR RELATIONSHIPS
How is the compound interest formula related to $f(x) = a(1 + r)^x$?

The graph below shows $10 at 5% simple interest and at 5% interest compounded quarterly.

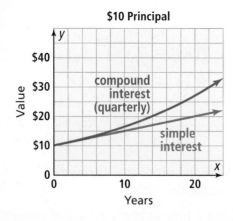

$10 Principal

APPLICATION

EXAMPLE 2 **Exponential Models of Growth**

Kimberly's family invested in a Certificate of Deposit (CD) for her when she was born. The interest is compounded quarterly.

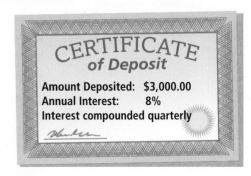

CERTIFICATE
of Deposit

Amount Deposited: $3,000.00
Annual Interest: 8%
Interest compounded quarterly

A. **What is the value of the CD at the end of five years?**

Use the compound interest formula.

USE STRUCTURE
Use the order of operations when entering your numbers on a calculator. How can the omission of parentheses change your answer?

$A = P\left(1 + \frac{r}{n}\right)^{nt}$

$= 3{,}000\left(1 + \frac{0.08}{4}\right)^{4t}$ — The principal amount is 3,000. The rate of interest is 8%, or 0.08. The number of times per year the interest is calculated is 4.

$= 3{,}000(1 + 0.02)^{4t}$

$= 3{,}000(1.02)^{4t}$ — The 8% interest is paid over 4 periods, so 2% interest is paid each period.

$= 3{,}000(1.02)^{4(5)}$

$= 4{,}457.84$

At the end of five years, the value of the CD will be $4,457.84.

B. **Will the value of Kimberly's CD be greater after 15 years if it is compounded annually rather than quarterly?**

Compare the exponential function you found in Part A with annual compounding ($n = 1$) over the same 15 years.

REASON
The simple interest formula is $A = P(1 + rt)$. How is simple interest similar to annual compounding? How is it different?

Quarterly:

$A = 3{,}000(1.02)^{4t}$

$= 3{,}000(1.02)^{4 \times 15}$

$= 3{,}000(1.02)^{60}$

$= \$9{,}843.09$

Annually:

$A = P\left(1 + \frac{r}{n}\right)^{nt}$

$= 3{,}000\left(1 + \frac{0.08}{1}\right)^{1(15)}$ — Since the interest is only compiled once per year, the entire 8% interest is paid one time.

$= 3{,}000(1.08)^{15}$

$= \$9{,}516.51$

The value of Kimberly's CD will be less if the interest is compounded annually rather than quarterly.

 Try It! **2. a.** What will be the difference after 15 years if the interest is compounded semiannually rather than quarterly?

b. What will be the difference after 15 years if the interest is compounded monthly rather than quarterly?

APPLICATION

EXAMPLE 3 — Exponential Decay

A video is labeled a fan favorite if it receives at least 1,000 views per day. Amelia posts a video that gets 8,192 views on the first day. The number of views decreases by 25% each day after that. In how many days total will the video stop being a fan favorite?

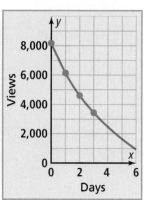

USE STRUCTURE
How does the exponential decay function differ from the exponential growth function?

You can model **exponential decay** with a function of the form $f(x) = a \cdot b^x$, where $a > 0$ and $0 < b < 1$.

The **decay factor** is 1 minus the decay rate.

$$f(x) = a \cdot b^x$$
$$f(x) = a(1 - r)^x$$

↑
r is the decay rate.

Step 1 Model the situation.

Let x = time in years, a = initial amount, and r = decay rate.

$f(x) = a(1 - r)^x$

$= 8{,}192(1 - 0.25)^x$ ⟵ The decay factor is written as a decimal less than 1.

$= 8{,}192(0.75)^x$

Step 2 Write an equation to find x if $f(x) = 1{,}000$.

$1{,}000 = 8{,}192(0.75)^x$

Step 3 Estimate the solution of the equation using a graphing calculator.

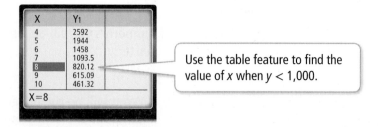

Use the table feature to find the value of x when $y < 1{,}000$.

The video will stop being a fan favorite in 8 days.

 Try It! 3. Suppose the number of views decreases by 20% per day. In how many days will the number of views per day be less than 1,000?

APPLICATION    **EXAMPLE 4**   **Exponential Models of Decay**

The number of pika in a region is decreasing. How does the decrease in the pika population for years 1 to 5 compare to the population for years 6 to 10?

Write an exponential decay function to model the situation.

$$f(x) = a(1 - r)^x$$
$$= 144(1 - 0.08)^x$$
$$f(x) = 144(0.92)^x$$

Pika population are decreasing by 8% each year.

Initial population: 144 pikas

Find the average rate of change for each interval.

Year 1 to Year 5: $1 \leq x \leq 5$

$f(1) \approx 132$ $f(5) \approx 95$

$\dfrac{95 - 132}{5 - 1} = \dfrac{-37}{4} = -9.25$

Year 6 to Year 10: $6 \leq x \leq 10$

$f(6) \approx 87$ $f(10) \approx 63$

$\dfrac{63 - 87}{10 - 6} = \dfrac{-24}{4} = -6$

For years 1 to 5, the pika population decreases by an average of 9.25 pikas per year. For years 6 to 10 the pika population decreases by an average of 6 pikas per year. The average rate of change for the pika population decreases as years increase.

 Try It!   **4.** How would the average rate of change over the same intervals be affected if the population increased at a rate of 8%?

APPLICATION   **EXAMPLE 5**   **Exponential Growth and Decay**

Rich is comparing the cost of maintaining his car with the depreciating value of the car. When will the cost and value be the same?

Value: starts at $20,000, decreases by 15% per year.

Maintenance cost: $500 the first year, increases by 28% per year.

Formulate ◀   Write the exponential functions.

Value of the car: $f(x) = 20(0.85)^x$

Cost of maintenance: $g(x) = 0.5(1.28)^x$

Compute ◀   Solve by graphing.

Find the point of intersection: (9, 4.5).

Interpret ◀   The value of the car and the cost of maintenance are both about $4,500 at 9 years.

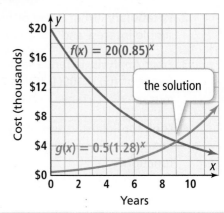

 Try It!   **5.** Explain how to use tables on a graphing calculator to answer this question.

CONCEPT SUMMARY Exponential Growth and Decay

	Exponential Growth	Exponential Decay	Compound Interest
ALGEBRA	$f(x) = a \cdot b^x$ $f(x) = a(1 + r)^x$	$f(x) = a \cdot b^x$ $f(x) = a(1 - r)^x$	$f(x) = a \cdot b^x$ $A = P\left(1 + \dfrac{r}{n}\right)^{nt}$
NUMBERS	$f(x) = 4(1 + 0.5)^x$	$f(x) = 4(1 - 0.5)^x$	$A = 5\left(1 + \dfrac{0.12}{2}\right)^{2t}$
WORDS	initial value: 4 growth rate: 50% growth factor: 1.5	initial value: 4 decay rate: 50% decay factor: 0.5	principal: 5 annual interest rate: 12% periods per year: 2
GRAPHS	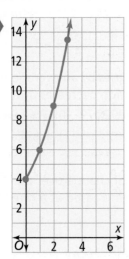	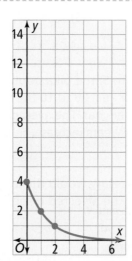	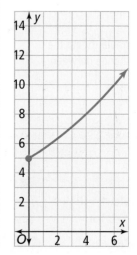

Do You UNDERSTAND?

1. **ESSENTIAL QUESTION** What kinds of situations can be modeled with exponential growth or exponential decay functions?

2. **Vocabulary** What is the difference between simple interest and *compound interest*?

3. **Error Analysis** LaTanya says that the growth factor of $f(x) = 100(1.25)^x$ is 25%. What mistake did LaTanya make? Explain.

4. **Look for Relationships** Why is the growth factor $1 + r$ for an exponential growth function?

Do You KNOW HOW?

Write an exponential growth or decay function for each situation.

5. initial value of 100 increasing at a rate of 5%

6. initial value of 1,250 increasing at a rate of 25%

7. initial value of 512 decreasing at a rate of 50%

8. initial value of 10,000 decreasing at a rate of 12%

9. What is the difference in the value after 10 years of an initial investment of $2,000 at 5% annual interest when the interest is compounded quarterly rather than annually?

PRACTICE & PROBLEM SOLVING

 Scan for Multimedia Practice Tutorial

Additional Exercises Available Online

UNDERSTAND

10. Look for Relationships How is an exponential growth function of the form $f(x) = a(1 + r)^x$ related to an exponential function of the form $f(x) = a \cdot b^x$?

11. Generalize What is the asymptote of the graph of an exponential growth or exponential decay function? Explain your reasoning.

12. Error Analysis Describe and correct the error a student made in writing an equation to find the annual value of an investment of $1,000 at 4% annual interest compounded semiannually.

$$A = 1{,}000(1+0.04)^{4t}$$
$$= 1{,}000(1.04)^{4t}$$

✗

13. Use Appropriate Tools Describe how you could use a graphing calculator to estimate the value of x when $f(x) = 8(1.25)^x$ equals 15.

14. Higher Order Thinking In Example 2, you used the formula $A = P\left(1 + \frac{r}{n}\right)^{nt}$ to solve problems involving compound interest.

a. How is the growth factor of a function that models compound interest affected as n increases? Explain.

b. Copy and complete the table.

n	$A = 3{,}000\left(1 + \dfrac{0.08}{n}\right)^{5n}$
12	▪
365	▪
1,000	▪
10,000	▪
100,000	▪

c. What is the relationship between the value of the function and the change in the growth factor as n increases? Explain.

PRACTICE

Write an exponential growth function to model each situation. SEE EXAMPLE 1

15. initial value: 20
growth factor: 1.25

16. initial value: 100
growth factor: 1.05

Compare each investment to an investment of the same principal at the same rate compounded annually. SEE EXAMPLE 2

17. principal: $8,000
annual interest: 6%
interest periods: 4
number of years: 20

18. principal: $10,000
annual interest: 3.5%
interest periods: 2
number of years: 5

Write an exponential decay function to model each situation. Then estimate the value of x for the given value of $f(x)$. SEE EXAMPLE 3

19. initial value: 100
decay factor: 0.95
$f(x) = 60$

20. initial value: 5,000
decay factor: 0.7
$f(x) = 100$

Write an exponential decay function to model each situation. Compare the average rates of change over the given intervals. SEE EXAMPLE 4

21. initial value: 50
decay factor: 0.9
$1 \le x \le 4$ and
$5 \le x \le 8$

22. initial value: 25
decay factor: 0.8
$2 \le x \le 4$ and
$6 \le x \le 8$

Write an exponential function to model the data in each table. Identify the growth or decay factor.
SEE EXAMPLES 1–4

23.

x	$f(x)$
0	4
1	2
2	1
3	$\frac{1}{2}$
4	$\frac{1}{4}$

24.

x	$f(x)$
0	100
1	110
2	121
3	133.1
4	146.41

Model each pair of situations with exponential functions f and g. Find the approximate value of x that makes $f(x) = g(x)$. SEE EXAMPLE 5

25. f: initial value of 100 decreasing at a rate of 5%
g: initial value of 20 increasing at a rate of 5%

26. f: initial value of 40 increasing at a rate of 25%
g: initial value of 10,000 decreasing at a rate of 16%

APPLY

27. Model With Mathematics A plant will become invasive when the number of plants reaches 10,000. Model the situation with an exponential growth function. How many years will it take for the plant to become invasive? Explain how you found the solution.

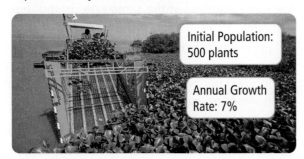

Initial Population: 500 plants

Annual Growth Rate: 7%

28. Look for Relationships Joshua invests $500 at the interest rate shown. Felix invests $1,000 in an account with the same compounding, but at 6% interest rate. Model each investment with an exponential growth function. Whose money will double first? Explain.

7.8%

Investment Special!

Annual Interest Rate: 7.8%
Interest Period: 2 per year

29. Make Sense and Persevere Write and graph exponential functions to model the number of students at School A and at School B as a function of number of years. In about how many years will the number of students at both schools be approximately the same? Explain how you can use a graph to determine the answer.

School A

240 students
decreasing at
an annual rate of 2%

School B

180 students
increasing at
an annual rate of 3%

ASSESSMENT PRACTICE

30. Classify each function as an exponential growth function or an exponential decay function.

$f(x) = 2(1.02)^x$

$f(x) = 5000(3)^x$

$f(x) = 7500(0.91)^x$

$f(x) = 189(1 - 0.25)^x$

$f(x) = 2485(1 + 0.25)^x$

31. SAT/ACT Which function models the value in x years of an investment at 3% annual interest compounded quarterly?

Ⓐ $150(1 - 0.03)^{4x}$

Ⓑ $150(1 + 0.03)^{4x}$

Ⓒ $150(1 - 0.03)^x$

Ⓓ $150(1 + 0.0075)^{4x}$

Ⓔ $150(1 - 0.0075)^x$

32. Performance Task Isabel has $10,000 to invest. She is choosing between the three investment opportunities shown.

Investment	Annual Interest	Number of Interest Periods
A	4%	1
B	4%	4
C	4.2%	1

Part A Write a function for each investment to model its value in x years.

Part B Suppose Isabel only wants to invest her money for five years. Which investment will have the greatest value in five years?

Part C Which investment will make Isabel a millionaire first?

5-4

Geometric Sequences

SavvasRealize.com

I CAN... identify and describe geometric sequences.

VOCABULARY
• geometric sequence

EXPLORE & REASON

A seating plan is being designed for Section 12 of a new stadium.

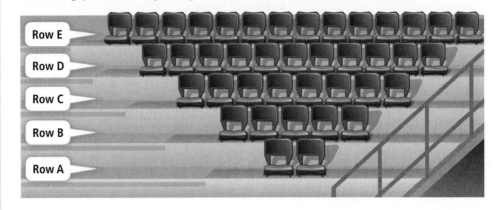

Row E
Row D
Row C
Row B
Row A

A. Describe the pattern.

B. Write an equation for this pattern.

C. **Use Structure** Row Z of Section 12 must have at least 75 seats. If the pattern continues, does this seating plan meet that requirement? Justify your answer.

? ESSENTIAL QUESTION

How are geometric sequences related to exponential functions?

EXAMPLE 1   Identify Arithmetic and Geometric Sequences

Is each sequence an arithmetic or a geometric sequence?

A **geometric sequence** is a number sequence in which each term after the first term is found by multiplying the previous term by a common ratio.

Look for a common difference or a common ratio between consecutive terms.

STUDY TIP
The common ratio is the fixed number used to find terms in a geometric sequence. The common ratio cannot be zero.

A. $3, 2, \frac{4}{3}, \frac{8}{9}, \frac{16}{27}, \ldots$

> no common difference

> Divide the second term by the first term in each consecutive pair to find the *common ratio*.

$2 - 3 = -1 \qquad \frac{4}{3} - 2 = -\frac{2}{3}$

$2 \div 3 = \frac{2}{3} \qquad \frac{4}{3} \div 2 = \frac{2}{3} \qquad \frac{8}{9} \div \frac{4}{3} = \frac{2}{3} \qquad \frac{16}{27} \div \frac{8}{9} = \frac{2}{3}$

The sequence does not have a common difference, but has a common ratio of $\frac{2}{3}$, so it is a geometric sequence.

> There is a common difference.

B. $3, 4.5, 6, 7.5, 9, \ldots$

$4.5 - 3 = 1.5 \qquad 6 - 4.5 = 1.5 \qquad 7.5 - 6 = 1.5 \qquad 9 - 7.5 = 1.5$

The sequence has a common difference of 1.5, so it is an arithmetic sequence.

 Try It!   **1.** Is each sequence an arithmetic or a geometric sequence? Explain.

a. 1, 2.2, 4.84, 10.648, 23.4256, ...   **b.** 1, 75, 149, 223, 297, ...

EXAMPLE 2 Write the Recursive Formula For a Sequence

What recursive formula describes the geometric sequence 8, 12, 18, 27, 40.5, …?

Recursive formula:

$$a_n = r\,(a_{n-1})$$

nth term common ratio previous term

Find the common ratio.

$$\frac{12}{8} = \frac{18}{12} = \frac{27}{18} = \frac{40.5}{27} = \frac{3}{2}$$

The common ratio is $\frac{3}{2}$.

$a_n = \frac{3}{2}(a_{n-1})$ ········· Substitute $\frac{3}{2}$ for r.

The recursive formula is $a_n = \frac{3}{2}(a_{n-1})$, where the initial condition is $a_1 = 8$.

☑ **Try It!** 2. Write the recursive formula for the geometric sequence 3,072, 768, 192, 48, 12, ….

 EXAMPLE 3 Use the Explicit Formula

What is the 10th term in the sequence shown in Example 2?

Explicit formula:

$$a_n = a_1(r)^{n-1}$$

nth term first term common ratio

The first term is 8. The common ratio is $\frac{3}{2}$.

$$a_{10} = 8\left(\frac{3}{2}\right)^9$$
$$= 307.546875$$

The 10th term in the sequence is 307.55 rounded to the nearest hundredth.

☑ **Try It!** 3. What is the 12th term of the sequence described?
Initial condition is 3.
Recursive formula is $a_n = 6(a_{n-1})$.

CONCEPTUAL
UNDERSTANDING

EXAMPLE 4   Connect Geometric Sequences and Exponential Functions

The number of subscribers to a blog doubles each week.

How can the trend in subscribers be modeled?

Class Blog

In our first week, we had 5 subscribers!

The number of subscribers doubles each week, so an exponential function models the situation. The initial number of subscribers is 5, and that number doubles each week.

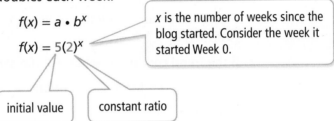

$f(x) = a \cdot b^x$

$f(x) = 5(2)^x$

x is the number of weeks since the blog started. Consider the week it started Week 0.

initial value   constant ratio

The trend can also be modeled as a geometric sequence with an initial value of 5 and a common ratio of 2.

$a_n = a_1(r)^{n-1}$

$a_n = 5(2)^{n-1}$ .... Substitute 5 for a_1, 2 for r.

The number of subscribers changes by a constant ratio, so both an exponential function and a geometric sequence can model the situation.

 Try It!   4. How many subscribers will there be in Week 9 if the initial number of subscribers is 10?

APPLICATION   **EXAMPLE 5**   **Apply the Recursive and Explicit Formulas**

The number of people attending the annual Town International Food Festival has decreased 20% each year since the first year.

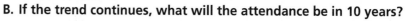

A. How can the attendance for the first 5 years be modeled?

The attendance is declining at a constant rate of 20%, so a geometric sequence can model the trend.

Find the common ratio. The common ratio is the decay factor here.

$$1 - r$$
$$1 - 0.2 = 0.8$$

Write a recursive formula to describe the trend.

$$a_n = r(a_{n-1})$$
$$a_n = 0.8(a_{n-1}) \quad \text{......... Substitute 0.8 for } r.$$

The recursive formula is $a_n = 0.8(a_{n-1})$, where the attendance at the first festival is $a_1 = 1{,}250$.

B. If the trend continues, what will the attendance be in 10 years?

Use the explicit formula to find the attendance in year 10.

$$a_n = a_1(r)^{n-1}$$
$$a_{10} = 1{,}250(0.8)^{10-1}$$
$$a_{10} = 1{,}250(0.8)^9$$

Use a calculator to evaluate the expression.

$1250 \times (4/5)^9$
167.77216

Attendance in 10 years will be about 168 people.

GENERALIZE
How is the form of a geometric sequence related to the types of questions that can be answered efficiently using that form?

 Try It!   **5.** The formula $a_n = 1.5(a_{n-1})$ with an initial value of 40 describes a sequence. Use the explicit formula to determine the 5th term of the sequence.

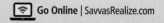

CONCEPT SUMMARY Explicit and Recursive Formulas

Explicit formula	Recursive formula
ALGEBRA $a_n = a_1(r)^{n-1}$	$a_n = r(a_{n-1})$
nth term, first term, common ratio	nth term, common ratio, previous term
Initial condition: a_1 is the first term	
NUMBERS $a_n = 2(3)^{n-1}$ $a_1 = 2$	$a_n = 3(a_{n-1})$

GRAPH

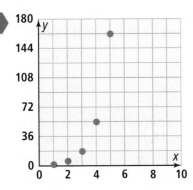

Do You UNDERSTAND?

1. **ESSENTIAL QUESTION** How are geometric sequences related to exponential functions?

2. **Vocabulary** How are *geometric sequences* similar to arithmetic sequences? How are they different?

3. **Error Analysis** For a geometric sequence with $a_1 = 3$ and a common ratio r of 1.25, Jamie writes $a_n = 1.25 \cdot (3)^{n-1}$. What mistake did Jamie make?

4. **Generalize** Is a sequence geometric if each term in the sequence is x times greater than the preceding term?

Do You KNOW HOW?

Determine whether the sequence is an arithmetic or a geometric sequence. If it is geometric, what is the common ratio?

5. 30, 6, 1.2, 0.24, 0.048, …

6. 0.5, 2, 8, 32, 148, …

Write the recursive formula for each geometric sequence.

7. 640, 160, 40, 10, 2.5, …

8. 2, 5, 12.5, 31.25, 78.125, …

9. What is the recursive formula for a sequence with the following explicit formula? $a_n = 1.25 \cdot (3)^{n-1}$

10. A sequence has an initial value of 25 and a common ratio of 1.8. How can you write the sequence as a function?

UNDERSTAND

11. Make Sense and Persevere Explain how to write a formula to describe the sequence 1, 3, 9, 27, 81, 243, ...

12. Look for Relationships How are geometric sequences related to exponential growth and decay functions? Explain your reasoning.

13. Error Analysis Describe and correct the error a student made when writing a recursive formula from an explicit formula.

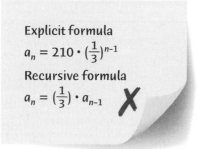

Explicit formula
$$a_n = 210 \cdot \left(\tfrac{1}{3}\right)^{n-1}$$
Recursive formula
$$a_n = \left(\tfrac{1}{3}\right) \cdot a_{n-1}$$ ✗

14. Use Appropriate Tools Explain how you could use a graphing calculator to determine whether the data in the table represents a geometric sequence.

n	a_n
1	20
2	90
3	405
4	1822.5
5	8201.25

15. Higher Order Thinking In Example 5, a geometric sequence is written as a function.

a. How is the domain of a function related to the numbers in the sequence?

b. How is the range of the function related to the numbers in the sequence?

16. Mathematical Connections A pendulum swings 80 cm on its first swing, 76 cm on its second swing, 72.2 cm on its third swing, and 68.59 cm on its fourth swing.

a. If the pattern continues, what explicit formula can be used to find the distance of the nth swing?

b. Use your formula to find the distance of the 10th swing.

PRACTICE

Determine whether the sequence is a geometric sequence. If it is, write the recursive formula.
SEE EXAMPLES 1 AND 2

17. 8, 12, 18, 27, 40.5, ...

18. 3, $\frac{3}{2}$, $\frac{3}{4}$, $\frac{3}{8}$, $\frac{3}{16}$, ...

19. $\frac{1}{27}$, $\frac{1}{9}$, $\frac{1}{3}$, 1, 3, ...

20. $\frac{10}{3}$, $\frac{8}{3}$, 2, $\frac{4}{3}$, $\frac{2}{3}$, ...

21. 1, 1, 2, 3, 5, ...

22. 2, $\frac{8}{3}$, $\frac{32}{9}$, $\frac{128}{27}$, $\frac{512}{81}$, ...

23. 1, 1.2, 1.4, 1.6, 1.8, ...

24. $\frac{1}{2}$, 2, 8, 32, 128, ...

25. 9, 18, 36, 74, 144, ...

26. $\frac{4}{5}$, 4, 20, 100, 500, ...

Write the recursive formula for the sequence represented by the explicit formula. SEE EXAMPLE 3

27. $a_n = \frac{1}{5}(10)^{n-1}$

28. $a_n = 1.1(6)^{n-1}$

29. $a_n = \frac{2}{3}(5)^{n-1}$

30. $a_n = 0.4(8)^{n-1}$

Write an explicit formula for each sequence represented by the recursive formula. SEE EXAMPLE 5

31. $a_n = \frac{4}{5}(a_{n-1})$, $a_1 = 100$

32. $a_n = 8(a_{n-1})$, $a_1 = 1$

33. $a_n = \frac{5}{9}(a_{n-1})$ $a_1 = 10$

34. $a_n = 6(a_{n-1})$ $a_1 = 7$

Write each geometric sequence using function notation.
SEE EXAMPLE 4

35. $a_n = \frac{3}{4}(a_{n-1})$, $a_1 = 20$

36. $a_n = 3(a_{n-1})$, $a_1 = 7$

37. $a_n = 2a_{n-1}$, $a_1 = 4$

38. $a_n = \frac{2}{3}a_{n-1}$, $a_1 = 99$

Write a function to model each geometric sequence in the table.

39.

n	a_n
1	9
2	3
3	1
4	$\frac{1}{3}$
5	$\frac{1}{9}$

40.

n	a_n
1	18
2	54
3	162
4	486
5	1,458

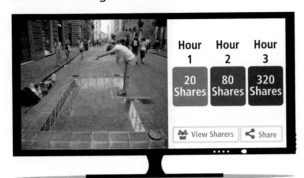

APPLY

41. Make Sense and Persevere A new optical illusion is posted to the Internet. Write a recursive formula to describe the pattern. Then, write the explicit formula that can be used to find the number of times the optical illusion is shared after eight hours?

Hour 1	Hour 2	Hour 3
20 Shares	80 Shares	320 Shares

View Sharers   Share

42. Construct Arguments Write the recursive formula for a geometric sequence that models the data in the table. Use the explicit formula to determine whether there will be 1,000 participants by the tenth year of the Annual Clean-Up Day.

Annual Clean-up Day

Year	Participants
1	16
2	24
3	36
4	54
5	81

43. Model With Mathematics The number of bacteria in the sample shown decreases by a factor of $\frac{2}{3}$ every hour. Write a geometric sequence to model the pattern. How many hours will it take for the number of bacteria to decrease below 1,000?

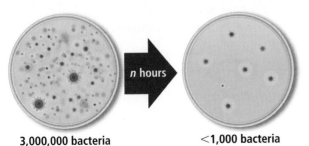

3,000,000 bacteria   <1,000 bacteria

ASSESSMENT PRACTICE

44. Is each sequence shown a geometric sequence? Select *Yes* or *No*.

	Yes	No
6, 18, 30, 42, 54, …	❏	❏
2, 3, $\frac{9}{2}$, $\frac{27}{4}$, $\frac{81}{8}$, …	❏	❏
1024, 256, 64, 16, 4, …	❏	❏
243, 162, 81, 54, 27, …	❏	❏

45. SAT/ACT What is the explicit formula for the sequence 360, 180, 90, 45, 22.5, …?

Ⓐ $a_n = \frac{1}{2}(360)^{n-1}$

Ⓑ $a_n = \frac{1}{2}(a_{n-1})$

Ⓒ $a_n = 360(a_{n-1})$

Ⓓ $a_n = 360\left(\frac{1}{2}\right)^{n-1}$

Ⓔ $a_n = 360 + \frac{1}{2}(a_{n-1})$

46. Performance Task A computer program generates the patterns shown each time the program loops.

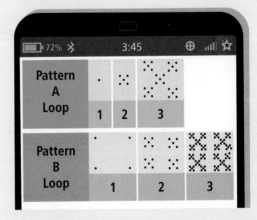

Part A Write the recursive formula for the geometric sequence that models each pattern.

Part B How are the geometric sequences for patterns A and B related?

Part C If pattern B has *x* dots at loop *n*, how many dots does pattern A have at loop *n*? Explain.

5-5

Transformations of Exponential Functions

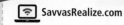
SavvasRealize.com

I CAN... perform, analyze, and use transformations of exponential functions.

MODEL & DISCUSS

A radio station uses the function $f(x) = 100(3)^x$ to model the growth of Band A's fan base.

A. What would the graph of the function look like for Band B with a fan base growing twice as fast as Band A's fan base?

B. Compare and contrast the two graphs.

C. **Look for Relationships** Suppose Band C starts with a fan base of 200 fans that is growing twice as fast as Band A's fan base. Compare and contrast this new function with the previous two functions.

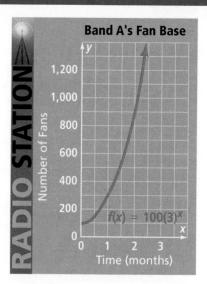

? **ESSENTIAL QUESTION**   How do changes in an exponential function relate to translations of its graph?

CONCEPTUAL UNDERSTANDING

👆 **EXAMPLE 1**   Vertical Translations of Graphs of Exponential Functions

How does the value of k affect the graph of $f(x) = 2^x + k$?

Compare the graphs of $g(x) = 2^x + 3$ and $j(x) = 2^x - 3$ to the graph of $f(x) = 2^x$.

x	$f(x) = 2^x$	$g(x) = 2^x + 3$	$j(x) = 2^x - 3$
-2	$\frac{1}{4}$	$3\frac{1}{4}$	$-2\frac{3}{4}$
-1	$\frac{1}{2}$	$3\frac{1}{2}$	$-2\frac{1}{2}$
0	1	4	-2
1	2	5	-1
2	4	7	1

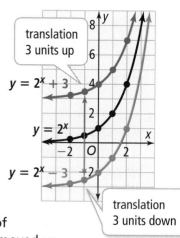

The graph of $f(x) = 2^x + k$ is a vertical translation of the graph of $f(x) = 2^x$. If k is positive, the graph is moved up. If k is negative, the graph is moved down.

☑ **Try It!**   **1. a.** How does the graph of $g(x) = 2^x + 1$ compare to the graph of $f(x) = 2^x$?

b. How does the graph of $j(x) = 2^x - 1$ compare to the graph of $f(x) = 2^x$?

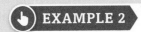
EXAMPLE 2 **Horizontal Translations of Graphs of Exponential Functions**

A. Compare the graph of $g(x) = 2^{x-h}$ with the graph of $f(x) = 2^x$ when $h > 0$. What effect does h have on the graph of g?

Let $h = 5$. Compare the graph of $g(x) = 2^{x-5}$ to the graph of $f(x) = 2^x$.

COMMON ERROR
Remember that the graph is translated right when h is positive and left when h is negative. This is the opposite of the effect of subtraction of a positive on a number line.

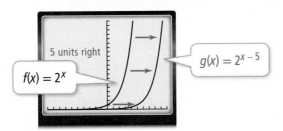

When $h > 0$, the graph is translated h units to the right. The graph of $g(x)$ is a translation of $f(x)$ to the right by 5 units.

B. Compare the graph of $j(x) = 2^{x-h}$ with the graph of $f(x) = 2^x$ when $h < 0$. What effect does h have on the graph of j?

Let $h = -3$. Compare the graph of $j(x) = 2^{x+3}$ to the graph of $f(x) = 2^x$.

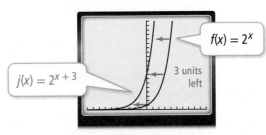

When $h < 0$, the graph is translated h units to the left. The graph of $j(x)$ is a translation of $f(x)$ to the left by 3 units.

 Try It! **2.** Compare the graph of each function with the graph of $f(x) = 2^x$. What effect does h have on the graph of each?

    a. $g(x) = 2^{x+2}$ **b.** $j(x) = 2^{x-2}$

EXAMPLE 3 Compare Two Different Transformations of $f(x) = 2^x$

How can you compare the properties of *g*, given in the table, to the properties of *j*, given in the graph? Both functions are translations of *f*.

x	$f(x) = 2^x$	*g(x)*
−2	0.25	2.25
−1	0.5	2.5
0	1	3
1	2	4
2	4	6

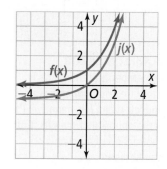

USE STRUCTURE
The range of $f(x) = 2^x$ is $f(x) > 0$. How do different transformations of $f(x) = 2^x$ affect the range of the function?

Step 1 Compare *g* to *f*.

The *y*-intercept of the graph of *f* is 1.
The *y*-intercept of the graph of *g* is 3.
The *y*-values for *g* are 2 units greater than the corresponding *y*-values for *f*. The asymptote of *f* is $y = 0$. So, the asymptote of *g* is 2 units greater, $y = 2$.

Since the asymptote of *g* is $y = 2$, the range of *g* is $y > 2$, as compared to the range of *f*, which is $y > 0$.

Step 2 Compare *j* to *f*.

The asymptote of *f* is $y = 0$.
The asymptote of *j* is $y = -1$.
The asymptote of *j* is 1 unit less than the asymptote of *f*.

Since the asymptote of *j* is $y = -1$, the range of *j* is $y > -1$, as compared to the range of *f*, which is $y > 0$.

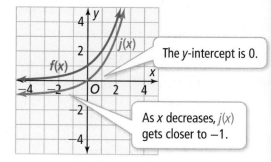

The *y*-intercept is 0.

As *x* decreases, *j(x)* gets closer to −1.

Step 3 Compare *g* to *j*.

The graph of *g* is the graph of *f* translated 2 units up, while the graph of *j* is the graph of *f* translated 1 unit down.

So, the graph of *g* is the graph of *j* translated 3 units up. Thus, the asymptote of *g* is 3 units greater than the asymptote of *j* and the *y*-values of *g* are 3 units greater than the *y*-values of *j*.

 Try It! **3. a.** The graph of the function *b* is a vertical translation of the graph of $a(x) = 3^x$, and has a *y*-intercept of 0. How does the graph of $c(x) = 3^x + 1$ compare to the graph of *b*?

b. How does the graph of $m(x) = 3^x - 3$ compare to the graph of $p(x) = 3^x + 4$?

CONCEPT SUMMARY Translations of Exponential Functions

	Vertical Translations	Horizontal Translations
ALGEBRA	$f(x) = a^x + k$	$f(x) = a^{(x-h)}$
NUMBERS	$f(x) = 0.5^x$ $g(x) = 0.5^x + 3$ $j(x) = 0.5^x - 3$	$f(x) = 0.5^x$ $g(x) = 0.5^{x+3}$ $j(x) = 0.5^{x-3}$
GRAPHS	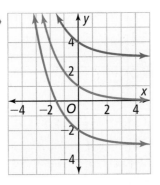	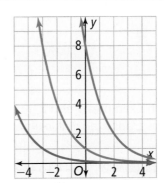

Do You UNDERSTAND?

1. **ESSENTIAL QUESTION** How do changes in an exponential function relate to translations of its graph?

2. **Communicate Precisely** How is the effect of k on the graph of $a^x + k$ similar to the effect of h on the graph of a^{x-h}? How is it different?

3. **Error Analysis** Tariq graphs $g(x) = 2^x + 6$ by translating the graph of $f(x) = 2^x$ six units right. What mistake did Tariq make?

4. **Reason** As the value of k switches from a positive to a negative number, what is the effect on the graph of $f(x) = 2^x + k$?

5. **Use Structure** The general form of vertical translations of exponential functions is $f(x) = a^x + k$. The general form of horizontal translations of exponential functions is $f(x) = a^{x-h}$. Why do you think one involves addition and one involves subtraction?

Do You KNOW HOW?

Compare the graph of each function to the graph of $f(x) = 2^x$.

6. $g(x) = 2^x + 1$

7. $p(x) = 2^{x-1}$

8. $j(x) = 2^x - 4$

9. $g(x) = 2^{x+1}$

10. Compare the function represented by the graph of $g(x) = 2^x - 3$ to the function represented by the table.

x	j(x)
−2	1.25
−1	1.5
0	2
1	3
2	5

Compare the graph of each function to the graph of $f(x) = 0.4^x$.

11. $g(x) = 0.4^{x+1}$

12. $p(x) = 0.4^{x-1}$

13. $j(x) = 0.4^x + 1$

14. $g(x) = 0.4^x - 1$

UNDERSTAND

15. Make Sense and Persevere Let $f(x) = a^x$. Describe two ways you could identify the value of k in the transformation implied by $g(x) = a^x + k$ from the graphs of f and g.

16. Error Analysis Describe and correct the error a student made in analyzing the transformation $g(x) = a^{x-h}$.

> The graph of $g(x) = a^{x-h}$ is the graph of $f(x) = a^x$ translated h units to the left. ✗

17. Higher Order Thinking In Examples 1 and 2, the graph of $f(x) = 2^x$ was translated vertically and horizontally.

  a. Compare the graph of $g(x) = 2^{x+3} + 4$ to the graph of $f(x) = 2^x$.

  b. In general, when the graph of an exponential function is translated both vertically and horizontally, what is the effect on the asymptote?

  c. In general, when the graph of an exponential function is translated both vertically and horizontally, what is the effect on the domain and the range?

18. a. Use Appropriate Tools Copy and complete the table. Compare the graphs of f and g.

x	$f(x) = 4^{\frac{1}{2}x}$	$g(x) = 4^x$
-2		
-1		
0		
2		
4		

  b. What point do the functions have in common?

  c. Describe the asymptote of each function.

PRACTICE

Compare the graph of each function to the graph of $f(x) = 2^x$. SEE EXAMPLES 1–3

19. $g(x) = 2^x - 6$

20. $p(x) = 2^{x+4}$

21. $g(x) = 2^{x-1}$

22. $j(x) = 2^x + \frac{3}{4}$

Find the value of k or h in each of the graphs.
SEE EXAMPLES 1–3

23.

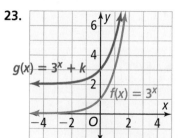

$g(x) = 3^x + k$

$f(x) = 3^x$

24.

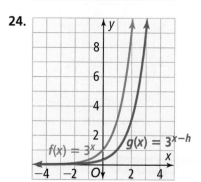

$f(x) = 3^x$

$g(x) = 3^{x-h}$

Graph each function and its transformation.
SEE EXAMPLES 1–3

25. $f(x) = 4^x$
    $g(x) = 4^x + k$ for $k = -4$

26. $f(x) = 0.5^x$
    $g(x) = 0.5^{x-h}$ for $h = -5$

Compare the y-intercepts, asymptotes, and ranges for the graphs of f and g. SEE EXAMPLE 3

27. $f(x) = 4^x$

x	$g(x)$
-2	3.0625
-1	3.25
0	4
1	7
2	19

28.

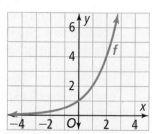

f

The graph of g is a horizontal translation 3 units to the left of the graph of $f(x) = 2^x$.

PRACTICE & PROBLEM SOLVING

APPLY

29. Reason How are graphs of $f(x) = 2^{x-h}$ similar and different for positive and negative values of h?

30. Communicate Precisely How does the graph of $f(x) = 2^{x+2}$ compare to the graph of $g(x) = 2^x + 2$?

31. Compare the function represented by the graph of $g(x) = 2^{x+0.5}$ to the graph of the function represented by the table.

x	j(x)
−2	0.088
−1	0.177
0	0.354
1	0.707
2	1.414

32. Model With Mathematics The function in the graph models an online gaming tournament that is expected to start with 400 players, with half of the players being eliminated in each round.

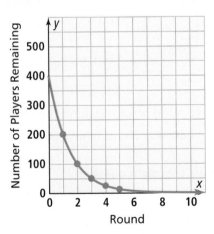

a. Describe how the graph will change if the starting number of players is 600 instead of 400. Explain your reasoning.

b. Describe how the graph will change if the starting number of players is 800 instead of 400?

ASSESSMENT PRACTICE

33. Consider the function $f(x) = 0.5^x$.

a. Graph $f(x)$, $g(x) = 0.5^x + k$ for $k = -1$, and $j(x) = 0.5^{x-h}$ for $h = 1$ in the same coordinate plane.

b. What are the y-intercepts of the graphs of g and j?

34. SAT/ACT The graph of g is a translation 4 units to the right of the graph of $f(x) = 5^x$. What is g?

Ⓐ $g(x) = 5^x + 4$

Ⓑ $g(x) = 5^x - 4$

Ⓒ $g(x) = 5^{x+4}$

Ⓓ $g(x) = 5^{x-4}$

Ⓔ $g(x) = 5^{4x}$

35. Performance Task Darnell is thinking about investing $500 in a savings plan. The graph shows how Darnell's $500 will grow if he invests his money in the plan today.

Part A How will the graph change if Darnell selects the same savings plan, but waits 5 years to invest his $500?

Part B If Darnell waits 5 years, in approximately how many years will his investment reach $1,000? Explain your reasoning.

Part C Suppose that instead of $500, Darnell invests $1,000 in the savings plan today. Describe how the graph will change. How can you use the transformed graph to estimate how many years will it take for his investment to reach $7,500?

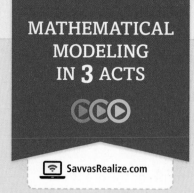

▶ Big Time Pay Back

Most people agree that investing your money is a good idea. Some people might advise you to put money into a bank savings account. Other people might say that you should invest in the stock market. Still others think that buying bonds is the best investment option.

Is a bank savings account a good way to let your money grow? Just how much money can you make from a savings account? In the Mathematical Modeling in 3 Acts lesson, you'll see an intriguing situation about an investment option.

Scan for Multimedia

ACT 1 Identify the Problem

1. What is the first question that comes to mind after watching the video?
2. Write down the main question you will answer about what you saw in the video.
3. Make an initial conjecture that answers this main question.
4. Explain how you arrived at your conjecture.
5. Write a number that you know is too small.
6. Write a number that you know is too large.
7. What information will be useful to know to answer the main question? How can you get it? How will you use that information?

ACT 2 Develop a Model

8. Use the math that you have learned in this Topic to refine your conjecture.

ACT 3 Interpret the Results

9. Is your refined conjecture between the highs and lows you set up earlier?
10. Did your refined conjecture match the actual answer exactly? If not, what might explain the difference?

Video

MATHEMATICAL MODELING IN 3 ACTS

SavvasRealize.com

Topic Review

? TOPIC ESSENTIAL QUESTION

1. How do you use exponential functions to model situations and solve problems?

Vocabulary Review

Choose the correct term to complete each sentence.

2. A population's growth can be modeled by a(n) _____ function of the form $f(x) = a \cdot b^x$, where $a > 0$ and $b > 1$.

3. An exponential function repeatedly multiplies an initial amount by the same positive number, called the _____.

4. A(n) _____ is a number sequence formed by multiplying a term in the sequence by a fixed nonzero number, or a common ratio, to find the next term.

5. _____ is interest that is paid both on the principal and on the interest that has already been paid.

6. As x or y gets larger in absolute value, the graph of the exponential function gets closer to the line called a(n) _____.

- geometric sequence
- constant ratio
- simple interest
- decay factor
- compound interest
- exponential decay
- exponential growth
- exponential function
- asymptote
- growth factor

Concepts & Skills Review

LESSON 5-1 ▶ Rational Exponents and Properties of Exponents

Quick Review

If the nth root of a is a real number and m is an integer, then $a^{\frac{1}{n}} = \sqrt[n]{a}$ and $a^{\frac{m}{n}} = (\sqrt[n]{a})^m$.

Power of a Power: $(a^m)^n = a^{mn}$

Power of a Product: $(a \cdot b)^m = a^m b^m$

Product of Powers: $a^m \cdot a^n = a^{m+n}$

Quotient of Powers: $\frac{a^m}{a^n} = a^{m-n}$, $a \neq 0$

Example

How can you use the Power of a Power Property to solve $64^{x-3} = 16^{2x-1}$?

Rewrite the equation so both expressions have the same base.

$64^{x-3} = 16^{2x-1}$ → $6x - 18 = 8x - 4$
$(2^6)^{x-3} = (2^4)^{2x-1}$ $-18 = 2x - 4$
$2^{6x-18} = 2^{8x-4}$ $-14 = 2x$
        $-7 = x$

The solution is -7.

Practice & Problem Solving

Write each radical using rational exponents.

7. $\sqrt{8}$ 8. $\sqrt[3]{12}$

Solve each equation.

9. $\left(6^{\frac{x}{2}}\right)\left(6^{\frac{x}{3}}\right) = 6^6$ 10. $36^{4x-1} = 6^{x+2}$

11. **Make Sense and Persevere** Describe two ways to express the edge length of a cube with a volume of 64 cm^3.

12. **Model With Mathematics** Use rational exponents to express the relationship between the dollar values of two prizes in a contest.

Prize	Value
Bicycle	$256
Luxury vehicle	$65,536

LESSON 5-2　Exponential Functions

Quick Review

An exponential function is the product of an initial amount and a **constant ratio** raised to a power. Exponential functions are expressed using $f(x) = a \cdot b^x$, where a is a nonzero constant, $b > 0$, and $b \neq 1$.

Example

Find the initial amount and the constant ratio of the exponential function represented by the table.

x	$f(x)$	
0	3	The initial amount is 3.
1	12	$12 \div 3 = 4$
2	48	$48 \div 12 = 4$
3	192	$192 \div 48 = 4$
4	768	$768 \div 192 = 4$

The constant ratio is 4.

In $f(x) = a \cdot b^x$, substitute 3 for a and 4 for b.

The function is $f(x) = 3(4)^x$.

Practice & Problem Solving

Graph each exponential function.

13. $f(x) = 2.5^x$ 14. $f(x) = 5(2)^x$

15. Write the exponential function for this table.

x	0	1	2	3
$f(x)$	0.5	1	2	4

16. **Make Sense and Persevere** Write an equation for an exponential function that models the expected number of bacteria as a function of time. Graph the function. If the pattern continues, in which month will the bacteria exceed 45,000,000?

Month	Number of Bacteria
0	2,500
1	7,500
2	22,500
3	67,500
4	202,500

LESSON 5-3　Exponential Growth and Decay

Quick Review

An **exponential growth function** can be written as $f(x) = a(1 + r)^x$. An exponential decay function can be written as $f(x) = a(1 - r)^x$.

Example

Chapter City has a population of 18,000 and grows at an annual rate of 8%. What is the estimated population of Chapter City in 6 years?

Let $x =$ time in years, $a =$ initial amount, and $r =$ growth rate.

$f(x) = a(1 + r)^x$

$\quad = 18,000(1 + 0.08)^x$

The function is $f(x) = 18,000(1.08)^x$.

Find the expected population in 6 years.

$f(6) = 18,000(1.08)^6 \approx 28,563.74$

After 6 years, the population is expected to be about 28,564.

Practice & Problem Solving

17. **Make Sense and Persevere** An exponential function of the form $f(x) = b^x$ includes the points (2, 36), (3, 216), and (4, 1,296). What is the value of b?

Write an exponential growth or decay function to model each situation.

18. initial value: 50, growth factor: 1.15

19. initial value: 200, decay factor: 0.85

Construct Arguments Compare each investment to an investment of the same principal at the same rate compounded annually.

20. principal: $12,000
    annual interest: 5%
    interest periods: 2
    number of years: 10

21. principal: $20,000
    annual interest: 2.5%
    interest periods: 4
    number of years: 15

Geometric Sequences

Quick Review

A **geometric sequence** is a number sequence in which each term after the first term is found by multiplying the previous term by a common ratio.

Explicit formula: $a_n = a_1(r)^{n-1}$

Recursive formula: $a_n = r(a_{n-1})$

Example

What are the explicit and recursive formulas for the geometric sequence 9, 22.5, 56.25, 140.625, 351.5625, ... ?

$\dfrac{22.5}{9} = \dfrac{56.25}{22.5} = \dfrac{140.625}{56.25}$

$= \dfrac{351.5625}{140.625} = \dfrac{5}{2}$ ⎯⎯⎯ Find the common ratio.

The common ratio is $\dfrac{5}{2}$. The first term is 9.

The explicit formula is $a_n = 9\left(\dfrac{5}{2}\right)^{n-1}$

The recursive formula is $a_n = \dfrac{5}{2}(a_{n-1})$, $a_1 = 9$.

Practice & Problem Solving

Determine if the sequence is a geometric sequence. If it is, write the explicit and recursive formulas.

22. $5, \dfrac{5}{2}, \dfrac{5}{4}, \dfrac{5}{8}, \dfrac{5}{16}, \dots$

23. 2, 5, 8, 11, 14, ...

24. 8, 16, 32, 64, 128, ...

25. $\dfrac{1}{5}, \dfrac{2}{5}, \dfrac{4}{5}, \dfrac{8}{5}, \dfrac{16}{5}, \dots$

Translate each explicit formula to recursive form.

26. $a_n = 2.2(4)^{n-1}$

27. $a_n = 6(3.5)^{n-1}$

28. Write the explicit and recursive formula for a geometric sequence modeled in the table. Will the number of signatures reach 7,000 by the end of the second week? Explain.

Petition to Turn Parking Lot into Park

Day	Number of Signatures
1	40
2	60
3	90
4	135

Transformations of Exponential Functions

Quick Review

The graph of $g(x) = a^x + k$ is the graph of a^x translated up when $k > 0$ and translated down when $k < 0$.

The graph of $g(x) = a^{x-h}$ is the graph of a^x translated right when $h > 0$ and translated left when $h < 0$.

Practice & Problem Solving

Compare the graph of each function to the graph of $f(x) = 3^x$.

29. $g(x) = 3^x - 5$

30. $j(x) = 3^x + 10$

31. $g(x) = 3^{x-2}$

32. $j(x) = 3^{x+3}$

Graph each function and its transformation.

33. $f(x) = 1.5^x$, $g(x) = 1.5^x + k$ for $k = 2$

34. $f(x) = 4^x$, $g(x) = 4^x - k$ for $k = 0.5$

Example

Compare the graphs of $g(x) = 3^x - 2$ and $f(x) = 3^x$.

x	f(x)	g(x)
−2	$\dfrac{1}{9}$	$-\dfrac{17}{9}$
−1	$\dfrac{1}{3}$	$-\dfrac{5}{3}$
0	1	−1
1	3	1
2	9	7

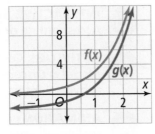

The graph of $g(x)$ is translated 2 units down from the graph of $f(x)$.

Foundations of Geometry

? TOPIC ESSENTIAL QUESTION

What are some of the fundamentals of geometry?

Topic Overview

enVision® STEM Project
Design a Tablet

6-1 Measuring Segments and Angles

6-2 Basic Constructions

6-3 Midpoint and Distance

6-4 Inductive Reasoning

Mathematical Modeling in 3 Acts:
The Mystery Spokes

6-5 Conditional Statements

6-6 Deductive Reasoning

6-7 Writing Proofs

6-8 Indirect Proof

Topic Vocabulary

- angle bisector
- biconditional
- conditional
- conjecture
- construction
- contrapositive
- converse
- counterexample
- deductive reasoning
- inductive reasoning
- inverse
- Law of Detachment
- Law of Syllogism
- negation
- proof
- perpendicular bisector
- postulate
- theorem
- truth table
- truth value

Digital Experience

INTERACTIVE STUDENT EDITION
Access online or offline.

ACTIVITIES Complete *Explore & Reason, Model & Discuss*, and *Critique & Explain* activities. Interact with Examples and Try Its.

ANIMATION View and interact with real-world applications.

PRACTICE Practice what you've learned.

 Go online | SavvasRealize.com

▶ The Mystery Spokes

Some photos are taken in such a way that it is difficult to determine exactly what the picture shows. Sometimes this is because the photo is a close up of an object, and you do not see the entire object. Other times, it might be because the photographer used special effects when taking the photo.

You can often use clues from the photo to determine what is in the photo and also what the rest of the object might look like. What clues would you look for? Think about this during the Mathematical Modeling in 3 Acts lesson.

▶ **VIDEOS** Watch clips to support *Mathematical Modeling in 3 Acts Lessons* and **enVision**® *STEM Projects.*

🔑 **CONCEPT SUMMARY** Review key lesson content through multiple representations.

☑ **ASSESSMENT** Show what you've learned.

A-Z **GLOSSARY** Read and listen to English and Spanish definitions.

🔓 **TUTORIALS** Get help from *Virtual Nerd*, right when you need it.

🔧 **MATH TOOLS** Explore math with digital tools and manipulatives.

▶ Video

Did You Know?

The **golden ratio**, $(1 + \sqrt{5}) : 2$, has been explored in mathematics for over 2400 years. A golden rectangle has sides in the golden ratio.

$$(1 + \sqrt{5}) : 2$$

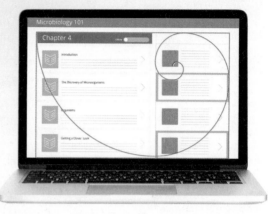

Microbiology 101

Chapter 4

Golden rectangles are used in webpage design to allocate space for content areas.

The main door of the Taj Mahal, in Agra, India, is in the shape of a **golden rectangle**.

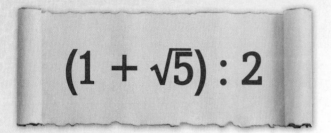

▶ Your Task: Design a Tablet

The tablet market is growing quickly. Each quarter, more than 38 million tablets are shipped around the world. By 2019, yearly shipping is expected to surpass 189 million. In this project, you'll design a new tablet using the golden ratio.

Go Online | SavvasRealize.com

6-1

Measuring Segments and Angles

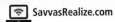
SavvasRealize.com

I CAN... use properties of segments and angles to find their measures.

VOCABULARY

- collinear points
- line
- plane
- point
- postulate

 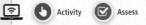
EXPLORE & REASON

A teacher labels two points on the number line.

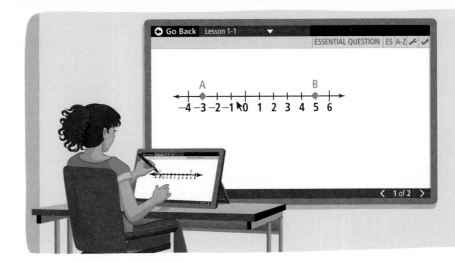

A. What are some methods for finding the distance between points *A* and *B*?

B. **Construct Arguments** Which method of finding the distance is the best? Explain.

ESSENTIAL QUESTION   How are the properties of segments and angles used to determine their measures?

CONCEPT Undefined Terms

Undefined terms are terms whose meanings are accepted without formal definition. The terms point, line, and plane are undefined terms that are the basic building blocks of geometry.

Description	Diagram	Notation
A **point** is a location and has no size.	•*P*	*P*
A **line** is an infinite number of points on a straight path that extends in two opposite directions with no end and has no thickness.	•*A* •*B* ℓ	line ℓ $\overleftrightarrow{AB}$
A **plane** is an infinite number of points and lines on a flat surface that extends without end and has no thickness.	•*X* *Ẏ* *Ż* *M*	plane *M* plane *XYZ*

CONCEPT Defined Terms

In geometry, new terms are defined using previously defined or known terms.

Description	Diagram	Notation
A segment is the part of a line that consists of two points, called *endpoints* and all points between them.	A ●———————● B	$\overline{AB}$
A ray is the part of a line that consists of one *endpoint* and all the points of the line on one side of the endpoint.	M ●———————●——→ N	$\overrightarrow{MN}$
Opposite rays are rays with the same endpoint that lie on the same line.	←——●——●——●——→ S T U	$\overrightarrow{TS}$ and $\overrightarrow{TU}$
An angle is formed by two rays with the same endpoint. Each ray is a side of the angle and the common endpoint is the vertex of the angle.	R ... 2 ... Q ... P	$\angle Q$ $\angle PQR$ $\angle 2$

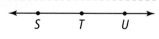 **EXAMPLE 1** Find Segment Lengths

How can you find the length of $\overline{CD}$?

The length of a segment is a positive real number. You can use the number line to find the length of $\overline{CD}$.

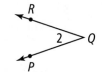

> The notation *CD* represents the length of $\overline{CD}$.

There are 3 units between *C* and *D*, so $CD = 3$.

To find the length of a segment, count the units of length between the endpoints. The length of $\overline{CD}$ is 3.

COMMUNICATE PRECISELY
Think about how notation and symbols are used. How might the notation for a segment and for the length of a segment help you remember their meaning?

☑ **Try It!** 1. Refer to the figure in Example 1. How can you find the length of $\overline{AC}$?

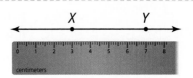

POSTULATE 6-1 Ruler Postulate

Every point on a line can be paired with a unique real number. This number is called the *coordinate* of the point.

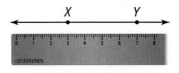

The coordinate of *X* is 3.
The coordinate of *Y* is 7.

CONCEPT Distance on a Line

The distance between any two points *X* and *Y* is the absolute value of the difference of their coordinates.

$$XY = |7 - 3| = 4$$
$$XY = |3 - 7| = 4$$

CONCEPTUAL
UNDERSTANDING

 EXAMPLE 2   Find the Length of a Segment

What is *KL*?   A **postulate** is a statement that is assumed to be true.

Use the Ruler Postulate to find the coordinates of *K* and *L*.

STUDY TIP
Remember, when finding distance between two points, take the absolute value of the difference because distance is positive.

$$KL = |16 - 12| = 4 \quad \text{or} \quad KL = |12 - 16| = 4$$

✓ **Try It!**   **2.** Refer to the figure in Example 2.

   a. What is *JK*?   **b.** What is *KM*?

POSTULATE 6-2 Segment Addition Postulate

If points *A*, *B*, and *C* are on the same line with *B* between *A* and *C*, then *AB* + *BC* = *AC*.

If...

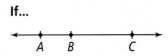

Then... *AB* + *BC* = *AC*

EXAMPLE 3 Use the Segment Addition Postulate

Points *F*, *G*, and *H* are collinear. **Collinear points** lie on the same line.
If *GH* = 16, what is *FH*?

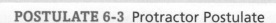

F   G   H

3x − 1   2x + 2

Step 1 Use the expression for *GH* to find *x*.

$$GH = 16$$
$$2x + 2 = 16$$
$$2x = 14$$
$$x = 7$$

Step 2 Find *FH*.

$$FH = FG + GH$$
$$= 5x + 1$$
$$= 5(7) + 1$$
$$= 36$$

Apply the Segment Addition Postulate.

COMMON ERROR
Be sure to answer the question that is posed. You may state the value of the variable *x* as the answer, but you use this answer to find *FH*.

✓ **Try It!** **3.** Points *J*, *K*, and *L* are collinear.

J   K   L

3n   5n − 7

a. If *JL* = 25, what is *n*?   **b.** What is *JK*? *KL*?

POSTULATE 6-3 Protractor Postulate

Given $\overrightarrow{BA}$ and a point *C* not on $\overrightarrow{BA}$, a unique real number from 0 to 180 can be assigned to $\overrightarrow{BC}$.

0 is assigned to $\overrightarrow{BA}$.
180 is assigned to $\overrightarrow{BD}$.

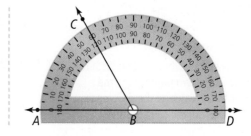

 EXAMPLE 4 Use the Protractor Postulate to Measure an Angle

STUDY TIP
Remember, the measure of ∠*BEC* is denoted as *m*∠*BEC*.

What is *m*∠*BEC*?

Since $\overrightarrow{EA}$ lines up with 0 on the top scale, use the top scale for all of the other rays in the figure.

By the Protractor Postulate, real numbers are assigned to $\overrightarrow{EB}$ and $\overrightarrow{EC}$.

47 is assigned to $\overrightarrow{EB}$.   105 is assigned to $\overrightarrow{EC}$.

You can subtract *m*∠*AEB* from *m*∠*AEC* to find *m*∠*BEC*.

$$m∠BEC = |105 − 47| = 58$$

CONTINUED ON THE NEXT PAGE

EXAMPLE 4 CONTINUED

 Try It! **4.** Refer to the figure in Example 4.

      a. What is $m\angle AEC$?   **b.** What is $m\angle BED$?

POSTULATE 6-4 Angle Addition Postulate

If point D is in the interior of $\angle ABC$, then $m\angle ABD + m\angle DBC = m\angle ABC$.

If...

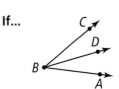

Then... $m\angle ABD + m\angle DBC = m\angle ABC$

APPLICATION

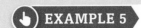 **EXAMPLE 5**   **Use the Angle Addition Postulate to Solve Problems**

A lighting designer is finalizing the lighting plan for an upcoming production. The spotlight can rotate 25° to the left or right from the shown starting position. The beam of light from the spotlight forms a 22° angle. Can the designer use the spotlight to light each of the objects on the stage?

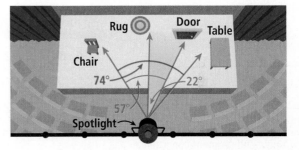

Formulate ◀   Draw and label a diagram to represent the beam angle, the angles given and the unknown angles.

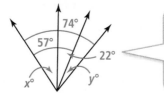

> Use the Angle Addition Postulate to find the angles the light must rotate to the left and right to light the chair and table.

Compute ◀   Write and solve equations to find x and y.

     $x + 22 = 57$ $y + 57 = 74$
         $x = 35$ $y = 17$

Interpret ◀   The spotlight can rotate 25° to the right or left, so the designer can use the spotlight to light the table but cannot light the chair.

 Try It! **5.** Refer to Example 5. Can the lighting designer use a spotlight with a 33° beam angle that can rotate 25° to the left and right to light all of the objects on the stage?

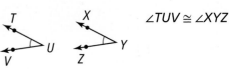

CONCEPT Congruent Segments and Congruent Angles

Segments that have the same length are congruent segments.

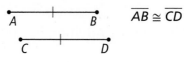

$\overline{AB} \cong \overline{CD}$

$\overline{PQ} \cong \overline{RS}$

The same number of *tick marks* shows congruent segments.

Angles that have the same measure are congruent angles.

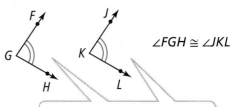

$\angle TUV \cong \angle XYZ$

$\angle FGH \cong \angle JKL$

The same number of *arc marks* shows congruent angles.

 EXAMPLE 6 Use Congruent Angles and Congruent Segments

A. If $m\angle XWZ = 127$, what is $m\angle YWV$?

$m\angle XWY + m\angle YWV + m\angle VWZ = m\angle XWZ$

$32 + m\angle YWZ + 32 = 127$

$m\angle YWV = 63$

Apply the Angle Addition Postulate.

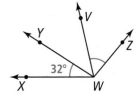

B. What is *HF*?

Apply the Segment Addition Postulate and substitute congruent segment lengths.

$HF = HG + GF$

$HF = AH + BC$

$HF = 11 + 8 = 19$ cm

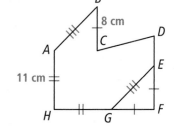

Try It! **6. a.** If $m\angle NOP = 31$ and $m\angle NOQ = 114$, what is $m\angle ROQ$?

b. In the figure in Part B above, suppose $CD = 11.5$ cm, $DE = 5.3$ cm, and the perimeter of the figure is 73.8 cm. What is *GE*?

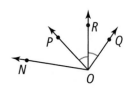

CONCEPT SUMMARY Measuring Segments and Angles

Ruler Postulate	Protractor Postulate
WORDS Every point on a line can be paired with a unique real number. This number is called the *coordinate* of the point.	Given $\overrightarrow{KL}$ and a point J not on $\overrightarrow{KL}$, a unique real number from 0 to 180 can be paired with $\overrightarrow{KJ}$.

DIAGRAM

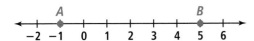

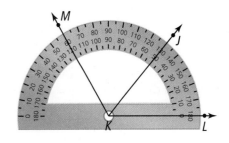

SYMBOLS

$JK = 5$ $KL = 4$ $JL = 9$

$JK + KL = JL$

$m\angle JKL = 50$ $m\angle JKM = 70$

$m\angle JKL + m\angle JKM = 120$

☑ Do You UNDERSTAND?

1. **ESSENTIAL QUESTION** How are the properties of segments and angles used to determine their measures?

2. **Error Analysis** Ella wrote $AB = |-1 + 5| = 4$. Explain Ella's error.

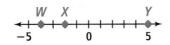

3. **Vocabulary** What does it mean for segments to be congruent? What does it mean for angles to be congruent?

4. **Make Sense and Persevere** Suppose M is a point in the interior of $\angle JKL$. If $m\angle MKL = 42$ and $m\angle JKL = 84$, what is $m\angle JKM$?

Do You KNOW HOW?

Find the length of each segment.

```
W  X              Y
+-+--+--+-+-+-+-+-+-+-+
  -5        0        5
```

5. $\overline{WX}$ 6. $\overline{WY}$

7. Points A, B, and C are collinear and B is between A and C. Given $AB = 12$ and $AC = 19$, what is BC?

8. Given $m\angle JML = 80$ and $m\angle KML = 33$, what is $m\angle JMK$?

UNDERSTAND

9. **Reason** The coordinate of point *M* on a number line is 11. If *MN* = 12, what are the possible coordinates for *N* on the number line?

10. **Construct Arguments** How can you use the Segment Addition Postulate to show that *AE* = *AB* + *BC* + *CD* + *DE*?

11. **Higher Order Thinking** If points *C*, *D*, and *E* are on a line and *CD* = 20 and *CE* = 32, what are the possible values of *DE*?

12. **Error Analysis** Benito wrote the equations shown about the figure. Explain Benito's errors.

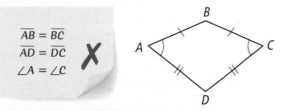

$$\overline{AB} = \overline{BC}$$
$$\overline{AD} = \overline{DC}$$
$$\angle A = \angle C$$

13. **Make Sense and Persevere** Point *Y* is in the interior of ∠*XWZ*. Given that $\overrightarrow{WX}$ and $\overrightarrow{WZ}$ are opposite rays, and *m*∠*XWY* = 4(*m*∠*YWZ*), what is *m*∠*YWZ*?

14. **Mathematical Connections** The area of *ABED* is 49 square units. Given *AG* = 9 units and *AC* = 10 units, what fraction of the area of *ACIG* is represented by the shaded region? Give your answer in simplest form.

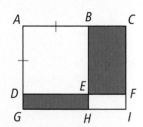
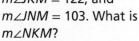

15. **Look for Relationships** In the diagram at the right, *m*∠*LMN* = 116, *m*∠*JKM* = 122, and *m*∠*JNM* = 103. What is *m*∠*NKM*?

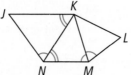

PRACTICE

Find the length of each segment. SEE EXAMPLES 1 AND 2

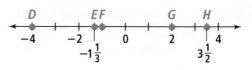

16. $\overline{DF}$ 17. $\overline{DE}$ 18. $\overline{FG}$

19. $\overline{FH}$ 20. $\overline{GH}$ 21. $\overline{EH}$

Points *A*, *B*, *C*, *D*, and *E* are collinear. SEE EXAMPLE 3

A	B	C	D	E
x + 7	2*x*	3*x* − 1	2*x* + 3	

22. If *AC* = 16, what is *x*?

23. What is *AB*?

24. What is *BD*?

25. What is *CE*?

Use the figure shown for Exercises 26–28.
SEE EXAMPLES 4 AND 5

26. If *m*∠*POQ* = 24 and *m*∠*POR* = 59, what is *m*∠*QOR*?

27. If *m*∠*POQ* = 19, *m*∠*QOR* = 31, and *m*∠*ROS* = 15, what is *m*∠*POS*?

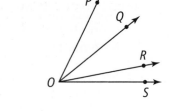

28. If *m*∠*QOS* = 46, *m*∠*POR* = 61, and *m*∠*POQ* = 28, what is *m*∠*ROS*?

Suppose *EG* = 3, *EB* = 8, *AF* = 7, *m*∠*EBG* = 19, *m*∠*EGF* = 28, and *m*∠*CAE* = 51. Find each value.
SEE EXAMPLE 6

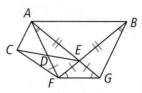

29. *EF*   30. *AG*   31. *AD*

32. *m*∠*EFG*   33. *m*∠*CAF*   34. *DF*

35. Points *P*, *Q*, *R*, and *S* are collinear. Point *Q* is between *P* and *R*, *R* is between *Q* and *S*, and $\overline{PQ} \cong \overline{RS}$. If *PS* = 18 and *PR* = 15, what is the value of *QR*?

PRACTICE & PROBLEM SOLVING

  Practice Tutorial

Mixed Review Available Online

APPLY

36. Make Sense and Persevere Dave is driving to Gilmore to visit his friend. If he wants to stop for lunch when he is about halfway there, in which town should he plan to stop? Explain.

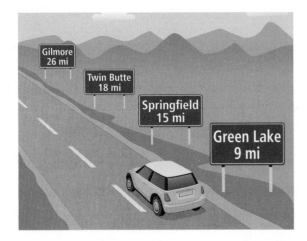

37. Reason A city planning commission must determine whether to approve the construction of a new building. The company wants to build in an area of the city that has a height limitation of 310 feet. The plans show that the first floor of the building is 20 ft high and each of the next 15 floors have a height of 11 ft, including the space between each floor needed for electrical, plumbing, and other systems. If the plan meets all other city code requirements, should the city commission approve the building plan? Explain.

38. Reason The city planning committee wants one tree planted every 20 ft along Dayton Avenue. If the perimeter of the plot of land is 234 ft, about how many trees will be planted? Explain.

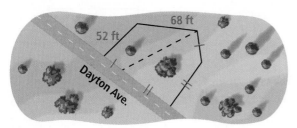

ASSESSMENT PRACTICE

39. In the diagram, $FH = 2FG$, $GH = HI$, and $FI = IK$. Which of the following statements must be true? Select all that apply.

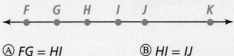

Ⓐ $FG = HI$ Ⓑ $HI = IJ$

Ⓒ $IK = 3FG$ Ⓓ $FH = GI$

Ⓔ $HJ = JK$ Ⓕ $HK = 2GI$

40. SAT/ACT Point C is in the interior of $\angle ABD$, and $\angle ABC \cong \angle CBD$. If $m\angle ABC = \left(\frac{5}{2}x + 18\right)$ and $m\angle CBD = (4x)$, what is $m\angle ABD$?

Ⓐ 12   Ⓑ 36   Ⓒ 48   Ⓓ 72   Ⓔ 96

41. Performance Task The American Institute of Architects is located in a historical building called "The Octagon" in Washington, DC. Octagonal houses became popular in the United States in the mid-1800s.

Part A Design your own plan for one floor of an octagonal-shaped house. Your plan should include at least four rooms, two walls of equal length, and two angles with equal measure. Draw your floor plan using the scale 1 cm = 1 m. Write the measures of the angles and lengths of the walls on your plan, and use appropriate marks to show congruent angles and segments. Label all the points in your diagram where the walls intersect.

Part B Write equations that show congruent angles and segments in your plan.

6-2

Basic Constructions

SavvasRealize.com

I CAN... use a straightedge and compass to construct basic figures.

VOCABULARY
- angle bisector
- construction
- perpendicular bisector

EXPLORE & REASON

Using a compass, make a design using only circles like the one shown.

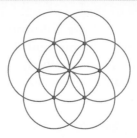

A. What instructions can you give to another student so they can make a copy of your design?

B. Make Sense and Persevere Use a ruler to draw straight line segments to connect points where the circles intersect. Are any of the segments that you drew the same length? If so, why do you think they are?

? ESSENTIAL QUESTION   How are a straightedge and compass used to make basic constructions?

CONCEPTUAL UNDERSTANDING

EXAMPLE 1   Copy a Segment

How can you copy a segment using only a straightedge and compass?

A straightedge is a tool for drawing straight lines. A compass is a tool for drawing arcs and circles of different sizes and can be used to copy lengths.

Step 1   To copy $\overline{AB}$, first use a straightedge to draw line ℓ. Mark point M on line ℓ.

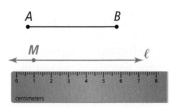

STUDY TIP
Remember, with constructions, only use a ruler as a straightedge, not as a measuring tool.

Step 2   Place the compass point at A, and open the compass to length AB.

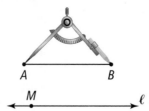

Step 3   Using the same setting, place the compass point at M, and draw an arc through line ℓ. Mark point N at the intersection.

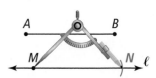

The constructed segment MN is a copy of $\overline{AB}$. A copy of a line segment is a type of *construction*. A **construction** is a geometric figure made with only a straightedge and compass.

 Try It!   **1.** How can you construct a copy of $\overline{XY}$?

X ———————————————————— Y

 **EXAMPLE 2** **Copy an Angle**

How can you construct a copy of ∠A?

Step 1 Mark a point X. Use a straightedge to draw a ray with endpoint X.

Step 2 Place the compass point at A. Draw an arc that intersects both rays of ∠A. Label the points of intersection B and C.

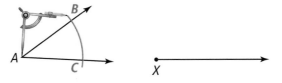

Step 3 Without changing the setting, place the compass point at X and draw an arc intersecting the ray. Mark the point Y at the intersection.

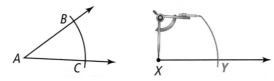

Step 4 Place the compass point at C, and open the compass to the distance between B and C.

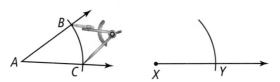

Step 5 Without changing the setting, place the compass point at Y and draw an arc. Label the point Z where the two arcs intersect. Use a straightedge to draw $\overrightarrow{XZ}$.

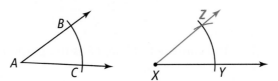

The constructed angle, ∠YXZ, is a copy of ∠A.

STUDY TIP
You can use a protractor to confirm that the two angles are congruent.

 Try It! **2.** How can you construct a copy of ∠B?

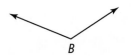

EXAMPLE 3   Construct a Perpendicular Bisector

How can you construct the perpendicular bisector of $\overline{AB}$?

A **perpendicular bisector** of a segment is a line, segment, or ray that is perpendicular to the segment and divides the segment into two congruent segments.

You can use a straightedge and compass to construct the perpendicular bisector of a segment.

Step 1 With a setting greater than $\frac{1}{2}AB$, place the compass point at A. Draw arcs above and below $\overline{AB}$.

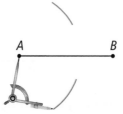

Step 2 With the same setting, place the compass point at B. Draw arcs above and below $\overline{AB}$.

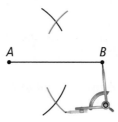

Step 3 Label the points of intersection of the arcs E and F. Use a straightedge to draw $\overleftrightarrow{EF}$.

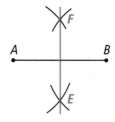

The constructed line, $\overleftrightarrow{EF}$, is the perpendicular bisector of $\overline{AB}$.

USE APPROPRIATE TOOLS
Consider the tools you can use to verify that a segment bisects another segment. What tool can you use?

Try It!   **3.** How can you construct the perpendicular bisector of $\overline{JK}$?

Activity   Assess

EXAMPLE 4 **Construct an Angle Bisector**

How can you construct the *angle bisector* of ∠A?

An **angle bisector** is a ray that divides an angle into two congruent angles. You can use a straightedge and compass to construct an angle bisector.

Step 1 Place the compass point at *A*. Draw an arc intersecting both rays of ∠A. Label the points of intersection *B* and *C*.

Step 2 Place the compass point at *B*. Draw an arc in the interior of ∠A. With the same setting, place the compass point at *C* and draw an arc intersecting the arc drawn from *B*.

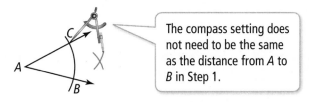

The compass setting does not need to be the same as the distance from *A* to *B* in Step 1.

COMMON ERROR
Be sure to set the compass greater than $\frac{1}{2}$ the distance from *A* to *C*.

Step 3 Label the point of intersection of the two arcs *D*. Use a straightedge to draw $\overrightarrow{AD}$.

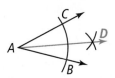

The constructed ray, $\overrightarrow{AD}$, is the bisector of ∠A.

Try It! **4.** How can you construct the angle bisector of ∠G?

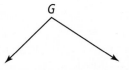

APPLICATION  **EXAMPLE 5**   **Use Constructions**

An artist wants to center-align a new sculpture with the bay window in the museum lobby. He also wants to center-align it with the entrance. Where should the sculpture be placed?

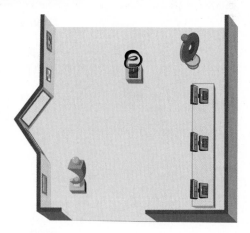

Formulate ◀ If the sculpture is center-aligned with the bay window, it lies on the angle bisector of the bay window. If it is center-aligned with the entrance, it lies on the perpendicular bisector of the entrance.

Compute ◀ Construct the angle bisector of the bay window and the perpendicular bisector of the entrance.

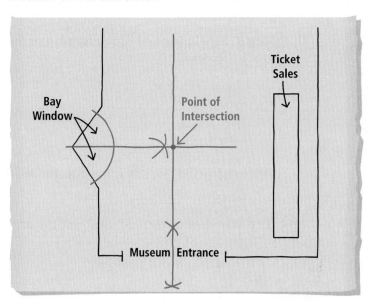

Interpret ◀ The center of the sculpture should be placed at the point of intersection of the angle bisector of the bay window and the perpendicular bisector of the museum entrance.

✓ **Try It!** 5. Where should the sculpture be placed if it is to be center-aligned with the museum entrance and the center of the ticket sales desk?

CONCEPT SUMMARY Constructions

WORDS A **construction** is a geometric figure that can be made using only a straightedge and compass.

Straightedge
- is used to draw segments, lines and rays.

Compass
- is used to draw circles and arcs.
- is used to measure and copy length.

DIAGRAMS Construction of an Angle Bisector

Step 1

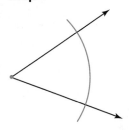

Step 2

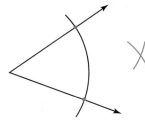

Step 3

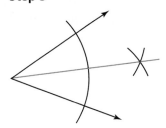

Use a compass to make arcs.   Use a straightedge to draw the bisector.

Do You UNDERSTAND?

1. **ESSENTIAL QUESTION** How are a straightedge and compass used to make basic constructions?

2. **Error Analysis** Chris tries to copy ∠T but is unable to make an exact copy. Explain Chris's error.

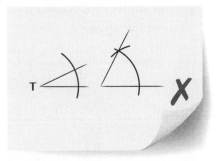

3. **Vocabulary** What is the difference between a line that is perpendicular to a segment and the perpendicular bisector of a segment?

4. **Look for Relationships** Darren is copying △ABC. First, he constructs $\overline{DE}$ as a copy of $\overline{AB}$. Next, he constructs ∠D as a copy of ∠A, using $\overline{DE}$ as one of the sides. Explain what he needs to do to complete the copy of the triangle.

Do You KNOW HOW?

Construct a copy of each segment, and then construct its perpendicular bisector.

5.

6.

Construct a copy of each angle, and then construct its bisector.

7.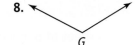

8.

9. A new sidewalk is perpendicular to and bisecting the existing sidewalk. At the point where new sidewalk meets the fence around the farmer's market, a gate is needed. At about what point should the gate be placed?

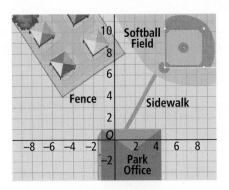

UNDERSTAND

PRACTICE

10. **Use Appropriate Tools** How could you use a compass to determine if two segments are the same length?

11. **Higher Order Thinking** You can divide a segment into *n* congruent segments by bisecting segments repeatedly. What are some of the possible values of *n*? Give a rule for *n*.

12. **Make Sense and Persevere** In the figure shown, suppose m∠ABC = *n* and m∠ABD = 2(m∠DBC). The angle bisector of ∠DBC is $\overrightarrow{BE}$. What is m∠EBC?

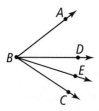

13. **Make Sense and Persevere** There are other methods for making constructions, such as paper folding. Follow the steps to use paper folding to construct the perpendicular bisector of a segment.

- On a sheet of paper, draw $\overline{FG}$.
- Fold the paper so that *F* is on top of *G*.
- Crease the paper along the fold.
- Unfold the paper. The crease line represents the perpendicular bisector.

Why must *F* and *G* be aligned when you fold the paper?

14. **Error Analysis** Adam is asked to construct the bisector of ∠R. Explain the error in Adam's work.

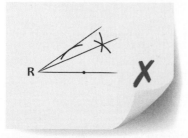

Copy the segments. SEE EXAMPLE 1

15.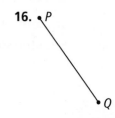

16.

Copy the angles. SEE EXAMPLE 2

17.

18.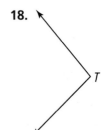

Copy and bisect the segments.
SEE EXAMPLE 3

19. A

20. V

Copy and bisect the angles. SEE EXAMPLE 4

21.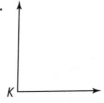

22.

23. Where is the intersection of the perpendicular bisector of $\overline{GF}$ and the angle bisector of ∠E?
SEE EXAMPLE 5

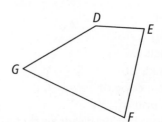

PRACTICE & PROBLEM SOLVING

APPLY

24. Communicate Precisely The quilt block is designed from a square using only perpendicular bisectors and angle bisectors. Write instructions for constructing the pattern in square *ABCD*. You may find it helpful to name some additional points.

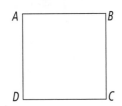

25. Mathematical Connections A school gym is divided for a fair by bisecting its width and its length. Each half of the length is then bisected, forming 8 sections in all. What are the dimensions and area of each section?

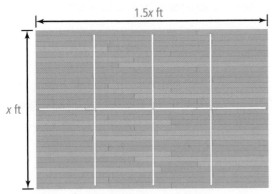

1.5*x* ft

x ft

Perimeter = 300 ft

26. Model With Mathematics A sixth wind turbine will be placed near the intersections of the bisector of ∠*BCD* and the perpendicular bisectors of $\overline{AE}$ and $\overline{ED}$. What is a possible location for the sixth turbine?

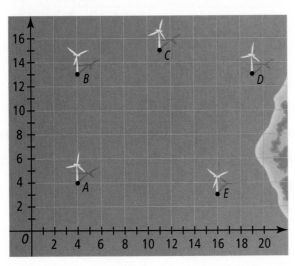

ASSESSMENT PRACTICE

27. The angle bisector of ∠*NPM* is $\overrightarrow{PQ}$. Write an equation to describe the relationship between *m*∠*NPM* and *m*∠*QPM*

28. SAT/ACT A perpendicular bisector of $\overline{DC}$ is $\overleftrightarrow{AB}$, and a perpendicular bisector of $\overline{AB}$ is $\overline{DC}$. The intersection of $\overline{AB}$ and $\overline{DC}$ is at *E*. Which equation is true?

Ⓐ *AB* = *CD*

Ⓑ *CE* = *CD*

Ⓒ *DE* = *CE*

Ⓓ *AE* = *DE*

Ⓔ *EB* = *CD*

29. Performance Task Reducing or enlarging images can be useful when you need a smaller or larger version of a picture or graph for a report or poster.

Part A Use a compass and straightedge to draw a polygon with at least 3 sides.

Part B Make a reduced version of your figure with sides that are half the length of the original figure. First, select one of the sides, bisect it, and then copy one of the halves. Next, copy one of the angles that is adjacent. Repeat until you have a reduced version of your figure.

Part C Think about how you can double the length of the line segment. Make an enlarged version of your figure with sides that are twice the length of the original figure. Describe how you made the enlarged figure.

6-3

Midpoint and Distance

I CAN... use the midpoint and distance formulas to solve problems.

VOCABULARY
• midpoint

👆 **MODEL & DISCUSS**

LaTanya is decorating her living room and draws a floorplan to help look at placement.

A. LaTanya wants to hang a picture at the center of the back wall. How do you find the point at the center between A and B?

B. Communicate Precisely LaTanya wants to place a lamp halfway between the chairs at points C and D. How can you find the point where the lamp should go?

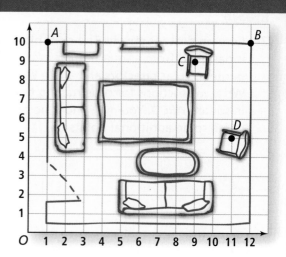

❓ **ESSENTIAL QUESTION** How are the midpoint and length of a segment on the coordinate plane determined?

CONCEPT Midpoint Formula

A **midpoint** of a segment is the point that divides the segment into two congruent segments. The midpoint of $\overline{PQ}$ with $P(x_1, y_1)$ and $Q(x_2, y_2)$, is:

$$M = \left(\frac{x_1 + x_2}{2}, \frac{y_1 + y_2}{2}\right)$$

👆 **EXAMPLE 1** Find a Midpoint

What is the midpoint of $\overline{AB}$?

Substitute the coordinates of the endpoints of $\overline{AB}$ into the Midpoint Formula.

$$M = \left(\frac{-3 + 4}{2}, \frac{2 + (-2)}{2}\right)$$

$$= \left(\frac{1}{2}, 0\right)$$

The midpoint of $\overline{AB}$ is $\left(\frac{1}{2}, 0\right)$.

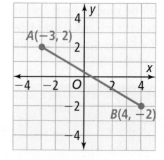

COMMON ERROR
Finding the midpoint is like finding the average of the x-coordinates and the y-coordinates, so be sure to add the coordinates before dividing by 2.

✓ **Try It!** **1.** Find the midpoint for each segment with the given endpoints.

    a. $C(-2, 5)$ and $D(8, -12)$ **b.** $E(2.5, -7)$ and $F(-6.2, -3.8)$

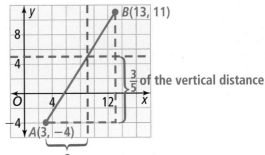

EXAMPLE 2 **Partition a Segment**

LOOK FOR RELATIONSHIPS
Think about how number lines are related to the x- and y-axes. How can you relate partitioning on a number line to partitioning on a coordinate plane?

What are the coordinates of the point $\frac{3}{5}$ of the way from A to B?

Step 1 Find $\frac{3}{5}$ of the horizontal and vertical distances from A to B.

$\frac{3}{5}$ of the vertical distance

Horizontal distance:
$\frac{3}{5}|13 - 3| = \frac{3}{5}(10) = 6$

Vertical distance:
$\frac{3}{5}|11 - (-4)| = \frac{3}{5}(15) = 9$

$\frac{3}{5}$ of the horizontal distance

Step 2 Add the horizontal distance to the x-coordinate and the vertical distance to the y-coordinate of point $A(3, -4)$.

$$(3 + 6, -4 + 9) = (9, 5)$$

The coordinates of the point $\frac{3}{5}$ of the way from A to B are $(9, 5)$.

Try It! 2. Find the coordinates of each point described.

a. $\frac{7}{10}$ of the way from A to B. **b.** $\frac{4}{5}$ of the way from B to A.

CONCEPTUAL UNDERSTANDING

EXAMPLE 3 **Derive the Distance Formula**

How can you find the distance between $P(x_1, y_1)$ and $Q(x_2, y_2)$ on the coordinate plane?

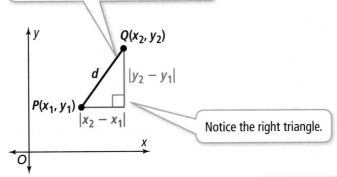

The distance d relies on the horizontal and vertical change from P to Q.

Notice the right triangle.

STUDY TIP
Recall that the square of any quantity is always nonnegative, so absolute value bars are not needed when an expression is squared.

$d^2 = |x_2 - x_1|^2 + |y_2 - y_1|^2$
Apply the Pythagorean Theorem, $c^2 = a^2 + b^2$.

$d = \sqrt{|x_2 - x_1|^2 + |y_2 - y_1|^2}$

The length of $\overline{PQ}$ is the distance between points P and Q,
$d = \sqrt{(x_2 - x_1)^2 + (y_2 - y_1)^2}$.

CONTINUED ON THE NEXT PAGE

EXAMPLE 3 CONTINUED

 Try It! **3.** Tavon claims that $d = \sqrt{(x_1 - x_2)^2 + (y_1 - y_2)^2}$ can also be used to find distance between two points. Is he correct? Explain.

CONCEPT Distance Formula

The distance d between two points $P(x_1, y_1)$ and $Q(x_2, y_2)$ is:

$$d(P, Q) = \sqrt{(x_2 - x_1)^2 + (y_2 - y_1)^2}$$

APPLICATION **EXAMPLE 4** **Find the Distance**

A pitcher throws a ball to a batter, who hits the ball to the shortstop. If the ball travels in a straight line between each, what is the total distance traveled by the ball? Round your answer to the nearest tenth of a foot.

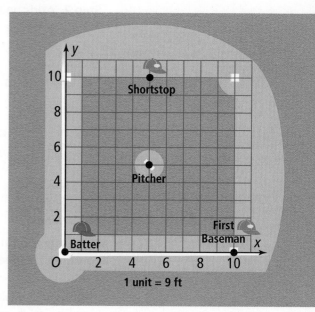

Formulate ◄ Represent the pitcher at point $P(5, 5)$, the batter at point $B(0, 0)$, and the shortstop at point $S(5, 10)$.

Compute ◄ Use the Distance Formula to find each distance.

$d \text{ (pitcher to batter)} = \sqrt{(0 - 5)^2 + (0 - 5)^2}$

Use the Distance Formula with $P(5, 5)$ and $B(0, 0)$.

$= \sqrt{(-5)^2 + (-5)^2}$

$= \sqrt{25 + 25}$

$= \sqrt{50}$

≈ 7.1

$d \text{ (batter to shortstop)} = \sqrt{(5 - 0)^2 + (10 - 0)^2}$

Use the Distance Formula with $B(0, 0)$ and $S(5, 10)$.

$= \sqrt{5^2 + 10^2}$

$= \sqrt{25 + 100}$

$= \sqrt{125}$

≈ 11.2

Interpret ◄ The total distance the ball traveled is about $7.1 + 11.2 = 18.3$ units, or about $(18.3)(9) = 164.7$ ft.

 Try It! **4.** How far does the shortstop need to throw the ball to reach the first baseman? Round your answer to the nearest tenth of a foot.

CONCEPT SUMMARY Midpoint and Distance on the Coordinate Plane

MIDPOINT

$$M = \left(\frac{x_1 + x_2}{2}, \frac{y_1 + y_2}{2}\right)$$

DISTANCE

$$d = \sqrt{(x_2 - x_1)^2 + (y_2 - y_1)^2}$$

EXAMPLE

The endpoints of $\overline{PQ}$ are $P(-3, 4)$ and $Q(1, 7)$.

$$M = \left(\frac{-3 + 1}{2}, \frac{4 + 7}{2}\right)$$

$$= \left(-1, \frac{11}{2}\right)$$

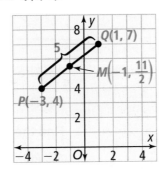

$$d = \sqrt{(-3 - 1)^2 + (4 - 7)^2}$$

$$= \sqrt{(-4)^2 + (-3)^2}$$

$$= \sqrt{25}$$

$$= 5$$

Do You UNDERSTAND?

1. **ESSENTIAL QUESTION** How are the midpoint and length of a segment on the coordinate plane determined?

2. **Error Analysis** Corey calculated the midpoint of $\overline{AB}$ with $A(-3, 5)$ and $B(1, 7)$. What is Corey's error?

$$M\left(\frac{-3 + 5}{2}, \frac{1 + 7}{2}\right)$$

$$M(1, 4) \quad \bigtimes$$

3. **Vocabulary** If M is the midpoint of $\overline{PQ}$, what is the relationship between PM and MQ? Between PM and PQ?

4. **Reason** Is it possible for $\overline{PQ}$ to have two distinct midpoints, $M_1(a, b)$ and $M_2(c, d)$? Explain.

Do You KNOW HOW?

$\overline{PQ}$ has endpoints at $P(-5, 4)$ and $Q(7, -5)$.

5. What is the midpoint of $\overline{PQ}$?

6. What are the coordinates of the point $\frac{2}{3}$ of the way from P to Q?

7. What is the length of $\overline{PQ}$?

8. A chair lift at a ski resort travels along the cable as shown.

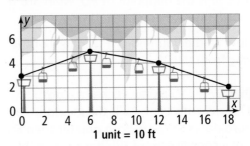

1 unit = 10 ft

How long is the cable? Round your answer to the nearest whole foot.

UNDERSTAND

9. Use Structure Point K is $\frac{1}{n}$ of the way from $J(4, -5)$ to $L(0, -7)$.

   a. What are the coordinates of K if $n = 4$?

   b. What is a formula for the coordinates of K for any n?

10. Error Analysis Describe and correct the error a student made in finding the midpoint of $\overline{CD}$ with $C(-4, 5)$ and $D(-1, -4)$.

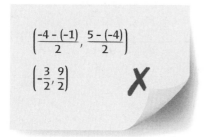

$$\left(\frac{-4-(-1)}{2}, \frac{5-(-4)}{2}\right)$$

$$\left(-\frac{3}{2}, \frac{9}{2}\right) \quad ✗$$

11. Mathematical Connections Point M is the midpoint of $\overline{FG}$. Can you determine the value of a? Explain.

$G(2a, 3b + 3)$

$M(3, 5)$

$F(b + 1, a + 2)$

12. Reason Suppose $\overline{PQ}$ has one endpoint at $P(0, 0)$.

   a. If $(2, 5)$ is the midpoint of $\overline{PQ}$, what are the coordinates of point Q?

   b. How would you find Q if $(2, 5)$ is $\frac{1}{4}$ of the way from P to Q?

13. Higher Order Thinking $\overline{PQ}$ has a length of 17 units with $P(-4, 7)$. If the x- and y-coordinates of Q are both greater than the x- and y-coordinates of P, what are possible integer value coordinates of Q? Explain.

14. Make Sense and Persevere Suppose $\overline{PQ}$ has $P(a, b)$ and midpoint $M(c, d)$. What is an expression for PM? Use the expression for PM to find an expression for PQ.

PRACTICE

Find the coordinates of each given point on $\overline{AB}$.
SEE EXAMPLE 2

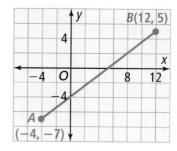

15. The point $\frac{3}{10}$ of the way from A to B.

16. The point $\frac{1}{4}$ of the way from B to A.

Find the midpoint of $\overline{PQ}$. SEE EXAMPLE 1

17. $P(3, 5)$, $Q(-2, 13)$

18. $P(-2, 2.5)$, $Q(1.4, 4)$

19. $P\left(4\frac{1}{3}, 3\frac{1}{6}\right)$, $Q\left(-2\frac{1}{5}, 3\frac{2}{3}\right)$

Cameron, Arthur, and Jamie are playing soccer. Their locations are recorded by a motion tracking system. The distance between grids is 5 meters.
SEE EXAMPLES 3 AND 4

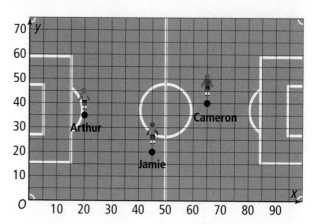

20. How far apart are Arthur and Jamie? Round to the nearest tenth of a meter.

21. Who is closer to Cameron? Explain.

22. The soccer ball is located at the point $(35, 60)$. Who is closest to the soccer ball?

Practice | Tutorial

Mixed Review Available Online

23. Model With Mathematics A university is building a new student center that is two-thirds the distance from the arts center to the residential complex. What are the coordinates of the new center? Explain.

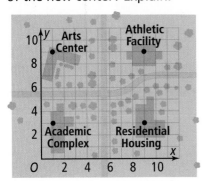

24. Mathematical Connections A lighthouse casts a revolving beam of light as far as the pier. What is the area that the light covers?

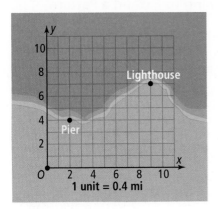

1 unit = 0.4 mi

25. Make Sense and Persevere A ship captain is attempting to contact a deep sea diver.

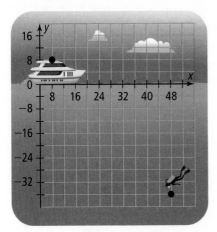

If the maximum range for communication is 60 meters, will he be able to communicate with the diver based on their current positions? Explain.

26. $\overline{AB}$ has an endpoint at $A(1, -2)$ and midpoint $C(3, 2)$. Graph $\overline{AB}$ and point C.

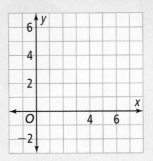

27. SAT/ACT $\overline{RS}$ has an endpoint at $R(6, -4)$ and length 17. Which of the following cannot be the coordinates of S?

Ⓐ (14, 11)

Ⓑ (6, 13)

Ⓒ (−9, −12)

Ⓓ (23, 13)

Ⓔ (23, −4)

28. Performance Task A parade route must start and end at the intersections shown on the map. The city requires that the total distance of the route cannot exceed 3 miles. A proposed route is shown.

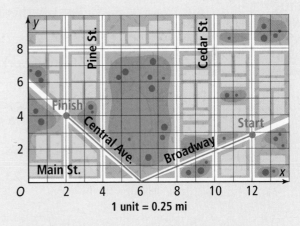

1 unit = 0.25 mi

Part A Why does the proposed route not meet the requirement?

Part B Assuming that the roads used for the route are the same and the end point is the same, at what intersection could the parade start so the total distance is as close to 3 miles as possible?

Part C The city wants to station video cameras halfway down each road in the parade. Using your answer to Part B, what are the coordinates of the locations for the cameras?

6-4
Inductive Reasoning

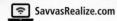

I CAN... use inductive reasoning to make conjectures about mathematical relationships.

VOCABULARY
- conjecture
- counterexample
- inductive reasoning

EXPLORE & REASON

When points on a circle are connected, the line segments divide the circle into a number of regions, as shown.

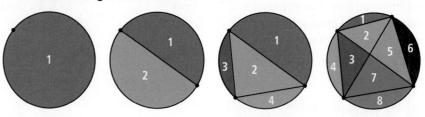

A. How does the number of regions change when another point is added?

B. Look for Relationships Using the pattern you observed, make a prediction about the number of regions formed by connecting 5 points on a circle. Make a drawing to test your prediction. Is your prediction correct?

? ESSENTIAL QUESTION

How is inductive reasoning used to recognize mathematical relationships?

EXAMPLE 1 Use Inductive Reasoning to Extend a Pattern

Inductive reasoning is a type of reasoning that reaches conclusions based on a pattern of specific examples or past events. How can you use inductive reasoning to determine what appears to be the next two terms in each sequence?

A. 88, 82, 76, 70, 64,...

> Look for a pattern. Observe that the terms decrease and the difference of the first two terms is 6.

STUDY TIP
When looking for a pattern, remember to always test subsequent terms to be sure that you have found the correct rule.

Test whether the pattern continues with subsequent terms.

$$82 - 6 = 76 \qquad 76 - 6 = 70 \qquad 70 - 6 = 64$$

The rule works. Use the pattern to find the next two terms.

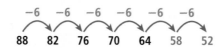

The next two terms in the sequence appear to be 58 and 52.

B. 3, 5, 9, 15, 23,...

> Look for a pattern. Observe that the terms increase by successive multiples of 2.

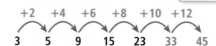

The next two terms in the sequence appear to be 33 and 45.

✓ Try It!

1. What appear to be the next two terms in each sequence?

    a. 800, 400, 200, 100,...   **b.** 18, 24, 32, $\frac{128}{3}$,...

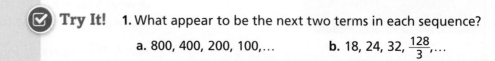

EXAMPLE 2 **Use Inductive Reasoning to Make a Conjecture**

A **conjecture** is an unproven statement or rule that is based on inductive reasoning. What conjecture can be made about the number of dots in the *n*th term of this geometric pattern?

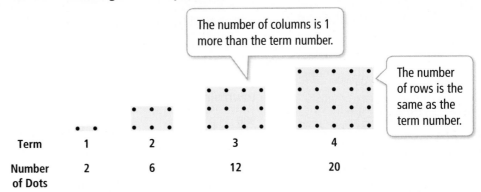

The number of columns is 1 more than the term number.

The number of rows is the same as the term number.

Term	1	2	3	4
Number of Dots	2	6	12	20

Write an algebraic expression to generalize the pattern for the *n*th term. Since the number or rows in the pattern is equivalent to the term number, use the n to represent the number of rows.

MODEL WITH MATHEMATICS
You can write an algebraic expression to represent a geometric pattern. What expressions can you write for the *n*th term?

n + 1 columns

n rows

Term   *n*

The total number of dots is the product of the number of rows and the number of columns.

Conjecture: The *n*th term of the sequence will contain $n(n + 1)$, or $n^2 + n$ dots.

Try It!   **2. a.** How many dots are in the 5th and 6th terms of the pattern?

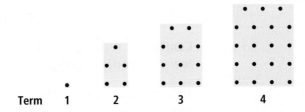

Term	1	2	3	4

b. What conjecture can you make about the number of dots in the *n*th term of the pattern?

APPLICATION   **EXAMPLE 3**   Use a Conjecture to Make a Prediction

Based on the data in the table, how many residents would you expect to vote in the 7th town council election?

Town Council Elections Voter Turnout

Year	Total Residents	Voters
1	3,511	386
2	3,790	414
3	4,085	451
4	4,907	544
5	5,562	623
6	7,014	767
7	7,786	?

Formulate ◀ Look for a pattern by comparing the ratios $\frac{\text{number of voters}}{\text{number of residents}}$ for each year. Then use the pattern to make a conjecture about the number of residents who will vote in the 7th town election.

Compute ◀

$\frac{386}{3,511} \approx 0.110$ $\frac{414}{3,790} \approx 0.109$

$\frac{451}{4,085} \approx 0.110$ $\frac{544}{4,907} \approx 0.111$

$\frac{623}{5,562} \approx 0.112$ $\frac{767}{7,014} \approx 0.109$

> The number of voters each year is about 11% of the total residents.

Use the pattern to predict the number of voters in the 7th election.

$7,786 \cdot 0.11 = 856.46$

Interpret ◀ About 856 people can be expected to vote in the 7th town council election.

 Try It!   **3.** Based on the data, about how many members would you expect the chess club to have in its 5th year?

Year	1	2	3	4
Club Members	10	13	17	22

CONCEPTUAL UNDERSTANDING   **EXAMPLE 4**   Find a Counterexample to Show a Conjecture is False

Why does a *counterexample* show that a conjecture is false?

Conjecture: A polygon with diagonals has two fewer diagonals as sides.

> A **counterexample** is an example that shows a statement or conjecture is false.

To find a counterexample, you must find a polygon that has a number of diagonals that is not two fewer than the number of its sides.

CONSTRUCT ARGUMENTS
For a conjecture to be true, it must be true for every possible case, so if a counterexample is found, the conjecture is false.

4 sides
2 diagonals

5 sides
5 diagonals

> You only need to find one counterexample to show that a statement is false. A counterexample exists, so the conjecture is false.

 Try It!   **4.** What is a counterexample that shows the statement, *the sum of two composite numbers must be a composite number*, is false?

Go Online | SavvasRealize.com

 **EXAMPLE 5** Test a Conjecture

For each conjecture, test the conjecture with several more examples or find a counterexample to disprove the conjecture.

A. A polygon with four congruent sides is a square.

A square has four congruent sides and four right angles.

Think: Is it possible to draw a polygon with four congruent sides but not four right angles?

This rhombus has four congruent sides and no right angles.

A counterexample exists, so this conjecture is false.

B. If a number is a multiple of 9, then the sum of its digits is a multiple of 9.

To test the conjecture, list some multiples of 9 and find the sum of the digits of each multiple.

Multiples of 9	Sums of the Digits
$9 \cdot 12 = 108$	$1 + 0 + 8 = 9$
$9 \cdot 313 = 2{,}817$	$2 + 8 + 1 + 7 = 18$
$9 \cdot 1{,}105 = 9{,}945$	$9 + 9 + 4 + 5 = 27$

The sums 9, 18, and 27 are multiples of 9.

The conjecture is true for the three cases tested.

COMMON ERROR
You may think that finding examples that support a conjecture shows that it is true. Remember that you must show that a conjecture is true for all cases, not just a few.

 Try It! **5.** For each conjecture, test the conjecture with several more examples or find a counterexample to disprove it.

a. For every integer n, the value of n^2 is positive.

b. A number is divisible by 4 if the last two digits are divisible by 4.

WORDS ▸ Inductive Reasoning

- leads to a conjecture by observing patterns.
- uses specific examples to make a generalization.

- does not show that a conjecture is true, so a conjecture could be disproven by a counterexample.

DIAGRAM ▸

Pattern

$$0^2 + 0 + 11 = 11$$
$$1^2 + 1 + 11 = 13$$
$$2^2 + 2 + 11 = 17$$
$$3^2 + 3 + 11 = 23$$
$$4^2 + 4 + 11 = 31$$

→

Generalization

As the pattern continues, the sum is a prime number.

→

Conjecture

If n is a whole number, then $n^2 + n + 11$ is a prime number.

Counterexample: If $n = 11$, $11^2 + 11 + 11 = 143$ is divisible by 11, so the sum is not always prime.

☑ Do You UNDERSTAND?

1. **ESSENTIAL QUESTION** How is inductive reasoning used to recognize mathematical relationships?

2. **Error Analysis** Esteban made the following drawing and then stated this conjecture: "The altitude of a triangle always lies inside of or along the side of the triangle." What error did Esteban make?

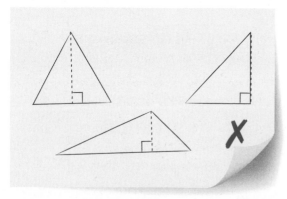

3. **Vocabulary** What type of statement results from inductive reasoning?

Do You KNOW HOW?

4. What appear to be the next three numbers in the pattern?

   4, 11, 18, 25,…

5. What conjecture can you make about the number of regions created by n unique diameters?

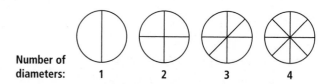

Number of diameters: 1   2   3   4

6. Can you find four examples that are true or a counterexample for the following statement?

   For every integer n, the value of $n^2 + 1$ is odd.

UNDERSTAND

7. Mathematical Connections Abby notices that for the first twenty perfect squares, each square is either a multiple of 5, one less than a multiple of 5, or one more than a multiple of 5.

1	4	9	16	25
36	49	64	81	100
121	144	169	196	225
256	289	324	361	400

She writes the following statement.

> If n is a natural number, then n^2 can be written as $5k - 1$, $5k$, or $5k + 1$, where k is a whole number.

What type of statement did Abby make? Has she shown that her statement is true for all values of n? Explain.

8. Error Analysis Danielle tests the following conjecture.

> If two angles share a common vertex, then they are adjacent.

Her work is shown below. What error does Danielle make?

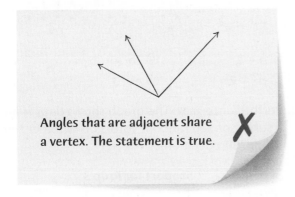

Angles that are adjacent share a vertex. The statement is true. ✗

9. Higher Order Thinking Consider the following conjecture.

> There are no prime numbers between 7,608 and 7,620.

How could you show that this statement is true or false? Would it still be a conjecture if you do not find a counterexample? Explain.

PRACTICE

For each sequence, what appear to be the next three numbers? SEE EXAMPLE 1

10. 101, 89, 77, 65,...   **11.** 9, 6, 4, $\frac{8}{3}$,...

12. Observe the pattern made by the figures. Can you write a conjecture about the number of triangles formed by connecting one vertex of a polygon with n sides to each of the other vertices? SEE EXAMPLE 2

Number
of Sides: 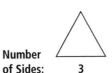 3   4   5   6

The table shows the number of students in the senior class and the number of seniors who have their driver's license. SEE EXAMPLE 3

Year	2014	2015	2016	2017
Number of Seniors	341	367	309	382
Seniors With a License	222	240	199	246

13. What pattern can you find between the number of seniors and the seniors who have a driver's license?

14. The class of 2018 has 413 seniors. How many seniors in the class of 2018 do you think will have a driver's license?

15. Can you find a counterexample for the following statement? SEE EXAMPLE 4

> A trapezoid cannot have more than one right angle.

16. Support the following conjecture with 4 examples or disprove it with a counterexample. SEE EXAMPLE 5

> The quotient of two rational numbers is a rational number.

APPLY

17. Model With Mathematics Data from four identical trials on a new sleep herb are shown in the table.

Group	Number of Subjects	Number Who Reported Better Sleep
A	250	55
B	170	35
C	210	48
D	190	40

a. What conjecture can you make about the effectiveness of the herb?

b. The next trial will have 1,000 subjects. What is a reasonable prediction for the next trial?

18. Make Sense and Persevere Deshawn is given the following conjecture.

The first and third digits of a three-digit number are the same. If the second digit is equal to the sum of the first and third digits, then the number must be divisible by 11.

How can he determine whether the conjecture is true?

19. Generalize A graphic designer wants to know the number of regions that are formed when circles overlap in a particular way. Can she find a rule that describes how the number of regions increases when another circle is added to the design? How many regions would a design with 6 circles create?

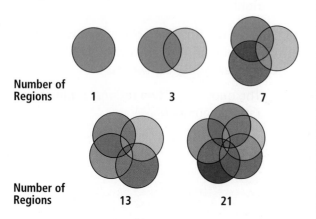

Number of Regions: 1   3   7

Number of Regions: 13   21

ASSESSMENT PRACTICE

20. Consider the conjecture, "Any number divisible by 2 is also divisible by 4." Is each number a counterexample of the conjecture? Select *Yes* or *No*.

	Yes	No
12	☐	☐
19	☐	☐
22	☐	☐
28	☐	☐
30	☐	☐

21. SAT/ACT Which number is next in the following sequence?

1, 2, 2, 4, 8, 32,...

Ⓐ 64   Ⓑ 84   Ⓒ 106   Ⓓ 256

22. SAT/ACT How many dots are in the nth term of the following sequence?

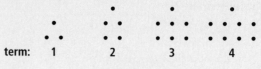

term: 1   2   3   4

Ⓐ $n + 2$ Ⓑ $2n + 1$
Ⓒ $n^2 + 2$ Ⓓ $n + 3$

23. Performance Task The graph shows data from a survey of 300 random voters on whether they support Proposition 3.

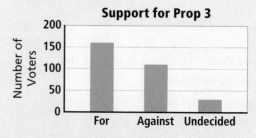

Part A Make a conjecture about the likelihood of Proposition 3 passing and explain your reasoning.

Part B If 7,500 people vote in the next election, how many people would you expect to vote for Proposition 3?

The Mystery Spokes

Some photos are taken in such a way that it is difficult to determine exactly what the picture shows. Sometimes it's because the photo is a close up part of an object, and you do not see the entire object. Other times, it might be because the photographer used special effects when taking the photo.

You can often use clues from the photo to determine what is in the photo and also what the rest of the object might look like. What clues would you look for? Think about this during the Mathematical Modeling in 3 Acts lesson.

Scan for
Multimedia

ACT 1 Identify the Problem

1. What is the first question that comes to mind after watching the video?

2. Write down the main question you will answer about what you saw in the video.

3. Make an initial conjecture that answers this main question.

4. Explain how you arrived at your conjecture.

5. Write a number that you know is too small.

6. Write a number that you know is too large.

ACT 2 Develop a Model

7. Use the math that you have learned in this Topic to refine your conjecture.

ACT 3 Interpret the Results

8. Is your refined conjecture between the highs and lows you set up earlier?

9. Did your refined conjecture match the actual answer exactly? If not, what might explain the difference?

6-5
Conditional Statements

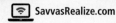
SavvasRealize.com

I CAN... write conditionals and biconditionals and find their truth values.

VOCABULARY
- biconditional
- conclusion
- conditional
- contrapositive
- converse
- hypothesis
- inverse
- negation
- truth table
- truth value

EXPLORE & REASON

If-then statements show a cause and effect. The table shows some if-then statements.

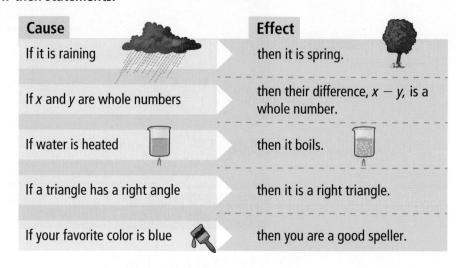

Cause	Effect
If it is raining	then it is spring.
If x and y are whole numbers	then their difference, $x - y$, is a whole number.
If water is heated	then it boils.
If a triangle has a right angle	then it is a right triangle.
If your favorite color is blue	then you are a good speller.

A. Construct Arguments Determine whether each effect is always true for the given cause, or is not necessarily true for the given cause. For the effects that are not necessarily true, how could you change them to make them always true?

B. Write some if-then statements of your own. Write two statements that are always true and two statements that are not necessarily true.

ESSENTIAL QUESTION   How do if-then statements describe mathematical relationships?

CONCEPT Conditional Statement

A **conditional** is an *if-then* statement that relates a **hypothesis**, the part that follows *if*, to a **conclusion**, the part that follows *then*.

Conditionals can be represented as $p \rightarrow q$, read as "If p, then q," where p represents the hypothesis and q represents the conclusion.

EXAMPLE 1   Write a Conditional Statement

Write each statement as a conditional.

A. You can register to vote if you are at least 18 years old.

Identify the hypothesis and conclusion.

> The conclusion gives the outcome or result.

> The hypothesis follows "if" and gives the condition.

You can register to vote **if you are at least 18 years old.**

Conditional: If you are at least 18 years old, then you may register to vote.

COMMON ERROR
Remember that in everyday language, the hypothesis does not necessarily come before the conclusion.

CONTINUED ON THE NEXT PAGE

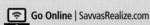 Go Online | SavvasRealize.com

EXAMPLE 1 CONTINUED

B. A square must have four congruent sides.

Identify the hypothesis and conclusion.

The hypothesis is that a polygon is a square.

The conclusion is that the polygon has four congruent sides.

A square must have four congruent sides.

Conditional: If a polygon is a square, then it has four congruent sides.

 Try It! **1.** Write each statement as a conditional.

   a. A triangle with all angles congruent is equilateral.

   b. Alberto can go to the movies if he washes the car.

CONCEPTUAL UNDERSTANDING

EXAMPLE 2 Find a Truth Value of a Conditional

The **truth value** of a statement is "true" (T) or "false" (F) according to whether the statement is true or false, respectively. A **truth table** lists all the possible combinations of truth values for two or more statements.

Truth Table for $p \rightarrow q$

A conditional with a false hypothesis has a value of true, regardless of the conclusion.

Hypothesis p	Conclusion q	Conditional $p \rightarrow q$
T	T	T
T	F	F
F	T	T
F	F	T

Only a conditional with a true hypothesis and a false conclusion has a value of false.

How can you determine the truth value of each conditional?

A. If a number is even, then it is divisible by 2.

An even number is always divisible by two, so when the hypothesis is true, the conclusion is always true.

The conditional is true.

MAKE SENSE AND PERSEVERE
To determine the truth value of a conditional, consider all of the options for the hypothesis and for the conclusion. For example, assume the hypothesis is true, then determine whether the conclusion must also always be true.

B. If a quadrilateral has two pairs of congruent angles, then it is a parallelogram.

Assume the hypothesis, a quadrilateral that has two pairs of congruent angles, is true. To decide whether the conclusion is true, determine whether the quadrilateral must be a parallelogram.

An isosceles trapezoid has two pairs of congruent angles, but is not a parallelogram. The conclusion is false.

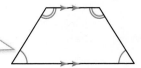

In this example, the hypothesis of the conditional is true and the conclusion is false, so this conditional is false.

CONTINUED ON THE NEXT PAGE

EXAMPLE 2 CONTINUED

 Try It! **2.** What is the truth value of each conditional? Explain your reasoning.

    a. If a quadrilateral has a right angle, then it is a rectangle.

    b. If X is the midpoint of $\overline{AB}$, then X lies on $\overline{AB}$.

CONCEPT Related Conditional Statements

Definition	Symbols	Words
A conditional has a hypothesis and a conclusion.	$p \rightarrow q$	If p, then q.
The **converse** reverses the hypothesis and the conclusion of a conditional.	$q \rightarrow p$	If q, then p.
The **negation** of a statement has the opposite meaning of the original statement.	$\sim p$	not p
The **inverse** is obtained by negating both the hypothesis and the conclusion of a conditional.	$\sim p \rightarrow \sim q$	If not p, then not q.
The **contrapositive** is obtained by negating and reversing both the hypothesis and the conclusion of a conditional.	$\sim q \rightarrow \sim p$	If not q, then not p.

EXAMPLE 3   Write and Evaluate the Truth Value of a Converse

Write and determine the truth value of the converse of the conditional.

If you play the trumpet, then you play a brass instrument.

To write the converse, reverse the hypothesis and conclusion.

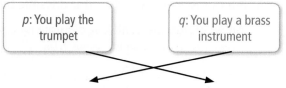

p: You play the trumpet q: You play a brass instrument

If you play a brass instrument, **then** you play the trumpet.

If you play a brass instrument, then you may play a brass instrument that is not a trumpet. The converse is false.

STUDY TIP
To remember that the converse switches the order back and forth, remember that a *conversation* goes back and forth between two people.

 Try It! **3.** Write and determine the truth value of the converse of the conditional.

    a. If a polygon is a quadrilateral, then it has four sides.

    b. If two angles are complementary, then their angle measures add to 90.

👆 **EXAMPLE 4** Write and Evaluate the Truth Value of an Inverse and a Contrapositive

Write and determine the truth value of the inverse and contrapositive of the conditional.

If two whole numbers are both even, then their sum is even.

COMMUNICATE PRECISELY
Consider how you can use clear and accurate reasoning to determine a truth value. What can you reason about a conditional if the conclusion is not true?

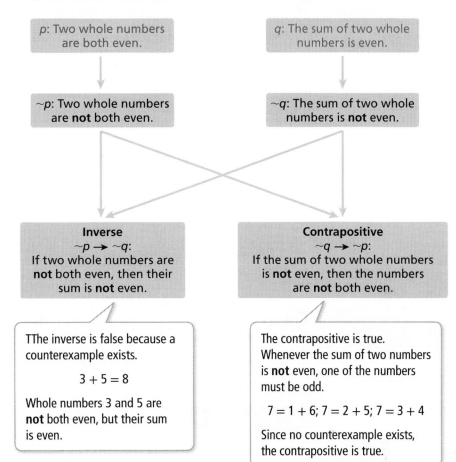

p: Two whole numbers are both even.

q: The sum of two whole numbers is even.

~p: Two whole numbers are **not** both even.

~q: The sum of two whole numbers is **not** even.

Inverse
~p → ~q:
If two whole numbers are **not** both even, then their sum is **not** even.

Contrapositive
~q → ~p:
If the sum of two whole numbers is **not** even, then the numbers are **not** both even.

TThe inverse is false because a counterexample exists.

$3 + 5 = 8$

Whole numbers 3 and 5 are **not** both even, but their sum is even.

The contrapositive is true. Whenever the sum of two numbers is **not** even, one of the numbers must be odd.

$7 = 1 + 6; 7 = 2 + 5; 7 = 3 + 4$

Since no counterexample exists, the contrapositive is true.

☑ **Try It!** 4. Write the converse, the inverse, and the contrapositive. What is the truth value of each?

If today is a weekend day, then tomorrow is Monday.

CONCEPT Biconditional Statements

A **biconditional** is the combination of a conditional, $p → q$, and its converse, $q → p$. The resulting compound statement $p ↔ q$ is read as "p if and only if q."

When p and q have the same truth value, the biconditional is true. When they have opposite truth values, it is false.

p	q	$p ↔ q$
T	T	T
T	F	F
F	T	F
F	F	T

APPLICATION

EXAMPLE 5 Write and Evaluate a Biconditional

A marine biologist writes this conditional: "If a seahorse gives birth, then it is a male." Since it is true that, among seahorses, only the males can become pregnant and give birth, should the marine biologist state this as a biconditional in a paper she is writing?

Formulate ◀ Identify the hypothesis p and the conclusion q of the conditional.

Combine the conditionals $p \rightarrow q$ and $q \rightarrow p$ in the form $p \leftrightarrow q$ to write the biconditional.

Then evaluate the truth value of the biconditional.

Compute ◀ p: **A seahorse gives birth.**

q: **A seahorse is male.**

Biconditional $p \leftrightarrow q$: A seahorse gives birth if and only if it is male.

Determine the truth value of the biconditional.

$p \rightarrow q$: If a seahorse gives birth, then it is male. T

$q \rightarrow p$: If a seahorse is male, then it gives birth. F

> If each of the combined conditionals is true, then the biconditional is true.

Interpret ◀ The biconditional is not true; the biologist should not include the statement as a biconditional in her paper.

 Try It! 5. Write a biconditional for the following conditional. What is its truth value?

If two lines intersect at right angles, then they are perpendicular.

EXAMPLE 6 Identify the Conditionals in a Biconditional

What are the two conditionals implied by the biconditional?

A triangle is equilateral if and only if it has three congruent sides.

Identify the two statements in the biconditional

p: A triangle is equilateral.

q: A triangle has three congruent sides.

Write the two conditionals.

$p \rightarrow q$: If a triangle is equilateral, then it has three congruent sides.

$q \rightarrow p$: If a triangle has three congruent sides, then it is equilateral.

STUDY TIP
Remember that because the conditionals that form a true biconditional are also true, you can choose either part of the biconditional as the hypothesis and the other part as the conclusion.

Try It! 6. What are the two conditionals implied by the biconditional?

The product of two numbers is negative if and only if the numbers have opposite signs.

CONCEPT SUMMARY Conditional Statements

STATEMENT	Conditional	Converse	Inverse	Contrapositive	Biconditional
SYMBOLS	$p \rightarrow q$	$q \rightarrow p$	$\sim p \rightarrow \sim q$	$\sim q \rightarrow \sim p$	$p \leftrightarrow q$
WORDS	If p, then q.	If q, then p.	If not p, then not q.	If not q, then not p.	p if and only if q.

Do You UNDERSTAND?

1. **ESSENTIAL QUESTION** How do if-then statements describe mathematical relationships?

2. **Error Analysis** Allie was asked to write the inverse of the following conditional.

   If it is sunny, then I use sunscreen.

   What error did Allie make?

   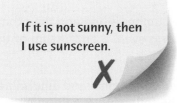

   If it is not sunny, then I use sunscreen. ✗

3. **Vocabulary** Which term is used to describe the opposite of a statement?

4. **Generalize** How do you write the converse of a conditional? How do you write the contrapositive of a conditional?

5. **Communicate Precisely** Explain how the inverse and the contrapositive of a conditional are alike and how they are different.

Do You KNOW HOW?

6. Write the following statement as a biconditional.

   A prime number has only 1 and itself as factors.

For Exercises 7–9, use the following conditional.

   If a rectangle has an area of 12 m², then it has sides of length 3 m and 4 m.

7. What is the hypothesis? What is the conclusion?

8. Assume the hypothesis is false. What is the truth value of the conditional? Assume the hypothesis is true. What would be a counterexample?

9. What are the converse, the inverse, and the contrapositive? What are their truth values?

10. What two conditionals are implied by the following biconditional?

   "The city can build new roads if and only if the sales tax is raised to 10%."

UNDERSTAND

11. Construct Arguments Why is the following conditional logically true?

> If 20 is a multiple of 3, then 101 is a perfect square.

12 Higher Order Thinking Write a true biconditional and show that both implied conditionals are true.

13. Error Analysis Jacy was asked to write the following statement as a conditional.

> Water freezes if it is below 0°C.

What error did she make? What is the correct conditional?

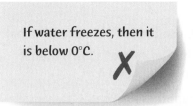

If water freezes, then it is below 0°C. ✗

14. Higher Order Thinking Write a true biconditional about angle bisectors.

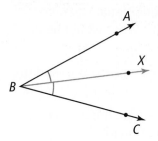

15. Reason Can an inverse and the contrapositive both have false truth values? Explain.

16. Reason If a biconditional is true, what are the truth values of the hypothesis and conclusion of the conditional? Explain.

17. Look for Relationships Emma found a counterexample to a given conditional. What are the truth values of the hypothesis and the conclusion? Explain.

18. Mathematical Connections Write the Pythagorean Theorem as a conditional. Then write a biconditional to include the Converse of the Pythagorean Theorem.

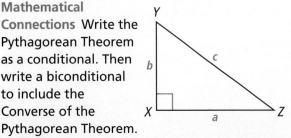

PRACTICE

Write each statement as a conditional.
SEE EXAMPLE 1

19. My hair will be shorter if I cut it.

20. A number that is divisible by 6 is divisible by 3.

21. Movie tickets are half-price on Tuesdays.

Find the truth value of each conditional. Explain your reasoning or show a counterexample.
SEE EXAMPLE 2

22. If a pair of lines is parallel, then they do not intersect.

23. If the product of two numbers is positive, then the numbers are both positive.

Write the negation of the hypothesis and the negation of the conclusion for each conditional.
SEE EXAMPLES 3 and 4

24. If the sum of the interior angle measures of a polygon is 180, then the polygon is a triangle.

25. If one whole number is odd and the other whole number is even, then the sum of the two numbers is odd.

Write each related conditional and determine each truth value for the following conditional.
SEE EXAMPLES 3 and 4

> If an angle measures 100, then it is obtuse.

26. converse   **27.** contrapositive

28. inverse

29. An employee at an animal shelter wrote the true conditional "If 47% of the dogs at the shelter are female, then 53% of the dogs are male." Can he rewrite this as a true biconditional? Explain. SEE EXAMPLE 5

Write two conditionals from each biconditional.
SEE EXAMPLE 6

30. A month has exactly 28 days if and only if it is February.

31. Two angles are complementary if and only if their measures add up to 90.

32. The area of a square is s^2 if and only if the perimeter of the square is $4s$.

APPLY

33. Model With Mathematics In general, a person is 1% shorter in the evening than in the morning. Use your height to write a conditional that uses this fact.

34. Communicate Precisely In the year 1881, three different men were president of the United States—Rutherford B. Hayes, James Garfield, and Chester A. Arthur.

  a. Use this fact to write a conditional and a biconditional.

  b. There was one other year in which three different men were president of the United States. In 1841, Martin Van Buren, William Henry Harrison, and John Tyler were president. Using this information, determine the truth value of the conditional and the biconditional you wrote for part (a).

35. Reason The sign shows the hours for an art museum.

MO ART Modern Art Museum
HOURS

Monday	Closed	
Tuesday	10:00 AM	8:00 PM
Wednesday	10:00 AM	6:00 PM
Thursday	10:00 AM	8:00 PM
Friday	9:00 AM	6:00 PM
Saturday	9:00 AM	6:00 PM
Sunday	12:00 AM	5:00 PM

  a. Write a conditional to describe the hours of the museum on Mondays.

  b. Write a conditional to describe the hours of the museum on Thursdays.

  c. Write the converse, inverse, and contrapositive of the conditional you wrote in part (b). Then give the truth value for each statement.

  d. Can each conditional you wrote for parts (a) and (b) be written as a true biconditional? Why or why not? If so, give each biconditional.

ASSESSMENT PRACTICE

36. Consider the conditional $p \rightarrow q$, where p is true and q is false. Copy and complete the table to show the truth value of each statement.

Statement	Truth Value
Conditional	F
Converse	
Inverse	
Contrapositive	

37. SAT/ACT Which represents the contrapositive of $p \rightarrow q$?

  Ⓐ $p \leftrightarrow q$

  Ⓑ $q \rightarrow p$

  Ⓒ $\sim p \rightarrow \sim q$

  Ⓓ $\sim q \rightarrow \sim p$

  Ⓔ $\sim q \leftrightarrow \sim p$

38. Performance Task A group of students drew several different right triangles and found the measures of the two non-right angles. Their findings are shown in the table.

Angle Measure	Angle Measure	Sum
27	63	90
41	49	90
70	20	90
33	57	90

Part A Make a conjecture about the sum of two non-right angles in a right triangle. Write the conjecture in the form of a conditional.

Part B Construct several right triangles, and then measure the angles of each triangle. Do your measurements support your conjecture, or were you able to find a counterexample?

Part C Write the converse, the inverse, and the contrapositive of your conditional. Then, write a biconditional. Is the biconditional true? Explain.

6-6
Deductive Reasoning

SavvasRealize.com

I CAN... use deductive reasoning to draw conclusions.

VOCABULARY
• deductive reasoning
• Law of Detachment
• Law of Syllogism

CRITIQUE & EXPLAIN

A deck of 60 game cards are numbered from 1 to 15 on one of four different shapes (triangle, circle, square, and pentagon). A teacher selects five cards and displays four of the cards.

She tells her class that all of the cards she selected have the same shape and asks them to draw a conclusion about the fifth card.

Chen	Carolina
The fifth card is 11.	The fifth card has a circle.

A. Describe how each student might have reached his or her conclusion. Is each student's conclusion valid? Explain.

B. Make Sense and Persevere What are other possibilities of the fifth card? What could the teacher say to narrow the possibilities?

? ESSENTIAL QUESTION   How is deductive reasoning different from inductive reasoning?

CONCEPTUAL UNDERSTANDING

EXAMPLE 1   Determine Whether a Statement Is True

STUDY TIP
Recall that in a conditional $p \rightarrow q$, p is the hypothesis and q is the conclusion.

Given that a conditional and its conclusion are true, can you use deductive reasoning to determine whether the hypothesis is true?

You are given the facts that $p \rightarrow q$ is true and q is true. Make a truth table for the conditional $p \rightarrow q$.

Deductive reasoning is a process of reasoning using given and previously known facts to reach a logical conclusion.

p	q	$p \rightarrow q$
T	T	T
T	F	F
F	T	T
F	F	T

When $p \rightarrow q$ and q are true, p can be true or false.

You cannot determine whether the hypothesis is true.

 Try It!   **1.** Given that a conditional and its hypothesis are true, can you determine whether the conclusion is true?

CONCEPT Law of Detachment

The **Law of Detachment** is a law
of logic that states if a conditional
statement and its hypothesis are
true, then its conclusion is also true.

If... $p \rightarrow q$ and p are true.

Then... q is true.

 **EXAMPLE 2** Apply the Law of Detachment to Draw Real-World
and Mathematical Conclusions

Assume that each set of given information is true.

**A. If Alicia scores 85 or greater on her test, she will earn an A as her final
grade. Alicia scores 89 on her test. What can you logically conclude?**

To apply the Law of Detachment, determine the truth value
of $p \rightarrow q$ and p.

> $p \rightarrow q$: If Alicia scores 85 or greater on her test,
> then she will earn an A as her final grade.

This given conditional
is true.

> p: Alicia scores 85 or greater on her test.

The hypothesis is true
because $89 > 85$.

The conditional and its hypothesis are true,
so by the Law of Detachment, the conclusion q is true.

You can conclude that Alicia will earn an A as her final grade.

REASON

If you cannot assume that given
information is true, you can use
deductive reasoning to determine
whether the conditional and the
hypothesis are true.

**B. If point D is in the interior of $\angle ABC$, then
$m\angle ABC = m\angle ABD + m\angle DBC$. What can you
logically conclude about $m\angle ABC$?**

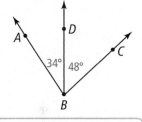

Determine the truth value of $p \rightarrow q$ and p.

> $p \rightarrow q$: If point D is in the interior of $\angle ABC$,
> then $m\angle ABC = m\angle ABD + m\angle DBC$.

> p: Point D is in the interior of $\angle ABC$.

The conditional is true by the
Angle Addition Postulate.

By the Law of Detachment, the conclusion
q is true.

This given hypothesis is true.

You can conclude that $m\angle ABC = m\angle ABD + m\angle DBC$.

 Try It! **2.** Assume that each set of given information is true.

a. If two angles are congruent, then the measures of the two
angles are equal to each other. Angle 1 is congruent to $\angle 2$.
What can you logically conclude about the measures of
$\angle 1$ and $\angle 2$?

b. If you finish the race in under 30 minutes, then you win a
prize. You finished the race in 26 minutes. What can you
logically conclude?

CONCEPT Law of Syllogism

The **Law of Syllogism** is a law of logic that states that given two true conditionals with the conclusion of the first being the hypothesis of the second, there exists a third true conditional having the hypothesis of the first and the conclusion of the second.

If... $p \rightarrow q$ and $q \rightarrow r$ are true.

Then... $p \rightarrow r$ is true.

ⓘ **EXAMPLE 3** Apply the Law of Syllogism to Draw Real-World and Mathematical Conclusions

Assume that each set of conditionals is true. What can you conclude using the Law of Syllogism?

A. If Kenji plays the trumpet, then he plays a brass instrument. If he plays a brass instrument, he is a member of the marching band.

To apply the Law of Syllogism, determine whether the conclusion of one statement is the hypothesis of the other statement.

$p \rightarrow q$: If Kenji plays the trumpet, then he plays a brass instrument.

$q \rightarrow r$: If he plays a brass instrument, then he is a member of the marching band.

> The conclusion of one statement is the hypothesis of the other statement.

Conclusion: If Kenji plays the trumpet, then he is a member of the marching band.

B. If points A, B, and C are collinear and B is between A and C, then $\overrightarrow{BA}$ and $\overrightarrow{BC}$ are opposite rays. If $\overrightarrow{BA}$ and $\overrightarrow{BC}$ are opposite rays, then $AB + BC = AC$. What can you conclude?

Apply the Law of Syllogism, determine whether the conclusion of one statement is the hypothesis of the other statement.

$p \rightarrow q$: If points A, B, and C are colinear and B is between A and C, then $\overrightarrow{BA}$ and $\overrightarrow{BC}$ are opposite rays.

$q \rightarrow r$: If $\overrightarrow{BA}$ and $\overrightarrow{BC}$ are opposite rays, then $AB + BC = AC$.

> The conclusion of one statement is the hypothesis of the other statement.

COMMON ERROR
You may confuse the hypotheses and conclusions of the given conditionals in writing the third conditional. Recall that the statement that is part of each conditional is not part of the conclusion.

Conclusion: If points A, B, and C are colinear and B is between A and C, then $AB + BC = AC$.

 Try It! **3.** Assume that each set of conditionals is true. Use the Law of Syllogism to draw a conclusion.

a. If an integer is divisible by 6, it is divisible by 2. If an integer is divisible by 2, then it is an even number.

b. If it is a holiday, then you do not have to go to school. If it is Labor Day, then it is a holiday.

APPLICATION 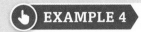 **EXAMPLE 4** **Apply the Laws of Detachment and Syllogism to Draw Conclusions**

What conclusions can you draw from the following true statements?

> **If you are climbing a mountain at an altitude of 28,500 feet or higher, then you are on the tallest mountain above sea level on Earth. If you are on the tallest mountain above sea level on Earth, then you are on Mount Everest. You are climbing a mountain at an altitude of 29,000 feet.**

Identify conditional statements and use the laws of logic to draw a conclusion.

Use the Law of Detachment

$p \rightarrow q$: If you are climbing a mountain at an altitude of 28,500 feet or higher, then you are on the tallest mountain above sea level on Earth.

> This given conditional is true.

p: You are climbing a mountain at an altitude of 28,500 feet or higher.

> p is true because $29,000 > 28,500$.

By the Law of Detachment, the conclusion q is true.

You are on the tallest mountain above sea level on Earth.

Use the Law of Syllogism

$p \rightarrow q$ If you are climbing a mountain at an altitude of 28,500 feet or higher, then you are on the tallest mountain above sea level on Earth.	$q \rightarrow r$ If you are on the tallest mountain above sea level on Earth, then you are on Mount Everest.
$p \rightarrow q$ is true.	$q \rightarrow r$ is true.

$p \rightarrow r$
If you are climbing a mountain at an altitude of 28,500 feet or higher, then you are on Mount Everest.

$p \rightarrow r$ is true by the Law of Syllogism.

Use the Law of Syllogism and the Law of Detachment

$p \rightarrow r$: If you are climbing a mountain at an altitude of 28,500 feet or higher, then you are on Mount Everest.

> $p \rightarrow r$ is true by the Law of Syllogism.

p: You are climbing a mountain at an altitude of 28,500 feet or higher.

> p is true because $29,000 > 28,500$.

By the Law of Detachment, the conclusion r: is true

You are on Mount Everest.

 Try It! 4. Martin walks his dog before dinner every day. Martin is now eating his dinner. Using the Law of Detachment and the Law of Syllogism, what conclusions can you draw from these true statements?

Concept Summary · Assess

WORDS | Law of Detachment

If a conditional statement and its hypothesis are true, then its conclusion is also true.

Law of Syllogism

Given two true conditionals with the conclusion of the first being the hypothesis of the second, there exists a third true conditional having the hypothesis of the first and the conclusion of the second.

SYMBOLS | If... $p \rightarrow q$ and p are true.

Then... q is true.

If... $p \rightarrow q$ and $q \rightarrow r$ are true.

Then... $p \rightarrow r$ is true.

✓ Do You UNDERSTAND?

1. **ESSENTIAL QUESTION** How is deductive reasoning different from inductive reasoning?

2. **Error Analysis** Dakota writes the following as an example of using the Law of Detachment. What is her error?

> If my favorite team wins more than 55 games, they win the championship. My team won the championship, so they won more than 55 games. ✗

3. **Vocabulary** What are the differences between the Law of Detachment and the Law of Syllogism?

4. **Use Structure** How can representing sentences and phrases with symbols help you determine whether to apply the Law of Detachment or the Law of Syllogism?

Do You KNOW HOW?

Assume that each set of given information is true.

5. If you have a temperature above 100.4°F, then you have a fever. Casey has a temperature of 101.2°F. What can you conclude about Casey? What rule of inference did you use?

6. If points A, B, and C are collinear with B between A and C, then $AB + BC = AC$. Use the information in the figure shown. What can you conclude about AC?

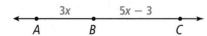

Assume that each set of conditionals is true. Use the Law of Syllogism to write a true conditional.

7. If you eat too much, you get a stomach ache. If you get a stomach ache, you want to rest.

8. If two numbers are odd, the sum of the numbers is even. If a number is even, then the number is divisible by 2.

Go Online | SavvasRealize.com

UNDERSTAND

9. Error Analysis Samantha writes the following as an example of using the Law of Syllogism. Explain Samantha's error.

> If an animal is a dog, then it is a mammal.
> If an animal is a dog, then it has four legs.
>
> I can conclude that if an animal has four legs, then it is a mammal.   ✗

10. Look for Relationships Make a truth table with statements p, q, r, $p \rightarrow q$, $q \rightarrow r$, and $p \rightarrow r$. How does the truth table support the validity of the Law of Syllogism and the Law of Detachment?

11. Mathematical Connections Consider the following conditional.

> If all four sides of a quadrilateral are of equal length, then its diagonals intersect at right angles.

Which of the following figures can you use with the conditional to apply the Law of Detachment to draw the conclusion that its diagonals intersect at right angles?

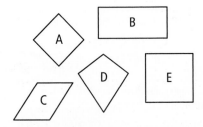

12. Higher Order Thinking Suppose you are given that a conditional is true but its conclusion is false. What can you conclude about the hypothesis? Explain your answer using the negation of the hypothesis and the conclusion with the Law of Detachment.

13. Look for Relationships To apply the Law of Detachment, a conditional statement and its hypothesis must both be true. Can you draw any conclusions if the conditional is true but the hypothesis is false? Explain.

PRACTICE

Determine the truth value of the following conditional. SEE EXAMPLE 1

14. If two adjacent angles form a right angle, then the angles are complementary.

Assume that each set of statements is true. Use the Law of Detachment to write a true statement. If the Law of Detachment cannot be used, explain why. SEE EXAMPLE 2

15. If you can play the piano, then you can play a musical instrument. Kiyo can play a musical instrument.

16. If the endpoints of a segment are $P(x_1, y_1)$ and $Q(x_2, y_2)$, then the coordinates of the midpoint are $M = \left(\frac{x_1 + x_2}{2}, \frac{y_1 + y_2}{2}\right)$. The endpoints of $\overline{CD}$ are $C(2, -4)$ and $D(-3, 5)$.

17. If the graph of a linear function has a positive slope, then the function is not decreasing. The slope of the graph is 0.

Assume that each set of conditionals is true. Use the Law of Syllogism to write a true conditional. If the Law of Syllogism cannot be used, explain why. SEE EXAMPLE 3

18. If $\overrightarrow{BD}$ bisects $\angle ABC$, then $\angle ABD \cong \angle DBC$. If $\angle ABD \cong \angle DBC$, then $m\angle ABD = m\angle DBC$.

19. If a whole number is even, then it is divisible by 2. If the sum of the digits of a whole number is divisible by 3, then the whole number is divisible by 3.

20. If Zachary eats pasta for dinner, then he goes to bed early. If it is Tuesday night, then Zachary eats pasta for dinner.

Use the Law of Detachment and the Law of Syllogism to draw conclusions from each set of true statements. SEE EXAMPLE 4

21. If it is Thursday, then Charles has baseball practice. If Charles has baseball practice, then he eats grilled chicken for dinner. It is the day after Wednesday.

22. If the length of a segment is PQ, then the distance from P to the midpoint of $\overline{PQ}$ is $\frac{1}{2}PQ$. If the endpoints of a segment are $P(x_1, y_1)$ and $Q(x_2, y_2)$, then the length of the segment is $PQ = \sqrt{(x_2 - x_1)^2 + (y_2 - y_1)^2}$. The endpoints of $\overline{PQ}$ are $P(3, -4)$ and $Q(-3, -12)$.

APPLY

23. **Model With Mathematics** Represent each true statement with symbols. Use symbols to write related contrapositives of the conditionals. Then use the Law of Detachment and the Law of Syllogism to draw a conclusion.

> If Avery draws a numbered card from 4 to 10, then his game piece moves to home base. If his game piece moves to home base, he wins the game. Avery does not win.

24. **Mathematical Connections** The chart describes the number of tickets needed to win prizes at a family fun center.

Numbers of Tickets	Prize Level	Sample Prizes
0–100	A	magnet, stickers
101–200	B	keychain, flashlight
201–300	C	earbuds, MP3 speaker

a. Write conditionals with sample prizes as the hypothesis and prize level as the conclusion. Write conditionals that relate the prize level to the number of tickets.

b. Ines wins an MP3 speaker. Use the Law of Detachment and Law of Syllogism to write true statements about Ines based on the conditionals you wrote in part (a).

25. **Reason** The table shows the main dishes served each day at a cafeteria.

Monday	hamburger, salad, pizza
Tuesday	hamburger, stir fry, pizza
Wednesday	fish and chips, stir fry, salad
Thursday	stir fry, salad, tacos
Friday	fish and chips, tacos, pizza

Suppose you know that Joshua has a salad and Nora has stir fry. Is that enough information to determine what day it is? If not, what other piece of information can help you?

ASSESSMENT PRACTICE

26. The following statements are true.

- If you are over 54 inches tall, you can ride on the roller coasters.
- If you can ride on the roller coasters, then you can go on the drop tower.
- Cindy is 56 inches tall.

Classify each of the following statements as *true* or *false*.

- If Cindy can go on the drop tower, then she can ride the roller coasters.
- Cindy can go on the drop tower.
- Cindy can ride the roller coasters.
- If Cindy rides on the roller coasters, then she goes on the drop tower.

27. **SAT/ACT** Which statement can you conclude from the given true statements?

If you ride your bike to school, you exercise. If you exercise, you are happy.

Ⓐ If you are happy, you exercise.

Ⓑ You exercise.

Ⓒ If you exercise, you ride your bike.

Ⓓ If you bike to school, you are happy.

28. **Performance Task** In a game of exploration, rolling a cube numbered from 1 to 6 simulates asset acquisition. Some rules are listed.

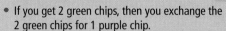

- If you roll an even number, you get 1 red chip.
- If you roll a factor of 6, you get 1 blue chip.
- If you roll a number greater than 3, you get 1 green chip.
- If you get 2 green chips, then you exchange the 2 green chips for 1 purple chip.
- If you get 2 red chips, then you exchange the 2 red chips for 1 purple chip.

Note that a roll can earn more than one chip.

Part A Jacinta rolls a 2, 5, 1, and then 3. What chips does she have?

Part B After four rolls, Kimberly has 1 purple chip, 1 green chip, 3 blue chips, and no red chips. What numbers could she have rolled?

6-7
Writing Proofs

I CAN... use deductive reasoning to prove theorems.

VOCABULARY
- paragraph proof
- proof
- theorem
- two-column proof

CRITIQUE & EXPLAIN

William solved an equation for *x* and wrote justifications for each step of his solution.

$6(14 + x) = 108$	Given
$84 + 6x = 108$	Distributive Property
$6x = 108 - 84$	Subtraction Property of Equality
$6x = 24$	Simplify
$x = 4$	Multiplication Property of Equality

A. Make Sense and Persevere Are William's justifications valid at each step? If not, what might you change? Explain.

B. Can you justify another series of steps that result in the same solution for *x*?

? ESSENTIAL QUESTION

How is deductive reasoning used to prove a theorem?

THEOREM 6-1 Vertical Angles Theorem

Vertical angles are congruent.

PROOF: SEE EXAMPLE 1.

If...

Then... $\angle 1 \cong \angle 2$ and $\angle 3 \cong \angle 4$

CONCEPTUAL UNDERSTANDING

EXAMPLE 1 Write a Two-Column Proof

A **theorem** is a conjecture that is proven. Prove the Vertical Angles Theorem.

Given: $\angle 1$ and $\angle 2$ are vertical angles

Prove: $\angle 1 \cong \angle 2$

A **proof** is a convincing argument that uses deductive reasoning. A **two-column proof**, in which the statements and reasons are aligned in columns, is one way to organize and present a proof.

COMMON ERROR
You may think that the proof is complete by stating that the measures of the angles are equal. You must explicitly state that the angles are congruent in order to complete the proof.

Statements	Reasons
1) $\angle 1$ and $\angle 2$ are vertical angles	1) Given
2) $m\angle 1 + m\angle 3 = 180$ and $m\angle 2 + m\angle 3 = 180$	2) Supplementary Angles
3) $m\angle 1 + m\angle 3 = m\angle 2 + m\angle 3$	3) Transitive Property of Equality
4) $m\angle 1 = m\angle 2$	4) Subtraction Property of Equality
5) $\angle 1 \cong \angle 2$	5) Definition of congruent angles

EXAMPLE 1 CONTINUED

 Try It! 1. Write a two-column proof.

Given: $\overrightarrow{BD}$ bisects $\angle CBE$.

Prove: $\angle ABD \cong \angle FBD$

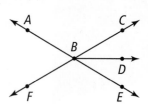

APPLICATION 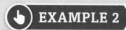 **EXAMPLE 2** Apply the Vertical Angles Theorem

The diagram shows how glass lenses change the direction of light rays passing through a telescope. What is the value of x, the angle formed by the crossed outermost light rays through the focal point?

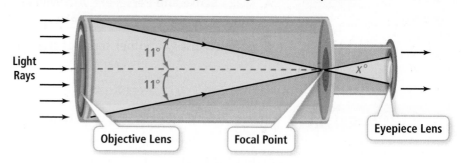

Formulate ◀ Draw and label a diagram to represent the telescope.

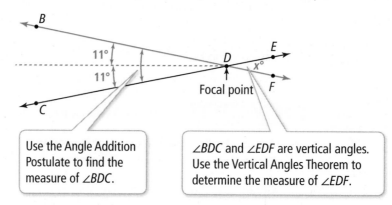

Use the Angle Addition Postulate to find the measure of $\angle BDC$.

$\angle BDC$ and $\angle EDF$ are vertical angles. Use the Vertical Angles Theorem to determine the measure of $\angle EDF$.

Compute ◀ $m\angle BDC = 11 + 11 = 22$ $\qquad\qquad m\angle EDF = m\angle BDC = 22$

Interpret ◀ The outermost light rays form a 22° angle as they leave the focal point, so the value of x is 22.

 Try It! 2. Find the value of x and the measure of each labeled angle.

a.

$(6x - 45)°$ $(4x + 5)°$

b.

$(8x - 20)°$ $(5x + 37)°$

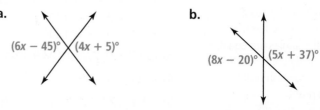

THEOREM 6-2 Congruent Supplements Theorem

If two angles are supplementary to congruent angles (or to the same angle), then they are congruent.

If... $m\angle1 + m\angle2 = 180$ and
$m\angle3 + m\angle2 = 180$

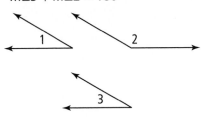

PROOF: SEE EXAMPLE 3.

Then... $\angle1 \cong \angle3$

THEOREM 6-3 Congruent Complements Theorem

If two angles are complementary to congruent angles (or to the same angle), then they are congruent.

If... $m\angle1 + m\angle2 = 90$ and
$m\angle3 + m\angle2 = 90$

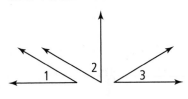

PROOF: SEE EXAMPLE 3 TRY IT.

Then... $\angle1 \cong \angle3$

PROOF

EXAMPLE 3 Write a Paragraph Proof

Write a paragraph proof of the Congruent Supplements Theorem.

Given: $\angle1$ and $\angle2$ are supplementary.
$\angle2$ and $\angle3$ are supplementary.

Prove: $\angle1 \cong \angle3$

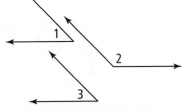

Another way to write a proof is a paragraph proof. In a **paragraph proof**, the statements and reasons are connected in sentences.

Proof: By the definition of supplementary angles, $m\angle1 + m\angle2 = 180$ and $m\angle2 + m\angle3 = 180$. Since both sums equal 180, $m\angle1 + m\angle2 = m\angle2 + m\angle3$. Subtract $m\angle2$ from each side of this equation to get $m\angle1 = m\angle3$. By the definition of congruent angles, $\angle1 \cong \angle3$.

> **STUDY TIP**
> It may be helpful to confirm that a paragraph proof is complete by underlining each statement and then circling the corresponding reason.

Try It! **3.** Write a paragraph proof of the Congruent Complements Theorem.

Given: $\angle1$ and $\angle2$ are complementary.
$\angle2$ and $\angle3$ are complementary.

Prove: $\angle1 \cong \angle3$

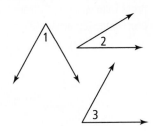

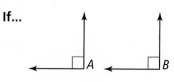

THEOREM 6-4

All right angles are congruent.

If...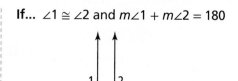

PROOF: SEE EXERCISE 9.

Then... $\angle A \cong \angle B$

THEOREM 6-5

If two angles are congruent and supplementary, then each is a right angle.

If... $\angle 1 \cong \angle 2$ and $m\angle 1 + m\angle 2 = 180$

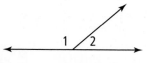

PROOF: SEE EXERCISE 11.

Then... $\angle 1$ and $\angle 2$ are right angles

THEOREM 6-6 Linear Pairs Theorem

The sum of the measures of a linear pair is 180.

If... $\angle 1$ and $\angle 2$ form a linear pair.

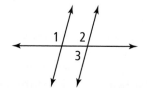

PROOF: SEE EXERCISE 12.

Then... $m\angle 1 + m\angle 2 = 180$

PROOF

EXAMPLE 4 Write a Proof Using a Theorem

Write a two-column proof.

Given: $m\angle 1 = m\angle 2$, $m\angle 1 = 105$

Prove: $m\angle 3 = 75$

Statements	Reasons
1) $m\angle 1 = m\angle 2$	1) Given
2) $m\angle 1 = 105$	2) Given
3) $m\angle 2 = 105$	3) Transitive Property of Equality
4) $\angle 2$ and $\angle 3$ are a linear pair	4) Definition of a linear pair
5) $m\angle 2 + m\angle 3 = 180$	5) Linear Pairs Theorem
6) $105 + m\angle 3 = 180$	6) Substitution Property of Equality
7) $m\angle 3 = 75$	7) Subtraction Property of Equality

CONSTRUCT ARGUMENTS
Consider the logical flow for writing a proof. How can you be sure that each step in a proof follows logically from the preceding step or steps?

 Try It! 4. Write a two-column proof.

Given: $m\angle 4 = 35$, $m\angle 1 = m\angle 2 + m\angle 4$

Prove: $m\angle 3 = 70$

 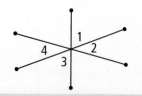

 CONCEPT SUMMARY Proofs

Proofs use given information and logical steps justified by **definitions, postulates, theorems,** and **properties** to reach a conclusion.

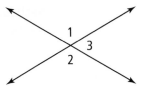

Given: ∠1 and ∠2 and are vertical angles

Prove: ∠1 ≅ ∠2

PROOF ▸ Two-Column Proof	
Statements	**Reasons**
1) ∠1 and ∠2 are vertical angles	**1)** Given
2) $m\angle 1 + m\angle 3 = 180$ and $m\angle 2 + m\angle 3 = 180$	**2)** Supplementary Angles
3) $m\angle 1 + m\angle 3 = m\angle 2 + m\angle 3$	**3)** Subst. Prop. of Equality
4) $m\angle 1 = m\angle 2$	**4)** Subtr. Prop. of Equality
5) ∠1 ≅ ∠2	**5)** Def. ≅ angles

PROOF ▸ Paragraph Proof

By Supplementary Angles, $m\angle 1 + m\angle 3 = 180$ and $m\angle 2 + m\angle 3 = 180$. By the Substitution Property of Equality, $m\angle 1 + m\angle 3 = m\angle 2 + m\angle 3$. Subtracting $m\angle 3$ from each side of the equation gives $m\angle 1 = m\angle 2$. Then by the definition of congruent angles, ∠1 ≅ ∠2.

☑ Do You UNDERSTAND?

1. **ESSENTIAL QUESTION** How is deductive reasoning used to prove a theorem?

2. **Error Analysis** Jayden states that based on the Congruent Supplements Theorem, if $m\angle 1 + m\angle 2 = 90$ and if $m\angle 1 + m\angle 3 = 90$, then ∠2 ≅ ∠3. What is the error in Jayden's reasoning?

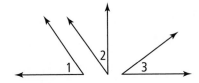

3. **Vocabulary** How is a theorem different from a postulate? How is a theorem different from a conjecture?

4. **Reason** If ∠2 and ∠3 are complementary, how could you use the Vertical Angles Theorem to find $m\angle 1$?

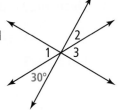

Do You KNOW HOW?

Use the figures to answer Exercises 5–7.

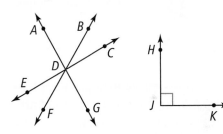

5. What statement could you write in a proof for $m\angle ADC$ using the Angle Addition Postulate as a reason?

6. Could you use the Vertical Angles Theorem as a reason in a proof to state $m\angle ADC = m\angle EDG$ or to state ∠ADC ≅ ∠EDG? Explain.

7. Given $m\angle ADC = 90$, what reason could you give in a proof to state ∠ADC ≅ ∠HJK?

8. The Leaning Tower of Pisa leans at an angle of about 4° from the vertical, as shown. What equation for the measure of x, the angle it makes from the horizontal, could you use in a proof?

UNDERSTAND

9. Construct Arguments Fill in the missing reasons for the proof of Theorem 6-4.

Given: ∠F and ∠G are right angles.

Prove: ∠F ≅ ∠G

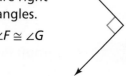

Statements	Reasons
1) ∠F and ∠G are right angles	1) Given
2) $m\angle F = 90$ and $m\angle G = 90$	2)
3) $m\angle F = m\angle G$	3)
4) ∠F ≅ ∠G	4)

10. Error Analysis A student uses the Vertical Angles Theorem and the definition of complementary angles to conclude $m\angle PTR = 50$ in the figure. What mistake did the student make?

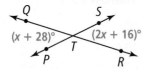

11. Construct Arguments Write a paragraph proof of Theorem 6-5. Given that ∠N and ∠M are congruent and supplementary, prove that ∠N and ∠M are right angles.

12. Construct Arguments Write a two-column proof of Theorem 6-6. Given that ∠ABC and ∠CBD are a linear pair, prove that ∠ABC and ∠CBD are supplementary.

13. Higher Order Thinking Explain how the Congruent Complements Theorem applies to the figure shown.

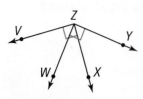

PRACTICE

Find the value of each variable and the measure of each labeled angle. **SEE EXAMPLES 1 AND 2**

14.
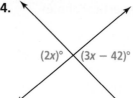

15.
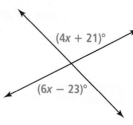

16.

17.
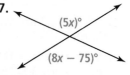

18. Write a paragraph proof. **SEE EXAMPLE 3**

Given: $m\angle ABC = 114$; $m\angle DHE = 25$; $m\angle EHF = 41$; ∠ABC and ∠GHF are supplementary.

Prove: $m\angle DHF \cong m\angle GHF$

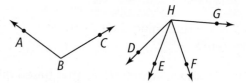

Write a two-column proof for each statement.
SEE EXAMPLE 4

19. Given: ∠1 and ∠2 are complementary.

$m\angle 1 = 23$

Prove: $m\angle 3 = 113$

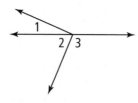

20. Given: $m\angle 2 = 30$

$m\angle 1 = 2m\angle 2$

Prove: $m\angle 3 + m\angle 4 = 90$

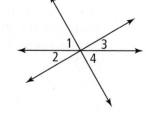

PRACTICE & PROBLEM SOLVING

APPLY

ASSESSMENT PRACTICE

21. Mathematical Connections The graph shows percentages of sales made by various divisions of a company in one year. What are the angles formed by the segments for each division? What are the missing percentages? Explain how you were able to determine each percentage.

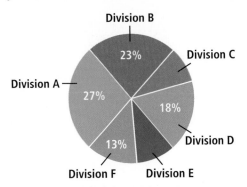

22. Use Structure A type of floor tiling is designed to give the illusion of a three-dimensional figure. Given that $m\angle 1 = 85$ and $m\angle 3 = 45$, what are the measures of the remaining angles?

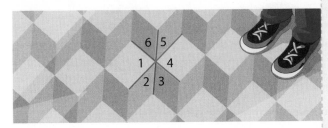

23. Reason Consider the angles formed by the garden gate. Using theorems from this lesson, what can you conclude from each of the following statements? State which theorem you applied to reach your conclusion.

a. $m\angle 1 = 90$ and $m\angle 2 = 90$.

b. $\angle 3$ and $\angle 4$ are vertical angles.

24. Consider the figure shown.

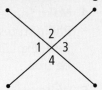

Classify each of the following statements as *always true*, *sometimes true*, or *never true*.

- $m\angle 1 + m\angle 4 = 180$
- $m\angle 1 + m\angle 2 + m\angle 3 = 180$
- $m\angle 2 + m\angle 4 = 180$
- $\angle 2 \cong \angle 3$
- $\angle 2 \cong \angle 4$
- $m\angle 3 = m\angle 4$

25. SAT/ACT Given $\angle ABC$ and $\angle DEF$ are supplementary and $\angle ABC$ and $\angle GHJ$ are supplementary, what can you conclude about the angles?

Ⓐ $m\angle DEF = m\angle GHJ$

Ⓑ $m\angle DEF + m\angle GHJ = 90$

Ⓒ $m\angle DEF + m\angle GHJ = 180$

Ⓓ $m\angle ABC = m\angle DEF$ and $m\angle ABC = m\angle GHJ$

26. Performance Task The figure shows lines that divide a designer window into different parts.

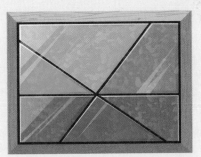

Part A Copy the figure onto a sheet of paper. Label each of the inner angles. Use a protractor to measure any two of the inner angles in the figure. Using your measurements, determine the measurements of the other angles.

Part B Choose two of the inner angles that you did not actually measure. How do you know the angle measures for these two angles? Write a two-column proof to show how you know their measures are correct.

6-8

Indirect Proof

SavvasRealize.com

I CAN... use indirect reasoning to write a proof.

VOCABULARY
• indirect proof

CRITIQUE & EXPLAIN

Philip presents the following number puzzle to his friends.

A. Make Sense and Persevere
Philip states that the number must be 7. Explain why this cannot be true.

B. Write your own number puzzle that has an answer of 5. Your friend says the answer is not 5. How do you use the statements of your puzzle to identify the contradiction?

The number is a prime number. The square of the number is less than 100 and greater than 10. The number is not a factor of 21. What is the number?

? ESSENTIAL QUESTION   What can you conclude when valid reasoning leads to a contradiction?

APPLICATION ⟶

EXAMPLE 1   Use Indirect Reasoning

Beth is having dinner with Sarah and one of Sarah's friends—Libby, Kelly, or Mercedes. Beth orders a chicken and spinach pizza to share for dinner.

 Libby is a vegetarian.

 Mercedes is at the library.

 Kelly is allergic to mushrooms.

Who is having dinner with Beth?

Use indirect reasoning to determine who is having dinner with Beth.

STUDY TIP
Use a flow chart or table to keep track of details if you have difficulty following the logic in an indirect reasoning problem.

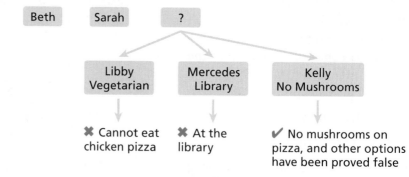

Beth must be having dinner with Sarah and Kelly.

 Try It! **1.** Use indirect reasoning to draw a conclusion in the following situation.

A bagel shop gives customers a free bagel on their birthday. Thato went to the bagel shop today but did not get a free bagel.

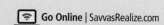 Go Online | SavvasRealize.com

CONCEPT Writing an Indirect Proof by Contradiction

A proof that uses indirect reasoning is an **indirect proof**. Use an indirect proof when a direct proof is impossible. Two types of indirect proof are proof by contradiction and proof by contrapositive.

Proof by Contradiction

A statement is given as a conditional $p \rightarrow q$.

> **Step 1** Assume p and $\sim q$ are true.
>
> **Step 2** Show that the assumption $\sim q$ leads to a contradiction.
>
> **Step 3** Conclude that q must be true.

PROOF **EXAMPLE 2** Write an Indirect Proof by Contradiction

Write an indirect proof of the following statement using proof by contradiction.

> **If Alani walks more than 8 kilometers over a two-day period, then she walks more than 4 kilometers on one or both days.**

Identify the hypothesis and conclusion.

> p: Alani walks more than 8 kilometers over a two-day period.
>
> q: She walks more than 4 kilometers on one or both days.

The statement has the form $p \rightarrow q$.

Step 1 Assume p and $\sim q$ are true.

> $\sim q$: Alani does not walk more than 4 kilometers on either day.

LOOK FOR RELATIONSHIPS
Consider what you can logically conclude from your assumption. What can you conclude from the negation?

Step 2 Show that the assumption $\sim q$ leads to a contradiction.

> If Alani does not walk more than 4 kilometers on either day, then the total distance she walks over the two-day period must be less than or equal to 8 kilometers. This contradicts the hypothesis, p.

Step 3 Conclude that q must be true.

> Because the assumption leads to a contradiction, q must be true.
>
> Alani walks more than 4 kilometers on one or both days.

✓ **Try It!** 2. Write an indirect proof for each statement using proof by contradiction.

> **a.** If today is a weekend day, then it is Saturday or Sunday.
>
> **b.** If you draw an angle that is greater than 90°, it must be obtuse.

CONCEPT Writing an Indirect Proof by Contrapositive

A conditional $p \rightarrow q$ and its contrapositive $\sim q \rightarrow \sim p$ are logically equivalent, so they have the same truth value.

If you prove the contrapositive, you have also proven the conditional.

Proof by Contrapositive

    Step 1 Assume $\sim q$ is true.

    Step 2 Show that the assumption leads to $\sim p$, which shows $\sim q \rightarrow \sim p$.

    Step 3 Conclude that $p \rightarrow q$ must be true.

CONCEPTUAL
UNDERSTANDING

 EXAMPLE 3　Write an Indirect Proof by Contrapositive

Write an indirect proof of the following statement using proof by contrapositive.

    For two positive integers n and m, if $nm > 16$, then either n or m is greater than 4 or both are greater than 4.

Write the negations of p and q.

    p: $nm > 16$

    $\sim p$: $nm \leq 16$ ← | This is the part of the contrapositive you prove.

    q: $n > 4$ or $m > 4$ or both are greater than 4

    $\sim q$: $n \leq 4$ and $m \leq 4$ | This is the part of the contrapositive you assume.

COMMON ERROR
Be careful not to make assumptions that are not given in the statements.

Step 1 Assume $\sim q$ is true.

    Assume $n \leq 4$ and $m \leq 4$.

Step 2 Show that the assumption leads to $\sim p$.

    $n \leq 4$ $m \leq 4$

    $nm \leq 4m$ $4m \leq 16$

| Use properties of inequality to write equivalent expressions of $n \leq 4$ and $m \leq 4$ as $nm \leq 16$.

    By the Transitive Property, $nm \leq 16$.

    Therefore, $\sim q \rightarrow \sim p$

Step 3 Conclude that $p \rightarrow q$ must be true.

    Proving the contrapositive proves the conditional. Therefore, for two positive integers n and m, if $nm > 16$, then either n or m is greater than 4 or both are greater than 4.

✅ **Try It!**　**3.** Write an indirect proof of each statement using proof by contrapositive.

    a. If today is Wednesday, then tomorrow is Thursday.

    b. If a whole number is between 1 and 4, it is a factor of 6.

CONCEPT SUMMARY Indirect Proof of $p \to q$

BY CONTRADICTION

Steps

1. Assume p and $\sim q$ are true.
2. Show that the assumption $\sim q$ leads to a contradiction.
3. Conclude that q must be true.

BY CONTRAPOSITIVE

Steps

1. Assume $\sim q$ is true.
2. Show that the assumption leads to $\sim p$, which shows $\sim q \to \sim p$.
3. Conclude that $p \to q$ must be true.

☑ Do You UNDERSTAND?

1. **? ESSENTIAL QUESTION** What can you conclude when valid reasoning leads to a contradiction?

2. **Vocabulary** What are the two types of indirect proof? How are they similar and how are they different?

3. **Error Analysis** Consider the figure below.

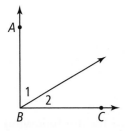

Consider the following conditional.

   If $\angle ABC$ is a right angle and, $m\angle 1 < 60$, then $m\angle 2 > 30$.

A student will prove the contrapositive as a way of proving the conditional. The student plans to assume $m\angle 2 < 30$ and then prove $m\angle 1 > 60$. Explain the error in the student's plan.

4. **Make Sense and Persevere** How do truth tables explain why proving the contrapositive also prove the original conditional statement?

5. **Generalize** Explain how you can identify the statement you assume and the statement you try to prove when writing a proof by contrapositive.

Do You KNOW HOW?

Use indirect reasoning to draw a conclusion in each situation.

6. Tamira only cuts the grass on a day that it does not rain. She cut the grass on Thursday.

7. Gabriela works at the library every Saturday morning. She did not work at the library this morning.

Write the first step of an indirect proof for each of the following statements.

8. $m\angle JKM = m\angle JKL - m\angle MKL$

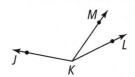

9. $\overline{PQ}$ is perpendicular to $\overline{ST}$.

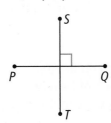

10. What can you conclude from the following situation using indirect reasoning? Explain.

   • Nadeem spent more than $10 but less than $11 for a sandwich and drink.

   • He spent $8.49 on his sandwich.

   • The cost for milk is $1.49.

   • The cost for orange juice is $2.49.

   • The cost for a tropical smoothie is $2.89.

   • The cost for apple juice is $2.59.

UNDERSTAND

11. **Construct Arguments** Write an indirect proof for this conditional statement about the given figure.

    If $\overline{NJ}$ is the perpendicular bisector of $\overline{KM}$, then $LM = 6$.

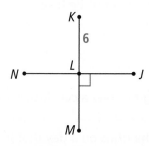

12. **Higher Order Thinking** Write an indirect proof about the given conditional using either contradiction or contrapositive. What is an advantage of the method you chose?

    Given that x is a whole number, if x and $3x$ are both less than 10, then $x \le 3$.

13. **Mathematical Connections** Write a proof by contrapositive to prove the following conditional about the figures.

    If $\angle TUV \cong \angle WXY$, then $x \ne y$.

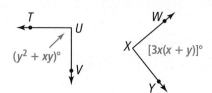

14. **Error Analysis** Consider the conditional, "If x^2 is even, then x is even." Anna uses the contrapositive to prove the conditional. What is Anna's error?

    Assume x is even. Then x can be written in the form $2k$, where k is an integer. Substitute this into x^2 to get $(2k)^2$, or $4k^2$. This expression can be written in the form $2m$, where m is an integer, which proves x^2 is even. ✗

PRACTICE

Use indirect reasoning to draw a conclusion in each situation. SEE EXAMPLE 1

15. Every student in Mr. Green's 2nd period class got an A on the math test. Paige got a B on the test.

16. Only students who studied at least 3 hours for the history test got an A on it. Derek studied 2 hours for the test.

Write the first step of an indirect proof of each statement. SEE EXAMPLE 2

17. $ST + TU + UV = 150$

18. Ray DE is the angle bisector of $\angle ADC$.

Identify the two statements that contradict each other in each set. SEE EXAMPLE 2

19.   I. $m\angle K + m\angle L = 150$

    II. $m\angle K - m\angle L = 20$

    III. $m\angle K = 180$

20.   I. $\angle S$ is an acute angle.

    II. $m\angle S = 80$

    III. $m\angle S + m\angle T = 40$

21. **Write an indirect proof for the following conditional about the figure.** SEE EXAMPLE 2

    If $\angle EFG$ and $\angle HFJ$ are vertical angles, then $x \ne 3y$.

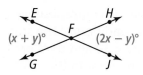

22. **Write a proof of the contrapositive to prove the following conditional about the figures.** SEE EXAMPLE 3

    If $AB + CD = EF$, then $EF = 14$.

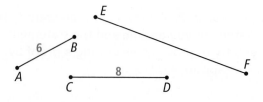

PRACTICE & PROBLEM SOLVING

APPLY

23. Model With Mathematics The lighthouse forms a right angle with the path of the boat.

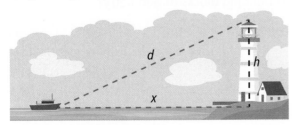

a. Write an equation relating *h*, *d*, and *x*.

b. Write an indirect proof of the statement by proving the contrapositive.

If *x* decreases, then *d* decreases.

24. Reason Friends eat the entire 6 slices of a pie. No slices are shared. Prove the following conditional by proving the contrapositive for the conditional.

If four friends share the pie, then at most two of the friends will have more than one slice of pie each.

25. Reason The library is at the midpoint between Nicky's home and the museum.

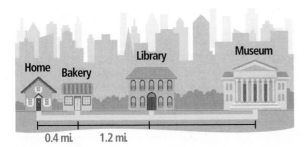

Nicky begins at her home and walks toward the museum. Write an indirect proof for this conditional: When she gets to the library, she will have less than 2 miles left to go.

ASSESSMENT PRACTICE

26. Does this pair of statements contradict each other? Explain.

∠P and ∠Q are both obtuse angles.

∠P and ∠Q are supplementary.

27. SAT/ACT If you write a proof of the following conditional by proving the contrapositive, what should your assumption be?

If $\overrightarrow{JK}$ is the angle bisector of ∠HJL, then $m\angle HJK + m\angle KJL = 90$.

Ⓐ $\overrightarrow{JK}$ is the angle bisector of ∠HJL.

Ⓑ $\overrightarrow{JK}$ is not the angle bisector of ∠HJL.

Ⓒ $m\angle HJK + m\angle KJL = 90$

Ⓓ $m\angle HJK + m\angle KJL \neq 90$

28. Performance Task Customers who eat lunch at a diner have the following meal choices:

Part A Write an indirect proof of the following conditional.

If a customer chooses a meal with a banana, then the customer also has a cheese sandwich.

Part B Write another conditional statement related to which meal a customer has at the diner. Then write an indirect proof of your conditional statement.

? TOPIC ESSENTIAL QUESTION

1. What are the fundamental building blocks of geometry?

Vocabulary Review

Choose the correct term to complete each sentence.

2. A statement accepted without proof is a _____.

3. Arriving at a conclusion by observing patterns is _____.

4. A _____ is the combination of a conditional and its converse.

5. According to the _____, if a conditional statement and its hypothesis are true, then its conclusion is also true.

6. A conjecture that has been proven is a _____.

7. A statement of the form *if not q, then not p* is a _____ of the conditional *if p, then q*.

8. You use _____ when you logically come to a valid conclusion based on given statements.

- biconditional
- conjecture
- contrapositive
- converse
- deductive reasoning
- inductive reasoning
- Law of Detachment
- Law of Syllogism
- postulate
- theorem

Concepts & Skills Review

LESSON 6-1 | **Measuring Segments and Angles**

Quick Review

If a **line segment** is divided into parts, the length of the whole segment is the sum of the lengths of its individual parts. **Congruent segments** have the same length.

Similarly, if an **angle** is divided into parts, the measure of the whole angle is the sum of the measures of the individual angles. **Congruent angles** have the same measure.

Example

Given $SU = 60$, find x.

$$ST + TU = SU$$
$$(6x - 24) + (2x + 20) = 60$$
$$8x - 4 = 60$$
$$8x = 64$$
$$x = 8$$

Practice & Problem Solving

Find each value.

9. $LN = 45$. Find x.

10. $RS = 27$. Find QS.

Find the measure of each angle.

11. $m\angle EBG = 60$; $m\angle FBG = 2m\angle EBF$; $m\angle EBF = $

12. $m\angle ABE = 64$; $m\angle DBE = $ ■

13. $m\angle GBH = 28$; $m\angle GBC = $ ■

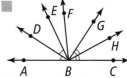

14. **Reason** Point K is located at 7 on a number line, and $JK = KL$. If the coordinate of L is 23, what is the coordinate of point J?

Quick Review

You can use a compass and a straightedge to copy segments and angles, and to construct the **angle bisector** of a given angle and the **perpendicular bisector** of a given line segment.

Any geometric figure that can be constructed using a compass and straightedge is a **construction**.

Example

Construct the angle bisector of ∠A.

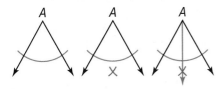

From the vertex, draw an arc that intersects both sides of the angle.

Next, using the same compass setting at each intersection, draw intersecting arcs within the angle.

Finally, draw the angle bisector from the vertex through the intersecting arcs.

Practice & Problem Solving

Copy each segment, and construct the perpendicular bisector.

15.

16.

Copy each angle, and construct its bisector.

17.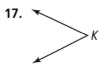

18.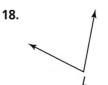

19. **Make Sense and Persevere** Why must the compass width be larger than half the segment width to draw a perpendicular bisector?

20. **Model With Mathematics** The sides of a roof meet at a 120° angle. A strip of wood extends down from the vertex so that it bisects the angle. Draw a diagram of the roof with the bisecting strip of wood.

Quick Review

The midpoint formula gives the coordinates of the **midpoint** between two points.

$$M = \left(\frac{x_1 + x_2}{2}, \frac{y_1 + y_2}{2} \right)$$

The distance formula gives the distance between two points on a coordinate plane.

$$d = \sqrt{(x_2 - x_1)^2 + (y_2 - y_1)^2}$$

Example

What are the coordinates of point K that is $\frac{2}{3}$ the distance from $J(8, 3)$ to $L(2, 6)$?

Horizontal distance: $\frac{2}{3}(x_2 - x_1) = \frac{2}{3}(2 - 8) = -4$

Vertical distance: $\frac{2}{3}(y_2 - y_1) = \frac{2}{3}(6 - 3) = 2$

$K(x, y) = (x_1 + (-4), y_1 + 2) = (8 - 4, 3 + 2) = (4, 5)$

Practice & Problem Solving

Find the midpoint and length of each segment.

21. $\overline{EF}$

22. $\overline{FG}$

23. $\overline{GH}$

24. $\overline{EH}$

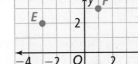

25. What are the coordinates of the point $\frac{2}{5}$ of the way from H to E on the grid?

26. **Make Sense of Problems** Sadie models her neighborhood on a coordinate plane so that her school is at (8, 12) and a store is at (14, 3). What are the coordinates of the point halfway between the school and the store?

Quick Review

Inductive reasoning is the process of reaching a conclusion by observing patterns. A **conjecture** is a conclusion reached through inductive reasoning.

You can use several examples to support a conjecture, or you can disprove it by finding a **counterexample**.

Example

Make a conjecture about the shape of the *n*th term of the pattern shown.

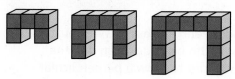

1st term: 2 blocks down each side, 3 blocks across

2nd term: 3 blocks down each side, 4 blocks across

3rd term: 4 blocks down each side, 5 blocks across

Conjecture: The *n*th term will have $n + 1$ blocks down each side and $n + 2$ blocks across.

Practice & Problem Solving

Use inductive reasoning to find the next two terms in each sequence.

27. 1, 2, 6, 24, 120, …   **28.** 3, 5, 8, 10, 13, …

29. 2, 5, 9, 14, 20, …   **30.** 17, 21, 25, 29, 33, …

Find a counterexample to disprove each statement, or support it with four examples.

31. All triangles have three congruent angles.

32. If p is an even number, then $p + 12$ is even.

33. Construct Arguments Explain why only one counterexample is sufficient to disprove a statement, but one example is not sufficient to prove a statement.

34. The table shows how much Jack saves in his bank account each week. At this rate, how much will he save on week 10?

Week	Savings ($)
1	1.75
2	3.50
3	5.25
4	7.00

Quick Review

A **conditional** $p \rightarrow q$ relates a **hypothesis** p to a **conclusion** q. The **converse** is $q \rightarrow p$, the **inverse** is $\sim p \rightarrow \sim q$, the **contrapositive** is $\sim q \rightarrow \sim p$ and a **biconditional** is $p \leftrightarrow q$.

Statements are logically equivalent if they have the same **truth value**. A conditional and its contrapositive are logically equivalent. A converse and an inverse are also logically equivalent.

Example

Find the truth value of the following conditional: All quadrilaterals have four congruent angles.

A parallelogram that is not a rectangle is an example of a quadrilateral. It is a counterexample because its angles are not all congruent. The truth value for the conditional is false.

Practice & Problem Solving

For each statement, write a conditional and the converse, inverse, and contrapositive.

35. A number that is a multiple of 4 is a multiple of 2.

36. Kona jogs 5 miles every Saturday morning.

Find the truth value of each conditional. Explain your reasoning or show a counterexample.

37. If a number is less than 4, then it is prime.

38. If $3x - 7 < 14$, then $x < 8$.

39. If it snows, then school will be cancelled.

40. Communicate Precisely A cafeteria only offers pudding on Tuesdays. Use this fact to write a biconditional about the pudding.

LESSON 6-6 › Deductive Reasoning

Quick Review

Deductive reasoning uses logical steps based on given facts to reach a conclusion and can be applied through laws of logic, such as the following.

- **Law of Detachment:** If $p \to q$ and p are true, then q is true.
- **Law of Syllogism:** If $p \to q$ and $q \to r$ are true, then $p \to r$ is true.

Example

Given the following, use the Law of Syllogism to write a true conditional.

- If $m\angle A < 90$, then $\angle A$ is acute.
- If $\angle A$ is acute, then it is not a right angle.

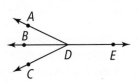

Conditional: If $m\angle A < 90$, then $\angle A$ is not a right angle.

Practice & Problem Solving

Assume the given information is true.

41. If $AB = BC$, then $DE = 2(AB)$. $AB = 6$ and $BC = 6$. What can you conclude?

42. If it is a sunny day, the water park is filled with people. If the water park is filled with people, the lines for each ride are long. Use the Law of Syllogism to write a true conditional.

43. **Communicate Precisely** An advertisement says if you use their toothpaste for more than a week, you will have fresher breath. You use the toothpaste ten days. If the advertisement is true, what can you conclude?

LESSON 6-7 & 6-8 › Writing Proofs and Indirect Proof

Quick Review

A **proof** uses deductive reasoning to explain why a conjecture is true. A conjecture that has been proven is a **theorem**.

For an indirect proof, assume the negation of what is to be proven, and then show that the assumption leads to a contradiction.

Example

Write a paragraph proof.

Given: $m\angle BDC + m\angle ADE = 180$

Prove: $\angle ADB \cong \angle BDC$

Proof: By definition of supplementary angles, $m\angle ADB + m\angle ADE = 180$. Since it is given that $m\angle BDC + m\angle ADE = 180$, by the Congruent Supplements Theorem, $\angle ADB \cong \angle BDC$.

Practice & Problem Solving

Find the value of each variable and the measure of each labeled angle.

44.
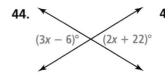
$(3x - 6)°$ $(2x + 22)°$

45.
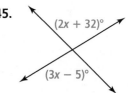
$(2x + 32)°$
$(3x - 5)°$

46. **Construct Arguments** Write a proof.

Given: $m\angle TUV = 90$

Prove: $x = 12$

$(4x)°$ $y°$

47. **Construct Arguments** Write an indirect proof by proving the contrapositive.

Given: $GJ = 48$

Prove: $x \neq 12$

$2x$ x
G H J

TOPIC 7

Parallel and Perpendicular Lines

? TOPIC ESSENTIAL QUESTION

What properties are specific to parallel lines and perpendicular lines?

Topic Overview

Topic Vocabulary

- flow proof

Digital Experience

INTERACTIVE STUDENT EDITION
Access online or offline.

ACTIVITIES Complete *Explore & Reason, Model & Discuss*, and *Critique & Explain* activities. Interact with Examples and Try Its.

ANIMATION View and interact with real-world applications.

PRACTICE Practice what you've learned.

 Go online | SavvasRealize.com

▶ **Parallel Paving Company**

Building roads consists of many different tasks. Once civil engineers have designed the road, they work with surveyors and construction crews to clear and level the land. Sometimes specialists have to blast away rock in order to clear the land. Once the land is leveled, the crews bring in asphalt pavers to smooth out the hot asphalt.

Sometimes construction crews will start work at both ends of the new road and meet in the middle. Think about this during the Mathematical Modeling in 3 Acts lesson.

TOPIC 7

▶ **VIDEOS** Watch clips to support *Mathematical Modeling in 3 Acts Lessons* and **enVision**® *STEM Projects.*

CONCEPT SUMMARY Review key lesson content through multiple representations.

ASSESSMENT Show what you've learned.

GLOSSARY Read and listen to English and Spanish definitions.

TUTORIALS Get help from *Virtual Nerd*, right when you need it.

MATH TOOLS Explore math with digital tools and manipulatives.

enVision® STEM

Video

Did You Know?

A roof is a critical component of shelter, one of humankind's most basic needs. Roofs vary depending on climate, local materials, and designs.

The front and back panels of a roof require a different, more complex, design than the rest of the roof and include vertical support beams called gable studs.

A roof's pitch determines the length of the rafters.

The weight of the roofing material affects the spacing of a roof's rafters and gable studs.

Bermuda has no fresh water other than falling rain, so roofs are designed to funnel rain down into underground holding tanks.

The weight of snow on a roof can be up to 21 lbs per square foot.

A green roof is topped with earth and plants, which cools the building in the summer and insulates it in the winter.

▶ Your Task: Build a Roof

You and your classmates will plan the construction of a roof, including the location and cost of its ridge-board, rafters, and gable studs. How does the cost of the roof change based on on its pitch and the spacing between rafters?

Go Online | SavvasRealize.com

7-1

Parallel Lines

I CAN... determine the measures of the angles formed when parallel lines are intersected by a transversal.

EXPLORE & REASON

The diagram shows two parallel lines cut by a transversal.

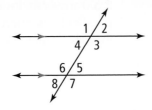

A. Look for Relationships What relationships among the measures of the angles do you see?

B. Suppose a different transversal intersects the parallel lines. Would you expect to find the same relationships with the measures of those angles? Explain.

? ESSENTIAL QUESTION

What angle relationships are created when parallel lines are intersected by a transversal?

EXAMPLE 1   Identify Angle Pairs

Identify the pairs of angles of each angle type made by the snowmobile tracks.

∠4 and ∠8, ∠1 and ∠5, ∠2 and ∠6, and ∠3 and ∠7 are corresponding angles.

STUDY TIP
Transversals can intersect either parallel or nonparallel lines. The types of angle pairs remain the same.

∠7 and ∠1, and ∠6 and ∠4 are alternate interior angles.

∠2 and ∠8, and ∠5 and ∠3 are alternate exterior angles.

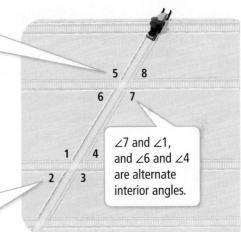

☑ Try It!

1. Which angle pairs include the named angle?

a. ∠4

b. ∠7

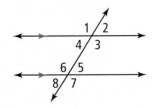

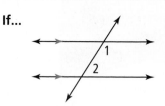
POSTULATE 7-1 Same-Side Interior Angles Postulate

If a transversal intersects two parallel lines, then same-side interior angles are supplementary.

If...

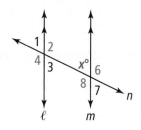

Then... $m\angle 1 + m\angle 2 = 180$

CONCEPTUAL UNDERSTANDING

 EXAMPLE 2 Explore Angle Relationships

How can you express each of the numbered angles in terms of x?

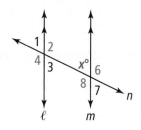

LOOK FOR RELATIONSHIPS
What patterns do you notice about the angles formed by two parallel lines cut by a transversal?

Angle 7 and the angle with measure x are vertical angles. Both $\angle 6$ and $\angle 8$ each form a linear pair with the angle with measure x and are therefore supplementary to it.

By Postulate 7-1 you know that $\angle 2$ and the angle with measure x are supplementary. From that you can make conclusions about $\angle 1$, $\angle 3$, and $\angle 4$ like you did with $\angle 6$, $\angle 7$, and $\angle 8$.

The angles equal to $x°$ are $\angle 1$, $\angle 3$, and $\angle 7$.
The angles that are supplementary to the angle with measure x have the measure $(180 - x)$. These are $\angle 2$, $\angle 4$, $\angle 6$, and $\angle 8$.

 Try It! 2. If $\angle 4 = 118°$, what is the measure of each of the other angles?

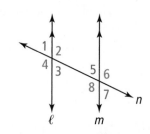

THEOREM 7-1 Alternate Interior Angles Theorem

If a transversal intersects two parallel lines, then alternate interior angles are congruent.

PROOF: SEE EXAMPLE 3.

If...

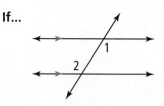

Then... $\angle 1 \cong \angle 2$

THEOREM 7-2 Corresponding Angles Theorem

If a transversal intersects two parallel lines, then corresponding angles are congruent.

PROOF: SEE EXAMPLE 3 TRY IT.

If...

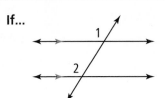

Then... $\angle 1 \cong \angle 2$

THEOREM 7-3 Alternate Exterior Angles Theorem

If a transversal intersects two parallel lines, then alternate exterior angles are congruent.

PROOF: SEE EXERCISE 10.

If...

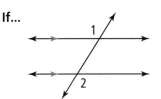

Then... $\angle 1 \cong \angle 2$

PROOF

EXAMPLE 3 Prove the Alternate Interior Angles Theorem

Prove the Alternate Interior Angles Theorem.

Given: $m \parallel n$

Prove: $\angle 1 \cong \angle 2$

Plan: Use the Same-Side Interior Angles Postulate to show $\angle 1$ is supplementary to $\angle 3$. Then show that angles 1 and 2 are congruent because they are both supplementary to the same angle.

Proof:

Statements	Reasons
1) $m \parallel n$	**1)** Given
2) $\angle 1$ and $\angle 3$ are supplementary	**2)** Same-Side Interior $\angle s$ Postulate
3) $m\angle 1 + m\angle 3 = 180$	**3)** Def. of supplementary angles
4) $m\angle 2 + m\angle 3 = 180$	**4)** Angle Addition Postulate
5) $m\angle 1 + m\angle 3 = m\angle 2 + m\angle 3$	**5)** Transitive Property of Equality
6) $m\angle 1 = m\angle 2$	**6)** Subtraction Property of Equality
7) $\angle 1 \cong \angle 2$	**7)** Def. of congruence

COMMON ERROR
Remember that for the proof to be complete, the last statement of the proof must match what you are trying to prove.

 Try It! **3.** Prove the Corresponding Angles Theorem.

Given: $m \parallel n$

Prove: $\angle 1 \cong \angle 2$

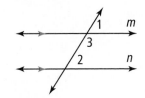

PROOF   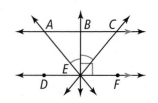 **EXAMPLE 4**   Use Parallel Lines to Prove an Angle Relationship

Use the diagram to prove the angle relationship.

Given: $\overline{AC} \parallel \overline{DF}$, and $\overline{BE} \perp \overline{DF}$, $\angle AEB \cong \angle CEB$

Prove: $\angle BAE \cong \angle BCE$

Proof:

Statements	Reasons
1) $\overline{AC} \parallel \overline{DF}$, $\overline{AC} \perp \overline{BE}$	1) Given
2) $\angle BED$, $\angle BEF$ are rt. angles	2) Def. of perpendicular
3) $m\angle BED = m\angle BEF = 90$	3) Def. of rt. angles
4) $m\angle AED + m\angle AEB = 90$, $m\angle CEF + m\angle CEB = 90$	4) Angle Addition Postulate
5) $\angle AEB \cong \angle CEB$	5) Given
6) $\angle AED \cong \angle CEF$	6) Congruent Complements Thm.
7) $\angle BAE \cong \angle AED$, $\angle BCE \cong \angle CEF$	7) Alt. Interior $\angle$s Thm.
8) $\angle BAE \cong \angle BCE$	8) Transitive Prop. of Congruence

MAKE SENSE AND PERSEVERE
Look for relationships in the diagram not listed as given information. What angle relationships are shown in the diagram?

 Try It! **4.** Given $\overline{AB} \parallel \overline{CD}$, prove that $m\angle 1 + m\angle 2 + m\angle 3 = 180$.

APPLICATION   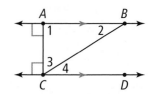 **EXAMPLE 5**   Find Angle Measures

The white trim shown for the wall of a barn should be constructed so that $\overline{AC} \parallel \overline{EG}$, $\overline{JA} \parallel \overline{HB}$, and $\overline{JC} \parallel \overline{KG}$. What should $m\angle 1$ and $m\angle 3$ be?

Formulate ◄ Look for relationships among the angles.

Compute ◄ By the Same-Side Interior Angles Postulate, $m\angle 1 + 68 = 180$.

$m\angle 1 = 180 - 68 = 112$

By the Corresponding Angles Theorem, $\angle EAB \cong \angle 2$ and $\angle 2 \cong \angle 3$, so $\angle 3 \cong \angle EAB$ by the Transitive Property of Congruence.

$m\angle 3 = 68$

Interpret ◄ So, $m\angle 1 = 112$ and $m\angle 3 = 68$.

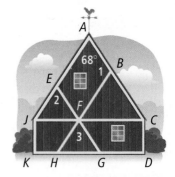

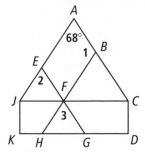

 Try It! **5.** If $m\angle EJF = 56$, find $m\angle FHK$.

Go Online | SavvasRealize.com

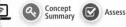

 CONCEPT SUMMARY Parallel Lines and Angle Pairs

There are four special angle relationships formed when parallel lines are intersected by a transversal.

POSTULATE 7-1 ▶ Same-Side Interior Angles Postulate

If...

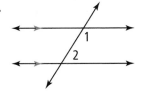

Then... $m\angle 1 + m\angle 2 = 180$

THEOREM 7-1 ▶ Alternate Interior Angles Theorem

If...

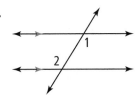

Then... $\angle 1 \cong \angle 2$

THEOREM 7-2 ▶ Corresponding Angles Theorem

If...

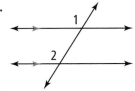

Then... $\angle 1 \cong \angle 2$

THEOREM 7-3 ▶ Alternate Exterior Angles Theorem

If...

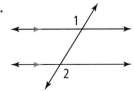

Then... $\angle 1 \cong \angle 2$

Do You UNDERSTAND?

1. **? ESSENTIAL QUESTION** What angle relationships are created when parallel lines are intersected by a transversal?

2. **Vocabulary** When a transversal intersects two parallel lines, which angle pairs are congruent?

3. **Error Analysis** What error did Leah make?

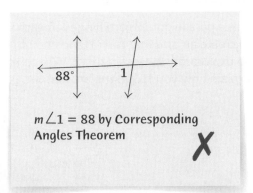

$m\angle 1 = 88$ by Corresponding Angles Theorem ✗

4. **Generalize** For any pair of angles formed by a transversal intersecting parallel lines, what are two possible relationships?

Do You KNOW HOW?

Use the diagram for Exercises 5–8.

Classify each pair of angles. Compare angle measures, and give the postulate or theorem that justifies it.

5. $\angle 2$ and $\angle 6$

6. $\angle 3$ and $\angle 5$

If $m\angle 1 = 71$, find the measure of each angle.

7. $\angle 5$

8. $\angle 7$

9. Elm St. and Spruce St. are parallel. What is $m\angle 1$?

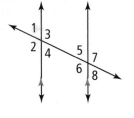

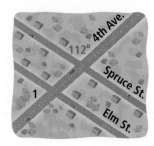

UNDERSTAND

PRACTICE

10. **Construct Arguments** Write a two-column proof of the Alternate Exterior Angles Theorem.

Given: $m \parallel n$

Prove: $\angle 1 \cong \angle 2$

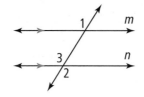

11. **Higher Order Thinking** Using what you know about angle pairs formed by parallel lines and a transversal, how are $\angle 1$, $\angle 2$, $\angle 3$, and $\angle 4$ related in the trapezoid? Explain.

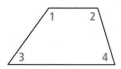

12. **Error Analysis** What error did Tyler make?

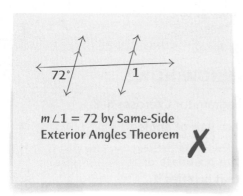

$m\angle 1 = 72$ by Same-Side Exterior Angles Theorem ✗

13. **Generalize** In the diagram shown, if $x + y = 180$, label the remaining angles as $x°$ or $y°$.

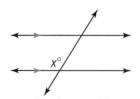

14. **Mathematical Connections** A transversal intersects two parallel lines. The measures of a pair of alternate interior angles are $5v$ and $2w$. The measures of a pair of same-side exterior angles are $10w$ and $5v$. What are the values of w and v?

Identify a pair of angles for each type. SEE EXAMPLE 1

15. same-side interior

16. corresponding

17. alternate exterior

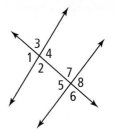

18. Which angles are supplementary to $\angle 1$? Which are congruent to $\angle 1$? SEE EXAMPLE 2

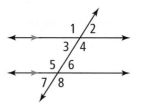

Find each angle measure. SEE EXAMPLE 3

19. $m\angle 1$

20. $m\angle 2$

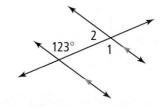

21. Opposite sides of a parallelogram are parallel. Prove that opposite angles of a parallelogram are congruent. SEE EXAMPLE 4

Given: $ABCD$ is a parallelogram

Prove: $\angle A \cong \angle C$, $\angle B \cong \angle D$

22. Three parallelograms are hinged at each vertex to create an arm that can extend and collapse for an exploratory spaceship robot. What is $m\angle 1$? Explain how you found the answer. SEE EXAMPLE 5

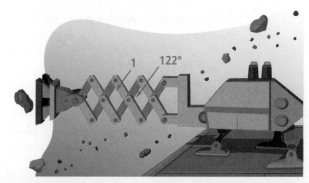

APPLY

23. Model With Mathematics A glazier is setting supports in parallel segments to prevent glass breakage during storms. What are the values of *x* and *y*? Justify your conclusions.

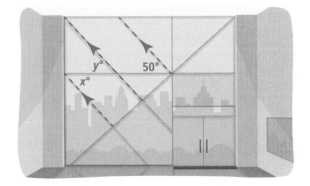

24. Reason In the parking lot shown, all of the lines for the parking spaces should be parallel. If *m*∠3 = 61, what should *m*∠1 and *m*∠2 be? Explain.

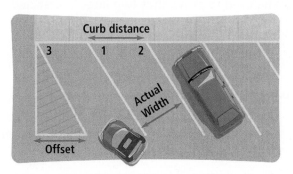

25. Communicate Precisely Margaret is in a boat traveling due west. She turned the boat 50° north of due west for a couple of minutes to get around a peninsula. Then she resumed due west again.

a. How many degrees would she turn the wheel to resume a due west course?

b. Name the pair of angles she used. Are the angles congruent or supplementary?

26. Parallel lines *m* and *n* intersect parallel lines *x* and *y*, representing two sets of intersecting railroad tracks. At what angles do the tracks intersect?

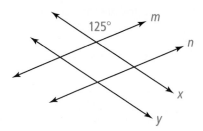

ASSESSMENT PRACTICE

27 Classify each angle as *congruent to* ∠1 or *congruent to* ∠2.

∠3   ∠4

∠5   ∠6

∠7   ∠8

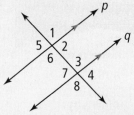

28. SAT/ACT In the diagram, *a* ∥ *b*. What is *m*∠1?

Ⓐ 28

Ⓑ 62

Ⓒ 90

Ⓓ 118

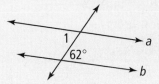

29. Performance Task Students on a scavenger hunt are given the map shown and several clues.

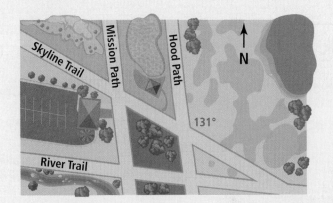

Part A The first clue states the following.

Skyline Trail forms a transversal with Hood Path and Mission Path. Go to the corners that form same side exterior angles north of Skyline Trail.

Which two corners does the clue mean? Use intersections and directions to explain.

Part B If the second clue states the following, what trail marker should they go to?

Hood and Mission Paths are parallel, and the northeast corner of Hood Path and Skyline Trail forms a 131° angle. The angle measure formed by the southwest corner of Skyline Trail and Mission Path is equal to the trail marker number on River Trail you must go to.

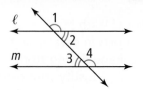
7-2
Proving Lines Parallel

SavvasRealize.com

I CAN... use angle relationships to prove that lines are parallel.

VOCABULARY
• flow proof

Juan analyzes the diagram to see if line ℓ is parallel to line m. His teacher asks if there is enough information to say whether the lines are parallel.

> Yes, if a transversal intersects two parallel lines, then alternate interior angles are congruent and corresponding angles are congruent. I have both angle relationships here, so the lines are parallel.

A. Make Sense and Persevere Why is Juan's statement correct or incorrect?

B. Can you use the Alternate Exterior Angles Theorem to prove that the lines are not parallel?

? **ESSENTIAL QUESTION** What angle relationships can be used to prove that two lines intersected by a transversal are parallel?

👆 **EXAMPLE 1** Understand Angle Relationships

Suppose two lines are not parallel. Can corresponding angles still be congruent?

Draw two nonparallel lines t and m and a transversal s. Draw line ℓ parallel to m that passes through the intersection of s and t.

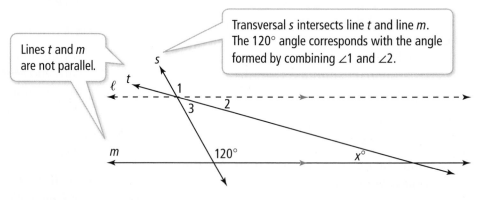

Lines t and m are not parallel.

Transversal s intersects line t and line m. The 120° angle corresponds with the angle formed by combining ∠1 and ∠2.

COMMUNICATE PRECISELY
Consider the conclusion in the example. What statement can you write that is logically equivalent to this statement?

Since ℓ ∥ m, m∠1 = 120 by the Corresponding Angles Theorem. By the Alternate Interior Angles Theorem, m∠2 = x. Since m∠1 + m∠2 = 120 + x, m∠1 + m∠2 > 120.

If two lines are not parallel, then corresponding angles are not congruent.

☑ **Try It!** **1.** Could ∠3 be supplementary to a 120° angle? Explain.

THEOREM 7-4 Converse of the Corresponding Angles Theorem

If two lines and a transversal form corresponding angles that are congruent, then the lines are parallel.

PROOF: SEE EXERCISE 8.

If...

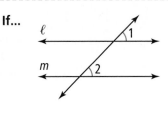

Then... $\ell \parallel m$

THEOREM 7-5 Converse of the Alternate Interior Angles Theorem

If two lines and a transversal form alternate interior angles that are congruent, then the lines are parallel.

PROOF: SEE EXAMPLE 2.

If...

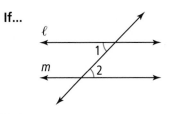

Then... $\ell \parallel m$

PROOF

🖑 **EXAMPLE 2** Write a Flow Proof of Theorem 7-5

Write a flow proof to prove the Converse of the Alternate Interior Angles Theorem.

In a **flow proof**, arrows show the logical connections between statements. Reasons are shown below the statements.

Given: $\angle 1 \cong \angle 2$

Prove: $\ell \parallel m$

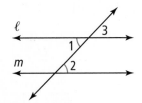

COMMON ERROR
You may incorrectly write all information along one line of the flow proof. Remember that you should have two separate arrows when two statements are needed to justify the next statement in a proof.

Proof:

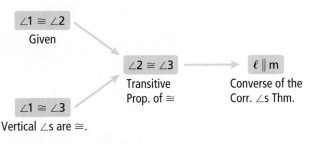

 Try It! **2.** Write a flow proof for Theorem 7-6, the Converse of the Same-Side Interior Angles Postulate.

THEOREM 7-6 Converse of the Same-Side Interior Angles Postulate

If two lines and a transversal form same-side interior angles that are supplementary, then the lines are parallel.

PROOF: SEE EXAMPLE 2 TRY IT.

If... $m\angle 1 + m\angle 2 = 180$

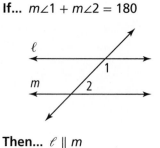

Then... $\ell \parallel m$

THEOREM 7-7 Converse of the Alternate Exterior Angles Theorem

If two lines and a transversal form alternate exterior angles that are congruent, then the lines are parallel.

PROOF: SEE EXERCISE 16.

If...

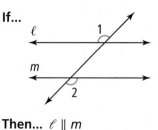

Then... $\ell \parallel m$

CONCEPTUAL
UNDERSTANDING

EXAMPLE 3   Determine Whether Lines Are Parallel

The edges of a new sidewalk must be parallel in order to meet accessibility requirements. Concrete is poured between straight strings. How does an inspector know that the edges of the sidewalk are parallel?

The inspector can first measure the angles of corners of the sidewalk.

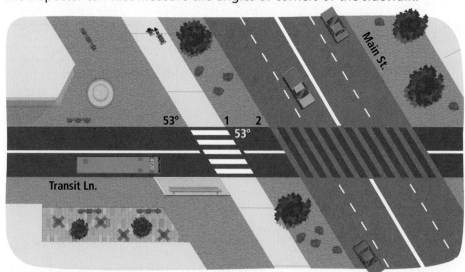

MAKE SENSE AND PERSEVERE
Think about what other theorems could be applied to determine parallel edges. What other measurements could the inspector make?

Since the two 53° angles are congruent, he can apply the Converse of the Alternate Exterior Angles Theorem. The edges of the sidewalk are parallel.

 Try It!   **3.** What is $m\angle 1$? What should $\angle 2$ measure in order to guarantee that the sidewalk is parallel to Main Street? Explain.

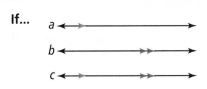

THEOREM 7-8

If two lines are parallel to the same line, then they are parallel to each other.

PROOF: SEE EXERCISE 17.

If...

a

b

c

Then... $a \parallel b$

THEOREM 7-9

If two lines are perpendicular to the same line, then they are parallel to each other.

PROOF: SEE EXERCISE 18.

If...

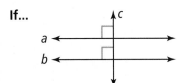

c

a

b

Then... $a \parallel b$

APPLICATION

EXAMPLE 4 **Solve a Problem With Parallel Lines**

A. When building a gate, how does Bailey know that the vertical boards *v* and *w* are parallel?

LOOK FOR RELATIONSHIPS
Look for different ways that parts of a diagram are put together as a whole. How can you use the labeled parts to determine a strategy for solving a problem?

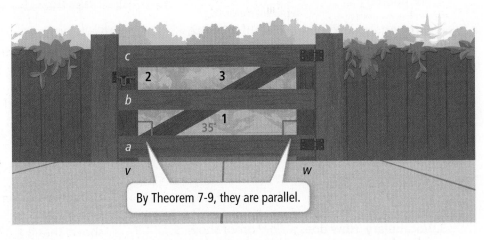

By Theorem 7-9, they are parallel.

B. What should ∠1 measure to ensure board *b* is parallel to board *a*?

Apply the Converse of the Same-Side Interior Angles Postulate.

$$35 + m\angle 1 = 180$$
$$m\angle 1 = 145$$

 Try It! **4. a.** Bailey also needs board *c* to be parallel to board *a*. What should ∠2 measure? Explain.

b. Is $b \parallel c$? Explain.

DIAGRAM

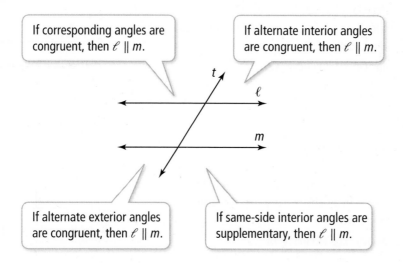

If corresponding angles are congruent, then $\ell \parallel m$.

If alternate interior angles are congruent, then $\ell \parallel m$.

If alternate exterior angles are congruent, then $\ell \parallel m$.

If same-side interior angles are supplementary, then $\ell \parallel m$.

☑ Do You UNDERSTAND?

1. ❓ **ESSENTIAL QUESTION** What angle relationships can be used to prove that two lines intersected by a transversal are parallel?

2. **Error Analysis** Noemi wrote, "If ∠1 ≅ ∠2, then by the Converse of the Same-Side Interior Angles Postulate, $\ell \parallel m$." Explain the error in Noemi's reasoning.

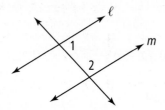

3. **Vocabulary** How does a *flow proof* show logical steps in the proof of a conditional statement?

4. **Reason** How is Theorem 7-9 a special case of the Converse of the Corresponding Angles Theorem?

Do You KNOW HOW?

Use the figure shown for Exercises 5 and 6.

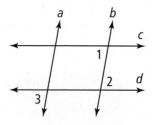

5. If ∠1 ≅ ∠2, which theorem proves that $c \parallel d$?

6. If $m\angle 2 = 4x - 6$ and $m\angle 3 = 2x + 18$, for what value of x is $a \parallel b$? Which theorem justifies your answer?

7. Using the Converse of the Same-Side Interior Angles Postulate, what equation shows that $g \parallel h$?

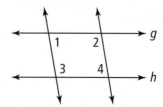

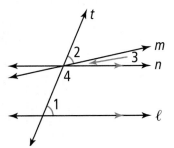
UNDERSTAND

8. Construct Arguments Write an indirect proof of the Converse of the Corresponding Angles Theorem following the outline below.

Given: $\angle 1 \cong \angle 2$

Prove: $\ell \parallel m$

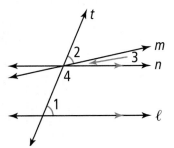

- Assume that lines ℓ and m are not parallel.
- Draw line n parallel to line ℓ.
- Conclude that $m\angle 3 > 0$.
- Use the Same-Side Interior Angles Postulate to arrive at the contradiction that $m\angle 1 \neq m\angle 2$.

9. Error Analysis What is the student's error?

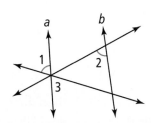

Given $\angle 1 \cong \angle 2$. By the Vertical Angles Thm., $\angle 1 \cong \angle 3$, so by the Transitive Property, $\angle 2 \cong \angle 3$. By the Converse of the Corresponding Angles Thm., $a \parallel b$.

10. Mathematical Connections Copy the figure below. Construct a line through P parallel to ℓ. (*Hint:* Copy either $\angle PCA$ or $\angle PCB$ so that one of the sides of the angle is parallel to ℓ.) What theorem justifies your construction?

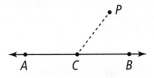

11. Higher Order Thinking The interior angles of a regular hexagon are congruent. Why are any pair of opposite sides parallel?

PRACTICE

For Exercises 12–15, use the given information. Which lines in the figure can you conclude are parallel? State the theorem that justifies each answer. SEE EXAMPLES 1 AND 3

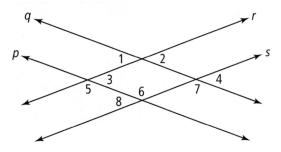

12. $\angle 2 \cong \angle 3$

13. $\angle 6 \cong \angle 7$

14. $\angle 1 \cong \angle 4$

15. $m\angle 5 + m\angle 8 = 180°$

16. Write a flow proof of the Converse of the Alternate Exterior Angles Theorem. SEE EXAMPLE 2

Use the figure for Exercises 17 and 18. SEE EXAMPLE 2

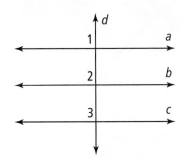

17. Given $a \parallel c$ and $b \parallel c$, write a flow proof of Theorem 7-8.

18. Given $a \perp d$ and $b \perp d$, write a flow proof of Theorem 7-9.

19. For what value of x is $f \parallel g$? Which theorem justifies your answer? SEE EXAMPLE 4

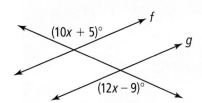

APPLY

20. Look for Relationships To make a puzzle, Denzel draws lines *a* and *b* to cut along on a square piece of posterboard. He wants to draw line *c* so that it is parallel to line *b*. What should the measure of ∠1 be? Explain.

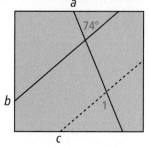

21. Reason A downhill skier is fastest when her skis are parallel. What should ∠1 be in order for the skier to maximize her speed through a gate? Which theorem justifies your answer?

22. Make Sense and Persevere Malia makes a fabric design by drawing diagonals between opposite corners. She wants to draw other lines parallel to one of the diagonal lines, as shown by the dashed lines.

a. What should ∠1 be in order for line *b* to be parallel to line *a*? Explain.

b. What should ∠2 be in order for line *c* to be parallel to line *b*? Explain.

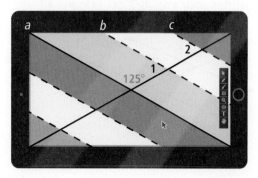

ASSESSMENT PRACTICE

23. In order for *c* ∥ *d*, ∠2 and ∠7 must be ___?___, and ∠3 and ∠5 must be ___?___.

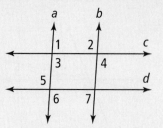

24. SAT/ACT Which statement must always be true?

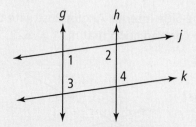

Ⓐ If ∠1 ≅ ∠2, then *g* ∥ *h*.

Ⓑ If ∠1 ≅ ∠3, then *g* ∥ *h*.

Ⓒ If ∠2 ≅ ∠4, then *j* ∥ *k*.

Ⓓ If ∠3 ≅ ∠4, then *j* ∥ *k*.

25. Performance Task The diagram shows part of a plan to arrange aisles in a store.

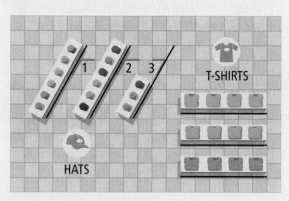

Part A The aisles are arranged so that *m*∠1 = 125. What should be the measures of the other labeled angles so that all three aisles will be parallel? Explain.

Part B Describe how theorems can be applied to make sure that the T-shirt aisles are parallel.

7-3

Parallel Lines and Triangle Angle Sums

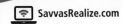

SavvasRealize.com

I CAN... solve problems using the measures of interior and exterior angles of triangles.

👆 EXPLORE & REASON

Two parallel lines never intersect. But, can two lines that intersect ever be parallel to the same line?

Draw point *P*. Then draw lines *a* and *b* that intersect at point *P* as shown.

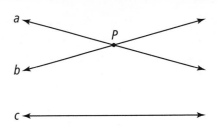

A. Place a pencil below the intersecting lines on your paper to represent line *c*. Rotate the pencil so that it is parallel to line *b*. Can you rotate the pencil so that it is parallel to line *a* at the same time as line *b*?

B. Look for Relationships Can you adjust your drawing of the two intersecting lines so you can rotate the pencil to be parallel to both lines?

❓ ESSENTIAL QUESTION   What is true about the interior and exterior angle measures of a triangle?

CONCEPTUAL UNDERSTANDING

👆 EXAMPLE 1   Investigate the Measures of Triangle Angles

What appears to be the relationship between the angle measures of a triangle?

Using pencil and paper, or scissors and paper, construct several triangles of different types. Number the angles.

  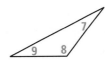

Trace the angles from each triangle and place the vertices together with the sides of the angles sharing a vertex and ray.

For each triangle shown, the angles combine to form a straight angle.

So, the sum of the angle measures of a triangle appears to be 180.

USE APPROPRIATE TOOLS
What tools might you use to confirm that the angles sum to 180°?

☑ Try It!   1. Given two angle measures in a triangle, can you find the measure of the third angle? Explain.

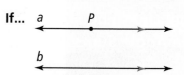
THEOREM 7-10

Through a point not on a line, there is one and only one line parallel to the given line.

PROOF: SEE EXERCISE 10.

If...

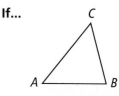

Then... line *a* is the only line parallel to line *b* through *P*.

THEOREM 7-11 Triangle Angle-Sum Theorem

The sum of the measures of all the angles of a triangle is 180.

PROOF: SEE EXAMPLE 2.

If...

Then... $m\angle A + m\angle B + m\angle C = 180$

PROOF   **EXAMPLE 2**   **Prove the Triangle Angle-Sum Theorem**

Prove the Triangle Angle-Sum Theorem.

Given: $\triangle ABC$

Prove: $m\angle 1 + m\angle 2 + m\angle 3 = 180$

STUDY TIP
When using a geometric figure in a proof, you can construct additional parts to help with the proof, such as parallel lines, angle bisectors, and midpoints.

Plan: Draw a line through *C*, because a straight angle measures 180. This line should be parallel to the line containing $\overline{AB}$ so that an alternate interior angle relationship is formed.

Proof:

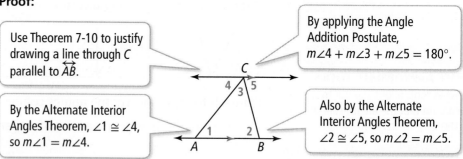

Use Theorem 7-10 to justify drawing a line through *C* parallel to $\overleftrightarrow{AB}$.

By the Alternate Interior Angles Theorem, $\angle 1 \cong \angle 4$, so $m\angle 1 = m\angle 4$.

By applying the Angle Addition Postulate, $m\angle 4 + m\angle 3 + m\angle 5 = 180°$.

Also by the Alternate Interior Angles Theorem, $\angle 2 \cong \angle 5$, so $m\angle 2 = m\angle 5$.

By substitution, $m\angle 1 + m\angle 3 + m\angle 2 = 180$. Therefore, using the Commutative Property of Addition, $m\angle 1 + m\angle 2 + m\angle 3 = 180$.

Try It!   **2.** How does Theorem 7-10 justify the construction of the line through *C* that is parallel to $\overleftrightarrow{AB}$?

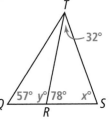

EXAMPLE 3 Use the Triangle Angle-Sum Theorem

What are the values of x and y?

Write and solve an equation that relates the measures of the angles of △TRS.

$$32 + 78 + x = 180$$
$$x = 70$$

> Use the Triangle Angle-Sum Theorem.

To find the value of y, notice that ∠QRS is a straight angle.

$$m\angle QRT + m\angle TRS = 180$$
$$y + 78 = 180$$
$$y = 102$$

> Apply the Angle Addition Postulate.

The value of x is 70 and the value of y is 102.

☑ Try It! **3.** What are the values of x and y in each figure?

a.

b.

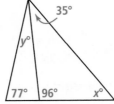

THEOREM 7-12 Triangle Exterior Angle Theorem

The measure of each exterior angle of a triangle equals the sum of the measures of its two remote interior angles.

PROOF: SEE EXERCISE 13.

If...

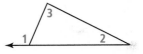

Then... $m\angle 1 = m\angle 2 + m\angle 3$

EXAMPLE 4 Apply the Triangle Exterior Angle Theorem

What is the missing angle measure in each figure?

A.

B.

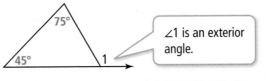

> ∠1 is an exterior angle.

> ∠2 is a remote interior angle.

COMMON ERROR
Be careful when writing an equation to solve for the unknown angle measure. The unknown value can be an addend or the sum.

$$m\angle 1 = 45 + 75$$
$$m\angle 1 = 120$$

> Use the Exterior Angles Theorem.

$$109 = 51 + m\angle 2$$
$$58 = m\angle 2$$

CONTINUED ON THE NEXT PAGE

 Try It! **4.** What is the value of *x* in each figure?

a.
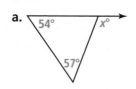

b.
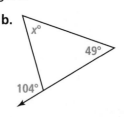

 EXAMPLE 5 **Apply the Triangle Theorems**

Cheyenne built this display for her ornament collection. Each shelf is parallel to the base. She recalls only the angle measures shown in the diagram. Now she wants to build another just like it. What are the measures of ∠1, ∠2, and ∠3?

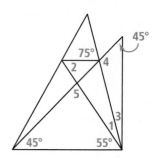

Formulate ◄ Begin by writing equations for the unknown angle measures. Since the bottom and top shelves are parallel, apply the Corresponding Angles Theorem.

$$55 + m\angle 1 = 75$$

Apply the Triangle Exterior Angle Theorem.

$$m\angle 1 + m\angle 2 = 75$$

Use the Triangle Angle-Sum Theorem.

$$45 + 45 + (m\angle 1 + m\angle 3 + 55) = 180$$

Compute ◄ Solve for $m\angle 1$, $m\angle 2$, and $m\angle 3$.

$$55 + m\angle 1 = 75 \qquad m\angle 1 + m\angle 2 = 75$$
$$m\angle 1 = 20 \qquad 20 + m\angle 2 = 75$$
$$m\angle 2 = 55$$
$$45 + 45 + (m\angle 1 + m\angle 3 + 55) = 180$$
$$45 + 45 + (20 + m\angle 3 + 55) = 180$$
$$m\angle 3 + 165 = 180$$
$$m\angle 3 = 15$$

Interpret ◄ The measures of the angles are $m\angle 1 = 20$, $m\angle 2 = 55$, and $m\angle 3 = 15$.

 Try It! **5.** What are the measures of ∠4 and ∠5? Explain.

CONCEPT SUMMARY Angle Measures of Triangles

WORDS | **Interior Angle Measures** | **Exterior Angle Measure**

The sum of the measures of all the angles of a triangle is 180.

The measure of each exterior angle of a triangle equals the sum of the measures of its two remote interior angles.

DIAGRAM

$m\angle A + m\angle B + m\angle C = 180$

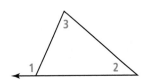

$m\angle 1 = m\angle 2 + m\angle 3$

Do You UNDERSTAND?

1. **ESSENTIAL QUESTION** What is true about the interior and exterior angle measures of a triangle?

2. **Error Analysis** Chiang determined that the value of x is 103 and the value of y is 132 in the figure below. What mistake did Chiang make?

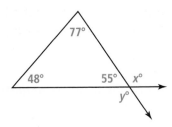

3. **Vocabulary** The word *remote* means distant or far apart. What parts of a figure are *remote interior angles* distant from?

4. **Look for Relationships** Use the Triangle Angle-Sum Theorem to answer the following questions. Explain your answers.

   a. What are the measures of each angle of an equiangular triangle?

   b. If one of the angle measures of an isosceles triangle is 90, what are the measures of the other two angles?

Do You KNOW HOW?

What is the value of x in each figure?

5.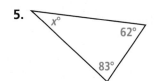

6.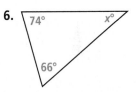

What is the value of x in each figure?

7.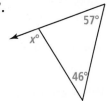

8.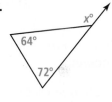

9. Write an equation relating the measures of ∠1, ∠2, and ∠3. Write another equation relating the measures of ∠1, ∠2, and ∠4.

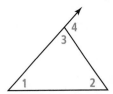

✏ PRACTICE & PROBLEM SOLVING

UNDERSTAND

10. Construct Arguments Write a proof for Theorem 7-10.

11. Higher Order Thinking Marisol claims that each pair of remote interior angles in a triangle has two exterior angles. Do you agree? Use a diagram to support your answer.

12. Error Analysis A student was asked to find the value of x. What error did the student make?

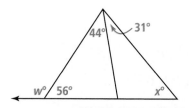

By the Linear Pairs Theorem,
$w + 56 = 180$, so $w = 124$.
By the Triangle Exterior Angle
Theorem, $w = x + 31$, or
$124 = x + 31$, so $x = 93$.

13. Reason Prove the Triangle Exterior Angle Theorem.

14. Mathematical Connections What are the values of x, y, and z? Use theorems to justify each answer.

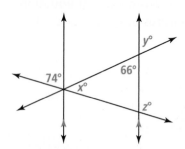

15. Use Structure Write and solve an equation to find the value of x. What is the measure of each labeled angle?

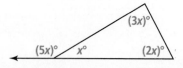

PRACTICE

What are the values of the variables in each figure? SEE EXAMPLES 1–3

16.

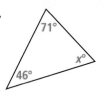

17.

18.

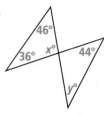

19.

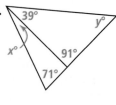

What is the value of x in each figure? SEE EXAMPLE 4

20.

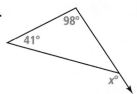

21.

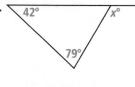

22.

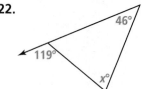

23.

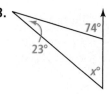

For Exercises 24–27, find the measure of each angle. SEE EXAMPLE 4

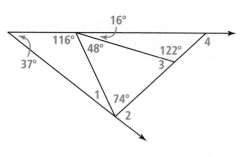

24. ∠1

25. ∠2

26. ∠3

27. ∠4

28. A pennant is in the shape of an isosceles triangle. One leg of the triangle is fastened to a stick. The stick forms an 84° angle with the other leg. What is the measure of each remote interior angle in the triangle?

APPLY

29. Model With Mathematics Pilar is making a replacement set of sails for a sailboat.

a. What equation can Pilar use that relates the values of w and x?

b. What equation can Pilar use that relates the values of y and z?

30. Reason An artist painting from a photo begins with a geometric sketch to match angle measures. What is the value of z?

31. Look for Relationships Use the figure shown.

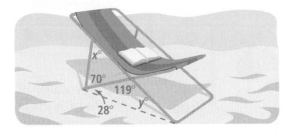

a. What is the value of x?

b. What is the value of y?

c. The chair can lay farther back so that the 70° angle changes to 86° and $x°$ changes to 36°. How does this affect the 119° angle?

ASSESSMENT PRACTICE

32. What are the values of x, y, and z?

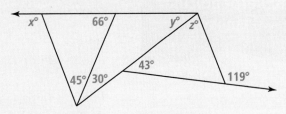

33. SAT/ACT What is the value of x?

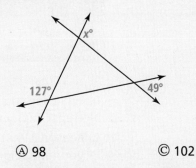

Ⓐ 98   Ⓒ 102

Ⓑ 106   Ⓓ 176

34. Performance Task A tablet case is supported at the back. The measure of the slant angle of the tablet can be changed, but $m\angle 2 = m\angle 3$ for any slant that is chosen.

Part A A user adjusts the case so that $m\angle 2 = 42$. What are the measures of the other angles?

Part B Is it possible to slant the tablet case so that $m\angle 1 = m\angle 5$? If so, explain how. If not, explain why it is not possible.

Part C A user wants to slant the tablet case so that $m\angle 1 = 2(m\angle 5)$. What should the measure of each of the five angles be?

7-4

Slopes of Parallel and Perpendicular Lines

I CAN... use slope to solve problems about parallel and perpendicular lines.

👆 MODEL & DISCUSS

Pilar and Jake begin climbing to the top of a 100-ft monument at the same time along two different sets of steps at the same rate. The tables show their distances above ground level after a number of steps.

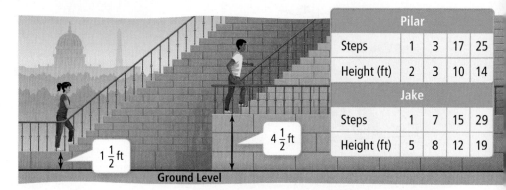

Pilar				
Steps	1	3	17	25
Height (ft)	2	3	10	14

Jake				
Steps	1	7	15	29
Height (ft)	5	8	12	19

A. How many feet does each student climb after 10 steps? Explain.

B. Will Pilar and Jake be at the same height after the same number of steps? Explain.

C. **Reason** What would you expect the graphs of each to look like given your answers to parts A and B? Explain.

❓ ESSENTIAL QUESTION

How do the slopes of lines that are parallel to each other compare? How do the slopes of lines that are perpendicular to each other compare?

CONCEPTUAL UNDERSTANDING

👆 EXAMPLE 1 > Slopes of Parallel Lines

A hill and a gondola line 20 ft above the ground that goes up the hill both have slope $\frac{1}{2}$. What is the geometric relationship between the hill and the gondola line?

Model the hill and gondola line on a coordinate plane where x represents the horizontal distance from the base of the hill and y represents the vertical distance from the base of the hill.

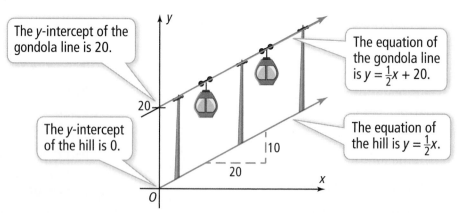

The y-intercept of the gondola line is 20.

The equation of the gondola line is $y = \frac{1}{2}x + 20$.

The y-intercept of the hill is 0.

The equation of the hill is $y = \frac{1}{2}x$.

MODEL WITH MATHEMATICS
Would you describe a different relationship between the slopes of parallel lines if the y-intercept for the hill were not at (0, 0)?

Because the slope of the hill is $\frac{1}{2}$, the hill gains one foot of height for every two feet of horizontal distance. The same is true for the gondola. It never gets any closer or farther away from the hill.

Conjecture: If two linear equations have the same slope, then the graphs of the equations are parallel.

CONTINUED ON THE NEXT PAGE

EXAMPLE 1 CONTINUED

 Try It! **1.** Suppose another line for a chair lift is placed at a constant distance c below the gondola line. What is an equation of the new line? Is the new line also parallel to the hill? Explain.

THEOREM 7-13

Two non-vertical lines are parallel if and only if their slopes are equal.

Any two vertical lines are parallel.

PROOF: SEE INTEGRATED MATHEMATICS II LESSON 9-5.

If... p and q are both not vertical

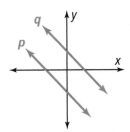

Then... $p \parallel q$ if and only if the slope of line p = slope of line q

If... p and q are both vertical

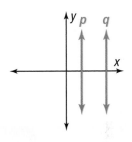

Then... $p \parallel q$

 EXAMPLE 2 **Check Parallelism**

Are lines k and n parallel?

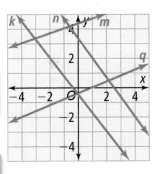

> **COMMON ERROR**
> Be sure that the first numbers in both subtraction expressions are the coordinates of the same point.

Step 1 Find the slope of line k.

$$m = \frac{-3 - 2}{2 - (-2)} = -\frac{5}{4}$$

Line k passes through $(-2, 2)$ and $(2, -3)$.

Step 2 Find the slope of line n.

$$m = \frac{-2 - 2}{4 - 1} = -\frac{4}{3}$$

Line n passes through $(1, 2)$ and $(4, -2)$.

Step 3 Compare the slopes.

Parallel lines have equal slope, but $-\frac{5}{4} \neq -\frac{4}{3}$. Thus, lines k and n are not parallel.

 Try It! **2.** Are lines m and q parallel?

THEOREM 7-14

Two non-vertical lines are perpendicular if and only if the product of their slopes is −1.

A vertical line and a horizontal line are perpendicular to each other.

PROOF: SEE INTEGRATED MATHEMATICS II LESSON 9-4.

If... p and q are both not vertical

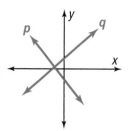

Then... $p \perp q$ if and only if the product of their slopes is −1

If... one of p and q is vertical and the other is horizontal

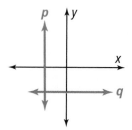

Then... $p \perp q$

EXAMPLE 3   Check Perpendicularity

Are lines j and k perpendicular?

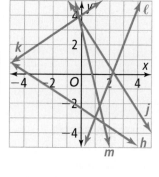

Step 1 Find the slope of line j.

$$m = \frac{2 - 5}{1 - (-1)} = -\frac{3}{2}$$

Line j passes through $(-1, 5)$ and $(1, 2)$.

Step 2 Find the slope of line k.

$$m = \frac{4 - 2}{0 - (-3)} = \frac{2}{3}$$

Line k passes through $(-3, 2)$ and $(0, 4)$.

Step 3 Compare the slopes.

Perpendicular lines have slopes with a product of −1, and $-\frac{3}{2} \cdot \frac{2}{3} = -1$. Thus, lines j and k are perpendicular.

STUDY TIP
Look for two points on each line where you can easily read the coordinates of the points from the graph.

Try It!   **3. a.** Are lines h and ℓ perpendicular?

b. Are lines k and m perpendicular?

EXAMPLE 4   Write Equations of Parallel and Perpendicular Lines

A. What is an equation of the line through P that is parallel to ℓ?

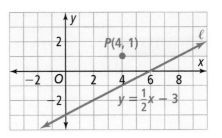

Step 1 Identify the slope of the parallel line.

The slope of ℓ is $\frac{1}{2}$. Parallel lines have equal slope, so the slope of the parallel line is $\frac{1}{2}$.

Step 2 Solve for the y-intercept of the parallel line.

$y = mx + b$

$1 = \frac{1}{2}(4) + b$ ← Use the point (4, 1).

$b = -1$

Step 3 Write an equation of the line.

$y = \frac{1}{2}x - 1$

The line parallel to ℓ passing through P is $y = \frac{1}{2}x - 1$.

GENERALIZE

If the slope of a line is $\frac{a}{b}$, what is the slope of any line perpendicular to it? How do you know?

B. What is the equation of the line through P that is perpendicular to ℓ?

Step 1 Identify the slope of the perpendicular line.

The slope of ℓ is $\frac{1}{2}$. Perpendicular lines have slopes with a product of −1, so the slope of the perpendicular line is −2.

Step 2 Solve for the y-intercept of the perpendicular line.

$y = mx + b$

$1 = -2(4) + b$ ← Use the point (4, 1).

$b = 9$

Step 3 Write the equation of the line.

$y = -2x + 9$

The line perpendicular to ℓ passing through P is $y = -2x + 9$.

✅ **Try It!**   **4.** What are equations of lines parallel and perpendicular to the given line k passing through point T?

a. $y = -3x + 2$; T(3, 1)   **b.** $y = \frac{3}{4}x - 5$; T(12, −2)

CONCEPT SUMMARY Slopes of Parallel and Perpendicular Lines

Parallel Lines	**Perpendicular Lines**
DIAGRAMS 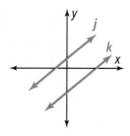	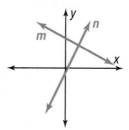
SYMBOLS $j \parallel k$ if and only if the slopes are the same.	$m \perp n$ if and only if the product of the two slopes is -1.

Do You UNDERSTAND?

1. **ESSENTIAL QUESTION** How do the slopes of lines that are parallel to each other compare? How do the slopes of lines that are perpendicular to each other compare?

2. **Error Analysis** Katrina said that the lines $y = -\frac{2}{3}x + 5$ and $y = -\frac{3}{2}x + 2$ are perpendicular. Explain Katrina's error.

3. **Reason** Give an equation for a line perpendicular to the line $y = 0$. Is there more than one such line? Explain.

4. **Communicate Precisely** What are two different if-then statements implied by Theorem 7-13?

5. **Error Analysis** Devin said that $\overleftrightarrow{AB}$ and $\overleftrightarrow{CD}$ for $A(-2, 0)$, $B(2, 3)$, $C(1, -1)$, and $D(5, -4)$ are parallel. Explain and correct Devin's error.

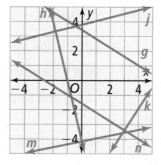

slope of $\overleftrightarrow{AB}$: $\dfrac{3-0}{2-(-2)} = \dfrac{3}{4}$

slope of $\overleftrightarrow{CD}$: $\dfrac{-1-(-4)}{5-1} = \dfrac{3}{4}$

slopes are equal, so $\overleftrightarrow{AB} \parallel \overleftrightarrow{CD}$ ✗

Do You KNOW HOW?

Use the diagram for Exercises 6–9.

6. Are lines g and n parallel?

7. Are lines j and m parallel?

8. Are lines n and k perpendicular?

9. Are lines h and j perpendicular?

10. What is an equation for the line parallel to $y = -x + 7$ that passes through $(7, -2)$?

11. What is an equation for the line perpendicular to $y = 3x - 1$ that passes through $(-9, -2)$?

12. The graph of a roller coaster track goes in a straight line through coordinates $(10, 54)$ and $(42, 48)$, with coordinates in feet. A support beam runs parallel 12 feet below the track. What equation describes the support beam?

UNDERSTAND

13. Look for Relationships What are the equations of lines *m* and *q*?

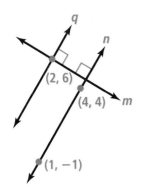

14. Reason Why can you not say that two vertical lines have equal slope? Why can you not say that the product of the slopes of a vertical and horizontal line is −1?

15. Higher Order Thinking Lines *k* and *n* intersect on the *y*-axis.

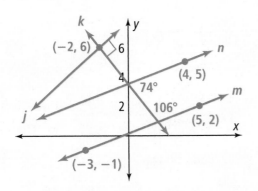

a. What is the equation of line *k* in slope-intercept form?

b. What is the equation of line *j* in slope-intercept form?

16. Construct Arguments Line *m* passes through points *X* and *Y*. Line *n* passes through points *X* and *Z*. If *m* and *n* have equal slope, what can you conclude about points *X*, *Y*, and *Z*? Explain.

17. Error Analysis Shannon says that the lines $y = -3x - 4$, $y = -\frac{1}{3}x + 6$, $y = -4x - 5$, and $y = \frac{1}{4}x - 5$ could represent the sides of a rectangle. Explain Shannon's error.

PRACTICE

Compare the slopes of the lines for $y = f(x)$ and $y = g(x)$ to determine if each pair of lines is parallel.
SEE EXAMPLE 1

18.

x	f(x)	g(x)
0	20	22
1	35	37
2	50	52
3	65	67

19.

x	f(x)	g(x)
0	5	10
1	7	15
2	9	20
3	11	25

Determine if each pair of lines is parallel.
SEE EXAMPLE 2

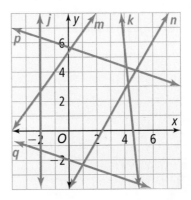

20. *j* and *k*   **21.** *m* and *n*   **22.** *p* and *q*

Determine if each pair of lines is perpendicular.
SEE EXAMPLE 3

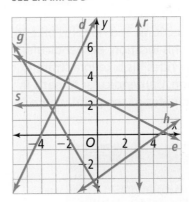

23. *d* and *e*   **24.** *g* and *h*   **25.** *r* and *s*

Write the equations for the lines parallel and perpendicular to the given line *j* that passes through *Q*. SEE EXAMPLE 4

26. $y = -4x + 1$; $Q(6, -1)$

27. $y = \frac{3}{2}x + 4$; $Q(-1, 1)$

APPLY

28. Model With Mathematics The table shows locations of several sites at a high school campus. A landscaper wants to connect two sites with a path perpendicular to the path connecting the cafeteria and the library. Which two sites should he connect?

Locations	
Cafeteria (5, 5)	Library (11, 14)
Office (4, 12)	Gym (15, 8)
Woodshop (11, 6)	Art Studio (3, 16)

29. Make Sense and Persevere Are the steepest parts of the two water slides parallel? Explain.

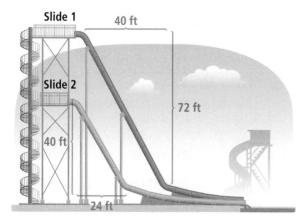

Slide 1   40 ft
Slide 2
72 ft
40 ft
24 ft

30. Mathematical Connections Teo rides his bike in a straight line from his location, perpendicular to path A, and Luke rides his bike in a straight line from his location, perpendicular to path B. What are the coordinates of the point where they meet?

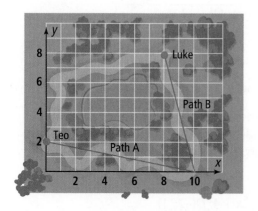

ASSESSMENT PRACTICE

31. $\overleftrightarrow{AB} \perp \overleftrightarrow{BC}$ for $A(-3, 2)$ and $C(2, 7)$. Which of the following could be the coordinates of B? Select all that apply.

Ⓐ (8, 0)   Ⓓ (1, 3)

Ⓑ (−2, 2)   Ⓔ (−1, −1)

Ⓒ (−4, 5)   Ⓕ (−3, 7)

32. SAT/ACT Line k passes through $(2, -3)$ and $(8, 1)$. Which equation represents a line that is parallel to k?

Ⓐ $y = -\frac{2}{3}x - \frac{5}{3}$ Ⓒ $y = \frac{3}{2}x - 6$

Ⓑ $y = \frac{2}{3}x - \frac{13}{3}$ Ⓓ $y = -\frac{3}{2}x$

33. Performance Task A knight travels in a straight line from the starting point to Token 1. The knight can only make right-angle turns to get to Tokens 2 and 3.

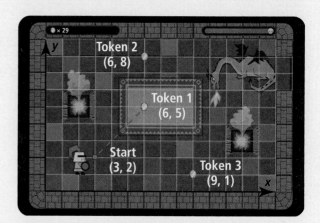

Part A Since the knight can only make right-angle turns, what are the slopes of the straight line paths the knight can travel?

Part B What equations describe a path that the knight can follow from the starting point to reach the tokens for the arrangement shown?

Part C What is the fewest number of turns that the knight can take in order to get all three tokens?

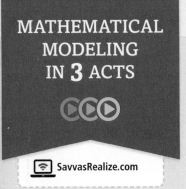

MATHEMATICAL MODELING IN 3 ACTS

SavvasRealize.com

Scan for Multimedia

Parallel Paving Company

Building roads consists of many different tasks. Once civil engineers have designed the road, they work with surveyors and construction crews to clear and level the land. Sometimes specialists have to blast away rock in order to clear the land. Once the land is leveled, the crews bring in asphalt pavers to smooth out the hot asphalt.

Sometimes construction crews will start work at both ends of the new road and meet in the middle. Think about this during the Mathematical Modeling in 3 Acts lesson.

ACT 1 Identify the Problem

1. What is the first question that comes to mind after watching the video?

2. Write down the main question you will answer about what you saw in the video.

3. Make an initial conjecture that answers this main question.

4. Explain how you arrived at your conjecture.

5. What information will be useful to know to answer the main question? How can you get it? How will you use that information?

ACT 2 Develop a Model

6. Use the math that you have learned in this Topic to refine your conjecture.

ACT 3 Interpret the Results

7. Did your refined conjecture match the actual answer exactly? If not, what might explain the difference?

1. What properties are specific to parallel lines and perpendicular lines?

Vocabulary Review

Choose the correct term to complete each sentence.

2. Angles that are outside the space between parallel lines and that lie on the same side of a transversal are _____.

3. A _____ intersects coplanar lines at distinct points.

4. Two angles inside a triangle that correspond to the nonadjacent exterior angle are the _____.

5. _____ lie on the same side of a transversal of parallel lines and are in corresponding positions relative to the parallel lines.

6. Angles between parallel lines that are nonadjacent and that lie on opposite sides of a transversal are _____.

7. Angles between parallel lines that are on the same side of a transversal are _____.

- alternate exterior angles
- alternate interior angles
- corresponding angles
- exterior angle of a triangle
- remote interior angles
- same-side exterior angles
- same-side interior angles
- transversal

Concepts & Skills Review

LESSONS 7-1 & 7-2   **Parallel Lines and Proving Lines Parallel**

Quick Review

When two **parallel lines** are intersected by a **transversal**, the angle pairs that are formed have special relationships. These angle pairs are either congruent or supplementary angles.

Example

Which angles are supplementary to $\angle 3$?

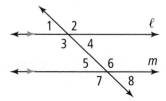

$\angle 1, \angle 4, \angle 5, \angle 8$

Practice & Problem Solving

Use the figure for Exercises 8–10.

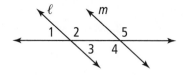

8. Suppose $\ell \parallel m$. What is the measure of each angle if $m\angle 2 = 138$?

   a. $m\angle 1$ b. $m\angle 3$ c. $m\angle 4$

9. If $m\angle 1 = 3x - 3$ and $m\angle 5 = 7x + 23$, for what value of x is $\ell \parallel m$?

10. **Reason** The transversal that intersects two parallel lines forms corresponding angles with measures $m\angle 1 = 3x - 7$ and $m\angle 2 = 2x + 12$. What is the measure of each angle?

Parallel Lines and Triangle Angle Sums

Quick Review

The interior and exterior angle measures of a triangle have the following properties.

- The sum of the interior angles of every triangle is 180°.

- The measure of each **exterior angle of a triangle** equals the sum of the measures of the two corresponding **remote interior angles**.

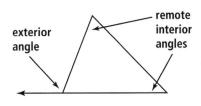

exterior angle   remote interior angles

Example

What is $m\angle 1$?

$m\angle 1 = 36 + 127$

$m\angle 1 = 163$

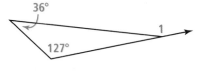

36°   127°   1

Practice & Problem Solving

What is the value of x in each figure?

11.
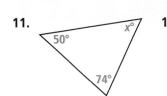
50° $x°$ 74°

12.
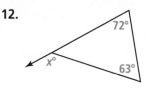
72° $x°$ 63°

13.
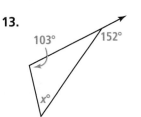
103°   152° $x°$

14.
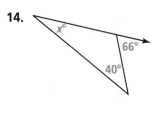
$x°$ 66°   40°

15. **Make Sense and Persevere** During a storm, a tree is blown against a building so that it forms a triangle with remote interior angles of 90° and 52°. What is the measure of the corresponding exterior angle formed by the leaning tree?

Slopes of Parallel and Perpendicular Lines

Quick Review

Two non-vertical lines are parallel if they have the same slope. Two vertical lines are parallel to each other.

Two non-vertical lines are perpendicular if the product of the slopes is −1. A vertical line is perpendicular to a horizontal line.

Example

What is the equation of a line that is parallel to the line $y = 3x - 9$ and passes through (6, 12)?

The slope of the line is 3.
Solve for the y-intercept of the parallel line:

$$y = mx + b$$
$$12 = (3)(6) + b$$
$$b = -6$$

The equation of the parallel line is $y = 3x - 6$.

Practice & Problem Solving

Use the figure for Exercises 16–17. Show the calculations you use to answer each question.

16. Are lines p and q parallel?

17. Are lines w and t perpendicular?

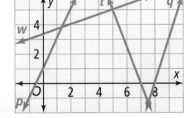

18. **Reason** Theorem 7-4 states that two non-vertical lines are perpendicular if and only if the product of their slopes is −1. Why are vertical lines excluded?

19. **Use Structure** Write an equation for each line that passes through (2, 7) and is parallel or perpendicular to the line $y = -3x - 6$.

Transformations

Topic Overview

enVision® STEM Project
Create an Animation

Mathematical Modeling in 3 Acts:
The Perplexing Polygon

Topic Vocabulary

- composition of rigid motions
- glide reflection
- point symmetry
- reflectional symmetry
- rigid motion
- rotational symmetry

 Go online | SavvasRealize.com

Digital Experience

INTERACTIVE STUDENT EDITION
Access online or offline.

ACTIVITIES Complete *Explore & Reason*, *Model & Discuss*, and *Critique & Explain* activities. Interact with Examples and Try Its.

ANIMATION View and interact with real-world applications.

PRACTICE Practice what you've learned.

▶ The Perplexing Polygon

Look around and you will see shapes and patterns everywhere you look.
The tiles on a floor are often all the same shape and fit together to
form a pattern. The petals on a flower often make a repeating pattern
around the center of the flower. When you look at snowflakes under
a microscope, you can notice that they are made up of repeating
three-dimensional crystals. Think about the patterns you have seen during
the Mathematical Modeling in 3 Acts lesson.

▶ **VIDEOS** Watch clips to support
Mathematical Modeling in 3 Acts Lessons
and **enVision**® *STEM Projects.*

CONCEPT SUMMARY Review
key lesson content through
multiple representations.

ASSESSMENT Show what
you've learned.

A-Z **GLOSSARY** Read and listen to
English and Spanish definitions.

TUTORIALS Get help from
Virtual Nerd, right when you need it.

MATH TOOLS Explore math
with digital tools and manipulatives.

Did You Know?

Polygonal modeling uses polygons to model the surfaces of three-dimensional objects. Animators use vertices and edges to define polygons (usually triangles or quadrilaterals), and they use multiple polygons to create more complex shapes.

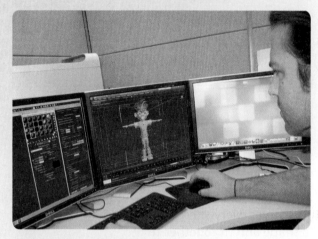

The phenakistoscope was invented nearly **200 years ago**. When the viewer looks through a slot, a sequence of images appears to show moving figures.

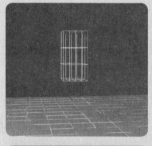

An animated character represents hundreds of hours of work. An animator builds a *mesh* of polygons connected through shared vertices and edges. A rigger links the mesh to a system of joints and control handles. To represent a curved surface in a realistic way, the animator uses a mesh of many small polygons. Then the animator programs the joints and handles so that the character moves realistically. Finally, an artist provides surface texture and shading.

▶ Your Task: Create an Animation

Starting with the pixels (points) of a simple geometric figure, you and your classmates will use translations and reflections to move the figure through a series of frames.

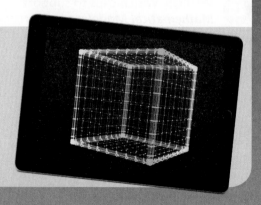

8-1
Reflections

SavvasRealize.com

I CAN... draw and describe the reflection of a figure across a line of reflection.

VOCABULARY
• rigid motion

EXPLORE & REASON

The illustration shows irregular pentagon-shaped tiles covering a floor.

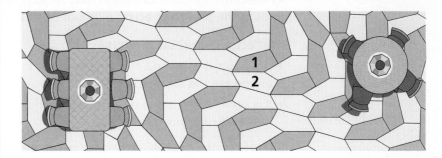

A. Which tiles are copies of tile 1. Explain.

B. Communicate Precisely If you were to move tile 1 from the design, what actions would you have to do so it completely covers tile 2?

C. Which tiles are *not* copies of tile 1? Explain.

? ESSENTIAL QUESTION ▶ How are the properties of reflection used to transform a figure?

EXAMPLE 1   Identify Rigid Motions

A rigid motion is a transformation that preserves length and angle measure. Is the transformation a rigid motion? Explain.

Although angle measure is preserved, the image is smaller than the preimage, so the transformation involves a change in length.

The transformation is not a rigid motion because the length is not preserved.

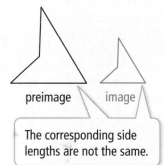

The corresponding side lengths are not the same.

STUDY TIP
Recall that a transformation is a function that maps a given figure called the preimage onto the resulting figure, the image.

 Try It!   **1.** Is each transformation a rigid motion? Explain.

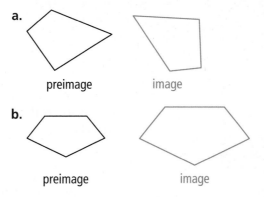

CONCEPT Reflections

A reflection is a transformation that reflects each point in the preimage across a line of reflection.

A reflection has these properties:

- If a point A is on line m, then the point and its image are the same point (that is, $A' = A$).
- If a point B is not on line m, line m is the perpendicular bisector of $\overline{BB'}$.

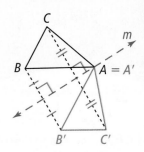

The reflection of $\triangle ABC$ across line m can be written as $R_m(\triangle ABC) = \triangle A'B'C'$.

A reflection is a rigid motion so length and angle measures are preserved.

CONCEPTUAL UNDERSTANDING

👆 **EXAMPLE 2** Reflect a Figure Across a Line

How can you reflect $\triangle FGH$ across line ℓ?

Use the properties of reflections to draw the image of $\triangle FGH$.

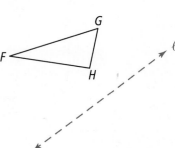

MAKE SENSE AND PERSEVERE
For any point not on the line of reflection, the line of reflection is the perpendicular bisector of the segment between corresponding preimage and image points.

Step 1 Draw lines through points F, G, and H that are perpendicular to line ℓ.

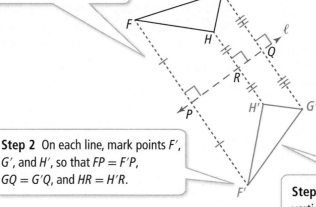

Step 2 On each line, mark points F', G', and H', so that $FP = F'P$, $GQ = G'Q$, and $HR = H'R$.

Step 3 Connect the vertices to draw $\triangle F'G'H'$.

☑ **Try It!** **2.** What is the reflection of $\triangle LMN$ across line n?

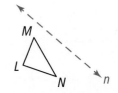

EXAMPLE 3 — Reflect a Figure on a Coordinate Plane

Quadrilateral *FGHJ* has coordinates *F*(0, 3), *G*(2, 4), *H*(4, 2), and *J*(−2, 0).

A. Graph and label *FGHJ* and $R_{x\text{-axis}}(FGHJ)$. What is a general rule for reflecting a point across the *x*-axis?

Step 1 Graph *FGHJ*.

Step 2 Find *F′*, *G′*, *H′*, and *J′* and draw *F′G′H′J′*.

> Because *J* is on the line of reflection, *J′* = *J*.

$R_{x\text{-axis}}(0, 3) = (0, -3)$

$R_{x\text{-axis}}(2, 4) = (2, -4)$

$R_{x\text{-axis}}(4, 2) = (4, -2)$

$R_{x\text{-axis}}(-2, 0) = (-2, 0)$

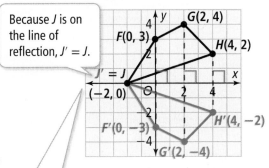

> The *x*-axis is the line of reflection, so it is the perpendicular bisector of $\overline{FF'}$, $\overline{GG'}$, and $\overline{HH'}$.

The reflection of any point (*x*, *y*) across the *x*-axis is the point (*x*, −*y*).

$$R_{x\text{-axis}}(x, y) = (x, -y)$$

B. Graph and label *FGHJ* and $R_{y\text{-axis}}(FGHJ)$. What is a general rule for reflecting a point across the *y*-axis?

Step 1 Graph *FGHJ*.

Step 2 Find *F′*, *G′*, *H′*, and *J′* and draw *F′G′H′J′*.

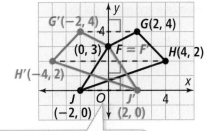

$R_{y\text{-axis}}(0, 3) = (0, 3)$

$R_{y\text{-axis}}(2, 4) = (-2, 4)$

$R_{y\text{-axis}}(4, 2) = (-4, 2)$

$R_{x\text{-axis}}(-2, 0) = (2, 0)$

> The *y*-axis is the line of reflection, so it is the perpendicular bisector of $\overline{GG'}$, $\overline{HH'}$, and $\overline{JJ'}$.

COMMON ERROR
Remember, when the *y*-axis is the line of reflection, the image points must have the same distances from the *x*-axis and on a line perpendicular to the *y*-axis, so the *y*-coordinate stays the same and the *x*-coordinate is the opposite.

The reflection of any point (*x*, *y*) across the *y*-axis is the point (−*x*, *y*).

$$R_{y\text{-axis}}(x, y) = (-x, y)$$

 Try It! **3.** Triangle *ABC* has vertices *A*(−5, 6), *B*(1, −2), and *C*(−3, −4). What are the coordinates of the vertices of △*A′B′C′* for each reflection?

a. $R_{x\text{-axis}}$ **b.** $R_{y\text{-axis}}$

CONCEPT Reflecting Points Across the x–axis and y-axis

When any point $P(x, y)$ on the coordinate plane is reflected across the x-axis, its image is $P'(x, -y)$.

When any point $P(x, y)$ on the coordinate plane is reflected across the y-axis, its image is $P'(-x, y)$.

EXAMPLE 4   Describe a Reflection on the Coordinate Plane

What reflection maps △KLM to its image?

Step 1 Write the coordinates of the preimage and the image.

$K(-3, 5)$ $L(1, 3)$ $M(-5, 1)$

$K'(5, -3)$ $L'(3, 1)$ $M'(1, -5)$

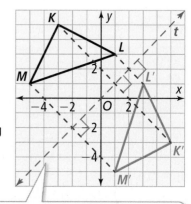

Step 2 Find the midpoints of the segments connecting two pairs of corresponding points.

Midpoint of $\overline{KK'}$:

$\left(\dfrac{-3 + 5}{2}, \dfrac{5 + (-3)}{2}\right) = (1, 1)$

Midpoint of $\overline{MM'}$:

$\left(\dfrac{-5 + 1}{2}, \dfrac{1 + (-5)}{2}\right) = (-2, -2)$

> The line of reflection is the perpendicular bisector of the segments that connect corresponding vertices of the preimage and image.

STUDY TIP
When providing a rule, you must clearly define the line of reflection. Be certain that the line of reflection is the perpendicular bisector of segments between preimage and image points.

Step 3 Write the equation of the line through the midpoints.

Find the slope.

$m = \dfrac{1 - (-2)}{1 - (-2)}$

$= 1$

Use point slope form.

$y - 1 = 1 \cdot (x - 1)$

$y = x$

The transformation is a reflection across the line $y = x$. You can write this reflection rule as $R_{y = x} (\triangle KLM) = (\triangle K'L'M')$ or $R_m (x, y) \rightarrow (y, x)$, where m is the line $y = x$.

Try It! **4.** What is a reflection rule that maps each triangle to its image?

a. $C(3, 8)$, $D(5, 12)$, $E(4, 6)$ and $C'(-8, -3)$, $D'(-12, -5)$, $E'(-6, -4)$

b. $F(7, 6)$, $G(0, -4)$, $H(-5, 0)$ and $F'(-5, 6)$, $G'(2, -4)$, $H'(7, 0)$

APPLICATION

EXAMPLE 5 **Use Reflections**

In a billiards game, a player must hit the white cue ball so that the cue ball hits the red ball without touching the yellow ball. Where should the cue ball bounce off the top rail so that it hits the red ball?

Consider the top rail as a line of reflection and find the reflection of the red ball.

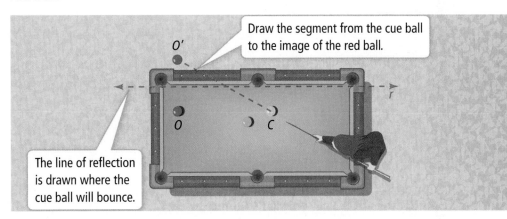

Draw the segment from the cue ball to the image of the red ball.

The line of reflection is drawn where the cue ball will bounce.

Reflect the segment from the cue ball to the red ball across the line of reflection.

MAKE SENSE AND PERSEVERE
What do you notice about the angles formed by the line of reflection and the path of the cue ball? Which are congruent?

The player should aim at point P, where the two segments intersect.

Try It! **5.** Student A sees the reflected image across the mirror of another student who appears to be at B'. Trace the diagram and show the actual position of Student B.

B'
•

——————————————— mirror

•
A

WORDS A reflection is a transformation that reflects each point in the preimage across a line of reflection.

DIAGRAM

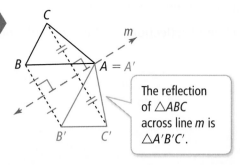

The reflection of △ABC across line m is △A'B'C'.

SYMBOLS $R_m(\triangle ABC) = \triangle A'B'C'$

$R_m(A) = A'$

Line m is the perpendicular bisector of $\overline{BB'}$ and $\overline{CC'}$.

Do You UNDERSTAND?

1. **ESSENTIAL QUESTION** How are the properties of reflection used to transform a figure?

2. **Error Analysis** Oscar drew the image of a triangle reflected across the line $y = -1$. What mistake did Oscar make?

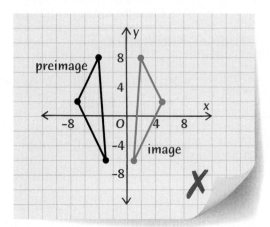

3. **Vocabulary** One meaning of the word *rigid* is "not bendable," and another is "unable to be changed." How do those meanings correspond to the definition of rigid motion?

4. **Communicate Precisely** How can you determine whether the transformation of a figure is a rigid motion?

5. **Generalize** Describe the steps you must take to identify the path an object will follow if it bounces off a surface and strikes another object.

Do You KNOW HOW?

6. Does the transformation shown appear to be a rigid motion? Explain.

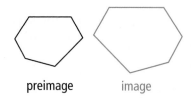

preimage   image

What are the coordinates of each image?

7. $R_{x\text{-axis}}(-5, 3)$ 8. $R_{x\text{-axis}}(1, 6)$

9. Write a reflection rule that maps each triangle to its image.

   a. $J(1, 0)$, $K(-5, 2)$, $L(4, -4)$ and $J'(-9, 0)$, $K'(-3, 2)$, $L'(-12, -4)$

   b. $P(8, 6)$, $Q(-4, 12)$, $R(7, 7)$ and $P'(8, -20)$, $Q'(-4, -26)$, $R'(7, -21)$

10. Squash is a racket sport like tennis, except that the ball must bounce off a wall between returns. Trace the squash court. At what point on the front wall should player 1 aim in order to reach the rear wall as far from player 2 as possible?

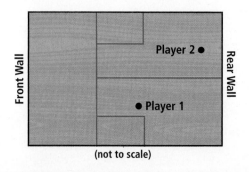

(not to scale)

UNDERSTAND

11. **Look for Relationships** Becky draws a triangle with vertices $A(6,7)$, $B(9,3)$, and $C(4, -2)$ on a coordinate grid. She reflects the triangle across the line $y = 4$ to get $\triangle A'B'C'$. She then reflects the image across the line $x = 3$ to get $\triangle A''B''C''$.

   a. What are the coordinates of $\triangle A'B'C'$ and $\triangle A''B''C''$?

   b. Write a rule for each reflection.

12. **Use Structure** Under a transformation, a preimage and its image are both squares with side length 3. The image, however, is rotated with respect to the preimage. Is the transformation a rigid motion? Explain.

13. **Error Analysis** Jacob is playing miniature golf. He states that he cannot hit the ball from the start, bounce it off the back wall once, and reach the hole in one shot. Is Jacob correct? Trace and label a diagram to support your answer.

14. **Higher Order Thinking** For the miniature golf hole in Exercise 13, Jacob wants to bounce the ball off the back wall and then the right wall. Draw a diagram to show how Jacob can hit the ball so that it reaches the hole after two bounces.

15. **Mathematical Connection** Dana reflects point $A(2, 5)$ across line ℓ to get image point $A'(6, 1)$. What is an equation for line ℓ?

16. **Look for Structure** Can a figure be reflected across three lines of reflection so the image is the original figure? Explain.

PRACTICE

For Exercises 17 and 18, does each transformation appear to be a rigid motion? Explain. SEE EXAMPLE 1

17.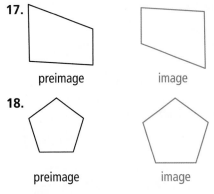

   preimage   image

18.

   preimage   image

For Exercises 19–24, suppose m is the line with equation $x = -5$, line n is the line with equation $y = 1$, line g is the line with equation $y = x$, and line h is the line with equation $y = -2$. Given $A(9, -3)$, $B(6, 4)$, and $C(-1, -5)$, what are the coordinates of the vertices of $\triangle A'B'C'$ for each reflection? SEE EXAMPLES 2 AND 3

19. $R_{x\text{-axis}}$ 20. $R_{y\text{-axis}}$

21. R_m 22. R_n

23. R_g 24. R_h

For Exercises 25–28, what is a reflection rule that maps each triangle and its image? SEE EXAMPLE 4

25. $D(3, 6)$, $E(-4, -3)$, $F(6, 1)$ and $D'(1, 6)$, $E'(8, -3)$, $F'(-2, 1)$

26. $G(9, 12)$, $H(-2, -15)$, $J(3, 8)$ and $G'(9, -2)$, $H'(-2, 25)$, $J'(3, 2)$

27. $K(7, -6)$, $L(9, -3)$, $M(-4, 6)$ and $K'(7, -4)$, $L'(9, -7)$, $M'(-4, -16)$

28.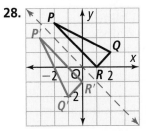

29. Trace the diagram below. Where does the shopper in a dressing room see her image in each mirror? SEE EXAMPLE 5

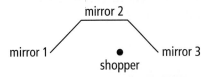

APPLY

30. Look for Relationships Which of the numbered stones shown cannot be mapped to another with a rigid motion?

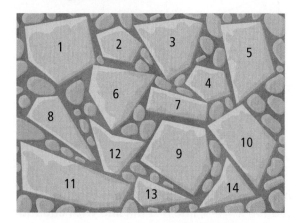

31. Use Structure Reese is inside a shop and sees the sign on the window from the back. Draw the letters as they would appear from the outside of the shop. Is the transformation a rigid motion?

32. Make Sense and Persevere Look at the floor plan below. Abdul sees the image of a clock in the mirror on the door.

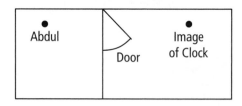

a. Trace the diagram. Where is the line of reflection? Explain.

b. Where is the clock located? Explain.

c. Find where Abdul's image is located relative to the line of reflection. Can Abdul see himself in the mirror? Explain.

ASSESSMENT PRACTICE

33. Classify whether each pair of figures appears to be a *rigid motion* or *not a rigid motion*.

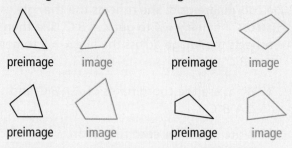

preimage   image   preimage   image

preimage   image   preimage   image

34. SAT/ACT Consider the following reflection.

Preimage: $A(3, 9)$, $B(2, -7)$, $C(6, 14)$

Image: $A'(-25, 9)$, $B'(-24, -7)$, $C'(-28, 14)$

Suppose p is the line with equation $x = 11$, q is the line with equation $x = 22$, r is the line with equation $x = -11$, and s is the line with equation $x = -22$. What is the rule for the reflection?

Ⓐ $R_p(x, y)$ Ⓒ $R_r(x, y)$
Ⓑ $R_q(x, y)$ Ⓓ $R_s(x, y)$

35. Performance Task Sound echoes from a solid object in the same way that light reflects from a mirror. A hiker at point A shouts the word *hello*. The hiker at point B first hears the shout directly and later hears the echo.

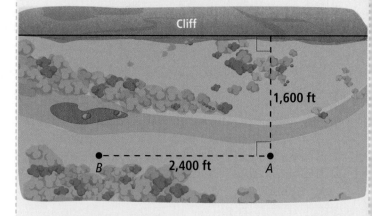

Part A Trace the diagram. Show the path taken by the sound the hiker at point B hears echoing from the cliff.

Part B Sound travels at about 1,000 feet per second. After how long does the hiker at point B hear the shout directly? After how long does he hear the echo? Show your work.

8-2

Translations

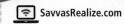
I CAN... describe the properties of a figure before and after translation.

VOCABULARY
• composition of rigid motions

EXPLORE & REASON

Draw a copy of *ABCD* on a grid. Using another color, draw a copy of *ABCD* on the grid in a different location with the same orientation, and label it *QRST*.

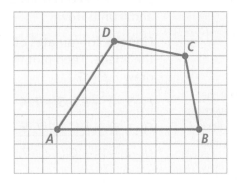

A. On another sheet of paper, write instructions that describe how to move *ABCD* to the location of *QRST*.

B. Exchange instructions with a partner. Follow your partner's instructions to draw a third shape *EFGH* in another color on the same grid. Compare your drawings. Do your drawings look the same? Explain.

C. **Communicate Precisely** What makes a set of instructions for this Explore & Reason a good set of instructions?

ESSENTIAL QUESTION

What are the properties of a translation?

CONCEPT Translations

A translation is a transformation in a plane that maps all points of a preimage the same distance and in the same direction.

The translation of $\triangle ABC$ by x units along the x-axis and by y units along the y-axis can be written as $T_{\langle x, y \rangle}(\triangle ABC) = \triangle A'B'C'$.

A translation has the following properties:

If $T_{\langle x, y \rangle}(\triangle ABC) = \triangle A'B'C'$, then

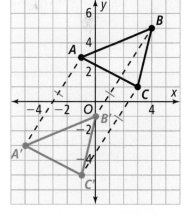

• $\overline{AA'} \parallel \overline{BB'} \parallel \overline{CC'}$.

• $\overline{AA'} \cong \overline{BB'} \cong \overline{CC'}$.

• $\triangle ABC$ and $\triangle A'B'C'$ have the same orientation.

A translation is a rigid motion, so length and angle measure are preserved.

EXAMPLE 1   Find the Image of a Translation

What is the graph of $T_{\langle 7, -4 \rangle}(\triangle EFG) = \triangle E'F'G'$?

The subscript $\langle 7, -4 \rangle$ indicates that each point of $\triangle EFG$ is translated 7 units right and 4 units down.

Find the coordinates of the vertices of the image. Then plot the points and draw $\triangle E'F'G'$.

$E(-5, 4) \rightarrow E'(-5 + 7, 4 - 4) = E'(2, 0)$

$F(-1, 5) \rightarrow F'(-1 + 7, 5 - 4) = F'(6, 1)$

$G(-2, -1) \rightarrow G'(-2 + 7, -1 - 4) = G'(5, -5)$

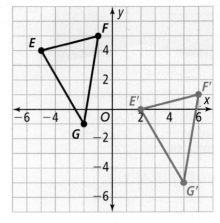

COMMON ERROR
Do not misunderstand that the translation only maps the vertices of the preimage to the vertices of the image. The translation maps $\triangle EFG$ onto $\triangle E'F'G'$.

Try It!   1. What are the vertices of $\triangle E'F'G'$ for each translation?

a. $T_{\langle 6, -7 \rangle}(\triangle EFG) = \triangle E'F'G'$ b. $T_{\langle 11, 2 \rangle}(\triangle EFG) = \triangle E'F'G'$

EXAMPLE 2   Write a Translation Rule

What translation rule maps $STUV$ onto $S'T'U'V'$?

Use one pair of corresponding vertices to determine the change in the horizontal and vertical directions between the preimage to its image.

Use the vertex $S(-5, 6)$ and its image $S'(-6, 2)$.

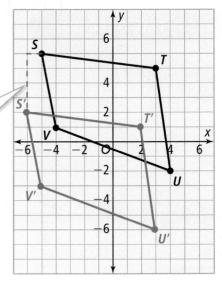

Change in the horizontal direction x:
$-6 - (-5) = -1$

Change in the vertical direction y:
$2 - 6 = -4$

The translation maps every (x, y) point to $(x - 1, y - 4)$, so this translation rule is $T_{\langle -1, -4 \rangle}$. You can verify the rule on the remaining vertices.

Try It!   2. What translation rule maps $P(-3, 1)$ to its image $P'(2, 3)$?

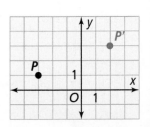

Go Online | SavvasRealize.com

CONCEPT Composition of Rigid Motions

A **composition of rigid motions** is a transformation with two or more rigid motions in which the second rigid motion is performed on the image of the first rigid motion.

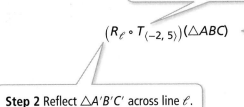

Step 1 Translate $\triangle ABC$ left 2 units and up 5 units.

$$(R_\ell \circ T_{\langle -2,\ 5\rangle})(\triangle ABC)$$

This notation uses a small open circle to indicate a composition of rigid motions on $\triangle ABC$.

Step 2 Reflect $\triangle A'B'C'$ across line ℓ.

APPLICATION

👆 **EXAMPLE 3**   **Compose Translations**

In learning a new dance, Kyle moves from position A to position B and then to position C. What single transformation describes Kyle's move from position A to position C?

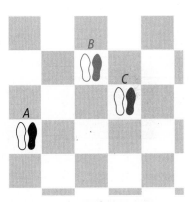

Formulate ◄

Let $(0, 0)$ represent position A.
The translation from A to B is $T_{\langle 2,\ 2\rangle}(x, y)$.
The translation from B to C is $T_{\langle 1,\ -1\rangle}(x, y)$.
Kyle's final position is the composition of those two translations.

Compute ◄

Find $T_{\langle 1,\ -1\rangle} \circ T_{\langle 2,\ 2\rangle}(x, y)$.

$$T_{\langle 2,\ 2\rangle}(x, y) = (x + 2, y + 2)$$

$$T_{\langle 1,\ -1\rangle}(x + 2, y + 2) = (x + 3, y + 1)$$

First, apply $T_{\langle 2,\ 2\rangle}$. Then apply $T_{\langle 1,\ -1\rangle}$ to the result.

Interpret ◄

The translation $T_{\langle 3,\ 1\rangle}(A)$ represents a single transformation that maps Kyle's move from position A to position C.

✅ **Try It!**   **3.** What is the composition of the transformations written as one transformation?

   a. $T_{\langle 3,\ -2\rangle} \circ T_{\langle 1,\ -1\rangle}$

   b. $T_{\langle -4,\ 0\rangle} \circ T_{\langle -2,\ 5\rangle}$

CONCEPTUAL UNDERSTANDING

👆 **EXAMPLE 4** Relate Translations and Reflections

How is a composition of reflections across parallel lines related to a translation?

Step 1 Reflect △ABC across the y-axis. The image is △A'B'C'.

Step 2 Reflect △A'B'C' across line m. The image is △A"B"C".

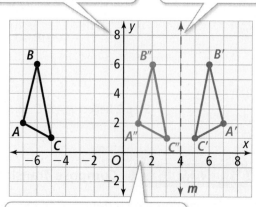

STUDY TIP
After the first reflection, the orientation of the figure is reversed. After the second reflection, the orientation of the figure returns to that of the preimage.

Notice that the distance between corresponding points on the y-axis and line m is 4 units and $BB'' = AA'' = CC'' = 8$ units.

If △ABC is translated 8 units to the right, its image is also △A"B"C".

So, $(R_m \circ R_{y\text{-axis}})(\triangle ABC) = T_{\langle 8, 0\rangle}(\triangle ABC)$.

☑ **Try It!** 4. Suppose n is the line with equation $y = 1$. Given △DEF with vertices $D(0, 0)$, $E(0, 3)$, and $F(3, 0)$, what translation image is equivalent to $(R_n \circ R_{x\text{-axis}})(\triangle DEF)$?

THEOREM 8-1

A translation is a composition of reflections across two parallel lines.

• Both reflection lines are perpendicular to the line containing a preimage point and its corresponding image point.

• The distance between the preimage and the image is twice the distance between the two reflection lines.

PROOF: SEE EXAMPLE 5.

If... $T(ABC) = A''B''C''$

$AA'' = BB'' = CC'' = 2d$

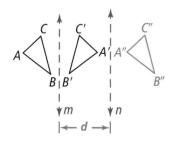

Then... $(R_n \circ R_m)(ABC) = A''B''C''$

👆 **EXAMPLE 5** ▷ **Prove Theorem 8-1**

Given: A translation T, with $T(C) = C''$

Prove: There exist parallel lines m and n such that $T = R_n \circ R_m$.

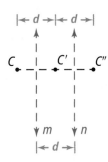

Plan: The given information says the translation T maps C to C''. First find a composition of reflections that maps C to C''. Then show that this composition of reflections is equivalent to the translation T for *any* point. (There are several cases to consider. One case is shown below.)

Proof: Let C' be the midpoint of $\overline{CC''}$, and let $CC' = C'C'' = d$. Let m be the perpendicular bisector of $\overline{CC'}$ and n be the perpendicular bisector of $\overline{C'C''}$.

By the properties of reflections $R_m(C) = C'$ and $R_n(C') = C''$, so $(R_n \circ R_m)(C) = C''$. Also, the distance between n and m is d and the distance between C and C'' is $2d$.

Now pick another point B and show that $(R_n \circ R_m)(B) = T(B)$. To do this, show that $\overline{BB''} = \overline{CC''} = 2d$, and $\overline{BB''} \parallel \overline{CC''}$.

First reflect across m. Call the image B'. Let the distance from B to m and the distance from m to B' be x.

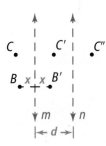

Now reflect B' across n. Call the image B''. Since the distance between m and n is d, the distance between B' and n is $d - x$. By the properties of reflections, the distance between n and B'' is also $d - x$.

So $BB'' = x + x + (d - x) + (d - x) = 2d$.

Since $\overline{CC''}$ and $\overline{BB''}$ are both perpendicular to m and n, they are parallel to each other.

Therefore $(R_n \circ R_m)(B) = T(B)$.

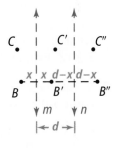

CONSTRUCT ARGUMENTS
The choice of C and C'' were arbitrary. Why does this mean that this proof is valid for *any* translation?

 Try It! **5.** Suppose the point B you chose in the Proof of Theorem 8-1 was between lines m and n. How would that affect the proof? What are the possible cases you need to consider?

Concept Summary   Assess

| **WORDS** | A translation is a transformation that maps all points the same distance and in the same direction. | A composition of two reflections across parallel lines is a translation. |

GRAPH

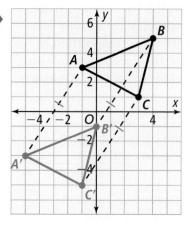

DIAGRAM

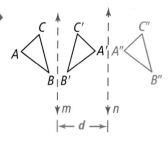

SYMBOLS

$T_{\langle -4, -6\rangle}(\triangle ABC) = \triangle A'B'C'$

$\overline{AA'} \parallel \overline{BB'} \parallel \overline{CC'}$

$\overline{AA'} \cong \overline{BB'} \cong \overline{CC'}$

$T(ABC) = (R_n \circ R_m)(ABC)$

$AA'' = BB'' = CC'' = 2d$

Do You UNDERSTAND?

1. **ESSENTIAL QUESTION** What are the properties of a translation?

2. **Error Analysis** Sasha says that for any $\triangle XYZ$, the reflection over the y-axis composed with the reflection over the x-axis is equivalent to a translation of $\triangle XYZ$. Explain Sasha's error.

3. **Vocabulary** Write an example of a composition of rigid motions for $\triangle PQR$.

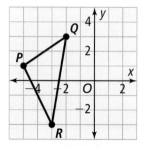

4. **Make Sense and Persevere** What are the values of x and y if $T_{\langle -2, 7\rangle}(x, y) = (3, -1)$?

Do You KNOW HOW?

For Exercises 5 and 6, the vertices of $\triangle XYZ$ are $X(1, -4)$, $Y(-2, -1)$, and $Z(3, 1)$. For each translation, give the vertices of $\triangle X'Y'Z'$.

5. $T_{\langle -4, -3\rangle}(\triangle XYZ)$ 6. $T_{\langle 5, -3\rangle}(\triangle XYZ)$

7. What is the rule for the translation shown?

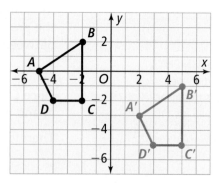

For Exercises 8 and 9, write composition of translations as one translation.

8. $T_{\langle 7, 8\rangle} \circ T_{\langle -3, -4\rangle}$ 9. $T_{\langle 0, 3\rangle} \circ T_{\langle 4, 6\rangle}$

10. How far apart are two parallel lines m and n such that $T_{\langle 12, 0\rangle}(\triangle JKL) = (R_n \circ R_m)(\triangle JKL)$?

Go Online | SavvasRealize.com

UNDERSTAND

11. Error Analysis Hugo graphed $\triangle PQR$ and $(R_t \circ T_{\langle 3, 1 \rangle})(\triangle PQR)$ where the equation of line t is $y = 2$. His translation and reflection were both correct. What mistake did Hugo make?

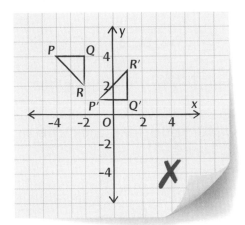

12. Mathematical Connections Suppose line k has equation $x = 3$. Compare the areas of $ABCD$ and $A''B''C''D'' = (T_{\langle 1, 2 \rangle} \circ R_k)(ABCD)$. Justify your answer.

13. Make Sense and Persevere A robot travels from position A to B to C to D. What composition of rigid motions represents those moves?

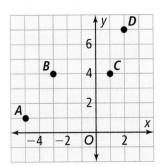

14. Higher Order Thinking How can you describe the complete transformation to a person who cannot see the transformations below?

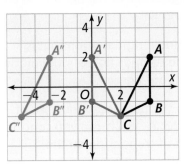

PRACTICE

For Exercises 15–17, give the coordinates of the image. SEE EXAMPLE 1

15. $T_{\langle 3, -1 \rangle}(\triangle ABC)$ for $A(5, 0)$, $B(-1, 2)$, $C(6, -3)$

16. $T_{\langle -4, 0 \rangle}(\triangle DEF)$ for $D(3, 3)$, $E(-2, 3)$, $F(0, 2)$

17. $T_{\langle -10, -5 \rangle}(\triangle GHJ)$ for $G(0, 0)$, $H(3, 6)$, $J(12, -1)$

18. What is the rule for the rigid motion?
SEE EXAMPLE 2

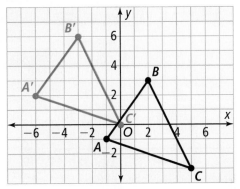

19. Write a composition of translations that is equivalent to $T_{\langle 8, -5 \rangle}(x, y)$. SEE EXAMPLE 3

20. Given $\triangle XYZ$, line n with equation $x = -2$, and line p with equation $x = 2$, write a translation that is equivalent to $R_n \circ R_p$.
SEE EXAMPLE 4

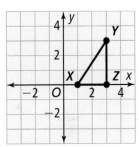

For Exercises 21–24, write each composition of translations as one translation. SEE EXAMPLE 3

21. $T_{\langle -3, 3 \rangle} \circ T_{\langle -2, 4 \rangle}$ **22.** $T_{\langle -4, -3 \rangle} \circ T_{\langle 3, 1 \rangle}$

23. $T_{\langle 5, -6 \rangle} \circ T_{\langle -7, 5 \rangle}$ **24.** $T_{\langle 8, -2 \rangle} \circ T_{\langle -4, 9 \rangle}$

For Exericses 25–28, write each composition of reflections as one translation. Suppose k is the line with equation $x = -3$, ℓ is the line with equation $x = -2$, m is the line with equation $x = 1$, n is the line with equation $x = -1$, p is the line with equation $y = 1$, q is the line with equation $y = 3$, s is the line with equation $y = 2$, and t is the line with equation $y = -4$. SEE EXAMPLE 4

25. $R_k \circ R_\ell$ **26.** $R_m \circ R_n$

27. $R_p \circ R_q$ **28.** $R_s \circ R_t$

29. The distance between vertical lines a and b is 6 units and a is left of b. If $T_{\langle x, 0 \rangle}(\triangle JKL) = (R_b \circ R_a)(\triangle JKL)$, what is the value of x?
SEE EXAMPLE 5

APPLY

30. Communicate Precisely Benjamin walks from his house to Timothy's house and then to school. Describe Benjamin's walk as a composition of translations. If Benjamin walks from his house directly to school, what translation describes his walk?

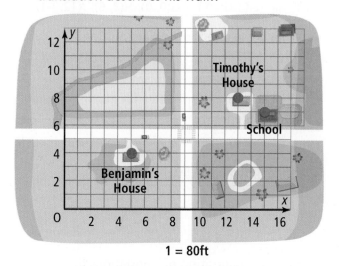

1 = 80ft

Use the map for Exercises 31 and 32.

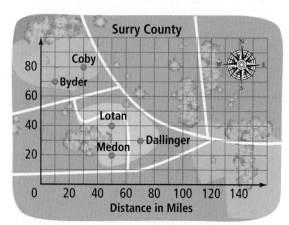

31. Model With Mathematics The Surry County sheriff's patrol route starts in Coby. The composition of rigid motions $T_{\langle -20, 10 \rangle} \circ T_{\langle 40, -50 \rangle}$ describes her route. How would you describe the sheriff's route in words?

32. Reason What composition of rigid motions describes a car trip starting in Medon, stopping in Dallinger, and then going on to Byder?

ASSESSMENT PRACTICE

33. Does each of the rigid motions below result in $\triangle A''B''C''$? Select *Yes* or *No*.

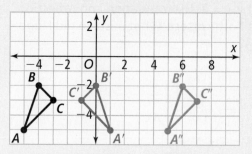

Suppose *a* is the line with equation $x = 6$, *b* is the line with equation $x = 3$, and *c* is the line with equation $x = -2$.

	Yes	No
$T_{\langle 0, 10 \rangle}(\triangle ABC)$	☐	☐
$T_{\langle 10, 0 \rangle}(\triangle ABC)$	☐	☐
$(R_{y\text{-axis}} \circ R_a)(\triangle ABC)$	☐	☐
$(R_b \circ R_c)(\triangle ABC)$	☐	☐

34. SAT/ACT Suppose the equation of line *m* is $x = -7$ and the equation of line *n* is $x = 7$. Which is the equivalent to the composition $T_{\langle -1, 3 \rangle} \circ T_{\langle -6, 4 \rangle}$?

Ⓐ R_m Ⓒ R_n

Ⓑ $T_{\langle -7, 7 \rangle}$ Ⓓ $T_{\langle -6, 4 \rangle} \circ T_{\langle -1, 3 \rangle}$

35. Performance Task Rectangle *WXYZ* has a perimeter of 16 units and an area of 15 square units.

Part A Graph *WXYZ* on a sheet of graph paper. Write a composition of rigid motions describing two reflections of *WXYZ* across parallel lines of your choosing. Graph and label the parallel lines $W'X'Y'Z'$ and $W''X''Y''Z''$.

Part B Write a single rigid motion that is equivalent to the composition of rigid motions in Part B. Justify your answer.

Part C Compare the perimeter and area of *WXYZ* and $W''X''Y''Z''$. What can you conclude about the effect of translation on the properties of figures?

8-3
Rotations

SavvasRealize.com

I CAN... draw and describe the rotation of a figure about a point of rotation for a given angle of rotation.

👆 **CRITIQUE & EXPLAIN**

Activity   Assess

Filipe says that the next time one of the hands of the clock points to 7 will be at 7:00 when the hour hand points to 7. Nadia says that it will be at 5:35 when the minute hand points to 7.

A. Whose statement is correct? Explain.

B. **Communicate Precisely** Suppose the numbers on the clock face are removed. Write instructions that another person could follow to move the minute hand from 2 to 6.

❓ **ESSENTIAL QUESTION**   What are the properties that identify a rotation?

👆 **EXAMPLE 1** **Draw a Rotated Image**

How can you perform a 75° rotation of △XYZ about point P?

To rotate △XYZ 75° about point P, each point in the triangle must rotate 75°. Then the measure of the angle formed by each preimage point, point P, and the corresponding image point is 75°.

STUDY TIP
Unless otherwise stated, rotations are always performed counterclockwise.

Use a ruler and protractor to draw 75° angles from each vertex on △XYZ with point P, and mark image points that are the same distance from P.

Step 1 To rotate X, draw $\overline{PX}$ to form one side of a 75° angle.

Step 2 Measure the angle and draw the other side, PX'. Mark point X' so PX' = PX.

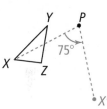

Step 3 Repeat Step 1 and Step 2 for Y and Z in order to locate points Y' and Z'.

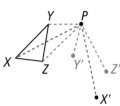

Step 4 Connect the image points to form △X'Y'Z'.

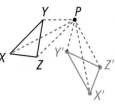

 Try It! **1.** Do you think a rotated image would ever coincide with the original figure? Explain.

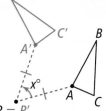

CONCEPT Rotations

A rotation $r_{(x°, P)}$ is a transformation that rotates each point in the preimage about a point P, called the center of rotation, by an angle measure of $x°$, called the angle of rotation. A rotation has these properties:

• The image of P is P' (that is, $P' = P$).

• For a preimage point A, $PA = PA'$ and $m\angle APA' = x°$.

A rotation is a rigid motion, so length and angle measure are preserved. Note that a rotation is counterclockwise for a positive angle measure.

CONCEPT Rotations in the Coordinate Plane

Rules can be used to rotate a figure 90°, 180°, and 270° about the origin O in the coordinate plane.

$$r_{(90°, O)} (x, y) = (-y, x) \qquad r_{(180°, O)} (x, y) = (-x, -y) \qquad r_{(270°, O)} (x, y) = (y, -x)$$

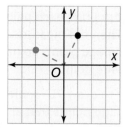 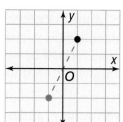 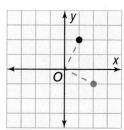

EXAMPLE 2   Draw Rotations in the Coordinate Plane

What is $r_{(90°, O)}$ ABCD?

A rotation of 90° about the origin follows the rule $(x, y) \rightarrow (-y, x)$.

Determine the vertices of the image.

$A(3, 5) \rightarrow A'(-5, 3)$

$B(1, 7) \rightarrow B'(-7, 1)$

$C(-2, 4) \rightarrow C'(-4, -2)$

$D(2, -1) \rightarrow D'(1, 2)$

Draw $A'B'C'D'$ on the coordinate plane.

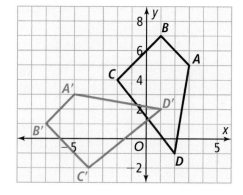

LOOK FOR RELATIONSHIPS
Compare the distance of each vertex from the origin for the preimage and image. What relationships must they have?

Try It! 2. The vertices of $\triangle XYZ$ are $X(-4, 7)$, $Y(0, 8)$, and $Z(2, -1)$.

a. What are the vertices of $r_{(180°, O)}(\triangle XYZ)$?

b. What are the vertices of $r_{(270°, O)}(\triangle XYZ)$?

APPLICATION

 **EXAMPLE 3** Use Rotations

The first drummer in a drumline is at the 20 yard line and the sixth drummer is at the 35 yard line. The drumline rotates counterclockwise 180° about the sixth drummer and then rotates 135° clockwise about the first drummer. Where does the sixth drummer stand after the rotations? Describe the change in position as a composition of rotations.

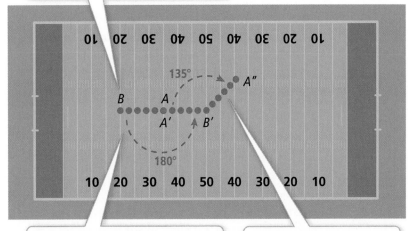

Represent the first drummer as point *B* and the sixth drummer as point *A*.

First, rotate the drumline 180° counterclockwise about point *A*.

Second, rotate the drumline 135° clockwise about point *B*.

COMMUNICATE PRECISELY
Think about how the notation used represents the information shown. What information do you need to identify in order to use the notation?

The sixth drummer stands at the position labeled *A″*. The drumline is first transformed by the rotation $r_{(180°, A)}$ and then by the rotation $r_{(-135°, B′)}$.

 Try It! **3. a.** Suppose the drumline instead turns counterclockwise about *B′*. How many degrees must it rotate so that the sixth drummer ends in the same position?

b. Can the composition of rotations be described by $r_{(45°, A)}$ since 180° − 135° = 45°? Explain.

CONCEPTUAL
UNDERSTANDING

👆 **EXAMPLE 4**   Investigate Reflections and Rotations

LOOK FOR RELATIONSHIPS
Consider how properties of the transformations are related. What properties would you consider in determining the number of reflections needed?

Can you find a sequence of reflections that result in the same image as a rotation?

The image of *JKLM* rotated about point *T* is *WXYZ*. Try to reflect *JKLM* one or more times so that the image aligns with *WXYZ*.

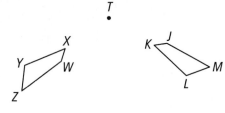

Step 1 Draw line *p* through point *T* and reflect *JKLM* across *p* to form *J'K'L'M'*.

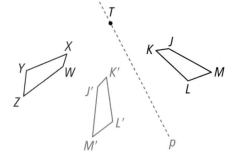

Step 2 Think about how to reflect *J'K'L'M'* to form *WXYZ*. Connect corresponding points in *J'K'L'M'* and *WXYZ* and then find each midpoint.

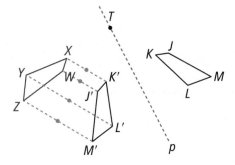

Step 3 The midpoints appear to be collinear with *T*. Draw line *q* through the midpoints and *T*. The reflection of *J'K'L'M'* across *q* is *WXYZ*.

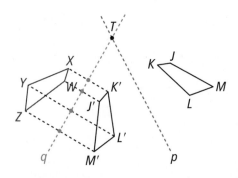

✅ **Try It!**   4. Perform the same constructions shown, except draw line *p* so that it does not pass through *T*. Do you get the same results? Explain.

THEOREM 8-2

Any rotation is a composition of reflections across two lines that intersect at the center of rotation.

The angle of rotation is twice the angle formed by the lines of reflection.

If... 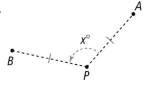   **Then...**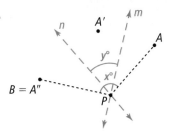

PROOF: SEE EXAMPLE 5. $y = \frac{1}{2}x$

PROOF → **EXAMPLE 5** Prove Theorem 8-2

Prove Theorem 8-2.

Given: $r_{(x°, P)}(A) = B$

Prove: There exist two lines m and n such that $(R_n \circ R_m)(A) = r_{(x°, P)}(A)$ equals B, and the measure of the angle formed by lines m and n is $\frac{1}{2}x$.

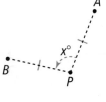

Proof:

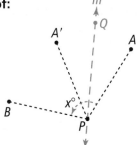   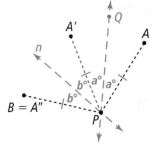

> **LOOK FOR RELATIONSHIPS**
> Think about how to construct lines to help you in the proof. What properties does the angle bisector preserve as a line of reflection?

Mark a point Q anywhere except on $\vec{PA}$. Then draw line m through Q and P. Reflect A across m to image A'. The reflection line is an angle bisector of $\angle APA'$. Let $m\angle APQ = m\angle A'PQ = a$.

Construct the angle bisector n of $\angle BPA'$. Reflect A' across n to image A''. Since a reflection is rigid motion, $PA = PA' = PA'' = PB$. So $A'' = B$. The congruent angles formed measure b. Therefore, $r_{(x°, P)}(A) = (R_n \circ R_m)(A)$.

The angle of rotation $x°$ has a measure equal to $a + a + b + b$, or $2(a + b)$. The angle formed by lines m and n has a measure equal to $a + b$, or $\frac{1}{2}x$.

 Try It! 5. Suppose point Q is closer to point B or even outside of $\angle APB$. Does the relationship still hold for the angle between the reflection lines and the angle between the preimage and the image? Explain.

🔑 CONCEPT SUMMARY Properties of Rotations

WORDS A rotation is a transformation that rotates each point in the preimage about the center of rotation through the angle of rotation.

Any rotation is a composition of reflections across two intersecting lines.

DIAGRAMS

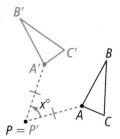

SYMBOLS

$r_{(x°, P)}(\triangle ABC) = \triangle A'B'C'$
$PA = PA', PB = PB', PC = PC'$
$m\angle APA' = m\angle BPB' = m\angle CPC' = x°$

$r_{(x°, P)}(A) = (R_n \circ R_m)(A) = B$
$y° = \frac{1}{2}x°$

✅ Do You UNDERSTAND?

1. **ESSENTIAL QUESTION** What are the properties that identify a rotation?

2. **Error Analysis** Isabel drew the diagram below to show the rotation of $\triangle DEF$ about point T. What is her error?

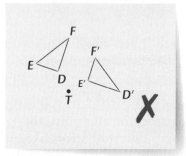

3. **Vocabulary** How is the *center of rotation* related to the *center of a circle*?

4. **Construct Arguments** In the diagram, $\triangle A''B''C''$ is the image of reflections of $\triangle ABC$ across lines p and q. It is also the image of a rotation of $\triangle ABC$ about R. What is the angle of rotation? Explain.

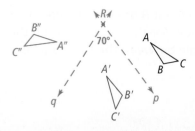

Do You KNOW HOW?

Trace each figure and draw its rotated image.

5. $r_{(90°, P)}(\overline{MN})$

6. $r_{(120°, T)}(\triangle ABC)$

Give the coordinates of each image.

7. $r_{(180°, O)}(\overline{GH})$ for $G(2, -9)$, $H(-1, 3)$

8. $r_{(90°, O)}(\triangle XYZ)$ for $X(0, 3)$, $Y(1, -4)$, $Z(5, 2)$

Trace each figure and construct two lines of reflection such that the composition of the reflections across the lines maps onto the image shown.

9.

10.

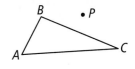
PRACTICE & PROBLEM SOLVING

UNDERSTAND

11. Construct Arguments When you rotate a figure, does every point move the same distance? Explain.

12. Error Analysis Shannon says that $\triangle X'Y'Z'$ is a rotation of $\triangle XYZ$ about P. What is the correct transformation from $\triangle XYZ$ to $\triangle X'Y'Z'$?

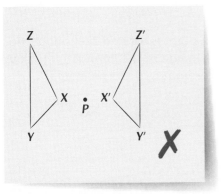

13. Mathematical Connections Points A' and B' are the images of points A and B after a 270° rotation about the origin. If the slope of $\overleftrightarrow{AB}$ is −3, what is the slope of $\overleftrightarrow{A'B'}$? Explain.

14. Use Structure The diagram shows $r_{(90°,\ O)}(ABCD)$. What are the coordinates of $ABCD$?

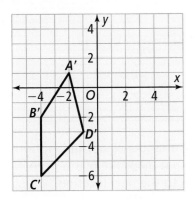

15. Higher Order Thinking In the diagram, $r_{(180°,\ O)}(\triangle ABC) = \triangle A'B'C'$. Describe a composition of a rotation and a translation that results in the same image.

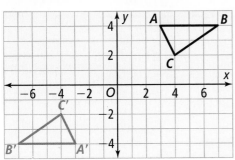

PRACTICE

For Exercises 16–18, trace each figure and draw its rotated image. SEE EXAMPLES 1 AND 3

16. $r_{(80°,\ P)}(\triangle ABC)$

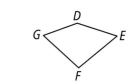

17. $r_{(110°,\ Q)}(\triangle DEFG)$

18. $r_{(175°,\ R)}(\triangle HJK)$

For Exercises 19–22, give the coordinates of each image. SEE EXAMPLE 2

19. $r_{(90°,\ O)}(\triangle DEF)$ for $D(0, 5)$, $E(−2, 8)$, $F(−3, −5)$

20. $r_{(270°,\ O)}(WXYZ)$ for $W(4, −2)$, $X(7, 3)$, $Y(1, 11)$, $Z(−4, 6)$

21. $r_{(180°,\ O)}(\triangle STU)$ for $S(−2, −6)$, $T(−5, 3)$, $U(1, 0)$

22. $r_{(360°,\ O)}(JKLM)$ for $J(−4, 7)$, $K(1, 5)$, $L(6, 1)$, $M(3, −9)$

23. Trace the point and triangle. Draw the image $r_{(160°,\ T)}(\triangle XYZ)$. Then draw two reflections that result in the same image. SEE EXAMPLES 4 AND 5

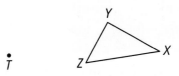

24. Find the angle of rotation for the rotation about point S that is the composition $R_n \circ R_m$. Then trace the figure and draw the image.

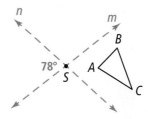

APPLY

25. Make Sense and Persevere What rotation must the driver gear make for gear A to rotate 90° clockwise? Explain how you found your answer.

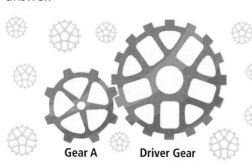

Gear A   Driver Gear

26. Reason Luis is programming an animation for a countdown timer where points flash in sequence, one at a time, around in a circle. He calculates that the coordinates of the first four points in his sequence are (6, 0), (5.5, 2.3), (4.2, 4.2), and (2.3, 5.5). He can find the rest of the coordinates by rotating the first four points by 90°, 180°, and 270°. What are the coordinates of the points that complete the sequence around in a circle?

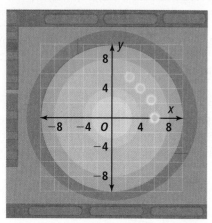

27. Communicate Precisely Lourdes created the design below by rotating △ABF, quadrilateral BCEF, and △CDE. Describe the rotations she used. How do you determine the angles of rotation?

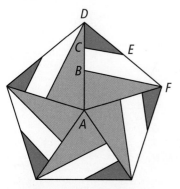

ASSESSMENT PRACTICE

28. Quadrilateral J′K′L′M′ is the image of JKLM rotated about point P. What completes each statement?

$\overline{KP}$ ___?___ $\overline{K'P'}$

$\overline{LM}$ ___?___ $\overline{L'M'}$

$\overline{JJ'}$ ___?___ $\overline{KK'}$

m∠KPK′ ___?___ m∠LPL′

29. SAT/ACT A point is rotated 270° about the origin. The image of the point is (−11, 7). What are the coordinates of the preimage?

Ⓐ (7, −11)

Ⓑ (−7, −11)

Ⓒ (7, 11)

Ⓓ (11, 7)

30. Performance Task Movers need to move the pianos as shown in the diagram.

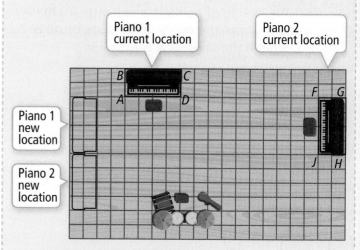

Part A Describe a sequence of rigid motions for each piano that maps the piano from its current location to the new location.

Part B Describe a single rotation for each piano that maps the piano from its current location to the new location. (*Hint:* You can find two reflections to determine the center of rotation.)

8-4

Classification of Rigid Motions

I CAN... identify different rigid motions used to transform two-dimensional shapes.

VOCABULARY

• glide reflection

👆 CRITIQUE & EXPLAIN

Two students are trying to determine whether compositions of rigid motions are commutative. Paula translates a triangle and then reflects it across a line. When she reflects and then translates, she gets the same image. She concludes that compositions of rigid motions are commutative.

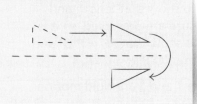

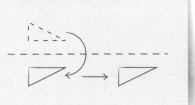

Keenan rotates a triangle and then reflects it. When he changes the order of the rigid motions, he gets a different image. He concludes that compositions of rigid motions are not commutative.

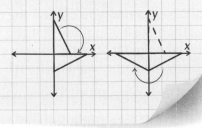

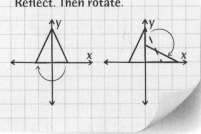

A. Should Paula have used grid paper? Explain.

B. Communicate Precisely Do you agree with Paula or with Keenan? Explain.

❓ ESSENTIAL QUESTION

How can rigid motions be classified?

THEOREM 8-3

The composition of two or more rigid motions is a rigid motion.

If...

M: QRST → Q'R'S'T' and
N: Q'R'S'T' → Q"R"S"T" are rigid motions.

Then...

(N ∘ M): QRST → Q"R"S"T"
is a rigid motion.

PROOF: SEE EXAMPLE 1.

PROOF   **EXAMPLE 1**   Prove Theorem 8-3

Write a paragraph proof of Theorem 8-3.

Given: *T* and *S* are rigid motions.

Prove: *S* ∘ *T* is a rigid motion.

Plan: Let *P*, *Q*, and *R* be any three noncollinear points in the preimage. You want to show that length and angle measure are preserved, so it is sufficient to show that $PQ = P''Q''$ and $m\angle PQR = m\angle P''Q''R''$.

Proof: Since *T* and *S* are rigid motions, $PQ = P'Q'$, $P'Q' = P''Q''$, $m\angle PQR = m\angle P'Q'R'$, and $m\angle P'Q'R' = m\angle P''Q''R''$.

By the Transitive Property of Equality, $PQ = P''Q''$ and $m\angle PQR = m\angle P''Q''R''$.

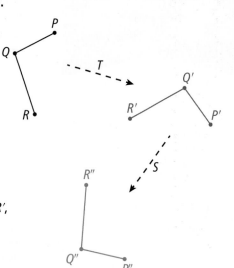

S ∘ *T* is a rigid motion because it preserves length and angle measure.

Try It!   1. Describe how you can use the reasoning used to prove Theorem 8-3 to show that the theorem is true when composing three rigid motions. Can your strategy be extended to include any number of rigid motions?

CONCEPTUAL UNDERSTANDING   **EXAMPLE 2**   Explore Glide Reflections

A. Is there a rigid motion that maps △*ABC* to △*A'B'C'*?

Observe that $m\angle A = m\angle A'$, $m\angle B = m\angle B'$, and $m\angle C = m\angle C'$.

Also, $AB = A'B'$, $AC = A'C'$, and $BC = B'C'$.

Length and angle measure are preserved, so the transformation is a rigid motion.

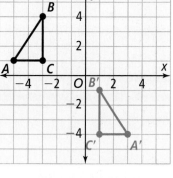

B. Does a reflection, translation, or rotation map △*ABC* to △*A'B'C'*?

USE STRUCTURE
Each rigid motion has specific properties. What properties should you consider for each type?

Check whether a translation maps △*ABC* to △*A'B'C'*.

Use the point *B*(−3, 4) and its image *B'*(1, −1) .

The translation rule that maps *B* onto *B'* is $T_{\langle 4, -5\rangle}$. This rule does not map *A* to *A'*.

The rigid motion is not a translation.

Check whether a rotation maps △*ABC* to △*A'B'C'*.

Since orientation of the triangle is not preserved, the rigid motion is not a rotation.

Check whether a reflection maps △*ABC* to △*A'B'C'*.

There is no line of reflection that produces the image, so the rigid motion is not a reflection.

CONTINUED ON THE NEXT PAGE

EXAMPLE 2 CONTINUED

C. **What composition of two rigid motions maps △ABC to △A'B'C'?**

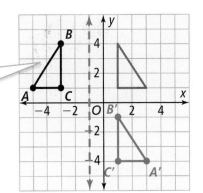

> Because △ABC has a clockwise orientation and △A'B'C' has a counterclockwise orientation, orientation is not preserved. This means that one of the rigid motions must be a reflection.

Reflect △ABC across *k*, the line with equation $x = -1$.

Then translate the image down 5 units.

$$(T_{\langle 0, -5 \rangle} \circ R_k)(\triangle ABC) = \triangle A'B'C'$$

The composition of a reflection followed by a translation in a direction parallel to the line of reflection is a rigid motion called a **glide reflection**.

USE STRUCTURE
Often there is more than one composition of rigid motions that maps a preimage to its image. What is another composition of rigid motions that maps △ABC to △A'B'C'?

 Try It! 2. Draw the perpendicular bisector of $\overline{BB'}$. Is that line also the perpendicular bisector of $\overline{AA'}$ and $\overline{CC'}$? Use your answer to explain why a reflection alone can or cannot map △ABC to △A'B'C'.

APPLICATION

👆 **EXAMPLE 3** **Find the Image of a Glide Reflection**

A digital artist is reproducing a tire tread pattern from a partial tire print from a crime scene by applying a glide reflection. She uses the rule $T_{\langle 0, 0.1 \rangle} \circ R_{y\text{-axis}}$ to generate a pattern. Confirm that her rule can be applied to the partial pattern that was taken from the crime scene.

COMMON ERROR
The notation tells you the order in which you should use the transformations. Remember that in the composition $T_{\langle 0, 0.1 \rangle} \circ R_{y\text{-axis}}$, the reflection is performed first.

Step 1 Apply the first rigid motion.

Reflect the outlined preimage across the line $x = 0$.

Step 2 Apply the second rigid motion.

Translate the reflection 0.1 unit up.

The rule appears to map the pieces of the partial pattern onto itself.

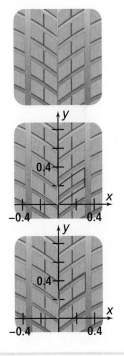

 Try It! 3. Quadrilateral *RSTV* has vertices $R(-3, 2)$, $S(0, 5)$, $T(4, -4)$, and $V(0, -2)$. Use the rule $T_{\langle 1, 0 \rangle} \circ R_{x\text{-axis}}$ to graph and label the glide reflection of *RSTV*.

THEOREM 8-4

Any rigid motion is either a translation, reflection, rotation, or glide reflection.

If... M is a rigid motion

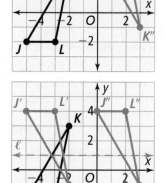

Then... $M = R_\ell$ or
$M = T_{\langle x, y \rangle}$ or
$M = r_{(n°, P)}$ or
$M = T_{\langle x, y \rangle} \circ R_\ell$

You will prove this in a more advanced course.

COROLLARY TO THEOREM 8-4

Any rigid motion can be expressed as a composition of reflections.

PROOF: SEE EXERCISE 11.

If... M is a rigid motion

Then... $M = R_\ell$ or $M = R_\ell \circ R_m$
or $M = R_\ell \circ R_m \circ R_n$

EXAMPLE 4   Determine a Glide Reflection

What is the glide reflection that maps $\triangle JKL$ to $\triangle J''K''L''$?

To determine the glide reflection, you can work backward.

Step 1 Determine the translation.

First determine the translation that vertically aligns J'' with J and L'' with L. It is 5 units horizontally and 0 units vertically.

STUDY TIP
The vertices of the preimage and of the image are equidistant from the line of reflection.

Step 2 Determine the line of reflection.

The vertices of an image and preimage are the same distance from the line ℓ with equation $y = 1$, so ℓ is the line of reflection. If you reflect $\triangle J'K'L'$ across ℓ, you map back to the original triangle, $\triangle JKL$.

Step 3 Write the complete glide reflection.

$$\left(T_{\langle 5, 0 \rangle} \circ R_\ell\right)(\triangle JKL) = \triangle J'K'L', \text{ where } \ell \text{ is the line } y = 1$$

 Try It!   **4.** What is the glide reflection that maps each of the following?

a. $\triangle ABC \rightarrow \triangle A'B'C'$ given $A(-3, 4)$, $B(-4, 2)$, $C(-1, 1)$, $A'(1, 1)$, $B'(2, -1)$, and $C'(-1, -2)$.

b. $\overline{RS} \rightarrow \overline{R'S'}$ given $R(-2, 4)$, $S(2, 6)$, $R'(4, 0)$, and $S'(8, -2)$.

CONCEPT SUMMARY Types of Rigid Motions

REFLECTION

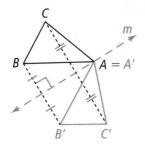

$$R_m(\triangle ABC) = \triangle A'B'C'$$

TRANSLATION

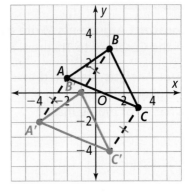

$$T_{\langle -2,\ -3\rangle}(\triangle ABC) = \triangle A'B'C'$$

ROTATION

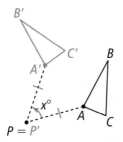

$$r_{(x°,\ P)}(\triangle ABC) = \triangle A'B'C'$$

GLIDE REFLECTION

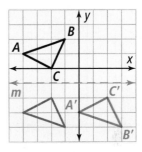

$$(T_{\langle 4,\ 0\rangle} \circ R_m)(\triangle ABC) = \triangle A'B'C'$$

Do You UNDERSTAND?

1. **ESSENTIAL QUESTION** How can rigid motions be classified?

2. Is it correct to say that the composition of a translation followed by a reflection is a glide reflection? Explain.

3. **Error Analysis** Tamika draws the following diagram as an example of a glide reflection. What error did she make?

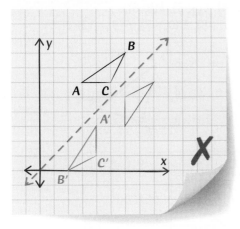

Do You KNOW HOW?

Use the figures for Exercises 4–7. Identify each rigid motion as a translation, a reflection, a rotation, or a glide reflection.

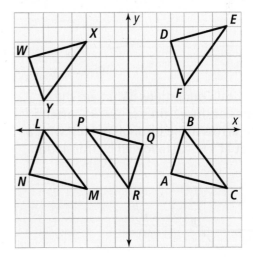

4. $\triangle WYX \rightarrow \triangle NLM$ 5. $\triangle DFE \rightarrow \triangle WYX$

6. $\triangle WYX \rightarrow \triangle ABC$ 7. $\triangle NLM \rightarrow \triangle QRP$

UNDERSTAND

8. Construct Arguments Write a paragraph proof of the Corollary to Theorem 8-4.

9. Error Analysis Damian draws the diagram for the glide reflection $(T_{\langle 0, 7 \rangle} \circ R_{y\text{-axis}})(ABCD)$. What error did he make?

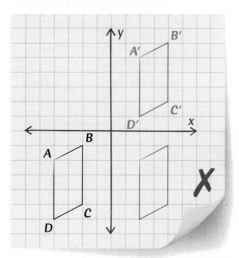

10. Higher Order Thinking What are the reflection and translation for the glide reflection shown? Sketch the intermediate image.

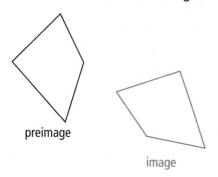

preimage

image

11. Mathematical Connections What are the coordinates of the vertices of $\triangle A'B'C'$ after a reflection across a line through point P with a y-intercept at $y = -2$, followed by translation $T_{\langle 3, 3 \rangle}$?

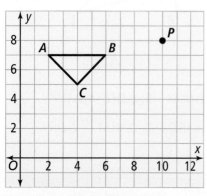

PRACTICE

12. What are two rigid motions with a composition that maps $\triangle JKL$ to $\triangle J'K'L'$? SEE EXAMPLES 1 AND 2

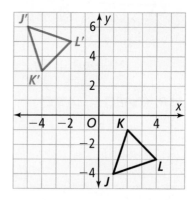

For Exercises 13–17, given $A(6, -4)$, $B(3, 8)$, and $C(-7, 9)$, determine the coordinates of the vertices of $\triangle A'B'C'$ for each glide reflection. Suppose p is the line with equation $x = -3$, q is the line with equation $y = 9$, and r is the line with equation $y = -2$. SEE EXAMPLE 3

13. $(T_{\langle 0, -2 \rangle} \circ R_{y\text{-axis}})(\triangle ABC) = \triangle A'B'C'$

14. $(T_{\langle 4, 0 \rangle} \circ R_{x\text{-axis}})(\triangle ABC) = \triangle A'B'C'$

15. $(T_{\langle 0, 8 \rangle} \circ R_p)(\triangle ABC) = \triangle A'B'C'$

16. $(T_{\langle -5, 0 \rangle} \circ R_q)(\triangle ABC) = \triangle A'B'C'$

17. $(T_{\langle 7, 0 \rangle} \circ R_r)(\triangle ABC) = \triangle A'B'C'$

For Exercises 18–21, write a rule for each glide reflection that maps $\triangle DEF$ to $\triangle D'E'F'$. SEE EXAMPLE 4

18. $D(7, -2)$, $E(3, 9)$, $F(8, 6)$;
$D'(-5, 1)$, $E'(-1, 12)$, $F'(-6, 9)$

19. $D(-5, 8)$, $E(1, 4)$, $F(6, 3)$;
$D'(-3, 8)$, $E'(3, 12)$, $F'(8, 13)$

20. $D(0, 4)$, $E(6, 3)$, $F(9, 8)$;
$D'(-6, -8)$, $E'(0, -7)$, $F'(3, -12)$

21.

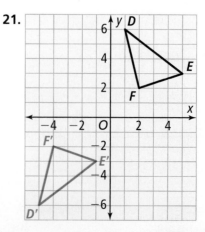

APPLY

22. **Look for Relationships** The diagram shows one section of concrete being stamped with a pattern. The design can be described by two glide reflections from triangle 1 to triangle 5. Write the rules for each glide reflection.

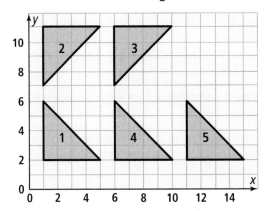

23. **Model With Mathematics** Each parking space in the figure can be the image of another parking space as a glide reflection. What is the rule that maps the parking space where the red car is parked to the parking space where the blue car is parked?

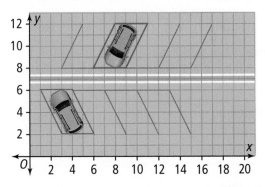

24. **Look for Relationships** Starting from tile 1, quadrilateral tiles are embedded into a wall following a pattern of glide reflections. If the pattern continues, what are the shapes and locations of the next two tiles the builder will place in the wall? Explain.

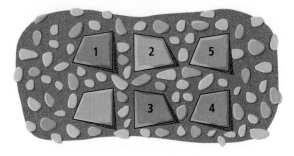

ASSESSMENT PRACTICE

25. Match each rigid motion with its image.

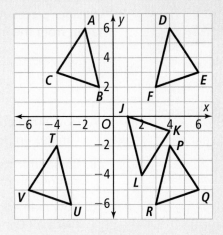

I. $r_{(180°, (0, 1))}(\triangle ABC)$ A. $\triangle ABC$

II. $(T_{\langle 0, 8\rangle} \circ R_{y\text{-axis}})(\triangle TUV)$ B. $\triangle DFE$

III. $(T_{\langle 2, 0\rangle} \circ R_{y\text{-axis}})(\triangle DFE)$ C. $\triangle LJK$

IV. $R_{y\text{-axis}}(\triangle TUV)$ D. $\triangle PRQ$

26. **SAT/ACT** Suppose m is the line with equation $y = 3$. Given $A(7, 1)$, $B(2, 9)$, and $C(3, -5)$, what are the coordinates of the vertices of $\triangle A'B'C'$ for $(T_{\langle -4, 0\rangle} \circ R_m)(\triangle ABC) = \triangle A'B'C'$?

Ⓐ $A'(11, 4)$, $B'(6, 12)$, $C'(7, -2)$

Ⓑ $A'(11, 5)$, $B'(-6, -3)$, $C'(7, 11)$

Ⓒ $A'(3, 4)$, $B'(-2, 12)$, $C'(-1, -2)$

Ⓓ $A'(3, 5)$, $B'(-2, -3)$, $C'(-1, 11)$

27. **Performance Task** Glide reflections are used to print a design across a length of wrapping paper.

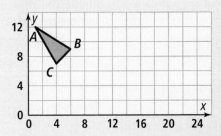

Part A Copy the diagram and draw image $\triangle A'B'C' = (T_{\langle 0, -2\rangle} \circ R_\ell)(\triangle ABC)$, where ℓ is the line with equation $x = 5$.

Part B Translate $\triangle ABC$ 7 units to the right to print $\triangle DEF$ and 14 units to right to print $\triangle GHJ$. What glide reflections of $\triangle DEF$ and $\triangle GHJ$ result in the same arrangement of figures as in Part A? Draw these images to create the wrapping paper pattern.

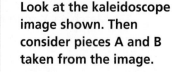
8-5
Symmetry

SavvasRealize.com

I CAN... identify different types of symmetry in two-dimensional figures.

VOCABULARY
- point symmetry
- reflectional symmetry
- rotational symmetry

EXPLORE & REASON

Look at the kaleidoscope image shown. Then consider pieces A and B taken from the image.

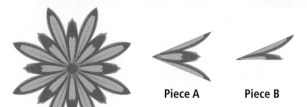

Piece A   Piece B

A. How are piece A and piece B related? Describe a rigid motion that you can use on piece B to produce piece A.

B. Communicate Precisely Describe a composition of rigid motions that you can use on piece A to produce the image.

C. How many rigid motions did you need to produce the image from piece A? Can you think of another composition of rigid motions to produce the image starting with piece A?

ESSENTIAL QUESTION   How can you tell whether a figure is symmetric?

CONCEPTUAL UNDERSTANDING

EXAMPLE 1   Identify Transformations for Symmetry

What transformations can be used to map the figure onto itself? Why can some figures be mapped onto themselves?

A figure has symmetry if a rigid motion can map the figure onto itself.

STUDY TIP
To identify reflectional symmetry, fold a figure so one half lines up with the other.

Reflectional symmetry is a symmetry for which a reflection maps the figure onto itself. The line of reflection for a reflection symmetry is called the line of symmetry.

The reflections R_m and R_n map the figure onto itself. Observe that lines m and n both divide the figure into two pieces with the same size and shape.

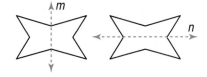

A figure has **rotational symmetry** if its image is mapped onto the preimage after a rotation of less than 360°.

The rotation $r_{(180°, P)}$ maps the figure onto itself.

Try It!   **1.** What transformations map each figure onto itself?

a.

b.

Go Online | SavvasRealize.com

EXAMPLE 2 | Identify Lines of Symmetry

How many lines of symmetry does a regular hexagon have?

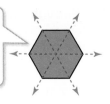

Each line through opposite vertices creates equal halves.

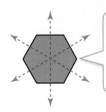

Each line through midpoints of opposite sides creates equal halves.

COMMON ERROR
Remember that lines of symmetry are not necessarily horizontal or vertical lines.

A regular hexagon has six lines of symmetry.

 Try It! **2.** How many lines of symmetry does each figure have? How do you know whether you have found them all?

a.

b.

 EXAMPLE 3 | Identify Rotational Symmetry

For what angles of rotation does the figure map onto itself?

A. an equilateral triangle

Find the angles of rotation about the center that map △*ABC* onto itself.

USE STRUCTURE
Think about how a regular polygon can be divided. How can you divide a regular polygon into pieces of the same size and shape?

- A rotation of 120° creates an identical image with vertex *B* at the top.

- A rotation of 240° creates an identical image with vertex *C* at the top.

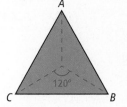

B. a parallelogram

- Only a rotation of 180° maps the figure onto itself.

The type of symmetry for which there is rotation of 180° that maps a figure onto itself is called **point symmetry**. A parallelogram has 180° rotational symmetry, or point symmetry.

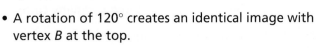 **Try It!** **3.** What are the rotational symmetries for each figure? Does each figure have point symmetry?

a.

b.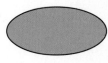

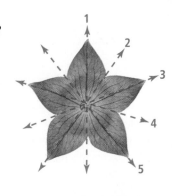

EXAMPLE 4 ▸ **Determine Symmetries**

What type(s) of symmetry does each figure have?

A. • A line through the center of a petal is a line of reflection. Since there are 5 petals, there are 5 lines of symmetry.

• Since 360° ÷ 5 = 72°, there is rotational symmetry at multiples of 72°.

The flower has reflectional symmetry with 5 lines of symmetry and rotational symmetry for angles of 72°, 144°, 216°, and 288°.

COMMON ERROR
You may think a rectangular figure has reflectional symmetry along the diagonal. Recognize that a rectangular shape may only have horizontal or vertical lines of symmetry.

B. • No lines of symmetry can be drawn.

• Rotating the card 180° about its center creates an identical image.

The card has 180° rotational symmetry, or point symmetry.

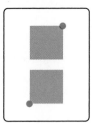

Try It! **4.** What symmetries does a square have?

APPLICATION

EXAMPLE 5 ▸ **Use Symmetry**

A company CEO wants a new logo that looks the same for each rotation of 30° and uses the three company colors. What are some possible logo designs?

Formulate ◀ Consider the different elements of the design.

Start with a polygon that has the specified rotational symmetry, which means a polygon that maps to itself at each 30° rotation.

The colors will have to be used carefully to achieve symmetry.

Compute ◀ To find the number of sides for the polygon, find the number of 30° rotations in a full circle.

360° ÷ 30° = 12

You need a regular 12-gon (dodecagon).

Then, consider how the colors can be used so that each section is the same.

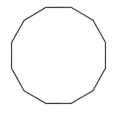

Interpret ◀ Three possible designs are shown.

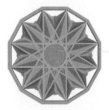  

 Try It! **5.** What is a possible design for a circular logo that looks the same for each 60° rotation and uses at least two colors?

CONCEPT SUMMARY Symmetry

	Reflectional Symmetry	Rotational Symmetry
WORDS	• A figure that maps onto itself when it is reflected over a line has reflectional symmetry. • A line of symmetry is a line of reflection when a figure is reflected onto itself.	• A figure that maps onto itself when it is rotated about its center by an angle measuring less than 360° has **rotational symmetry**. • A figure with 180° rotational symmetry has **point symmetry**.
DIAGRAM		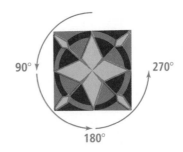

☑ Do You UNDERSTAND?

1. **ESSENTIAL QUESTION** How can you tell whether a figure is symmetric?

2. **Error Analysis** For the figure below, Adam was asked to draw all lines of reflection. His work is shown. What error did Adam make?

3. **Vocabulary** What type of symmetry does a figure have if it can be mapped onto itself by being flipped over a line?

4. **Communicate Precisely** What does it mean for a figure to have 60° rotational symmetry?

5. **Construct Arguments** Is it possible for a figure to have rotational symmetry and no reflectional symmetry? Explain or give examples.

Do You KNOW HOW?

Find the number of lines of symmetry for each figure.

6.

7.

Describe the rotational symmetry of each figure. State whether each has point symmetry.

8.

9.

Identify the types of symmetry of each figure. For each figure with reflectional symmetry, identify the lines of symmetry. For each figure with rotational symmetry, identify the angles of rotation that map the figure onto itself.

10.

11.

UNDERSTAND

PRACTICE

12. **Construct Arguments** Is it possible for a figure to have reflectional symmetry and no rotational symmetry? Explain or give examples.

13. **Reason** Explain how you would find the angles of rotational symmetry for the figure shown.

14. **Mathematical Connections** A figure that has 180° rotational symmetry also has point symmetry. Write a conditional to relate those facts. Then, write the converse, inverse, and contrapositive.

15. **Look for Relationships** If a figure has 90° rotational symmetry, what other symmetries must it have?

16. **Error Analysis** Yumiko's work is shown below. What error did she make?

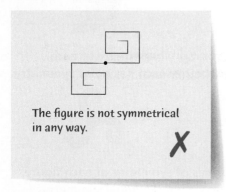

The figure is not symmetrical in any way.   **X**

17. **Higher Order Thinking** Three types of rigid motion are translations, rotations, and reflections.

A frieze pattern is a linear pattern that repeats, and it has translational symmetry. An example is shown below.

Find and name some occurrences of frieze patterns in the real world.

For Exercises 18 and 19, find all transformations that can be used to map each figure onto itself. SEE EXAMPLE 1

18.

19.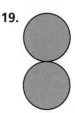

20. How many lines of symmetry does a regular five-pointed star have? SEE EXAMPLE 2

For Exercises 21 and 22, describe the rotational symmetries of each figure. SEE EXAMPLE 3

21.

22.

23. What types of symmetry does the figure have? Explain. SEE EXAMPLE 4

24. When drawn in the style shown, the number 808 has horizontal and vertical reflectional symmetry, as well as 180° rotational symmetry.

What are some other combinations of numbers or letters with symmetry? Find at least three other combinations, and identify the types of symmetry for each. SEE EXAMPLE 5

PRACTICE & PROBLEM SOLVING

APPLY

25. Reason How would you decide which flags show reflection symmetry? Rotational symmetry? No symmetry?

Canada

Sweden

Jamaica

Saint Kitts and Nevis

26. Look for Relationships Make observations about the structure of each snowflake, and describe the types of symmetry that a snowflake can have.

27. Make Sense and Persevere Describe the symmetries of each molecule shown.

a. benzene

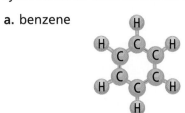

b. water

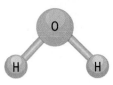

c. hydrogen peroxide

ASSESSMENT PRACTICE

28. Which types of symmetry does the figure display? Select all that apply.

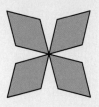

Ⓐ reflectional symmetry across a vertical line

Ⓑ reflectional symmetry across a horizontal line

Ⓒ 120° rotational symmetry

Ⓓ 180° rotational symmetry

29. SAT/ACT Which letter can be mapped onto itself by a 180° rotation about its center?

30. Performance Task A client wants a graphic designer to create an emblem that has rotational symmetry of 90° and 180°. The client needs the colors of the emblem to be red, yellow, and blue. The emblem should also include the first letter of the company name, X.

Part A The designer begins his design with a polygon. What polygons can he use?

Part B If a figure has rotational symmetry of 90° and 180°, what type of reflectional symmetry does the figure have?

Part C Create two possible designs for the client.

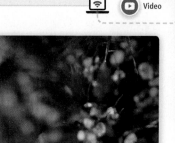

The Perplexing Polygon

Look around and you will see shapes and patterns everywhere you look. The tiles on a floor are often all the same shape and fit together to form a pattern. The petals on a flower often make a repeating pattern around the center of the flower. When you look at snowflakes under a microscope, you'll notice that they are made up of repeating three-dimensional crystals. Think about this during the Mathematical Modeling in 3 Acts lesson.

Scan for Multimedia

ACT 1 ⟩ Identify the Problem

1. What is the first question that comes to mind after watching the video?

2. Write down the main question you will answer about what you saw in the video.

3. Make an initial conjecture that answers this main question.

4. Explain how you arrived at your conjecture.

5. What information will be useful to know to answer the main question? How can you get it? How will you use that information?

ACT 2 ⟩ Develop a Model

6. Use the math that you have learned in this Topic to refine your conjecture.

ACT 3 ⟩ Interpret the Results

7. Did your refined conjecture match the actual answer exactly? If not, what might explain the difference?

Topic Review

? TOPIC ESSENTIAL QUESTION

1. What are properties of the four types of rigid motion?

Vocabulary Review

Choose the correct term to complete each sentence.

2. A(n) _____ is a transformation about a point with a given angle measure.

3. Reflections, translations, rotations, and glide reflections are the four types of _____.

4. A line that a figure is reflected across so that it maps onto itself is called a(n) _____.

5. The composition of a reflection and a translation is called a(n) _____.

6. The set of points that a transformation acts on is called the _____.

7. The result of a transformation is called the _____.

- composition of rigid motions
- glide reflection
- image
- line of reflection
- line of symmetry
- preimage
- rigid motion
- rotation
- translation

Concepts & Skills Review

LESSON 8-1 | **Reflections**

Quick Review

A **rigid motion** is a transformation that preserves length and angle measure.

A reflection is a transformation that reflects a point across a line of reflection m such that the image of a point A on m is A, and for a point B not on m, line m is the perpendicular bisector $\overline{BB'}$.

A reflection is a rigid motion.

Example
What is the reflection of $\triangle ABC$ across ℓ?

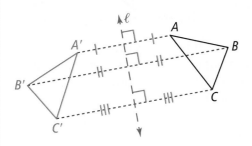

Practice & Problem Solving

8. Does the transformation appear to be a rigid motion?

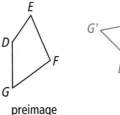

preimage   image

For Exercises 9 and 10, the vertices of $\triangle HJK$ are $H(-3, 2)$, $J(-1, -3)$, and $K(4, 3)$. What are the coordinates of the vertices of $\triangle H'J'K'$ for each reflection?

9. $R_{y\text{-axis}}$

10. $R_{x\text{-axis}}$

11. **Communicate Precisely** Given the coordinates of two points and the equation of a line, how can you check that one point is the image of the other point reflected across the line?

LESSON 8-2 Translations

Quick Review

A translation is a transformation that maps all points the same distance and in the same direction, so that for any two points A and B, $AA' = BB'$.

A translation is a rigid motion. Any translation can be expressed as a composition of two reflections across two parallel lines.

Example

What is the graph of $T_{\langle 3, -2\rangle}(\triangle LMN)$?

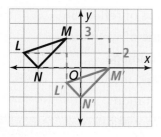

Practice & Problem Solving

For Exercises 12 and 13, the vertices of $\triangle PQR$ are $P(-4, 3)$, $Q(-2, 3)$, and $R(1, -3)$. What are the coordinates of the vertices of $\triangle P'Q'R'$ for each translation?

12. $T_{\langle -3, 2\rangle}$ **13.** $T_{\langle 4, -5\rangle}$

14. What is the translation shown?

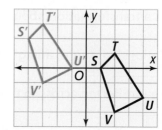

15. Make Sense and Persevere Given reflections R_h and R_k, where h is a line with equation $x = -3$ and k is a line with equation $x = 2$, how can you determine the distance of the translation resulting from the composition $R_k \circ R_h$?

LESSON 8-3 Rotations

Quick Review

A rotation is a transformation that rotates a point about the center of rotation P by the angle of rotation $x°$ such that the image of P is P, $PA = PA'$, and $m\angle APA' = x$.

A rotation is a rigid motion. Any rotation can be expressed as a composition of reflections across two intersecting lines.

Example

What is the 150° rotation of $\overline{XY}$ about P?

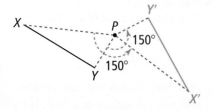

Practice & Problem Solving

For Exercise 16 and 17, the vertices of $\triangle ABC$ are $A(2, -2)$, $B(-3, -2)$, and $C(-1, 3)$. What are the coordinates of the vertices of $\triangle A'B'C'$ for each rotation?

16. $r_{(90°, O)}$ **17.** $r_{(270°, O)}$

18. Draw two lines of reflection so the composition of the reflections across the lines is equivalent to the rotation shown.

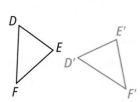

19. Use Structure If two lines intersect at a right angle at point P, what rotation is equivalent to the composition of the reflections across the two lines?

Classification of Rigid Motions

Quick Review

A **glide reflection** is the composition of a reflection followed by a translation.

Any rigid motion is either a translation, reflection, rotation, or glide reflection. As a result, any rigid motion can be expressed as a combination of reflections.

Example

What is a glide reflection that maps △GHJ to △KLM?

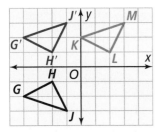

First reflect △GHJ across the x-axis to get △G'H'J'. Then translate △G'H'J' by 4 units to the right to get △KLM. The glide reflection is $T_{\langle 4, 0 \rangle} \circ R_{x\text{-axis}}$.

Practice & Problem Solving

For Exercises 20 and 21, the vertices of △LMN are L(−2, 4), M(1, 2), and N(−3, −5). Suppose j is a line with equation x = 3 and k is a line with equation y = −2. what are the coordinates of the vertices of △L′M′N′ for each glide reflection?

20. $T_{\langle -2, 4 \rangle} \circ R_j$

21. $T_{\langle 2, -3 \rangle} \circ R_k$

22. What is a glide reflection for the transformation shown?

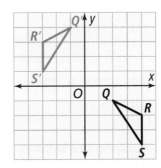

23. Make Sense and Persevere Is there more than one way to describe a glide reflection as a composition of a reflection and then a translation? Explain.

Symmetry

Quick Review

A figure has **symmetry** if a rigid motion can map the figure to itself. If the rigid motion is a reflection, then the symmetry is **reflectional symmetry**. If the rigid motion is a rotation, then the symmetry is **rotational symmetry**.

When the angle of rotation is 180°, the rotational symmetry is called **point symmetry**.

Example

How many lines of symmetry does the figure have?

You can draw a line of reflection through each vertex and the center of the star. There are six lines of symmetry.

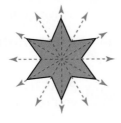

Practice & Problem Solving

24. Describe the transformations that can be used to map the figure onto itself.

For Exercises 25 and 26, describe all the symmetries of each figure. If the figure has reflectional symmetry, identify all the lines of symmetry. If the figure has rotational symmetry, give the angles of rotation.

25.

26.

27. Communicate Precisely Suppose a figure has at least two lines of symmetry. Explain why the figure must have rotational symmetry.

? TOPIC ESSENTIAL QUESTION

What relationships between sides and angles of triangles can be used to prove triangles congruent?

Topic Overview

enVision® STEM Project
Design a Bridge

Topic Vocabulary

- chord
- congruence transformation
- congruent

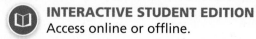

Digital Experience

INTERACTIVE STUDENT EDITION Access online or offline.

ACTIVITIES Complete *Explore & Reason, Model & Discuss*, and *Critique & Explain* activities. Interact with Examples and Try Its.

ANIMATION View and interact with real-world applications.

PRACTICE Practice what you've learned.

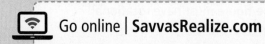

Go online | SavvasRealize.com

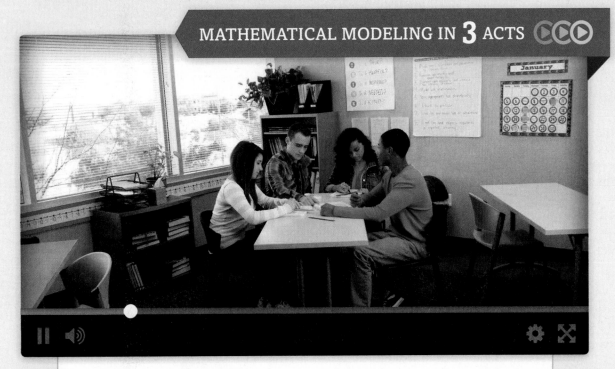

MATHEMATICAL MODELING IN 3 ACTS

▶ Check It Out!

Maybe you've played this game before: you draw a picture. Then you try to get a classmate to draw the same picture by giving step-by-step directions but without showing your drawings.

Try it with a classmate. Draw a map of a room in your house or a place in your town. Then give directions to a classmate to draw the map that you drew. How similar are they? Think about your results during the Mathematical Modeling in 3 Acts lesson.

TOPIC 9

VIDEOS Watch clips to support *Mathematical Modeling in 3 Acts Lessons* and **enVision®** *STEM Projects.*

CONCEPT SUMMARY Review key lesson content through multiple representations.

ASSESSMENT Show what you've learned.

GLOSSARY Read and listen to English and Spanish definitions.

TUTORIALS Get help from *Virtual Nerd*, right when you need it.

MATH TOOLS Explore math with digital tools and manipulatives.

Did You Know?

The Tacoma Narrows Bridge, in Washington, collapsed in high winds a few months after it opened in 1940. The bridge was rebuilt in 1950 using a truss for stabilization.

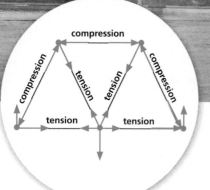

A bridge works by balancing compression (pressing inward) and tension (pressing outward), distributing the load onto the bridge supports.

The design of a truss is based on the strength of a triangle. It distributes a load from a narrow point to a wider base.

BRIDGE LOAD =
Weight of **bridge** + Weight of **people** + Weight of **vehicles** + Weight of **precipitation**

▶ Your Task: Design a Bridge

You and your classmates will analyze different truss bridge designs and how congruent triangles are used in each construction. What type of truss would you use in a bridge design, and why?

9-1

Congruence

SavvasRealize.com

I CAN... use a composition of rigid motions to show that two objects are congruent.

VOCABULARY
• congruence transformation
• congruent

 EXPLORE & REASON

Some corporate logos are distinctive because they make use of repeated shapes.

A designer creates two versions of a new logo for the Bolt Company. Version 1 uses the original image shown at the right and a reflection of it. Version 2 uses reduced copies of the original image.

A. Make a sketch of each version.

B. Communicate Precisely The owner of the company says, "I like your designs, but it is important that the transformed image be the same size and shape as the original image." What would you do to comply with the owner's requirements?

C. What transformations can you apply to the original image that would produce logos acceptable to the owner? Explain.

? ESSENTIAL QUESTION What is the relationship between rigid motions and congruence?

CONCEPTUAL UNDERSTANDING

 EXAMPLE 1 **Understand Congruence**

Suppose there is a rigid motion that maps one figure to another. Why does that show that the two figures are congruent?

Figure *ABCDEF* has the following lengths and angle measures, and *GHIJKL* is the image of *ABCDEF* after the rigid motion $T_{\langle 2, -5 \rangle} \circ R_\ell$.

$AB = 3$	$BC = 1$	$CD = 1$
$DE = 2$	$EF = 2$	$FA = 3$

All angles in figure *ABCDEF* are right angles.

Because rigid motions preserve length and angle measure, *GHIJKL* has the following lengths and angle measures.

$GH = 3$	$HI = 1$	$IJ = 1$
$JK = 2$	$KL = 2$	$LG = 3$

All angles in figure *GHIJKL* are right angles.

Since rigid motions preserve measures of corresponding sides and angles, the two figures are *congruent*.

STUDY TIP
Recall that angles with the same measure are congruent, and segments with the same length are congruent.

✓ **Try It!** **1.** A 90° rotation about the origin maps △*PQR* to △*LMN*. Are the triangles congruent? Explain.

CONCEPT Congruence

Figures that have the same size and shape are said to be *congruent*. Two figures are **congruent** if there is a rigid motion that maps one figure to the other.

A rigid motion is sometimes called a **congruence transformation** because it maps a figure to a congruent figure.

Use the ≅ symbol to show that two figures are congruent. Since R_m ($\triangle ABC$) = $\triangle DEF$, $\triangle ABC \cong \triangle DEF$.

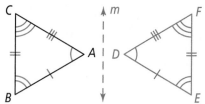

👆 **EXAMPLE 2** Verify Congruence

Given $\triangle XYZ \cong \triangle ABC$, what composition of rigid motions maps $\triangle XYZ$ to $\triangle ABC$?

First rotate $\triangle XYZ$ 180° about point Z. Next translate the image three units to the right.

$$(T_{\langle 3, 0 \rangle} \circ r_{(180°, Z)})(\triangle XYZ) = \triangle ABC$$

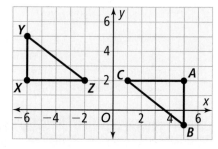

LOOK FOR RELATIONSHIPS
Think of other solutions. Can you identify another composition of rigid motions that maps one triangle to the other?

The composition $T_{\langle 3, 0 \rangle} \circ r_{(180°, Z)}$ maps $\triangle XYZ$ to $\triangle ABC$.

 Try It! 2. Use the graph shown.

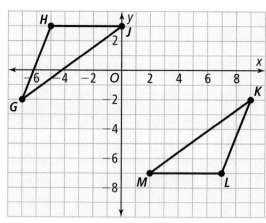

a. Given $\triangle GHJ \cong \triangle KLM$, what is one composition of rigid motions that maps $\triangle GHJ$ to $\triangle KLM$?

b. What is another composition of rigid motions that maps $\triangle GHJ$ to $\triangle KLM$?

EXAMPLE 3   **Identify Congruent Figures**

Given △ABC, △EFG, and △JKL, which triangles are congruent?

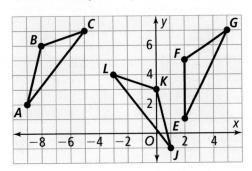

Find a composition of rigid motions to map △ABC to △JKL.

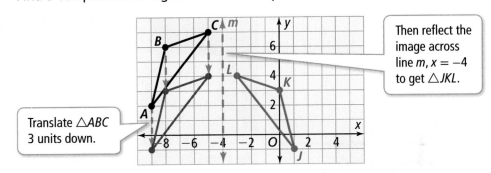

Then reflect the image across line m, x = −4 to get △JKL.

Translate △ABC 3 units down.

The composition of rigid motions $R_m \circ T_{\langle 0, -3 \rangle}$ maps △ABC to △JKL. Therefore, △ABC ≅ △JKL.

Observe that AC and EG are the longest side in each corresponding triangle, and AC ≠ EG, so there is no single rigid motion or composition of rigid motions that maps △ABC to △EFG. Therefore, they are not congruent.

STUDY TIP
To show that two figures are not congruent, you only need to find one corresponding pair of sides or angles that do not have the same measure.

✓ Try It!   **3.** Use the graph shown.

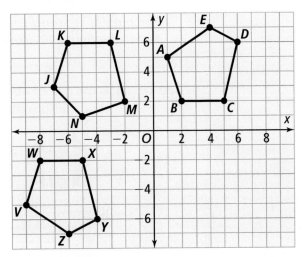

a. Are ABCDE and JKLMN congruent? If so, describe a composition of rigid motions that maps ABCDE to JKLMN. If not, explain.

b. Are ABCDE and VWXYZ congruent? If so, describe a composition of rigid motions that maps ABCDE to VWXYZ. If not, explain.

EXAMPLE 4 — Determine Congruence

Which pairs of objects are congruent? If a pair of objects is congruent, describe a composition of rigid motions that maps one to the other.

A.

The puzzle pieces are congruent. A reflection across a vertical line maps one puzzle piece to the other.

B.

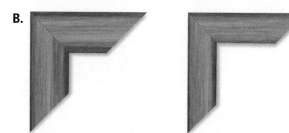

The frame corners are not congruent. The diagonal segment at the corner of the left frame is longer than the diagonal segment at the corner of the right frame, so the two frame corners are not the same size.

C.

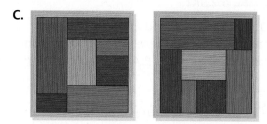

The puzzles are congruent. Translate the preimage puzzle on the left, rotate the figure 90° clockwise, and then reflect over a vertical line.

Try It! 4. Is the pair of objects congruent? If so, describe a composition of rigid motions that maps one object onto the other.

a.

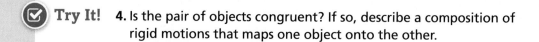

b.

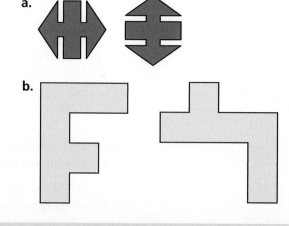

APPLICATION

EXAMPLE 5 Apply Congruence

A boat builder plans to connect two pieces of wood by using a puzzle joint as shown. For a successful joint, each unit must be congruent.

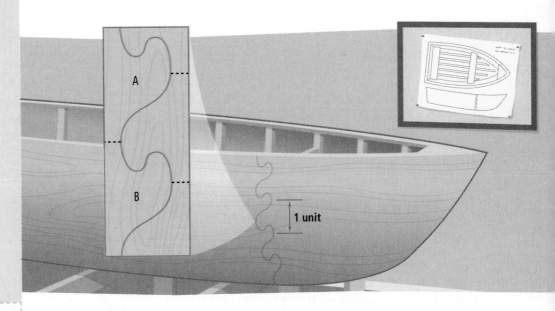

1 unit

Given Unit A, what composition of rigid motions maps Unit A to Unit B?

Unit B is a translation of Unit A. Unit B has the same size, shape, and orientation as Unit A. The only difference is that it is farther down.

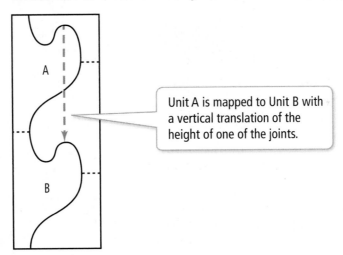

Unit A is mapped to Unit B with a vertical translation of the height of one of the joints.

Try It! 5. Is Unit C congruent to Unit A? If so, describe the sequence of rigid motions that maps Unit A to Unit C.

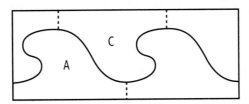

CONCEPT SUMMARY Congruent Figures

WORDS If two figures are congruent, a composition of rigid motions maps one figure to another.

DIAGRAM Since $R_n(\triangle PQR) = \triangle P'Q'R'$, $\triangle PQR \cong \triangle P'Q'R'$.

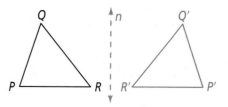

Do You UNDERSTAND?

1. **ESSENTIAL QUESTION** What is the relationship between rigid motions and congruence?

2. **Error Analysis** Taylor says *ABCD* and *EFGH* are congruent because he can map *ABCD* to *EFGH* by multiplying each side length by 1.5 and translating the result to coincide with *EFGH*. What is Taylor's error?

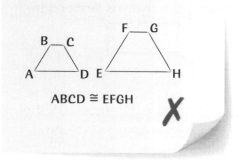

ABCD ≅ EFGH ✗

3. **Vocabulary** Why is a rigid motion also called a congruence transformation?

4. **Reason** For any two line segments that are congruent, what must be true about the lengths of the segments?

5. **Construct Arguments** A composition of rigid motions maps one figure to another figure. Is each intermediate image in the composition congruent to the original and final figures? Explain.

6. **Communicate Precisely** Describe how you can find a rigid motion or composition of rigid motions to map a segment to a congruent segment and an angle to a congruent angle.

Do You KNOW HOW?

7. Given *ABCD* ≅ *EFGH*, what rigid motion, or composition of rigid motions maps *ABCD* to *EFGH*?

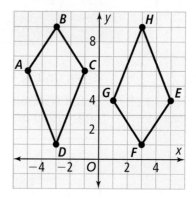

8. Which triangles are congruent?

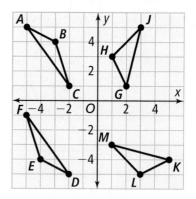

9. Are Figure A and Figure B congruent? If so, describe a composition of rigid motions that maps Figure A to Figure B. If not, explain.

Figure A   Figure B

PRACTICE & PROBLEM SOLVING

UNDERSTAND

10. Reason If △JKL ≅ △RST, give the coordinates for possible vertices of △RST. Justify your answer by describing a composition of rigid motions that maps △JKL to △RST.

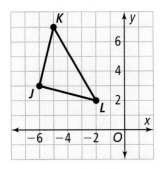

11. Error Analysis Yuki says that if all lines are congruent, then all line segments must be congruent. Is Yuki correct? Explain.

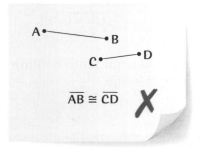

$\overline{AB} \cong \overline{CD}$ ✗

12. Mathematical Connections Given square JKLM and $(T_{\langle -6, 4 \rangle} \circ T_{\langle 1, 5 \rangle})(JKLM) = RSTU$, what is the area of RSTU?   144 cm²

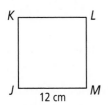

12 cm

13. Higher Order Thinking Are $\overrightarrow{AB}$ and $\overrightarrow{CD}$ congruent? If so, describe a composition of rigid motions that maps any ray to any other ray. If not, explain. Are any two rays congruent? Explain.

PRACTICE

14. Given $R_m(\triangle PQR) = \triangle P'Q'R'$, do △P'Q'R' and △PQR have equal perimeters? Explain.
SEE EXAMPLE 1

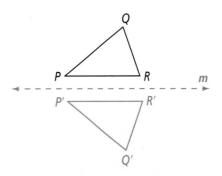

15. Given WXYZ ≅ WTUV, describe a composition of rigid motions that maps WXYZ to WTUV.
SEE EXAMPLE 2

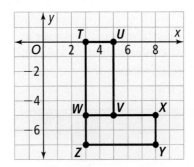

16. Are ABCD and EFGH congruent? If so, describe a composition of rigid motions that maps ABCD to EFGH. If not, explain. SEE EXAMPLE 3

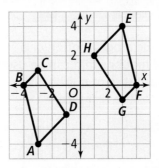

17. Which objects are congruent? For any congruent objects, describe a composition of rigid motions that maps the preimage to the image. SEE EXAMPLES 4 AND 5

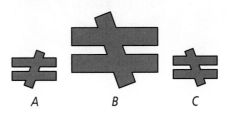

A   B   C

PRACTICE & PROBLEM SOLVING

APPLY

18. Communicate Precisely Using a 3D printer, Emery makes the chocolate mold shown by copying different shapes.

a. Which of the designs in the mold appear to be congruent?

b. Describe a composition of rigid motions that maps the congruent shapes.

19. Reason Are the illustrations of the shoes in the advertisement congruent? If so, describe a composition of rigid motions that maps the left shoe to the right shoe.

20. Use Structure Describe a rigid motion or a composition of rigid motions that can be used to make sure that each slice of quiche is the same size and shape as the first slice.

ASSESSMENT PRACTICE

21. The transformation $T_{\langle 3, 8 \rangle} \circ r_{(90°, A)}$ maps $\triangle ABC$ to $\triangle DEF$.

Triangle ABC is ____?____ to $\triangle DEF$ because $T_{\langle 3, 8 \rangle} \circ r_{(90°, A)}$ is a ____?____ .

22. SAT/ACT A board game token is shown.

Which is congruent to the token?

Ⓐ 　　Ⓒ

Ⓑ 　　Ⓓ

23. Performance Task The fabric pattern shown is based on the original image.

Part A Identify any images in the pattern that appear to be congruent to the original image.

Part B Describe a composition of rigid motions that maps the original image to each congruent image in the pattern.

Part C For any images in the pattern that are not congruent to the original image, explain how you know they are not congruent.

9-2

Isosceles and Equilateral Triangles

🖥 **SavvasRealize.com**

I CAN... apply theorems about isosceles and equilateral triangles to solve problems.

EXPLORE & REASON

Cut out a triangle with two sides of equal length from a sheet of paper and label its angles 1, 2, and 3. Trace the outline of your triangle on another sheet of paper and label the angles.

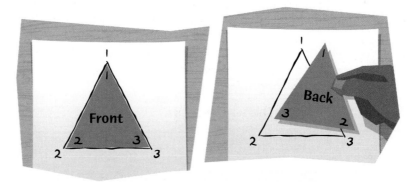

A. In how many different ways can you flip, slide, or turn the triangle so that it fits exactly on the outline?

B. **Look for Relationships** How do the angles and sides of the outline correspond to the angles and sides of the triangle?

C. How would your answer to Part A change if all three sides of the triangle were of equal length?

❓ ESSENTIAL QUESTION

How are the side lengths and angle measures related in isosceles triangles and in equilateral triangles?

CONCEPTUAL UNDERSTANDING

👆 **EXAMPLE 1**   **Understand Angles of Isosceles Triangles**

STUDY TIP
The rigid motion that maps $\overline{BC}$ to $\overline{BA}$ must map point B to itself. A reflection across a line that contains point B maps point B to itself.

How are the base angles of an isosceles triangle related?

Draw isosceles triangle ABC.

Because $\overline{BC} \cong \overline{BA}$, there is a rigid motion that maps $\overline{BC}$ onto $\overline{BA}$. Draw the angle bisector $\overleftrightarrow{BD}$ of $\angle ABC$, so that $m\angle DBC = m\angle DBA$.

$R_{\overleftrightarrow{BD}}(B) = B$

$R_{\overleftrightarrow{BD}}(D) = D$

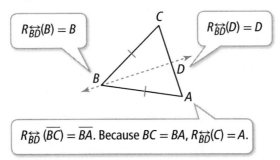

$R_{\overleftrightarrow{BD}}(\overline{BC}) = \overline{BA}$. Because $BC = BA$, $R_{\overleftrightarrow{BD}}(C) = A$.

Since the reflection maps $\triangle BCD$ to $\triangle BAD$, $m\angle BCA = m\angle BAC$. Therefore, $\angle BCA \cong \angle BAC$.

☑ **Try It!**   **1.** Copy isosceles $\triangle ABC$. Reflect the triangle across line BC to create the image $\triangle C'B'A'$. What rigid motion maps $\triangle C'B'A'$ onto $\triangle ABC$? Can you use this to show that $\angle A \cong \angle C$? Explain.

THEOREM 9-1 Isosceles Triangle Theorem and the Converse

If two sides of a triangle are congruent, then the angles opposite those sides are congruent.

If... $\overline{AB} \cong \overline{BC}$,
Then... $\angle ACB \cong \angle BAC$.

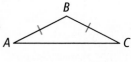

If two angles of a triangle are congruent, then the sides opposite those angles are congruent.

If... $\angle ACB \cong \angle BAC$,
Then... $\overline{AB} \cong \overline{BC}$.

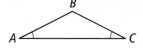

PROOF: SEE EXERCISE 17.

APPLICATION

EXAMPLE 2   Use the Isosceles Triangle Theorem

An architect is designing a community park between N. First St. and S. First St. The pathways on either side of the pool will be equal in length and will provide effective access and circulation around the pool. To protect the landscaping and to minimize erosion, the architect will place

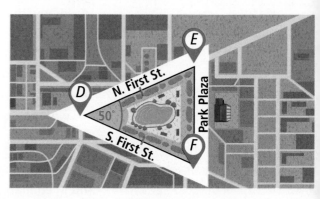

a triangular section of triangular cobblestones at the corners along Park Plaza. What angle measure should the architect specify for the corners in her design?

The park is in the shape of an isosceles triangle. Find $m\angle F$ and $m\angle E$.

$$m\angle D + m\angle E + m\angle F = 180$$

$$50 + m\angle F + m\angle F = 180$$

$$m\angle F = 65$$

> The base angles of the isosceles triangle are congruent by the Isosceles Triangle Theorem, so $m\angle E = m\angle F$.

The landscape architect should specify that the angles at the corners measure 65°.

STUDY TIP
Confirm your solution by using your original equation. In this example, the three angles of $\triangle ABC$ are 65°, 65°, and 50°, and the sum is 180°.

 Try It!   2. What is the value of x?

a.

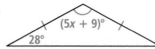
$(5x + 9)°$
$28°$

b.

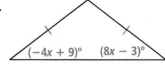
$(-4x + 9)°$ $(8x - 3)°$

👆 **EXAMPLE 3** Use the Converse of the Isosceles Triangle Theorem

What are the lengths of all three sides of the triangle?

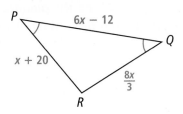

COMMON ERROR
Be careful not to set the expressions for the length of a leg and the length of the base equal to each other. Remember that the congruent legs are opposite the congruent base angles.

Step 1 Find the value of x.

$$x + 20 = \frac{8x}{3}$$
$$3x + 60 = 8x$$
$$12 = x$$

> Because $\angle P \cong \angle Q$, the sides opposite $\angle P$ and $\angle Q$ are also congruent.

Step 2 Substitute 12 for x to determine the side lengths.

$PR = x + 20$	$PQ = 6x - 12$	$QR = \frac{8x}{3}$
$= 12 + 20$	$= 6(12) - 12$	$= \frac{8(12)}{3}$
$= 32$	$= 60$	$= 32$

 Try It! **3.** Use the figure shown.

    a. What is the value of x?

    b. What are the lengths of all three sides of the triangle?

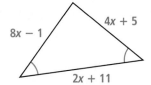

THEOREM 9-2

If a line or line segment bisects the vertex angle of an isosceles triangle, then it is also the perpendicular bisector of the opposite side.

If...   **Then...**

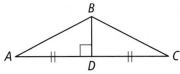

$\overline{AB} \cong \overline{BC}$ and $m\angle ABD = m\angle CBD$ $\overline{BD} \perp \overline{AC}$ and $\overline{AD} \cong \overline{DC}$

PROOF: SEE EXERCISE 13.

APPLICATION   👆 **EXAMPLE 4**   **Use Perpendicular Bisectors to Solve Problems**

A prefabricated house is delivered to a foundation in two symmetric halves that are assembled on-site. Along the planned route to the site, the truck must pass under a bridge that has a clearance height of 17 feet. Should the trucker plan a different route for delivering the house? Explain.

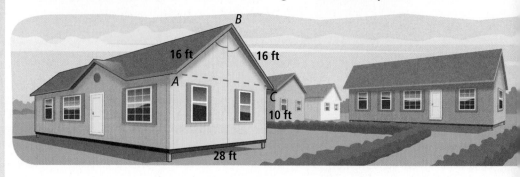

CONSTRUCT ARGUMENTS
Consider the information the figure provides about △*ABC*. What other information given in the figure is needed?

Draw a diagram to represent the roof.

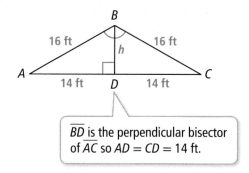

$\overline{BD}$ is the perpendicular bisector of $\overline{AC}$ so $AD = CD = 14$ ft.

Use the Pythagorean Theorem to find the height *h*.

$$h^2 + 14^2 = 16^2$$
$$h^2 = 60$$
$$h = \sqrt{60} \approx 7.7$$

The house is approximately 17.7 feet tall, so the total height that the truck must clear is greater than 17.7 ft. The trucker should plan a different route to the site.

 Try It!   **4.** Use the figure shown.

a. What is $m\angle RSQ$?

b. What is *PR*?

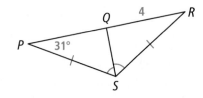

CONCEPT Equilateral Triangles

An equilateral triangle is equiangular.

An equiangular triangle is equilateral.

If... $\angle A \cong \angle B \cong \angle C$, **then...** $\overline{AB} \cong \overline{BC} \cong \overline{AC}$.

If... $\overline{AB} \cong \overline{BC} \cong \overline{AC}$, **then...** $\angle A \cong \angle B \cong \angle C$.

EXAMPLE 5 **Prove that Equilateral Triangles are Equiangular**

A. Prove that equilateral triangles are equiangular.

Given: $\overline{DE} \cong \overline{EF} \cong \overline{DF}$

Prove: $\angle D \cong \angle E \cong \angle F$

Plan: Use the fact that an equilateral triangle is also an isosceles triangle to show that all three angles are congruent.

Proof:

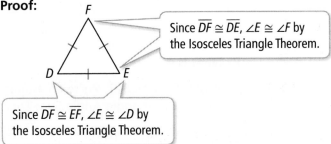

Since $\overline{DF} \cong \overline{DE}$, $\angle E \cong \angle F$ by the Isosceles Triangle Theorem.

Since $\overline{DF} \cong \overline{EF}$, $\angle E \cong \angle D$ by the Isosceles Triangle Theorem.

Since $\angle D \cong \angle E$ and $\angle E \cong \angle F$, $\angle D \cong \angle E \cong \angle F$.

B. Prove that equiangular triangles are equilateral.

Given: $\angle G \cong \angle H \cong \angle J$

Prove: $\overline{GH} \cong \overline{HJ} \cong \overline{GJ}$

Plan: Use a strategy similar to the one in part A by applying the Converse of the Isosceles Triangle Theorem.

Proof:

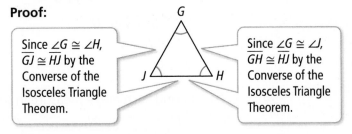

Since $\angle G \cong \angle H$, $\overline{GJ} \cong \overline{HJ}$ by the Converse of the Isosceles Triangle Theorem.

Since $\angle G \cong \angle J$, $\overline{GH} \cong \overline{HJ}$ by the Converse of the Isosceles Triangle Theorem.

Since $\overline{GJ} \cong \overline{HJ}$ and $\overline{GH} \cong \overline{HJ}$, $\overline{GH} \cong \overline{HJ} \cong \overline{GJ}$.

 Try It! **5.** What rotation can be used to show the angles of an equilateral triangle are congruent?

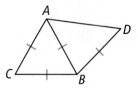 **EXAMPLE 6** **Find Angle Measures in Isosceles and Equilateral Triangles**

A. If $m\angle CBD = 130$, what is $m\angle BAD$?

Step 1 Find $m\angle ABD$.

$$m\angle ABC + m\angle ABD = m\angle CBD$$

$$60 + m\angle ABD = 130$$

$$m\angle ABD = 70$$

> Since $\triangle ABC$ is equilateral, $m\angle ABC = 60$.

> **COMMON ERROR**
> You may think you have solved the problem after finding one angle measure. Make sure you provide the measure of the angle asked for in the question.

Step 2 Use the Isosceles Triangle Theorem to find $m\angle BAD$.

$$m\angle ABD + m\angle BDA + m\angle BAD = 180$$

$$70 + m\angle BAD + m\angle BAD = 180$$

$$m\angle BAD = 55$$

> Since $\triangle ABD$ is isosceles, $m\angle BDA = m\angle BAD$.

B. What is $m\angle U$?

Step 1 Find $m\angle SVT$. Write an equation using the Triangle Angle-Sum Theorem.

$$m\angle S + m\angle STV + m\angle SVT = 180$$

$$72 + m\angle SVT + m\angle SVT = 180$$

$$2m\angle SVT = 108$$

$$m\angle SVT = 54$$

> Since $\triangle STV$ is isosceles, $m\angle STV = m\angle SVT$.

Step 2 Find $m\angle U$. Write an equation using the Triangle Exterior Angle Theorem.

$$m\angle SVT = m\angle VTU + m\angle U$$

$$54 = m\angle U + m\angle U$$

$$54 = 2m\angle U$$

$$m\angle U = 27$$

> Since $\triangle VTU$ is isosceles, $m\angle VTU = m\angle U$.

 Try It! **6.** Find each angle measure in the figure.

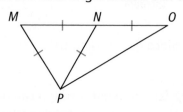

a. $m\angle PNO$ **b.** $m\angle NOP$

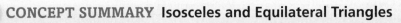

CONCEPT SUMMARY Isosceles and Equilateral Triangles

ISOSCELES TRIANGLES	PERPENDICULAR BISECTOR	EQUILATERAL TRIANGLES
If... $\overline{AB} \cong \overline{BC}$	If... 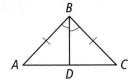 $\overline{AB} \cong \overline{BC}$ and $m\angle ABD = m\angle CBD$	If... $\overline{AB} \cong \overline{BC} \cong \overline{AC}$
Then... $\angle ACB \cong \angle BAC$	Then... 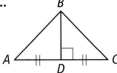 $\overline{BD} \perp \overline{AC}$ and $AD = DC$	Then... $\angle A \cong \angle B \cong \angle C$

Do You UNDERSTAND?

1. **ESSENTIAL QUESTION** How are the side lengths and angle measures related in isosceles triangles and in equilateral triangles?

2. **Error Analysis** Nate drew the following diagram to represent an equilateral triangle and an isosceles triangle. What mistake did Nate make?

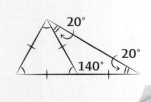

3. **Vocabulary** How can you distinguish the base of an isosceles triangle from a leg?

4. **Reason** Is it possible for the vertex of an isosceles triangle to be a right angle? Explain why or why not, and state the angle measures of the triangle, if possible.

5. **Communicate Precisely** Describe five rigid motions that map equilateral triangle △PQR onto itself.

Do You KNOW HOW?

For Exercises 6 and 7, find the unknown angle measures.

6.

7.

For Exercises 8 and 9, find the lengths of all three sides of the triangle.

8.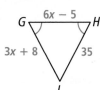

9.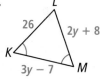

10. What is $m\angle ABD$ in the figure shown?

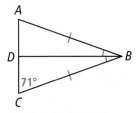

11. A light is suspended between two poles as shown. How far above the ground is the light? Round to the nearest tenth of a foot.

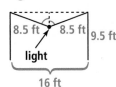

UNDERSTAND

PRACTICE

12. **Mathematical Connections** What are the measures of ∠1 and ∠2? Explain.

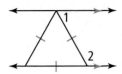

13. **Construct Arguments** Use the properties of rigid motions to write a proof of Theorem 9-2.

Given: $\overline{PQ} \cong \overline{QR}$ and
$m\angle PQS = m\angle RQS$

Prove: $\overline{QS} \perp \overline{PR}$ and
$PS = SR$

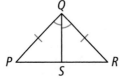

14. **Look for Relationships** Prove that ∠BAD ≅ ∠BCD and ∠ABC ≅ ∠CDA.

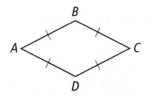

15. **Error Analysis** Amaya is asked to find the side lengths of the triangle shown. What is her error?

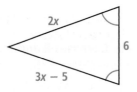

From the top leg and the base, 2x = 6, so x = 3. Substitute x into the expression for the bottom leg's length to get 3(3) − 5 = 4.

16. **Higher Order Thinking** Deondra draws points at (1, 5) and (1, −1) on a coordinate plane. Each point will be a vertex of an isosceles right triangle. What are two possible points in the second quadrant that she can specify as a vertex of her triangle? Explain.

17. Use rigid motions to write a proof of the Converse of the Isosceles Triangle Theorem.
SEE EXAMPLE 1

Given: ∠J ≅ ∠L

Prove: JK ≅ KL

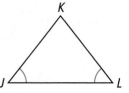

Find the unknown angle measures in each triangle.
SEE EXAMPLE 2

18.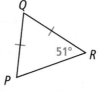

19.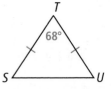

Find the lengths of all three sides of each triangle.
SEE EXAMPLE 3

20.

21.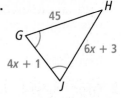

Use the figure shown for Exercises 22 and 23.
SEE EXAMPLE 4

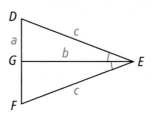

22. What is m∠DEG if m∠DFE = 70?

23. What is the value of b if a = 8 and c = 24?

24. Prove that ∠ABC is a right angle.
SEE EXAMPLE 5

Given: $\overline{AD} \cong \overline{BD} \cong \overline{CD}$

Prove: m∠ABC = 90

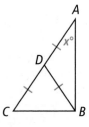

25. Given m∠PSR = 134, what is the measure of ∠SQR?
SEE EXAMPLE 6

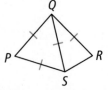

APPLY

26. Make Sense and Persevere Each of the five points on a star produced for a flag is an isosceles triangle with leg length 6 cm and base length 4.2 cm. What is the total height *h* of each star? Round to the nearest tenth of a centimeter.

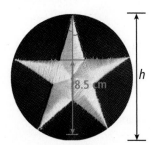

27. Use Structure The front of the tent below has the shape of an equilateral triangle.

   a. What is the side length of the triangle? Round to the nearest tenth of a foot.

   b. Explain the method you use to calculate the length.

28. Look for Relationships For a crane to lift the beam shown below, the beam and the two support cables must form an isosceles triangle with height *h*. If the distance between the cables along the beam is 18 ft and the height *h* is 8 ft, what is the total length of the two cables? Round to the nearest tenth of a foot.

ASSESSMENT PRACTICE

29. Consider the following triangle.

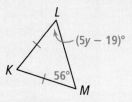

   a. Write an equation you can solve to find the value of *y*.

   b. What is $m\angle K$?

30. SAT/ACT Given $m\angle ABC = 114$, what is $m\angle BAD$?

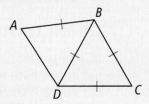

   Ⓐ 54   Ⓒ 60

   Ⓑ 63   Ⓓ 72

31. Performance Task Emaan designs the birdhouse shown below.

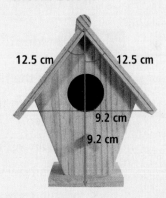

Part A What is the total height of the birdhouse? Show your work.

Part B If Emaan decides to change the design by increasing each side of the roof from 12.5 cm to 15.2 cm, what will be the new height of the birdhouse? All other labeled dimensions on the birdhouse will remain unchanged.

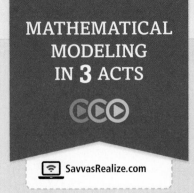

MATHEMATICAL MODELING IN **3** ACTS

 Video

▶ Check It Out!

Maybe you've played this game before: you draw a picture. Then you try to get a classmate to draw the same picture by giving step-by-step directions but without showing your drawings.

Try it with a classmate. Draw a map of a room in your house or a place in your town. Then give directions to a classmate to draw the map that you drew. How similar are they? Think about this during the Mathematical Modeling in 3 Acts lesson.

Scan for Multimedia

ACT 1 ▸ Identify the Problem

1. What is the first question that comes to mind after watching the video?

2. Write down the main question you will answer about what you saw in the video.

3. Make an initial conjecture that answers this main question.

4. Explain how you arrived at your conjecture.

5. What information will be useful to know in order to answer the main question? How can you get it? How will you use that information?

ACT 2 ▸ Develop a Model

6. Use the math that you have learned in this Topic to refine your conjecture.

ACT 3 ▸ Interpret the Results

7. Did your refined conjecture match the actual answer exactly? If not, what might explain the difference?

9-3

Proving and Applying the SAS and SSS Congruence Criteria

 SavvasRealize.com

I CAN... use SAS and SSS to determine whether triangles are congruent.

CONCEPTUAL
UNDERSTANDING

GENERALIZE
Consider the relationship between corresponding parts of any pair of congruent triangles. How do the corresponding sides and angles compare to each other?

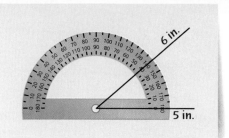

🖐 EXPLORE & REASON

Make five triangles that have a 5-inch side, a 6-inch side, and one 40° angle.

A. How many unique triangles can you make?

B. Construct Arguments How are the unique triangles different from each other?

❓ ESSENTIAL QUESTION How are SAS and SSS used to show that two triangles are congruent?

🖐 EXAMPLE 1   Explore the Side-Angle-Side (SAS) Congruence Criterion

Given two triangles with two pairs of sides congruent and the included angles congruent, verify that the triangles are congruent.

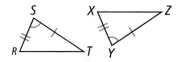

To prove that the triangles are congruent, show that a rigid motion maps △RST to △XYZ.

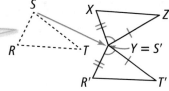

Translate △RST so point S maps to point Y.

Since the translation maps S to Y, Y = S′.

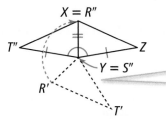

Rotate △R′S′T′ about point Y, so S″R″ coincides with YX.

Since rotation preserves length, R″S″ = RS = XY, so X = R″.

Then reflect △R″S″T″ across XY.

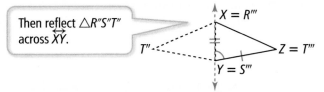

Since reflection preserves angle measure and length, $m\angle R'''S'''T''' = m\angle RST = m\angle XYZ$, so $\overline{S'''T'''}$ coincides with $\overrightarrow{YZ}$. Additionally, $S'''T''' = ST = YZ$, so Z coincides with T‴.

Because the vertices of △R‴S‴T‴ coincide with the vertices of △XYZ, there exists a rigid motion that maps △RST to △XYZ. By the definition of congruence, △RST ≅ △XYZ.

CONTINUED ON THE NEXT PAGE

EXAMPLE 1 CONTINUED

 Try It! 1. What rigid motion or composition of rigid motions shows that △UVW maps to △XYZ?

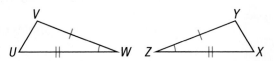

THEOREM 9-3 Side-Angle-Side (SAS) Congruence Criterion

If two sides and the included angle of one triangle are congruent to two sides and the included angle of another triangle, then the two triangles are congruent.

PROOF: SEE EXAMPLE 1.

If...

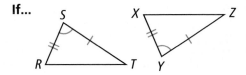

Then... △RST ≅ △XYZ

THEOREM 9-4 Corresponding Parts of Congruent Triangles are Congruent (CPCTC)

If two triangles are congruent, then each pair of corresponding sides is congruent and each pair of corresponding angles is congruent.

PROOF: SEE EXERCISE 13.

If... △ABC ≅ △XYZ

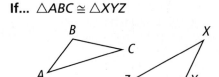

Then... $\overline{AB} \cong \overline{XY}$, $\overline{BC} \cong \overline{YZ}$, $\overline{AC} \cong \overline{XZ}$, ∠A ≅ ∠X, ∠B ≅ ∠Y, and ∠C ≅ ∠Z.

APPLICATION

 **EXAMPLE 2** Apply the SAS Congruence Criterion

Allie cuts two triangles from a rectangular piece of metal along the dashed line to make earrings. How can Allie show that the earrings are the same size and shape?

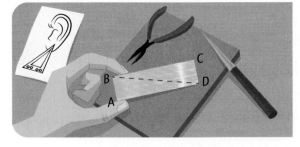

Draw diagrams to represent the earrings.

Because the sheet is a rectangle, $m\angle A = m\angle C = 90$, so ∠A ≅ ∠C.

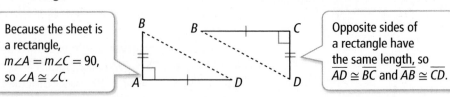

Opposite sides of a rectangle have the same length, so $\overline{AD} \cong \overline{BC}$ and $\overline{AB} \cong \overline{CD}$.

By SAS, △ABD ≅ △CDB.

By CPCTC, all the corresponding sides and angles of the earrings are congruent, so the earrings are the same size and shape.

CONTINUED ON THE NEXT PAGE

EXAMPLE 2 CONTINUED

 Try It! **2.** Given that $\overline{AB} \parallel \overline{CD}$ and $\overline{AB} \cong \overline{CD}$, how can you show that $\angle B \cong \angle D$?

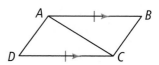

THEOREM 9-5 Side-Side-Side (SSS) Congruence Criterion

If three sides of one triangle are congruent to three sides of another triangle, then the two triangles are congruent.

If...

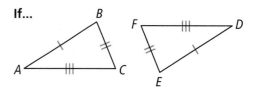

PROOF: SEE EXAMPLE 3.

Then... $\triangle ABC \cong \triangle DEF$

PROOF

 **EXAMPLE 3** Prove the Side-Side-Side (SSS) Congruence Criterion

Prove the SSS Congruence Criterion.

Given: $\overline{AB} \cong \overline{DE}$, $\overline{BC} \cong \overline{EF}$, $\overline{AC} \cong \overline{DF}$

Prove: $\triangle ABC \cong \triangle DEF$

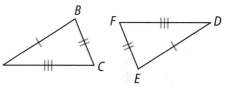

Proof: First, translate $\triangle ABC$ so point B maps to point E. Since the translation maps B to E, $E = B'$.

Then rotate $\triangle A'B'C'$ about point E so the image $\overline{B''C''}$ coincides with $\overline{EF}$. It appears that A'' coincides with D'', but this needs to be proven.

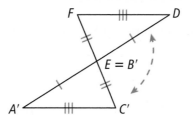

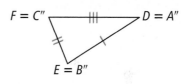

STUDY TIP
Use indirect reasoning to show that A'' must coincide with D.

To show that A'' does coincide with D, assume that A'' does not coincide.

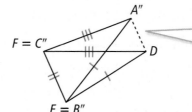

Draw $\overline{A''D}$. Then $\overline{A''D}$ is the base of two isosceles triangles, $\triangle FA''D$ and $\triangle EDA''$.

By the Isosceles Triangle Theorem, $\angle FA''D \cong \angle FDA''$ and $\angle EA''D \cong \angle EDA''$. From the diagram, observe that $m\angle FA''D > m\angle EA''D$ and $m\angle FDA'' < m\angle EDA''$.

$m\angle FA''D > m\angle EA''D$
$m\angle FDA'' > m\angle EA''D$
$m\angle FDA'' > m\angle EDA''$

Substitute $m\angle FDA''$ for $m\angle FA''D$, and substitute $m\angle EDA''$ for $m\angle EA''D$.

This contradicts the observation that $\angle FDA'' < \angle EDA''$. Therefore, A'' must coincide with D. Since $D = A''$, $E = B''$, and $F = C''$, there exists a rigid motion that maps $\triangle ABC$ to $\triangle DEF$, so $\triangle ABC \cong \triangle DEF$.

CONTINUED ON THE NEXT PAGE

EXAMPLE 3 CONTINUED

  Activity Assess

 Try It! 3. Show that there is a rigid motion that maps △PQR to △STU.
Hint: Be sure to consider a reflection when mapping △PQR to △STU.

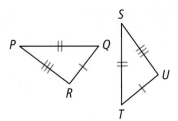

EXAMPLE 4 **Determine Congruent Triangles**

A. Which of the following pairs are congruent by SAS or SSS?

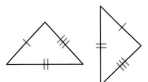

Congruent by SSS

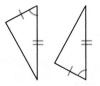

Congruent by SAS

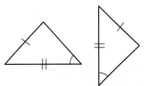

Cannot be determined

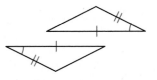

Congruent by SAS

COMMON ERROR
It may not be enough to identify two pairs of congruent sides and one pair of congruent angles. Recall that to apply SAS, the congruent angle pair must be the included angles.

B. What additional information is needed to show △ABC ≅ △DEF by SAS? By SSS?

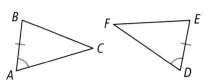

To show △ABC ≅ △DEF by SAS, you need $\overline{AC} \cong \overline{DF}$.

To show △ABC ≅ △DEF by SSS, you need $\overline{AC} \cong \overline{DF}$ and $\overline{BC} \cong \overline{EF}$.

 Try It! 4. a. Is △STU congruent to △XYZ? Explain.

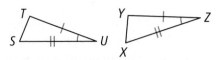

b. Is any additional information needed to show △DEF ≅ △GHJ by SAS? Explain.

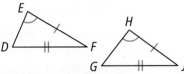
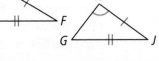

Go Online | SavvasRealize.com

THEOREM 9-3 Side-Angle-Side (SAS)

If...

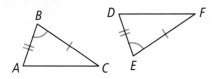

$\overline{AB} \cong \overline{DE}$, $\overline{BC} \cong \overline{EF}$, and $\angle B \cong \angle E$

Then... $\triangle ABC \cong \triangle DEF$

THEOREM 9-5 Side-Side-Side (SSS)

If...

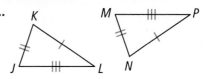

$\overline{JK} \cong \overline{MN}$, $\overline{JL} \cong \overline{MP}$, and $\overline{KL} \cong \overline{NP}$

Then... $\triangle JKL \cong \triangle MNP$

Do You UNDERSTAND?

1. **ESSENTIAL QUESTION** How are SAS and SSS used to show that two triangles are congruent?

2. **Error Analysis** Elijah says $\triangle ABC$ and $\triangle DEF$ are congruent by SAS. Explain Elijah's error.

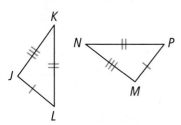

3. **Construct Arguments** Suppose $\overline{PR} \cong \overline{ST}$ and $\angle P \cong \angle S$. Ron wants to prove $\triangle PQR \cong \triangle STU$ by SAS. He says that all he needs to do is show $\overline{RQ} \cong \overline{SU}$. Will this work? Explain.

4. **Reason** How would you decide what theorem to use to prove $\angle JKL \cong \angle MNP$? Explain.

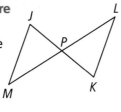

5. **Make Sense and Persevere** Suppose that $\overline{JK}$ and $\overline{LM}$ bisect each other. Is there enough information to show that $\triangle JPM \cong \triangle KPL$? Explain.

Do You KNOW HOW?

For Exercises 6–8, which pairs of triangles are congruent by SAS? By SSS?

6.

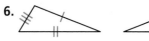

7.

8.

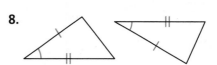

For Exercises 9–11, are the triangles congruent? Explain.

9.

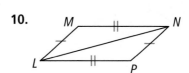

10.

11.

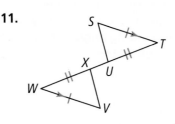

UNDERSTAND

12. Error Analysis Zhang says △ABC is congruent to △ADC. Explain the error in Zhang's work.

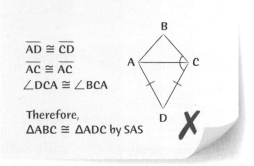

$\overline{AD} \cong \overline{CD}$

$\overline{AC} \cong \overline{AC}$

$\angle DCA \cong \angle BCA$

Therefore,
△ABC ≅ △ADC by SAS ✗

13. Construct Arguments Given △ABC ≅ △XYZ, use a rigid motion to prove Theorem 9-4, Corresponding Parts of Congruent Triangles are Congruent.

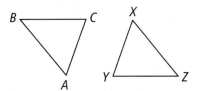

14. Mathematical Connections Is △JKL congruent to △MNL? Explain.

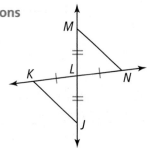

15. Make Sense and Persevere Why is △ABC ≅ △GHJ?

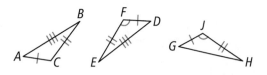

16. Higher Order Thinking Given quadrilaterals ABCD and LMNO, and $\overline{AC} \cong \overline{LN}$, how can you show that the corresponding angles of the quadrilaterals are congruent?

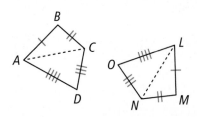

PRACTICE

17. Prove △ACE is an isosceles triangle.
SEE EXAMPLES 1 AND 2

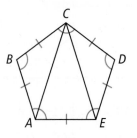

18. What is m∠RTS? Justify your answer.
SEE EXAMPLES 1 AND 2

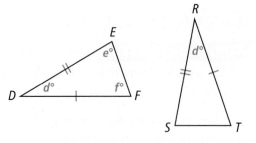

19. What additional information is needed to show that △PQR ≅ △STU by SSS? SEE EXAMPLE 3

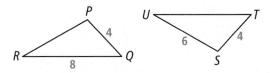

20. What additional information is needed to show that △ABC ≅ △DEF? SEE EXAMPLE 3

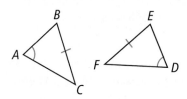

21. Is △RSV ≅ △UTV? Explain.
SEE EXAMPLE 4

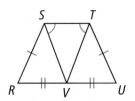

22. Is △PQR ≅ △PSR? Explain.
SEE EXAMPLE 4

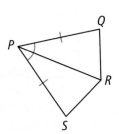

APPLY

23. Critique Reasoning Kathryn runs from the northwest corner to the southeast corner of a rugby field and Mia runs from the northeast corner to the southwest corner. Mia says she ran farther. Is she correct? Explain.

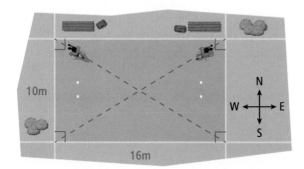

24. Reason Following the route shown, what is the total distance traveled by the architectural tour if it ends where it started? What properties and theorems did you use to find the distance?

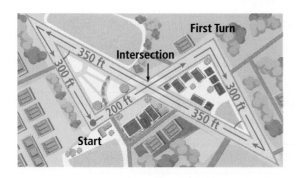

25. Make Sense and Persevere Justice and Leah both made a triangular scarf. Do the scarves have the same size and shape? What do you notice about the information that is given?

ASSESSMENT PRACTICE

26. Which sets of congruent parts are sufficient to conclude that △FGH ≅ △JKL? Select *Yes* or *No*.

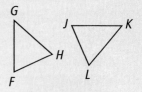

	Yes	No
$\overline{FG} \cong \overline{JK}$, $\overline{GH} \cong \overline{KL}$, $\overline{FH} \cong \overline{JL}$		
$\overline{FG} \cong \overline{JK}$, $\overline{FH} \cong \overline{JL}$, $\angle FHG \cong \angle JLK$		
$\overline{GH} \cong \overline{KL}$, $\overline{FG} \cong \overline{JK}$, $\angle FGH \cong \angle JKL$		
$\overline{GH} \cong \overline{KL}$, $\overline{FH} \cong \overline{JL}$, $\angle FHG \cong \angle JLK$		

27. SAT/ACT Consider △DEF and △PQR. Which additional piece of information would allow you to conclude that △DEF ≅ △PQR?

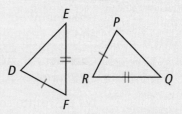

Ⓐ $\angle D \cong \angle P$ Ⓒ $\angle D \cong \angle Q$

Ⓑ $\angle E \cong \angle Q$ Ⓓ $\angle F \cong \angle R$

28. Performance Task In a marching band show, Kayden and Latoya start 10 yards apart. Kayden marches the path in blue and Latoya marches the path in green.

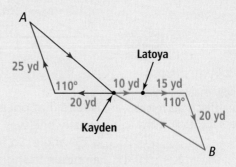

Part A Are the triangles formed by the paths congruent? Explain.

Part B Are the angle measures that Kayden and Latoya turn at points *A* and *B* the same? Explain.

9-4

Proving and Applying the ASA and AAS Congruence Criteria

I CAN... determine congruent triangles by comparing two angles and one side.

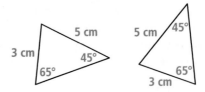

EXPLORE & REASON

Are these triangles congruent?

5 cm   5 cm   45°
3 cm   45°   65°
65°   3 cm

A. **Make Sense and Persevere** Assume the triangles are *not* congruent. What contradictions can you find to contradict your assumption? Explain.

B. Is it sufficient to say that the triangles are congruent because of the contradictions you found? Explain.

? ESSENTIAL QUESTION

How are ASA and AAS used to show that triangles are congruent?

CONCEPTUAL UNDERSTANDING

EXAMPLE 1   Explore the ASA Congruence Criterion

How many possible triangles can you determine when given two angles and the included side of a triangle?

Consider $\overrightarrow{AB}$, $\overrightarrow{AE}$, and $\overrightarrow{BG}$, where $\overrightarrow{AB}$ and $\overrightarrow{AE}$ form a 25° angle.

Let $\overrightarrow{BG}$ rotate counterclockwise about point B to form a 68° angle, a 57° angle, and a 45° angle. The rays will intersect to form some triangles.

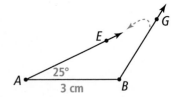

When $m\angle B$ changes, the second and third side lengths and third angle measure always change.

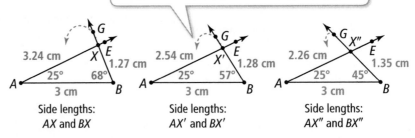

Side lengths: AX and BX

Side lengths: AX' and BX'

Side lengths: AX" and BX"

LOOK FOR RELATIONSHIPS
Think about how change in one part of a figure affects the rest of the figure. Does the result follow a pattern?

Notice that once the 25° angle, and the side of length 3 cm are set, there is exactly one way to complete the triangle with a 68° angle, a 57° angle, or a 25° angle. So for each unique combination of AB, $m\angle A$, and $m\angle B$, there is a unique triangle.

☑ Try It!   1. What is the relationship between △AXB and △AYB?

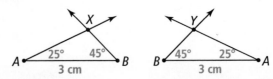

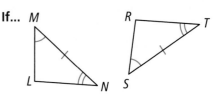

THEOREM 9-6 Angle-Side-Angle (ASA) Congruence Criterion

If two angles of one triangle and the included side are congruent to two angles and the included side of another triangle, then the two triangles are congruent.

PROOF: SEE EXAMPLE 2.

If...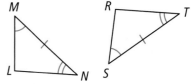

Then... $\triangle MLN \cong \triangle SRT$

PROOF → 👆 **EXAMPLE 2** **Prove the Angle-Side-Angle (ASA) Congruence Criterion**

Given two triangles with two pairs of angles congruent and the included sides congruent, prove the triangles are congruent.

Given: $\angle LMN \cong \angle RST$, $\angle LNM \cong \angle RTS$, $\overline{MN} \cong \overline{ST}$

Prove: $\triangle MLN \cong \triangle SRT$

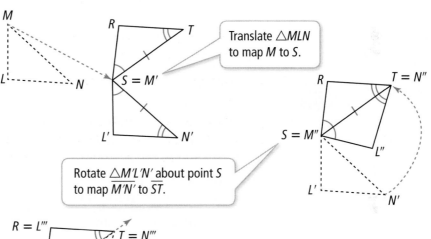

Translate $\triangle MLN$ to map M to S.

Rotate $\triangle M'L'N'$ about point S to map $\overline{M'N'}$ to $\overline{ST}$.

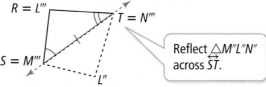

Reflect $\triangle M''L''N''$ across $\overleftrightarrow{ST}$.

STUDY TIP
When all vertices coincide, there exists a rigid motion that maps one triangle to the other. By definition, the triangles are congruent.

Because angle measures are preserved with reflections, $\overrightarrow{M'''L'''}$ coincides with $\overrightarrow{SR}$ and $\overrightarrow{N'''L'''}$ coincides with $\overrightarrow{TR}$. The intersection of $\overrightarrow{SR}$ and $\overrightarrow{TR}$ is at both R and L'''. Since the intersection of two rays is unique, R and L''' coincide.

Therefore, $\triangle MLN \cong \triangle SRT$.

☑ **Try It!** **2.** Describe a series of transformations that shows $\triangle JKL \cong \triangle MNO$.

APPLICATION

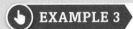 **EXAMPLE 3** **Apply the Angle-Side-Angle (ASA) Congruence Criterion**

A technician installs cables from a cell phone tower to the ground. To pass inspection, both cables must be the same length. Does this installation meet the cable-length requirement? Explain.

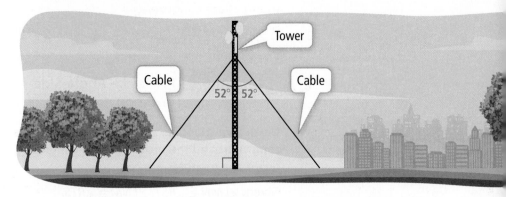

Formulate ◀ The ground, tower, and cables form two triangles, △ABX and △CBX.

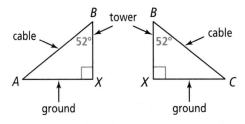

Compute ◀ All right angles are congruent, so ∠AXB ≅ ∠CXB. By the Reflexive Property of Congruence, $\overline{BX} \cong \overline{BX}$. Also, m∠ABX = 52° and m∠CBX = 52°, so ∠ABX ≅ ∠CBX.

Two angles and the included side of △ABX are congruent to two angles and the included side of △CBX. Therefore, △ABX ≅ △CBX by ASA.

By CPCTC, $\overline{AB} \cong \overline{CB}$. So, both cables are the same length.

Interpret ◀ The cable lengths do meet the inspection requirement.

✓ **Try It!** **3. a.** Are △JKL and △MNO congruent? Explain.

　　　b. Are △JKL and △PQR congruent? Explain.

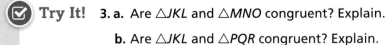

📶 **Go Online** | SavvasRealize.com

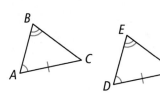

EXAMPLE 4 **Investigate the Angle-Angle-Side (AAS) Congruence Criterion**

Given △ABC, is the triangle determined by ∠A, ∠B, and the non-included side $\overline{AC}$ unique?

Assume that △ABC is not unique. Then there must exist △DEF such that △ABC ≇ △DEF, ∠A ≅ ∠D, ∠B ≅ ∠E, and $\overline{AC}$ ≅ $\overline{DF}$.

By the Triangle Angle-Sum Theorem, m∠C = 180 − m∠A − m∠B and m∠F = 180 − m∠D − m∠E. Since ∠A ≅ ∠D and ∠B ≅ ∠E, m∠C = 180 − m∠D − m∠E = m∠F, so ∠C ≅ ∠F.

Therefore, by ASA, △ABC ≅ △DEF, and the assumption is false. A unique triangle is determined by ∠A and ∠B and the non-included side $\overline{AC}$.

Try It! **4.** Using the figures shown, describe a sequence of rigid motions that maps △JKL to △QRP.

THEOREM 9-7 Angle-Angle-Side (AAS) Congruence Criterion

If two angles and a nonincluded side of one triangle are congruent to two angles and a nonincluded side of another triangle, then the two triangles are congruent.

If...

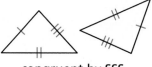

Then... △UVW ≅ △XYZ

PROOF: SEE EXERCISE 16.

EXAMPLE 5 Use Triangle Congruence Criteria

A. State whether each pair of triangles is congruent by SAS, SSS, ASA, or AAS, or if the congruence cannot be determined.

COMMON ERROR
Be careful not to just assume that triangles are congruent when given two pairs of congruent angles and one pair of congruent sides. The congruent sides must be corresponding sides.

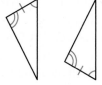

congruent by ASA

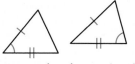

congruent by SSS

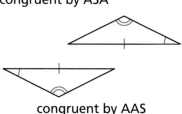

congruent by AAS

cannot be determined

CONTINUED ON THE NEXT PAGE

LESSON 9-4 Proving and Applying the ASA and AAS Congruence Criteria   **391**

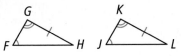
EXAMPLE 5 CONTINUED

B. Prove that $\overline{FH} \cong \overline{JL}$.

    Given: $\overline{GH} \cong \overline{KL}$, $\angle GFH \cong \angle KJL$,
        and $\angle FGH \cong \angle JKL$

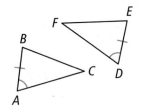

    Prove: $\overline{FH} \cong \overline{JL}$

Statements	Reasons
1) $\angle F \cong \angle J$, $\angle G \cong \angle K$, $\overline{GH} \cong \overline{KL}$	1) Given
2) $\triangle FGH \cong \triangle JKL$	2) AAS
3) $\overline{FH} \cong \overline{JL}$	3) CPCTC

> When triangle congruence applies, you can conclude the remaining sides and angles are congruent by CPCTC.

 Try It! **5. a.** What additional information is needed to show $\triangle ABC \cong \triangle DEF$ by ASA?

        b. What additional information is needed to show $\triangle ABC \cong \triangle DEF$ by AAS?

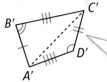

 EXAMPLE 6   **Determine Congruent Polygons**

USE STRUCTURE
Consider the diagonals of a polygon. Can any polygon be divided into a figure composed of triangles?

All sides and angles of *ABCD* are congruent to the corresponding sides and angles of *A′B′C′D′*. Is *ABCD* congruent to *A′B′C′D′*?

Each polygon can be divided into two triangles by the diagonals shown.

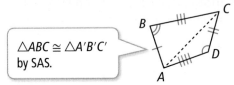

$\triangle ABC \cong \triangle A'B'C'$ by SAS.

$\triangle ADC \cong \triangle A'D'C'$ by SAS.

Since $\triangle ABC \cong \triangle A'B'C'$, there is a rigid motion that maps $\triangle ABC$ to $\triangle A'B'C'$. Consider this rigid motion applied to $\triangle ADC$. Side $\overline{AC}$ maps to $\overline{A'C'}$ since $\overline{AC}$ is shared by both $\triangle ABC$ and $\triangle ADC$.

Now suppose that this rigid motion maps *D* to some point other than *D′*. Call that point *E*. Since $\triangle A'D'C'$ and $\triangle A'EC'$ are congruent to $\triangle ADC$, $\triangle A'D'C' \cong \triangle A'EC'$. Since $\angle C'A'E \cong \angle C'A'D'$, *E* lies on $\overleftrightarrow{A'D'}$. By a similar argument, *E* lies on $\overleftrightarrow{C'D'}$. So *E* must be the point *D′*.

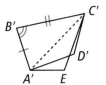

Since the rigid motion that maps $\triangle ABC$ to $\triangle A'B'C'$ also maps *ABCD* to *A′B′C′D′*, *ABCD* is congruent to *A′B′C′D′*.

 Try It! **6.** Given $ABCD \cong EFGH$, what is the value of *x*?

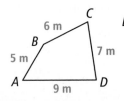

CONCEPT SUMMARY Triangle Congruence

| THEOREM 9-6 | Angle-Side-Angle (ASA) |

If...

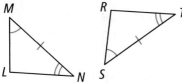

$\overline{MN} \cong \overline{ST}$, $\angle M \cong \angle S$, and $\angle N \cong \angle T$

Then... $\triangle MLN \cong \triangle SRT$

| THEOREM 9-7 | Angle-Angle-Side (AAS) |

If...

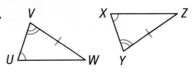

$\overline{VW} \cong \overline{YZ}$, $\angle U \cong \angle X$, and $\angle V \cong \angle Y$

Then... $\triangle UVW \cong \triangle XYZ$

☑ Do You UNDERSTAND?

1. **ESSENTIAL QUESTION** How are ASA and AAS used to show that triangles are congruent?

2. **Error Analysis** Why is Terrell's conclusion incorrect?

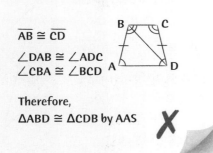

$\overline{AB} \cong \overline{CD}$

$\angle DAB \cong \angle ADC$
$\angle CBA \cong \angle BCD$

Therefore,
$\triangle ABD \cong \triangle CDB$ by AAS ✗

3. **Reason** How can you tell which property of triangle congruence shows $\triangle RST \cong \triangle UVW$?

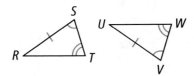

4. **Make Sense and Persevere** Is there a congruence relationship that is sufficient to show that $\triangle MNO \cong \triangle TUV$? Explain.

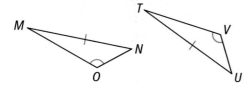

Do You KNOW HOW?

For Exercises 5 and 6, find the value of x.

5.

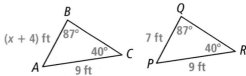

6.

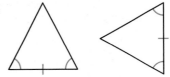

For Exercises 7 and 8, state whether the triangles are congruent and by which theorem.

7.

8.

9. Why is $LMNO \cong PQRS$?

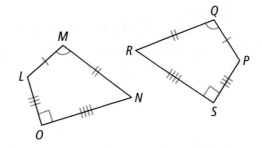

UNDERSTAND

10. Error Analysis Stacy says there is not enough information to prove △ACX ≅ △BCX. Explain why Stacy's statement is incorrect.

Given: ∠AXC ≅ ∠BXC, ∠ACX ≅ ∠BCX
Prove: △ACX ≅ △BCX

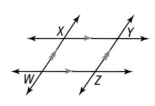

Not enough information ✗

11. Mathematical Connections Given $\overleftrightarrow{WZ} \parallel \overleftrightarrow{XY}$ and $\overleftrightarrow{WX} \parallel \overleftrightarrow{ZY}$, write a two-column proof to show $\overline{WX} \cong \overline{YZ}$.

12. Use Structure Given the figure shown, write a two-column proof to prove ∠CAE ≅ ∠CEA.

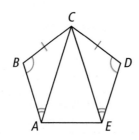

13. Reason How might you decide what additional piece of information you need to prove △JKL ≅ △NOM?

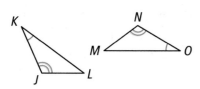

14. Higher Order Thinking Describe a composition of rigid motions that maps $\overline{DE}$ to $\overline{JK}$, $\overline{EF}$ to $\overline{KL}$, and ∠D to ∠J. Why does this composition show that there is no angle-side-side congruence criterion?

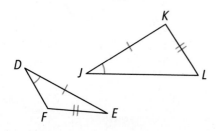

PRACTICE

15. Carpenters build a set of triangular roof supports, each with the measurements shown. How can the carpenters be sure all the slanted beams are the same length? SEE EXAMPLES 1–3

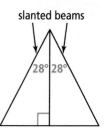

slanted beams

16. Prove the Angle-Angle-Side Congruence Criterion. SEE EXAMPLE 4

Given: ∠P ≅ ∠S, ∠Q ≅ ∠T, $\overline{QR} \cong \overline{TU}$

Prove: △PQR ≅ △STU

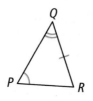

17. Write a proof. SEE EXAMPLE 5

Given: ∠A ≅ ∠C, $\overline{BX} \cong \overline{DX}$

Prove: $\overline{AX} \cong \overline{CX}$

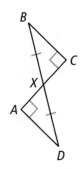

18. Is ABCD ≅ GHJK? Explain. SEE EXAMPLE 6

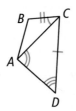 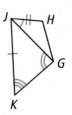

19. If ABCD ≅ EFGH, are all corresponding parts congruent? Explain. SEE EXAMPLE 6

APPLY

20. Look for Relationships Climbers want to determine a halfway point up a vertical cliff. If the top and bottom are parallel, why is point *P*, where the ropes intersect, halfway up the cliff?

21. Use Appropriate Tools Keisha, Dwayne, and Lonzell are planning for a new bridge to replace the old bridge. The new bridge will start at point *B*, where Dwayne is standing, and end at point *C*, where Keisha is standing. Lonzell walks to point *D* and then walks parallel to the river until he reaches point *E*, where he sees Dwayne and Keisha are aligned. Why is the distance from *E* to *B* the length of the new bridge?

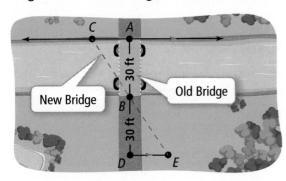

22. Construct Arguments The Robotics Club wants to divide their robot battle arena into two congruent arenas for a tournament. Paxton says that if they build a wall perpendicular to and bisecting $\overline{PO}$ from *M*, then the arenas will be congruent. Is Paxton correct? Explain.

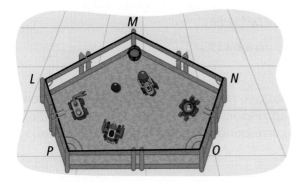

ASSESSMENT PRACTICE

23. Given the figure shown, copy and complete the table to identify the congruent pairs.

∠W	∠Y
	∠ZXY
∠WXZ	
	$\overline{XZ}$
$\overline{WZ}$	

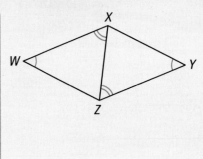

24. SAT/ACT Given △*LMN* ≅ △*QRS*, what is the value of *x*?

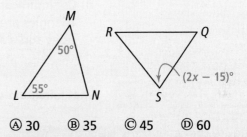

Ⓐ 30   Ⓑ 35   Ⓒ 45   Ⓓ 60

25. Performance Task Gregory wants to make four congruent triangular flags using as much of the rectangular canvas shown as possible.

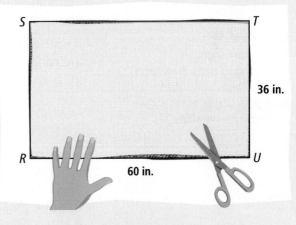

Part A Draw and label a diagram to show how Gregory should cut the fabric.

Part B Explain why the flags are congruent.

Part C Is there another way Gregory can cut the fabric to make 4 congruent triangular flags using the same amount of fabric? Explain.

9-5

Congruence in Right Triangles

SavvasRealize.com

I CAN... identify congruent right triangles.

CRITIQUE & EXPLAIN

Seth and Jae wrote the following explanations of why the two triangles are congruent.

 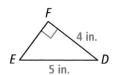

Seth

There are two pairs of congruent sides, $\overline{AB} \cong \overline{DE}$ and $\overline{AC} \cong \overline{DF}$, and a pair of congruent right angles, $\angle C \cong \angle F$. So $\triangle ABC \cong \triangle DEF$ by SSA.

Jae

The lengths of $\overline{BC}$ and $\overline{EF}$ are 3 in., since these are 3-4-5 right triangles. There are three pairs of congruent sides, $\overline{AB} \cong \overline{DE}$, $\overline{AC} \cong \overline{DF}$, and $\overline{BC} \cong \overline{EF}$. So $\triangle ABC \cong \triangle DEF$ by SSS.

A. Do you think either student is correct? Explain.

B. Communicate Precisely Describe when you can state that two right triangles are congruent if you are only given two pairs of congruent sides and a right angle in each triangle.

ESSENTIAL QUESTION

What minimum criteria are needed to show that right triangles are congruent?

CONCEPTUAL UNDERSTANDING

EXAMPLE 1   Investigate Right Triangle Congruence

When any two pairs of corresponding sides are congruent, can you show that two right triangles $\triangle ABC$ and $\triangle DEF$ are congruent? Explain.

Given that right triangles have one pair of congruent corresponding angles with right angles, look to see what else is congruent.

STUDY TIP
To visualize congruent corresponding parts, draw copies of $\triangle ABC$ and $\triangle DEF$. Then mark the triangles to show the congruent relationships.

- If both pairs of corresponding legs are congruent, use SAS with $\overline{AC} \cong \overline{DF}$, $\angle C \cong \angle F$, and $\overline{BC} \cong \overline{EF}$.

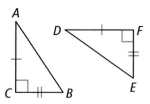

- If one pair of corresponding legs is congruent along with the hypotenuses, apply the Pythagorean Theorem to show that the other pair of corresponding legs is also congruent.

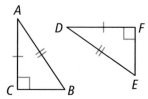

$$BC = \sqrt{AB^2 - AC^2} = \sqrt{DE^2 - DF^2} = EF$$

The right triangles are congruent by SSS.

 Try It!   **1.** Can you show that two right triangles are congruent when any one pair of corresponding acute angles is congruent and any one pair of corresponding legs is congruent? Explain.

THEOREM 9-8 Hypotenuse-Leg (HL) Theorem

If the hypotenuse and one leg of a right triangle are congruent to the hypotenuse and leg of another right triangle, then the triangles are congruent.

If...

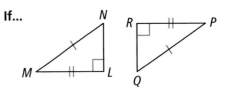

PROOF: SEE EXERCISE 9.

Then... $\triangle MNL \cong \triangle PQR$

APPLICATION

✋ EXAMPLE 2 Use the Hypotenuse-Leg (HL) Theorem

Ashton is washing windows using a 10-foot ladder. For the first window, the ladder reaches the window when he places the base of the ladder at the rose bush. How can he determine where to place the ladder to be sure it reaches the last window?

The ground, the ladder, and the side of the house form a right triangle, $\triangle RAH$. When Ashton moves the ladder, there will be another right triangle, $\triangle SBK$.

COMMON ERROR
Remember that the triangles must be right triangles in order to use the HL Theorem. Be sure the situation, like this one, describes right triangles.

Ashton wants $AH = BK$. If the two triangles are congruent, then he knows $\overline{AH} \cong \overline{BK}$ by CPCTC.

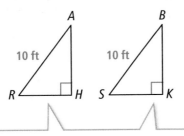

To make sure the triangles are congruent, Ashton can place the base of the ladder so that $RH = SK$.

If $RH = SK$, then $\triangle RAH \cong \triangle SBK$ by the HL Theorem.

Thus, by placing the base of the ladder the same distance away from the house as the rose bush, the ladder will reach the last window.

✓ Try It! 2. What information is needed in order to apply the Hypotenuse-Leg (HL) Theorem?

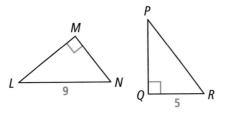

PROOF → **EXAMPLE 3**   Write a Proof Using the Hypotenuse-Leg (HL) Theorem

Write a proof to show that a triangle is isosceles.

Given: $\overline{FD} \perp \overline{AB}$, $\overline{FE} \perp \overline{AC}$, $\overline{AE} \cong \overline{AD}$, $\overline{FC} \cong \overline{FB}$

Prove: $\triangle ABC$ is isosceles.

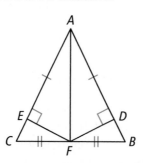

Statement	Reason
1) $\overline{FD} \perp \overline{AB}$, $\overline{FE} \perp \overline{AC}$	1) Given
2) $m\angle FDA = m\angle FDB = 90$, $m\angle FEA = m\angle FEC = 90$	2) Def. of $\perp$
3) $\triangle FEA$, $\triangle FDA$, $\triangle FEC$, and $\triangle FDB$ are rt. triangles	3) Def. of rt. triangle
4) $\overline{AE} \cong \overline{AD}$	4) Given
5) $\overline{AF} \cong \overline{AF}$	5) Refl. Prop. of Congruence
6) $\triangle FEA \cong \triangle FDA$	6) HL Theorem
7) $\overline{EF} \cong \overline{DF}$	7) CPCTC
8) $\overline{FC} \cong \overline{FB}$	8) Given
9) $\triangle FDB \cong \triangle FEC$	9) HL Theorem
10) $\angle ECF \cong \angle DBF$	10) CPCTC
11) $\overline{AC} \cong \overline{AB}$	11) Converse of Isosc. Triangle Thm.
12) $\triangle ABC$ is isosceles.	12) Def. of isosc. triangle

LOOK FOR RELATIONSHIPS
Consider what properties can be used to identify congruent parts in two triangles. What property shows that a common side is congruent to itself?

 Try It!   **3.** Write a proof to show that two triangles are congruent.

Given: $\overline{JL} \perp \overline{KM}$, $\overline{JK} \cong \overline{LK}$

Prove: $\triangle JKM \cong \triangle LKM$

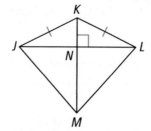

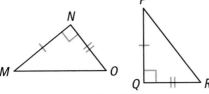

CONCEPT SUMMARY Congruence of Right Triangles

Triangle congruence theorems apply to right triangles.

THEOREM 9-3 Side-Angle-Side (SAS)

If...

$\overline{MN} \cong \overline{PQ}$ and $\overline{NO} \cong \overline{QR}$

Then... $\triangle MNO \cong \triangle PQR$

THEOREM 9-6 Angle-Side-Angle (ASA)

If...

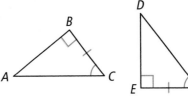

$\overline{BC} \cong \overline{EF}$ and $\angle C \cong \angle F$

Then... $\triangle ABC \cong \triangle DEF$

THEOREM 9-7 Angle-Angle-Side (AAS)

If...

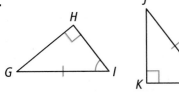

$\overline{GI} \cong \overline{JL}$ and $\angle I \cong \angle L$

Then... $\triangle GHI \cong \triangle JKL$

THEOREM 9-8 Hypotenuse-Leg (HL) Theorem

If...

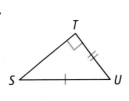

Then... $\triangle STU \cong \triangle XYZ$

☑ Do You UNDERSTAND?

1. **ESSENTIAL QUESTION** What minimum criteria are needed to show that right triangles are congruent?

2. **Error Analysis** Yama stated that $\triangle KLM \cong \triangle PLN$ by the HL Theorem. What mistake did Yama make?

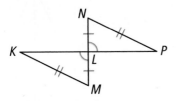

3. **Use Structure** What are the three conditions that two triangles must meet in order to apply the HL Theorem?

4. **Reason** The HL Theorem is a side-side-angle theorem for right triangles. Why does it prove congruence for two right triangles but not prove congruence for two acute triangles or for two obtuse triangles?

Do You KNOW HOW?

What information is needed to prove the triangles are congruent using the Hypotenuse-Leg (HL) Theorem?

5.

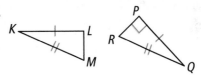

6.

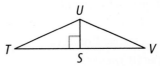

What information would be sufficient to show the two triangles are congruent by the Hypotenuse-Leg (HL) Theorem?

7.

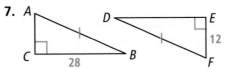

8.

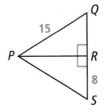

UNDERSTAND

9. Construct Arguments Follow the steps to prove the HL Theorem.

Given: Right triangles $\triangle MNL$ and $\triangle PQR$, $\overline{MN} \cong \overline{PQ}$, $\overline{ML} \cong \overline{PR}$

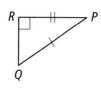

Prove: $\triangle MNL \cong \triangle PQR$

• Show that there is a rigid motion that maps L to R and M to P so that N' and Q are on opposite sides of $\overleftrightarrow{PR}$.

• Then show that $\triangle PQN'$ is isosceles.

• Show that $\triangle M'N'L' \cong \triangle PQR$, so $\triangle MNL \cong \triangle PQR$.

10. Mathematical Connections Consider the figures.

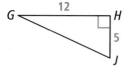 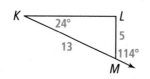

Describe the steps you would have to take before you could use the HL Theorem to prove $\triangle GHJ \cong \triangle KLM$.

11. Error Analysis Mohamed wrote the paragraph proof to show that $\triangle DEG \cong \triangle EFG$. What mistake did he make?

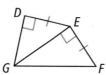

> $\triangle DEG$ and $\triangle EFG$ are right triangles. The figure shows $\overline{DE} \cong \overline{EF}$, AND $\overline{EG} \cong \overline{EG}$ by the Reflexive Property. Therefore, by the HL theorem, $\triangle DEG \cong \triangle EFG$. ✗

12. Higher Order Thinking Suppose $\triangle ABC$ is an equilateral triangle. Use the HL Theorem to explain why any segment perpendicular to a side from the opposite vertex produces two congruent triangles. Would the same be true if $\triangle ABC$ were an isosceles triangle that was not equilateral? Explain.

PRACTICE

For Exercises 13–16, you are given a theorem and a congruence statement. What additional information is needed to prove that the triangles are congruent? SEE EXAMPLE 1

13. By using ASA, given $\overline{AC} \cong \overline{EF}$ $\angle C \cong \angle F$

14. By using AAS, given $\angle B \cong \angle D$ $\overline{BC} \cong \overline{DF}$ or $\overline{AC} \cong \overline{EF}$

15. By using SAS, given $\overline{AB} \cong \overline{DE}$ $\overline{AC} \cong \overline{EF}$

16. By using HL, given $\overline{CB} \cong \overline{DF}$ $\overline{AC} \cong \overline{EF}$ or $\overline{AB} \cong \overline{ED}$

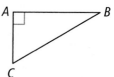
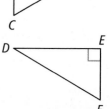

For Exercises 17–18, what information would be sufficient to show that the triangles are congruent by the HL Theorem? SEE EXAMPLE 2

17. $GL = 9$ and $HK = 15$

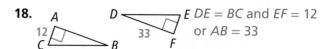

18. $DE = BC$ and $EF = 12$ or $AB = 33$

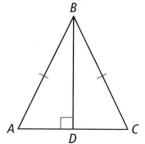

For Exercises 19–20, write a proof using the HL Theorem to show that the triangles are congruent. SEE EXAMPLE 3

19. Given: $\overline{AB} \cong \overline{CB}$, $\overline{AC} \perp \overline{DB}$

Prove: $\triangle ABD \cong \triangle CBD$

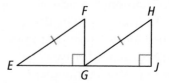

20. Given: $\overline{EF} \cong \overline{GH}$, G is the midpoint of $\overline{EJ}$

Prove: $\triangle EFG \cong \triangle GHJ$

PRACTICE & PROBLEM SOLVING

APPLY

21. Make Sense and Persevere Part of a truss bridge consists of crossbeam $\overline{KM}$ and a perpendicular beam $\overline{LN}$. What beams could an engineer measure in order to show $\triangle KLN \cong \triangle MLN$ using the HL Theorem?

22. Construct Arguments Raul wants to verify that the steps built by a carpenter are uniform by checking that $\triangle ABC \cong \triangle CDE$. The carpenter assures him they are because $\overline{AB} \cong \overline{CD}$ and $\overline{BC} \cong \overline{DE}$.

a. Explain why Raul cannot use the HL Theorem to prove $\triangle ABC \cong \triangle CDE$.

b. Is there another theorem that Raul can apply to prove $\triangle ABC \cong \triangle CDE$? If so, state the theorem. If not, explain why not.

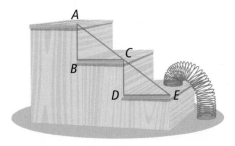

23. Communicate Precisely What are the fewest measurements that a homeowner could make to be certain that the front windows shown below are congruent?

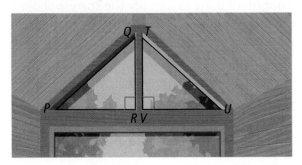

ASSESSMENT PRACTICE

24. Match each set of congruence statements with the theorem that can be used to prove that the two triangles are congruent.

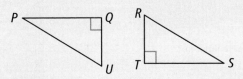

I. $\overline{PQ} \cong \overline{ST}$ and $\overline{QU} \cong \overline{TR}$ A. ASA

II. $\overline{PU} \cong \overline{SR}$ and $\overline{QU} \cong \overline{TR}$ B. AAS

III. $\overline{QU} \cong \overline{TR}$ and $\angle U \cong \angle R$ C. SAS

IV. $\overline{QU} \cong \overline{TR}$ and $\angle P \cong \angle S$ D. HL

25. SAT/ACT Which statement proves the triangles are congruent using the HL Theorem?

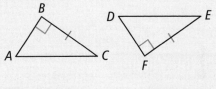

Ⓐ $\angle A \cong \angle D$ Ⓒ $\angle B \cong \angle F$

Ⓑ $\overline{AB} \cong \overline{DF}$ Ⓓ $\overline{AC} \cong \overline{DE}$

26. Performance Task Holly makes the origami figure shown. Assume that every angle that appears to be a right angle is a right angle.

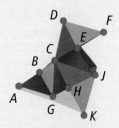

Part A What can Holly measure so that she can use the HL Theorem to prove that $\triangle ABG \cong \triangle CBG$?

Part B Holly measures to find that $HK = DE$ and $HJ = EC$. Is it possible for her to apply the HL Theorem to prove that $\triangle JHK \cong \triangle CED$? Explain.

Part C Choose two other triangles on the figure. Describe what Holly could measure to prove the triangles are congruent by using the HL Theorem.

Congruence in Overlapping Triangles

SavvasRealize.com

I CAN... use triangle congruence to solve problems with overlapping triangles.

CONTINUED ON THE NEXT PAGE

EXPLORE & REASON

Look at the painting shown.

A. How many triangles can you find?

B. Make Sense and Persevere What strategy did you use to count the triangles? How well did your strategy work?

? ESSENTIAL QUESTION
Which theorems can be used to prove that two overlapping triangles are congruent?

CONCEPTUAL UNDERSTANDING

EXAMPLE 1   Identify Corresponding Parts in Triangles

Figure *ABCD* is a rectangle with diagonals $\overline{AC}$ and $\overline{BD}$. Why is it important to identify corresponding parts of overlapping triangles?

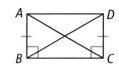

Consider △*ABC* and △*DCB*. Identify the corresponding sides and angles in the two triangles by first determining congruent parts.

Two segments, $\overline{AB}$ and $\overline{DC}$, have the same length.

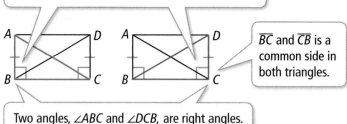

$\overline{BC}$ and $\overline{CB}$ is a common side in both triangles.

Two angles, ∠*ABC* and ∠*DCB*, are right angles.

Use what you know about congruent parts to identify the corresponding vertices. Then use the corresponding vertices to identify the corresponding angles and sides.

COMMON ERROR
Be careful to name corresponding segments correctly. While $\overline{BC}$ is congruent to itself, $\overline{BC}$ corresponds to $\overline{CB}$ in the two triangles.

Corresponding angles:

∠*ACB* and ∠*DBC*
∠*CBA* and ∠*BCD*
∠*BAC* and ∠*CDB*

Corresponding sides:

$\overline{AC}$ and $\overline{DB}$
$\overline{CB}$ and $\overline{BC}$
$\overline{BA}$ and $\overline{CD}$

Once you identify the corresponding angles and sides, you can determine if the triangles are congruent.

CONTINUED ON THE NEXT PAGE

EXAMPLE 1 CONTINUED

 Try It! 1. What are the corresponding sides and angles in △FHJ and △KHG?

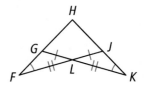

EXAMPLE 2 Use Common Parts of Triangles

Is ∠EGD ≅ ∠EFH?

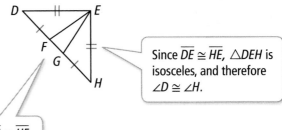

Since $\overline{DE} \cong \overline{HE}$, △DEH is isosceles, and therefore ∠D ≅ ∠H.

Since $\overline{FG} \cong \overline{FG}$ and $\overline{DF} \cong \overline{HG}$, $\overline{DG} \cong \overline{HF}$ by the Segment Addition Postulate.

Because $\overline{DE} \cong \overline{HE}$, ∠D ≅ ∠H, and $\overline{DG} \cong \overline{HF}$, △EDG ≅ △EHF by SAS. By CPCTC, ∠EGD ≅ ∠EFH.

 Try It! 2. Are $\overline{VW}$ and $\overline{ZY}$ congruent? Explain.

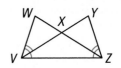

EXAMPLE 3 Prove That Two Triangles Are Congruent

Write a proof to show that △BFE is congruent to △CEF.

Given: $\overline{AB} \cong \overline{DC}$, $\overline{AF} \cong \overline{DE}$, and ∠A ≅ ∠D

Prove: △BFE ≅ △CEF

Proof: Given that $\overline{AF} \cong \overline{DE}$ and $\overline{FE} \cong \overline{FE}$, $\overline{AE} \cong \overline{DF}$ by the Segment Addition Postulate. Since $\overline{AB} \cong \overline{DC}$ and ∠A ≅ ∠D, △ABE ≅ △DCF by SAS.

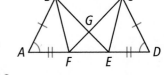

MAKE SENSE AND PERSEVERE
There are often multiple ways to complete a proof. How could you use SSS triangle congruence in this proof?

This means that by CPCTC, $\overline{BE} \cong \overline{CF}$ and ∠BEA ≅ ∠CFD. Therefore, by SAS, △BFE ≅ △CEF.

 Try It! 3. Write a proof to show that △SRV ≅ △TUW.

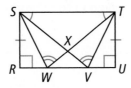

APPLICATION → **EXAMPLE 4** ▸ **Separate Overlapping Triangles**

A city runs three triangular bus routes to various attractions. How can you draw a separate triangle for each route? Are any of the routes the same length?

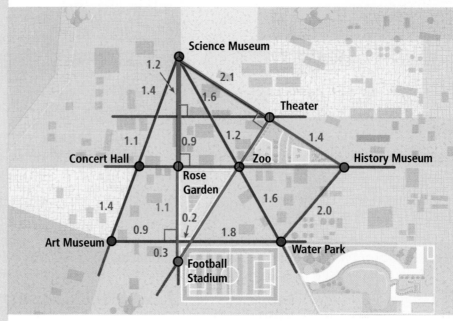

Green Route Stops:
Science Museum
Theater
History Museum
Zoo
Rose Garden
Science Museum

Purple Route Stops:
Water Park
Art Museum
Concert Hall
Science Museum
Zoo
Water Park

Red Route St
Football Stad
Zoo
Theater
Science Muse
Rose Garden
Football Stad

Use the map and the list of locations for each route to help you draw the triangles. Add length and angle information to your diagrams.

By HL, the triangles representing the green route and the red route are congruent. Therefore, the green route and the red route are the same length.

☑ **Try It!** **4.** A new route will stop at the History Museum, Water Park, Zoo, Science Museum, and Theater. Draw a triangle to represent the new route. Include any length or angle information that is given in the diagram.

CONCEPT SUMMARY Congruence in Overlapping Triangles

All congruence criteria can be applied to overlapping triangles.

THEOREM 9-5
Side-Side-Side (SSS)

If...

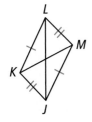

Then... △KLM ≅ △MJK and
△LMJ ≅ △JKL

THEOREM 9-7
Angle-Angle-Side (AAS)

If...

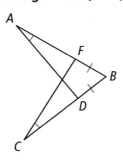

Then... △ABD ≅ △CBF

THEOREM 9-8
Hypotenuse-Leg (HL) Theorem

If...

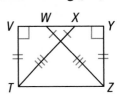

Then... △VXT ≅ △YWZ

Do You UNDERSTAND?

1. **ESSENTIAL QUESTION** Which theorems can be used to prove two overlapping triangles are congruent?

2. **Construct Arguments** How could you prove that △ACD ≅ △ECB?

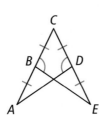

3. **Error Analysis** Nicholas wrote a proof to show that △EFD ≅ △DGE. Explain Nicholas's error. Is it possible to prove the triangles congruent? Explain.

Since $\overline{EF} \cong \overline{DG}$, ∠F ≅ ∠G, and $\overline{ED} \cong \overline{ED}$, by SAS, △EFD ≅ △DGE. ✗

4. **Use Structure**
Quadrilateral *JKLM* is a rectangle. Which triangles are congruent to △JKL? Explain.

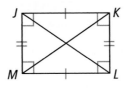

Do You KNOW HOW?

5. What are the corresponding sides and angles in △WXV and △XWY?

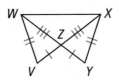

In Exercises 6–9, name a side or angle congruent to each given side or angle.

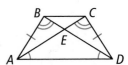

6. ∠CDA

7. $\overline{DB}$

8. ∠FGH

9. $\overline{HJ}$

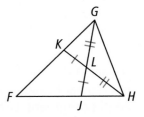

For Exercises 10 and 11, name a theorem that can be used to prove that each pair of triangles is congruent.

10. △GJL and △KHL   11. △NQM and △PMQ

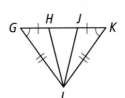   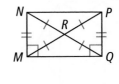

UNDERSTAND

12. Construct Arguments Write a proof to show that $\overline{AF} \cong \overline{GB}$.

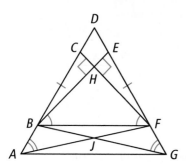

13. Mathematical Connections Explain why $\triangle ABF \cong \triangle GDE$.

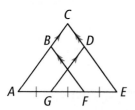

14. Error Analysis Dyani wrote a proof to show that $\angle XWY \cong \angle YZX$. What is her error?

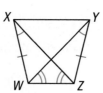

Since $\angle WXZ \cong \angle ZYW$, $\angle XZW \cong \angle YWX$, and $\overline{XW} \cong \overline{YZ}$, by AAS, $\triangle XWZ \cong \triangle YZW$. Therefore, by CPCTC, $\angle XWY \cong \angle YZX$. ✗

15. Higher Order Thinking Hexagon *ABCDEF* is a regular hexagon with all sides and angles congruent. List all sets of congruent triangles with vertices that are also vertices of the hexagon, and list all sets of congruent quadrilaterals with vertices that are also vertices of the hexagon.

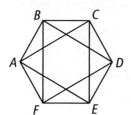

PRACTICE

16. What are the corresponding parts of $\triangle CAE$ and $\triangle DAB$? SEE EXAMPLE 1

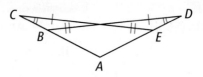

For Exercises 17–20, identify which side or angle is congruent to each given part. SEE EXAMPLE 2

17. $\angle JGK$

18. $\overline{HL}$

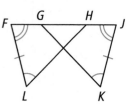

19. $\angle WYZ$

20. $\overline{XV}$

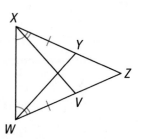

21. Write a proof to show triangles $\triangle MRO$ and $\triangle PQN$ are congruent. SEE EXAMPLE 3

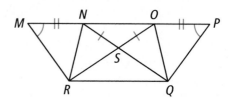

22. Write a proof to show that $\triangle BCE \cong \triangle CBD$. SEE EXAMPLE 3

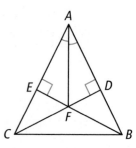

23. Draw separate diagrams showing $\triangle AEC$ and $\triangle DBG$. SEE EXAMPLE 4

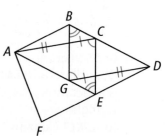

APPLY

24. Construct Arguments Parker wants to place red trim along the seams, $\overline{AC}$ and $\overline{BD}$, of a patio umbrella. He assumes they are the same length. Is he correct? Explain.

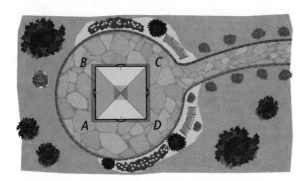

25. Reason A student is checking whether the design she drew is symmetric. Can she determine whether $\overline{MN}$ and $\overline{PN}$ are the same length? Explain.

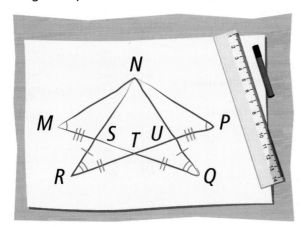

26. Look for Relationships The support for a drop tower ride is shown in the diagram. What is the width of the support? Round to the nearest hundredth.

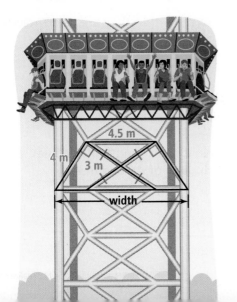

ASSESSMENT PRACTICE

27. Which statements are true? Select all that apply.

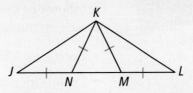

Ⓐ $\overline{KN} \cong \overline{KL}$

Ⓒ $\angle KJN \cong \angle KLM$

Ⓑ $\triangle KMJ \cong \triangle KNL$

Ⓓ $\overline{MJ} \cong \overline{NL}$

28. SAT/ACT Which theorem could you use to prove $\triangle ABD \cong \triangle DCA$?

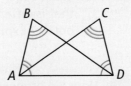

Ⓐ SAS

Ⓒ SSS

Ⓑ AAS

Ⓓ AAA

29. Performance Task The diagram shows running trails at a park.

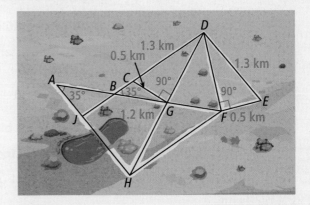

Part A Lucy ran the triangular route represented by $\triangle BDF$. Kaitlyn starts from point H and wants to run the same distance as Lucy. What triangular route can Kaitlyn run? Explain.

Part B Draw separate triangles to represent the routes the two girls ran. Label as many side lengths and angle measures as you can determine.

Part C Can you determine the distances that the girls ran? Explain.

9-7

Polygons in the Coordinate Plane

SavvasRealize.com

I CAN... use the coordinate plane to analyze geometric figures.

EXPLORE & REASON

Players place game pieces on the board shown and earn points from the attributes of the piece placed on the board.

• 1 point for a right angle

• 2 points for a pair of parallel sides

• 3 points for the shortest perimeter

A. Which game piece is worth the greatest total points? Explain.

B. Make Sense and Persevere Describe a way to determine the perimeters that is different from the way you chose. Which method do you consider better? Explain.

? ESSENTIAL QUESTION   How are properties of geometric figures represented in the coordinate plane?

CONCEPTUAL UNDERSTANDING

EXAMPLE 1   Connect Algebra and Geometry Through Coordinates

What formulas can you use to identify properties of figures on the coordinate plane?

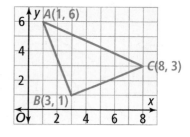

A. Which formula can you use to find *AB*?

Use the Distance Formula to find segment length.

$$AB = \sqrt{(3-1)^2 + (1-6)^2} = \sqrt{29}$$

B. What point bisects $\overline{AB}$?

Use the Midpoint Formula to find a segment bisector.

$$\text{midpoint of } \overline{AB} = \left(\frac{1+3}{2}, \frac{6+1}{2}\right) = \left(2, \frac{7}{2}\right)$$

COMMON ERROR
Recall that the slope of a line is the ratio of the difference in the *y*-coordinates to the difference in the *x*-coordinates. Be careful not to reverse the ratio.

C. Why do slopes of $\overline{AB}$ and $\overline{BC}$ show that $m\angle ABC = 90°$?

Use the slopes of the two segments to show that they are perpendicular.

$$\text{slope of } \overline{AB} = \frac{1-6}{3-1} = -\frac{5}{2}$$

$$\text{slope of } \overline{BC} = \frac{3-1}{8-3} = \frac{2}{5}$$

The product of the slopes is −1. So $\overline{AB} \perp \overline{BC}$, and $m\angle ABC = 90°$.

☑ Try It!   **1.** Given △*ABC* in Example 1, what is the length of the line segment connecting the midpoints of $\overline{AC}$ and $\overline{BC}$?

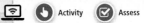

EXAMPLE 2   **Classify a Triangle on the Coordinate Plane**

A. Is △XYZ equilateral, isosceles, or scalene?

Find the length of each side.

$$XY = \sqrt{(5-1)^2 + (8-2)^2} = \sqrt{52}$$

$$YZ = \sqrt{(8-5)^2 + (6-8)^2} = \sqrt{13}$$

$$XZ = \sqrt{(8-1)^2 + (6-2)^2} = \sqrt{65}$$

No two sides are congruent. The triangle is scalene.

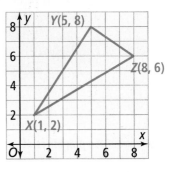

B. Is △XYZ a right triangle?

If △XYZ is a right triangle, then $\overline{XZ}$ is the hypotenuse because it is the longest side, and XY, YZ, and XZ satisfy the Pythagorean Theorem.

$$\left(\sqrt{52}\right)^2 + \left(\sqrt{13}\right)^2 \stackrel{?}{=} \left(\sqrt{65}\right)^2$$

$$65 = 65 \checkmark$$

Triangle XYZ is a right triangle.

 Try It!   **2.** The vertices of △PQR are P(4, 1), Q(2, 7), and R(8, 5).

     a. Is △PQR equilateral, isosceles, or scalene? Explain.

     b. Is △PQR a right triangle? Explain.

EXAMPLE 3   **Classify a Parallelogram on the Coordinate Plane**

What type of parallelogram is RSTU?

Determine whether RSTU is a rhombus, a rectangle, or a square. First calculate ST and SR:

$$ST = \sqrt{(2-8)^2 + (8-4)^2} = \sqrt{52}$$

$$RS = \sqrt{(2-1)^2 + (8-5)^2} = \sqrt{10}$$

Since not all side lengths are equal, RSTU is not a rhombus or a square.

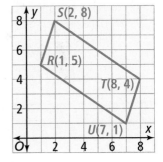

Check for right angles by finding the slopes.

$$\text{slope of } \overline{ST} = \frac{4-8}{8-2} = -\frac{2}{3}$$

$$\text{slope of } \overline{RS} = \frac{8-5}{2-1} = 3$$

MAKE SENSE AND PERSEVERE
Consider other formulas you use on the coordinate plane. What are some ways to show that a quadrilateral is not a rectangle or a rhombus?

The product of the slopes is not −1, so $\overline{ST}$ and $\overline{RS}$ are not perpendicular. At least one angle is not a right angle, and RSTU is not a rectangle. Therefore, quadrilateral RSTU is a parallelogram that is neither a square, nor a rhombus, nor a rectangle.

 Try It!   **3.** The vertices of a parallelogram are A(−2, 2), B(4, 6), C(6, 3), and D(0, −1).

     a. Is ABCD a rhombus? Explain.

     b. Is ABCD a rectangle? Explain.

EXAMPLE 4   Classify Quadrilaterals as Trapezoids and Kites on the Coordinate Plane

A. Is *ABCD* a trapezoid?

A trapezoid has exactly one pair of parallel sides. Use the slope formula to determine if only one pair of opposite sides is parallel.

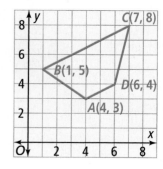

$$\text{slope of } \overline{AB} = \frac{5-3}{1-4} = -\frac{2}{3}$$

$$\text{slope of } \overline{BC} = \frac{8-5}{7-1} = \frac{1}{2}$$

$$\text{slope of } \overline{CD} = \frac{4-8}{6-7} = \frac{4}{1}$$

$$\text{slope of } \overline{AD} = \frac{4-3}{6-4} = \frac{1}{2}$$

COMMUNICATE PRECISELY
Think about the properties of a trapezoid. Why do you need to find the slopes for all four sides?

Since only the slopes of $\overline{BC}$ and $\overline{AD}$ are equal, $\overline{BC} \parallel \overline{AD}$, and only one pair of opposite sides is parallel. Therefore, quadrilateral *ABCD* is a trapezoid.

B. Is *JKLM* a kite?

A kite has two pairs of consecutive congruent sides and no opposite sides congruent. Use the Distance Formula to find the lengths of the sides.

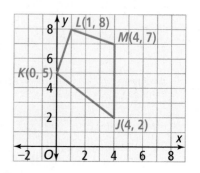

$$JK = \sqrt{(0-4)^2 + (5-2)^2} = 5$$

$$KL = \sqrt{(1-0)^2 + (8-5)^2} = \sqrt{10}$$

$$LM = \sqrt{(4-1)^2 + (7-8)^2} = \sqrt{10}$$

$$MJ = \sqrt{(4-4)^2 + (2-7)^2} = 5$$

Consecutive pair $\overline{KL}$ and $\overline{LM}$ and consecutive pair $\overline{JK}$ and $\overline{MJ}$ are congruent. No opposite pair is congruent, so *JKLM* is a kite.

✓ **Try It!**   **4.** Is each quadrilateral a kite, trapezoid, or neither?

a.
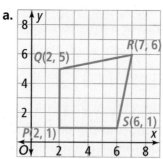

b.
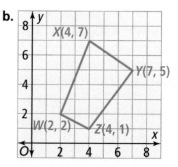

APPLICATION   👆 **EXAMPLE 5**   **Find Perimeter and Area**

Dylan draws up a plan to fence in a yard for his chickens. The distance between grid lines is 1 foot.

A. Is 30 feet of fencing enough to enclose the yard?

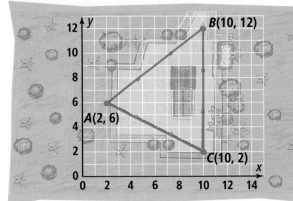

Find the lengths of the sides.

$$AB = \sqrt{(2 - 10)^2 + (6 - 12)^2} = 10 \text{ ft}$$

$$BC = \sqrt{(10 - 10)^2 + (12 - 2)^2} = 10 \text{ ft}$$

$$AC = \sqrt{(2 - 10)^2 + (6 - 2)^2} = \sqrt{80} \text{ ft}$$

Find the perimeter of the yard.

$$P = 10 + 10 + \sqrt{80}$$

$$\approx 28.9 \text{ ft}$$

The perimeter is about 28.9 feet, which is less than 30 feet. Dylan has enough fencing material.

B. For a healthy flock, each chicken needs at least 8 square feet of space. What is the maximum number of chickens Dylan can put in the yard?

The yard is an isosceles triangle. To find the area, you need the height of the triangle. The height of $\triangle ABC$ is BX, where X is the midpoint of $\overline{AC}$.

Find the midpoint of $\overline{AC}$.

$$X = \left(\frac{2 + 10}{2}, \frac{6 + 2}{2}\right) = (6, 4)$$

Find the height of $\triangle ABC$.

$$BX = \sqrt{(10 - 6)^2 + (12 - 4)^2} = \sqrt{80} \text{ ft}$$

Then find the area of the yard.

$$\text{area of } \triangle ABC = \frac{1}{2}(\sqrt{80})(\sqrt{80}) = 40 \text{ ft}^2$$

Divide 40 by 8 to find the number of chickens.

$$40 \div 8 = 5$$

Dylan can keep as many as 5 chickens in the yard.

CONSTRUCT ARGUMENTS

Consider the properties of an isosceles triangle. What property of an isosceles triangle justifies that $\overline{BX}$ is a height of the triangle?

 Try It!   **5.** The vertices of *WXYZ* are *W*(5, 4), *X*(2, 9), *Y*(9, 9), and *Z*(8, 4).

     a. What is the perimeter of *WXYZ*?

     b. What is the area of *WXYZ*?

CONCEPT SUMMARY Connecting Algebra and Geometry

You can use algebra to determine properties of and to classify geometric figures on the coordinate plane.

WORDS
Use the Distance Formula to find the lengths of segments to classify figures.

Use the Slope Formula to determine whether two lines or segments are parallel or perpendicular.

Use the Midpoint Formula to determine if a point bisects a segment.

GRAPH

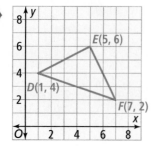
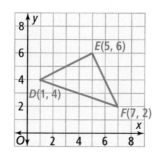
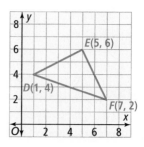

NUMBERS

$DE = \sqrt{(5-1)^2 + (6-4)^2}$
$= \sqrt{20}$

slope of $\overline{DE} = \dfrac{6-4}{5-1}$
$= \dfrac{1}{2}$

midpoint of $\overline{DF}$
$= \left(\dfrac{1+7}{2}, \dfrac{4+2}{2}\right) = (4, 3)$

Do You UNDERSTAND?

1. **ESSENTIAL QUESTION** How are properties of geometric figures represented in the coordinate plane?

2. **Error Analysis** Chen is asked to describe two methods to find *BC*. Why is Chen incorrect?

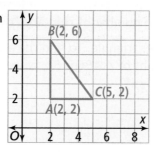

The only possible method is to use the Distance Formula because you only know the endpoints of $\overline{BC}$.

3. **Communicate Precisely** Describe three ways you can determine whether a quadrilateral is a parallelogram given the coordinates of the vertices.

Do You KNOW HOW?

Use *JKLM* for Exercises 4–6.

4. What is the perimeter of *JKLM*?

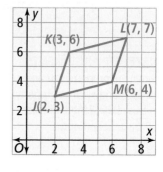

5. What is the relationship between $\overline{JL}$ and $\overline{KM}$? Explain.

6. What type of quadrilateral is *JKLM*? Explain.

Use △*PQR* for Exercises 7 and 8.

7. What kind of triangle is *PQR*? Explain.

8. What is the area of *PQR*?

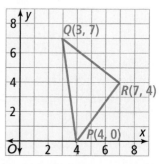

Go Online | SavvasRealize.com

UNDERSTAND

9. Error Analysis What error did Kelley make in finding the area of △PQR?

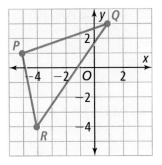

$$\text{Area} = \frac{1}{2}bh = \frac{1}{2}(PR)(PQ) = \frac{1}{2}\sqrt{26}\sqrt{40}$$

The area of △PQR is about 16.12 square units.

10. Mathematical Connections Find the equation of the line that passes through point R and is perpendicular to line m.

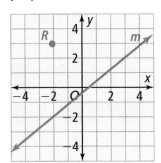

$$y = -\frac{5}{4}x + \frac{1}{2}$$

11. Construct Arguments Prove △ABC ≅ △DEF.

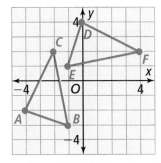

12. Communicate Precisely Given the coordinates of the vertices, how can you show that a quadrilateral is a kite without using the Distance Formula?

13. Higher Order Thinking Let line p be the perpendicular bisector of $\overline{AB}$ that has endpoints and $A(x_1, y_1)$ and $B(x_2, y_2)$. Describe the process for writing a general equation in slope-intercept form for line p.

PRACTICE

Use the figure shown for Exercises 14–17. SEE EXAMPLE 1

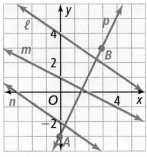

14. Which lines are parallel? $\ell \parallel n$

15. Which lines are perpendicular? $m \perp p$

16. What is the length of $\overline{AB}$? $\sqrt{45}$ units

17. What is the midpoint of $\overline{AB}$? $\left(\frac{3}{2}, 0\right)$

Use the figure shown for Exercises 18–23.

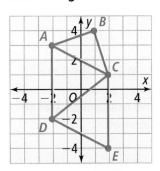

18. Is △ABC a scalene, isosceles, or equilateral triangle? Is it a right triangle? Explain. SEE EXAMPLE 2

19. Is △ADC a scalene, isosceles, or equilateral triangle? Is it a right triangle? Explain. SEE EXAMPLE 2

20. What type of parallelogram is ACED? Explain. SEE EXAMPLE 3

21. What type of quadrilateral is ABCD? How do you know? SEE EXAMPLE 4

22. Find the area and perimeter of △ABC. SEE EXAMPLE 5

23. Find the area and perimeter of ABCD. SEE EXAMPLE 6

Three vertices of a quadrilateral are P(−2, 3), Q(2, 4), and R(1, 0). SEE EXAMPLE 3

24. Suppose PQRS is a parallelogram. What are the coordinates of vertex S? What type of parallelogram is PQRS? (−3, −1); rhombus

25. Suppose PQSR is a parallelogram. What are the coordinates of vertex S? What type of parallelogram is PQSR? (5, 1); parallelogram

APPLY

26. Use Appropriate Tools An architect overlays a coordinate grid on her plans for attaching a greenhouse to the side of a house. She wants to locate point *D* so that *ABCD* is a trapezoid and $\overline{CD}$ is perpendicular to the house. What are the coordinates for point *D*?

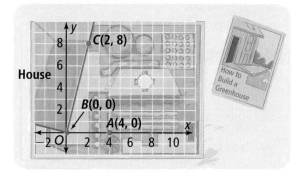

27. Model With Mathematics Yuson thinks the design she made is symmetric across the dashed line she drew. How can she use coordinates to show that her design is symmetric?

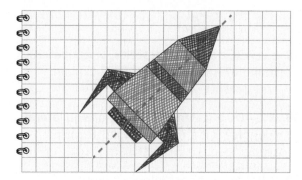

28. Construct Arguments The map shows the regions that Anna and Richard have explored. Each claims to have explored the greater area. Who is correct? Explain.

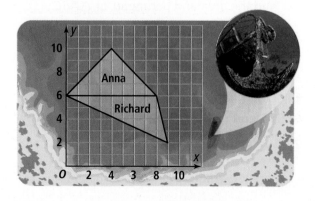

ASSESSMENT PRACTICE

29. Triangle *ABC* has vertices *A*(2, 5), *B*(6, 8), and *C*(5, 1). Determine whether each statement about △*ABC* is true. Select *Yes* or *No*.

	Yes	No
$\overline{AB} \cong \overline{AC}$	☐	☐
$BC = AB \sqrt{2}$	☐	☐
The midpoint of *BC* is (5.5, 4).	☐	☐
The perimeter is 12.5 units.	☐	☐

30. SAT/ACT Quadrilateral *JKLM* has vertices *J*(1, −2), *K*(7, 1), *L*(8, −1), and *M*(2, −4). Which is the most precise classification of *JKLM*?

Ⓐ rectangle

Ⓑ rhombus

Ⓒ trapezoid

Ⓓ kite

31. Performance Task Dana draws the side view of a TV stand that has slanted legs. Each unit in his plan equals half of a foot.

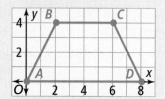

Part A Dana thinks his TV stand is in the shape of isosceles trapezoid. Is he correct? Explain.

Part B Dana adds an additional support by connecting the midpoints of the legs. How long is the support?

Part C Dana decides he wants to make the TV stand a half foot higher by placing *B* at (2, 5) and *C* at (6, 5). How much longer will the legs and support connecting the midpoints be?

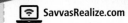
9-8

Chords

SavvasRealize.com

I CAN... relate the length of a chord to its central angle and the arc it intercepts.

VOCABULARY
• chord

👆 **EXPLORE & REASON**

Use the diagram to answer the questions.

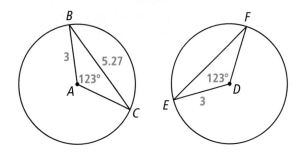

A. What figures in the diagram are congruent? Explain.

B. Look for Relationships How can you find *EF*?

❓ **ESSENTIAL QUESTION**   How are chords related to their central angles and intercepted arcs?

CONCEPTUAL UNDERSTANDING

👆 **EXAMPLE 1**   **Relate Central Angles and Chords**

A chord is a segment whose endpoints are on a circle.
Why is $\overline{RS} \cong \overline{UT}$?

STUDY TIP
Refer to the diagram as you read the proof. Note which parts of the triangles are congruent.

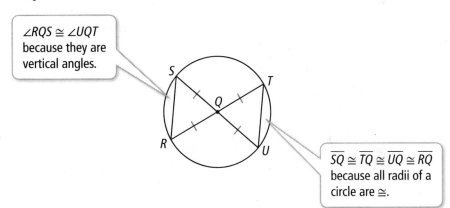

∠RQS ≅ ∠UQT because they are vertical angles.

$\overline{SQ} \cong \overline{TQ} \cong \overline{UQ} \cong \overline{RQ}$ because all radii of a circle are ≅.

By the SAS Congruence Theorem, △QRS ≅ △QUT. Therefore $\overline{RS} \cong \overline{UT}$ because they are corresponding parts of congruent triangles.

☑ **Try It!**   **1.** Why is ∠BAC ≅ ∠DAE?

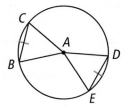

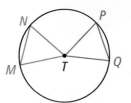

THEOREM 9-9 AND THE CONVERSE

Theorem

If two chords in a circle or in congruent circles are congruent, then their central angles are congruent.

Converse

If two central angles in a circle or in congruent circles are congruent, then their chords are congruent.

PROOF: SEE EXERCISES 12 AND 13.

If... $\overline{MN} \cong \overline{PQ}$
Then... $\angle MTN \cong \angle PTQ$

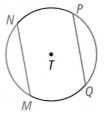

If... $\angle MTN \cong \angle PTQ$
Then... $\overline{MN} \cong \overline{PQ}$

THEOREM 9-10 AND THE CONVERSE

Theorem

If two arcs in a circle or in congruent circles are congruent, then their chords are congruent.

Converse

If two chords in a circle or in congruent circles are congruent, then their arcs are congruent.

PROOF: SEE EXAMPLE 2 AND EXAMPLE 2 TRY IT.

If... $\overset{\frown}{MN} \cong \overset{\frown}{PQ}$
Then... $\overline{MN} \cong \overline{PQ}$

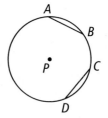

If... $\overline{MN} \cong \overline{PQ}$
Then... $\overset{\frown}{MN} \cong \overset{\frown}{PQ}$

PROOF

EXAMPLE 2 Relate Arcs and Chords

Write a proof of Theorem 9-10.

Given: $\overset{\frown}{AB} \cong \overset{\frown}{CD}$

Prove: $\overline{AB} \cong \overline{CD}$

MAKE SENSE AND PERSEVERE
Think about other strategies you can use. How could you use congruent triangles to prove the relationship?

Plan: Use the relationship between central angles and arcs by drawing the radii $\overline{PA}$, $\overline{PB}$, $\overline{PC}$, and $\overline{PD}$.

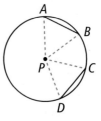

Proof: Since $\overset{\frown}{AB} \cong \overset{\frown}{CD}$, you know that $m\overset{\frown}{AB} = m\overset{\frown}{CD}$. And since the measure of a central angle is equal to the measure of its arc, $m\angle APB = m\overset{\frown}{AB}$ and $m\angle CPD = m\overset{\frown}{CD}$. By substitution, $m\angle APB = m\angle CPD$ and $\angle APB \cong \angle CPD$. So, by the Converse of Theorem 9-9, $\overline{AB} \cong \overline{CD}$.

 Try It! **2.** Write a flow proof of the Converse of Theorem 9-10.

THEOREM 9-11 AND THE CONVERSE

Theorem

If chords are equidistant from the center of a circle or the centers of congruent circles, then they are congruent.

Converse

If chords in a circle or in congruent circles are congruent, then they are equidistant from the center or centers.

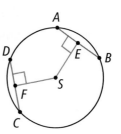

If... $\overline{SE} \cong \overline{SF}$, Then... $\overline{AB} \cong \overline{CD}$
If... $\overline{AB} \cong \overline{CD}$, Then... $\overline{SE} \cong \overline{SF}$

PROOF: SEE EXAMPLE 3 AND EXAMPLE 3 TRY IT.

PROOF

EXAMPLE 3   **Relate Chords Equidistant from the Center**

Write a proof of Theorem 9-11.

Given: $\odot P$ with $\overline{AB} \perp \overline{PE}$,
$\overline{CD} \perp \overline{PF}$,
$\overline{PE} \cong \overline{PF}$

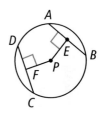

> **COMMON ERROR**
> Be sure to construct the triangles with corresponding parts that yield the desired conclusion.

Prove: $\overline{AB} \cong \overline{CD}$

Plan: Construct triangles by drawing the radii $\overline{PA}$, $\overline{PB}$, $\overline{PC}$, and $\overline{PD}$. Then show that the triangles are congruent in order to apply CPCTC.

Proof:

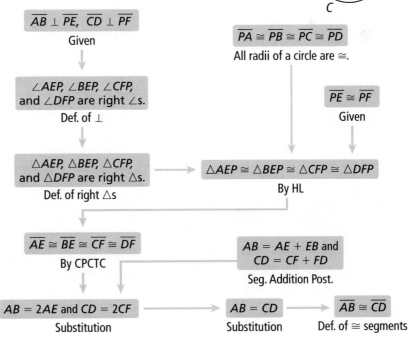

 Try It!   **3.** Write a flow proof of the Converse of Theorem 9-11.

EXAMPLE 4   Construct a Regular Hexagon Inscribed in a Circle

How do you draw a regular hexagon inscribed in ⊙P?

Step 1 Mark point Q on the circle.

Step 2 Set the compass the radius of the circle. Place the compass point at Q and draw an arc through the circle.

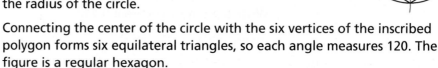

Step 3 Keep the compass setting. Move the compass point to the intersection of the arc and the circle. Draw another arc through the circle. Each point of intersection is a vertex of the hexagon. Continue this way until you have five arcs.

Step 4 Draw chords connecting consecutive points on the circle.

The side lengths of the resulting figure are all congruent because they have the same length as the radius of the circle.

Connecting the center of the circle with the six vertices of the inscribed polygon forms six equilateral triangles, so each angle measures 120. The figure is a regular hexagon.

 Try It!   **4.** Construct an equilateral triangle inscribed in a circle.

THEOREM 9-12 AND THE CONVERSE

Theorem

If a diameter is perpendicular to a chord, then it bisects the chord.

Converse

If a diameter bisects a chord (that is not a diameter), then it is perpendicular to the chord.

PROOF: SEE EXERCISES 15 AND 16.

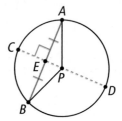

If... $\overline{CD}$ is a diameter, $\overline{AB} \perp \overline{CD}$
Then... $\overline{AE} \cong \overline{BE}$

If... $\overline{CD}$ is a diameter, $\overline{AE} \cong \overline{BE}$
Then... $\overline{AB} \perp \overline{CD}$

THEOREM 9-13

The perpendicular bisector of a chord contains the center of the circle.

PROOF: SEE EXERCISE 28.

If...

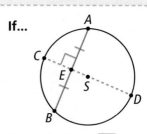

Then... S is on $\overline{CD}$

APPLICATION

EXAMPLE 5 Solve Problems Involving Chords of Circles

An engineer is designing a service tunnel to accommodate two trucks simultaneously. If the tunnel can accommodate a width of 18 ft, what is the greatest truck height that the tunnel can accommodate? Subtract 0.5 ft to account for fluctuations in pavement.

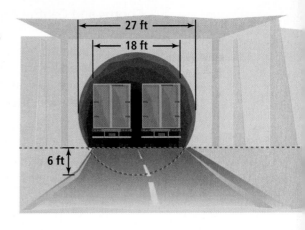

Formulate ◀ Draw and label a sketch to help solve the problem.

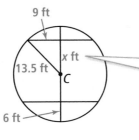

Let x be the distance from the center to the greatest height. The radius is 13.5 ft.

Compute ◀ Write and solve an equation for x.

$$9^2 + x^2 = 13.5^2$$

Use the Pythagorean Theorem.

$$x^2 = 13.5^2 - 9^2$$
$$x = \sqrt{13.5^2 - 9^2}$$
$$x \approx 10.06$$

Add the distance from the ground to the center $13.5 - 6 = 7.5$ to x and subtract 0.5 ft to account for fluctuations in pavement.

$$7.5 + 10.06 - 0.5 = 17.06$$

Interpret ◀ The greatest height that the tunnel can accommodate is about 17.06 ft.

 Try It! 5. Fresh cut flowers need to be in at least 4 inches of water. A spherical vase is filled until the surface of the water is a circle 5 inches in diameter. Is the water deep enough for the flowers? Explain.

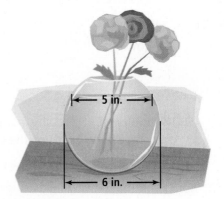

CONCEPT SUMMARY Chords

Chords and Central Angles	Chords and Arcs
WORDS Two chords in a circle or in congruent circles are congruent if and only if the central angles of the chords are congruent.	Two chords in a circle or in congruent circles are congruent if and only if the chords intercept congruent arcs.
DIAGRAMS 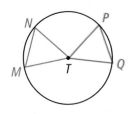	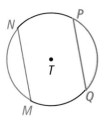
$\angle MTN \cong \angle PTQ$ if and only if $\overline{MN} \cong \overline{PQ}$.	$\overset{\frown}{MN} \cong \overset{\frown}{PQ}$ if and only if $\overline{MN} \cong \overline{PQ}$.

☑ Do You UNDERSTAND?

1. **ESSENTIAL QUESTION** How are chords related to their central angles and intercepted arcs?

2. **Error Analysis** Sasha writes a proof to show that two chords are congruent. What is her error?

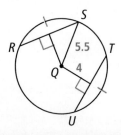

$\angle APB \cong \angle CPD$ Vert. $\angle$s $\cong$
$\overset{\frown}{AB} \cong \overset{\frown}{CD}$ Intercepted by $\cong \angle$s
$\overline{AB} \cong \overline{DC}$ Chords intercept $\cong$ arcs

3. **Vocabulary** Explain why all diameters of circles are also chords of the circles.

4. **Reason** Given $\overset{\frown}{RS} \cong \overset{\frown}{UT}$, how can you find UT?

Do You KNOW HOW?

For Exercises 5–10, in $\odot P$, $m\overset{\frown}{AB} = 43°$, and $AC = DF$. Find each measure.

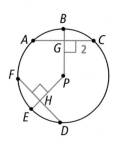

5. DF

6. $m\overset{\frown}{ABC}$

7. FH

8. $m\overset{\frown}{DE}$

9. AC

10. $m\overset{\frown}{DF}$

11. For the corporate headquarters, an executive wants to place a company logo that is six feet in diameter with the sides of the H five feet tall on the front wall. What is the width x of the crossbar for the H?

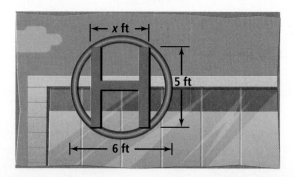

UNDERSTAND

12. Construct Arguments Write a paragraph proof of Theorem 9-9.

Given: $\overline{AB} \cong \overline{CD}$

Prove: $\angle AEB \cong \angle CED$

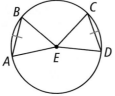

13. Construct Arguments Write a two-column proof of the Converse of Theorem 9-9.

Given: $\angle AEB \cong \angle CED$

Prove: $\overline{AB} \cong \overline{CD}$

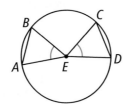

14. Error Analysis What is Ashton's error?

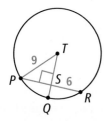

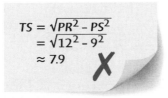

$$TS = \sqrt{PR^2 - PS^2}$$
$$= \sqrt{12^2 - 9^2}$$
$$\approx 7.9 \quad ✗$$

15. Construct Arguments Write a proof of Theorem 9-12.

Given: $\overline{LN}$ is a diameter of $\odot Q$; $\overline{LN} \perp \overline{KM}$

Prove: $\overline{KP} \cong \overline{MP}$

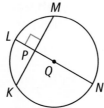

16. Construct Arguments Write a proof of the Converse of Theorem 9-12.

Given: $\overline{LN}$ is a diameter of $\odot Q$; $\overline{KP} \cong \overline{MP}$

Prove: $\overline{LN} \perp \overline{KM}$

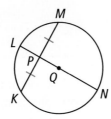

17. Higher Order Thinking $\triangle ABP \sim \triangle CDE$. How do you show that $\overparen{AB} \cong \overparen{CD}$?

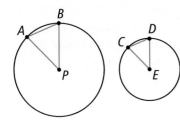

PRACTICE

For Exercises 18–21, in $\odot B$, $m\angle VBT = m\overparen{PR} = 90$, and $QR = TU$. SEE EXAMPLES 1 AND 2

18. Find $m\angle PBR$. 90

19. Find $m\overparen{TV}$. 90

20. Which angle is congruent to $\angle QBR$? $\angle TBU$

21. Which segment is congruent to $\overline{TV}$? $\overline{PR}$

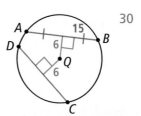

22. Construct a square inscribed in a circle. How is drawing an inscribed square different from drawing an inscribed hexagon or triangle? SEE EXAMPLE 4

23. Find CD. SEE EXAMPLE 3

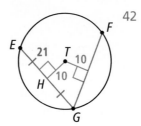

30

24. Find FG. SEE EXAMPLE 3

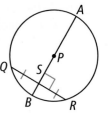

42

25. A chord is 12 cm long. It is 30 cm from the center of the circle. What is the radius of the circle? SEE EXAMPLE 5 ≈30.59 cm

26. The diameter of a circle is 39 inches. The circle has two chords of length 8 inches. What is the distance from each chord to the center of the circle? ≈19.09 in.

27. A chord is 4 units from the center of a circle. The radius of the circle is 5 units. What is the length of the chord? 6

28. Write a proof of Theorem 9-13.

Given: $\overline{QR}$ is a chord in $\odot P$; $\overline{AB}$ is the perpendicular bisector of $\overline{QR}$.

Prove: $\overline{AB}$ contains P.

APPLY

29. Mathematical Connections Nadia designs a water ride and wants to use a half-cylindrical pipe in the construction. If she wants the waterway to be 8 ft wide when the water is 2 ft deep, what is the diameter of the pipe?

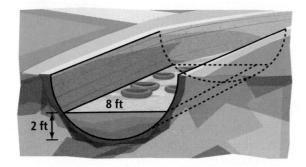

30. Model With Mathematics A bike trail has holes up to 20 in. wide and 5 in. deep. If the diameter of the wheels of Anna's bike is 26 in., can she ride her bike without the wheels hitting the bottom of the holes? Explain.

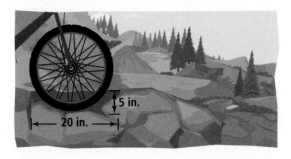

31. Make Sense and Persevere The bottom of a hemispherical cake has diameter 8 in.

a. If the cake is sliced horizontally in half so each piece has the same height, would the top half fit on a plate with diameter 6 in.? Explain.

b. If the cake is sliced horizontally in thirds so each piece has the same height, would the top third fit on a plate with diameter 5 in.? Explain.

ASSESSMENT PRACTICE

32. Which must be true? Select all that apply.

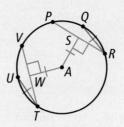

Ⓐ $\overset{\frown}{QR} \cong \overset{\frown}{TU}$ Ⓒ $VW = AS$

Ⓑ $PR = TV$ Ⓓ $PS = SR$

33. SAT/ACT The radius of the semicircle is r, and $CD = \frac{3}{4} \cdot AB$. What is the distance from the chord to the diameter?

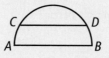

Ⓐ $\frac{5}{4}r$ Ⓑ $\frac{\sqrt{7}}{4}r$ Ⓒ $\frac{\sqrt{7}}{4}\pi r$ Ⓓ $\frac{5}{4}\pi r$

34. Performance Task The radius of the range of a radar is 50 miles. At 1:00 P.M., a plane enters the radar screen flying due north. At 1:04 P.M. the aircraft is due east of the radar. At 1:08 P.M., the aircraft leaves the screen. The plane is moving at 8 miles per minute.

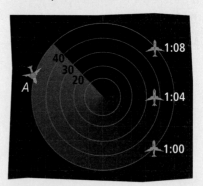

Part A What distance does the plane fly on the controller's screen?

Part B What is the distance of the plane from the radar at 1:04 P.M.?

Part C Another plane enters the screen at point A at 1:12 P.M. and flies in a straight line at 9 miles per minute. If it gets no closer than 40 miles from the radar, at what time does it leave the screen? Explain.

Topic Review

? TOPIC ESSENTIAL QUESTION

1. What relationships between sides and angles of triangles can be used to prove triangles congruent?

Vocabulary Review

Choose the correct term to complete each sentence.

2. Figures that have the same size and shape are said to be _____.

3. The side of an isosceles triangle that is opposite the vertex is called the _____.

4. A rigid motion is sometimes called a _____ because it maps a figure to a figure with the same shape and size.

5. The legs of an isosceles triangle form an angle called the _____.

- base
- base angle
- congruence transformation
- congruent
- leg
- vertex

Concepts & Skills Review

LESSON 9-1 ▸ Congruence

Quick Review

Two figures are **congruent** if there is a rigid motion, or sequence of rigid motions, that maps one figure to the other.

Example

Figure 1 is translated right to form Figure 2. Are the figures congruent?

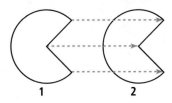

Yes, a translation is a congruence transformation.

Practice & Problem Solving

For Exercises 6 and 7, determine if Figure A and Figure B are congruent. If so, describe the sequence of rigid motions that maps Figure A to Figure B. If not, explain.

6.

A   B

7.

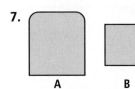

A   B

8. **Reason** If a figure is reflected across the same line twice, is the resulting image congruent to that figure? Explain.

Quick Review

Two sides of a triangle are congruent if and only if the angles opposite those sides are also congruent.

A line that bisects the **vertex** angle of an isosceles triangle is the perpendicular bisector of the opposite side.

Example

What is the measure of ∠C?

The sides opposite ∠A and ∠C are congruent, so ∠A ≅ ∠C; m∠A is 75°, so m∠C is 75°.

Practice & Problem Solving

Find the unknown angle measures for each triangle.

9. 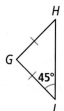   10.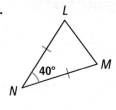

11. **Use Structure** A zipper bisects the vertex of the front of the tent, which is in the shape of an equilateral triangle, forming two triangles. What are the angle measures of the resulting triangles?

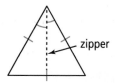

Quick Review

Two triangles are congruent if two sides and the included angle of one triangle are congruent to two sides and the included angle of the other triangle (SAS).

Two triangles are congruent if three sides of one triangle are congruent to three sides of the other triangle (SSS).

Corresponding parts of congruent triangles are congruent (CPCTC).

Example

Show that the triangles are congruent.

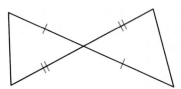

They are congruent by SAS, because they have two pairs of congruent sides and the included angles are vertical angles and so are congruent.

Practice & Problem Solving

Which pairs of triangles are congruent by SAS or SSS? Explain.

12.

13.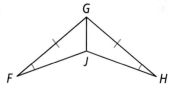

14. **Make Sense and Persevere** The paths of a ping-pong ball during two separate serves intersect at the center of the table. How many pairs of congruent triangles can you find?

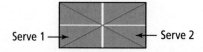

Proving and Applying the ASA and AAS Congruence Criteria

Quick Review

Two triangles are congruent if two angles of one triangle and the included side are congruent to two angles and the included side of the other triangle (ASA).

Two triangles are congruent if two angles and a nonincluded side of one triangle are congruent to two angles and a nonincluded side of the other triangle (AAS).

Example

Show that the triangles are congruent.

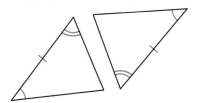

They are congruent by ASA because they have two pairs of congruent angles that have a congruent side between the angles.

Practice & Problem Solving

State whether each pair of triangles is congruent by SAS, SSS, ASA, AAS, or the congruence cannot be determined. Justify your answer.

15. 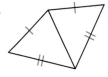   16.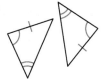

17. **Generalize** Are two triangles with two pairs of congruent angles and one pair of congruent sides always congruent? Explain.

18. **Make Sense and Persevere** Are the triangles congruent? If they are, by which congruence criterion? Explain.

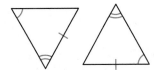

Congruence in Right Triangles

Quick Review

If the hypotenuse and one leg of a right triangle are congruent to the hypotenuse and leg of another triangle, then the triangles are congruent (HL).

Example

Show that the triangles are congruent.

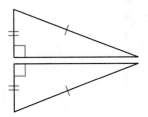

They are congruent by HL because the triangles are right triangles, and the hypotenuses and one pair of legs are congruent.

Practice & Problem Solving

Prove that the pair of triangles is congruent.

19.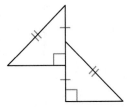

20. **Communicate Precisely** Triangle *ABC* is an isosceles triangle with the vertex bisected by a line segment. Draw the triangle and prove that the resulting triangles are congruent.

Quick Review

If two triangles are overlapping, all congruence criteria—AAS, ASA, HL, SAS, and SSS—can still be applied.

To identify congruent overlapping triangles, first identify the parts of each triangle. Then test if any of the congruence criteria hold.

Example

Given rectangle *ABCD*, how can you prove that ∠*ADB* ≅ ∠*BCA*?

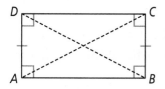

Opposite sides of a rectangle are congruent, so $\overline{AD} \cong \overline{BC}$. All right angles are congruent, so ∠*DAB* ≅ ∠ *CBA*. By the Reflexive Property, $\overline{AB} \cong \overline{BA}$. Thus, △*ADB* ≅ △*BCA* by SAS, and ∠*ADB* ≅ ∠*BCA* by CPCTC.

Practice & Problem Solving

For Exercise 21, prove that the pair of triangles is congruent. For Exercise 22, which pairs are of triangles are congruent? Explain.

21. 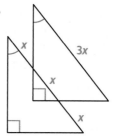   **22.**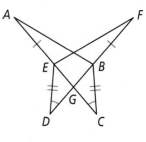

23. Make Sense and Persevere Describe where to place point *E* along $\overline{AC}$ such that △*ABD* ≅ △*CBE*. Then explain why the triangles are congruent.

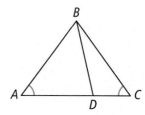

Polygons in the Coordinate Plane

Quick Review

When a geometric figure is represented in a coordinate plane, you can use slope, distance, and midpoints to analyze properties of the figure.

Example

Is △ABC an isosceles triangle? Explain.

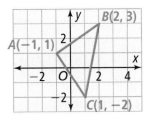

A triangle is isosceles if two sides are congruent. Use the Distance Formula to find the side lengths.

$$AB = \sqrt{(2-(-1))^2 + (3-1)^2} = \sqrt{13}$$
$$BC = \sqrt{(1-2)^2 + (-2-3)^2} = \sqrt{26}$$
$$CA = \sqrt{(1-(-1))^2 + (-2-1)^2} = \sqrt{13}$$

Since $AB = CA$, △ABC is isosceles.

Practice & Problem Solving

For Exercises 24–27, determine whether each figure is the given type of figure.

24. $F(-2, 4)$, $G(0, 0)$, $H(3, 1)$; right triangle

25. $A(7, 2)$, $B(3, -1)$, $C(3, 4)$; equilateral triangle

26. $J(-4, -4)$, $K(-7, 0)$, $L(-4, 4)$, $M(-1, 0)$; rhombus

27. What are the area and perimeter of $PQRS$?

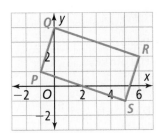

28. **Make Sense and Persevere** Parallelogram $WXYZ$ has coordinates $W(a, b)$, $X(c, d)$, $Y(f, g)$, and $Z(h, j)$. What equation can you use to determine whether $WXYZ$ is a rhombus? Explain.

Chords

Quick Review

Chords in a circle have the following properties:

• Two chords in the same circle with the same length have congruent central angles, have congruent arcs, and are equidistant from the center of the circle.

• Chords are bisected by the diameter of the circle that is perpendicular to the chord.

Example

What is the radius of ⊙T?

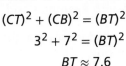

Since $\overline{CT} \perp \overline{AB}$, $\overline{CT}$ bisects $\overline{AB}$. So, $CB = 7$. Use the Pythagorean Theorem to find the radius.

$$(CT)^2 + (CB)^2 = (BT)^2$$
$$3^2 + 7^2 = (BT)^2$$
$$BT \approx 7.6$$

The radius of ⊙T is about 7.6.

Practice & Problem Solving

For Exercises 29–31, the radius of ⊙T is 7. Find each value. Round to the nearest tenth.

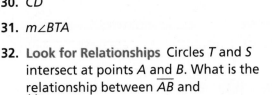

29. FH

30. CD

31. $m\angle BTA$

32. **Look for Relationships** Circles T and S intersect at points A and B. What is the relationship between $\overline{AB}$ and $\overleftrightarrow{TS}$? Explain.

33. A contractor cuts off part of a circular countertop so that it fits against a wall. What should be the length x of the cut? Round to the nearest tenth.

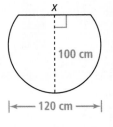

? TOPIC ESSENTIAL QUESTION

How do you use statistics to model situations and solve problems?

Topic Overview

enVision® STEM Project:
Take an Energy Survey

10-1 Analyzing Data Displays

10-2 Comparing Data Sets

10-3 Interpreting the Shapes of Data Displays

10-4 Standard Deviation

10-5 Two-Way Frequency Tables

Mathematical Modeling in 3 Acts:
Text Message

Topic Vocabulary

- conditional relative frequency
- joint frequency
- joint relative frequency
- marginal frequency
- marginal relative frequency
- normal distribution
- standard deviation
- variance

Digital Experience

 INTERACTIVE STUDENT EDITION
Access online or offline.

 **ACTIVITIES** Complete *Explore & Reason, Model & Discuss*, and *Critique & Explain* activities. Interact with Examples and Try Its.

 ANIMATION View and interact with real-world applications.

 PRACTICE Practice what you've learned.

 Go online | **SavvasRealize.com**

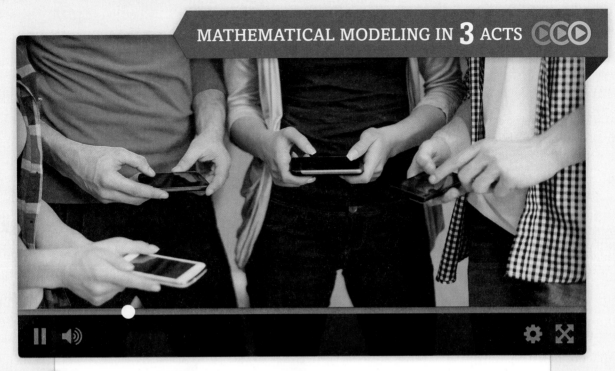

▶ Text Message

Text messages used be just that: text only. Now you can send multimedia messages (or MMS) with emojis, images, audio, and videos. Did you know Finland was the first country to offer text messaging to phone customers?

Some people send and receive so many texts that they use textspeak to make typing faster. RU 1 of them? You will see one person keep track of his text messages in this Modeling Mathematics in 3 Acts lesson.

TOPIC 10

VIDEOS Watch clips to support *Mathematical Modeling in 3 Acts Lessons* and **enVision®** *STEM Projects.*

CONCEPT SUMMARY Review key lesson content through multiple representations.

ASSESSMENT Show what you've learned.

GLOSSARY Read and listen to English and Spanish definitions.

TUTORIALS Get help from *Virtual Nerd*, right when you need it.

MATH TOOLS Explore math with digital tools and manipulatives.

Did You Know?

The average energy consumption in U.S. households is many times greater than countries in the rest of the world.

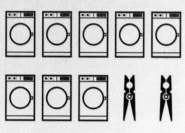

About 80% of American homes have a clothes dryer, which uses around **12% of the home's electricity** to dry about 300 loads of laundry each year.

Total Annual Energy Consumption for Select Countries (in million tons of oil equivalent)

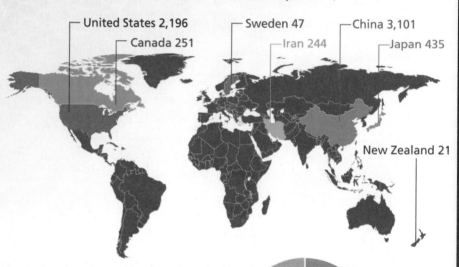

United States 2,196
Canada 251
Sweden 47
Iran 244
China 3,101
Japan 435
New Zealand 21

In the United States, petroleum, natural gas, and coal have provided most of the energy for more than 100 years.

About **86%** of the world's energy is supplied by fossil fuels.

In 2013, winds generated almost 3% of the world's electricity. World-wide, wind-generated power grows at a rate of about 17% per year.

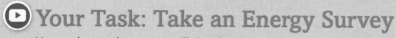

▶ Your Task: Take an Energy Survey

You and your classmates will develop a survey, and then gather and analyze data looking for ways to reduce energy consumption.

10-1

Analyzing Data Displays

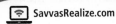

I CAN... organize and understand data using dot plots, histograms, and box plots.

👆 MODEL & DISCUSS

MARKET RESEARCHERS WANTED!

A clothing company is designing a new line of shirts. Look around your classroom and collect data about the color of top worn by each student. If a student's top has multiple colors, choose the most prevalent one.

A. Explain why you chose to organize the data the way that you did.

B. How do you think the company could use these data?

C. Use Appropriate Tools How would you display these data in a presentation?

❓ ESSENTIAL QUESTION

What information about data sets can you get from different data displays?

APPLICATION →

👆 EXAMPLE 1 Represent and Interpret Data in a Dot Plot

Manuel plans to buy a new car with the gas mileage shown. To determine if the gas mileage of this car is good, he gathers data on the estimated city driving fuel efficiency, in miles per gallon, of several other cars. How does the fuel efficiency of the car he wants to buy compare to the fuel efficiency of the other cars he researched?

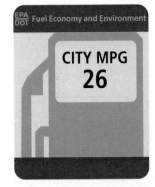

EPA DOT Fuel Economy and Environment

CITY MPG 26

25	45	26	35	31	26	30	28
29	26	28	26	27	27	28	28

CONSTRUCT ARGUMENTS
Why is a dot plot a good way to show individual values? What kind of data do other types of displays show?

Manuel wants to compare individual values, so a dot plot is a good way to show that information.

Create a dot plot of the data by first drawing a number line that represents the range of the data. Plot each value from the table as a dot above the number line.

> These data are a *cluster* because they are positioned close together.

> The data point at 45 is an *outlier* because it lies outside of most other data in the set.

20 21 22 23 24 25 26 27 28 29 30 31 32 33 34 35 36 37 38 39 40 41 42 43 44 45 46 47 48 49 50
City Fuel Efficiency (mpg)

Use the dot plot to interpret the data.

The dot plot shows that most of the values are clustered between 25 and 28.

The car Manuel plans to buy has about the same city fuel efficiency as comparable cars.

☑ Try It! 1. What might account for the outlier?

EXAMPLE 2 Represent and Interpret Data in a Histogram

A marketing team is about to launch a campaign for a new product that is targeted at adults aged 25–34 years. The team is researching the age range of viewers of a certain TV show to decide whether to advertise during the show. The data show the ages of a random sample of 30 viewers of the show. Based on the findings, should the marketing team launch their campaign during this particular show?

14	21	22	17	24	20	26	15	20	22	14	24	26	15	17
21	32	30	16	31	25	25	19	16	21	37	17	20	15	16

Histograms are often used to represent data over ranges of numbers.

To create a histogram, first decide on an appropriate interval for the data.

Create a frequency table to organize the data.

Age Range	Frequency
0–4	
5–9	
10–14	II
15–19	JHT JHT
20–24	JHT JHT
25–29	IIII
30–34	III
35–39	I
40–44	

Remember that the intervals must be consistent.

Use the frequency table to create a histogram.

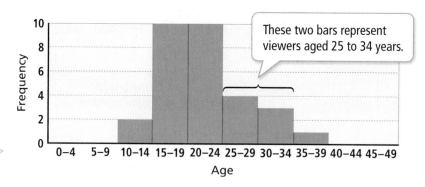

These two bars represent viewers aged 25 to 34 years.

COMMON ERROR
Be careful not to misinterpret the intervals. Each interval represents 5 possible values. Since the intervals start at 0, they are 0–4, 5–9, 10–14, and so on.

Use the histogram to interpret the data.

The histogram reveals that fewer than 25% of the viewers are between the ages of 25 and 35.

Based on this information, the marketing team should not launch their campaign during this particular show.

✓ **Try It!** 2. What age group would be a good match for products advertised on this TV show? Explain.

👆 **EXAMPLE 3**   Represent and Interpret Data in a Box Plot

Students at a local high school organized a fundraiser for charity. Kaitlyn, the student council president, announces that more than half of the students raised over $50 each. The amounts of money raised by a random sample of 24 students is shown. Do the data support Kaitlyn's claim?

$59	$42	$25	$38	$45	$54	$68	$32
$26	$54	$50	$45	$42	$48	$50	$25
$45	$36	$55	$27	$31	$32	$49	$54

Kaitlyn's claim is about the distribution of values, so a box plot will reveal the information needed.

A *box plot* shows the distribution of data using a 5-number summary.

The *minimum* value is the least value in the set.

The *maximum* value is the greatest value in the set.

The *median* is the middle value in the set when the numbers are arranged from least to greatest.

The *first quartile* is the middle number between the minimum value and the median. The *third quartile* is the middle number between the median and the maximum value.

List the data from least to greatest to identify each of these values.

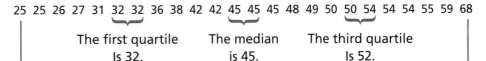

25 25 26 27 31 32 32 36 38 42 42 45 45 45 48 49 50 50 54 54 54 55 59 68

The first quartile Is 32.   The median is 45.   The third quartile Is 52.

The minimum value is 25.   The maximum value is 68.

Create a box plot of the data.

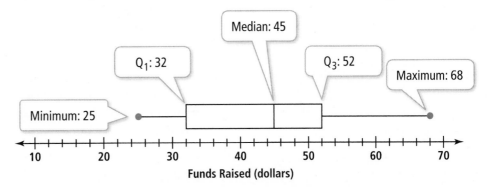

Median: 45

Q₁: 32

Q₃: 52

Maximum: 68

Minimum: 25

Funds Raised (dollars)

VOCABULARY
The interquartile range, *IQR*, represents the range of the middle 50% of the data. Subtract the Q_1 value from the Q_3 value to find the IQR. In this example the IQR is $52 - 32$, or 20.

Use the box plot to interpret the data. The box plot shows that, based on the sample, the median amount of money collected was $45. Since half of this population collected $45 or less, the data do not support Kaitlyn's claim.

 Try It!   3. Suppose Kaitlyn wants to make the statement that 25% of the students raised over a certain amount. What is that amount? Explain.

CONCEPTUAL
UNDERSTANDING

 EXAMPLE 4 Choose a Data Display

Helena's dance team scores 68 points at a competition. The scores for all of the teams that competed are shown.

66	89	81	75
90	79	82	68
80	82	65	80
81	66	81	83

A. Helena wants to know what place her team finished. Should Helena use a dot plot, histogram, or box plot to display the data?

Compare the features of the three types of data displays.

- A dot plot has dots for each value in the data. It shows clusters of data and outliers.

- A histogram groups values in a data set into ranges or intervals. Individual values are not displayed but trends are observable.

- A box plot shows center and spread of a data set. A box plot does not show individual data but summarizes the data using 5 key pieces of information.

Helena is interested in displaying individual scores. A dot plot will display the data in a way that is most helpful to Helena.

B. What place did Helena's team finish in the competition?

Create and analyze a dot plot of the data.

65 66 67 68 69 70 71 72 73 74 75 76 77 78 79 80 81 82 83 84 85 86 87 88 89 90
Dance Competition Scores

A dot plot reveals that Helena's team score was low compared to the other teams. Only three teams scored lower, so Helena's team placed 13th out of 16.

> **CONSTRUCT ARGUMENTS**
> What would be a good display choice if Helena wanted to compare her team's score with the median?

✓ **Try It!** 4. Which data display should Helena use if she wants to know what percent of the teams scored higher than her team? Explain.

CONCEPT SUMMARY Data Displays

Dot Plots	Histograms	Box Plots
WORDS Dot plots display each data value from a set of data. They show clusters, gaps, and outliers in a data set.	Histograms do not show individual values, but show clearly the shape of the data. The data are organized into intervals. The bars show the frequency, or number of times, that the data within that interval occur.	Box plots show the center (median) and spread of a distribution. Box plots provide the following information about a data set: minimum, maximum, and median values, and the first and third quartile.

GRAPHS

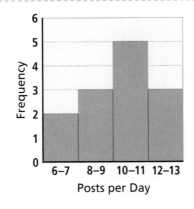

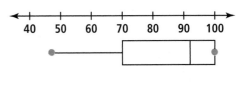

Do You UNDERSTAND?

1. **ESSENTIAL QUESTION** What information about data sets can you get from different data displays?

2. **Communicate Precisely** How is a dot plot different from a box plot? How are they similar?

3. **Use Appropriate Tools** If you want to see data values grouped in intervals, which data display should you choose? Explain.

4. **Error Analysis** Taylor says you can determine the mean of a data set from its box plot. Is Taylor correct? Explain your reasoning.

5. **Use Structure** Can you determine the minimum and maximum values of a data set simply by looking at its dot plot? Histogram? Box plot? Explain.

Do You KNOW HOW?

Use the data set shown for exercises 6–11.

7	5	8	15	4
9	10	1	12	8
13	7	11	8	10

6. Make a dot plot for the data. What information does the display reveal about the data set?

7. Make a histogram for the data. What information does the display reveal about the data set?

8. Make a box plot for the data. What information does the display reveal about the data set?

Identify the most appropriate data display to answer each question about the data set. Justify your response.

9. What is the median of the data set?

10. How many data values are greater than 7?

11. How many values fall in the interval 10 to 12?

UNDERSTAND

12. Reason A data set is represented by the box plot shown. Between which two values would the middle 50% of the data be found? Explain.

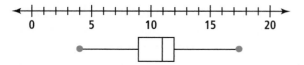

13. Generalize Write a scenario for which a dot plot would be the best display for a data set. Explain your thinking.

14. Error Analysis Describe and correct the errors a student made in analyzing the histogram shown.

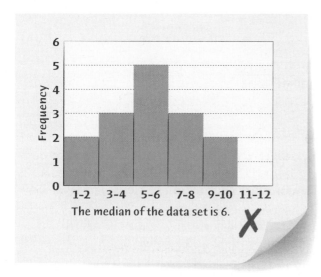

The median of the data set is 6. ✗

15. Higher Order Thinking The box plot represents a data set with 12 values. The minimum, first quartile, median, third quartile, and maximum values are 6, 8, 10, 12, and 14, respectively.

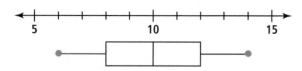

a. Is it possible to create a dot plot for the data set using just the box plot and the values given? Explain.

b. Is it possible to create a histogram using just the box plot and the values given? Explain.

PRACTICE

For each data set, create the data display that best reveals the answer to the question. Explain your reasoning. SEE EXAMPLES 1–4

16. What is the median value of the data set?

40	47	43	35
42	32	40	47
49	46	50	42
48	43	34	45

17. What is the frequency of the data value 83?

85	81	83	84	83	80
84	86	76	83	82	83
82	82	84	89	85	83

18. How many data values are between 7 and 9?

9.6	5.5	8.4	9.1	6.7
7.2	11.5	9.2	5.2	7.6
11.1	6.1	7.2	14.8	12.5
8.4	10.5	10.2	8.4	13.5

Choose whether a dot plot, histogram, or box plot is the most appropriate data display to answer each question about a data set. Explain.
SEE EXAMPLE 4

19. How many data values are greater than any given value in the data set?

20. What are the frequencies for each interval of 5 points?

21. 25% of the data values are less than which value?

Consider the data set represented by the dot plot. Create a different data display that better reveals the answer to each question. SEE EXAMPLES 1–4

22. How many data values are in the interval between 8 and 10 inclusive?

23. What is the first quartile of the data set?

APPLY

24. Model With Mathematics Isabel knits scarves and sells them online. The table shows the prices of the scarves she sold last month. At what prices were the middle 50% of the scarves sold? Create a data display that will reveal the answer.

Prices of Scarves ($)				
35	32	60	80	36
90	45	76	96	92
100	120	60	38	75
36	36	100	100	100
95	58	100	85	40

25. Make Sense and Persevere Lucy usually pays between $0.40 and $0.60 per ounce for her favorite shampoo. She gathers prices of the same shampoo at different stores near her home. Prices are shown in dollars in the table. Create a data display that allows Lucy to easily compare the price she is paying to the other prices. How does the price she is currently paying compare?

Shampoo Pricing Comparison				
0.55	0.95	0.29	0.65	0.39
0.99	0.42	1.10	0.99	0.75
0.65	0.99	0.34	0.85	0.99
0.95	0.75	0.95	0.50	0.75

26. Use Structure Aaron scores 82 points at his karate tournament. He wants to compare his score to the others in the competition to see how many competitors scored higher than he did. The table shows all scores for the competition. What type of data display is appropriate to answer his question? Create the data display and analyze Aaron's performance.

Karate Scores					
78	66	82	86	72	70
74	86	30	80	89	80
82	68	100	84	84	42
86	82	80	94	78	82

ASSESSMENT PRACTICE

27. Consider a box plot. Does a box plot display the features of a data set listed below? Select Yes or No.

	Yes	No
Median of the data set	☐	☐
Individual values in the data set	☐	☐
Outliers	☐	☐
Minimum of the data set	☐	☐

28. SAT/ACT From which display(s) can the median of a data set be determined?
Ⓐ Dot plot only
Ⓑ Box plot only
Ⓒ Dot plot and box plot
Ⓓ Histogram and box plot
Ⓔ Dot plot, histogram, and box plot

29. Performance Task A group of students use a stopwatch to record times for a 100-yard dash. Tell whether each student should choose a dot plot, a histogram, or a box plot to display the data. Explain your reasoning. Then create the display.

12.5	13.5	14.1	12.8	13.4
14.0	11.5	14.2	13.9	14.4
13.3	14.5	13.2	13.6	12.0
14.5	13.5	14.4	14.1	13.9

Part A Neil wants a data display that clearly shows the shape of the data distribution.

Part B Yuki wants a display that shows the spread of data above and below the median.

Part C Thato wants a display that groups the data by intervals.

Part D Edwin wants a display that he could use to find the mean of the data set.

10-2
Comparing Data Sets

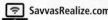 SavvasRealize.com

I CAN... use measures of center and spread to compare data sets.

Activity   Assess

CRITIQUE & EXPLAIN

The prices of paintings sold at two galleries in the last month are shown. Stacy and Diego both have a painting they want to sell.

- Stacy wants Gallery I to sell her painting because it has the highest sales price.

- Diego wants Gallery II to sell his painting because it has the most consistent sales prices.

A. Do you agree with Stacy or Diego? Explain your reasoning.

B. Reason What reason(s) could there be for the differences in sales prices between the two galleries and for the outlier in Gallery I?

Gallery I
$500 $800 $1,200
$750 $550 $15,000

Gallery II
$2,800 $3,500 $3,000
$2,750 $3,100

? ESSENTIAL QUESTION How can you use measures of center and spread to compare data sets?

EXAMPLE 1 Compare Data Sets Displayed in Dot Plots

Sawyer has narrowed his car search down to two different types of cars. To make an informed decision, he gathers data on estimated highway fuel efficiency (mpg) of the two different types of cars. The dot plots show the data for each type.

Type 1

30 31 32 33 34 35 36 37 38 39 40 41 42 43 44 45 46 47 48 49 50 51 52 53 54 55
Highway Fuel Efficiency (mpg)

Type 2

30 31 32 33 34 35 36 37 38 39 40 41 42 43 44 45 46 47 48 49 50 51 52 53 54 55
Highway Fuel Efficiency (mpg)

VOCABULARY
An *outlier* is a data value that is very different from the others. In the data set for Type 2, 51 appears to be an outlier.

A. If highway fuel efficiency is the most important feature to Sawyer, which type of car should Sawyer purchase?

The data displays suggest that Type 2 cars have better highway fuel efficiency. The data for Type 1 car are clustered from 33 to 38 and the data for Type 2 cars are clustered from 35 to 44.

Based on this data display, Sawyer should purchase a car in the Type 2 category.

CONTINUED ON THE NEXT PAGE

Go Online | SavvasRealize.com

EXAMPLE 1 CONTINUED

B. Sawyer wants more information about the fuel efficiency of each type of car, so he calculates the mean and the mean absolute deviation (MAD) of the two data sets. How can these measures help him make a more informed decision?

Mean Fuel Efficiency

    Type 1 Cars: 35.75 mpg
    Type 2 Cars: 40.25 mpg

The mean fuel efficiency of Type 2 cars is greater than the mean fuel efficiency of Type 1 cars.

Sawyer also wants to consider how much his data vary to determine reliability. The mean absolute deviation (MAD) is the mean of the differences between each value in a data set and the mean of the data set. The MAD helps you determine how much data vary within a particular data set.

To calculate mean absolute deviation, calculate the absolute value of the difference between each data point and the mean. Then find the mean of those differences.

MAD for Type 1 Cars (mean: 35.75)
$|33 - 35.75| = 2.75$
$|34 - 35.75| = 1.75$
$|35 - 35.75| = 0.75$
$|36 - 35.75| = 0.25$
$|37 - 35.75| = 1.25$
$|38 - 35.75| = 2.25$
$|41 - 35.75| = 5.25$

> Multiply each difference by the number of times it appears in the data set.

$2.75(2) + 1.75(3) + 0.75(3) + 0.25(3) + 1.25(2) + 2.25(2) + 5.25 = 26$

The sum of all of the differences between the data points and the mean is 26. Divide that by the number of data points to find the MAD.

$26 \div 16 \approx 1.63$

The MAD of Type 1 cars is about 1.63.

Use a similar process to find the MAD of Type 2 cars. The MAD of Type 2 cars is about 2.94.

So, while the mean fuel efficiency for Type 2 cars is greater than for Type 1 cars, there is more variation with Type 2 cars. This could mean that the expected fuel efficiency is less reliable for Type 2 cars.

 Try It! **1.** How does the outlier in the second data set affect the mean and the MAD?

> **EXAMPLE 2** Compare Data Sets Displayed in Box Plots

Kaitlyn and Philip go to neighboring high schools, and both are sponsoring charity fundraisers. Kaitlyn claims that students at her school are raising more for charity than the students at Philip's school. The amounts raised by a random sample of 30 students at each school are shown in the box plots below. Do the data support Kaitlyn's claim?

Kaitlyn's High School

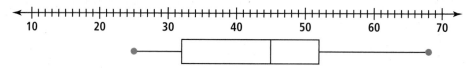

Philip's High School

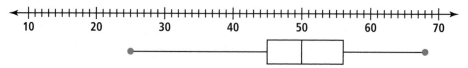

Analyze the distribution of values in each data set.

	Kaitlyn's High School	Philip's High School
Minimum Value	25	25
Maximum Value	68	68
First Quartile	32	45
Median	45	50
Third Quartile	52	56
Interquartile Range (IQR)	20	11

USE STRUCTURE

Recall that the interquartile range (IQR) is the difference of the third and first quartiles and represents the spread of the middle 50% of the data values. How does the structure of a box plot represent the IQR?

While the minimum and maximum amount of money raised at each school was the same, the spread of data points between the minimum and maximum values varies.

- The sample data show that 50% of the students at Kaitlyn's school raised between $32 and $52. At Philip's school, 50% of the students in the sample raised between $45 and $56.

- Based on the data, 50% of the students at Kaitlyn's school raised $45 or more; At Philip's school, 50% raised $50 or more.

The data do not support Kaitlyn's claim. Instead, they suggest that individual students at Philip's school raised more money than individual students at Kaitlyn's school.

 Try It! **2.** How does the IQR compare to the range for each school?

APPLICATION

EXAMPLE 3 Compare Data Sets Displayed in Histograms

A marketing team compares the ages of a random sample of 30 viewers of two popular new shows to decide which product to advertise during each show. During which show should the marketing team advertise a product that is targeted at adults aged 20–29?

Show 1

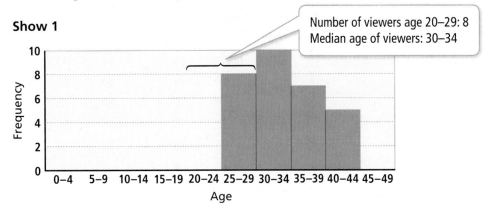

> Number of viewers age 20–29: 8
> Median age of viewers: 30–34

COMMON ERROR
When comparing histograms of data sets, be sure the intervals of the histogram are the same.

Show 2

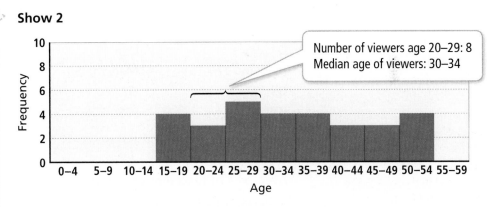

> Number of viewers age 20–29: 8
> Median age of viewers: 30–34

From the data displays, you can make several observations about the data collected by the marketing team.

- Of the 30 viewers in the sample, each show has 8 viewers between the ages of 20 and 29.

- Show 1 has no viewers between the ages of 20 and 24.

- Show 2 has viewers in each subsection of the target range; 20–24 and 25-29.

- Show 2 also has viewers in the age brackets just above and just below the target range, who are potential customers.

Based on this sample, the marketing team should advertise during Show 2 because that show has broader appeal.

 Try It! **3.** If the marketing team wants to advertise a product that is targeted at adults 25–34, during which show should they advertise? Explain.

CONCEPTUAL UNDERSTANDING →

EXAMPLE 4 **Make Observations With Data Displays**

Nadia collected data from 15 classmates about the number of text messages they send on school days and the number of text messages they send on non-school days. Nadia organized her data in the tables below. How can you use a box plot to compare the data that she collected?

Average # of texts sent on school days		
14	23	18
17	19	26
4	9	0
19	22	25
8	15	16

Average # of texts sent on non-school days		
80	45	50
50	60	75
20	40	0
75	50	60
30	40	50

USE APPROPRIATE TOOLS
You may want to enter the data into a spreadsheet so you can easily sort and perform calculations.

Step 1: Calculate the five-number summary for each set of data.

School Day Texts

Minimum: 0

Maximum: 26

Q1: 9

Median: 17

Q3: 22

IQR: 13

Non-School Day Texts

Minimum: 0

Maximum: 80

Q1: 40

Median: 50

Q3: 60

IQR: 20

Step 2: Use the information to create a box plot to represent each set of data.

Average # of texts sent on school days

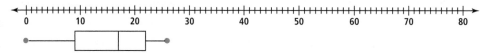

Average # of texts sent on non-school days

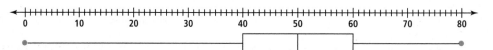

Step 3: Use the data displays to make observations about the data sets.

- Students send far more texts on non-school days than on school days.
- There is more variation in the number of texts sent on non-school days than on school days.
- One person does not send any texts on non-school days. This represents an outlier because it is far from the other data values.

 Try It! **4. a.** Provide a possible explanation for each of the observations that was made.

b. Make 2 more observations about the data that Nadia collected.

CONCEPT SUMMARY Comparing Data Sets

You can compare data sets using statistical measures of center and measures of variability or spread.

DOT PLOTS Dot plots show how a particular data point fits in with the rest of the data.

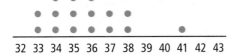 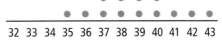

For a more specific measure of variance, find the mean absolute deviation.

BOX PLOTS Box plots show the minimum, maximum, and measures of center of the data.

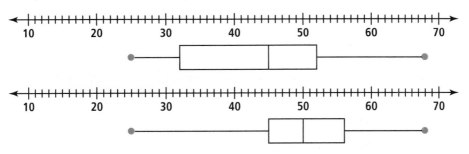

HISTOGRAMS Histograms allow you to easily compare data ranges.

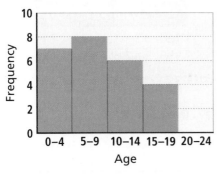 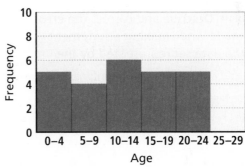

Do You UNDERSTAND?

1. **ESSENTIAL QUESTION** How can you use measures of center and spread to compare data sets?

2. **Communicate Precisely** How are the MAD and the IQR similar? How are they different?

3. **Reason** When comparing two sets of data, it is common to look at the means. Why might the MAD be a useful piece of information to compare in addition to the mean?

4. **Error Analysis** Val says that if the minimum and maximum values of two data sets are the same, the median will be the same. Is Val correct? Explain.

Do You KNOW HOW?

Use the two data sets.

Data Set A					Data Set B				
86	87	98	85	90	80	89	70	75	87
94	89	83	76	84	88	75	87	89	81
83	90	87	87	86	84	87	88	81	87

5. How do the means compare?

6. How do the MADs compare?

7. How do the medians compare?

8. How do the IQRs compare?

9. Which measures of center and spread are better for comparing data sets A and B? Explain.

UNDERSTAND

10. Reason The mean of the data set represented by the histogram is 12. What is a reasonable estimate for the median? Explain your reasoning.

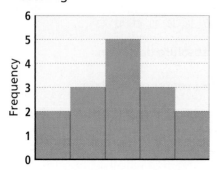

11. Construct Arguments The means of two data sets are the same, but the median of one data set is much smaller than the median of the other data set. What conclusions can you make about the sets from this information?

12. Error Analysis Describe and correct the errors a student made when making a statement based on the data set represented by the dot plot.

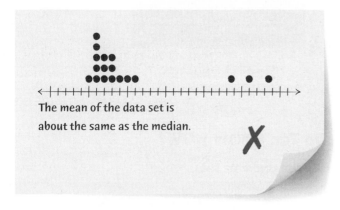

The mean of the data set is about the same as the median. ✗

13. Communicate Precisely How are the IQR and the range of a data set similar in terms of comparing data sets? How are they different?

14. Higher Order Thinking Two data sets each have a median of 10. The first data set has an IQR of 22 and the second data set has an IQR of 8.

  a. What conclusions can you make about the data sets? Explain.

  b. Is it possible to also make a prediction about the MADs from the information given? Explain.

PRACTICE

For each pair of data sets, compare the means and the MADs, and then the medians and the IQRs. Decide which measures are better for comparing the data sets. Explain your reasoning.
SEE EXAMPLES 1–4

15.

Data Set A			
5	6	5	4
5	4	5	6
6	5	4	5
4	5	6	5

Data Set B			
5	9	2	5
6	1	5	8
3	5	5	4
5	7	4	6

16.

Data Set A				
3.0	2.8	3.2	3.3	3.2
3.4	3.3	2.9	3.0	4.5
4.8	3.1	3.2	4.9	3.1

Data Set B				
1.9	3.3	1.5	3.2	3.1
3.4	3.0	3.2	3.4	1.6
3.2	3.6	3.5	3.1	3.3

17. Data Set A

70 71 72 73 74 75 76 77 78 79 80 81 82 83 84 85

Data Set B

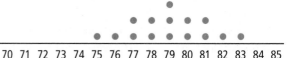

70 71 72 73 74 75 76 77 78 79 80 81 82 83 84 85

18. A researcher claims that students tend to have more apps on their smart phones than adults. Do the data support the researcher's claim? Explain. SEE EXAMPLE 2

Number of Apps

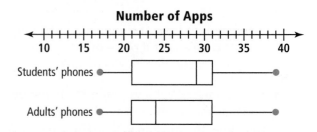

PRACTICE & PROBLEM SOLVING

APPLY

19. Model With Mathematics The mean score on last year's math final exam was 82, with MAD of 3.5 points. Scores for this year's exam are shown in the table. How do the scores for the two years compare?

Math Final Exam Scores				
85	82	88	84	85
84	86	70	95	86
99	71	85	92	79
88	85	91	82	85
86	75	84	78	100

20. Make Sense and Persevere The points of each player on Parker's basketball team for the season are shown in the table. The points of an opposing team are represented by the box plot. How does Parker's team compare?

Points per Player				
35	32	60	80	36
90	45	76	96	92
100	120	60	38	75

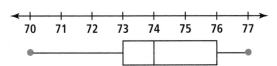

21. Use Structure The label on the cereal box says the weight is 12 ounces. The dot plots show weights of two random samples of 16 boxes packaged on two different machines. How can you compare the data sets to see if there is a problem with one of the machines?

Machine A

11.5 11.6 11.7 11.8 11.9 12.0 12.1 12.2 12.3 12.4 12.5

Machine B

11.5 11.6 11.7 11.8 11.9 12.0 12.1 12.2 12.3 12.4 12.5

ASSESSMENT PRACTICE

22. The table shows the number of minutes Dylan and Kyle spent on their homework each night over the past 5 nights.

Based on this data, which of the following statements are true? Select all that apply.

Dylan	Kyle
45	30
40	35
80	50
60	70
20	30

Ⓐ The median of Kyle's data is greater than the median of Dylan's data.

Ⓑ On average, Dylan spends more time on homework than Kyle.

Ⓒ The mean is greater than the median in both groups.

Ⓓ The IQR of the data is greater for Kyle.

23. SAT/ACT The histograms that correspond to two data sets look identical. What conclusion can you make about the data sets.

Ⓐ The data points in each set are the same.

Ⓑ The mean of each of the data sets is the same.

Ⓒ The median of each of the data sets is the same.

Ⓓ none of these

24. Performance Task A consumer group tested battery life times for two different smart phones. Results are shown in the tables below.

Phone A				
10.0	14.2	12.0	15.1	16.0
14.0	0.9	14.2	9.5	15.0
14.2	15.0	9.5	12.5	14.2
13.0	15.0	14.2	11.0	9.0

Phone B				
12.5	13.0	14.0	13.5	15.0
14.0	14.0	12.0	15.0	12.8
12.8	15.0	13.0	15.2	16.0
14.0	13.6	14.2	13.8	15.1

Part A Find the mean and MAD for each data set.

Part B Find the median and IQR for each data set.

Part C Create data displays that will allow you to compare the two data sets.

Part D Which cell phone battery is likely to last longer? Explain your reasoning.

10-3
Interpreting the Shapes of Data Displays

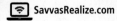
SavvasRealize.com

I CAN... interpret shapes of data displays representing different types of data distributions.

A meteorologist looks at measures of center to summarize the last 10 days of actual high temperatures.

SUN 75° MON 73° TUE 72° WED 75° THU 73° FRI 75° SAT 76° SUN 90° MON 95° TUE 95°
Average High 80°

A. Find the median, mean, and mode of the data.

B. Which of the three measures of center seems to be the most accurate in describing the data? Explain.

C. Communicate Precisely How can you describe the data?

ESSENTIAL QUESTION ⟩ How does the shape of a data set help you understand the data?

CONCEPTUAL UNDERSTANDING ⟶

EXAMPLE 1 Interpret the Shape of a Distribution

The histograms show the weights of all of the dogs entered in two different categories in a dog show. Consider each data set. What inferences can you make based on the shape of the data?

The histogram is *symmetric* and shows the data are evenly distributed around the center.

The mean and median of the data are equal or almost equal.

Based on the data, you can infer that most of the dogs in this category weigh between 30 and 59 pounds.

GENERALIZE
The mean includes all the values in the data set for its calculation. Should the mean always be used to make an inference when the data are evenly distributed?

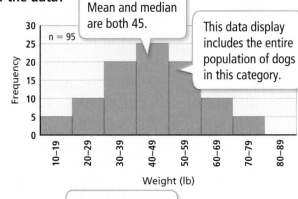

Mean and median are both 45.

This data display includes the entire population of dogs in this category.

The histogram shows the data are *skewed right*. The mean is greater than the median.

Based on the data, you can infer that most of the dogs in this category weigh less than 30 pounds.

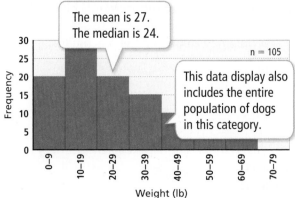

The mean is 27. The median is 24.

This data display also includes the entire population of dogs in this category.

☑ **Try It!** 1. Suppose a third category of dogs has a mean of 40 lb and a median of 32 lb. What can you infer about the shape of the histogram for the dogs in this category?

APPLICATION

EXAMPLE 2 Interpret the Shape of a Skewed Data Display

Customers of a bagel shop complained that some bagels weigh less than the amount on the label. A quality control manager randomly sampled 30 bagels and weighed them. Based on this sample, is a change in the process for making bagels warranted?

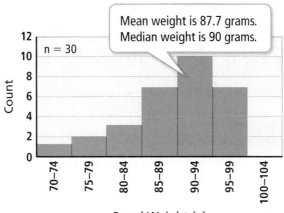

Mean weight is 87.7 grams.
Median weight is 90 grams.

COMMON ERROR
You may think that a conclusion can be made based on this sample. However, because the sample size is small, it is difficult to ensure that the sample is representative of the entire population.

The shape of the data display is skewed left. That is common when the mean of a data set is less than the median of a data set.

Because the mean of the sample is less than the advertised weight, the quality control manager wants to recommend some changes to the production process. However, because the sample consists of only 30 bagels, the manager decides to generate another random sample.

Try It! 2. How do skewed data affect the mean in this context?

EXAMPLE 3 Compare Shapes of Skewed Data Displays

The manager generates a second random sample of 30 bagels. Is a change in the process for making bagels warranted based on this sample? How does this sample compare to the previous sample?

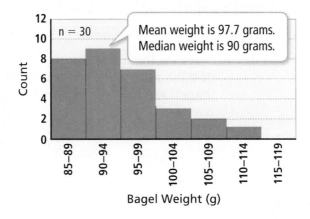

Mean weight is 97.7 grams.
Median weight is 90 grams.

CONTINUED ON THE NEXT PAGE

EXAMPLE 3 CONTINUED

The shape of this data display is skewed right. This often occurs when the mean of the data is greater than the median of the data. In this example, the mean is greater than the advertised weight and greater than the mean weight from the first sample.

Based only on this sample, the manager could recommend changes. However, because this sample gives opposite results from the first sample, the manager now has conflicting findings about the mean weights of the bagels.

 Try It! **3.** What does the shape of the histogram for the second sample tell you about the data?

 EXAMPLE 4 **Interpret the Shape of a Symmetric Data Display**

REASON
How does the increased sample size affect the inferences that are made about the population?

The quality control manager generates a third random sample that contains twice as many data points. A histogram that represents this third, larger sample is shown below. Based on this sample, is a change in the process for making bagels warranted?

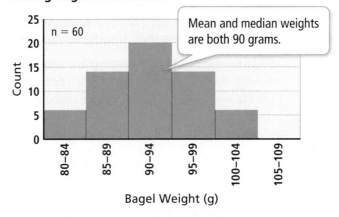

The data points are symmetrically distributed around the center. In this sample, the mean and median weights are the same.

Based on this larger sample, the quality control manager determines that the process of making bagels does not need to change because the data are centered around the advertised weight of 90 grams.

 Try It! **4.** Suppose the quality control manager adds another 10 bagels to the third sample. If 5 of the bagels are 78 g each, and 5 of the bagels are 106 g each, would that affect the mean and median weights? Explain.

Go Online | SavvasRealize.com

CONCEPTUAL
UNDERSTANDING   ✋ **EXAMPLE 5**   Comparing the Shapes of Data Sets

Jennifer is considering job offers from three different school districts. The histograms show the salary ranges for similar positions in each school district. What do the shapes of the data tell Jennifer about the teacher salaries in each district?

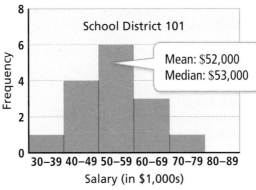

The data from teachers with similar positions in School District 101 have salaries that center around the mean. This indicates that the salaries of the teachers are fairly evenly distributed.

Mean: $52,000
Median: $53,000

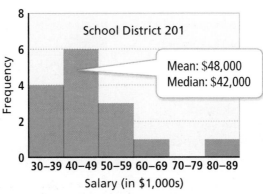

The data from teachers in School District 201 is skewed right. Most of the teachers in that district have salaries that are lower than the mean. This indicates that there are only a few teachers that make a higher salary.

Mean: $48,000
Median: $42,000

COMMON ERROR
When data displays are "skewed right," the "tail" of the graph goes toward the right. When data displays are "skewed left," the tail goes to the left.

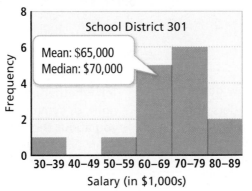

The data from teachers in School District 301 is skewed left. Most of the teachers with similar positions have salaries that are higher than the mean. This indicates that there are more teachers that make a higher salary.

Mean: $65,000
Median: $70,000

If Jennifer's starting salary is the same at each school district, she should strongly consider School District 101 or School District 301. Based on the data represented here, these districts have more potential for Jennifer to advance her salary.

 Try It!   **5.** Suppose a fourth school district offers Jennifer a job. School District 401 has a mean salary of $57,000 and a median salary of $49,000. Should Jennifer consider accepting the job offer with School District 401? Explain.

CONCEPT SUMMARY Interpreting the Shapes of Data Displays

WORDS The shape of a data display reveals a lot about the data set.

In a **symmetric** data display, the data points are evenly spread on either side of the center. The mean is equal (or approximately equal) to the median.

In a **skewed** data display, the data points are unevenly spread on either side of the center (median). A data display can be skewed right or skewed left. The mean and median are not equal.

GRAPHS This data set is symmetric. There are a similar number of data points greater than and less than the mean.

Cost of City Parking

$n = 250$

The mean is $25 per day.

One family with 5 pets skewed the data to the right. The very small sample size makes inferences unreliable.

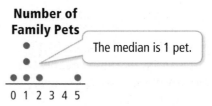

Number of Family Pets

The median is 1 pet.

0 1 2 3 4 5

Do You UNDERSTAND?

1. **ESSENTIAL QUESTION** How does the shape of a data set help you understand the data?

2. **Use Structure** How are the shapes of dot plots, histograms, and box plots similar? How are they different?

3. **Error Analysis** Nicholas says that the display for a skewed data distribution is symmetrical about the mean. Is Nicholas correct? Explain your reasoning.

Do You KNOW HOW?

Tell whether each display is skewed left, skewed right, or symmetric. Interpret what the display tells you about the data set.

4.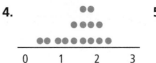

5.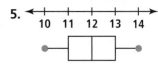

6.

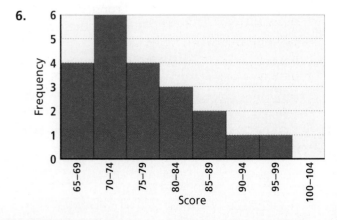

Go Online | SavvasRealize.com

PRACTICE & PROBLEM SOLVING

UNDERSTAND

7. Construct Arguments A student in your class does not understand why the mean is less than the median when a data display is skewed left. How can you explain this relationship to the student?

8. Look for Relationships Two data sets have the same median. If one data set is skewed right and the other is skewed left, how are the means of the two data sets related?

9. Error Analysis Describe and correct the error(s) a student made in interpreting the shape of a box plot.

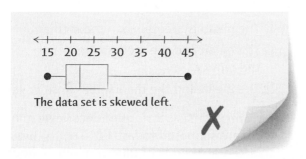

The data set is skewed left. ✗

10. Reason Two data sets both have a mean of 10. The first set has a MAD of 1.5, and the second has a MAD of 3. How are the shapes of the data displays similar? How are they different?

11. Higher Order Thinking Data display A is symmetric with a mean of 50 and a MAD of 5. Data display B is symmetric with a mean of 75 and a MAD of 5.

a. How are the data displays similar? How are they different?

b. If the shapes of the displays are not identical, how could values in data set B be changed so that the displays are exactly the same?

12. Make Sense and Persevere The data represent the average number of hours 12 students spend on homework each night. Create two different data sets that could be represented by the display.

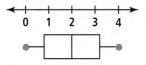

PRACTICE

Compare each pair of data displays. Tell whether each display is skewed left, skewed right, or symmetric. SEE EXAMPLES 1–3

13. Data Set A

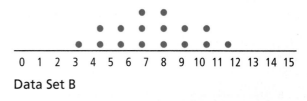

Data Set B

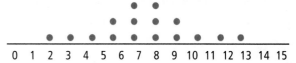

14. Data Set A

Data Set B

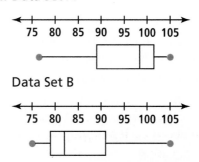

Interpret the shape of each display for the given context and make an inference based on a measure of center. SEE EXAMPLES 4 AND 5

15. The data represent amounts raised by students for a charity.

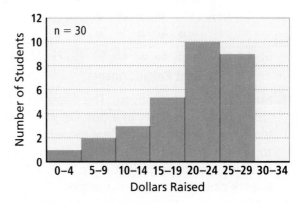

16. The data represent thousands of points scored in a video game tournament.

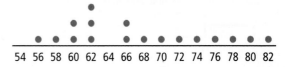

APPLY

17. Mathematical Connections The displays represent house prices in a town over two consecutive years. What do the displays tell you about the change in house prices in the two years?

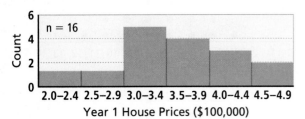

Year 1 House Prices ($100,000)

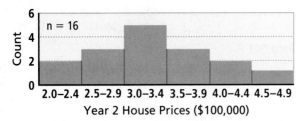

Year 2 House Prices ($100,000)

18. Make Sense and Persevere Amelia gathered data about the heights of students at her school. Based on the displays, what inferences can you make about each sample?

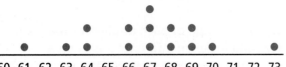

Student Heights (inches)

Student Heights (inches)

19. Make Sense and Persevere The displays show scores on two versions of a test. On which test is a randomly selected student more likely to get a higher score? On which version is a randomly selected student more likely to have a score close to the mean? Explain.

Test 1

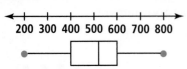

Test 2

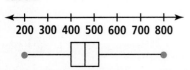

ASSESSMENT PRACTICE

20. A data display is symmetrical about the data value 10. Select all that apply.

Ⓐ The mean is about 10.

Ⓑ The median is about 10.

Ⓒ The mean must be greater than the median.

Ⓓ The median must be greater than the mean.

Ⓔ The majority of data values in the data set are greater than 10.

21. SAT/ACT The shape of a data set is relatively symmetrical. What does that indicate about the measures of center?

Ⓐ The mean is less than the median.

Ⓑ The mean is greater than the median.

Ⓒ The mean and the median are exactly the same.

Ⓓ The mean and the median are close in value.

22. Performance Task Strings of decorative mini lights are supposed to last 1,000 hours, with an acceptable error of plus or minus 50 hours. Data from two quality control tests are given.

Mini Lights Lifespan

TEST 1				
975	1,025	950	950	975
1,050	925	1,050	1,025	1,050
1,000	1,075	975	950	1,025

TEST 2				
975	1,000	1,025	1,000	1,000
1,025	1,000	950	975	1,025
1,000	975	1,050	1,000	1,000

Part A Find the mean, MAD, median, and IQR for each data set.

Part B Select the type of data display that you think will best allow you to compare the data sets. Explain your reasoning. Create the data displays.

Part C Interpret and compare the shapes of the data displays. What do the displays tell you about the quality of the mini lights?

10-4

Standard Deviation

I CAN... quantify and analyze the spread of data.

VOCABULARY
• normal distribution
• standard deviation
• variance

✋ MODEL & DISCUSS

A meteorologist compares the high temperatures for two cities during the past 10 days.

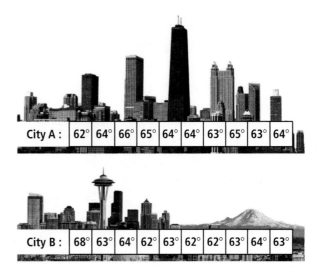

City A : | 62° | 64° | 66° | 65° | 64° | 64° | 63° | 65° | 63° | 64°

City B : | 68° | 63° | 64° | 62° | 63° | 62° | 62° | 63° | 64° | 63°

A. Create a data display for each city's high temperatures.

B. Use Structure What does the shape of each data display indicate about the data set and the measures of center?

❓ ESSENTIAL QUESTION

Why does the way in which data are spread out matter?

✋ EXAMPLE 1 | Interpret the Variability of a Data Set

The makers of a certain brand of light bulbs claim that the average life of the bulb is 1,200 hours. The life spans, in hours, of a sample of Brand A light bulbs are shown. How close to the claim were the light bulbs in this sample?

| 1,150 | 1,231 | 1,305 | 1,080 | 1,125 | 1,295 | 1,127 | 1,184 | 1,099 | 1,123 |
| 1,204 | 1,345 | 1,173 | 1,126 | 1,220 | 1,245 | 1,283 | 1,225 | 1,185 | 1,275 |

A. **What type of data display will provide the best view of the data?**

The numbers in the data set span a large range of numbers. To understand how these numbers relate to the claimed mean, create a histogram.

USE STRUCTURE
How does the shape of the distribution help you identify the mean?

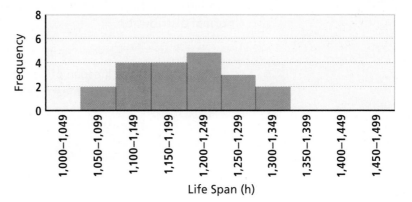

CONTINUED ON THE NEXT PAGE

B. What does the display reveal about the data?

The data forms a bell-shaped curve. Data that is in this shape is said to have a **normal distribution**.

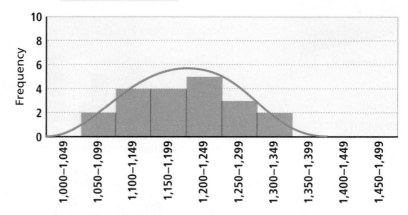

LOOK FOR RELATIONSHIPS
Most data values in a normally distributed set are clustered around the mean. The farther from the mean, the fewer data values there are.

When data are normally distributed, the most useful measure of spread is the **standard deviation**. Standard deviation is a measure that shows how data vary, or deviate, from the mean.

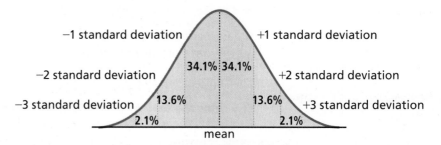

In a normal distribution,

- About 68% of data fall within one standard deviation of the mean.

- About 95% of data fall within two standard deviations of the mean.

- About 99.7% of data fall within three standard deviations of the mean.

The standard deviation for this sample of lightbulbs is 75.5 hours.

The mean of this data set is 1,200. Light bulbs with a life span between 1,124.5 hours and 1,275.5 hours lie within one standard deviation of the mean. In a large sample drawn randomly among such light bulbs, we would always expect about 68% of the life spans to be within one standard deviation of the mean thanks to the predictive power of the normal distribution.

 Try It! **1.** What is the lifespan of light bulbs that are within 2 standard deviations of the mean? Within 3 standard deviations of the mean?

CONCEPTUAL
UNDERSTANDING

EXAMPLE 2 **Calculate the Standard Deviation of a Sample**

The table shows the number of cars sold by an auto sales associate over an eight-week period. How much variability do the data show?

| 18 | 25 | 18 | 10 | 17 | 15 | 18 | 15 |

You can find the variability by solving for the standard deviation for a sample, using the formula $s = \sqrt{\dfrac{\sum(x - \bar{x})^2}{n - 1}}$. To calculate it, follow these steps.

Step 1 Find the mean of the data by finding the sum of the data points and dividing by 8. The notation $\bar{x}$ is used to indicate the mean.

$\bar{x} = 17$

Step 2 Find the difference between each data value, x, and the mean, $\bar{x}$. Then square each difference.

> **COMMON ERROR**
> Remember to square the differences between each data value and the mean. Otherwise, the sum of the differences will be zero.

x	18	25	18	10	17	15	18	15
$\bar{x}$	17	17	17	17	17	17	17	17
$x - \bar{x}$	1	8	1	−7	0	−2	1	−2
$(x - \bar{x})^2$	1	64	1	49	0	4	1	4

Step 3 Find the variance.

The **variance** of a total population, often noted σ^2, is the mean of the squares of the differences between each data value and the mean. When finding the variance of a sample, often noted s^2, dividing by n provides too small an estimate of the variance of the population. This is because data points from the sample are likely to cluster more closely around the sample mean than the population mean. If you divide by $n - 1$ instead of n, you get a slightly bigger number that is closer to the true population variance.

$s^2 = \dfrac{1 + 64 + 1 + 49 + 0 + 4 + 1 + 4}{7}$

$s^2 \approx 17.71$

> In this sample, $n = 8$ so we divide by $n - 1$, or 7.

Step 4 Take the square root of the variance to find the standard deviation, s.

$s \approx \sqrt{17.71}$

$s \approx 4.21$

> Since only whole cars can be sold, it makes sense to round the standard deviation to 4.

The standard deviation is about 4 cars and the mean is about 17 cars, so there is some variability in the data. The sales associate will sell between 13 and 21 cars about 68% of the time because those values are one standard deviation from the mean.

Try It! **2.** The table shows the number of cars sold by the auto sales associate over the next eight-week period. How much variability do the data show?

| 12 | 14 | 29 | 10 | 17 | 16 | 18 | 16 |

👆 **EXAMPLE 3**   Find Standard Deviation of a Population

The table displays the number of points scored by a football team during each of their regular season games.

24	13	10	21	18	3
27	18	20	14	7	27

A. What are the mean and standard deviation for this data set?

Find the mean of the data by finding the sum and dividing by 16.

$\bar{x} \approx 16.8$

Find the variance. Use n as the denominator because the data represent the full population.

> **STUDY TIP**
> Use the Greek letter σ (sigma) for standard deviation when working with *populations*. Use s when working with *samples*.

$$\sigma^2 = \frac{\sum(x - \bar{x})^2}{n}$$

$$\sigma^2 \approx \frac{51.36 + 14.69 + 46.69 + 17.36 + 1.36 + 191.36 + 103.36 + 1.36 + 10.03 + 8.03 + 96.69 + 103.36}{12}$$

$\sigma^2 \approx 53.8$

> In this example, divide by n because you are working with the entire population of games.

Find the standard deviation by taking the square root of the variance.

$\sigma \approx \sqrt{53.8}$

$\sigma \approx 7.3$

The mean number of points that the team scored was about 17. The standard deviation is about 7.3. This means that the team scored between about 10 and 25 points in about 68 percent of their games.

B. The team played in two post-season games, scoring 7 points in one and 14 points in the other. How do these games affect the overall mean and standard deviation of the number of points scored all season?

Use graphing technology to find the mean and standard deviation.

Enter all 14 scores as a list in the graphing calculator.

Use the STAT menu, to find the mean and standard deviation.

When the team includes their post-season games, the mean number of points scored decreases to about 15.9. The standard deviation remains about 7.3.

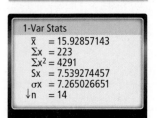

✅ **Try It!**   **3.** What was the range of points that the team scored in 95% of their regular season games?

APPLICATION   **EXAMPLE 4**   **Compare Data Sets Using Standard Deviation**

The histograms show the life spans of a sample of light bulbs from 2 companies. The first shows a sample from Brand A and the second from Brand B. The red lines indicate the mean and each standard deviation from the mean. Compare the distributions of life spans for the two light bulb brands.

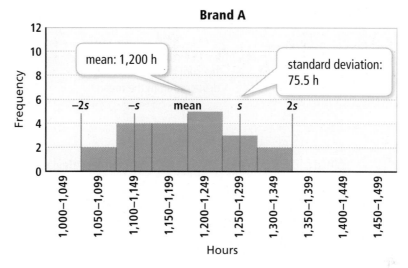

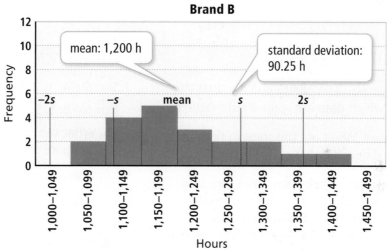

Both brands of light bulbs have an average life of about 1,200 hours.

USE STRUCTURE
How does the shape of each graph help you compare the standard deviations?

The standard deviation for the data set for Brand A is less than the standard deviation for Brand B. This suggests that Brand A light bulbs show less variability in their life spans.

Since their light bulbs are more consistently closer to the mean, Brand A light bulbs are more predictable in their life spans than Brand B.

 Try It!   **4.** Compare Brand C, with mean 1,250 hours and standard deviation 83 hours, to Brands A and B.

CONCEPT SUMMARY Standard Deviation

WORDS › Standard deviation is a measure of spread, or variability. It indicates by how much the values in a data set deviate from the mean. It is the square root of the variance. The variance is the average of the squared deviations from the mean. When data are normally distributed (in a bell curve), the mean and the standard deviation describe the data set completely.

ALGEBRA ›

Standard Deviation of a Sample

$$s = \sqrt{\frac{\sum(x - \bar{x})^2}{n - 1}}$$

the sum of the squares of the deviation from the mean

Standard Deviation of a Population

$$s = \sqrt{\frac{\sum(x - \bar{x})^2}{n}}$$

DIAGRAM ›

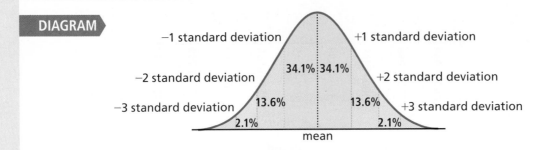

−1 standard deviation   +1 standard deviation

34.1% 34.1%

−2 standard deviation   +2 standard deviation

−3 standard deviation   13.6%   13.6%   +3 standard deviation

2.1%   2.1%

mean

Do You UNDERSTAND?

1. **ESSENTIAL QUESTION** › Why does the way in which data are spread out matter?

2. **Generalize** What are the steps in finding standard deviation?

3. **Error Analysis** Marisol says that standard deviation is a measure of how much the values in a data set deviate from the median. Is Marisol correct? Explain.

4. **Use Structure** If you add 10 to every data value in a set, what happens to the mean, range, and standard deviation. Why?

Do You KNOW HOW?

Sample A: 1, 2, 2, 5, 5, 5, 6, 6

Sample B: 5, 9, 9, 10, 10, 10, 11, 11

5. What can you determine by using range to compare the spread of the two data sets?

6. Find the standard deviation for each data set.

7. How can you use standard deviation to compare the spread of each data set?

8. Based on the histogram, what data values are within one standard deviation of the mean?

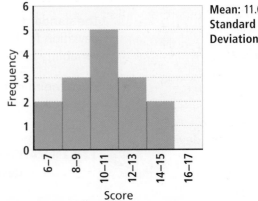

Mean: 11.05
Standard
Deviation: 2.40

✏ PRACTICE & PROBLEM SOLVING

UNDERSTAND

9. Generalize Two data sets have the same number of values. The first data set has a mean of 7.2 and a standard deviation of 1.25. The second data set has a mean of 7.2 and a standard deviation of 2.5.

   a. How can you tell which data set is more spread out?

   b. How is the shape of a histogram for the first data set different from the shape of a histogram for the second data set?

10. Error Analysis Describe and correct the errors a student made in calculating the standard deviation of a data set.

$$\sigma^2 = \frac{(-4) + 2 + (-1) + (-3) + 5 + 1}{6} = \frac{0}{6} = 0$$

$$\sigma = \sqrt{0} = 0 \qquad ✗$$

11. Use Appropriate Tools The screen shows statistics for a data set that has been entered into a graphing calculator. Does 8.7 fall within 2 standard deviations of the mean of the data set? Explain.

```
1-Var Stats
 x̄   = 13.14035088
 Σx  = 2247
 Σx² = 32883
 Sx  = 4.443522436
 σx  = 4.43051063
↓n   = 171
```

12. Higher Order Thinking A data set has data one standard deviation below the mean at 76.2 and data one standard deviation above the mean at 105.4.

   a. What is the mean of the data set?

   b. What is the standard deviation of the data set?

   c. What end values of the data are two standard deviations from the mean?

PRACTICE

Find and use the mean and the standard deviation to compare the variability of each pair of sample data sets. SEE EXAMPLES 1, 2, AND 4

13. Data Set A: 6, 9, 1, 2, 3, 4, 4, 5

   Data Set B: 10, 5, 5, 2, 3, 7, 4, 8

14.

Data Set A	Data Set B
21.25	41.50
42.25	29.25
2.00	39.75
40.50	40.00
19.75	38.25
57.75	51.25
39.25	42.00
78.75	31.00
38.50	37.75
62.25	49.00

15. Find and use the mean and standard deviation to compare the variability of the populations represented in the dot plots. SEE EXAMPLES 3–4

Data Set A

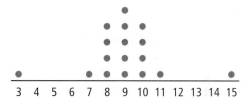

Data Set B

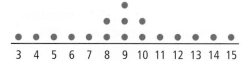

Data values in normally distributed data sets A and B are integers from 0 to 30 inclusive. Identify the range of values that satisfies each description. SEE EXAMPLE 2

Data Set A: mean: 12; standard deviation: 2

Data Set B: mean: 18; standard deviation: 3

16. All data values within 2 standard deviations from the mean of data set A

17. All data values more than 2 standard deviations from the mean of data set A

18. All data values within 1 standard deviation of the mean of data set B

PRACTICE & PROBLEM SOLVING

APPLY

19. Make Sense and Persevere The data display shows the number of runners with finishing times under 7 hours for all marathons run in a given year. How could you estimate the number of runners who had finishing times less than 2 standard deviations below the mean?

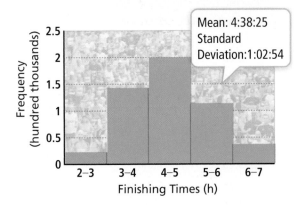

> Mean: 4:38:25
> Standard Deviation: 1:02:54

20. Make Sense and Persevere Last year, twelve hydrangea bushes had a mean of 14 blooms each, with a standard deviation of 2. The dot plot shows the number of blooms on the same bushes this year after a new plant food is used. What conclusions can you draw about the use of the new plant food and the number of blooms?

Hydrangeas with New Plant Food

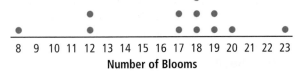

Number of Blooms

21. Make Sense and Persevere On a standardized test with the given statistics, about 68% of the scores fall within 1 standard deviation of the mean and about 95% of the scores fall within two standard deviations of the mean.

Mean Score: 450   **Standard Deviation:** 125

Total Number of Test Takers: 78,000

What is your score if you can say that you scored above the middle 95% of the people who took the test? How many test takers can say that?

ASSESSMENT PRACTICE

22. Consider a data set with a mean of 5.72 and a standard deviation of 1.55. Are the numbers within one standard deviation of the mean? Select *Yes* or *No*.

	Yes	No
7.51	❑	❑
4.18	❑	❑
4.16	❑	❑
10.00	❑	❑

23. SAT/ACT The variance for a data set with 8 items is 144. What is the standard deviation?

Ⓐ 4

Ⓑ 8

Ⓒ 12

Ⓓ none of these

24. Performance Task The table shows the top ten average driving distances in 2015 for male and female professional golfers. The mean for men is 310.9 yards, and the mean for women is 267.2 yards.

Men Average Drive(yd)	Women Average Drive(yd)
317.7	274.4
315.2	269.4
313.7	269.2
311.6	267.6
309.9	267.1
309.8	266.2
309.0	265.3
308.2	265.1
307.7	264.0
306.1	263.0

Part A Find the range for each data set. What do the ranges tell you about gender and average driving distance?

Part B Calculate the standard deviation for each sample. How can you use standard deviation to better understand the relationship between gender and average driving distance?

Part C How would histograms for the top ten men's and women's average driving distances be similar? How would they be different?

10-5

Two-Way Frequency Tables

SavvasRealize.com

I CAN... organize data in two-way frequency tables and use them to make inferences.

VOCABULARY
• conditional relative frequency
• joint frequency
• joint relative frequency
• marginal frequency
• marginal relative frequency

👆 EXPLORE & REASON

Baseball teams at a high school and a college play at the same stadium. Results for every game last season are given for both teams. There were no ties.

Baseball Season Results at Mountain View Stadium

★ ☆ Wins! ☆ ★	HOME	AWAY
WEST MOUNTAIN HIGH SCHOOL	11 OUT OF 16	08 OUT OF 14
BIG MOUNTAIN COLLEGE	18 OUT OF 26	18 OUT OF 30

A. How could you organize the data in table form?

B. Look for Relationships How would you analyze the data to determine whether the data support the claim that the team that plays at home is more likely to win?

❓ ESSENTIAL QUESTION

How can you use two-way frequency tables to analyze data?

APPLICATION →

👆 EXAMPLE 1   Interpret a Two-Way Frequency Table

Owners of a major food chain are planning to add a vegetarian item to its menu. Customers were asked to choose one of two vegetarian items. The results are shown in the table. What trends do the results suggest?

A **joint frequency** is at the joint of a column and a row.

A **marginal frequency** is at the margin, or edge of a column or row.

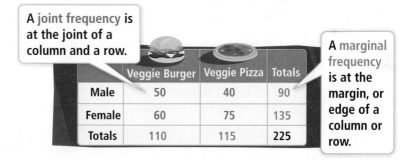

	Veggie Burger	Veggie Pizza	Totals
Male	50	40	90
Female	60	75	135
Totals	110	115	225

STUDY TIP
A two-way frequency table can show possible relationships between two sets of categorical data.

Joint frequencies indicate the frequency of a single option for one category; for example, the frequency of males choosing a veggie burger.

Marginal frequencies indicate the total frequency for each option or category, such as the total frequency of female respondents.

The joint frequencies suggest that male customers prefer veggie burgers over veggie pizzas, and female customers prefer veggie pizzas over veggie burgers.

The marginal frequencies suggest that all of the respondents showed only a slight preference for veggie pizza over a veggie burger. They also indicate that more females than males were surveyed.

☑ Try It!   1. What do the marginal frequencies tell you about the number of male and female respondents?

APPLICATION   👍 **EXAMPLE 2**   Interpret a Two-Way Relative Frequency Table

What do the survey results reveal about male and female customer preferences for veggie burgers?

Joint relative frequency is the ratio, or percent, of the joint frequency to the total.

Marginal relative frequency is the ratio, or percent, of the marginal frequency to the total.

COMMON ERROR
Divide each frequency by the total count, found in the bottom right corner of the two-way frequency table. Express relative frequency as a fraction, decimal, or percent.

	Veggie Burger	Veggie Pizza	Totals
Male	$\frac{50}{225} \approx 22\%$	$\frac{40}{225} \approx 18\%$	$\frac{90}{225} = 40\%$
Female	$\frac{60}{225} \approx 27\%$	$\frac{75}{225} \approx 33\%$	$\frac{135}{225} = 60\%$
Totals	$\frac{110}{225} \approx 49\%$	$\frac{115}{225} \approx 51\%$	$\frac{225}{225} = 100\%$

Of the customers surveyed, about 22% were males who selected veggie burgers and about 27% were females who selected veggie burgers. So, a greater percent of females than males selected veggie burgers.

✅ **Try It!**   **2.** How can you tell whether a greater percent of customers surveyed selected veggie burger or veggie pizza?

CONCEPTUAL UNDERSTANDING   👍 **EXAMPLE 3**   Calculate Conditional Relative Frequency

Using data from Examples 1 and 2, a marketing team concludes that females prefer veggie burgers more than men do. Do the survey results support this conclusion?

Conditional relative frequency is the ratio of the joint frequency and the related marginal frequency.

Calculating the conditional relative frequency for each row will adjust for differences in the number of male and female customers surveyed.

CONSTRUCT ARGUMENTS
What do the conditional relative frequencies tell you about associations between gender and menu item choice?

	Veggie Burger	Veggie Pizza	Totals
Male	$\frac{50}{90} \approx 56\%$	$\frac{40}{90} \approx 44\%$	$\frac{90}{90} = 100\%$
Female	$\frac{60}{135} \approx 44\%$	$\frac{75}{135} \approx 56\%$	$\frac{135}{135} = 100\%$

$$\text{Conditional relative frequency} = \frac{\text{joint frequency}}{\text{marginal frequency}}$$

The results do not support this conclusion. The conditional relative frequencies show that while about 56% of the males surveyed prefer veggie burgers, only about 44% of the females prefer veggie burgers.

✅ **Try It!**   **3.** What conclusion could the marketing team make about male and female preferences for veggie pizza? Justify your answer.

EXAMPLE 4 Interpret Conditional Relative Frequency

The marketing team also concludes that there is a greater variation between the percent of men and women who like veggie pizza than there is for those who prefer veggie burgers. Do the survey results support this conclusion?

Calculating the conditional relative frequency for each column allows you to analyze male and female preferences within each food choice category.

The conclusion is supported by the survey results. Conditional relative frequencies show that of the customers who prefer veggie pizza, 65% are female and only 35% are male. Of those who prefer veggie burgers, 55% are female and 45% are male.

	Veggie Burger	Veggie Pizza
Male	$\frac{50}{110} \approx 45\%$	$\frac{40}{115} \approx 35\%$
Female	$\frac{60}{110} \approx 55\%$	$\frac{75}{115} \approx 65\%$
Totals	$\frac{110}{110} = 100\%$	$\frac{115}{115} = 100\%$

 Try It! **4.** What conclusion could you draw if the percentages for male and female customers were the same across the rows in this table?

EXAMPLE 5 Interpret Data Frequencies

A random sample of spectators entering a stadium were asked whether they were cheering for the Bears or the Tigers in a championship game. The sample was categorized according to gender and team.

	Cheering for Bears	Cheering for Tigers	Total
Male	72	65	137
Female	49	44	93
Totals	121	109	230

A. What does the joint relative frequency $\frac{65}{230}$ represent in this context?

Joint relative frequency is the ratio of the joint frequency to the total.

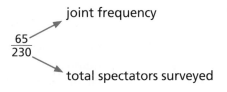

Find the joint frequency 65 in the table. You can see that 65 males cheered for the Tigers, so $\frac{65}{230}$ represents the ratio of male Tigers fans to the total number of people surveyed.

B. What does the conditional relative frequency $\frac{49}{93}$ represent in this context?

Conditional relative frequency is the ratio of the joint frequency to the related marginal frequency.

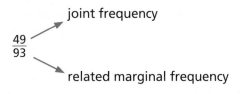

The number $\frac{49}{93}$ represents the ratio of female Bears fans to the number of females surveyed.

 Try It! **5.** What does the conditional relative frequency $\frac{72}{137}$ represent in this context?

🔑 CONCEPT SUMMARY Two-Way Frequency Tables

WORDS ▷ Two-way frequency tables show relationships between two sets of categorical data. Entries can be frequency counts or relative frequencies. Entries in the body of the table are **joint frequencies** (counts) or **joint relative frequencies** (ratios). Entries in the totals column or row are **marginal frequencies** or **marginal relative frequencies**.

Conditional relative frequencies show the frequency of responses for a given condition, or the ratio of the joint frequencies to the corresponding marginal frequency.

TABLES ▷

Movie Time Preferences

	Afternoon	Evening	Totals
Student	$\frac{90}{200} = 45\%$	$\frac{50}{200} = 25\%$	$\frac{140}{200} = 70\%$
Adult	$\frac{20}{200} = 10\%$	$\frac{40}{200} = 20\%$	$\frac{60}{200} = 30\%$
Totals	$\frac{110}{200} = 55\%$	$\frac{90}{200} = 45\%$	$\frac{200}{200} = 100\%$

> 20 of the 200 respondents, or 10%, were adults who prefer the afternoon show.

> 70% of the respondents were students.

Conditional Relative Frequency

	Afternoon	Evening	Totals
Student	$\frac{90}{140} \approx 64\%$	$\frac{50}{140} \approx 36\%$	$\frac{140}{140} = 100\%$
Adult	$\frac{20}{60} \approx 33\%$	$\frac{40}{60} \approx 67\%$	$\frac{60}{60} = 100\%$

> Of all of the adult respondents, 33% prefer afternoon shows.

Conditional Relative Frequency

	Afternoon	Evening
Student	$\frac{90}{110} \approx 82\%$	$\frac{50}{90} \approx 56\%$
Adult	$\frac{20}{110} \approx 18\%$	$\frac{40}{90} \approx 44\%$
Totals	$\frac{110}{110} = 100\%$	$\frac{90}{90} = 100\%$

> Of all of the respondents that prefer evening shows, 44% were adults.

☑ Do You UNDERSTAND?

1. **ESSENTIAL QUESTION** ▷ How can you use two-way frequency tables to analyze data?

2. **Communicate Precisely** How are joint frequencies and marginal frequencies similar? How are they different?

3. **Look for Relationships** How are conditional relative frequencies related to joint frequencies and marginal frequencies?

4. **Error Analysis** Zhang says that the marginal relative frequency for a given variable is 10. Could Zhang be correct? Explain your reasoning.

Do You KNOW HOW?

In a survey, customers select Item A or Item B. Item A is selected by 20 males and 10 females. Of 20 customers who select Item B, five are males.

5. Make a two-way frequency table to organize the data.

6. Make a two-way relative frequency table to organize the data.

7. Calculate conditional relative frequencies for males and females. Is it reasonable to conclude that males prefer Item A more than females do?

8. Calculate conditional relative frequencies for Item A and Item B. Is it reasonable to conclude that a customer who prefers Item B is more likely to be a female than a male?

✎ PRACTICE & PROBLEM SOLVING

UNDERSTAND

9. Reason An equal number of juniors and seniors were surveyed about whether they prefer lunch item A or B. Is it reasonable to infer from the table that more juniors prefer lunch item B while more seniors prefer lunch item A? Explain.

	Item A	Item B	Totals
Junior	0.1	0.4	0.5
Senior	0.3	0.2	0.5
Totals	0.6	0.4	1.0

10. Error Analysis Describe and correct the errors a student made when making a generalization based on a two-way frequency table.

Which subject do you prefer?			
	Math	Language Arts	Totals
Male	45	45	90
Female	30	30	60
Totals	75	75	150

Male students prefer math more than female students do.

11. Look for Relationships In a two-way relative frequency table, how are joint relative frequencies and marginal relative frequencies related?

12. Higher Order Thinking Students are surveyed to see how long they studied for a test.

- 10% of the students who studied 3 hours or more failed the test.
- 40% of the students who studied less than 3 hours passed the test.
- 2 students who studied 3 hours or more failed the test.
- 4 students who studied less than 3 hours passed the test.

a. Make a two-way frequency table that shows the association between hours spent studying and passing the test.

b. Does the association appear to be significant? Explain.

PRACTICE

In a survey, music club members select their preference between Song A or Song B. Song A is selected by 30 teens and 10 adults. Of 20 members who select Song B, five are teens. SEE EXAMPLES 1–4

Make a two-way frequency table to organize the data.

13. Is it reasonable to say that more people surveyed prefer Song A? Explain.

14. Is it reasonable to say that more adults than teens participated in the survey? Explain.

Calculate conditional relative frequencies.

15. Is it reasonable to say that teens prefer Song A more than adults do? Explain.

16. Is a member who prefers Song B significantly more likely to be an adult than a teen? Explain.

In the two-way frequency table, frequencies are shown on the top of each cell in blue, and relative frequencies are shown at the bottom in red. Most of the frequencies are missing. SEE EXAMPLES 1–5

High School Graduate?	Choice A	Choice B	Totals
Yes	16 / 0.08	___	___ / 0.56
No	___	24	___
Totals	___	___	___

17. Complete the table.

18. Calculate conditional relative frequencies for yes and no.

19. Calculate conditional relative frequencies for Choices A and B.

20. Is a high school graduate more likely to prefer Choice A or B? Explain.

21. Is someone who prefers Choice A more likely to be a high school graduate than not? Explain.

22. What does the joint relative frequency $\frac{64}{200}$ represent in this context?

23. What does the conditional relative frequency $\frac{96}{120}$ represent in this context?

Practice   Tutorial

Mixed Review Available Online

APPLY

24. Construct Arguments Is there a significant association between income and whether or not a voter supports the referendum? Justify your answer.

Do you support the referendum?			
Income	Yes	No	Totals
≤ $100,000	80	20	100
> $100,000	40	10	50
Totals	120	30	150

25. Make Sense and Persevere A gardener is only satisfied when a hydrangea bush has at least 14 blooms. How can you organize the data shown in the dot plots into two-way frequency tables to make inferences about the new plant food and the number of blooms?

Hydrangeas Without New Plant Food

Number of Blooms

Hydrangeas with New Plant Food

Number of Blooms

26. Construct Arguments Based on the survey data below, a marketing team for an airline concludes that someone between 18 and 24 years of age is more likely never to have flown on a commercial airliner than someone 25 years or older. Do you agree with this conclusion? Justify your answer.

Have you ever flown on a commercial airline?	Yes	No	Totals
18–24 yrs	198	81	279
25+ yrs	2,539	448	2,987
Totals	2,737	529	3,266

ASSESSMENT PRACTICE

27. Consider a two-way frequency table. Select all that apply.

Ⓐ The sum of all joint frequencies equals the total frequency.

Ⓑ The sum of all marginal frequencies equals the total frequency.

Ⓒ The sum of all marginal frequencies in a row equals the total frequency.

Ⓓ The sum of all joint frequencies in a column equals the marginal frequency at the bottom of the column.

Ⓔ A relative frequency is the ratio of a joint frequency and a marginal frequency.

28. SAT/ACT In a two-way frequency table, the joint frequency in a cell is 8 and the marginal frequency in the same row is 32. What is the conditional relative frequency for the cell?

Ⓐ 0.12

Ⓑ 0.20

Ⓒ 0.25

Ⓓ 0.40

Ⓔ 0.50

29. Performance Task A high school offers a prep course for students who are taking a retest for a college entrance exam.

• Of 25 students who took the prep course, 20 scored at least 50 points higher on the retest than on the original exam.

• Overall, 100 students took the retest and 50 students scored at least 50 points higher on the retest than on the original exam.

Part A Create a two-way frequency table to organize the data.

Part B Funding for the prep course may be cut because more students scored at least 50 points higher on the retest without taking the prep course. Do you agree with this decision? If not, how could you use a two-way frequency table to construct an argument to keep the funding?

MATHEMATICAL MODELING IN **3** ACTS

 SavvasRealize.com

▶ Text Message

Text messages used be just that: text only. Now you can send multimedia messages (or MMS) with emojis, images, audio, and videos. Did you know Finland was the first country to offer text messaging to phone customers?

Some people send and receive so many texts that they use textspeak to make typing faster. RU 1 of them? You will see one person keep track of his text messages in this Modeling Mathematics in 3 Acts lesson.

Scan for Multimedia

ACT 1 Identify the Problem

1. What is the first question that comes to mind after watching the video?

2. Write down the main question you will answer about what you saw in the video.

3. Make an initial conjecture that answers this main question.

4. Explain how you arrived at your conjecture.

5. What information will be useful to know to answer the main question? How can you get it? How will you use that information?

ACT 2 Develop a Model

6. Use the math that you have learned in this Topic to refine your conjecture.

ACT 3 Interpret the Results

7. Is your refined conjecture between the highs and lows you set up earlier?

8. Did your refined conjecture match the actual answer exactly? If not, what might explain the difference?

Topic Review

1. How do you use statistics to model situations and solve problems?

Vocabulary Review

Choose the correct term to complete each sentence.

2. _____ is a measure of spread that reflects how the data vary from the mean.

3. _____ indicate the frequency of a single option for one category.

4. A(n) _____ is a data distribution that forms a bell-shaped curve.

5. _____ is the ratio of the joint frequency and the related marginal frequency.

- conditional relative frequency
- joint frequencies
- normal distribution
- standard deviation
- joint relative frequency

Concepts & Skills Review

LESSON 10-1 | **Analyzing Data Displays**

Quick Review

Dot plots show counts of values within data sets. **Histograms** show the distribution of values within a data set in ranges or intervals. **Box plots** show the center and spread of a distribution using a five-number summary.

Example

The table below shows a class's math test scores. Create a histogram of the data.

83	92	56	63	80	91	78	59
75	79	62	85	81	90	82	74
60	95	88	82	77	74	68	82

Break the scores into intervals of 10.

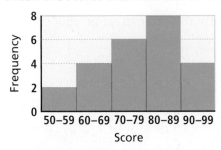

Practice & Problem Solving

6. **Generalize** In what situations would a box plot be the best display for a data set?

7. In what situations would a dot plot be the best display for a data set?

For the data set below, create the data display that best reveals the answer to the question. Explain your reasoning.

8. What is the frequency of the data value 35?

30	33	35	39
37	35	31	36
39	30	35	35

Choose the most appropriate data display to answer each question about a data set. Explain.

9. What are the frequencies for each interval of 2 points?

10. How many data values are less than any given value in the data set?

Quick Review

You can compare data sets using statistical measures of center and measures of spread. The shape of the data in data displays indicates the relationship between measures of center. The mean absolute deviation (MAD) describes how much the data values vary from the mean of a data set. It is the mean of the absolute deviations.

Example

Micah would like to purchase a new golf club. He gathers data on the average driving distance (in yards) of two different types of clubs. The dot plots show the data for each type.

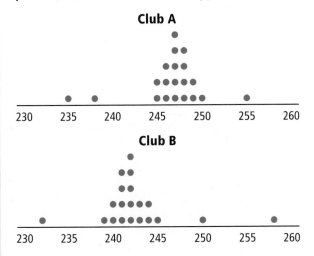

Club A

Club B

If Micah is most interested in increasing his driving distance, which golf club should he purchase?

The data show that Club A has better driving distance. Most of the dots in the data display for Club A golf clubs are clustered from 245 to 250 yd, and the dots in the data display for Club B golf clubs are clustered from 239 to 245 yd. Therefore, Micah should purchase Club A.

Practice & Problem Solving

11. Construct Arguments If the mean is greater than the median for a given data set, what does that indicate about the data?

12. For the given data sets, compare the means and the MADs, and then the medians and the IQRs. Decide which measures are better for comparing the data sets. Explain your reasoning.

Data Set A			
3	8	7	5
7	1	4	9
5	4	2	6
4	1	4	3

Data Set B			
4	6	2	5
3	7	8	6
8	2	9	3
6	2	8	6

13. Model With Mathematics Last year's school basketball team had a mean average score of 78 with a mean absolute deviation of 4.5 points. The scores for this year's team are shown in the table. How do the scores for the two years compare?

83	65	90	88	75	82
68	78	80	82	94	73
78	85	80	81	74	88

Quick Review

When the shape of a data display is **symmetric**, the data values are evenly spread on either side of the center. The mean is close to the median. When the shape of a data display is **skewed**, the data display is skewed right or skewed left. The mean and median are not equal.

Example

The histogram shows the heights of players on a football team. The mean height is 59 in. What inferences can you make about the shape of the data?

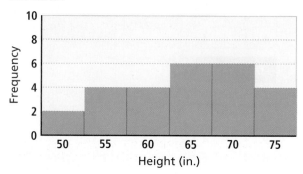

The histogram shows the data are skewed to the left. The mean is less than the median.

Based on the data, you can infer that most of the players are taller than 59 in.

Practice & Problem Solving

14. Look for Relationships One data set has a median that is less than the mean, while a second data set has a median that is greater than the mean. What does this mean for the graph of the data sets?

Tell whether each display is skewed left, skewed right or symmetric.

15.   **16.**

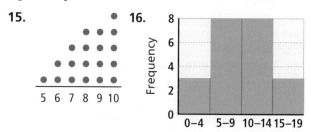

Interpret the shape of the display for the given context and make an inference based on a measure of center.

17. The data are average minutes spent playing video games each day.

18. The displays represent car sales at a dealership over two consecutive months. What do the displays tell about the change in car sales in the two months?

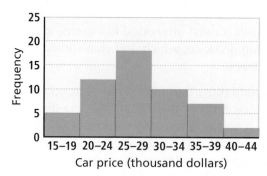

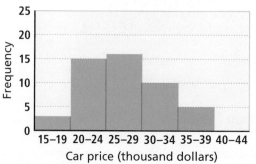

LESSON 10-4 — Standard Deviation

Quick Review

Standard deviation indicates by how much the values in a data set deviate from the mean. It is the square root of the **variance**, the mean of the squared deviations from the mean.

Example

The table shows the number of hot dogs sold per day by a street vendor over a two-week period. How much variability do the sample data show?

40	28	18	36	52	41	29
24	30	27	51	34	42	35

Mean: $\bar{x} \approx 35$; variance: $s^2 \approx 95.41$; standard deviation: $s \approx 9.77$

The standard deviation is relatively large, so the data show quite a bit of variability. Typically, the vendor sells between 25 and 45 hot dogs per day.

Practice & Problem Solving

19. **Reason** The mean of a data set is 50.5 and the standard deviation is about 9.6. Does 70.5 fall within 2 standard deviations of the mean of the data set? Explain.

Find and use the mean and the standard deviation to compare the variability of the data sets.

20. **Sample A:** 15, 12, 8, 18, 16, 13, 14, 10;
    Sample B: 16, 19, 11, 9, 8, 10, 15, 11

21. **Make Sense and Persevere** A normally distributed sample of bank accounts shows a mean of $22,000 and a standard deviation of $1,275. How much money would be in an account that contains more than the middle 95% of the accounts? How many accounts would meet that requirement?

LESSON 10-5 — Two-Way Frequency Tables

Quick Review

Two-way frequency tables show relationships between two sets of categorical data. **Joint frequencies** indicate the frequency of one category. **Marginal frequencies** indicate the total frequency for each category.

Example

A teacher asked her students to choose between the museum or the zoo for a class trip. The results are shown in the table. What trends do the results suggest?

	Museum	Zoo	Totals
Male	5	7	12
Female	12	6	18
Totals	17	13	30

The joint frequencies suggest that males prefer the zoo and females prefer the museum. The marginal frequencies suggest that all respondents showed a slight preference for going to the museum.

Practice & Problem Solving

In a survey, TV viewers can choose between two movies. 40 men and 10 women choose the action movie that is featured. Of the 30 people who chose the comedy, 20 are women and 10 are men.

22. Make a two-way frequency table to organize the data. Is it reasonable to say that more people surveyed prefer action movies? Explain.

23. **Construct Arguments** According to the data below, is there a significant association between age and a person's news source? Justify your answer.

Where do you get most of your news?			
Age	TV	Internet	Totals
≤ 30	50	80	130
> 30	30	40	70
Totals	80	120	200

Visual Glossary

English

Acute triangle   An acute triangle has three acute angles.

Example

Adjacent angles   Adjacent angles are two coplanar angles that have a common side and a common vertex but no common interior points.

Example

$\angle 1$ and $\angle 2$ are adjacent. $\angle 3$ and $\angle 4$ are *not* adjacent.

Alternate interior (exterior) angles   Alternate interior (exterior) angles are nonadjacent interior (exterior) angles that lie on opposite sides of the transversal.

Example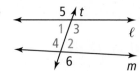

$\angle 1$ and $\angle 2$ are alternate interior angles, as are $\angle 3$ and $\angle 4$. $\angle 5$ and $\angle 6$ are alternate exterior angles.

Angle   An angle is formed by two rays with the same endpoint. The rays are the *sides* of the angle and the common endpoint is the *vertex* of the angle.

Example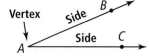

This angle could be named $\angle A$, $\angle BAC$, or $\angle CAB$.

Angle bisector   An angle bisector is a ray that divides an angle into two congruent angles.

Example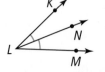

$\overrightarrow{LN}$ bisects $\angle KLM$.
$\angle KLN \cong \angle NLM$.

Spanish

Triángulo acutángulo   Un triángulo acutángulo tiene los tres ángulos agudos.

Ángulos adyacentes   Los ángulos adyacentes son dos ángulos coplanarios que tienen un lado común y el mismo vértice, pero no tienen puntos interiores comunes.

Ángulos alternos internos (externos)   Los ángulos alternos internos (externos) son ángulos internos (externos) no adyacentes situados en lados opuestos de la transversal.

Ángulo   Un ángulo está formado por dos semirrectas que convergen en un mismo extremo. Las semirrectas son los *lados* del ángulo y los extremos en común son el *vértice*.

Bisectriz de un ángulo   La bisectriz de un ángulo es una semirrecta que divide al ángulo en dos ángulos congruentes.

English

Spanish

Arithmetic sequence   A number sequence formed by adding a fixed number to each previous term to find the next term. The fixed number is called the *common difference*.

Progresión aritmética   En una progresión aritmética la diferencia entre términos consecutivos es un número constante. El número constante se llama la diferencia común.

Example   4, 7, 10, 13, … is an arithmetic sequence with a common difference of 3.

Causation   When a change in one quantity causes a change in a second quantity. A correlation between quantities does not always imply causation.

Causalidad   Cuando un cambio en una cantidad causa un cambio en una segunda cantidad. Una correlación entre las cantidades no implica siempre la causalidad.

Chord   A chord of a circle is a segment whose endpoints are on the circle.

Cuerda   Una cuerda de un círculo es un segmento cuyos extremos son dos puntos del círculo.

Example

$\overline{HD}$ and $\overline{HR}$ are chords of $\odot C$.

Collinear points   Collinear points lie on the same line.

Puntos colineales   Los puntos colineales son los que están sobre la misma recta.

Example

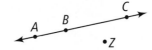

Points A, B, and C are collinear, but points A, B, and Z are noncollinear.

Common difference   The difference between consecutive terms of an arithmetic sequence.

Diferencia común   La diferencia común es la diferencia entre los términos consecutivos de una progresión aritmética.

Example   The common difference is 3 in the arithmetic sequence 4, 7, 10, 13, …

Compass   A compass is a tool for drawing arcs and circles of different sizes and can be used to copy lengths.

Compás   El compás es un instrumento que se usa para dibujar arcos y círculos de diferentes tamaños, y que se puede usar para copiar longitudes.

Complementary angles   Two angles are complementary angles if the sum of their measures is 90.

Ángulos complementarios   Dos ángulos son complementarios si la suma de sus medidas es igual a 90.

Composition of rigid motions   A composition of rigid motions is a transformation with two or more rigid motions in which the second rigid motion is performed on the image of the first rigid motion.

Composición de movimientos rígidos   Una composición de movimientos rígidos es una transformación de dos o más movimientos rígidos en la que el segundo movimiento rígido se realiza sobre la imagen del primer movimiento rígido.

Example

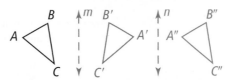

If you reflect $\triangle ABC$ across line m to get $\triangle A'B'C'$ and then reflect $\triangle A'B'C'$ across line n to get $\triangle A''B''C''$, you perform a composition of rigid motions.

English

Spanish

Compound inequalities   Two inequalities that are joined by *and* or *or*.

Desigualdades compuestas   Dos desigualdades que están enlazadas por medio de una *y* o una *o*.

Examples $5 < x$ and $x < 10$
$14 < x$ or $x \leq -3$

Compound interest   Interest paid on both the principal and the interest that has already been paid.

Interés compuesto   Interés calculado tanto sobre el capital como sobre los intereses ya pagados.

Example   For an initial deposit of $1,000 at a 6% interest rate with interest compounded quarterly, the function $y = 1000\left(\frac{0.06}{4}\right)^{4x}$ gives the account balance y after x years.

Conditional   A conditional is an *if-then* statement that relates a hypothesis, the part that follows if, to a conclusion, the part that follows then.

Condicional   Un enunciado condicional es del tipo *si . . ., entonces. . . .*

Example   *If* you act politely, *then* you will earn respect.

Conditional relative frequency   The ratio of the joint frequency and the related marginal frequency.

Frecuencia relativa condicional   La razón de la frecuencia conjunta y la frecuencia marginal relacionada.

Example

	Afternoon	Evening	Totals
Student	$\frac{90}{140} = 64\%$	$\frac{50}{140} = 36\%$	$\frac{140}{140} = 100\%$
Adult	$\frac{20}{60} = 33\%$	$\frac{40}{60} = 67\%$	$\frac{60}{60} = 100\%$

Congruence transformation   A congruence transformation maps a figure to a congruent figure. A rigid motion is sometimes called a congruence transformation.

Transformación de congruencia   En una transformación de congruencia, una figura es la imagen de otra figura congruente. Los movimientos rígidos son llamados a veces transformaciones de congruencia.

Congruent angles   Congruent angles are angles that have the same measure.

Ángulos congruentes   Los ángulos congruentes son ángulos que tienen la misma medida.

Congruent figures   Two figures are congruent if there is a rigid motion that maps one figure to the other.

Figuras congruentes   Dos figuras son congruentes si hay un movimiento rígido en el que una figura es imagen de la otra.

Example

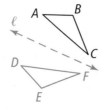

Since the reflection across line ℓ maps $\triangle ABC$ to $\triangle DEF$, $\triangle ABC$ and $\triangle DEF$ are congruent figures.

English

Congruent polygons   Congruent polygons are polygons that have corresponding sides congruent and corresponding angles congruent.

Spanish

Polígonos congruentes   Los polígonos congruentes son polígonos cuyos lados correspondientes son congruentes y cuyos ángulos correspondientes son congruentes.

Example

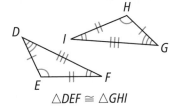

$$\triangle DEF \cong \triangle GHI$$

Congruent segments   Congruent segments are segments that have the same length.

Segmentos congruentes   Los segmentos congruentes son segmentos que tienen la misma longitud.

Example

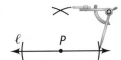

$$\overline{AB} \cong \overline{CD}$$

Conjecture   A conjecture is an unproven statement or rule that is based on inductive reasoning.

Conjetura   Una conjetura es una afirmación o regla no demostrada, que está fundamentada en un razonamiento inductivo.

Example   As you walk down the street, you see many people holding unopened umbrellas. You make the conjecture that the forecast must call for rain.

Constant ratio   The number that an exponential function repeatedly multiplies an initial amount by.

Razón constante   El número por el que una función exponencial multiplica repetidamente a una cantidad inicial.

Example   In an exponential function of the form $f(x) = ab^x$, b is the constant ratio.

Construction   A construction is a geometric figure made with only a straightedge and compass.

Construcción   Una construcción es una figura geométrica trazada solamente con una regla sin graduación y un compás.

Example

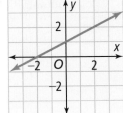

The diagram shows the construction (in progress) of a line perpendicular to a line ℓ through a point P on ℓ.

Continuous   A graph that is unbroken.

Continua   Una gráfica continua es una gráfica ininterrumpida.

Example

English

Spanish

Contrapositive   The contrapositive is obtained by negating and reversing the hypothesis and the conclusion of a conditional. The contrapositive of the conditional "if p, then q" is the conditional "if not q, then not p." A conditional and its contrapositive always have the same truth value.

Contrapositivo   El contrapositivo se obtiene al negar e intercambiar la hipótesis y la conclusión de un condicional. El contrapositivo del condicional "si p, entonces q" es el condicional "si no q, entonces no p". Un condicional y su contrapositivo siempre tienen el mismo valor verdadero.

Example   **Conditional:** If a figure is a triangle, then it is a polygon.
Contrapositive: If a figure is not a polygon, then it is not a triangle.

Converse   The converse reverses the hypothesis and conclusion of a conditional.

Expresión recíproca   La expresión recíproca intercambia la hipótesis y la conclusión de un condicional.

Example   The converse of "If I was born in Houston, then I am a Texan" would be "If I am a Texan, then I am born in Houston."

Coordinate(s) of a point   The coordinate of a point is its distance and direction from the origin of a number line. The coordinates of a point on a coordinate plane are in the form (x, y), where x is the x-coordinate and y is the y-coordinate.

Coordenada(s) de un punto   La coordenada de un punto es su distancia y dirección desde el origen en una recta numérica. Las coordenadas de un punto en un plano de coordenadas se expresan como (x, y), donde x es la coordenada x, e y es la coordenada y.

Example

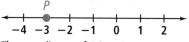

The coordinate of P is -3.

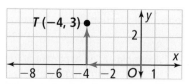

The coordinates of T are $(-4, 3)$.

Coordinate plane   The coordinate plane is formed by two number lines, called the axes, intersecting at right angles. The x-axis is the horizontal axis, and the y-axis is the vertical axis. The two axes meet at the origin, $O(0, 0)$. The axes divide the plane into four *quadrants*.

Plano de coordenadas   El plano de coordenadas se forma con dos rectas numéricas, llamadas *ejes*, que se cortan en ángulos rectos. El eje x es el eje horizontal y el eje y es el eje vertical. Los dos ejes se unen en el *origen*, $O(0, 0)$. Los ejes dividen el plano de coordenadas en cuatro *cuadrantes*.

Example

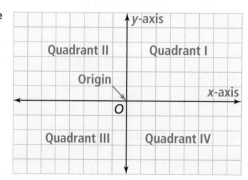

English

Corollary A corollary is a theorem that can be proved easily using another theorem.

Example **Theorem:** If two sides of a triangle are congruent, then the angles opposite those sides are congruent.
Corollary: If a triangle is equilateral, then it is equiangular.

Correlation coefficient A number from −1 to 1 that tells you how closely the equation of the line of best fit models the data. It is represented by the variable, *r*.

Example

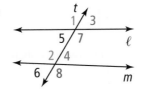

The correlation coefficient is approximately 0.94.

Corresponding angles Corresponding angles lie on the same side of the transversal *t* and in corresponding positions relative to ℓ and *m*.

Example

∠1 and ∠2 are corresponding angles, as are ∠3 and ∠4, ∠5 and ∠6, and ∠7 and ∠8.

Counterexample A counterexample is an example that shows a statement or conjecture is false.

Example **Statement:** All apples are red.
Counterexample: A Granny Smith Apple is green.

D

Decay factor 1 minus the decay rate in an exponential function when $0 < b < 1$.

Example The decay factor of the function $y = 5(0.3)^x$ is 0.3.

Deductive reasoning Deductive reasoning is a process of reasoning using given and previously known facts to reach a logical conclusion.

Example Based on the fact that the sum of any two even numbers is even, you can deduce that the product of any whole number and any even number is even.

Spanish

Corolario Un corolario es un teorema que se puede probar fácilmente usando otro teorema.

Coeficiente de correlación Número de −1 a 1 que indica con cuánta exactitud la línea de mejor encaje representa los datos. Se representa con la variable *r*.

Ángulos correspondientes Los ángulos correspondientes están en el mismo lado de la transversal *t* y en las correspondientes posiciones relativas a ℓ y *m*.

Contraejemplo Un contraejemplo es un ejemplo que demuestra que una afirmación o conjetura es falsa.

Factor de decremento 1 menos la tasa de decremento en una función exponencial si $0 < b < 1$.

Razonamiento deductivo El razonamiento deductivo es un proceso de razonamiento en el que se usan hechos dados y previamente conocidos para llegar a una conclusión lógica.

Discrete   A graph composed of isolated points.

Discreta   Una gráfica discreta es compuesta de puntos aislados.

Example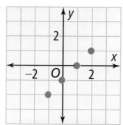

Distance between two points on a line   The distance between two points on a line is the absolute value of the difference of the coordinates of the points.

Distancia entre dos puntos de una línea   La distancia entre dos puntos de una línea es el valor absoluto de la diferencia de las coordenadas de los puntos.

Example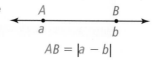

$$AB = |a - b|$$

Distance from a point to a line   The distance from a point to a line is the length of the perpendicular segment from the point to the line.

Distancia desde un punto hasta una recta   La distancia desde un punto hasta una recta es la longitud del segmento perpendicular que va desde el punto hasta la recta.

Example

The distance from point P to a line ℓ is PT.

Domain (of a relation or function)   The possible values for the input of a relation or function.

Dominio (de una relación o función)   Posibles valores de entrada de una relación o función.

Example   In the function $f(x) = x + 22$, the domain is all real numbers.

E

Elements (of a set)   Members of a set.

Elementos   Partes integrantes de un conjunto.

Example   Cats and dogs are elements of the set of mammals.

Equiangular triangle   An equiangular triangle is a triangle whose angles are all congruent.

Triángulo equiángulo   Un triángulo equiángulo es un triángulo cuyos ángulos son todos congruentes.

Example Each angle of the triangle is a 60° angle.

Equidistant   A point is equidistant from two objects if it is the same distance from the objects.

Equidistante   Un punto es equidistante de dos objetos si la distancia entre el punto y los objetos es igual.

Example 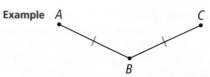 Point B is equidistant from points A and C.

English

Equivalent statements   Equivalent statements are statements with the same truth value.

Example   The following statements are equivalent:
If a figure is a square, then it is a rectangle.
If a figure is not a rectangle, then it is not a square.

Explicit formula   An explicit formula expresses the nth term of a sequence in terms of n.

Example   Let $a_n = 2n + 5$ for positive integers n.
If $n = 7$, then $a_7 = 2(7) + 5 = 19$.

Exponential decay   A situation modeled with a function of the form $y = ab^x$, where $a > 0$ and $0 < b < 1$.

Example $y = 5(0.1)^x$

Exponential function   The function $f(x) = b^x$, where $b > 0$ and $b \neq 1$.

Example

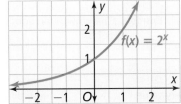

Exponential growth   A situation modeled with a function of the form $y = ab^x$, where $a > 0$ and $b > 1$.

Example $y = 100(2)^x$

Extrapolation   The process of predicting a value outside the range of known values.

Family of functions   A group of functions that use the same common operation in their equation forms.

Example $f(x) = 3x + 7$ and $f(x) = \frac{2}{3}x - 9$ are members of the linear family of functions.

Function   A relation in which each element of the domain corresponds with exactly one element in the range.

Example   Earned income is a function of the number of hours worked. If you earn \$4.50/h, then your income is expressed by the function $f(h) = 4.5h$.

Function notation   A method for writing variables as a function of other variables.

Example $f(x) = 3x - 8$ is in function notation.

Spanish

Enunciados equivalentes   Los enunciados equivalentes son enunciados con el mismo valor verdadero.

Fórmula explícita   Una fórmula explícita expresa el n-ésimo término de una progresión en función de n.

Decremento exponencial   Para $a > 0$ y $0 < b < 1$, la función $y = ab^x$ representa el decremento exponencial.

Función exponencial   La función $f(x) = b^x$, donde $b > 0$ y $b \neq 1$.

Incremento exponencial   Para $a > 0$ y $b > 1$, la función $y = ab^x$ representa el incremento exponencial.

Extrapolación   Proceso que se usa para predecir un valor por fuera del ámbito de los valores dados.

Familia de funciones   Un grupo de funciones que usan la misma operación común en su forma de ecuación.

Función   Una relación en la cual cada elemento del dominio se corresponde con exactamente un elemento del rango.

Notación de una función   Un método para escribir variables como una función de otras variables.

English	Spanish

G

Geometric sequence   A number sequence formed by multiplying a term in a sequence by a fixed number to find the next term.

Progresión geométrica   Tipo de sucesión numérica formada al multiplicar un término de la secuencia por un número constante, para hallar el siguiente término.

Example $9, 3, 1, \frac{1}{3}, \ldots$ is an example of a geometric sequence.

Glide reflection   A glide reflection is the composition of a reflection followed by a translation in a direction parallel to the line of reflection.

Reflexión deslizada   Una reflexión por deslizamiento es la composición de una reflexión seguida de una traslación en una dirección paralela a la recta de reflexión.

Example

The red G in the diagram is a glide reflection image of the black G.

Growth factor   1 plus the growth rate in an exponential function when $b > 1$.

Factor incremental   1 más la tasa de incremento en una función exponencial si $b > 1$.

Example   The growth factor of $y = 7(1.3)^x$ is 1.3.

I

Identity   An equation that is true for every value.

Identidad   Una ecuación que es verdadera para todos los valores.

Example $5 - 14x = 5\left(1 - \frac{14}{5}x\right)$ is an identity because it is true for any value of x.

Indirect reasoning   Indirect reasoning is a type of reasoning in which all possiblities are considered and then all but one are proved false. The remaining possibility must be true.

Razonamiento indirecto   Razonamiento indirecto es un tipo de razonamiento en el que se consideran todas las posibilidades y se prueba que todas son falsas, a excepción de una. La posibilidad restante debe ser verdadera.

Example   Eduardo spent more than $60 on two books at a store. Prove that at least one book costs more than $30.
Proof: Suppose neither costs more than $30. Then he spent no more than $60 at the store. Since this contradicts the given information, at least one book costs more than $30.

Inductive reasoning   Inductive reasoning is a type of reasoning that reaches conclusions based on a pattern of specific examples or past events.

Razonamiento inductivo   El razonamiento inductivo es un tipo de razonamiento en el cual se llega a conclusiones con base en un patrón de ejemplos específicos o sucesos pasados.

Example   You see four people walk into a building. Each person emerges with a small bag containing food. You use inductive reasoning to conclude that this building contains a restaurant.

Interpolation   The process of estimating a value between two known quantities.

Interpolación   Proceso que se usa para estimar el valor entre dos cantidades dadas.

English

Spanish

Intersection   The intersection of two or more geometric figures is the set of points the figures have in common.

Intersección   La intersección de dos o más figuras geométricas es el conjunto de puntos que las figuras tienen en común.

Example 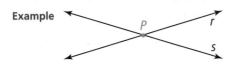 The intersection of lines *r* and *s* is point *P*.

Inverse   The inverse is obtained by negating both the hypothesis and the conclusion of a conditional. The inverse of the conditional "if *p*, then *q*" is the conditional "if not *p*, then not *q*."

Inverso   El inverso es la negación de la hipótesis y de la conclusión de un condicional. El inverso del condicional "si *p*, entonces *q*" es el condicional "si no *p*, entonces no *q*".

Example   **Conditional:** If a figure is a square, then it is a parallelogram.
Inverse: If a figure is not a square, then it is not a parallelogram.

Isosceles trapezoid   An isosceles trapezoid is a trapezoid whose nonparallel opposite sides are congruent.

Trapecio isósceles   Un trapecio isosceles es un trapecio cuyos lados opuestos no paralelos son congruentes.

Example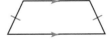

J

Joint frequency   The frequency of a single option for one category.

Frecuencia conjunta   La frecuencia de una única opción por categoría.

Example

	Afternoon	Evening	Totals
Student	90	50	140
Adult	20	40	60
Totals	110	90	200

90, 50, 20, and 40 are joint frequencies.

Joint relative frequency   The ratio, or percent, of the joint frequency to the total.

Frecuencia relativa conjunta   La razón, o porcentaje, de la frecuencia conjunta al total.

Example

	Afternoon	Evening	Totals
Student	$\frac{90}{200} = 45\%$	$\frac{50}{200} = 25\%$	$\frac{140}{200} = 70\%$
Adult	$\frac{20}{200} = 10\%$	$\frac{40}{200} = 20\%$	$\frac{60}{200} = 30\%$
Totals	$\frac{110}{200} = 55\%$	$\frac{90}{200} = 45\%$	$\frac{200}{200} = 100\%$

45%, 25%, 10%, and 20% are joint relative frequencies.

L

Law of Detachment   The Law of Detachment is a law of logic that states if a conditional statement and its hypothesis are true, then its conclusion is also true. Symbolically, if $p \rightarrow q$ and *p* are true, then *q* is true.

Regla de eliminación del condicional   La ley de eliminación del condicional es una regla lógica que establece que si un enunciado condicional y su hipótesis son ambos verdaderos, entonces la conclusión también será verdadera. Desde un punto de vista simbólico, si $p \rightarrow q$ y *p* son verdaderos, entonces *q* es verdadero.

English

Spanish

Law of Syllogism   The Law of Syllogism is a law of logic that states that given two true conditionals with the conclusion of the first being the hypothesis of the second, there exists a third true conditional having the hypothesis of the first and the conclusion of the second. Symbolically, if $p \rightarrow q$ and $q \rightarrow r$ are true, then $p \rightarrow r$ is true.

Ley del silogismo hipotético   La ley del silogismo hipotético es una regla lógica que establece que si se tienen dos condicionales verdaderos en los que la conclusión del primero es la hipótesis del segundo, existe un tercer condicional verdadero compuesto por la hipótesis del primero y la conclusión del segundo. Desde un punto de vista simbólico, si $p \rightarrow q$ y $q \rightarrow r$ son verdaderos, entonces $p \rightarrow r$ es verdadero.

Example   Suppose the following statements are true.
- If Renaldo works 20 hours this week, he earns $200.
- If Renaldo earns $200, he buys a new guitar.

Then the following is true.
- If Renaldo works 20 hours this week, he buys a new guitar.

Line   A line is undefined. You can think of a line as a straight path that extends in two opposite directions without end and has no thickness. A line contains infinitely many points. In spherical geometry, you can think of a line as a great circle of a sphere.

Recta   Una recta es indefinida. Se puede pensar en una recta como un camino derecho que se extiende en direcciones opuestas sin fin ni grosor. Una recta tiene un número infinito de puntos. En la geometría esférica, se puede pensar en una recta como un gran círculo de una esfera.

Example

Line of best fit   The most accurate trend line on a scatter plot showing the relationship between two sets of data.

Recta de mayor aproximación   La línea de tendencia en un diagrama de puntos que más se acerca a los puntos que representan la relación entre dos conjuntos de datos.

Example

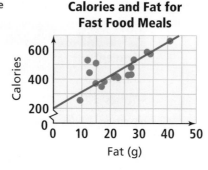

Linear function   A function whose graph is a line is a linear function. You can represent a linear function with a linear equation.

Función lineal   Una función cuya gráfica es una recta es una función lineal. La función lineal se representa con una ecuación lineal.

Example

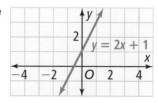

English

Linear inequality in two variables An inequality in two variables whose graph is a region of the coordinate plane that is bounded by a line. Each point in the region is a solution of the inequality.

Example

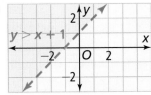

Linear pair A linear pair is a pair of adjacent angles whose noncommon sides are opposite rays.

Example

∠1 and ∠2 are a linear pair.

Linear regression A method used to calculate the line of best fit.

Literal equation An equation expressed in variables.

Example 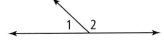 $4x + 2y = 18$ is a literal equation.

M

Marginal frequency The total frequency for each option or category.

Example

	Afternoon	Evening	Totals
Student	90	50	140
Adult	20	40	60
Totals	110	90	200

140, 60, 110, and 90 are marginal frequencies.

Marginal relative frequency The ratio, or percent, of the marginal frequency to the total.

Example

	Afternoon	Evening	Totals
Student	$\frac{90}{200} = 45\%$	$\frac{50}{200} = 25\%$	$\frac{140}{200} = 70\%$
Adult	$\frac{20}{200} = 10\%$	$\frac{40}{200} = 20\%$	$\frac{60}{200} = 30\%$
Totals	$\frac{110}{200} = 55\%$	$\frac{90}{200} = 45\%$	$\frac{200}{200} = 100\%$

70%, 30%, 55%, and 45% are marginal relative frequencies.

Spanish

Desigualdad lineal con dos variables Una desigualdad lineal es una desigualdad de dos variables cuya gráfica es una región del plano de coordenadas delimitado por una recta. Cada punto de la región es una solución de la desigualdad.

Par lineal Un par lineal es un par de ángulos adjuntos cuyos lados no comunes son semirrectas opuestas.

Regresión lineal Método que se utiliza para calcular la línea de mejor ajuste.

Ecuación literal Ecuación que se expresa con variables.

Frecuencia marginal La frecuencia total para cada opción o categoría.

Frecuencia relativa marginal La razón, o porcentaje, de la frecuencia marginal al total.

English

Spanish

Measure of an angle   Consider $\overrightarrow{OD}$ and a point C on one side of $\overrightarrow{OD}$. Every ray of the form $\overrightarrow{OC}$ can be paired one to one with a real number from 0 to 180. The measure of $\angle COD$ is the absolute value of the difference of the real numbers paired with $\overrightarrow{OC}$ and $\overrightarrow{OD}$.

Medida de un ángulo   Toma en cuenta $\overrightarrow{OD}$ y un punto C a un lado de $\overrightarrow{OD}$. Cada semirrecta de la forma $\overrightarrow{OC}$ puede ser emparejada exactamente con un número real de 0 a 180. La medida de $\angle COD$ es el valor absoluto de la diferencia de los números reales emparejados con $\overrightarrow{OC}$ y $\overrightarrow{OD}$

Example

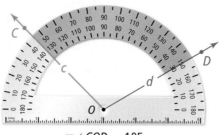

$$m\angle COD = 105$$

Midpoint of a segment   A midpoint of a segment is the point that divides the segment into two congruent segments.

Punto medio de un segmento   El punto medio de un segmento es el punto que divide el segmento en dos segmentos congruentes.

Example   Midpoint of $\overline{AB}$

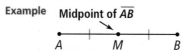

N

Negation   The negation of a statement has the opposite meaning of the original statement.

Negación   La negación de un enunciado tiene el sentido opuesto del enunciado original.

Example   **Statement:** The angle is obtuse.
Negation: The angle is not obtuse.

Negative association   When y-values tend to decrease as x-values increase, the two data sets have a negative association.

Asociación negativa   Cuando los valores de y tienden a disminuir a medida que los valores de x aumentan, los dos conjuntos de datos tienen una asociación negativa.

Example

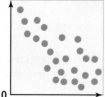

Negative correlation   When data with a negative association are modeled with a line, there is a negative correlation.

Correlación negativa   Cuando los datos que tienen una asociación negativa se representan con una línea, hay una correlación negativa.

Example

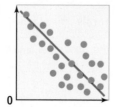

English

Spanish

No association   When there is no general relationship between *x*-values and *y*-values, the two data sets have no association.

Sin asociación   Cuando no existe ninguna relación general entre los valores de *x* y los valores de *y*, los dos conjuntos de datos no tienen ninguna asociación.

Example

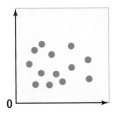

Normal distribution   A normal distribution shows data that vary randomly from the mean in the pattern of a bell-shaped curve.

Distribución normal   Una distribución normal muestra, con una curva en forma de campana, datos que varían alcatoriamente respecto de la media.

Example

Distribution of Test Scores

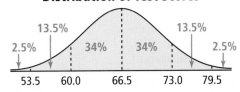

In a class of 200 students, the scores on a test were normally distributed. The mean score was 66.5 and the standard deviation was 6.5. The number of students who scored greater than 73 percent was about 13.5% + 2.5% of those who took the test.
16% of 200 = 32
About 32 students scored 73 or higher on the test.

O

Obtuse triangle   An obtuse triangle has one obtuse angle.

Triángulo obtusángulo   Un triángulo obtusángulo tiene un ángulo obtuso.

Example

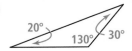

Opposite angles   Opposite angles of a quadrilateral are two angles that do not share a side.

Ángulos opuestos   Los ángulos opuestos de un cuadrilátero son dos ángulos que no comparten lados.

Example

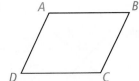

$\angle A$ and $\angle C$ are opposite angles, as are $\angle B$ and $\angle D$.

Opposite rays   Opposite rays are collinear rays with the same endpoint. They form a line.

Semirrectas opuestas   Las semirrectas opuestos son semirrectas colineales con el mismo extremo. Forman una recta.

Example

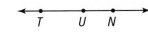

$\overrightarrow{UT}$ and $\overrightarrow{UN}$ are opposite rays.

English

Spanish

Opposite sides   Opposite sides of a quadrilateral are two sides that do not share a vertex.

Lados opuestos   Los lados opuestos de un cuadrilátero son dos lados que no tienen un vértice en común.

Example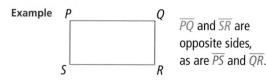

$\overline{PQ}$ and $\overline{SR}$ are opposite sides, as are $\overline{PS}$ and $\overline{QR}$.

Orientation   Two figures have opposite orientation if a reflection is needed to map one onto the other. If a reflection is not needed to map one figure onto the other, the figures have the same orientation.

Orientación   Dos figuras tienen orientación opuesta si una reflexión es necesaria para trazar una sobre la otra. Si una reflexión no es necesaria para trazar una figura sobre la otra, las figuras tienen la misma orientación.

Example   R Я   The two R's have opposite orientation.

Parallel lines   Two lines are parallel if they lie in the same plane and do not intersect. Parallel lines have the same slope. The symbol ∥ means "is parallel to."

Rectas paralelas   Dos rectas son paralelas si están en el mismo plano y no se cortan. Las rectas paralelas tienen la misma pendiente. El símbolo ∥ significa "es paralelo a".

Example $\ell \parallel m$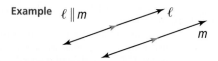

The red symbols indicate parallel lines.

Parallelogram   A parallelogram is a quadrilateral with two pairs of parallel sides. You can choose any side to be the *base*. An *altitude* is any segment perpendicular to the line containing the base drawn from the side opposite the base. The *height* is the length of an altitude.

Paralelogramo   Un paralelogramo es un cuadrilátero con dos pares de lados paralelos. Se puede escoger cualquier lado como la *base*. Una *altura* es un segmento perpendicular a la recta que contiene la base, trazada desde el lado opuesto a la base. La *altura*, por extensión, es la longitud de una altura.

Example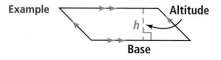

Perpendicular bisector   The perpendicular bisector of a segment is a line, segment, or ray that is perpendicular to the segment and divides the segment into two congruent segments.

Mediatriz   La mediatriz de un segmento es una recta, segmento o semirrecta que es perpendicular al segmento y que divide al segmento en dos segmentos congruentes.

Example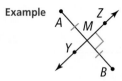

$\overleftrightarrow{YZ}$ is the perpendicular bisector of $\overline{AB}$. It is perpendicular to $\overline{AB}$ and intersects $\overline{AB}$ at midpoint M.

Perpendicular lines   Perpendicular lines are lines that intersect and form right angles. Two lines are perpendicular if the product of their slopes is −1. The symbol ⊥ means "is perpendicular to."

Rectas perpendiculares   Las rectas perpendiculares son rectas que se cortan y forman ángulos rectos. Dos rectas son perpendiculares si el producto de sus pendientes es −1. El símbolo ⊥ significa "es perpendicular a".

Example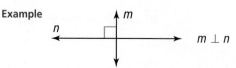

$m \perp n$

English	Spanish

Pi Pi (π) is the ratio of the circumference of any circle to its diameter. The number π is irrational and is approximately 3.14159.

Pi Pi (π) es la razón de la circunferencia de cualquier írculo a su diámetro. El número π es irracional y se aproxima a $\pi \approx 3.14159$.

Example
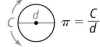

Plane A plane is undefined. You can think of a plane as a flat surface that extends without end and has no thickness. A plane contains infinitely many lines.

Plano Un plano es indefinido. Se puede pensar en un plano como una superficie plana sin fin, ni grosor. Un plano tiene un número infinito de rectas.

Example
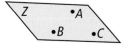
Plane *ABC* or plane *Z*

Point A point is undefined. You can think of a point as a location. A point has no size.

Punto Un punto es indefinido. Puedes imaginarte a un punto como un lugar. Un punto no tiene dimensión.

Example • *P*

Point-slope form A linear equation of a nonvertical line written as $y - y_1 = m(x - x_1)$. The line passes through the point (x_1, y_1) with slope *m*.

Forma punto-pendiente La ecuación lineal de una recta no vertical que pasa por el punto (x_1, y_1) con pendiente *m* está dada por $y - y_1 = m(x - x_1)$.

Example An equation with a slope of $-\frac{1}{2}$ passing through $(2, -1)$ would be written $y + 1 = -\frac{1}{2}(x - 2)$ in point-slope form.

Point symmetry Point symmetry is the type of symmetry for which there is a rotation of 180° that maps a figure onto itself.

Simetría central La simetría central es un tipo de simetría en la que una figura se ha rotado 180° sobre sí misma.

Example
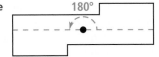

Polygon A polygon is a closed plane figure formed by three or more segments. Each segment intersects exactly two other segments, but only at their endpoints, and no two segments with a common endpoint are collinear. The *vertices* of the polygon are the endpoints of the sides. A *diagonal* is a segment that connects two nonconsecutive vertices. A polygon is *convex* if no diagonal contains points outside the polygon. A polygon is *concave* if a diagonal contains points outside the polygon.

Polígono Un polígono es una figura plana compuesta por tres o más segmentos. Cada segmento interseca los otros dos segmentos exactamente, pero únicamente en sus puntos extremos y ningúno de los segmentos con extremos comunes son colineales. Los *vértices* del polígono son los extremos de los lados. Una *diagonal* es un segmento que conecta dos vértices no consecutivos. Un polígono es *convexo* si ninguna diagonal tiene puntos fuera del polígono. Un polígono es *cóncavo* si una diagonal tiene puntos fuera del polígono.

Example
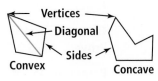

English	Spanish

Positive association   When *y*-values tend to increase as *x*-values increase, the two data sets have a positive association.

Asociación positiva   Cuando los valores de *y* tienden a aumentar a medida que los valores de *x* aumentan, los dos conjuntos de datos tienen una asociación positiva.

Example

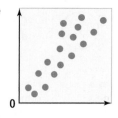

Positive correlation   When data with a positive association are modeled with a line, there is a positive correlation.

Correlación positiva   Cuando los datos que tienen una asociación positiva se representan con una línea, hay una correlación positiva.

Example

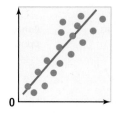

Postulate   A postulate is an accepted statement of fact.

Postulado   Un postulado es un enunciado que se acepta como un hecho.

Example   **Postulate:** Through any two points there is exactly one line.

Proof   A proof is a convincing argument that uses deductive reasoning. A proof can be written in many forms. In a two-column proof, the statements and reasons are aligned in columns. In a paragraph proof, the statements and reasons are connected in sentences. In a flow proof, arrows show the logical connections between the statements. In a coordinate proof, a figure is drawn on a coordinate plane and the formulas for slope, midpoint, and distance are used to prove properties of the figure. An indirect proof involves the use of indirect reasoning.

Prueba   Una prueba es un argumento convincente en el cual se usa el razonamiento deductivo. Una prueba se puede escribir de varias maneras. En una *prueba de dos columnas*, los enunciados y las razones se alinean en columnas. En una *prueba de párrafo*, los enunciados y razones están unidos en oraciones. En una *prueba de flujo*, hay flechas que indican las conexiones lógicas entre enunciados. En una *prueba de coordenadas*, se dibuja una figura en un plano de coordenadas y se usan las fórmulas de la pendiente, punto medio y distancia para probar las propiedades de la figura. Una *prueba indirecta* incluye el uso de razonamiento indirecto.

Example

Given: $\triangle EFG$, with right angle $\angle F$
Prove: $\angle E$ and $\angle G$ are complementary.

Paragraph Proof: Because $\angle F$ is a right angle, $m\angle F = 90$. By the Triangle Angle-Sum Theorem, $m\angle E + m\angle F + m\angle G = 180$. By substitution, $m\angle E + 90 + m\angle G = 180$. Subtracting 90 from each side yields $m\angle E + m\angle G = 90$. $\angle E$ and $\angle G$ are complementary by definition.

English

Range (of a relation or function)   The possible values of the output, or dependent variable, of a relation or function.

Example   In the function $y = |x|$, the range is the set of all nonnegative numbers.

Ratio   A ratio is a comparison of two quantities by division. An *extended ratio* is a comparison of three or more quantities by division.

Ray   A ray is the part of a line that consists of one *endpoint* and all the points of the line on one side of the endpoint.

Example

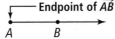

Reciprocal   The reciprocal of a number is 1 divided by that number.

Example $\frac{2}{5}$ and $\frac{5}{2}$ are reciprocals because $1 \div \frac{2}{5} = \frac{5}{2}$.

Recursive formula   A recursive formula defines the terms in a sequence by relating each term to the ones before it. It is composed of an initial value and a rule for generating the sequence.

Example   Let $a_n = 2.5a_{n-1} + 3a_{n-2}$.

If $a_5 = 3$ and $a_4 = 7.5$, then

$a_6 = 2.5(3) + 3(7.5) = 30$.

Reflection   A reflection across line r, called the *line of reflection*, is a transformation such that if a point A is on line r, then the image of A is itself, and if a point B is not on line r, then its image B' is the point such that r is the perpendicular bisector of $\overline{BB'}$. A reflection is a rigid motion.

Example

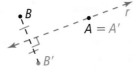

Reflectional symmetry   Reflectional symmetry is the type of symmetry for which there is a reflection that maps a figure onto itself. The reflection line is the *line of symmetry*. The line of symmetry divides a figure with reflectional symmetry into two congruent halves.

Example

Spanish

Rango (de una relación o función)   El conjunto de todos los valores posibles de la salida, o variable dependiente, de una relación o función.

Razón   Una razón es una comparación de dos cantidades usando la división. Una *razón extendida* es una comparación de tres o más cantidades usando la división.

Semirrecta   Una semirrecta es la parte de una recta que tiene un *extremo* de donde parten todos los puntos de la recta.

Recíproco   El recíproco de un número es 1 dividido entre ese número.

Fórmula recursiva   Una fórmula recursiva define los términos de una secuencia al relacionar cada término con los términos que lo anteceden. Está compuesta por un valor inicial y una regla para generar la secuencia.

Reflexión   Una reflexión a través de una línea r, llamada el *eje de reflexión*, es una transformación en la que si un punto A es parte de la línea r, la imagen de A es sí misma, y si un punto B no está en la línea r, su imagen B' es el punto en el cual la línea r es la bisectriz perpendicular de $\overline{BB'}$. Una reflexión es un movimiento rígido.

Simetría reflexiva   Simetría reflexiva es el tipo de simetría donde hay una reflexión que ubica una figura en sí misma. El eje de reflexión es *el eje de simetría*. El eje de simetría divide una figura con simetría reflexiva en dos mitades congruentes.

A reflection across the given line maps the figure onto itself.

English

Spanish

Regular polygon   A regular polygon is a polygon that is both equilateral and equiangular. Its *center* is the point that is equidistant from its vertices.

Polígono regular   Un polígono regular es un polígono que es equilateral y equiangular. Su *centro* es el punto equidistante de sus vértices.

Example

ABCDEF is a regular hexagon. Point *X* is its center.

Relation   Any set of ordered pairs.

Relación   Cualquier conjunto de pares ordenados

Example   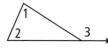 {(0, 0), (2, 3), (2, − 7)} is a relation.

Remote interior angles   Remote interior angles are the two nonadjacent interior angles corresponding to each exterior angle of a triangle.

Ángulos interiores remotos   Los ángulos interiores remotos son los dos ángulos interiores no adyacentes que corresponden a cada ángulo exterior de un triángulo.

Example

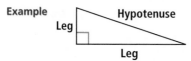

∠1 and ∠2 are remote interior angles of ∠3.

Residual   The difference between the *y*-value of a data point and the corresponding *y*-value of a model for the data set.

Residuo   La diferencia entre el valor de *y* de un punto y el valor de *y* correspondiente a ese punto en el modelo del conjunto de datos.

Right angle   A right angle is an angle whose measure is 90.

Ángulo recto   Un ángulo recto es un ángulo que mide 90.

Right triangle   A right triangle contains one right angle. The side opposite the right angle is the *hypotenuse* and the other two sides are the *legs*.

Triángulo rectángulo   Un triángulo rectángulo contiene un ángulo recto. El lado opuesto del ángulo recto es la *hipotenusa* y los otros dos lados son los *catetos*.

Example

Rigid motion   A rigid motion is a transformation that preserves distance and angle measure. A rigid motion is sometimes called a *congruence transformation*.

Movimiento rígido   Un movimiento rígido es una transformación en el plano que no cambia la distancia ni la medida del ángulo. Los movimientos rígidos se conocen a veces como *transformaciones de congruencia*.

Example   The four rigid motions are reflections, translations, rotations, and glide reflections.

Rotation   A rotation of *x* about a point *R*, called the *center of rotation*, is a transformation such that for any point *V*, its image is the point *V'*, where $RV = RV'$ and $m\angle VRV' = x$. The image of *R* is itself. The positive number of degrees *x* that a figure rotates is the *angle of rotation*. A rotation is a rigid motion.

Rotación   Una rotación de *x* sobre un punto *R*, llamado el *centro de rotación*, es una transformación en la que para cualquier punto *V*, su imagen es el punto *V'*, donde $RV = RV'$ y $m\angle VRV' = x$. La imagen de *R* es sí misma. El número positivo de grados *x* que una figura rota es el *ángulo de rotación*. Una rotación es un movimiento rígido.

Example

English

Spanish

Rotational symmetry   Rotational symmetry is the type of symmetry for which there is a rotation of 360° or less that maps a figure onto itself.

Simetría rotacional   La simetría rotacional es un tipo de simetría en la que una rotación de 360° o menos vuelve a trazar una figura sobre sí misma.

Example The figure has 120° rotational symmetry.

Same-side interior angles   Same-side interior angles lie on the same side of the transversal t and between ℓ and m.

Ángulos internos del mismo lado   Los ángulos internos del mismo lado están situados en el mismo lado de la transversal t y dentro de ℓ y m.

Example

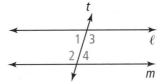

$\angle 1$ and $\angle 2$ are same-side interior angles, as are $\angle 3$ and $\angle 4$.

Scalene triangle   A scalene triangle has no congruent sides.

Triángulo escaleno   Un triángulo escaleno no tiene lados congruentes.

Example

Segment   A segment is the part of a line that consists of two points, called *endpoints*, and all points between them.

Segmento   Un segmento es la parte de una recta que tiene dos puntos, llamados *extremos*, entre los cuales están todos los puntos de esa recta.

Example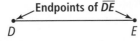

Segment bisector   A segment bisector is a line, segment, ray, or plane that intersects a segment at the midpoint.

Bisectriz de un segmento   La bisectriz de un segmento es una recta, segmento, semirrecta o plano que corta un segmento en el punto medio.

Example  ℓ bisects $\overline{KJ}$.

Sequence   An ordered list of numbers that often forms a pattern.

Progresión   Lista ordenada de números que muchas veces forma un patrón.

Example   −4, 5, 14, 23 is a sequence.

Set   A well-defined collection of elements.

Conjunto   Un grupo bien definido de elementos.

Example   The set of integers:
{. . . , −3, −2, −1, 0, 1, 2, 3, . . .}

English	Spanish
Simple interest Interest paid only on the principal.	**Interés simple** Intéres basado en el capital solamente.

Example The interest on $1,000 at 6% for
5 years is $1,000(0.06)5 = $300.

English	Spanish
Slope-intercept form The slope-intercept form of a linear equation is $y = mx + b$, where m is the slope of the line and b is the y-intercept.	**Forma pendiente-intercepto** La forma pendiente-intercepto es la ecuación lineal $y = mx + b$, en la que m es la pendiente de la recta y b es el punto de intersección de esa recta con el eje y.

Example $y = \frac{1}{2}x - 3$

In this equation, the slope is $\frac{1}{2}$ and the y-intercept is -3.

English	Spanish
Slope of a line The slope of a line is the ratio of its vertical change in the coordinate plane to the corresponding horizontal change. If (x_1, y_1) and (x_2, y_2) are points on a nonvertical line, then the slope is $\frac{y_2 - y_1}{x_2 - x_1}$. The slope of a horizontal line is 0, and the slope of a vertical line is undefined.	**Pendiente de una recta** La pendiente de una recta es la razón del cambio vertical en el plano de coordenadas en relación al cambio horizontal correspondiente. Si (x_1, y_1) y (x_2, y_2) son puntos en una recta no vertical, entonces la pendiente es $\frac{y_2 - y_1}{x_2 - x_1}$. La pendiente de una recta horizontal es 0, y la pendiente de una recta vertical es indefinida.

Example

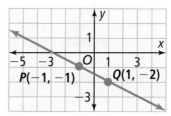

The line containing $P(-1, -1)$ and $Q(1, -2)$
has slope $\frac{-2 - (-1)}{1 - (-1)} = \frac{-1}{2} = -\frac{1}{2}$.

English	Spanish
Solution of an inequality in two variables Any ordered pair that makes the inequality true.	**Solución de una desigualdad con dos variables** Cualquier par ordenado que haga verdadera la desigualdad.

Example

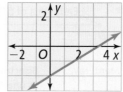

Each ordered pair in the yellow area and on the solid red line is a solution of $3x - 5y \leq 10$

English	Spanish
Solution of a system of linear inequalities Any ordered pair that makes all of the inequalities in the system true.	**Solución de un sistema de desigualdades lineales** Todo par ordenado que hace verdaderas todas las desigualdades del sistema.

Example

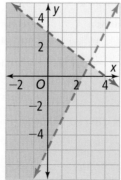

The shaded green area shows the solution of the system $\begin{matrix} y > 2x - 5 \\ 3x + 4y < 12 \end{matrix}$.

English

Standard deviation A measure of how data varies, or deviates, from the mean.

Example Use the following formula to find the standard deviation.

$$\sigma = \sqrt{\frac{\Sigma(x - \bar{x})^2}{n}}$$

Standard form of a linear equation The standard form of a linear equation is $Ax + By = C$, where A, B, and C are real numbers and A and B are not both zero.

Example $6x - y = 12$

Straight angle A straight angle is an angle whose measure is 180.

Example

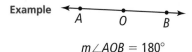

$$m\angle AOB = 180°$$

Straightedge A straightedge is a tool for drawing straight lines.

Subset A subset of a set consists of elements from the given set.

Example If $B = \{1, 2, 3, 4, 5, 6, 7\}$ and $A = \{1, 2, 5\}$, then A is a subset of B.

Supplementary angles Two angles are supplementary if the sum of their measures is 180.

Example

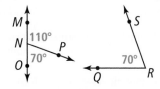

$\angle MNP$ and $\angle ONP$ are supplementary, as are $\angle MNP$ and $\angle QRS$.

Symmetry A figure has symmetry if there is a rigid motion that maps the figure onto itself. *See also* **point symmetry; reflectional symmetry; rotational symmetry.**

Example

A regular pentagon has reflectional symmetry and 72° rotational symmetry.

Spanish

Desviación típica Medida de cómo los datos varían, o se desvían, de la media.

Forma normal de una ecuación lineal La forma normal de una ecuación lineal es $Ax + By = C$, donde A, B y C son números reales, y donde A y B no son iguales a cero.

Ángulo llano Un ángulo llano es un ángulo que mide 180.

Regla sin graduación Una regla sin graduación es un instrumento para dibujar líneas rectas.

Subconjunto Un subconjunto de un conjunto consiste en elementos del conjunto dado.

Ángulos suplementarios Dos ángulos son suplementarios cuando sus medidas suman 180.

Simetría Una figura tiene simetría si hay un movimiento rígido que traza la figura sobre sí misma. *Ver también* **point symmetry; reflectional symmetry; rotational symmetry.**

English

Spanish

System of linear inequalities   Two or more linear inequalities using the same variables.

Example $y \leq x + 11$
$y < 5x$

Sistema de desigualdades lineales   Dos o más desigualdades lineales que usen las mismas variables.

Term of a sequence   A term of a sequence is any number in a sequence.

Término de una progresión   Un término de una secuencia es cualquier número de una secuencia.

Example   −4 is the first term of the sequence −4, 5, 14, 23.

Theorem   A theorem is a conjecture that is proven.

Teorema   Un teorema es una conjetura que se demuestra.

Example   The theorem "Vertical angles are congruent" can be proven by using postulates, definitions, properties, and previously stated theorems.

Transformation   A transformation is a change in the position, size, or shape of a geometric figure. The given figure is called the *preimage* and the resulting figure is called the *image*. A transformation *maps* a figure onto its image. *Prime notation* is sometimes used to identify image points. In the diagram, *X′* (read "*X* prime") is the image of *X*.

Transformación   Una transformación es un cambio en la posición, tamaño o forma de una figura. La figura dada se llama la *preimagen* y la figura resultante se llama la *imagen*. Una transformación *traza* la figura sobre su propia imagen. La *notación prima* a veces se utilize para identificar los puntos de la imagen. En el diagrama de la derecha, *X′* (leído *X* prima) es la imagen de *X*.

Example

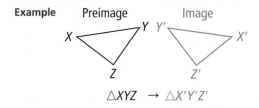

$\triangle XYZ \;\; \rightarrow \;\; \triangle X'Y'Z'$

Transformation of a function   A transformation of a function maps each point of its graph to a new location.

Transformación de una función   Una transformación de una función desplaza cada punto de su gráfica a una ubicación nueva.

Example   Transformations can be translations, rotations, reflections, or dilations.

Translation   A translation is a transformation that moves points the same distance and in the same direction. A translation is a rigid motion.

Traslación   Una traslación es una transformación en la que se mueven puntos la misma distancia en la misma dirección. Una traslación es un movimiento rígido.

Example

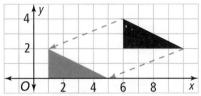

The blue triangle is the image of the black triangle under the translation $\langle -5, -2 \rangle$.

English

Translation of a function A transformation that shifts the graph of a function the same distance horizontally, vertically, or both.

Example

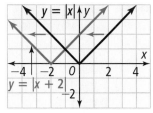

$y = |x + 2|$ is a translation of $y = |x|$.

Transversal A transversal is a line that intersects two or more lines at distinct points.

Example

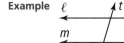

t is a transversal of ℓ and m.

Trapezoid A trapezoid is a quadrilateral with exactly one pair of parallel sides, the *bases*. The nonparallel sides are called the *legs* of the trapezoid. Each pair of angles adjacent to a base are *base angles* of the trapezoid. An *altitude* of a trapezoid is a perpendicular segment from one base to the line containing the other base. Its length is called the *height* of the trapezoid.

Example

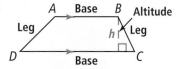

In trapezoid $ABCD$, $\angle ADC$ and $\angle BCD$ are one pair of base angles, and $\angle DAB$ and $\angle ABC$ are the other.

Trend line A line that models the data in a scatter plot by showing the general direction of the data.

Example

Positive   Negative

Spanish

Translación de una función Proceso de mover una gráfica horizontalmente, verticalmente o en ambos sentidos.

Transversal Una transversal es una línea que interseca dos o más líneas en puntos precisos.

Trapecio Un trapecio es un cuadrilátero con exactamente un par de lados paralelos, las *bases*. Los lados no paralelos se llaman los *catetos* del trapecio. Cada par de ángulos adyacentes a la base son los *ángulos de base* del trapecio. Una *altura* del trapecio es un segmento perpendicular que va de una base a la recta que contiene la otra base. Su longitud se llama, por extensión, la *altura* del trapecio.

Línea de tendencia Una línea que representa los datos en un diagrama de puntos y muestra la dirección general de los datos.

English

Spanish

Truth table A truth table is a table that lists all the possible combinations of truth values for two or more statements.

Tabla de verdad Una tabla de verdad es una tabla que muestra todas las combinaciones posibles de valores de verdad de dos o más enunciados.

Example

p	q	$p \rightarrow q$
T	T	T
T	F	F
F	T	T
F	F	T

Truth value The truth value of a statement is "true" (T) or "false" (F) according to whether the statement is true or false, respectively.

Valor verdadero El valor verdadero de un enunciado es "verdadero" (T) o "falso" (F) según el enunciado sea verdadero o falso, respectivamente.

Two-way frequency table A two-way frequency table is a table that displays frequencies in two different categories.

Tabla de frecuencias de doble entrada Una tabla de frecuencias de doble entrada es una tabla de frecuencias que contiene dos categorías de datos.

Example

	Male	Female	Totals
Juniors	3	4	7
Seniors	3	2	5
Totals	6	6	12

V

Variance The mean of the squares of the difference between each data value and the mean.

Varianza La media de los cuadrados de la diferencia entre cada valor de los datos y la media.

Example

x	18	25	18	10	17	15	18	15
$\overline{x}$	17	17	17	17	17	17	17	17
$x - \overline{x}$	1	8	1	−7	0	−2	1	−2
$(x - \overline{x})^2$	1	64	1	49	0	4	1	4

The variance is $s^2 = \dfrac{1 + 64 + 1 + 49 + 0 + 4 + 1 + 4}{7}$.

Vertical angles Vertical angles are two angles whose sides form two pairs of opposite rays.

Ángulos opuestos por el vértice Dos ángulos son ángulos opuestos por el vértice si sus lados son semirrectas opuestas.

Example $\angle 1$ and $\angle 2$ are vertical angles, as are $\angle 3$ and $\angle 4$.

Y

y-intercept The y-coordinate of a point where a graph crosses the y-axis.

Intercepto en y Coordenada y por donde la gráfica cruza el eje de las y.

Example The y-intercept of $y = 5x + 2$ is 2.

Z

Zero-Product Property For all real numbers a and b, if $ab = 0$, then $a = 0$ or $b = 0$.

Propiedad del producto cero Para todos los números reales a y b, si $ab = 0$, entonces $a = 0$ ó $b = 0$.

Index

slope of. *see* slope
 of symmetry, 350–351
 trend, 115–116
 vertical, 64–65

literal equations, 18–23

M

marginal frequency, 461

marginal relative frequency, 462

mathematical modeling
 absolute value equations, 43
 equations with variables on both
  sides, 17
 inequalities in one variable, 29

mean, 454

midpoints, 236, 239, 408

multiplication of exponents, 177–179

Multiplication Property of Equality, 152

N

negation, 252

negative association, 112–114

negative correlation, 114, 121, 122

no association, 113

normal distribution, 454

notations
 for angles, 220
 for compositions of rigid motions,
  329
 for lines, 219
 for planes, 219
 for points, 219
 for rays, 220
 for segments, 220

number line(s)
 absolute value on, 37
 segment lengths on, 220, 221
 solution of an inequality on, 24–25
 using, 219

numbers
 absolute value of, 38
 integers, 6, 63

O

one-to-one, 85

opposite rays, 220

opposite reciprocals, 72

or, compound inequalities containing, 32

ordered pair, 158

outlier, 438

overlapping triangles, 402–407

P

paragraph proofs, 267, 269

parallel line(s)
 angle pair relationships, 285–291
 checking, 307
 concept summary, 303
 perpendicular lines and, 70–76
 proving, 292–298
 transversals and, 285–291
 triangle angle sums and, 299–305

parallelograms, classification of, 409

parentheses, expressions in, 144

patterns, 104–105, 242–248

perimeter, 411

perpendicular bisectors
 construction of, 230, 232
 defined, 230
 of isosceles triangles, 373–374
 of reflections, 320–326

perpendicular line(s)
 equations of, 309
 parallel lines and, 70–76
 slopes of, 308–309

planes, 219

points
 collinear, 222
 coordinates of, 221, 225
 defined, 219
 endpoints, 220
 midpoints, 236, 239, 408

point-slope form of linear equations,
 57–62

point symmetry, 351

polygonal modeling, 318

polygons
 congruence of, 392
 in coordinate plane, 408–414
 dividing, 351
 modeling with, 318
 symmetry of, 352

population, standard deviation of, 456

positive association, 112

positive correlation, 114, 121

Postulates
 Angle Addition, 223
 defined, 221
 Protractor, 222–223, 225
 Ruler, 221, 225
 Same-Side Interior Angles, 286, 289
 Same-Side Interior Angles, Converse
  of, 294
 Segment Addition, 221

Power of a Power Property, 177–179

Power of a Product Property, 179

Product of Powers Property, 177–179

proofs
 for Alternate Interior Angles
  Theorem, 287
 for Angle-Side-Angle congruence
  criterion, 389
 for congruent triangles, 403
 for Converse of the Anterior Interior
  Angles Theorem, 293
 defined, 265, 269
 for equilateral triangles, 375
 for Hypotenuse-Leg (HL) Theorem,
  398
 indirect, 272–277
 paragraph, 267, 269
 parallel lines to prove angle
  relationships, 288
 Side-Side-Side Congruence Criterion,
  383–384
 for Triangle Angle-Sum Theorem,
  300
 two-column, 265–266, 268, 269
 writing, 265–272

property(ies)
 Multiplication Property of Equality,
  152
 Power of a Power Property, 177–179
 Power of a Product Property, 179
 Product of Powers Property,
  177–179
 Quotient of Powers Property, 180

Protractor Postulate, 222–223, 225

Pythagorean Theorem, 419

Q

quadrilaterals
 classification of, on coordinate
  plane, 410
 parallelogram as, 251, 409
 rectangle as, 252
 uses of, 318

quartiles, 433

Quotient of Powers Property, 180

R

range
 continuous, 84
 defined, 83
 discrete, 84
 of functions, 83–88, 208
 reasonable, 84

rate of change, 195

rational exponents, 177–183

rational numbers, integers as, 63

ratios, common, 186, 199

rays, 220, 230, 231, 233

reciprocal, defined, 71